W9-AQU-449

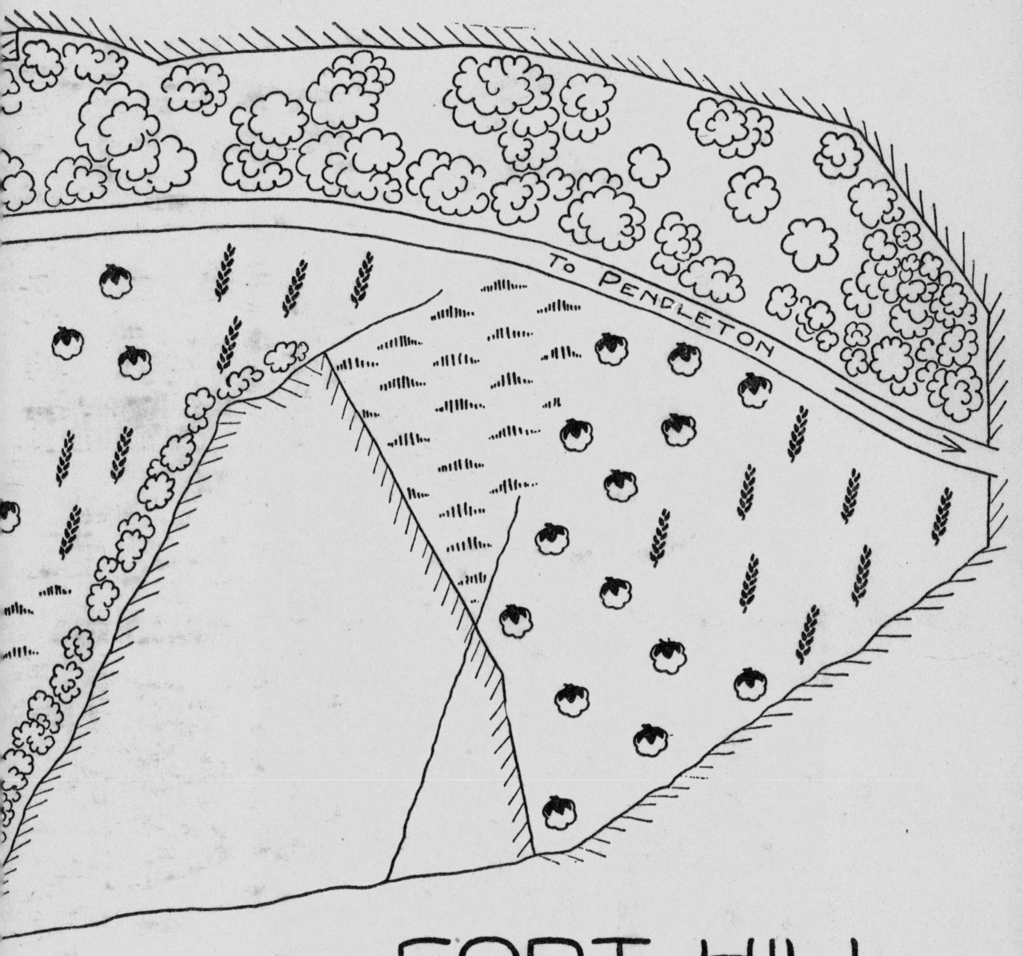

FORT HILL

JOHN C. CALHOUN

Nullifier, 1829-1839

JOHN C. CALHOUN, ABOUT 1838
by Rembrandt Peale

JOHN C. CALHOUN

NULLIFIER, 1829-1839

by

Charles M. Wiltse

THE BOBBS-MERRILL COMPANY, INC.

Publishers

INDIANAPOLIS NEW YORK

PRINTED IN THE UNITED STATES OF AMERICA

First Edition

TABLE OF CONTENTS

TABLE OF CONTENTS—*Continued*

LIST OF ILLUSTRATIONS

LIST OF ILLUSTRATIONS—*Continued*

JOHN C. CALHOUN
Nullifier, 1829-1839

CHAPTER I

THE MILLENNIUM OF MINNOWS

1

MARCH 4, 1829, was a day to remember. The unprecedented cold of the past two months had broken at last, and damp patches of earth in shady corners were all that remained of the snow that had blanketed Washington only two days before. The Potomac was still frozen and the trees were bare, but there was warmth and color enough for anyone in the cheering, pushing, eager crowds of people that gave to the unpaved streets and scattered houses of the overambitious Capital the aspect for once of a metropolis. From five hundred miles and more away they had descended upon the city like a great swarm of locusts, by stagecoach, cart, and wagon, on horseback and on foot. In broadcloth and homespun, in finery and tatters, in coonskin cap and silk topper, they were the People: a cross section of the citizenry of this vast sprawling nation, already showing as it closed its fortieth year extremes of poverty and wealth, of culture and condition, as great as its extremes of climate. On this one bright, exuberant, carefree day the extremes met, for Democracy had triumphed. The country had been saved from some terrible danger, the nature of which was obscure to all but the most astute politicians, and Andrew Jackson, the People's President, was about to be inaugurated.

The ceremonies began at dawn with an artillery salute befitting a military hero. People and vehicles already filled the streets. Many, indeed, had been in the streets all night, for rooming houses were long since filled to overflowing, and people slept where they could. Jackson himself was at the National Hotel, better known as Gadsby's Tavern, six blocks below the Capitol on Pennsylvania Avenue. There he was greeted a little before eleven by officers and soldiers of the Revolution. At eleven sharp the ranks of the old soldiers parted and the President-elect, on foot and bareheaded, moved slowly toward the Capitol. Personal friends and former military aides opened a path for him through the milling crowd.[1]

It was Jackson's victory and Jackson's day. Even those who

crowded into the newly remodeled semicircular gallery of the Senate chamber at an early hour were there to see the President-elect and no one else. If they watched at all when the tall, angular figure of the Vice President entered the room and took the chair, it was only to while away the time until the Hero himself should come. Yet John C. Calhoun of South Carolina, Vice President of the United States and Vice President-elect, was a man worth seeing in his own right, both for what he was and for what he had accomplished.

Though still a few days short of forty-seven, Calhoun was already a political veteran of twenty years. His features were sharply cut but without any particular distinction, his height was not unduly conspicuous among the many tall men in public life, and there was nothing extraordinary about the clipped shock of stiff, dark hair that bushed out over his rather large head. Yet there was an air about him, particularly in the brilliance of his dark, varicolored eyes, that stamped him at once as no ordinary man. When he spoke his face became animated and expressive, the words tumbled out with surprising rapidity and singular directness, and the hearer was presently aware of a mind bold, penetrating, and quick, impatient of thought processes less rapid than its own, and superbly, obstinately confident.[2]

At eleven o'clock, as Jackson was starting his triumphal march to the Capitol, Calhoun called the Senate to order and took the oath from General Samuel Smith of Maryland, President pro tempore of that body and a long-standing political foe of his own. Then he himself administered the oath to a dozen Senators who were starting new terms, among them lean and humorless Hugh Lawson White, rough-hewn frontier puritan from Tennessee; heavy-set, stooping, eccentric Littleton Waller Tazewell of Virginia, like Calhoun a reluctant convert to the Jackson cause, but thought by some to be the ablest man in the party; scholarly Edward Livingston of Louisiana who belonged to the Revolutionary generation and muttered words of wisdom through toothless gums; and suave, handsome Robert Y. Hayne of South Carolina, outstanding partisan of the Vice President and soon to be the acknowledged leader of the Jackson party in the Senate.

At eleven-thirty Andrew Jackson, grave, dignified, and impressive, with his erect, military bearing, his weather-beaten face, and his shock of straight white hair, took his seat in front of the secretary's desk. At the left were the foreign Ministers in their showy court costumes. At the right Chief Justice John Marshall and the black-robed Associate Justices of the Supreme Court took their places. Members of the House of Representatives crowded into the small Senate chamber, where they rubbed elbows with Cabinet members, editors, Army and Navy officers, and visiting notables of all degrees. Only the retiring President, John Quincy Adams, was absent, nursing his political wounds at his home on Meridian Hill. At noon Calhoun adjourned the Senate and the whole procession passed through the rotunda to the east portico of the Capitol.

2

Surrounding the popular military hero, in addition to the Vice President and members of the official party, were the old friends and personal advisers who were never far from his side and whose presence seemed essential to his well-being. Senator John H. Eaton of Tennessee, Jackson's biographer and most intimate friend, and Secretary of War-designate in the new Cabinet; Major William B. Lewis, Eaton's brother-in-law and often credited with being the brains behind the Jackson campaign; General Richard K. Call who had stood fast by Jackson's side in many an Indian campaign and could speak bluntly to his chief; Amos Kendall, gaunt, sharp-faced Kentucky editor who under financial pressure had abandoned Henry Clay to join the winning side and brought one of the most skillful pens in America to Jackson's service; and James A. Hamilton of New York who was both political and personal emissary of the absent Martin Van Buren.

Also in the portico, mingling with the official party, blocking doorways, standing on stairs, were the ladies of Washington. The soft curls of the previous season were largely gone, and hair was frizzed in a "most hideous fashion,"[3] but skirts were full and voluminous, bonnets were often large and decked with plumes, and colors were gay enough for anybody. In contrast to the sober black of the men, the women wore scarlet and purple and blue and yellow and white; nor were the Southern beauties behind their Northern sisters in lavish finery, although their husbands wore simple homespun in protest against the tariff of 1828. Emily Donelson, Jackson's niece, who was to be White House hostess for the next few stormy months, and her cousin, Mary Eastin, were there with small, determined Floride Calhoun, the Vice President's wife. In the same party were

Mrs. Samuel D. Ingham, whose husband had already been named Secretary of the Treasury, and the wives of Senators Hayne and Livingston. The group was conspicuously avoided by gorgeous Peggy Eaton, the tavernkeeper's daughter who had married Jackson's closest friend two months before.[4]

The Capitol grounds were one living mass of humanity. Jackson stepped forward on the portico and bowed to the People. A great shout of triumph went up from fifteen thousand throats.[5] The crowd surged toward the barricade, and on the portico above women were boosted up onto the sculptured bases of the pillars for a better view. When the roar had subsided to a babble, the President-elect read his brief inaugural message, no word of which was audible, pronounced the oath after the Chief Justice and kissed the Bible, then turned again to the multitude and bowed. Another shout rent the air and was answered by booming cannon on the near-by heights. More distant batteries at the forts took up the salute, which was echoed at last by still other guns on the plains near Alexandria. With difficulty the President and his party made their way back through the Capitol to the west entrance, where the procession formed again, moving slowly in the direction of the "Palace." Jackson, this time on horseback, was again swallowed by the multitude.

The inauguration impressed observers, even those hostile to the new President, as a sublime and majestic spectacle: the People in all their dignity and grandeur, for the moment assuming the mantle of their sovereignty. From the Capitol they followed their President to the Executive Mansion and went in to shake his hand. Then dignity, majesty, and grandeur were no more. A rough, ill-mannered, pushing mob jammed the rooms, stood on chairs, broke furniture. Jackson was all but crushed before those nearest to him could fight off the mob, but the none-too-robust old man was finally slipped out through the rear door and taken back to the peace and privacy of Gadsby's. At the White House the rooms became so full that people could move neither in nor out and fell to jostling and fighting among themselves. The building was cleared only by opening the windows, which were used as impromptu emergency exits, and by moving the refreshments outside. Thousands of dollars' worth of glass and china were broken; mud was trampled into the carpets; punches and ices, while they lasted, were freely spilled on floors and furniture. The genii, having been recklessly invoked, had got out of hand.

That evening there was a grand ball at Carusi's, as decorous and proper as the most aristocratic Federalist could have desired. Tickets sold for five dollars and could be purchased only by invitation of a board of managers, appointed by a self-created Jackson Central Committee. Strangers in the city might apply for tickets if they so desired, but the implication was clear that they must meet the necessary qualifications as to gentility. After the ordeal of the afternoon, the President and his family did not attend, the place of honor being occupied instead by Vice President Calhoun and his dark, vivacious, still pretty wife. The members of the new Cabinet and their ladies were also present, including Peggy Eaton who was roundly snubbed.

It was perhaps fitting that the inaugural ball should be presided over by Calhoun; for he had been admitted to the Jackson ranks only to lend intellectual weight and social prestige to a party whose rank and file were innocent of either. The association, although the Vice President was not yet clearly aware of it, was tenuous and had been intended from the start to be temporary.

3

The party that elected Andrew Jackson to the Presidency was made up of many and heterogeneous elements, but chief among them were the Radicals of William H. Crawford, manipulated since Crawford's retirement in 1825 by Martin Van Buren, erstwhile Senator and now Governor of New York. It was the Radicals who had given Jackson twenty of New York's thirty-six electoral votes and all of Virginia's twenty-four, and had been instrumental in carrying for the Hero the states of North Carolina, Georgia, and in part South Carolina as well. In the last-named state the Radicals and the personal following of Calhoun had been pitted against each other on almost even terms since 1820. They had agreed on Jackson, but the bitterness of the feeling between them was attested by Georgia's vote for Senator William Smith, the Radical leader in South Carolina, for Vice President in opposition to Calhoun. Jackson's personal popularity was also potent, as was the adroit way in which he managed to be on both sides of the tariff issue and other controversial questions of the day; but he could never have won the election without the support of the Radicals. The price of that support had been, since 1827, the elimination of John C. Calhoun at the earliest convenient moment.[6]

When Gargantuan William Harris Crawford of Georgia, who had forged the old Jeffersonian party into the first national political machine in the country's history, was shelved by illness after his unsuccessful campaign for the Presidency in 1824, it was to shrewd and capable Martin Van Buren that the mantle of party leadership descended. The Red Fox of Kinderhook brought to the task a mind both acute and subtle, a charming and likable personality, a rare ability to manage men for his own purposes, and a knowledge of the political process unequaled in his day. He realized that after the "corrupt bargain" charges of 1825 Jackson would be the man to beat, and with Crawford out of the running he saw no one among the Radicals able to perform that feat in a three-way race. But an enemy who could not be beaten could be joined; so Van Buren boldly took the Radicals into the Jackson camp and prepared to absorb the Jackson party into his own.

The new organization was based, as the Jeffersonian party of 1800 had been based, on an alliance between New York, Pennsylvania, and the South. The economic interests of these components, however, were now sharply divergent. With Pennsylvania committed to a high tariff, while the South in general and South Carolina in particular opposed the protective system to the verge of violence, it was necessary to assure each group that the Jackson party, appearances to the contrary notwithstanding, really stood for the favored measures. So Calhoun was brought into the fold to satisfy the South that Jackson did indeed favor tariff reform, while Van Buren and Eaton cast the deciding votes in the Senate that carried the tariff of 1828.

Calhoun's position in the party was anomalous from the start. He had been forced into the arms of Van Buren by a combination of circumstances, the ultimate tendency of which he had not been enough of a practical politician to foresee. Elected Vice President in 1824 as the running mate of both Adams and Jackson, he had been quickly read out of the Adams party by Henry Clay. For the Adams victory was based on a sectional alliance between New England and the West, with the tariff for the one and internal improvements for the other, and there was no place in it for the South, which wanted neither. Convinced by 1826 that the Union itself could not survive the sectional hostility engendered by the protective system, Calhoun was thus forced to cast in his lot with the opposition or to play a lone hand. His own Presidential ambitions forbade the latter course, and the Jackson managers, before the tariff of 1828, promised the reforms he sought. Jackson, furthermore, was publicly committed to a single term. Calhoun's own personal popularity was only a little less great than that of Jackson himself, and with the old Hero's blessing his path to the White House would be easy and certain.

After the tariff of 1828, reform at Jackson's hands seemed less sure; and after the General's overwhelming triumph at the polls, with its clear evidence that the Radicals had been reborn, the Presidential succession too became uncertain. Calhoun did not yet know that his own elimination was the condition Crawford had exacted for throwing his influence behind Jackson; but he did know that Crawford felt for him only a deep and all-pervading animosity, and that a surprising number of the old Crawford men had ridden to victory behind the Jackson banner.

From the very beginning Calhoun's relationship to the Jackson party was one of political expediency. He hoped thereby to secure the tariff reduction so impatiently demanded by the South, and he explained as much to Jackson himself well before the election of 1828.[7] It was not to secure tariff reduction, however, that Calhoun had been accepted by the Jacksonians, but only to give an appearance of reform until the votes were counted. With the election won his usefulness was over, and the longer he remained in a position of power the more dangerous he would be to the acknowledged heir apparent, Martin Van Buren.[8] Not only was Calhoun marked for the ax from the day he joined the party, but even the method that would be used to eject him was predetermined. His role in the Jackson ranks, in addition to quieting the South on the tariff, was to lend respectability to what conservatives held to be an uneducated rabble. When the time came to get rid of him, therefore, it would be necessary to destroy his character, so that the respectable could no longer have confidence in him, and his popularity, so that few would follow his exit. It was to be accomplished by deliberately perverting an honest discharge of duty into selfish duplicity, and by misrepresenting as high treason an ingenious political philosophy designed to defend a minority interest.

4

Calhoun did not reach Washington for the short session of Congress until just before Christmas 1828, having remained in South

Carolina until his *Exposition and Protest* against the tariff had been submitted to the legislature and the danger of radical measures against the protective system had been for the time being averted. He found his own partisans and those of Van Buren quarreling so openly that the election victory itself appeared to be in jeopardy. Tariff reform was more important in his eyes than the Presidential succession, and he would not risk the one by premature talk of the other.[9] Pugnacious Duff Green was instructed to deny in the columns of the *United States' Telegraph* that any disharmony existed; and it was privately agreed among the Calhoun men that if it should be necessary in order to preserve the degree of unity required for accomplishing the party program, Jackson should be supported for a second term.[10]

Van Buren also called for party harmony, but only because the time was not yet ripe for the purging of the Vice President. Although Duff Green was known to be partial to Calhoun, the little New York Governor's aides in Washington acquiesced in his re-election as public printer in February 1829 rather than risk a premature quarrel with the tall South Carolinian.[11] It was the last political victory Calhoun was to enjoy at the hands of the Jacksonians.

From early December on, the city swarmed with office seekers of all sorts and descriptions, whose party services ranged all the way from nominating Jackson in a local caucus to operating a major newspaper. The editors were in fact especially conspicuous, most notable among them being Amos Kendall of the *Kentucky Argus,* Isaac Hill of the *New Hampshire Patriot,* Mordecai Noah of the New York *Enquirer,* and Nathaniel Greene of the Boston *Statesman.*[12] All of them had been friendly to Calhoun during the campaign, so Duff Green urged their appointment to office, and the Vice President himself gave a dinner in their honor.[13] It was Green more than anyone else who beat the drums for wholesale proscription, arguing that public office was a perquisite of party and should go to those who had served the cause faithfully.[14] He did not realize how soon his policy would be turned against the candidate he favored.

As the number of office seekers in Washington grew, the Senate refused to confirm any of President Adams' appointments, and conservatives loudly bewailed in anticipation the abuse of the patronage by the Jacksonians.[15] No one really knew, however, what Jackson meant to do, unless perhaps it was Major Lewis or Senator Eaton.

Wild rumors of all descriptions floated about, including one of Jackson's death and others that he was too ill to live long.[16] He arrived in Rockville, Maryland, however, in remarkably good health and spirits after his long journey from Nashville. Delayed by excessive and enthusiastic crowds, Jackson stayed the night in Rockville. Early on the morning of February 11 he slipped out ahead of his entourage and drove to Washington with Senator Eaton in the latter's private carriage. He was met near the Western Market by the Jackson Central Committee, handsomely mounted for the occasion, and escorted to Gadsby's, while cannon were fired on the Mall.[17] For the next two weeks political speculation settled down to the serious business of Cabinet making, leaving the lesser offices for the time being in abeyance.

5

It was on the selection of the Cabinet that the rival interests and ambitions in the Jackson party tended to concentrate during the three months following the election, for it was generally believed that whoever controlled the Cabinet would control the President. Rumors were flying thick and fast by the time Congress met early in December 1828, and all of them had Van Buren as Secretary of State. The contribution of the Little Magician toward Jackson's election was too well and too widely understood to permit any doubt as to his reward, even on the part of those who least desired to see him in so influential a position. So general was the acceptance of the New Yorker for the first seat in the council chamber, indeed, that Van Buren's own intimates were inclined to suspect at times that it was intended as a disservice to their chief and questioned whether he ought to accept it. The duties of the State Department made it risky, and the propaganda they had themselves publicized at the time of Adams' election had made Secretaries of State unpopular as Presidential candidates. Some thought Van Buren should stay in Albany, while others believed he should ask instead for the Treasury Department, which had the "most valuable internal patronage" to dispense.[18]

Calhoun himself expressed interest only in the Treasury Department, all-important to him because of its connection with the tariff issue, but even there he named no individual. He hoped only that "an able sound man" would get the position in the interest of justice to the South.[19] His preferences, however, were undoubtedly expressed by James Hamilton, Jr., and Senator Hayne, who submitted identical lists to Van Buren.

For the State Department the South Carolinians professed satisfaction with Van Buren himself. For the Treasury, however, they wanted not the plodding, methodical Samuel D. Ingham who eventually got the job, but the infinitely abler Langdon Cheves of their own state who had once been Speaker of the House and later president of the Bank of the United States. Ingham was devoted body and soul to Calhoun while Cheves was no more than lukewarm, but Cheves had proved himself one of the most skillful financiers in the country and he was sound on the tariff, whereas Ingham would be under enormous pressure from his own high-tariff constituents in Pennsylvania. Second choice for the Treasury was Louis McLane, Radical Senator from Delaware, who was also first choice for the Navy Department. McLane, like Cheves, was understood to favor tariff reform, and his inclusion indicated a disposition on the part of the Calhoun faction to make peace with the Radicals. For the War Department the South Carolinians proposed John McLean of Ohio, the incumbent Postmaster General; and for Attorney General they were ready to accept William P. Barry of Kentucky, Philip P. Barbour of Virginia, or Levi Woodbury of New Hampshire. It was for Postmaster General that Hayne and Hamilton wanted Ingham, who had for years been chairman of the House Committee on Post Offices and Post Roads; and it was the Post Office that Ingham, with Calhoun's blessing, preferred.[20]

Van Buren professed to agree with this grouping, save that McLane, who was nearer to his own wing of the party, was his first choice for the Treasury, and he preferred to see Cheves, who might serve Calhoun's interest, in the relatively unimportant Navy post.[21] It is unlikely, however, that he would ever have accepted Ingham for the Post Office. The Treasury and Post Office Departments were the best sources of patronage in the government, and Van Buren's henchmen in Washington were particularly alert to see that these two above all did not fall under Calhoun's influence.[22]

Calhoun himself was not at any time consulted by Jackson or by any of Jackson's close advisers as to his preferences for Cabinet positions, and since his views were not asked, he would not offer them.[23] The Vice President was, however, a dinner guest of the President-elect on February 17. Jackson had been privately informed that Hayne, Hamilton, and other members of the South Carolina Congressional delegation would like to talk to him about the Cabinet, should he invite them to do so, and he took the occasion to extend such an invitation through Calhoun. Hayne and Hamilton called the next evening. They concentrated on the post most important to the Calhoun faction, urging Cheves for Secretary of the Treasury with McLane for second choice. Jackson replied that he would take no one who represented either extreme in the tariff controversy, and that in deference to the wishes of Pennsylvania he meant to give the place to Ingham. Thus were the two Carolinians neatly trapped. Having themselves recommended Ingham for the Post Office, they could not object to him for the Treasury, where his presence would clearly be a triumph for Calhoun.[24]

6

On February 19 the Cabinet was made known, to be greeted by mixed consternation, annoyance, and amusement. In addition to Van Buren and Ingham, the members of the charmed circle were John H. Eaton of Tennessee, Secretary of War; John P. Branch of North Carolina, Secretary of the Navy; and John McPherson Berrien of Georgia, Attorney General. In the Post Office John McLean of Ohio was retained from the Adams administration, but for the moment only. Supporters of the Vice President were openly critical, but Major William B. Lewis called the Cabinet decidedly favorable to the Secretary of State while James A. Hamilton made much of Calhoun's disappointment.[25]

Calhoun had reason to be disappointed. There were only two men in the Cabinet who could be considered friendly to his own aspirations —Ingham and McLean; and the latter withdrew to the comparative safety of the Supreme Court before the names were actually sent to the Senate. Even Ingham was not in the spot Calhoun had hoped to get for him. In the Post Office his unwearied industry and power of detail would have been valuable political assets. In the Treasury a low-tariff Pennsylvanian was in too tough a spot to be a political asset to anybody. It made little difference what stand Ingham might take, anyway, for with both Van Buren and Eaton—the two men who had sold out their bargain with the South to pass the tariff of

1828—in the Cabinet, there was little likelihood of tariff reform at Jackson's hands.[26]

Eaton's presence in the Cabinet served two purposes. Jackson required some intimate personal counselor, on whom he could implicitly rely, to be always at hand. Individualist to the core, with a mind not quick but grimly tenacious, Jackson neither liked nor profited by the give and take of group discussion. He did not like Cabinet meetings and so he held them only at rare intervals.[27] He did, however, like to think out loud, and because his thoughts in their initial form were often ungrammatical, sometimes violent, and occasionally absurd, he required a sympathetic ear. It was Van Buren's skill in adapting himself to share this role that was largely responsible for his success with the old General. To those who understood this trait of Jackson's character, it was certain that one of his Tennessee familiars would be in the Cabinet. In point of intellect, sagacity, and character, Hugh Lawson White, the junior Senator, was the Tennessean with the highest qualifications, and Jackson did indeed first offer the seat to White. He did it, however, in slightly equivocal terms, suggesting that if he did not wish the office he should pass the letter on to Eaton. The alternative choice was at the same time made known to the latter, who neatly finessed White into declining and then himself consented "with great reluctance and much difficulty, and persuasion."[28] More was involved in the selection, however, than merely attaching a personal friend to the President's official family. Jackson had long been committed to a policy of removing the Indians beyond the Mississippi. It was the War Department that would be responsible for the migration of the tribes, and Jackson wanted in that office someone firmly wedded to his own views. Berrien too was identified with the policy of Indian removal, through his efforts to secure eviction of the Creeks and Cherokees from Georgia, and it was this connection that had commended him to Jackson.[29]

It was Eaton, however, who had recommended Berrien for a Cabinet seat, and it was also Eaton who recommended Branch. Eaton and Branch had known each other since boyhood, had gone to college together, had been closely associated in the Senate, and until the glamorous Peggy O'Neale came between them they had been intimate friends.[30] With both Branch and Berrien Calhoun was on friendly terms, as he was with Eaton, but none of the three could be called in any sense his intimate or his political partisan. Berrien, fussy and precise, his waistcoat adorned with trinkets, had differed sharply with Calhoun over Indian policy and still shared the distrust of the Crawford Radical for the Vice President. Branch, if he was not altogether the "miserable old woman" that McLane thought him, yet was too enamored of his own rather mediocre talents to be other than repelled by such a mind as Calhoun's. That both Branch and Berrien became partisans of the Carolinian, and Eaton his mortal enemy, was owing to circumstances which have been reserved for another chapter.[31]

The Cabinet was completed early in March when John McLean, himself a Presidential candidate, concluded that a Supreme Court seat would be politically preferable to cleaning house in the Post Office for Van Buren's future benefit. With Ingham the intermediary, he asked for the vacant place on the bench which had been promised to William T. Barry of Kentucky. So with the consent of the Kentucky delegation in Congress Barry was named to be Postmaster General and McLean retired from political office, although not from politics. James A. Hamilton, who fancied himself as a more skillful intriguer than perhaps he was, took credit for the maneuver, and gloated: "Calhoun is cut up by this measure as is very manifest. He begins to feel that there is an influence beyond that he can hope to exercise." Nor was the significance of the step lost on the opposition. McLean, according to Senator John M. Clayton of Delaware, "was transferred to the Bench to make way for a 'whole hog' man and to leave the coast clear for the heir apparent to the throne."[32] In short, the composition of the Cabinet revealed only too clearly that Van Buren had already been designated as Jackson's successor, and McLean was too shrewd a politician to believe he could further Calhoun's pretensions or advance his own by remaining in the Jackson party.

7

The Cabinet was officially announced in the *Telegraph* on February 26, special note being taken of the fact that the Postmaster General was for the first time included in it. But the names had already been known for a week, and the storm had broken. Clay was incredulous, Webster amused, and Thomas Ritchie, who had done more than any other individual to swing the Virginia Radicals to Jackson, was disappointed and bewildered.[33] Even the thoroughgoing party men grumbled, and Calhoun's silence was eloquent. It seemed indeed, as one observer put it, that the millennium of minnows had come.[34] Stung by his critics, Jackson himself was soon defending the Cabinet, which he pronounced to be "one of the strongest . . . that ever have been in the United States." As for Eaton, the President showed scant appreciation of the record Calhoun had made in the same office when he declared that the War Department was better conducted under his friend than it had been since the days of General Knox.[35]

It was perhaps a gesture of appeasement when Jackson offered the British Mission to Tazewell and the French to Edward Livingston. Both declined, however, and these two key foreign posts went, on Van Buren's instigation, to members of the old Crawford party: the British Mission to McLane and the French to William C. Rives of Virginia.[36] Livingston's refusal was based on personal considerations; Tazewell's, officially at least, on the belief that he could accomplish nothing in England as long as the corn laws remained in force. The Virginia Senator's unwillingness to go to England was a further blow to Calhoun's influence and to his hopes for tariff reduction. "It does seem to me," he wrote Tazewell in April, "and the more I reflect on it, the more deeply am I impressed with the belief, that at London & Paris the death blow may be given to that odious system of monopoly which is now praying on the vitals of the community. With this view, I have felt much solicitude, that we should be ably and faithfully represented at both of these places; and a corresponding anxiety, that you should accept the proffered mission."[37] The subsequent appointment of McLane, although able and well qualified, did not satisfy the South, because it meant that Jackson did not intend to use the treaty power as an instrument of tariff reduction.[38]

On the secondary level Calhoun's friends were no more successful than they had been for Cabinet posts. He did, in fact, seek places for only two of his political henchmen. For Christopher Van Deventer, who had been his own Chief Clerk in the War Department, he sought the same position from Eaton; and for Virgil Maxcy, whose party services in Maryland were second only to those of Roger B. Taney, he sought the position of Treasurer of the United States. In the first instance James Hamilton, Jr., was the go-between, and was told by Eaton that the clerkship had already been offered to Colonel Gadsden, who was Jackson's own choice. Should Gadsden refuse it, however, the Secretary promised that it should go to Van Deventer. Calhoun himself called on Eaton on March 13 and was given the same assurance. Gadsden did in fact refuse the office, but Eaton's promise was not kept and Calhoun was given no explanation.[39]

In the case of Maxcy, Calhoun "took a deeper interest, than that of any other under the Admn." and spoke to the President "in the strongest terms, in relation to it." Jackson's reaction was completely favorable, both as to Maxcy's qualifications and as to his personal standing. The position nevertheless went, as appointments showed a strong tendency to go, to a Crawford Radical. Jackson, with the guileless frankness that so impressed all who came in contact with him, convinced Maxcy "that notwithstanding all his great appointments seem to be given to a certain class of politicians, yet he has not bestowed them with a view to favour Mr. V. B." The President avowed his impartiality between his Vice President and his Secretary of State with such sincerity that Maxcy was constrained to regard his obvious departures from neutrality as further proof of the adroitness of Van Buren. Calhoun agreed as to the quarter whence came the difficulty; but he felt that in the circumstances he could make no further effort in appointments.[40]

There was again marked bitterness between the partisans of Calhoun and those of Van Buren by the time the Vice President left Washington in mid-March.[41] Three appointments announced the day after the Senate adjourned—those of Isaac Hill, William B. Lewis, and Amos Kendall to be respectively second comptroller, second auditor, and fourth auditor—poured no oil on troubled waters;[42] and the arrival of Van Buren a week later left the Secretary of State and the "Kitchen Cabinet" in virtual control of the situation.

CHAPTER II

PETTICOAT POLITICS

1

VAN BUREN's plans for the political destruction of Calhoun were unexpectedly advanced by an occurrence on New Year's Day 1829. It was on that day that Senator John H. Eaton of Tennessee was married to Mrs. Margaret O'Neale Timberlake, daughter of a well-known Washington tavernkeeper and widow of a purser in the Navy.

The newspapers recorded the event briefly and without comment. The comment was reserved for the private correspondence of such as delighted in those things. Mrs. Margaret Bayard Smith, who wrote novels as well as gossipy letters and was herself one of the leaders of Washington society, did not mince words. "Tonight," she wrote on the fatal day, "Gen'l. Eaton, the bosom friend and almost adopted son of Gen'l. Jackson, is to be married to a lady whose reputation, her previous connection with him both before and after her husband's death, has totally destroyed. . . . She has never been admitted into good society, is very handsome and of not an inspiring character and violent temper. She is, it is said, irresistible and carries whatever point she sets her mind on." The "ladies," of course, refused to attend the wedding, and Jackson's friends were unhappy about the whole affair.[1]

More succinct, more suggestive, and at least equally revealing was the facetious commentary passed on to Van Buren by Churchill C. Cambreleng on the same day. "Poor Eaton is to be married tonight —to Mrs. T.!—There is a vulgar saying of some vulgar man, I believe Swift, on such unions—about using a certain household . . . . . . and then putting it on one's head. This last sentence prevents my subscribing my name to this——"[2]

The Calhouns were in the city but were not present at the wedding. They were probably not even invited. Eaton had already made the courtesy call that Senators paid to the Vice President at the beginning of a session of Congress. Calhoun returned the call—alone—while the Eatons were in Philadelphia on their honeymoon,[3] and there, for the moment, the matter rested. The ladies of Philadelphia had not heard the gossip, or perhaps they were simply curious, for they were reported to be "much pleased" with Mrs. Eaton's "intelligence and affability."[4]

Peggy Eaton was the sort of woman that men turn around to stare at and other women condemn on sight. She was of no more than medium height, straight and well-proportioned, with a lithe grace about her that was rhythm and beauty in itself. She had fair skin, bright blue eyes, a nose almost Greek in outline. Her thick brown hair had just a glint of red, and was swept back from her broad forehead in carefully artless ringlets. Free in manner and speech and full of zest for living, she could be as sharp of tongue as any virago when she chose to be.[5] She had been pampered and petted since childhood by the great and near great of the political world, who lived at O'Neale's Tavern. So she came to understand both politics and men, and she liked them both.

Having been born a tavernkeeper's daughter instead of a "lady," Peggy did not consider herself too rigidly bound by the mores of a class to which she did not belong. Her husband was at home when Senator Eaton, a wealthy widower who was rising in the political world with the rising fortunes of Andrew Jackson, first came to stay at O'Neale's. Timberlake was nostalgic for the sea, or perhaps weary of Peggy's temper. Some irregularity in the accounts of the last ship for which he had been purser prevented his reassignment, but Eaton courteously interceded with the Secretary of the Navy and all was forgiven. Eaton continued to stay at O'Neale's after Timberlake was safely at sea, and even brought Jackson there when the old gentleman was serving a term as Senator himself. To the chivalrous Jackson Peggy was as pure as she was beautiful, but there were other boarders, including at least one of Jackson's own entourage, who were far less high-minded.

There was gossip, which did not lessen when O'Neale's Tavern was sold to pay a bad debt and Eaton turned out to be the purchaser. Tongues were not stilled when Timberlake died, it was said by his own hand, on some remote foreign shore; and when Eaton married the widow with almost indecent haste, women whispered behind their hands and men shook their heads in consternation.[6]

2

It was some time before the composition of Jackson's Cabinet was made known that Senator and Mrs. Eaton called on the Calhouns. As luck would have it, the Vice President was not at home, and if the servant announced the names of the callers, Mrs. Calhoun did not hear them. She had never seen Peggy before, but recognized Eaton. Of course she had heard the gossip, friendly as she was with Mrs. Smith and others who lived more or less permanently in Washington, though she had not herself been in the city since the summer of 1826. There was nothing for it but to receive them graciously, and that she could do to perfection. She probably rejoiced in the opportunity, for now she could gratify her curiosity in the name of hospitality—she could get a good long look at the most-talked-of woman in Washington without in any way committing herself.

Floride Calhoun was small of stature, with black hair, dark eyes, and a flashing smile. She was beginning to grow a little stout, but that was not surprising in a woman of thirty-seven, who had borne eight children. Six of them were alive and thriving, the oldest seventeen already, the youngest not quite three. Since her stay in the Capital was to be short—she had really come only for the inauguration—all but the youngest of the children had been left at home in South Carolina, in charge of relatives,[7] and she was free to enjoy the social life of the city as she had never been before. She had been enjoying it, too, until this unlooked-for call of the Eatons forced her to make a decision of perhaps crucial importance.

The Eatons chatted for a while and then departed. When Calhoun returned the general question of Peggy and her standing in society was discussed by husband and wife, but without conclusions or any specific line of action being suggested. It was doubtless clear to both that the Eatons' call was in the nature of a challenge; for the Vice President occupied the highest social position in the city, and if his wife saw fit to accept the tavernkeeper's daughter, it would be difficult if not impossible for others to reject her. It meant throwing upon Floride Calhoun, who had been in the city only a month after an absence of almost three years, the responsibility for determining whether Peggy Eaton was or was not a virtuous woman.

After a night's sleep Floride decided that she had no basis for making such a judgment, and told her husband that she would not return the call. "She said," Calhoun wrote later, "that she considered herself in the light of a stranger in the place; that she knew nothing of Mrs. Eaton, or the truth, or falsehood of the imputations on her character; and that she conceived it to be the duty of Mrs. Eaton, if innocent, to open her intercourse with the ladies who resided in the place, and who had the best means of forming a correct opinion of her conduct, and not with those who, like herself, had no means of forming a correct judgment."[8]

Calhoun replied only that he approved her decision, although he foresaw the difficulties in which it would probably involve him. He was only too well aware of Eaton's relationship to Jackson and of Jackson's immense and immovable stubbornness where his personal feelings were enlisted. But he also knew from the experience of twenty years that his own wife was probably a match in stubbornness for any man living, once she had made up her mind. It is unlikely that he desired to overrule her decision; still less likely is it that he could have done so had he wished.

Mrs. Calhoun's decision was certainly justified by the general consensus of the ladies of Washington. Jackson made himself the champion of Peggy's virtue because it was not in his nature to go back on a friend, and because in battling for a woman whose honor was disputed he was battling again for his own beloved Rachel. Perhaps if Mrs. Jackson had lived there would have been no trouble. Certainly it was the opinion of James A. Hamilton, who was as close to Jackson as Eaton himself in those first months of 1829, that the "great mistake in relation to Mrs. Eaton" would not then have been made.[9] Before the Cabinet was chosen, John Branch, unaware that he was himself to have a seat in it which he would owe to Eaton, warned Jackson against elevating his friend to one of the departments. He knew that Mrs. Eaton would not be accepted in good society, and feared that her exclusion would embarrass the administration. He also appealed to Eaton not to accept a place if offered lest the President should suffer by it. But Eaton would hear none of it, and Jackson said that the rumors were slander and ought not to be noticed.[10]

To the peculiarly articulate Mrs. Smith, the refusal of the ladies of Washington to accept this slightly tarnished sister was a *"noble* stand." "Not even the President's wishes, in favour of his dearest, personal friend, can influence them to violate the respect due to virtue, by visiting one, who has left her straight and narrow path."[11] The lines were clearly drawn by inauguration day when Peggy was ignored by the ladies of the inner circle—Mrs. Calhoun, Mrs. Ingham, Mrs. Livingston, and the feminine members of the President's own household, fragile, titian-haired Emily Donelson and romantic Mary Eastin.

It is notable that up to the time the Calhouns left Washington for their South Carolina home on March 18, neither Eaton nor Jackson attributed any personal slight to them. Less than a week before his departure Calhoun had called on Eaton at the War Department to ask a favor, and it had been promised him with every evidence of cordiality.[12] The day after the Vice President's departure Jackson wrote to one of his intimates of the "secret" attack on Eaton's wife. He was at that time sure that the purpose was to keep his friend from the Cabinet, and equally sure that the prime mover in it all was Henry Clay.[13] Surely he was aware, since he was aware of all that concerned Peggy, that the Calhouns had not called on her, but it did not then occur to him that that was a mortal insult to himself.

It was only after Van Buren was established in the Capital, and in the old General's good graces, that the possibilities of the "Eaton Malaria" were fully realized; and even then the situation was not exploited to Calhoun's injury until the time was ripe.

3

Within a few days of Jackson's inauguration the swarms of visitors to the Capital were gone. So were the officeholders and political followers of the Adams-Clay machine, and most of the Representatives in Congress. The Senate remained in session until March 17 to act on Presidential appointments, but according to custom Calhoun withdrew as presiding officer of that body on March 12. The Vice President remained in the almost deserted city, however, until after the adjournment.

The Calhouns left Washington at noon on March 18. They went

WEBSTER REPLYING TO HAYNE

by George P. A. Healy

Washington
5th Jan'y 1830

My dear Maxcy, The Bill to which you refer is not yet reported, but there is no doubt that it will be shortly, and that in the shape you desire. The Attorney General is decidedly in favour of a Solicitor, and so, I understand, is the President. We have nothing worth communicating since you left here. Make my kindest respects to Mrs Maxcy, and your daughters.

Sincerely
J. C. Calhoun

Letter from Calhoun to Virgil Maxcy, January 5, 1830

by steamboat to Fredericksburg, thence by stage to Charlottesville, and on down the beautiful valley of Virginia, already alive and green with spring. The roads were at their miserable worst, and the travelers regretted long before they reached the Carolina highlands that they had not followed the lower route by boat from Baltimore to Norfolk. The trip took nearly three weeks, but was without accident, and its discomforts were quickly forgotten in the pleasure of reunion with a boisterous and growing family of children.[14]

The Calhoun home, near Pendleton, South Carolina, high in the foothills of the Blue Ridge, stood upon the top of a hill overlooking the Seneca River. Still known as Clergy Hall in 1829, the name of the estate was changed to the more familiar Fort Hill early in the following year, and will be so designated in this volume. The extensive alterations begun in the summer of 1826, when the Calhouns made Pendleton their permanent home, were almost completed. The house, reached by a winding tree-lined road carpeted with pine needles, was a fine example of the architectural style now so firmly associated with the ante-bellum South. Its pillared porticos with their gable roofs faced east and north, while to the west or rear of the house as it then was extended a low wing occupied by the servants. Gleaming white in its setting of pine, red oak, and cedar, Fort Hill was a landmark for miles around. The whole plantation, comprising about six hundred acres, was actually the property of "old Mrs. Calhoun," as she was affectionately called: Mrs. John Ewing Calhoun, Floride's mother and widow of John's first cousin.[15]

The Calhoun children were their father's particular pride. Andrew Pickens, the first-born, would be eighteen in the fall and was ready to go to college. The choice was left to him and he selected Yale, where he proposed to enter, as did most students from the more distant parts of the Union, with junior standing. Andrew was to go as far as Washington with his father when Calhoun returned to the Capital for the session of Congress. It proved to be impossible, however, for the Vice President to leave South Carolina before November, and inquiries indicated that the delay would cost the boy more time from his studies than could be made up. In the end the project was abandoned, and Andrew matriculated instead at South Carolina College.[16]

Next in age to Andrew was slender, round-faced Anna Maria, a sprightly child of twelve, who had her mother's buoyant tempera-

ment, sparkling dark eyes, and smooth black hair, and her father's quick and penetrating mind. Then came Patrick, a husky lad of eight; John Caldwell, just turning six; and Martha Cornelia, crippled since birth, who was barely five. The clan was completed by James Edward, at three still the baby of the family and the only one of the children who had been taken to Washington for Jackson's inauguration. He was not to be the baby much longer, for the ninth and last of the Calhoun children was on the way. It was another boy, born August 13, 1829,[17] and christened William Lowndes in honor of the gentle and generous friend whose untimely death seven years before had been so irreparable a blow to South Carolina and to the nation.

It was Floride's health after William's birth that prevented Calhoun from leaving South Carolina early enough to enter Andrew at Yale. It was presumably the same reason, added to financial considerations, that kept Floride from returning to Washington with her husband when Congress met. Even had she been fully recovered herself, it seems hardly likely that she would have attempted to go through a season in the Capital with an infant of only a few months to care for, and there is no evidence that she ever considered such a move. She probably never gave a thought to Peggy Eaton or the vexed question of who should call on whom. It took dour and caustic John Quincy Adams, who could not quite tear himself away from the scene of his former glory, to conclude that Mrs. Calhoun's absence when Congress met was a strategic withdrawal to avoid an unpleasant issue.[18]

4

When Martin Van Buren reached Washington a week after Calhoun's departure, he found the city divided into two camps on the question of Peggy Eaton's virtue.[19] The members of the Cabinet, and even the intimates of the President's household, were embroiled. The wives of Ingham and Berrien and the daughters of Branch would have nothing to do with Mrs. Eaton. Neither would Emily Donelson, whose husband was Jackson's secretary, nor Mary Eastin, who lived at the White House with the Donelsons. Postmaster General William T. Barry, who was not accompanied by his wife and was actually lodging with the Eatons, took Peggy's part. To him she seemed "an artless, sincere and friendly woman." She might have been imprudent, but he could not believe the rumors beyond that point. "If rumour were to be credited," he added charitably, "but few handsome ladies in the fashionable world in this city would be free from blemish."[20]

Van Buren perceived at once that in this battle there was no neutral ground. There was no doubt where Jackson's sympathies lay; and the Secretary of State, being a widower without daughters, was under none of the domestic compulsions that operated on his colleagues. Without hesitation, therefore, he determined to treat all the members of the Cabinet alike, which is to say he recognized Mrs. Eaton as having claims to virtue equal with those of Mrs. Ingham, Mrs. Berrien, and the Misses Branch.[21] For the next month or two Eaton's influence with the President was paramount, and Eaton's primary thought was to force the women of Washington to receive his wife. Calhoun was informed by the faithful Maxcy early in April that "the U. S. are governed by the Prest. The Prest. by the Secry. of War and the latter by his W—."[22] By May Duff Green had quarreled with Eaton, and shared the opinion of other Calhoun supporters close to the scene that Eaton was unfriendly to the Vice President.[23] June saw the ascendancy pass from Eaton to Van Buren. Among the means used by the Little Magician to bring Jackson into his own camp was "the most devoted and assiduous attention to Mrs. Eaton, and unceasing efforts to bring her into notice, especially with the families of the foreign ministers."[24]

Jackson himself spared no effort to get Peggy into society, and let it be clearly understood that "it would be a most acceptable service rendered him, if the members of his Cabinet would aid in promoting this object."[25] The President insisted that the scandal was repeated only by women, and that even they became silent when Eaton threatened to hold their husbands responsible.[26] It is a curious trait of Jackson's character that he could denounce in the strongest terms those "satelites of Clay" whom he still regarded as the originators of the scandal,[27] yet could at the same time be merely hurt when one of his own most intimate friends told him bluntly it was not scandal but truth. It was tough and outspoken General Richard K. Call, friend of Eaton and Lewis as well as of the President, who insisted that it was Jackson who had been deceived, and that Peggy was indeed unfit to associate with respectable females. "While living in the same house I had such evidences of her conduct, as to convince me of her want of virtue. . . ." Jackson merely endorsed Call's letter "to be filed with my private papers, as an evidence of the falibility of man and how far he will be carried by his prejudices."[28]

In the subsequent correspondence it developed that General Call had himself made advances toward Peggy some five years back, and still attributed his lack of success to Eaton's interference. He conceded that he had no direct personal knowledge such as would constitute positive proof, but he had eyes in his head, and he had talked about Peggy often enough with other credible witnesses who like Eaton, Jackson, and himself had lived at O'Neale's. Between the lines it was clear that he still thought Peggy a thoroughgoing jade, who had already been the ruin of Eaton and would in due time ruin Jackson as well.[29] It developed also that both Call and Lewis had tried to break the affair up, but that Peggy had outmaneuvered them. The net result, however, was merely to set Jackson the more stubbornly upon his course and make him the more determined to hush the gossiping tongues and force Peggy into society.

The worst of the stories, and the only one that could be pinned down, had to do with an abortion Peggy was supposed to have had while still Mrs. Timberlake, but at a time when her husband had been too long at sea. The tale rested on the testimony of a doctor, since deceased, who had told it to the Reverend J. N. Campbell, a popular Presbyterian pastor then of Washington but since removed to Philadelphia. Apparently in hopes of forewarning the President, who had once been a member of his congregation, Campbell had told the story to a brother pastor, the Reverend Ezra Styles Ely, whom he knew to be a friend of Jackson's. Sometime before the formation of the Cabinet Ely duly transmitted the message, but of course Jackson had branded it as false and malicious slander.

Campbell was of an evangelical turn of mind, however, and told the story also to Colonel Towson, who seems to have brought it once more to Jackson's attention. Jackson demanded proof, and Campbell was summoned. An initial interview was held by Major Donelson while the President was vacationing with Eaton at the Rip Raps, and a date for hearing was arranged. It took place on September 3, in the presence of Donelson and Towson. Then the Cabinet, except for Eaton, was ordered to an evening session at the White House, where both Campbell and Ely were present. Donelson read the documents in the case, Ely declared the story false, and Jackson pronounced Mrs. Eaton a virtuous and much persecuted woman.[30]

Eaton presently heard reports, possibly from Jackson himself, of Colonel Towson's agency in the affair, and threatened a challenge if he didn't get a satisfactory explanation. Towson tried to keep Campbell out of it; but Campbell, who seemed to be developing a martyr complex, insisted on staying in it. The Philadelphia clergyman sought an interview with Duff Green, at which he seems to have indicated that he would tell everything if anything happened to his friend the colonel. After some delay and not a few misunderstandings, Green persuaded Campbell to go himself to Eaton and tell his story, which was finally done, with Towson again present. Eaton, of course, already knew the story and who had been telling it.[31]

Eaton had already quarreled with Donelson, because the President's secretary would not undertake to force his wife to call upon Peggy.[32] By October he was quarreling with Branch because the latter's daughters had invited both Campbell and Ely to a party;[33] and to Berrien he actually issued a challenge, which did not, however, result in a meeting on the field of honor.[34] The President had to postpone his first state dinner until he could get the members of his official family on speaking terms with one another. The dinner was held on November 26 and was remarkable for the fact that all of the Cabinet ladies attended. The arrangements had been made with the most meticulous care to prevent an explosion. Jackson escorted Mrs. Ingham to the table, and Van Buren gave his arm to Emily Donelson. The disingenuous little secretary could not remember later how the other guests had been seated, but it is a safe guess that Mrs. Eaton was escorted by Sir Charles Vaughn, the bachelor British Minister. It was "certainly the most splendid entertainment" one member of the group, at least, had ever seen in Washington.[35] Yet just beneath the surface were taut nerves and a tension so great that the slightest false move by any of the principals in the affair would have touched off an explosion.

When Van Buren led off the round of Cabinet dinners shortly thereafter he evaded the issue by inviting and himself escorting Mrs. Thomas Mann Randolph, daughter of Thomas Jefferson. He need not have gone to such pains, for while his colleagues were pleased to be present, one and all, including Eaton, brought the regrets and the excuses of their ladies.[36]

5

By December the uneasy truce was crumbling and the President could no longer even pretend to conceal the breach in his Cabinet. The course of events, had it been fully known, might also have given some hint as to the manner in which the breach was to be used to purge the party of Calhoun's supporters. For though Branch and Berrien had both entered the Cabinet as friends of Eaton and at his instance, they were, by the fall of 1829, being lumped with Ingham as friends of the Vice President. From there it was but a step to associate the friends of Calhoun with the enemies of Peggy Eaton, and finally to shift to Calhoun personally responsibility for originating the Eaton scandals. A political motive was ready to hand, for was it not true that Eaton looked with disfavor on Calhoun's Presidential aspirations?

Just when the various steps in this logical progression were planted in Jackson's tenacious and unforgiving mind cannot be precisely determined, for it is not the sort of thing that would have been reduced to writing. We do know, however, that as late as July 5 it was still "the hired slanderers of Mr. Clay" who were seeking to injure the President by destroying Eaton. Fall found the poison working. The persecution of Peggy, Jackson wrote on November 24 to one of his Tennessee intimates, "was founded in political views, looking to the future. Jealousy arose that Eaton might not be a willing instrument to those particular views, that his popularity was growing and it was necessary to put him out of the Cabinet and destroy him regardless what injury it might do me or my administration." A month later he told another Tennessee familiar that "the case of Major Eaton was thought to present a fair opportunity of *destroying him,* and *injuring me,* by circulating, *secretly,* foul and insidious slanders against him and his family." This time he cast caution to the winds and referred to Calhoun by name.[37]

6

Calhoun got back to Washington just before the middle of December to find not only "society" but the Democratic party as well sharply divided on the Eaton question, and himself put forward by both sides as the leader of the "moral party" in opposition to Van Buren who headed the defenders of the "frail sisterhood."[38] Peggy was busily engaged in flattering the old General until it ran down "even to the hem of his garment like oil."[39] *Othello* was playing in Washington that week, with Cooper and the Blakes, and perhaps she already fancied herself in the role of Desdemona. If she did not see Calhoun as Iago, it was certainly no fault of Van Buren or of her husband.[40]

The "Eaton Malaria" reached its crisis on January 8, 1830, when Peggy was unmercifully snubbed at the Jackson Day ball. Eaton, furious and frustrated, made some savage remarks about other people's wives, and was himself threatened with a challenge.[41] The Cabinet did not meet because its members would not sit together; and the Secretary of State continued to hold the upper hand by controlling "all the pages on the back stairs," and by flattering "the Aaron's serpent among the President's desires, a settled purpose of making the lady . . . a person of reputation."[42] Then Baron Krudener, the Russian Minister, gave a ball; and in the absence of Mrs. Ingham, the ranking Cabinet wife, the Baron escorted Mrs. Eaton. Madam Huygens, wife of the Dutch Minister and most decidedly of the moral faction, found herself on the arm of the Secretary of War and her resentment smoldered. Presently there was a party at the Dutch Legation to which Mrs. Eaton was not invited. In quick succession came parties given by Ingham, Branch, and Berrien; and to none of them was Peggy Eaton asked. Jackson charged a conspiracy and prepared for a showdown in his official family.[43] It had become "too evident to be doubted, that the consequence of this dispute in the social and fashionable world, is producing great political effects, and may very probably determine who shall be successor to the present chief magistrate."[44]

Toward the end of January Jackson determined to force the issue and tell the recalcitrant Cabinet members to invite Mrs. Eaton, at least to their large general parties, or resign. Colonel Richard M. Johnson, Kentucky Congressman who had the rare quality of being personally liked by everyone, was sent as an unofficial emissary to test out the reaction. Johnson went first to Ingham, whom he visited at the Treasury Department on January 27, 1830. The President, he said, was "like a roaring lion" in his excitement and was determined to have harmony among his advisers. By harmony the President apparently meant social intercourse with Peggy Eaton on the part of the families of the other members of the Cabinet. Ingham flatly denied the right or the power of the President to regulate the social life of his family, and resented the attempt. That evening, by arrangement, Johnson met with Ingham, Branch, and Berrien at the home of the Attorney General, where the same ground was gone over and the same answer given.[45] It was probably on January 29 that Jackson himself interviewed the three dissidents, who denied any combination or conspiracy to injure either Eaton or Jackson. They disclaimed also either the ability or the wish to compel their wives to visit Mrs. Eaton or anyone else, and they most emphatically denied the right of the President to ask it.[46]

The trio did not resign and they were not removed, although to remove them was undoubtedly Jackson's intention at one time. Report had it that Senators Hugh Lawson White and Edward Livingston, both of them devoted wholly to the President, warned him that if anything untoward happened to Branch, the Senators from North Carolina would go into opposition and the still-pending appointments would be lost.[47] It is quite probable that there was some such intervention, but it would not have influenced Jackson in the slightest if his mind had been made up. It is most probable that Van Buren, on one of his early morning rides with the President, cautioned prudence and counseled delay. It was not Branch, nor Berrien, nor even Ingham that the little New Yorker was trying to eliminate—it was Calhoun. For that purpose more batteries were needed, lest the whole campaign fail.

CHAPTER III

THE MAGICIAN AT WORK

1

To THOSE contesting for the Presidential succession the policies to be pursued by the Jackson administration were as important as its personnel. The Calhoun and Van Buren factions into which the party was divided each sought to commit the President to its own program, and each group tried to build up the necessary pressure to carry its measures by means of sectional and special-interest alliances. The Jackson administrations will be more intelligible if these rival policy demands are clearly understood.

Jackson himself had no policy, although he had many and rich prejudices.[1] He had been swept into office after an astonishingly negative campaign. He was against many things, but what he intended to do about them was exceedingly vague. He had assured the South Carolinians privately that he meant to "quiet the public Mind in regard to the tariff,"[2] but he carefully avoided any further explanation. In his inaugural address he pledged his administration to favor equally "the great interests of agriculture, commerce, and manufactures" and to promote internal improvements so far as that could be done "by the constitutional acts of the federal government." He promised not to confuse the delegated powers with the reserved rights of the states, made equally noncommittal references to national defense and to the Indians, and came down hard on reform. The address was well received on all sides, because everybody could read into it whatever he wanted; but Jackson had in fact promised nothing at all except to clean house among the Federal officeholders.[3]

There was thus a period of nine months between the inauguration and the meeting of the new Congress in December in which the diverse elements in the party struggled for intellectual dominance as well as for political control. It was all to the advantage of Van Buren.

As a Cabinet officer he was on the ground, while Major Lewis, who actually lived in the White House, was constantly at the President's elbow. Calhoun and his principal aides, on the other hand, had no excuse to remain in Washington when Congress was not in session.

The legislative program for which Van Buren had of necessity to stand was relatively simple. He was against internal improvements at Federal expense, and he was against the recharter of the Bank of the United States. A dozen years earlier, New York had been as clamorous as the West for Federal assistance in the construction of roads and canals; but the funds had not been forthcoming and the Erie Canal had been financed exclusively by the state. The venture was paying handsome dividends, and New Yorkers in consequence were unalterably opposed to the investment of Federal money in any transportation scheme that might offer competition for the Western trade. As for the Bank, New York City was already replacing Philadelphia as the financial center of the nation; but the Bank of the United States, with its millions in government deposits and its substantial profits on government business, was located in Philadelphia. The elimination of the Bank, whatever the scheme that replaced it, could not fail to increase materially the banking activities and the commercial operations generally of New York. Opposition to internal improvements and opposition to the Bank were the basic economic interests of New York and were therefore the cornerstones of Van Buren's policy.

They were also about as far as his policy went. On the questions of Indian removal and the distribution of the surplus revenue he was content to follow Jackson's lead. On the public lands he was noncommittal but probably prepared to bargain. It was the tariff that gave Van Buren his most difficult problem and was the key to the role he played during the first formative and crucial year of Jackson's Presidency. For the Red Fox, as Calhoun liked to call him, had skillfully forged his party out of an alliance of "planters and plain republicans"— a union of Northern and Southern votes in opposition to the Adams-Clay alliance of New England and the West. With the two sections in opposite camps on the tariff issue, any position that Jackson took would be wrong, and it was therefore to Van Buren's interest to keep the President from taking any stand at all until the sectional leaders could agree on a program. If they could not agree, then the North-South alliance was doomed and the party would have to be rebuilt on some other basis.

2

The precarious nature of the existing sectional alignment was also clear to Calhoun's supporters. In that day of relatively primitive transportation, economic interests were largely geographical, but the way men earned their living exercised the same influence it has always exerted over the way they cast their ballots. The cotton planter, dependent for his livelihood on the sale of a raw material which he produced in overabundance, restricted by the immobility of his capital structure with its emphasis on land and labor, and hemmed in by the fearful burden of his slaves, could see no common ground with the manufacturer who required cheap raw materials and a high price for finished goods.

From the beginning the tariff had been a sectional issue, and since 1824 an explosive one, intensifying personal and regional antagonisms. Opposition to the protective system was identified with the South as a geographical region, and Calhoun was identified with both, which made his political prospects in the North very slim indeed. The West, however, was a different proposition. There were, to be sure, manufacturing interests in Kentucky and Ohio, but it was in the Middle Atlantic States and New England that the real industrial dominance lay. The wealth of the West was in its land, and a large portion of that land—too large a portion, many believed—was the property not of the states but of the Federal Government. The West, by and large, wanted a liberalization of land policy in the interest of the actual settler, and cheap transportation by way of roads and canals. To get these things, Western politicians might be willing to aid in reducing the tariff. The demands of South and West were not in any fundamental conflict, and the basis of a working alliance was clearly there. Toward the end of 1828 it was actively promoted by Calhoun's partisans, and it was actually realized, at least in part, by the tariff compromise of 1833. It might have reached fuller realization at an earlier date but for the adroit interference of Daniel Webster in the famous debate with Hayne. But this is getting ahead of our story.

While Calhoun, back in South Carolina, was putting the finishing touches on the *Exposition and Protest* that was to make him the acknowledged leader of the Southern State Rights party, his friend and partisan, Governor Ninian Edwards of Illinois, was preparing the ground in the West for a union of Southern and Western interests. In his annual message to the state legislature on December 2, 1828, Edwards called for a new and more liberal land policy. He prefaced his case with a long and elaborate analysis of the relative powers and rights of Federal and state governments in a vein that would have been familiar food in South Carolina, and concluded that the sale of the public lands from Washington under any terms was an infringement of the sovereignty of the states. His solution was retrocession of all public lands to the states in which they lay.[4]

Calhoun's *Exposition* and Edwards' message were thereafter the texts by which Duff Green, who was both Calhoun's editor and Edwards' brother-in-law, pointed out the mutual advantages to South and West of a political union whose fruits would be free lands and free trade. If the alliance should also make Calhoun President, Green would be the last to object.[5]

The policy Calhoun would pursue was thus as clearly limned as that of Van Buren and was based, like Van Buren's, on the economic interests of his state and section. He opposed the protective tariff for the same reason he had opposed it since 1824: because it worked unnecessary hardship upon the South, strained the loyalty of those who suffered by it, and in the end must work the destruction of the Union. Because he hoped to attach the Western states to the cause of tariff reduction, he favored a more generous policy in the disposal of the public lands. Since the West favored and the South opposed internal improvements at Federal expense, Calhoun avoided that issue as carefully as Van Buren avoided the tariff. He opposed all schemes to distribute the surplus revenue among the states lest new vested interests thereby be created to profit by the perpetuation of the protective system. On the Bank of the United States he was completely neutral, though associated with the Bank in the minds of many because he had drafted and steered through the House its original charter. For the time being he regarded the question of recharter as irrelevant and took no position on it. It was therefore possible for his leading partisans—Hayne in the Senate and McDuffie in the House—to be arrayed on opposite sides.

The strategy of the two champions was implicit in the situation. Van Buren would seek to make the destruction of the Bank the leading issue of the administration and would try to force Calhoun into opposition. Calhoun would use every means at his command to commit Jackson unequivocally to tariff reform, and would shed no tears if Van Buren then suffered the consequences of his tariff vote of 1828. Van Buren would also try to undermine his rival in the South by associating the latter with internal improvements. Calhoun, for his part, would try to force the New Yorker's hand on the land question, before Van Buren could make any use of it himself.

Each moved through the summer and fall of 1829 to associate the party with his own views. While Southern politicians pondered Calhoun's *Exposition,* James Hamilton, Jr., visited the North in a last effort to secure support for tariff reform. The Charleston *Mercury* pointedly declared that principles were more important than Presidential politics, and the colorful Hamilton warned Van Buren that the South expected more substantial accomplishments than "the miracle of making Mrs. E— an honest woman."[6] At the same time Calhoun restudied the vexed problem of internal improvements in the hope of finding some constitutional avenue of escape from his dilemma.[7]

The Secretary of State was on more certain ground. He ignored the tariff issue and concentrated his considerable abilities on a flank attack against the Bank of the United States. In this he received unexpected assistance from the man who for seven years had been the Bank's able and ubiquitous president—shrewd, autocratic, dapper Nicholas Biddle. The charter of the Bank was not due to expire until 1836, but Biddle thought it not too early to begin arousing the interest of the administration in renewal. Allegations—probably planted—were already common that the branch banks had used their influence against Jackson's election, and Jackson himself was generally believed to be hostile to the institution.[8] Biddle moved quickly to place Jackson partisans on the various branch bank directorates and opened a correspondence with William B. Lewis, the ostensible purpose of which was to assure the President that the administration of the Bank was in no way tinged with party feelings. From that point forward Biddle seems to have been deliberately led on to believe that he had nothing to fear, and that he and his Bank enjoyed the entire approbation of the party in power.

Biddle was assured of the President's esteem and confidence, and Jackson was quoted to other Bank officials as expressing his gratitude for the co-operation given to the Treasury. The Bank president was soon informed through one of his Congressmen that "the *old fellow* will do justice to the Bank in his message for the handsome manner in which it assisted the Govt. in paying the last installment of the National debt"; and numerous evidences of Jackson's friendly attitude were followed by an interview between Biddle and the President late in November.[9] Again Jackson professed no hostility to the Bank of the United States and listened attentively to Biddle's scheme for paying the public debt—a scheme that involved recharter. This time Jackson admitted to a distrust of all banks as institutions and confessed to certain constitutional scruples, but Biddle had no doubt that these could be overcome. What Biddle did not know was that as early as May Jackson had submitted an alternative bank scheme to Felix Grundy, who was scheduled to replace Eaton in the Senate from Tennessee, or that Cambreleng had advised a personal friend to sell his Bank stock because of the hostility of the administration.[10]

3

The strategy of the opposition continued to be to publicize and to foster by every available means the growing breach between the followings of Van Buren and Calhoun. The two Democratic leaders themselves publicly denied the existence of a breach, and privately each tried to make the other believe he had noticed nothing amiss. Gradually, however, Van Buren came to be looked on as the actual political leader of the party. It was with the Secretary of State rather than with the President that questions of politics and patronage were discussed, and in the long run it was his views that were followed. The inauguration of the proscriptive policy coincided with the departure of Calhoun and the arrival of Van Buren in the Capital, and with a few notable exceptions it was Van Buren's men who were appointed to the vacated offices. The total number of removals made by Jackson was probably not excessive by the standards of later days. Figures are available only for the so-called "civil list" which excluded postal employees as well as those in military service, but such as they are they show removal of something less than a thousand out of more than ten thousand Federal officeholders. The changes were enough, however, to give Van Buren a firm grip on the machinery of the party.[11]

As soon as he was sure of his own ascendancy over the President, Van Buren began to apply pressure against Calhoun's leading supporters in Washington—Duff Green and Secretary of the Treasury Samuel D. Ingham—but it was done so skillfully that even the hypersensitive Green did not recognize it at first for what it was. Although legally the printer to Congress, Green discovered suddenly one morning that he was no longer printer to the Post Office. He sought an explanation and was told by Barry that he had been dropped on Ingham's recommendation. It was, of course, all a misunderstanding; but it served to set Green and Ingham to quarreling with each other as only two high-strung, jealous, overworked males can quarrel. The Van Burenites were boundlessly delighted, and Calhoun had to mediate between the pair.[12]

Even more significant than the tug of war in Washington was the distribution of patronage in the states. In Massachusetts the Calhoun faction, led by Theodore Lyman, was ignored and the appointments went to the rival group of David Henshaw and George Bancroft, comparative newcomers to the Jackson fold. The losers complained in bewilderment that the party was being wrecked, then tried to block Henshaw's confirmation as Collector of the Port of Boston. Isaac Hill's *New Hampshire Patriot* took up the cudgels for Henshaw, and the Calhoun group was eventually frozen out of the party.[13] In Illinois and Missouri the recommendations of the Calhoun wing of the party were also ignored, despite Jackson's promises to Duff Green. Green learned, after it was too late, that the President had somehow been led to regard the Calhoun leader in the West, Governor Edwards, as his enemy.[14] Even in South Carolina Calhoun could not control the patronage of his party. David R. Williams, with whom the Vice President had served in Congress, made the situation unmistakably clear to Van Buren when he wrote that Calhoun's friends in his own state, though able and active, were few in number. "I am anxious to make this impression on you, that Mr. Calhoun holds influence here, only because his opponents are not properly recognized at Washington. A display then, adverse to him, will enable us to triumph over his friends here. . . ."[15]

Kept abreast of events by partisans in Washington, Calhoun understood his danger, and he did not need Judge McLean to tell him where the threat to his influence lay, but he still hoped for better things from the President. "That he is in principle true to the grounds on which he was elected," he wrote McLean in September 1829, "I do not doubt, but that he may by the arts and intrigue of him to whom you refer, surrounded by some unprincipled individuals, in whom he has improperly placed confidence, be led to act in opposition to the principles, on which he has been promoted, is not at all impossible. In fact I see many reasons to fear that such may be the fact, tho I am resolved, that nothing short of the clearest demonstration, shall convince me of it."[16] That there might be no mistake about it, he took pains to recall once more to Jackson's mind what South Carolina expected of him. The course of the administration to date was reviewed in the Charleston *Mercury* for September 30, concluding with a forecast which was also a warning. The President, predicted the editor, will "uphold the States . . . in their just powers, sedulously avoiding encroachments on their rights. . . . He will regard the preservation of the Union as the polar star of his conduct, and discarding local and sectional feeling, be governed only by equal justice to all the great interests of the nation. . . . Let him do so, and the people will uphold him. . . ." Duff Green devoted a column and a half to reprinting the article in the *Telegraph,* where Jackson could not miss it.[17]

4

Jackson's first annual message to Congress, delivered on December 8, 1829, indicated how completely the President had fallen in with the desires of Van Buren as to policy, and how far he had swung away from everything the South believed it had been promised in return for its votes. By way of renewing Calhoun's warning as to what South Carolina at least expected, Duff Green reprinted in the *Telegraph* for December 4 the annual message of Governor Stephen D. Miller, with its recapitulation of all of South Carolina's protests and its explicit expression of confidence that the tariff would be reduced. The President himself was deeply preoccupied at the moment with the affairs of Peggy Eaton, but his message was already in draft. It was not sent to the public printer the customary three or four days in advance, however, but arrived only barely in time to be printed in the newspapers on the day of its delivery.[18] The error, if error it was, meant that members of Congress were delayed in receiving copies of the message and its supporting documents. But it meant also that there could be no leak through Duff Green to any of the Calhoun faction, and so no chance that the President could be persuaded to change his mind.

The tariff question could not be avoided but was touched on with great caution. The President recommended nothing that in the long run could be satisfactory to South Carolina. The existing schedule of duties, he declared, had proved less beneficial to the manufacturers than had been hoped, and less harmful to agriculture and commerce than had been feared. Legislation such as this, however, which affected basic economic and sectional interests, should be altered only after the most careful consideration, divorced from local prejudices and partisan feeling. A beginning might safely be made by gradually reducing the duties on articles not coming into competition with domestic products. Only two such articles suggested themselves to the President: tea and coffee. On these he proposed some reduction in the existing tariff, but that was all.

The financial position of the government appeared to be excellent, and the public debt, already reduced to forty-eight million dollars, was being retired at the rate of about twelve million dollars a year. It would soon be necessary, therefore, to turn the surplus revenue into some useful channel, for Jackson could foresee no possible adjustment of the tariff that would not still bring more money into the Treasury than would be needed for the legitimate expenses of government. The most beneficial way to use the surplus would certainly be for the construction of roads and canals, but there were serious objections to such internal improvements by the Federal Government. Many thought them unconstitutional, and at best they were a fruitful source of legislative discord. Jackson therefore recommended that the surplus be distributed among the states in the ratio of their representation in Congress. If such a measure were unconstitutional, he proposed that it be specifically authorized by amendment.[19]

Then Jackson got to the core of the policy he had made his own—the issue that was most important to Van Buren, Kendall, and Lewis, and to which they meant to nail the battle flag of the administration. The clerks who read the message and the Senators and Representatives who listened were probably all of them weary by the time the critical point was reached, only four paragraphs from the end, but it was calculated to recapture wandering thoughts. The charter of the Bank of the United States, the President announced, would expire in 1836, but so great were the evils of sudden change in the financial world that the question of renewal could not be raised too soon. "Both the constitutionality and the expediency of the law creating this bank are well questioned by a large portion of our fellow citizens; and it must be admitted by all, that it has failed in the great end of establishing a uniform and sound currency."[20]

The message was quickly recognized as representing Van Buren's views, if it was not actually from his pen,[21] and members of the opposition speculated whether Jackson would recognize a line of it in ten days' time.[22] Within the party itself the document served only to emphasize the already existing cleavage. The Southern wing of the Democracy, though it praised the message, was soon forced to admit that there was no hope of tariff revision from Jackson.[23] Conservatives were shaken by the unprovoked attack on the Bank of the United States, six years before its charter was to expire and before the Bank itself had asked for renewal. Most shaken of all was Nicholas Biddle, who had been repeatedly assured, even while the message must have been in the writing, that the President was favorably disposed. Biddle decided to attribute to Jackson himself the views expressed, and to regard them "as the honest tho' erroneous notions of one who intends well";[24] but Alexander Hamilton, son of the old Federalist leader and brother of the man who probably wrote that part of Jackson's message, warned the Bank president to have no confidence in Van Buren. "As an aspirant to the Chief Magistracy, he is without principle, and totally destitute of sincerity." Hamilton had anticipated the unfavorable reference to the Bank but he realized that nothing could be done about it. His advice now was to be cautious and conciliatory.[25]

The advice was wasted. Jackson had already girded his loins for battle; and when the old Hero had marked his foe, he brooked neither caution nor conciliation. Both were evidences of weakness.

5

Calhoun did not take his seat as presiding officer of the Senate until December 14, 1829. He made no comments on the political situation as he found it on his arrival in the Capital and offered no criticism of the President's message, but he was plainly disturbed.[26] He did not know all the details, but the ascendancy of Van Buren was too clear to be missed. Jackson had been in poor health for some months, though only his intimates realized how seriously ill he really was,[27] and the Secretary of State seemed to handle the old gentleman like a ventriloquist's dummy. Even casual observers thought Calhoun could reach the Presidency only by the General's death, but that route seemed not unlikely.[28]

During the humid summer and fall months when Washington was deserted by all who could escape, Jackson had been adroitly turned against Calhoun; and before Congress met in December the President was ready to endorse Van Buren as his successor. He said as much to James A. Hamilton on December 3, but indicated also his awareness that Calhoun would not accept that eventuality without a struggle.[29] As the members of Congress gathered during the next few days, each looked at the portents and drew his own conclusions. Everywhere, among friends and foes, politicians and publicists, partisans and neutrals, the question was discussed, and there was little difference in the opinions reached. "The Secretary of State by his address, and attentions to *Madame,* Barry and the President, will undoubtedly give Calhoun and McClean much trouble. . . . I assure you the little fellow is managing with great address, and making friends on all sides."[30] "Van Buren is making rapid strides . . . the Crawfordites are falling in to him generally & rapidly . . . Calhoun is going down. . . ."[31]

Van Buren was too skillful a politician to rely on "address" or "attentions to *Madame*." None knew better than he that the real bricks and mortar of any political structure are patronage and perquisites —the offices at the disposal of the winner, the public funds to be expended by the party in power, and the legislation that may be passed for the benefit of special interests. The executive appointments of the Federal Government had been since April or May dispensed as Van Buren directed; and the patronage in New York State, still controlled by the Albany Regency, was being so distributed as to exclude all Jackson men who would not accept the Secretary of State as the successor.[32]

It was "circumstances connected with [New York] city and state politics" that first brought Van Buren's candidacy into the open, probably against his judgment. The announcement was made on December 19, 1829, by the New York *Courier and Enquirer*. Mordecai Noah's *Enquirer* had recently merged with the *Courier* of James Watson Webb, and the two were joint publishers of the enlarged paper. The arrangement was, however, that Noah, who was sympathetic toward Calhoun, was to have nothing to do with the paper's editorial policy, and he soon withdrew altogether.[33] Webb was deeply involved with the Van Buren faction, and after Jackson's first annual message he found it necessary to "settle beyond all manner of doubt the course to be pursued by this paper during the next presidential contest." The *Courier and Enquirer,* therefore, came out on December 19 with an editorial asserting flatly that Jackson would seek a second term and that Martin Van Buren of New York was the logical choice to succeed the General in 1836. He charged also that Duff Green and the *Telegraph* were opposed to the administration.[34]

Green was taken by surprise, but lost no time in aligning himself with the administration on its major policy issue, even before he quarreled with its candidate. On December 21 the *Telegraph* denounced the Bank of the United States and Green explained that "upon the expediency of re-chartering this bank, we differ with many of our political friends." In January he began publishing a series of anti-Bank articles, although he was himself in debt to the institution to the tune of some twelve thousand dollars.[35] The day following his first attack on the Bank, Green took issue with the *Courier and Enquirer*. Webb's editorial, he thought, could not fail to be regarded "as a formal and authorized annunciation of Mr. Van Buren, as a candidate for the Presidency. We regret it because its tendency will be to encourage the hopes of those who, relying on a division in the Republican party, calculate upon holding the balance of power. . . . The article is, in every sense, indiscreet, because it cannot benefit the individual whom it professes to serve, and is directly in conflict with his known opinions."[36] In both positions Green was correct. The opposition rejoiced to see this additional evidence of internal dissension in the Jackson ranks; while no less a Van Buren supporter than Major Lewis termed Webb's article "indiscreet and *ill-timed*" and calculated to do the little Secretary no good.[37]

Lewis was certainly in position to know whereof he spoke, for it was at this very time that he was persuading Jackson to commit himself on paper in Van Buren's behalf, and it would have wrecked his plans irrevocably if the jealous Hero had conceived the idea that the New Yorker was setting up shop for himself. By December Jackson's illness had begun to assume the character of confirmed dropsy, and his intimates became seriously alarmed. The thought of Calhoun taking over by default the machine they had built so painstakingly for Van Buren was distasteful in the extreme. In the belief that Jackson's name might still prove magic at the polls, even if the General himself were dead, Lewis got the President to write a letter endorsing Van Buren to one of his old friends, with the understanding that it was to be used if needed in a Presidential campaign. The letter, addressed to Judge Overton of Tennessee, minced no words:

"Permit me here to say of Mr. Van Buren that I have found him every thing that I could desire him to be, and believe him not only deserving *my* confidence, but the *confidence* of the *Nation.* Instead of his being selfish and intriguing, as has been represented by some of his opponents, I have ever found him frank, open, candid, and manly. As a Counsellor he is *able* and *prudent,* Republican in his principles and one of the most pleasant men to do business with I ever saw. He, my dear friend, is not only well qualified, but desires to fill the highest office in the gift of the people who, in him, will find a true friend and safe depository of their rights and liberty. I wish I could say as much for Mr. Calhoun and some of his friends. You know the confidence I once had in that gentleman. However, of *him* I desire not now to speak; but I have a right to believe that most of the troubles, vexations and difficulties I have had to encounter, since my arrival in this City, have been occasioned by his friends. But for the present let this suffice."[38]

All this was, of course, behind the scenes, but the external evidence as to the attitude and intentions of the President and the dominant element in his party continued to pile up. Virgil Maxcy, still without office, was roundly beaten for clerk of the House on December 7.[39] Jackson let Webb's editorial pass without comment. The Boston *Bulletin,* organ of the Henshaw faction in Massachusetts, accused Duff Green of deliberately misprinting the report of the Secretary of War to make Eaton look bad.[40] Former Senator Henry Baldwin of Pennsylvania, outspoken high-tariff man with whom Duff Green had recently been in acrimonious controversy, was named to the Supreme Court in January and was confirmed with only the two Senators from South Carolina voting against him.[41] At the same time a determined effort was being made by Van Buren's supporters to associate Calhoun, in Jackson's mind and in popular opinion, with the Bank of the United States.[42]

Calhoun was undoubtedly approached by some of the National Republicans, who realized that the defection of only a part of the South Carolinian's following in the Senate would throw the administration into a minority in the upper house;[43] but the Vice President was not yet ready to leave his party or to admit that he had been driven from it. He continued to believe that Jackson, whom he regarded as relatively weak and ignorant, was personally sound but under selfish influences which might yet be broken. There were, after all, enough gains on the Calhoun side of the ledger to give hope to one whose temperament was always sanguine where his own prospects were concerned. The Ingham faction had won the governorship in Pennsylvania;[44] and in the equally important state of Virginia Calhoun's popularity was so great that Thomas Ritchie dared not follow his inclination and bring the powerful Richmond *Enquirer* out for Van Buren.[45] In the Senate Tazewell was chairman of the Committee on Foreign Relations, and Hayne of the Committee on Naval Affairs; while the House Committee on Ways and Means, where revenue legislation including tariff revision would originate, continued to be headed by George McDuffie.

It was something in the nature of a defiance when on January 8, 1830, fifteenth anniversary of the famous battle that made Andrew Jackson President, and the day of Peggy Eaton's greatest humiliation, Duff Green reprinted excerpts from a recently issued American annual called the *Cabinet and Talisman*. From the sketch of Calhoun two paragraphs were quoted, including reference to the Vice President's "ardent patriotism" and his "stern and manly independence." "On important subjects," the sketch continued, "his opinions are formed with caution, and after indefatigable research; but once formed, he adheres to them with a firmness which nothing can shake. . . ."[46]

CHAPTER IV

THE GREAT DEBATE

1

On the subject of the protective tariff Calhoun's mind was fully made up, and he was not to be moved from the single overmastering purpose that had guided his course since 1824. By one means or another the tariff must be reduced before the Union itself was destroyed. It was clear from Jackson's first annual message that there would be no tariff reform initiated by the administration. The nullification doctrine, carefully formulated by Calhoun in the *South Carolina Exposition and Protest* of December 1828, was still a theory, to be put into action only as a last resort when all other means had failed. The day when it would be used was drawing closer, but there was still to be tried the time-honored method of political bargaining between interest groups.

The South, alone, was a hopeless minority, with interests sharply differentiated from those of the remainder of the country by the existence of slavery. Her salvation, and her very survival, were becoming more and more dependent on some form of sectional alliance as other regions outstripped her in population and territorial growth. The union of "planters and plain republicans" conceived by Van Buren in 1826 had for all practical purposes collapsed when the plain Republicans voted for the tariff of 1828. On that issue the South could not compromise, but neither could New England nor Pennsylvania. It was therefore to the West that the antitariff leaders turned when Jackson declined to make tariff reform an administration policy.[1]

In the West the paramount issue was land: cheap public land for settlers; no restrictions on settlement; and the extension, by fair means or foul, of the southwestern boundary to include Texas.[2] Jackson himself was deeply interested in the acquisition of Texas,[3] and was not unsympathetic toward the easing of land restrictions. It was therefore possible that a deal between West and South might win administration support in spite of Van Buren. The ground had already been carefully laid the previous winter, with just such a contingency in view. A little more than a week after the reading of the

President's message, Thomas Hart Benton of Missouri opened the fight in the Senate with a bill to graduate the price of the public lands.[4] Before it could be debated, however, a better opportunity was offered for getting the South and West together.

The occasion for the launching of the new alliance was a resolution offered by Senator Samuel A. Foote of Connecticut on December 29, 1829. Foote wanted the Senate Committee on Public Lands to "inquire into the expediency of limiting for a certain period the sales of the public lands to such lands only as have heretofore been offered for sale, and are subject to entry at the minimum price."[5] The resolution in itself was innocent enough and probably had no ulterior purpose behind it. Yet it served to touch off one of the most spectacular debates ever heard in the Senate—a debate that continued at intervals for five months, with more publicity than anything Congress had done since the Missouri Compromise, and with results almost if not quite as far-reaching.

The resolution was debated briefly on December 30, with Benton challenging even the reference to committee of what he termed "a resolution to inquire into the expediency of committing a great injury upon the new States in the West." After an interchange between Benton, Foote, and John Holmes of Maine, consideration was postponed, unusual as that procedure was where a mere resolution of inquiry was concerned.[6] The possibilities of Foote's resolution had been realized, but time for preparation was required. Before the discussion was resumed on January 13, a bill to grant pre-emption rights to settlers on the public lands had been debated briefly and passed by a strictly sectional vote of 29 to 12. The dominantly manufacturing states of New Jersey and Delaware lined up with New England, while New York and Maryland split.[7] It was the South and West against the East, with only the Senators from Pennsylvania and two or three from New England voting the party line rather than sectional interest. From this vote on pre-emption the Senate turned at once to Foote's resolution, but the discussion remained of an exploratory character. It was not until January 18, 1830, that the Great Debate got under way in earnest.

2

Benton led off for the West. He was a striking figure, of about average height and portly, with big head, thick sandy hair, and bushy side whiskers. Dignity and prodigious learning were his chief characteristics. He normally spoke softly, though with distinct emphasis; but when he worked himself into a passion of indignation he was like a vengeful demon, with lightning flashing from his gray eyes and words pouring from his lips with incredible fluency.[8] He began calmly enough, arguing that the resolution if acted on would check emigration to the West and restrict the settlement of the Western states. Only when he was well warmed to his subject did he launch his real thunderbolt. He accused New England and the other Northern manufacturing states of deliberately trying to limit the settlement of the West in order to keep at hand a supply a cheap labor for their factories. Adroitly the Missouri Senator, who had himself voted for the tariff of 1828 and had been a consistent supporter of the protective system, tied the resolution to the tariff and denounced them both as inimical to West and South alike. The tariff, by stimulating artificially the manufactures of the East, was a subsidy operating to prevent emigration to the West; the proposed restrictions on the sale of public lands would serve the same purpose by more direct means. "A most complex scheme of injustice, which taxes the South to injure the West, to pauperize the poor of the North." Then Benton brought his great learning to bear on the history of Western settlement; and wherever he found some subtle move to the injury of the West he loved, he found New England at the bottom of it. The action of Massachusetts in retaining her lands in Maine was contrasted with Virginia's generosity in giving up her own princely domain for the good of the whole. By the time Benton was ready to yield the floor he had built a strong case for the common interests of West and South and had cast doubts on the good faith of the Northeast.[9]

The next day John Holmes of Maine defended New England; and Levi Woodbury, staunch Jacksonian Senator from New Hampshire, tried to make peace between the sections. A motion to amend the original resolution was ruled out of order by Calhoun just before handsome, youthful-looking Robert Y. Hayne of South Carolina asked for the floor. Courteously but firmly Hayne thrust aside extraneous issues. The real question was one of the policy to be adopted toward the public lands. Congress had so far avoided a decision, but it could not be avoided much longer. The lands could be used to bring prosperity to the regions in which they lay, or they could be used to bring into the national Treasury an accumulation of revenue which would have no legitimate use and would therefore inevitably be used for purposes of corruption. He passed over lightly, as though it were unthinkable, the possibility that settlement of the West might be deliberately restricted in order to provide cheap labor for the factories of the East.

Hayne's solution for the public-land problem was a modification of that suggested by Governor Edwards in December of 1828. Settlers in the thirteen original colonies had received their lands for no more than a token payment: a penny or a peppercorn. Hayne wanted the new states to receive equally favorable terms. Since the lands had been pledged as security for the public debt, he would make no change in the law until the debt was paid. After that event, which all agreed was no more than four years distant, he thought the states should be free to dispose of the lands in whatever manner would be best suited to their needs. As fast as settlement in any state progressed beyond a given point—say when a specified percentage of the public lands had been disposed of—Hayne would sell the remainder of the lands to the state for a nominal sum, high enough to reimburse the Federal Government for its trouble, low enough so that the state would not be long in debt. He cited Ohio as a state that had already reached the point he referred to.[10]

Hayne's speech was more effective than Benton's because he had maintained throughout a conciliatory tone, had not attacked any person or section or class, and had offered a constructive solution for the problem under discussion. He had also indicated without being crude about it just what the South was willing to concede to the West in return for tariff reform. That the West would return the favor was implicit in Benton's somewhat heavy-handed opening broadside. The representatives in the Senate of those who profited by maintaining the protective system saw their danger and moved to counterattack.

Daniel Webster, who had been pleading a case in the Supreme Court, entered the Senate chamber while Hayne was speaking. He was urged by leading members of his party—Bell of New Hampshire, Chambers of Maryland, and his Massachusetts colleague, Nathaniel Silsbee—to make an immediate reply.[11] It was actually the following day, January 20, 1830, that Webster delivered what has come down to us as his first reply to Hayne. It was not, however, in any legitimate sense a reply at all, much less an answer to Hayne. It was a deliberately provocative attack on the South in general and South Carolina in particular, with every point carefully selected to be irritating.[12]

In so far as Webster was repelling charges against his section, they were charges leveled by Benton, not by Hayne; but he had his reasons for singling out the South Carolinian as his opponent. He denied categorically that New England had ever been hostile to the West; he credited the growth and prosperity of the Northwestern States to the exclusion of slavery by the Ordinance setting up the Northwest Territory and calmly attributed the Ordinance itself, which everyone knew to have been the work of Thomas Jefferson, to Nathan Dane of Massachusetts; and finally he seized upon the tariff, which he rightly said was at the bottom of the whole affair. Directing his remarks rather at Calhoun in the Vice President's chair than to Hayne or Benton, Webster recalled that the South had passed the tariff of 1816 while New England opposed, and that his section had continued to oppose the policy for another ten years. He made much of the Southern shift of ground and alluded in unmistakable terms to the excitement that had prevailed in South Carolina since 1827. "I know that there are some persons in the part of the country from which the honorable member comes, who habitually speak of the Union in terms of indifference, or even of disparagement. . . . They significantly declare, that it is time to calculate the value of the Union. . . ."[13]

What Webster had in fact done was not to reply to anybody, but adroitly to change the subject. Benton and Hayne had laid the basis for a political rapprochement of West and South based on tariff reduction and free or virtually free lands in the newer states. Such an alliance would necessarily exclude New England, just as the South had been consciously excluded by the deal between New England and the West in 1825—the deal that put Adams in the White House, Clay in the State Department, and the Tariff of Abominations on the statute books.[14] Like Hayne and Benton, Webster represented the economic interest of his section, and it was therefore up to him to block this new antitariff alliance if he could. The method he chose was a variation of the *argumentum ad hominem:* to discredit the South by crying "Treason!"[15]

3

Webster's purpose was to provoke the confident and impetuous Hayne into a debate on the constitutional issue at stake between the State Rights theorists and the advocates of national supremacy.

Benton followed Webster on January 20 and was entitled to the floor when the subject was resumed after other business was disposed of on Thursday, the twenty-first. When the hour came, however, Chambers of Maryland moved a postponement so that Webster might plead a case in the Supreme Court. After the unexpected and uncalled-for attack Webster had made on South Carolina the day before, Hayne was not disposed to be gracious and he exercised his privilege of objecting. Webster was then present; he presumed he could arrange to remain. "The gentleman had discharged his fire in the face of the Senate. He hoped he would now afford him the opportunity of returning the shot." Webster could do no less, and he arranged his affairs while Benton held the floor another half hour or so. Then Hayne began. According to a Congressman from New York, who had deserted his own seat in the House to listen, Hayne "bore down in a strain of eloquence, alternately grave, indignant, and witty, upon the Senator from Massachusetts, the like of which I have never witnessed, and which, as I thought, completely demolished him. Mr. Webster evidently suffered. He seemed uneasy in his seat; sometimes he took notes—then audibly dissented, anon assented, and, occasionally, leaned back in his chair."[16] After an hour or two, the Senate adjourned until Monday, January 25.

Over the long week end both men had ample time for preparation, but neither really needed it. Webster had maneuvered Hayne into a defense of nullification; but Hayne had been expounding, explaining, and defending nullification ever since Calhoun had devised the doctrine in the summer of 1828. Webster, for his part, meant to refute the arguments he knew Hayne would advance in terms of the same doctrine of national sovereignty that he had expounded over the past ten years in half a dozen leading cases before the Supreme Court—a doctrine that Chief Justice John Marshall had already read into the Constitution. Everyone knew what was coming, and both men undoubtedly received suggestions from their friends. One tale has Justice Story offering to help Webster prepare his speech and quotes the black-browed champion's reply: "Give yourself no uneasiness, Judge Story; I will grind him as fine as a pinch of snuff."[17] There were also rumors of consultations between Hayne and the Vice President,[18] and it would indeed have been amazing if there had not been consultations.

By Monday when the Senate met again, the impending clash had been widely advertised. The galleries and the floor itself were crowded, predominantly with gaily dressed ladies. They sat on the steps below the Vice President's chair, and they stood behind it. They crowded the aisles, and one politically minded belle even sat in Hayne's seat while the gallant South Carolina Senator was speaking from the floor.[19] Yet even Hayne's audience did not compare with the multitude that jammed the chamber to hear Webster deliver his second reply. Undoubtedly the greatest orator of his day, Webster was a legend in his own time; and as the period of the debate lengthened out, people came to hear him from as far away as Boston.[20]

Hayne finished what he had to say on January 25. He was still courteous and polished and his touch was deft, but he replied to Webster's attack on South Carolina and her political doctrines in kind. In his first speech Hayne had "questioned no man's opinion . . . impeached no man's motives . . . charged no party, or State, or section of the country, with hostility to any other."[21] But Webster had shown no such restraint, and so Hayne did in his second speech what he had been accused of doing in his first. He went back to the Alien and Sedition Laws of the elder Adams and to the vigorous protests of Virginia and Kentucky; he castigated New England and Federalism generally for the part they played in the War of 1812; he recalled in biting terms the Hartford Convention and Webster's attachment to the party that called it. And on the tariff he quoted with high words of praise Webster's own great antitariff speech of 1824. Even the subject of the peculiar institution of the South Hayne did not evade, but he made his discussion of it serve the purpose of casting the slave trade in the teeth of New England.

Through the wit and scorn and fire of the argument ran a persistent thread of constitutional reasoning, developed and built up at last to show that the so-called South Carolina doctrine was indeed the Republican creed of 1798 and, short of arms, was the last resort of freemen against despotic power. If the Federal Government had the exclusive right to prescribe its own limits, then it was in fact unlimited, the guarantees of the Constitution were worthless paper, and a partisan majority was absolute ruler of the land.

Hayne's conclusion was at once a repudiation of Webster's disunion insinuations and a stirring defense of South Carolina. "In all the efforts that have been made by South Carolina to resist the unconstitutional laws which Congress has extended over them, she has kept steadily in view the preservation of the Union, by the only means by which she believes it can be preserved—a firm, manly, and steady resistance against usurpation." The orator reviewed the measures that he held inimical to the interests of his state and that must soon "involve the whole South in irretrievable ruin," but denied that even these, disastrous as they had been, were the chief cause of complaint. The real issue was "the principle involved in the contest—a principle which, substituting the discretion of Congress for the limitations of the constitution, brings the States and the people to the feet of the Federal Government, and leaves them nothing they can call their own. . . ."[22]

A part of the lore of the Webster-Hayne debates is the tradition that Calhoun, from the Vice President's chair, sent notes and suggestions to Hayne.[23] There was no reason why he should not have done so, save perhaps his own strict interpretation of the functions and duties of the Vice President, but it is not likely that he did. There had been ample time for Calhoun to go over the whole ground with Hayne before the speech was made. The speech, moreover, gives every evidence of being carefully planned, not thrown together on the floor in the process of delivery. Though a shade less skilled in dialectics, Hayne was a more accomplished orator than Calhoun; he had his measure of conceit and would almost inevitably have resented and ignored any messages the Vice President might have been disposed to send him. More important still is the fact that Hayne slipped up on one essential point in the State Rights argument, which he would never have done had Calhoun really been coaching him from the side lines: he referred to the states and the Federal Government as joint parties to the constitutional compact, whereas the doctrine of state sovereignty could be logically defended only on the ground that the states alone were parties and the Federal Government the creature set up by them.[24]

4

Webster began his magnificent and justly famous second reply on January 26, concluding it the following day. Let no one doubt that the "Godlike Daniel" knew exactly what he was doing and what effect he meant to produce by it. He called his speech "in the strictest sense, unexpected, & occasional";[25] but he had spent much of the summer studying the constitutional argument, quite probably with Calhoun's *South Carolina Exposition and Protest* as a point of departure. He also took the precaution to ask Joseph Gales, senior editor of the *National Intelligencer,* to report the speech personally; and he spent almost a month revising the text as so reported before he consented to publication.[26] In short, Webster knew, and had probably known since the Missouri Compromise, that the economic interests of his section could be secured only by a theory of the Constitution that made the national legislature sovereign over the states. He had already won his case in the Supreme Court but he had yet to win it at the bar of public opinion. He was prepared to appeal to the public whenever a suitable opportunity offered; but the boldly proclaimed alliance of South and West to reduce the tariff and give away the public lands showed him that he could wait no longer, so he made his own opportunity.

The second reply to Hayne was addressed not to the Senate, nor even exclusively to the gallery. It was addressed to the people of the United States. It was a superb appeal to patriotism, so well done and so perfectly adapted to its purpose that it has been declaimed by schoolboys and Fourth of July orators ever since. The first day was devoted to refutation of the charges Hayne had advanced against Webster and against New England, and "considering the hardness of his case, he acquitted himself with honor."[27] Even as Hayne had quoted the Webster of 1824 to demolish the Webster of 1830, so Webster hurled at Hayne the Calhoun of 1816. At one point he shook his finger at the Vice President and addressed him directly in a deep rumbling voice that sent a shiver through the audience. So pointed was the allusion that Calhoun cut in to ask if he understood "the gentleman from Massachusetts to say that the person now occupying the chair of the Senate has changed his opinions on the subject of Internal Improvements?"[28] Webster quickly denied that he knew of any such change, but he had made his point as neatly as Hayne had done when Webster's tariff views were brought up.

It was the last third of Webster's speech—the final two hours on January 27—that was devoted to the constitutional question. All the rest had been no more than a build-up. It was for these two hours that he had so long and so carefully prepared. The immediate audience was small, though far larger than the Senate chamber should normally have held; but it served as a testing ground for the larger audience that lay scattered from Maine to Florida and from the Atlantic seaboard to the Great Plains, already being overrun by this restless, confident, enduring people. The farm hand in Illinois, the woodsman in Michigan, the factory worker in Rhode Island, the tradesmen, sailors, professors, idlers, and laborers of all descriptions and degrees who pursued their callings in the far corners of the land could not hear the vibrant thunder of a voice that carried conviction whether it uttered words or not. They could not be hypnotized by the great, sunken hazel eyes that made it all seem so clear and easy you failed to follow the reasoning. Many of them could not even read; but the message would reach them all, eventually.

Friend and foe alike, all who heard the speech knew it for a masterpiece, destined to be "preserved and admired by succeeding ages."[29] Few among them, perhaps, recognized that the thrilling final words —"Liberty *and* Union, now and forever, one and inseparable"—had been suggested by a similar phrase in Calhoun's tariff speech of 1816.[30]

The Vice President's gavel broke the spell. Hayne was on his feet in an instant and began his reply to Webster's constitutional argument; but the hour was late and the audience tired and surfeited. It was an anticlimax and Hayne cut his speech to a skeleton, only filling it out later for the record.

So far as the two giants were concerned the debate was over, and sentiment was divided as to which had the better of the exchange. Everyone agreed that each had added to his stature and increased his fame, but only those who were blinded by personal devotion or prejudice were so bold as to claim complete victory for either.[31] The question that lay back of it all, however, was by no means settled; and the debate continued at intervals until Foote's resolution was finally tabled on May 21. Before it was over, nearly every member of the Senate had aired his views and every leading topic of the day had been discussed. In furtherance of the alliance of South and West, McDuffie in the House introduced a bill to reduce the tariff on February 5, shortly after Benton in the Senate had reaffirmed the bargain in his reply to Webster.[32] Benton followed up on February 23, with a bill to abolish unnecessary duties and relieve the people from a sixteen-million-dollar tax burden.[33] There were varying opinions as to the ultimate success of the new sectional alignment, but little disagreement as to its existence or its purpose.[34] It had in fact been developed to a point that spelled danger for Martin Van Buren as well as for the New England manufacturers. The little Secretary could not permit such an alliance to receive the sanction of the administration, and he did not permit it.[35]

5

The Great Debate, as the contemporary papers were already calling it, had two distinct aspects. One of these was political: a realignment of parties and sections to favor the economic interests of the South and West, which its sponsors hoped might incidentally cut out Van Buren and put Calhoun in the White House. The other was ideological. This aspect of the debate was not anticipated by those who began it, but was forced on them by Webster and became in his hands a vehicle for defeating, at least in part, the political purpose intended.

It was primarily the portion of the debate in which Webster and Hayne were the principals that served to high light and contrast two rival theories of government. Others contributed at later stages, some of them brilliantly, but for our purposes the arguments of Webster and Hayne are of primary significance.[36] Webster wanted a central government strong enough to pass and enforce laws in the interest of the majority; Hayne wanted a government so checked and balanced that the interests of the minority would be secure. The distinction was as old as Aristotle and the terms of the argument as old as the Constitution of the United States, which each side interpreted in its own way. The debate was only a continuation of the discussions in the Constitutional Convention of 1787, of the issue between Hamilton and Jefferson, of the contest for power in the War of 1812, of the struggle over the Missouri Compromise. The whole ground was even then being reviewed by as distinguished a body of men as ever sat in a representative assembly, meeting in Richmond for the purpose of revising the Virginia State Constitution.[37] The major arguments had been worked over again and again in pamphlets, speeches, books, newspapers, and courts of law; but they remained real and important because the proponents on both sides saw their ultimate economic prosperity or ruin as the stake.

The prosperity of New England had in a short five years become identified with manufactures. Her once dominant financial interests had been subordinated to those of New York and Philadelphia, and in growing measure her ocean trade was also being absorbed by the sturdy adolescent colossus astride Manhattan Island; but each loss had been countered by further growth in manufactures, stimulated by successive additions to the tariff. The tariff had been enacted by the general government, but its constitutionality had been challenged. It was necessary to New England's prosperity that the power be upheld. So Webster argued that sovereignty, in the legal sense of power to make and enforce law, belonged to the general government and was exercised legitimately by the national legislature. To make his reasoning stand up, he had to argue that the government was not set up by a compact between the states but sprang directly from the people. His language was almost identical with the words of John Marshall's decision in M'Culloch vs. Maryland—language that Webster himself may well have used in pleading that very case. "The government of the Union is emphatically and truly a government of the people. In form and substance it emanates from them. Its powers are granted by them, and are to be exercised directly on them and for their benefit."[38] This historic decision had just preceded the contest over the admission of Missouri to the Union and had been savagely assailed in Virginia and the South, with Jefferson himself taking the lead.[39] For all the weight of authority and talent against it, the decision had not been upset, and Webster in 1830 could thus argue from precedent that his view was the law of the land. It followed naturally that if the government was created by and acted directly on the people, the will of the majority, as expressed through their representatives in Congress, must prevail.

The position Hayne took was essentially that of Jefferson and Madison in the Virginia and Kentucky Resolutions of 1798 and 1799; the position of John Taylor of Caroline who rationalized the case against the Supreme Court in M'Culloch vs. Maryland; the position Calhoun had taken in the *South Carolina Exposition and Protest.* It was also, ironically, the position Webster himself had taken at the time of the embargo. The theory of the dominant majority against which Hayne contended simply meant that any minority interest must combine with others to form a majority or must face eventual destruction. The planting interest which controlled South Carolina and the South in general could never hope to command a majority in the House of Representatives, even though the Missouri

Compromise gave it an uneasy equality in the Senate; and it was therefore doomed unless the sovereignty of the majority could be successfully challenged. So far, all challenges had failed, but now a combination offered that might for the time being put the actual power in Southern hands. So Webster, to block the combination, attacked once more the political philosophy of the minority. It was inevitable that his own concept of government should be challenged in turn.

The State Rights argument was in essence a defense of minority interests. Its proponents reasoned that the Constitution was a compact between the states, each of which had been sovereign and independent in its own right before the Constitution was ratified. By that compact a general government had been created, but it was a government of limited and specifically delegated powers: a confederacy rather than an organic state. Since it rested on a compact, the parties thereto had in the last resort the right to judge of infractions and to interpose their own original sovereignty whenever the joint agreement was violated by an unauthorized exercise of power on the part of the general government. The progressively rising tariffs had seriously impaired and now threatened to destroy the economic prosperity of the South. So the Southern leaders applied the State Rights formula, declared the tariff to be a violation of the compact, and threatened to interpose to prevent its enforcement if it were not modified by Congress.

Like the Missouri Compromise debates of a decade earlier, the contest arising out of Foote's resolution tended to emphasize sectional differences and antagonisms. For the principal contestants were separated by a geographical line that closely approximated the division established in 1820 between slave and free soil. North and South were arrayed in hostile camps, with the West holding the balance of power. So Hayne and Calhoun wooed the Congressional spokesmen of the West, while Webster sought to show that the theory of government which dominated the South was incompatible with the growth and security of a great nation.

Historically the State Rights argument rested on better ground than the opposing view. The framers of the Constitution had not meant to create a power state and had intended to leave local sovereignty as a check against the kind of arbitrary authority that had brought on the Revolution in the first place. At the time of its conception, and for some years thereafter, the Constitution was clearly regarded as a compact, even by those same interests that now denied it,[40] and the right of secession or withdrawal from the compact was explicitly recognized in one of the leading constitutional commentaries of the day.[41] But even though Webster's arguments were historically unsound, he found his audience—both the immediate auditors in the Senate chamber and the larger public beyond the confines of the Capitol—unusually sympathetic and almost eager to be convinced.[42] Before the end of May Gales and Seaton had printed forty thousand copies of Webster's speeches in the debate with Hayne, and at least twenty editions were known to have been printed elsewhere.[43] What the Constitution might originally have meant to its framers did not matter to the common people the country over, newly enfranchised, free, and already conscious of their destiny. They conceived themselves to be a nation, new but great and growing greater still. Behind Webster's ringing prose lay a Constitution compatible with their aspirations, and they accepted it as such. The transformation was complete when Madison himself, the very architect of the Federal structure, repudiated the plain meaning of his own Report of 1799 and compromised with Webster's version of the fundamental law.[44]

The kind of government for which Webster argued could not only establish and enforce a protective tariff; it could also free the slaves of the South whenever it should serve the interest of the majority to do so. Such a government the South could never accept; and so the Webster-Hayne debates, for all of Hayne's brilliance and persuasiveness and Calhoun's incisive logic, served only to identify Webster's cause with the perpetuation of the Union—which the South, by inference, was seeking to destroy. The South, of course, was actually seeking no such thing. Even while the debates were going on the South Carolina leaders were repeatedly urging moderation and insisting that disunion or secession was not even to be thought of. They wanted redress for what appeared to them intolerable grievances, but they wanted it to be legal and constitutional redress.[45]

Their reasoning was sound, but their cause was hopelessly lost; for it had been made to appear that they opposed the cause of Union and patriotism. It was Webster's triumph, but Van Buren moved quickly to guide the administration, which had been put in power with the aid of Southern antitariff votes and had backed Hayne throughout the contest, into Webster's intellectual camp.

CHAPTER V

VAN BUREN SETS THE STAGE

1

BY THE spring of 1830 the union of Southern and Western Democrats was so well advanced that the leaders of the alliance prepared to commit the party publicly to their platform. For this purpose an elaborate dinner was arranged for April 13, ostensibly to honor the memory of Thomas Jefferson. The list of active sponsors,[1] all friends and admirers of Jeffersonian principles, gave every indication of party harmony and seemingly no one suspected otherwise. No one, that is, but the wily little Secretary of State.

The Jefferson Day dinner of 1830 is another episode in the tangled relations of Jackson, Van Buren, and Calhoun so overlaid with myth and legend that the truth can only be conjectured.[2] Its purposes were many, but primary among them was to identify the Democratic party with the political philosophy of Thomas Jefferson. It was the Jeffersonian creed, with its emphasis on state sovereignty and individual liberty, that was to form the common ground in the alliance of South and West. The objectives of the alliance, including the ultimate one of putting Calhoun in the Presidency, could be more easily attained if the administration could be associated with these common principles. By the same token Van Buren's road to the White House lay in blocking the intended alliance and therefore in turning the President away from the views on which it was to rest.

By the time the dinner was announced on April 8 Van Buren's countermeasures had already taken effect. As soon as the Webster-Hayne debates had proceeded far enough to reveal the underlying purposes, the New York *Courier and Enquirer* had come out with an editorial denial that Van Buren was a candidate for 1832 and called on the *United States' Telegraph* to make a similar denial on Calhoun's behalf. Green replied that any discussion of the Presidential contest at that time would be premature, and the two editors were still engaged in an acrimonious controversy while the celebrated dinner was being arranged.[3] The episode served to bring into the open the bitterness between the Vice President and the Secretary of State and to convince Jackson that Calhoun was opposed to his re-election.[4]

While Jackson was still pondering this evidence of Calhoun's "disloyalty," Van Buren approached him with an account of the forthcoming celebration. On his own showing the New Yorker succeeded in convincing Jackson that there was something very suspicious about this sudden interest in Jefferson's birthday on the part of men who had never celebrated it before. The so-called Virginia doctrines, so ably sustained by Hayne in the recent debate, were represented by Van Buren as nothing but a mask, behind which lay the sinister figure of John C. Calhoun, bent on nullification; and had not Webster demonstrated that nullification and treason were one and the same?[5]

The dinner began at five o'clock in the great dining hall of Jesse Brown's Indian Queen Hotel, with close to a hundred guests in attendance. Despite Duff Green's cheerful report that men from all parts of the nation had "joined with the utmost cordiality and enthusiasm" to honor the Sage of Monticello, and that the gathering had been "free from all spirit of faction,"[6] the course of events did not run quite according to plan. As was customary at such banquets, the regular toasts prepared by the toast committee had been printed and were available for all to see before the festivities began. There were twenty-four of them on this occasion, all having something to do with Jefferson, his achievements, or his principles. Six of them were in fact direct quotations from Jefferson's first inaugural address. To some of them there was a State Rights twist, but not a single one of the scheduled twenty-four was nullification or overtly antitariff in sentiment. That impression was given currency shortly after the dinner because Van Buren had so persuaded the eight members of the Pennsylvania Congressional delegation who were present. After a consultation the Pennsylvanians had walked out in a body before the dinner began.[7] It remained current because both Van Buren and Benton insisted on it in their memoirs, Benton apparently having forgotten that he himself had been chairman of the committee that drew up the toasts.

The atmosphere was somewhat charged by the withdrawal of the Pennsylvanians before the guests sat down, but no further incident occurred. John Roane of Virginia, friend of Jefferson and lifelong Republican, was placed in the chair. Behind him was a full-length portrait of Washington, for whom he had been a Presidential elector;

and there were two busts of Jefferson conspicuously placed against a background of evergreens. The others at the speakers' table included the vice presidents for the occasion—Senators George M. Bibb of Kentucky, Levi Woodbury of New Hampshire, Felix Grundy of Tennessee; and Representatives Churchill C. Cambreleng of New York, William F. Gordon of Virginia, and Walter H. Overton of Louisiana—and the two honor guests of the evening, the President and Vice President of the United States.

When the dinner was over—an excellent dinner in which Jesse Brown had really outdone himself—the guests prepared to finish the evening drinking toasts and listening to speeches. The first toast was, of course, to Thomas Jefferson; the second was to the Declaration of Independence; and the third merely repeated the classic lines from Jefferson's tomb. The fourth toast was to the Kentucky Resolutions of 1798, and to this one Senator Bibb responded in a well-turned speech. It was patriotic to the core and glowed with enthusiasm for the Union, in the preservation of which alone he saw liberty and happiness. To preserve the Union, however, Bibb insisted that the rights and powers of the people and of the states must also be preserved. He ended with a volunteer toast to the Federal Constitution: the charter of limits between state and Federal powers. The fifth regular toast was to the Virginia Resolutions, to which Philip P. Barbour responded with a graceful tribute to the so-called Virginia doctrines.

The next toast was to Louisiana, which Jefferson had added to the Union. It was drunk to long-continued cheering and a burst of music from the Marine Band. When the hubbub had subsided, Benton responded for the West, the child of Louisiana and Virginia. He emphasized, as he had done in the Senate, the gratitude of the West to Virginia, and the common interests of West and South; and he left the impression with his hearers that the West too favored and would uphold the Virginia doctrines. As though to illustrate and expound the true meaning of those doctrines, the next six toasts were taken directly from Jefferson's first inaugural address. The thirteenth prepared toast was perhaps the high point on the list: "Republicans of the Jeffersonian faith, wherever found,—in the North, South, East, or West—all brethren of the same principles . . ." Levi Woodbury of New Hampshire responded, urging all sections to unite behind the Jeffersonian faith, in which alone he saw the true foundation of the Union.

The fourteenth toast was thoroughly innocuous—to the surviving associates of Jefferson—but it was followed by two that were definitely suggestive, if one happened to be looking for suggestions. The pair were opposite sides of the same shield: the "Basis of the Union: equality of rights and duties—of benefits and burthens"; and the "Bane of Union—oppression of minorities, unequal taxation, unequal distribution of public benefits." With the Great Debate still going on in the Senate, no one could fail to insert "tariff" and "internal improvements" in the proper places. At this point no speech was necessary, and none was made.

The next toast was a volunteer by Henry Hubbard of New Hampshire. He raised his glass to South Carolina, for her liberality to the family of Jefferson (the state had given land to the great Virginian's heirs, in token of her regard for his principles). The gesture was really only an excuse for a speech by Hayne, whose remarks were the complement of Benton's. Hayne ended with an unscheduled toast to Georgia, to which Representative James M. Wayne responded with a grateful acknowledgment of the vindication Georgia had at last won, through the eviction of the Cherokees, in her long fight for State Rights. After these two carefully planned interruptions, the regular toasts were resumed with the seventeenth, to liberty of speech and the press. The eighteenth was to Virginia, which was likened to the mother of the Gracchi in allusion to the Western States; and the nineteenth was drunk to freedom of industry.

With the twentieth toast, dangerous ground was once more approached; but no one refused to drink to the states, whose harmony was described as an overruling consideration. The twenty-first was perhaps the most pointed of all: "The States—Jefferson gave up the embargo in 1808 to restore harmony—can nothing be given up to restore harmony in 1830?" The twenty-second toast was to the memory of Washington, and the twenty-third to "Taxes—as many as necessary and no more . . ." The prepared toasts ended with one that could offend nobody: The daughter and descendants of Thomas Jefferson.

It was already ten o'clock and the festivities had been in progress for five hours when President Jackson rose to offer the first of something like eighty additional volunteer toasts. He had written it down on the back of the printed toast list, and he read it as the words were underscored: "Our *Federal* Union—*It must be preserved.*"[8] Tradition has it that the old General looked sternly and unflinchingly at Calhoun as he uttered this sentiment, and that the Vice President paled and was visibly disturbed. It may be so. Certainly Jackson was already convinced of Calhoun's "disloyalty" to his leadership, and Webster's replies to Hayne may indeed have convinced him that the Union was in danger, although they failed to convince Webster himself.[9] But the electrifying response to the President's toast, and its interpretation as a challenge to the nullifiers, seems not to have been perceived until a week or more after the event; and when it was noticed it was by the Adams-Clay press, representing a party not present at the dinner.

Calhoun responded to Jackson's toast with a sentiment he had been expressing in various forms and at frequent intervals for half a dozen years: "The Union—next to our liberty most dear. May we always remember that it can only be preserved by distributing equally the benefits and the burthens of the Union." Van Buren followed with what was in many ways the best of the volunteer toasts: "Mutual forbearance and reciprocal concession: through their agency the Union was established. The patriotic spirit from which they emanated will ever sustain it." Shortly after his own toast, Jackson withdrew; but the bulk of the guests stayed on until everyone present had offered at least one sentiment and it was doubtful if anyone present could be called exactly sober. In the small hours of the morning the dinner, designed to cement the political understanding of South and West on the principles of Jefferson, broke up.

2

The initial reactions to the Jefferson Day dinner fell into two categories, both dominated by wishful thinking. Everyone agreed that the intention had been to reorganize the party along Jeffersonian lines; but the opposition emphasized the withdrawal of the Pennsylvanians and predicted schism in the Jackson ranks, while the Republican spokesmen emphasized the harmonious agreement on principles and predicted still closer fusion of the diverse elements in the party.[10] A few days after the event opposition leaders had decided that the dinner "was not only a failure but has given great offense" and were now sure that the real purpose had been "to give a *State rights anti-tariff* tone & character to the whole party.—It was to found the party on *Southern* principles, & such principles as should exclude, not only their avowed political opponents, but Mr. Van Buren's friends also."[11] The opposition press, led by the *National Intelligencer,* took up the cry, and on re-examination found in the prepared toasts "a strong anti-tariff and rather anti-federal complexion." The President's toast was interpreted as a declaration that Jackson meant to enforce the tariff, which was represented as a rebuke to the South. The editors also noted, however, that the Union was uppermost in the minds of most of those present, including the Vice President and the Secretary of State, whose toasts were cited by way of proof.[12]

The day after the *Intelligencer* had expressed itself, Duff Green took issue, denying unequivocally that Jackson's toast was meant as a rebuke to anybody. The toast "was intended to speak to all parties. It calls as loudly upon the advocates of the tariff to relax unnecessary and oppressive restrictions, as it does on the South to submit with patience to the wholesome operations of public sentiment. It places the blessings of the federal union above the unjust exactions of the present tariff, and appeals to the patriotism of all sections to avoid collisions which weaken the bond of federal union." Green then proceeded to pursue the reasoning of Calhoun's toast, though without quoting it or referring to it. The Union was to be preserved, not by taunting or oppressing the South, but "by a careful, a candid, and liberal compromise of interest—an equalization of the benefits and burdens of the Government."[13]

The *Intelligencer* elaborated its interpretation of Jackson's toast on April 21, calling the whole affair political; and Green again defended his version, pointing out that the President's words were lifted almost verbatim from Senator Bibb's speech in response to the toasting of the Kentucky Resolutions. Green did not say so, but Calhoun's and Van Buren's toasts might well have been drawn from the same source. But the *Intelligencer* was not satisfied, and charged that Bibb had incorporated Jackson's sentiment when the speech was written down for publication.[14] In general the administration press accepted Green's interpretation, while the opposition press followed the *Intelligencer.* Neither Jackson nor Van Buren offered any comment, and the argument was finally dropped. Green then repeated the charges he had often made before that the strategy of the opposition was to split the Republican party by sowing tares between the Vice President and the Secretary of State.[15]

Whether the President's toast was consciously designed to align him with the consolidationists in opposition to the State Rights school or not can never be finally demonstrated; but its wording was ambiguous enough to serve that purpose, and in due time it was so used. Within six months Jackson himself was citing the toast as proof of his opposition to nullification.[16] Two years later, after the Jackson-Calhoun breach was irrevocable and nullification had actually been voted by South Carolina, the party line on the Jefferson Day dinner of 1830, like Athena from the head of Zeus, sprang full-grown from the fertile but twisted brain of Frank Blair. The *Globe* of November 30, 1832, announced that Calhoun had tried to rally the South to nullification in the debates on Foote's resolution and had tried to commit the President himself at the Jefferson Day dinner. The President, of course, had seen the whole treasonable plot "at the first glance" and had crushed it with his famous toast. By the time Benton told the story in the memoirs of his old age, he professed to believe that Calhoun's answering toast was conclusive proof of a plot to overthrow the Union.[17]

3

The real plot, if such it may be called, was a plot to isolate and ultimately to eliminate Calhoun. Van Buren had been working toward it for three years or more; and by April 1830 Jackson was a full party to it, if he had not been so from the start. Calhoun was not immediately aware that he was being read out of the party; but all indications pointed that way, and the Vice President himself was not to be left long in doubt.

Through the remainder of April and the early part of May the various threads that went into the weaving of the South-West alliance were gathered up and a final but unsuccessful attempt was made to knot them together. In the House of Representatives it was the vexed questions of tariff and internal improvements that furnished the necessary sounding board; in the Senate it continued to be Foote's resolution and the public lands. The internal improvement debate centered around a bill to authorize a government subscription to the stock of the Maysville, Washington, Paris and Lexington Turnpike

Company for the construction of a highway exclusively in Kentucky but joining with interstate routes; and the point of departure for renewal of the old tariff argument was a bill from the Committee on Manufactures to enforce the collection of duties. Calhoun's partisans sought to make the tariff the major issue, as McDuffie offered an amendment which would be in effect to substitute a bill to reduce the revenue for the measure on the floor.[18] Van Buren's following preferred the internal improvements issue, and the opposition to the Maysville Road bill was accordingly led by one of the favorite administration spokesmen, James K. Polk of Tennessee. On the surface both sides failed, because the Maysville Road bill was passed in the House on April 29, by a vote of 102 to 86;[19] while McDuffie's attempt to amend the revenue collection bill got nowhere, and the House reaffirmed in May its unwillingness to consider tariff reduction under any guise.[20] The Senate on May 7 passed Benton's bill to graduate the price of the public lands by the close vote of 24 to 22;[21] and a week later also passed the Maysville Road bill.[22] In the interval between the two votes the long-delayed nomination of Amos Kendall to be fourth auditor came to a vote in executive session. The Senate was full and the division was even, with Calhoun breaking the tie by an affirmative vote.[23]

The pattern of events was not yet fully clear, but the major elements in the pattern were beginning to take shape. The administration was definitely not going to do anything about the tariff; the combination of Senators from the South and West constituted a slim, but solid, majority; and Calhoun, by his vote to confirm Kendall, was still trying to get along with Jackson. He was already aware, however, of the danger to the Union in what was going on; and in a few days, at most, he would be aware also of his personal danger.

"The times are perilous," he wrote on May 12, "beyond any that I have ever witnessed. All of the great interests of the country are coming into conflict, and I must say, and with deep regret I speak it, that those to whom the vessel of state is entrusted seem either ignorant, or indifferent about the danger."[24] The next day Jackson sent to his Vice President a curt demand for an explanation of the latter's actions in 1818-1819, when Calhoun had been Secretary of War and Jackson the general who had led an army into Spanish territory in pursuit of a band of Seminoles.[25] The information on which the demand was based had been in Jackson's possession for more than a month,[26] but he had bided his time until after Kendall's nomination was confirmed before he used it.

On May 27 Jackson sent to the House a stinging veto of the Maysville Road bill, inspired and drafted by Van Buren.[27] May 28 saw a Senate tie on the nomination of Mordecai Noah to be Surveyor and Inspector for the Port of New York, with Calhoun again breaking the deadlock in favor of confirmation.[28] The following day Calhoun's loyal friend and supporter, Virgil Maxcy, was confirmed unanimously for the newly created position of Solicitor of the Treasury;[29] but in the House the bill to graduate the price of the public lands was tabled by a margin of fourteen votes.[30]

After Congress adjourned, the pattern emerged more sharply. In the veto of the Maysville Road bill Jackson had made a gesture toward the South which had to be accepted in good faith, and which made the failure to act on the tariff more palatable. It also strengthened Van Buren, whose measure it was, and weakened Calhoun, who had sought to avoid an issue on the question of internal improvements. The response of the South was immediately favorable but it was Van Buren rather than Calhoun who received the credit.[31] The opposition professed to believe that the veto was a *quid pro quo* to the South for a second term;[32] but from any point of view it was a shrewd political move. It went far to restore the confidence of the South in Jackson; it was pleasing to New York; and it issued to the West a challenge that would tend to weaken Clay and divert the rank and file from the blandishments of an alliance with the South in the interests of Calhoun. The South-West alliance was already stillborn because, while the parties to it could command at need a majority in the Senate, they had failed in the House on both ends of the bargain—the tariff and the public lands.

Calhoun's political fortunes had probably suffered as much as his policies. Though his votes to confirm Kendall and Noah showed his own desire to avoid a break with the administration, Jackson's challenge on the old Seminole campaign was conclusive that the President meant to force just such a break. The appointment of Maxcy, like a lucrative offer to Hayne's brother a month earlier,[33] did not necessarily mean any desire to conciliate the Vice President. In the context of time and place both were almost certainly intended as overtures to Calhoun's friends to the exclusion of Calhoun. It was his isolation rather than his appeasement that was the motive.

4

The letter Calhoun received from Andrew Jackson, handed to him by Major Donelson on the morning of May 13, 1830, could hardly have surprised him very much. The President enclosed a copy of a letter from William H. Crawford to Senator John Forsyth of Georgia, dated April 30, 1830. This letter stated explicitly that when Jackson's capture of the Spanish forts of St. Marks and Pensacola had been discussed in Monroe's Cabinet in 1818 Calhoun had urged that the General be reprimanded or punished. Crawford also insisted that a letter from Jackson to Monroe, offering to take possession of all of Florida on his own responsibility without committing the administration, had been before the Cabinet. Calhoun's course in the discussion, wrote the President, "being so different from what I had heretofore understood to be correct requires that it should be brought to your consideration. . . . My object in making this communication is to announce to you the great surprise which is felt, and to learn of you whether it be possible that the information given is correct; whether it can be, under all the circumstances of which you and I are both informed, that any attempt seriously to affect me was moved and sustained by you in the cabinet council, when, as is known to you, I was but executing the *wishes* of the government, and clothed with the authority to 'conduct the war in the manner I might judge best.' "[34]

The question had already been brought to Jackson's attention in 1827, and a protracted correspondence between the two men had dragged out into the summer of 1828, when it had been dropped by mutual consent. Calhoun was at that time still essential to the success of the Jackson ticket and a quarrel was to be avoided. By the spring of 1830 the Vice President was no longer politically necessary to the party and his presence in it, by his efforts to weld the South and West into a unit behind the old Virginia doctrines, had become inimical to Van Buren. The time had come to eject him and the charge that he had not sustained Jackson in 1818, but had actively sought to punish him, was simply the predetermined method by which the rupture was to be brought about.[35]

Jackson knew perfectly well the answer to his own question. Calhoun had given him the answer in July of 1828 and had made clear at that time his own awareness that the question itself had no other purpose than to produce a quarrel.[36] Jackson had known in 1818 that Calhoun regarded his seizure of the Spanish forts as exceeding his orders; and he had known—certainly since 1819—that the Secretary of War had favored some form of investigation into his conduct.[37] The whole matter had been recalled to his mind as recently as December 1829. On that occasion ex-President James Monroe, who had withdrawn from the Virginia Constitutional Convention in Richmond because of ill health, stopped over in Washington on his way back to New York. Jackson gave a small dinner in his honor at which the other guests were the members of the Cabinet, Major Lewis, Donelson, and Tench Ringgold, Marshal of the District of Columbia. Ringgold, who was also representing the ex-President in his financial claim against the government, took the occasion to inform Lewis that in the old Seminole campaign Monroe had defended Jackson against his entire Cabinet.[38] It was not strictly true but probably had the desired effect of disposing the administration favorably toward Monroe's claim. It also had the effect of recalling to Lewis, if he had forgotten, the earlier correspondence on that subject, which he had had a hand in procuring.

Although the parties concerned—and especially the silent partner, Martin Van Buren—steadfastly denied any plotting or scheming of any kind, the whole affair was too pat, and too well-timed, to have been anything else. The story that emerges from volumes of correspondence and personal narratives, many of which were designed deliberately to hide rather than to reveal the facts, is approximately as follows:[39]

In January 1827 Sam Houston, then a Representative in Congress from Tennessee, sent to Jackson a copy of a partially mutilated letter from Monroe to Calhoun, dated September 9, 1818, and dealing with the Seminole campaign. The letter had been stolen from Calhoun's file and, carefully edited by Houston, it was intended to arouse the old General's suspicions against the Vice President.[40] The Jackson party, under the guidance of Van Buren, was then busily engaged in trying to win over the Crawford Radicals, whose dislike for Calhoun was the primary bar to co-operation. Unless Houston was acting entirely on his own (and his letter to Jackson indicates that he was not) Van Buren and Cambreleng must have known when they called on Crawford in the spring of 1827 that the discussions in Monroe's Cabinet on the Seminole campaign could be so turned as to precipitate a quarrel between Jackson and Calhoun when the time was ripe. The matter was probably talked over with Crawford on this 1827 visit. In any event it was Crawford who took the lead in reopening the subject in December of that year, and he was undoubtedly the source of the hints that appeared in a Nashville paper at about the same time.

When James A. Hamilton, representing the Tammany Society of New York, attended the celebration of the anniversary of the Battle of New Orleans in the latter city on January 8, 1828, he discussed with Major Lewis the possibility of effecting a reconciliation between Jackson and Crawford. Close as he was to Van Buren, Hamilton undoubtedly knew that the price of Crawford's support was the elimination of Calhoun. If he had not already been informed as to the method to be used in achieving that end, the Nashville papers would have given him the necessary hint; but just to make sure, Lewis planted another seed. With Jackson's blessing, Hamilton then sought an interview with Crawford as he passed through Georgia on his way back to New York. Crawford was not at home, but he did see John Forsyth, who was then Governor of the state. Forsyth undertook to get from Crawford a statement as to what had actually passed in Monroe's Cabinet when Jackson's conduct of the Seminole campaign was under fire. On February 28, 1828, he wrote to Hamilton, quoting Crawford to the effect that "at a meeting of Mr. Monroe's Cabinet to discuss the course to be pursued towards Spain, in consequence of Gen. Jackson's proceedings in Florida during the Seminole War, Mr. Calhoun, the Secretary of the War Department, submitted to and urged upon the President the propriety of arresting and trying Gen. Jackson. . . ."[41]

Hamilton showed this letter to Major Lewis in the spring of 1828, but it had already been determined that no steps against Calhoun would be taken until after the election, so nothing further was done about it. Jackson had received the stolen letter on the same subject early in 1827, but he too had seen fit to do nothing about it for a year. In the spring of 1828 he opened a correspondence on the subject with Monroe and Calhoun, but was seemingly satisfied with the explanations he received. The election was coming on and the question was dropped, not to be taken up again until the winter of 1829-1830. By this date events had progressed to a point that made Calhoun's ejection from the party politically feasible—indeed, from Van Buren's point of view, essential—and the affair was pushed to its inevitable conclusion.

Major Lewis reported his conversation with Tench Ringgold to Eaton, and the two of them carried it to Jackson. According to Lewis the old General was incredulous, but this is hardly likely. His memory where an injury to himself, real or fancied, was concerned was tenacious; and he would certainly not have forgotten one of which he had been so often reminded. Lewis mentioned Forsyth's letter to Hamilton, and Jackson directed him to secure it. Forsyth, however, was now Senator from Georgia and available for consultation, and he suggested that Crawford be asked to make the necessary statement over his own signature. The statement was substantially as Forsyth had originally transmitted it to Hamilton, save that Crawford now denied having used the words "arresting and trying," and substituted "reprimanding." Curiously enough, although the preliminary discussion of the point apparently took place in December, Forsyth's letter to Crawford was dated April 16, just three days after the Jefferson Day dinner.

5

It was Crawford's reply that Jackson placed in Calhoun's hands on May 13, 1830, with his request for an explanation. Calhoun at once recognized in the correspondence a renewal of the earlier controversy, and was only too well aware of the motives and to a considerable extent of the persons behind it. He acknowledged the communication immediately, promising an answer as soon as he had time to prepare one. "In the mean time," he wrote, "I cannot repress the expression of my indignation at the affair; while, at the same time, I cannot but express my gratification that the secret and mysterious attempts which have been making by false insinuations, for years, for political purposes, to injure my character, are at length brought to light."[42] It was on a Thursday that Calhoun received and acknowledged Jackson's letter. As soon as the Senate rose for the week end on Saturday, May 15, he set out for a flying visit to Oak Hill, Monroe's Loudoun County estate, where the ex-President was already settled for the summer.[43] On Monroe's advice Calhoun also had a "full conversation" with William Wirt, Attorney General in the Cabinet that had passed on the Seminole controversy, and undoubtedly the most nearly objective member of it.[44]

In contrast to Calhoun's anxiety was Jackson's seeming glee at the plight of his Vice President. Calhoun, he wrote to Hamilton on May 18, would "either have to deny the truth of the statement, in Mr. Crawford's letter, or be in a delicate situation, if he admits the fact."[45] And Jackson knew from his correspondence on the subject in 1828 that Calhoun would admit enough of it to serve his turn.

Calhoun's explicit reply was dated May 29, 1830, the day after he had given the casting vote in the Senate to confirm Amos Kendall, one of the most sharply criticized of Jackson's appointees. He began by challenging the old General's right to call in question any part of his conduct while head of the War Department; and perhaps he should have let it go at that. On Monroe's advice, however, he entered into an elaborate explanation and a detailed refutation of Crawford's letter. Monroe could not believe that anything more than a misunderstanding was involved; and misunderstandings between rational men of good will can be dispelled by explanation. Calhoun knew better, and so he wrote with an eye to future publication, should that become necessary. He had little difficulty in demonstrating, by quotations from contemporary correspondence, that Jackson had understood from the beginning of the Seminole campaign what the War Department intended his orders to mean. It was almost as easy to show that by the middle of 1818 at the latest Jackson had been aware that both Monroe and Calhoun regarded his capture of the Spanish forts as a violation of orders; that both were ready to condone and justify it on grounds of necessity, if the necessity could be shown; but that the circumstances required investigation and the burden of proof was on the General. Jackson's own justification at the time had been in terms of his official orders, which he quoted so there could be no mistake, but which he interpreted to mean something quite at variance with the plain import of the language. Calhoun also pointed out that Crawford had done a neat about-face on the points at issue, which probably had more behind it than a change of mind. "I should be blind not to see that this whole affair is a political manoeuvre, in which the design is that you should be the instrument, and myself the victim, but in which the real actors are carefully concealed by an artful movement."

The case for Jackson ultimately rested on no more than his contention that he had been following not War Department orders but secret orders from the President, transmitted through John Rhea in answer to the General's highly unethical request of January 6, 1818. Monroe denied categorically that any such secret orders had ever been issued or that he had ever seen Jackson's letter requesting them until after the campaign was over. Calhoun and Wirt concurred with the ex-President that neither Jackson's letter nor its purport had ever been before the Cabinet. As the controversy dragged on, Jackson became more and more deeply entangled with his own story, which was in fact contradicted by everything he had said or done at the time. The definitive statement of Jackson's position was withheld during his lifetime, but was given by Blair to Benton, who inserted it in his memoirs, after Calhoun's death. The document bears the unmistakable stamp of the Blair-Kendall duo. Like earlier statements of the same version of the story, it is sheer, deliberate fabrication.[46]

Since the purpose of Jackson's challenge to Calhoun was to force a quarrel that would drive the latter out of the party, the President could not be, and was not, satisfied with the answer. He offered it to Van Buren for comment, but the wily Dutchman declined even to read it on the ground that he would undoubtedly be blamed for the whole imbroglio and he wanted to be able to deny any knowledge of it with a clear conscience.[47] More letters passed between President and Vice President, with Forsyth also participating, and each protagonist showed the correspondence to his "confidential friends." Calhoun left Washington the last day of May and was back in Pendleton within three weeks. Forsyth went home to Georgia shortly afterward, and Jackson himself left for Tennessee about the middle of June. But the change of scene in no way softened the controversy. Jackson grew increasingly bitter, as men are apt to do toward those they are bent upon injuring, and before the end of the summer he was blaming the South Carolinian for everything unpleasant and holding him for everything base. He had "led Hamilton and Hayne a stray" and was an "ambitious Demagogue" who would "sacrafice friends and country, and move heaven and earth, if he had the power, to gratify his unholy ambition."[48] Calhoun took note of Jackson's rising temper, and determined to keep his own "but not to yield the hundredth part of an inch."[49]

There was at least one council of caution behind Jackson, but he was already beyond reasoning with. It was Judge John Overton, one of the President's oldest friends, and he to whom the latter's preference for Van Buren had been confided in December, who tried to call a halt to the controversy. Overton pointed out that it was perfectly legitimate for Calhoun to aspire to the Presidency and that he would undoubtedly make a good President; that he differed from his colleagues in Monroe's Cabinet only in being more honest; and that Jackson and not Calhoun would be the sufferer if the correspondence were published. He urged, therefore, that Jackson drop it, and concluded by sending his regards to the Cabinet "including Mr. Calhoun, providi[n]g he may not chuse to fall out openly with you, feeling a hope you will not with him."[50]

6

Since December 1829, if not earlier, Jackson had held Calhoun personally responsible for the social failures of Peggy Eaton. The Seminole affair was shaping up at approximately the same time that the President faced a new Cabinet crisis over the refusal of some of his advisers to entertain the beautiful wife of his friend. Jackson's thinking was definitely on the fuzzy side in any instance that involved his emotions or his military fame, and it is not surprising that the "persecution" of Mrs. Eaton and the "duplicity" of Calhoun in relation to the bygone Florida campaign were presently merged in the old General's mind as a single gigantic plot to destroy his own reputation. Put thus baldly, it seems fantastic, and so it was; but Jackson continued to believe it until the day of his death, despite argument, cajolery, and the plain evidence of his own senses. In another year Calhoun's "plot" against Andrew Jackson would even be broadened in the latter's imagination until it became a plot against the Union itself.

Jackson discovered when he got back to Tennessee in the summer of 1830 that many of his own intimates, including men who had known Eaton all his life, were no more ready to pay homage to Peggy than were Ingham or Branch. To a logical mind this circumstance might have shaken, in some measure at least, the conviction Jackson had often expressed that the whole thing was an intrigue of his enemies; but he had been unmoved by the resistance of his nephew and secretary, and he was equally unmoved by the obduracy of his friends.[51] He had, he insisted, "long knew the hypocrite who was at the bottom of this, secretely wielding his pupits, afraid to act in open day";[52] and even those among his followers who thought him "wholy rong" dared not cross him.[53]

To a disinterested observer, had there been such, it was by no means clear how the alleged perpetrator of the plot was to profit by it; but Jackson himself had no trouble with the problem. Calhoun's aim, he was sure, was "to coerce me to abandon Eaton, and thereby bring on me disgrace for having appointed him, and thereby weaken me in the affections of the nation, and open the way to his perferment on my ruin."[54] As though in reprisal for some of the pet names bestowed on his favorite, Van Buren, Jackson began around the middle of 1830 to refer to Calhoun as the "great Political magician." By fall he was again threatening a Cabinet shake-up to get rid of all those who would not "harmonize" with Eaton.[55]

Only Donelson had the courage to remonstrate with his uncle, and was told for his pains that he too must go if he could not "harmonize." To the young secretary, who saw the President on more intimate terms than anyone else, and probably had a more genuine affection for him, it was all perfectly clear:

"An infatuation kept alive by the timidity of weak friends and the interests of the political party which have used Majr Eaton as an instrument first to obtain the confidence of the President and afterwards to controul him, has long since classed those who associated with Mrs. Eaton or who countenanced her pretensions to virtue and innocence, as the confidential friends of the President, and those who did not as secretly favoring the views of an opposition to his fame and character. The circumstances which ought to have removed this infatuation have confirmed it. It has now become a principle of the administration. . . .

"In conversation he will not reject the force of truth and honor. But in writing Mr. V and Mr. Lewis are his counsellors, and he will express no ideas that are not capable of perversion or material to the game which they have made the President play. . . ."[56]

7

The breach between Jackson and Calhoun, although it had been long anticipated, threw the political world into a ferment of speculation. Lines of cleavage that had already begun to appear were more sharply drawn, and men who had been uncommitted looked over the field and prepared to take sides. Duff Green, in the *Telegraph,* continued to deny any rivalry between Calhoun and Van Buren and insisted that he favored the re-election of Jackson; but in his private correspondence he admitted that he had no other choice if he wished to retain his lucrative post as public printer.[57] McLean and Calhoun drew closer together, with the Vice President's following in Congress blocking an investigation of McLean's administration of the Post Office;[58] while the old guard in Virginia prepared to repudiate both Jackson and the Richmond *Enquirer* and swing the state to Calhoun.[59] The National Republicans were jubilant and proclaimed the Jackson party already destroyed by its own internal dissension.[60]

But the seasoned politicians who were in control of the Jackson strategy knew exactly what they were about. They had set out to discredit Calhoun with the President and with the public, and to complete the infiltration of the party offices by the old Crawford Radicals. They anticipated such defections as that of the Virginia Senators, calculated the cost, and accepted the risk.

Late in March Joel R. Poinsett, recalled as Minister to Mexico, reached Washington, and by May had come to an understanding with the President. Poinsett was a South Carolinian who had never been particularly friendly toward Calhoun and might therefore become a useful instrument for attacking the Vice President in his own state.[61] In Massachusetts the faction that Calhoun had led into the party in 1828 was repudiated and cut adrift by summer;[62] while in neighboring New Hampshire Isaac Hill was chosen by the legislature to replace Levi Woodbury in the Senate of the United States—the same Senate that had a few weeks earlier pronounced Hill unfit to be second comptroller.[63] Thomas L. McKenny, who had edited a Calhoun paper in Washington during the campaign of 1824, was removed from his office as Superintendent of Indian Affairs and his earlier connection with the Vice President was emphasized.[64] As a gesture of appeasement toward the Virginians, Philip P. Barbour, former Radical Speaker of the House, was named to the Federal bench in that state.[65] In Illinois Calhoun's friends were excluded from the patronage and also lost the fall elections, perhaps as a consequence.[66]

Jackson's campaign for re-election, although there was no public admission of it for another six months, was in full swing by mid-summer of 1830.[67] It was agreed among the leaders that as quickly as it could be accomplished the *Telegraph* would be replaced by an official organ more in sympathy with their aims.[68] Van Buren's editor made overtures to Webster;[69] and the Little Magician himself, vacationing during August at Saratoga Springs, must have known that he had won his gamble.[70]

CHAPTER VI

CALHOUN IS PURGED

1

IN SOUTH CAROLINA, meanwhile, events were moving rapidly toward a crisis. Everyone believed in the reserved rights of the states; everyone believed that the tariff was oppressive and unjust. There was wide disagreement, however, as to how a state might exercise her reserved rights; as to whether the tariff was or was not unconstitutional; and as to what was to be done about it. One extreme, of which David R. Williams was the outstanding example, accepted the tariff as constitutional and saw no remedy but to go in for manufactures in South Carolina. The other extreme, led by young fire-eaters like Robert Barnwell Rhett, called for forcible resistance to the law. For three years or more the state had been in a ferment of political excitement. Like steam pressure building up in a boiler, the danger point had been reached and an explosion could be avoided only by opening a safety valve or removing the heat.

The nullification doctrine, ingeniously derived by Calhoun from the Virginia and Kentucky Resolutions of 1798 and 1799, was intended to be a safety valve. It was a conservative solution, designed to satisfy a majority and avoid either of the extremes of rebellion or submission. Calhoun himself, although he had written the *South Carolina Exposition and Protest* of December 1828 in which the doctrine was first set forth in detail, did not take an active part in propagating his theory or in leading the movement for which it formed the ideological basis. For the time being the Vice President concentrated on trying to put out the fire before the safety valve had to be opened. He confined his activities, therefore, during the first two years of Jackson's Presidency, to seeking tariff reduction.

The effective leadership of the nullification movement fell primarily to Hayne; McDuffie; James Hamilton, Jr., who was slated for the Governor's chair; youthful James H. Hammond, who established the *Southern Times* in January 1830; Patrick Noble, Calhoun's cousin and former law partner; and a handful of active but less widely known partisans. The constant endeavor of these men was to prevent violence or disorder, and their minds were steadily focused on the preservation of the Union. The *Southern Times* was their official organ, which never for a moment wavered in proclaiming these aims even while it kept perpetually before its readers the conviction that the tariff was unconstitutional and oppressive.[1]

The situation was further confused by the hopeless crossing of the older party lines, but by the summer of 1830 other differences had been largely merged, leaving two major groups. These were the State Rights and Union party, called by its opponents "Submissionists"; and the State Rights and Free Trade party, or "Nullifiers." The latter group included all shades of opinion, from the conservative Calhoun wing to those like Langdon Cheves, who favored outright secession if the rest of the South could be induced to go along, and Rhett, who was preaching revolution.[2] The Unionists were quite as firmly opposed to the tariff as were the Nullifiers, but they opposed also any form of state action except remonstrance and petition, relying on the justice of the general government for redress.

It was only too clear by the time Congress adjourned at the end of May 1830 that there would be no tariff reform at Jackson's hands, and leading Nullifiers pressed for immediate interposition by South Carolina to arrest the protective system.[3] The first step toward this end was the calling of a state convention, which required a two-thirds vote in the legislature. Convention or no convention thus came to be the issue in the state elections held in the fall of 1830. The campaign was in full swing by early summer.

Calhoun reaffirmed his own position with a Fourth of July toast at Pendleton: "Consolidation and disunion—the two extremes of our system: they are both equally dangerous, and ought both to be equally the object of our apprehension."[4] His lifelong purpose was to ameliorate the shock of sudden or violent change. He did not agree with Jefferson that the tree of liberty must now and again be watered by the blood of patriots; but he knew that revolts arose when minorities felt themselves to be oppressed. His opposition during his early Congressional career to the embargo and nonimportation acts was a consistent forerunner of his course with relation to the tariff. He opposed because the measures in question, though representing the will of the majority, had the effect of turning a whole class of citizens against their government. Yet always Calhoun sought to achieve his ends by legal means and shrank back from violence. As he conceived it, there was no violence implied in nullification. The state, through a properly elected convention, would declare the tariff acts null and void; and it would then be up to a jury in each individual case to refuse judgment on revenue bonds, acting under the law of the state.[5]

Excitement was running too high for such conservative methods to find favor. The local "Jacobin clubs" which Hamilton had organized to channel and direct the nullification vote became centers of political activity. Politics became the main business of life and candidates for the legislature spent full time electioneering.[6] The nullification press continued to insist on the peaceful and legal nature of the remedy; but as the excitement rose some of the younger men got out of hand. The conservative leaders redoubled their efforts lest sheer mob psychology render them helpless to control the situation.[7] The Unionists seized upon every extravagance and every ill-considered remark, regardless of source or circumstance, to argue that nullification was only a cloak of sophistry for rebellion. The Charleston *Courier,* leading organ of the party, repeated day after day for months on end that nullification and disunion were the same. The Unionist leaders, including James L. Petigru, Judge Daniel E. Huger, militant young Benjamin F. Perry, and Poinsett who acted or thought he acted under Jackson's orders, followed the same line incessantly.[8]

With the Senate debates on Foote's resolution for background, the controversy extended far beyond the boundaries of South Carolina; and finally James Madison himself felt called upon to deny that the famous resolutions of '98 and '99 implied the nullification doctrine or that any such theory could be sustained under the Constitution.[9] Calhoun's association with the leading Nullifiers was common knowledge, and his authorship of the *South Carolina Exposition* was widely suspected.[10] Friends and foes demanded that he take a public stand. Many of those closest to him, including Virgil Maxcy and Alexander Hamilton, thought his Presidential prospects were in jeopardy and urged him to stop the excitement among his followers for his own good.

Steadfastly he denied that it was in his power to arrest the course of events in his native state or that he would interfere if he could. He realized that it was not the tariff but slavery that was at stake. He saw the South as a permanent minority and knew that her only safety lay in her own ability to resist exploitation at the hands of the more populous sections of the Union. If their individual sovereignties could be preserved, the slave states could protect themselves. If the partisan majority in control of the general government were allowed to wield sovereign powers, then the South could continue to exist only on the sufferance of the stronger interest. "If, I really believed," Calhoun wrote to Maxcy as the campaign entered its climactic month, "that civil discord, revolution, or disunion would follow from the measures contemplated, I would not hesitate . . . to throw myself in the current with the view to arrest it at any hazard, but believing that the State, while she is struggling to preserve her reserved powers, is acting with devoted loyalty to the Union, no earthly consideration would induce me to do an act, or utter a sentiment, which would cast an imputation on her motives. . . ."[11]

2

The first real test of nullification strength came with the Charleston city elections early in September 1830. The canvass was spirited and the vote was close, but the Unionists elected the Intendant, or mayor, and all twelve of the Wardens, or aldermen. There was rejoicing in Boston, but the result was not a true indication of sentiment in South Carolina. For the convention issue had been dominant and, as the defeated candidate for mayor, Henry L. Pinckney of the *Mercury,* had himself pointed out at the start, the favored property holders of the city feared that a convention once called might not confine itself to the tariff. They were afraid the state constitution, under which the low-country parishes still had representation out of all proportion to their population, might be revised.[12]

The state elections followed in October and the Nullifiers won an undoubted majority. The shades of opinion were so numerous, however, and the various local pressures so great that no one could say until a test vote in the legislature was taken just how large the majority was. On the crucial issue—the calling of a state convention—it proved to be less than two thirds, and so the Unionist, or anticonvention, party claimed the victory for themselves.[13] Except for that single point, however, the Nullifiers took all the honors. James Hamilton, Jr., was elected Governor, with Patrick Noble as Lieutenant Governor. More important still, from the point of view of the Calhoun group, Stephen D. Miller was chosen to replace William Smith in the Senate. Miller was a conservative whose election as Governor two years earlier had been acquiesced in by Calhoun as a brake on his own hotheaded followers.[14] His selection as Senator at this time meant the splitting of the Radicals in South Carolina. He was not the first choice of the Nullifiers, who would rather have had McDuffie or even the relatively untried William C. Preston. But McDuffie was too valuable where he was to be promoted at so critical a juncture, and Preston could not be elected. Another consideration that was too important to pass up was the opportunity to bring into the nullification fold a substantial group of former Radicals, who could be counted on to follow Miller.[15]

The victorious party also used its power in the state legislature to drive through a series of resolutions relating to the crisis. The first three, passed unanimously, affirmed the attachment of the state to the Union and to the Constitution, declared that the latter instrument imposed certain limitations on the powers of the general government, and asserted the duty of the states to interpose when the Constitution was violated. A fourth resolution declared that the government was created by a compact among the states, each of which had a right to judge of infractions of the instrument. A fifth resolution pronounced that the Federal Government was then moving in the direction of absolutism. The sixth asserted the tariff to be a violation of the compact, which violation might be arrested by interposing the sovereignty of the state when no other recourse remained. All three of these nullification resolutions were passed by more than two thirds, with only the seventh resolution, calling for a convention, failing to muster that number. On the convention issue the vote was 23-18 in the state senate and 60-56 in the lower house. Governor Hamilton's inaugural address was a summation of the position and purposes of the Nullifiers.[16]

Calhoun himself seized the occasion to explain once more to his Northern supporters that the cause of South Carolina's unrest was neither political nor personal, but lay solely in the economic differences between the sections of the Union. "Till the South be convinced . . . that her labour & toil cannot be disposed of without control or responsibility by portions of the Union, having on these points, directly opposing interests, she cannot be at her ease. . . . She is anxious to give such construction to the Constitution as to reconcile her safety with the power of the majority, but if that majority insists that the two cannot be reconciled . . . the sincere and devoted friends of the Union in the South will, I deeply fear, have but a feeble foundation on which to stand."[17]

Other distinguished Southern statesmen besides Calhoun pleaded with members of the administration for a moderate and conciliatory policy before it was too late.[18] It was all to no avail. Van Buren was in the saddle and Jackson, if he had not already done so, would soon cast in his lot with the tariff states. The political power of New York and Pennsylvania was too great to risk, even to save the South. So tariff reform would be abandoned, the West would be placated for the loss of internal improvements by the destruction of the Bank of the United States, and the same sectional combination that had elected Adams in 1824 would re-elect Jackson in 1832.[19]

3

Calhoun remained in South Carolina until the adjournment of the legislature, stopping over in Columbia on his way to Washington. He did not reach the latter city until December 28, three weeks after Congress had convened.[20] In the interim Jackson's second annual message had been delivered and the tariff references were sharply pointed at the Vice President. Although the language was carefully conciliatory, the protection of industry was declared to be within the constitutional power of Congress. The right of the majority to rule was upheld, and the power of any state to nullify an act of the national legislature was categorically denied.[21]

The message, with its explicit warning to the Nullifiers, was reported on December 7, 1830, in the first issue of the Washington *Globe*. The new paper, edited by Francis Preston Blair, was a thoroughgoing Jackson organ, the real purpose of which was to supplant the *Telegraph* and aid in the elimination of Calhoun. Among themselves the Jacksonians made no bones about it.[22] So far as the general public was concerned, however, the inner circle played their cards very close to their respective chests. Even Blair was not aware of his mission until he got to Washington. In the *Kentucky Argus* he had opposed the Maysville veto and on his own showing, at least, he came to the Capital favoring Calhoun for the succession.[23] Duff Green had also been completely fooled by Kendall, who was responsible for the selection of his former partner for the work in hand.

Green had been told that the Kentucky editor was coming as an ally rather than as a rival, and seems to have been naïve enough to believe it.[24]

The cadaverous, hatchet-faced Blair—although only two inches under six feet in height, he weighed scarcely a hundred pounds and looked like a living skeleton—was a fitting instrument for those who employed him. To Blair was entrusted the enforcement of party discipline, and under his lash few strayed far from the fold. His blunt method of financing his paper might have brought a blush to the cheek of a twentieth-century racketeer. The *Globe* was delivered without preliminary inquiry to every Federal officeholder whose salary exceeded $1,000 a year, and in due course a bill for a twelve months' subscription followed. If the bill was not promptly paid the offender was informed that he could pay or surrender his job to someone who would. It was said that editorials for the *Globe* were sometimes dictated by Jackson himself, to be polished and refined by Kendall before publication.[25]

For a few weeks the deception was kept up and the policy of the *Globe* and the *Telegraph* appeared indistinguishable, even to Calhoun's partisans. By mid-January, however, the mask was off, and so was the velvet glove. Even Green realized, at last, that the establishment of the new paper was "preparatory to a development, on the part of a portion of the President's friends, in which it was anticipated that I could not cooperate."[26] The "development" was in fact clear from the President's message, even without the *Globe* to underline it. The South Carolinians could abandon Calhoun and tariff reform, or they could seek their ends outside the administration fold. They could expect no help from the protariff opposition party, nor after the Maysville veto even from the rest of the South. Although they still talked of modifying the land policy and winning support from the West, they realized that their own sovereignty must be their main reliance.[27]

Their case was not wholly without precedent. Jackson himself had lately withdrawn Federal troops from Georgia on demand of the Governor; and in the execution of a Cherokee Indian despite a Supreme Court ruling, the same truculent state had clearly nullified the twenty-fifth section of the Judiciary Act of 1789: the section that conferred upon the Supreme Court the right to review decrees of the state courts.[28] Even before Calhoun himself reached Washington, his followers had denounced the President's renewed recommendation for a distribution of the surplus revenue as "one of the most stupendous schemes of bribery ever devised by the wit of man" and had moved repeal of the twenty-fifth section of the Judiciary Act. The latter action would, as Judge Story exclaimed in horror, "enervate the whole power of the United States"; but that was precisely the intention.[29]

4

The quarrel between President and Vice President, meanwhile, was on everyone's tongue. No one was quite sure of the details, but the conspicuous absence of the tall Carolinian from White House functions gave eloquent confirmation. Calhoun probably talked freely among his intimates of his conviction that the Secretary of State was back of the whole affair. Whether for this cause or some other, the two were understood to have quarreled, and there was a widely current rumor that a challenge had passed between them.[30] The dispute was settled without bloodshed and Calhoun dined with Van Buren, but the gesture was misinterpreted as capitulation and a fresh outbreak threatened.[31]

It was at this point that the *Globe,* on January 22, 1831, announced that Jackson would not decline a second term. The language was that of an official press: ". . . we are permitted to say, that if it should be the will of the nation to call on the President to serve a second term in the Chief Magistracy, he will not decline the summons." The Van Buren press took up the cry, and Duff Green was soon in bitter controversy again. The opposition saw hope of victory if Calhoun could be brought over to their side and some form of alliance was undoubtedly offered, but without immediate effect.[32] The Vice President still hoped, even after what amounted to the opening gun in Jackson's second-term campaign, to reform his own party from within. It would not be for long. "The conquering Hero is again in the field," declared the *Globe* in its follow-up of a few days later, "and it must now be seen who are his friends and who are his foes."[33]

Duff Green was re-elected public printer on February 9 but the margin was close and the victory without political implications, save only that the Jacksonians did not have strength enough to elect Blair against both the National Republicans and the Nullifiers. The *Globe's* insinuation that personal interests and private feelings had been set aside in the common cause was not meant to be taken seriously. For if Calhoun could be forced into outright opposition, many of his more timorous followers would shrink back to the Jackson ranks under Blair's whiplash and the Vice President, once one of the most popular men in the nation, would stand alone.

5

The direct exchange of letters on the Seminole campaign between Jackson and Calhoun petered out in the fall of 1830, but those who stirred up the trouble were not disposed to let it drop until it had accomplished its purpose. Crawford continued to write letters—to Calhoun, Monroe, Adams, and other parties to the original discussions. Calhoun notified the Georgian caustically that he wanted no correspondence with him, but so many others were involved that Crawford found no lack of work for his pen. Adams spent the winter in Washington and visited Monroe in New York on the way.[34] Governor John Floyd of Virginia sought to make peace between Calhoun and Colonel John Williams of Tennessee, partly for political reasons and partly to gain access to Crawford's correspondence of December 1827.[35] Adams, Crowninshield, and Wirt went over the business together more than once; and Calhoun, in his extremity, so far put aside his reserve as to apply directly to Adams and Crowninshield for their recollections on the points in dispute.[36] He also continued to write to Monroe for additional or supplementary data as new angles to the argument developed.[37] Jackson was equally occupied, seeking some substantiation for his story of the Rhea letter. The aged and ailing Rhea proved anxious to oblige, even though he had no recollection of the circumstances himself.[38]

Calhoun's failure to call at the White House on New Year's Day 1831 was treated by mutual friends of the President and Vice President as the result of a personal disagreement which need not have political repercussions; and many of those close to Jackson deeply regretted the quarrel. All were clear, however, that if it came to an open breach they would have to stay with the President, and Calhoun himself so understood it.[39] He had every reason, therefore, not to publish the correspondence and he was determined to do so only if driven to it in self-defense. The Van Buren wing of the party was steadily driving him in that direction. Van Buren himself took no part whatever in the affair directly, but no one close to the scene doubted his ultimate agency—least of all Calhoun, who pointed out the remarkable coincidence "that every individual connected with it, is the correspondent and friend of a certain prominent individual, who made a visit to Georgia in 1827."[40] Rumors completely misrepresenting the nature of the dispute were industriously put into circulation and there were "whispers, wise looks & shrugging of shoulders."[41]

The whole affair, as Calhoun himself put it, was "a conspiracy for my destruction."[42] His alternatives were to allow an unfavorable public opinion to be built up against him without using the means of defense that was in his hands, or to publish the documents that would clear him of duplicity at the risk that his action would be construed as an attack on the administration and on Jackson personally. As late as February 3 it was understood by the inner circle that the President had agreed to a truce, and James A. Hamilton, told off to reply to Calhoun, queried Van Buren as to what course he should take if the Vice President did not publish.[43]

What further measures were taken to avoid this contingency do not appear from the record, but within a few days' time Calhoun had made up his mind. On February 12 a bundle of papers constituting the relevant correspondence was handed to John Quincy Adams by William D. Martin of the South Carolina Congressional delegation, undoubtedly one of those to whom the Vice President had left the final determination.[44] Calhoun, so Martin indicated, wanted Adams to examine the material and requested permission to publish the letters of the former President included in the collection. The permission was granted and the documents were returned the following morning, Colonel Towson having been sent to Adams' home for them.

The same papers, with a prefatory address to the public, were also handed to Secretary of War John H. Eaton by Senator Felix Grundy of Tennessee. Grundy expressed Calhoun's wish that the documents be shown to Jackson and indicated the Vice President's willingness to make any changes that might be desired, to all of which Eaton readily agreed. In short, Calhoun intended to publish a pamphlet to counteract the rumors and misrepresentations put afloat by Van Buren's coterie, but he wanted to do it in such a way that the President would not feel called on to reply. The whole matter could then be treated as a personal issue between the two principals, the correspondence could be dropped, and some semblance of harmony could be restored to the party. The manuscript was duly returned by Eaton with a few verbal changes and a memorandum in Grundy's hand which Calhoun followed in making his revisions. The pamphlet was then published by Duff Green, coming from the press in the very early morning of February 17, 1831.[45]

It was only after the storm had broken that Calhoun realized he had been tricked. Eaton had not submitted the manuscript to the General nor even mentioned to him the impending publication. Jackson was furious and the breach was irreparable. Calhoun had been careful to instruct his own editors not to attack Jackson personally in anything they might write, but to "direct the publick indignation against the contriver of this profligate intrigue."[46] His opponents would not have it so. For the better part of a week a violent controversy raged between the *Telegraph* and the *Globe*. Then on February 23 Blair denounced Green and Calhoun alike as opponents of the administration. For another ten days the *Globe* kept up a running editorial attack on the Vice President; then on March 5, apparently under instructions, tried to call a halt. It was too late. The Calhoun forces had stiffened, accepted the challenge, and seceded from the party.

The general reaction was about what might have been expected. The more violent Jacksonian editors followed the abusive lead of Blair; the moderates, like Ritchie, deplored the whole incident, with its inevitable disrupting tendency; and opposition editors, like Niles, thought Calhoun had "made out his case ably." The Calhoun press rejoiced in the triumph of its leader and the imminent downfall of the little Machiavelli who ruled from the State Department. Even the strongly anti-Calhoun Charleston *Courier*—or at least its Washington correspondent—thought that the Vice President had "attained a decided advantage" and predicted that Van Buren would be forced from the Cabinet.[47] Alexander Hamilton, notwithstanding the part his brother had played in the affair, thought the publication of the correspondence had "placed Calhoun before the people on triumphant ground." Clay thought both President and Vice President had lowered themselves by the controversy but that Calhoun "must be allowed to have attained the advantage." Even an occasional Jack-

CALHOUN, ABOUT 1832
by Chester Harding

Antitariff cartoon from the *United States Telegraph*, October 19, 1832

sonian noted that the "general impression . . . is favorable to Calhoun."[48]

Correspondence on the Seminole question continued to be published well into the fall, merging with other grievances as time went on. Van Buren, of course, made public denial of any knowledge or complicity, using Blair's friendly columns for the purpose. Ex-President Monroe, on his deathbed, signed a statement flatly contradicting Jackson's Rhea letter defense, and then died quietly on July 4, 1831. His statement was not published, but its existence was noised abroad and was probably enough to deter Jackson himself from further public participation in the controversy.[49] It no longer made any difference, for Calhoun had been effectively purged; and though he refused to join the ranks of the National Republicans, he was just as certainly in opposition.

CHAPTER VII

VICE PRESIDENT IN OPPOSITION AGAIN

1

THE day after official Washington had read Calhoun's pamphlet, Senator Littleton Waller Tazewell of Virginia, one of the ablest of the Vice President's supporters, moved to strike from the general appropriation bill then before the Senate all sums for compensation of diplomatic representatives in Turkey.[1] While the Senate was in recess in the early fall of 1829 three commissioners had been named by the President to negotiate a treaty with the Sublime Porte. Jackson, however, did not send the names to the Senate for confirmation when Congress reconvened, and up to the date of Tazewell's motion he had still not done so. There had not even been any official mention of the mission until an oblique reference in the President's message of December 6, 1830. The case was very similar to the Panama Mission of 1826, which had served as the vehicle for organizing an opposition to John Quincy Adams.[2] The Turkish Mission was now to be used for the same purpose against Jackson, and in part by the same men. For though Van Buren had conceived the earlier incident it was Tazewell who had led it; and Adams had believed then as Jackson believed now that Calhoun was the power behind the scenes.

Consideration of the issue was resumed on February 22, 1831, when Tazewell spoke at length, and the substance of his remarks was executive usurpation. The President and the Secretary of State were handled with neither gentleness nor tact. The toothless veteran Edward Livingston, in his mumbling voice, defended the administration and chided the Virginia Senator for putting himself in opposition. Livingston was answered by lean, hawk-nosed John Tyler, with Kane of Illinois and Forsyth taking part also before the debate was over. On February 25 Tazewell's motion was withdrawn and a proviso offered by Tyler, to the effect that nothing in the act should be construed as approving the President's action, was carried by a vote of 25 to 18.[3] Those voting in the affirmative included all the National Republicans, and from the Jackson side Hayne, Tazewell, Tyler, and Poindexter of Mississippi. The coincidence of this first factional attack on the administration with the publication of Calhoun's pamphlet was not lost on the opposition, who welcomed the accession of strength even while they distrusted both the men and the motives behind it.[4]

There was a further test of strength on March 1, when Calhoun wished the Senators "a very pleasant return to their homes" after announcing that he would not again attend at that session. As has always been the case in the hurried closing days of any session, the Senate met again in the evening; and the first business was the choice of a President pro tempore. The Jackson forces concentrated again on Samuel Smith of Maryland, who had held the post for many sessions past. The National Republicans voted for Samuel Bell of New Hampshire; the Calhoun forces supported Tazewell; and a few votes scattered. On the first ballot Tazewell had 3 votes to 12 for Bell and 17 for Smith; but on the third ballot the opposition concentrated its strength and the Virginia Senator was elected, with 21 votes out of 39 cast. Tazewell, still suffering from a recent illness, asked to be excused, and Smith was then chosen by a bare majority of 20 votes.[5] Although meaningless in itself, the balloting showed once more that with Calhoun's partisans in opposition the administration could not control the Senate.

The newspaper war between Green and Blair was still raging when Congress adjourned on March 3. For a time the controversy centered around the Seminole correspondence, with Green attacking Van Buren and the *Globe* repeating all of Jackson's charges against Calhoun. After the truculent Green had refused to let the matter drop when Blair showed a willingness to do so there was a subtle shift of ground. The ostensible basis of the quarrel was gradually lost sight of and Calhoun was presently being charged with nullification, disunion, and treason. On March 12 Blair recalled "the celebrated *Nullifying Dinner*" of the preceding April, and Jackson's toast was reinterpreted. Van Buren's New York *Courier and Enquirer* joined the chorus, followed by other Jackson papers, and all converged on Green in what he was not slow to recognize as a battle of extermination. Even Ritchie felt the sting of Blair's lash, and the Richmond *Enquirer* went over whole-hog to the party line. Soon Calhoun and his editor were being charged with having plotted Jackson's downfall even before his election and with having entered into a coalition with Clay and Webster. By April Kendall, Lewis, and the others of the inner circle had dropped their subscriptions to the *Telegraph,* and it was indeed war to the knife.[6]

In Jackson's own mind the quarrel with Calhoun continued to be bound up with the refusal of Washington—and Tennessee—society to accept Peggy Eaton, with opposition to his distribution scheme, with anticipated opposition to his Bank scheme, and in general with his personal prestige and his military fame. For every move and every whisper against himself, for every delay and every failure in carrying out his will, he blamed Calhoun, and was altogether as irrational and unreasonable as a child in a tantrum. For Jackson to believe that Calhoun meant to destroy the Union, that thought had only to be suggested to him. Blair saw to the suggestion, if others had not already planted it, and thereafter it became a fixed obsession which nothing could shake. When tried and trusted friends of his army days warned him against Eaton and Lewis and offered proof that the squabble with Calhoun had indeed, as the Vice President contended, been deliberately concocted, Jackson would not listen but launched once more into the most palpably absurd charges against the South Carolinian.[7] Throughout the summer the President continued to collect documents and depositions against Calhoun and to work on an elaborate exposé, which someone with sounder judgment than his own—probably Van Buren—persuaded him not to publish.[8]

2

Calhoun left Washington a few days after the adjournment of Congress, convinced that no reconciliation with Jackson was possible and desiring none.[9] His own strength appeared to rise rather than to diminish as the quarrel with Jackson progressed, and the only bar to his preferment was nullification. It was a bar that would not weigh heavily in the slaveholding states, and he soon convinced himself that he could carry the South in a Presidential contest. He had not yet definitely decided to be a candidate but with his oversanguine temperament it would not take much persuading. He found his Virginia supporters ready and willing to urge him on.[10]

Chief among these Virginia followers was gaunt, swarthy Governor John Floyd, one of the few statesman in the Old Dominion who did not have reservations about nullification. It was only natural that Calhoun should stop over in Richmond on his way home to talk over the turn of events with his political friends. Tyler had prepared the Governor for the impending visit and the Vice President was ceremoniously received on March 10, 1831. He spent that evening with Floyd and "a few friends." The next day the two men dined together, with three additional guests: William C. Preston of South Carolina; his cousin William B. Preston, who was also a nephew of Floyd; and Thomas W. Gilmer. The younger Preston and Gilmer were both prominent members of the Virginia legislature, and Gilmer was also editor of the influential *Virginia Advocate* of Charlottesville. The Jackson administration was discussed in detail, and there was cordial agreement on all points. After dinner some sixty others, mostly members of the legislature, came for the evening. "All went away highly gratified," wrote Floyd, "pleased and delighted with Mr. Calhoun. He has won upon all and I think nineteen twentieths will support him for the Presidency."[11]

When Calhoun set out for South Carolina on the twelfth, the impression he left behind him must have been fully as favorable as Floyd indicated. At least W. S. Archer, one of Van Buren's Virginia lieutenants, wrote in alarm to his chief that Virginia was turning against him and that the attacks on the Virginia Senators in the *Globe* must stop. With a dig at Van Buren's indirect methods he added, "If you have no control with this paper, as you tell me, get some one who has to do this." And he wanted Cambreleng to do likewise for the New York *Courier and Enquirer*.[12]

Everywhere along his route Calhoun found public sentiment in his favor.[13] Always susceptible to flattery, and always ready to discount obstacles and to magnify successes where his own prospects were concerned, he was the more firmly fixed in his belief that the South at least would support him. By the time he reached Columbia on March 17 he had worked the whole thing out in his mind, and was almost feverish with excitement when he talked to Hammond about his plans and prospects the next morning. Hammond, careful reporter that he was, wrote up the interview as soon as it was over.[14]

In Hammond's notes the positions Calhoun took were undoubtedly overstated, not by the editor but by the Vice President himself. In the first rush of his enthusiasm he invariably leaped farther ahead and stated more radical propositions than he was willing to sustain on mature reflection. That was the way his mind worked: the flash of insight, the instantaneous analysis of consequences, the impatient roughhewing of a course of action, without considering the practical difficulties in the way. Only later did he give heed to the obstacles in his path, modify and refine his views, and fix his ultimate direction. On that early morning of March 18, 1831, he saw again the glittering crown almost within his grasp and all his faculties were absorbed in contemplation of it.

The interview took place at seven in the morning, at the home of Judge Henry W. De Saussure, with only Hammond and later Martin present. Calhoun first offered his views on politics. He said that he had "dissolved all ties, political or otherwise," with Jackson. He would not join the National Republicans, but he believed the members of that party would support him against Jackson or Van Buren in spite of nullification if Clay should be unavailable. He thought it best that the South remain uncommitted to anything except her political philosophy.

The Vice President's real concern, however, was with the growing conflict of interests between the three great sections of the nation. He was convinced that the Union itself could not endure unless some means of resolving the conflict could be found, but he had worked out a solution in his own mind. For the West, he would by constitutional amendment set aside the public lands as a fund to pay for internal improvements. He meant by the term a planned system of roads, canals, and railroads to break the barrier of the Appalachians, and his views did not differ materially from those expressed in his early days in Congress and in his War Department reports. Hammond's notes do not indicate whether he meant this fund to be administered by the general government or by the states, but in the light of other expressions of opinion in the same period it is probable that he meant to give the lands to the states on condition that they were to be used for the purpose concerned.

The South, of course, was to have free trade, the benefits of which would also accrue to the West when the system of roads and canals should bring her produce to easy outlets on the Atlantic.

The North he would reconcile to a tariff for revenue only by the promise of cheap raw materials and an extended foreign market. As Hammond recorded it, Calhoun was willing "to single out some of the most important articles and giving them liberal protection, enhance their profits still further by lowering the duties upon all [or] nearly all the other articles of necessary consumption." These favored manufacturers would presumably exert their influence in favor of reducing all other duties. "He said," continued Hammond, "that the Northern manufacturers, if they took an extended view of things, must look to a foreign market and with that object it would be their desire and their most urgent interest, to cheapen everything in the country but their own peculiar manufactures."

As Calhoun and Hammond walked from the house together the Vice President "hinted pretty strongly that if things went right, he might be placed in nomination for the Presidency next fall." The young editor "told him candidly that such a step would be imprudent at this moment both at home and abroad, and should not be thought of at this time." Calhoun agreed and added that he meant "to throw himself entirely upon the South," to rise or fall with her principles. Clearly the balance of economic interests that formed the core of his political theory was already, in his mind, as much a part of "Southern principles" as was the compact theory of the Constitution.

3

After the publication of the Seminole correspondence and the open break between President and Vice President, it was a foregone conclusion that such of Calhoun's friends as remained in the administration would be ejected from it at the earliest possible moment. There had been more or less well-founded rumors of a Cabinet shake-up over the Eaton affair going back to the beginning of 1830, and the way had been paved for the dismissal of Ingham in December of that year by a vigorous attack in the pro-Jackson *Pennsylvania Inquirer.*[15] By March 1831 it had been noised about that Van Buren, weighed down by the burdens of his office, would resign, so that the way was also prepared for a complete reshuffling of the President's advisers.[16] The increasing bitterness of the partisan press left little doubt that a change was coming as soon as it could be made without making too many additional enemies for the administration, and the story actually broke on April 20. Again it was Van Buren who had conceived the method that was to be used to eliminate the friends of Calhoun.[17]

The basis of contention in the Cabinet had been from the beginning the attitude taken by the families of Ingham, Branch, and Berrien toward Mrs. Eaton. Ingham was from the start a Calhoun partisan, while Branch and Berrien had been literally driven into the Vice

President's camp by Jackson himself. The harmony which Jackson professed so ardently to desire and the political purge that was Van Buren's aim could both be accomplished by dismissing these three Secretaries. To do it openly, however, entailed too great a risk, even for Van Buren, and in itself would not have achieved all that he sought. What the Little Magician actually did, therefore, was to persuade Eaton that both of them should resign, which would give Jackson a reasonable excuse for changing the entire Cabinet. Jackson accepted the loss of his two favorites reluctantly, but he did accept it. Eaton's resignation was dated April 7, 1831, and Van Buren's April 11.[18]

The Secretary of War placed his action on the specious ground that he had entered the Cabinet in the first place against his own wishes, and had long meant to retire at the first favorable opportunity. Van Buren was more subtle. His retirement was attributed to the circumstance that his own name, prematurely and against his wishes, had been mentioned in connection with the Presidential succession; that Jackson had consented to run for a second term; and that it was therefore his duty to withdraw from a post in which his presence must be embarrassing. There must have been considerable uncertainty as to the proper course of action with respect to the other members of the Cabinet. Barry had been informed of the plan some time earlier, had offered to resign, and had been virtually commanded to remain, to carry on the role of confidential friend that had been Eaton's.[19] Jackson waited a week after receiving Van Buren's resignation, however, before he mentioned the matter at all to Ingham or Branch; and Berrien, who was out of the city on official business, was allowed to learn of it from the newspapers.

It was on April 18 that the President separately interviewed the Secretaries of the Treasury and of the Navy. Each was told that Eaton and Van Buren had resigned and was shown in confidence Van Buren's letter.[20] Neither Ingham nor Branch was stupid. Both understood perfectly well what was expected of them, but each professed to see no special course of action required of him personally. It was necessary, therefore, for Jackson to interview each of them again and to state specifically that he desired their resignations. Both then resigned on April 19, so wording their letters as to make it clear the action was involuntary.[21] When Berrien's turn came on his return to Washington in June, he also made the involuntary nature of his resignation a part of the record.[22] In each case Jackson expressed entire satisfaction with the work of the dismissed official, attributing the dismissal to the necessity of completely reorganizing his administration in consequence of the withdrawal of Van Buren and Eaton.

That, at least, was the reason the President assigned for public consumption. In private correspondence and among his intimates he traced the blowup to the unremitting efforts of certain designing politicians—meaning Calhoun and Green—to separate him from Eaton; and he was the more bitter because that purpose had actually been accomplished. He even quoted Calhoun as privately remarking, as the Vice President might well have done, that "Mrs. Eaton is the President."[23] Against his own Tennessee friends he vigorously defended Lewis and Kendall, and even went so far as to deny that they were partisans of Van Buren.

Van Buren himself recognized the step he had taken as "one of the most important . . . of my life," and he took care to inform his partisans in advance what was expected of them.[24] The New Yorker's reputation was such that no one doubted his agency in the Cabinet upheaval, but it was not until later that it became clear how the shift was to work to his advantage. With Calhoun out of the way, Van Buren no longer needed to be at the President's elbow to promote his own interests. His chances of the succession would be better if he was not in the Cabinet, better still if he were actually out of the country for a time, so that he could not be associated personally with any future controversies or intrigues. He arranged, therefore, for the recall of Louis McLane from England, and prepared to take over that post himself. He was probably not sure just what he would do after 1832. Some of his partisans wanted him to run for Vice President; others thought such a move would be a great mistake and preferred to see him return to the Senate from New York. Whatever he did, however, his Presidential prospects for 1836 were better for his being out of Jackson's Cabinet.[25]

The key figures in the new Cabinet were determined on from the start. Edward Livingston, who was to be the new Secretary of State, was directed on April 9 to come immediately to Washington;[26] and on the same day Jackson wrote to Senator Hugh Lawson White to ask him once more to take the War Department.[27] The inclusion of White would have served the double purpose of putting in the Cabinet another of Jackson's old Tennessee friends on whom he could implicitly rely, and of creating a Senate vacancy from Tennessee to which Eaton could be appointed. White's refusal[28] was therefore a double blow. The War Department was then offered to William Drayton of South Carolina, known as an opponent of Calhoun; and when he also refused, the position went to Lewis Cass, veteran Governor of Michigan Territory, whose views on Indian removal coincided with those of the President.[29] Louis McLane of Delaware was to be Secretary of the Treasury, to vacate the British Mission for Van Buren;[30] and Levi Woodbury of New Hampshire, who had surrendered his Senate seat for the vindication of Isaac Hill, was to be rewarded with the Navy Department. The Attorney Generalship gave Jackson some trouble. It was first offered to Philip P. Barbour of Virginia, who declined it.[31] James Buchanan was at one time considered, "he being a bachelor," as Duff Green put it with facetious reference to Peggy Eaton;[32] and various others were probably discussed. In the middle of June the job was finally offered to Roger Brooke Taney of Maryland, the intermediary being Francis Scott Key; and Taney accepted.[33]

The new Cabinet was undoubtedly stronger than the one it replaced and was far more pleasing to the rank and file of the Jackson party, who had tended to blame Eaton for the dissension.[34] To the South, however, the new line-up meant no improvement. Livingston, though he had been Senator from Louisiana, was a native of New York, and shared the intellectual outlook of the New York family to which he was allied. In the debates on Foote's resolution, moreover, he had committed himself to a construction of the Constitution that no slaveholder could accept. McLane had repaid the early confidence of the South Carolinians in his impartiality by identifying himself with Van Buren's cause. Cass was a pliant tool; and Woodbury, though he remained personally friendly to Calhoun, was in a position of no influence so far as the economic issues of the day were concerned. The nearest approach to a Southerner in the group was Taney, whose constitutional views were not those of the South. From this Cabinet, assuredly, there would be no pressure for tariff reform.

4

Calhoun's friends, meanwhile, were active, even though they were not unanimous as to what steps they should take. Alexander Hamilton thought Calhoun could be nominated for President by the Antimasons, who were to hold a September convention in Baltimore. Though the party rested on little but popular prejudice, it had developed enough strength in the three or four years of its existence to make the prospect worth considering. Hamilton offered to go himself as a delegate to look after Calhoun's interests, but felt that his hand would be strengthened if the South Carolinian could be placed in nomination by the Virginia legislature before that time.[35] Duff Green, in the first instance, wanted Virginia merely to renominate Calhoun for Vice President; but the more doctrinaire Virginians like Floyd would have none of it. They wanted Calhoun for President, standing solidly on the old Virginia doctrines, and they were not disposed to wait.[36] Tazewell and Tyler, shrewd and cautious both of them, wanted no Virginia nomination at all, lest it "turn the current that is now working in Calhoun's favour." They thought Jackson still too popular to be defeated and wanted Calhoun to wait another term.[37] But Gilmer agreed to set up a paper in Richmond devoted to the doctrines of 1798 and to Calhoun. Senator Poindexter stopped over in Virginia on his way home to Mississippi, and Warren R. Davis lingered on in Richmond until late in April.[38]

Less than a week after the Cabinet resignations were announced, the *Telegraph* published a lengthy biographical sketch of Calhoun written by Virgil Maxcy, which had all the earmarks of a campaign document. And as though by prearrangement, Governor Floyd noted in his diary that he would "shortly propose to the Confederacy the name of Mr. John C. Calhoun, of South Carolina, as a fit and proper person to fill the Presidential Chair." "Mr. Calhoun," he continued, "is a singularly strong minded man, the finest intellect, except Tazewell, I have ever met with, well educated, fine manners, forbearing and generous, he is bold, brave and truthful."[39] It was something of a tribute, coming as it did from one who, only five years earlier, had been a bitter political foe.

At about the same time the Calhoun sketch appeared in the *Telegraph,* Duff Green left his paper in charge of a subordinate and departed for New England, ostensibly to place his daughters in school there.[40] There can be little doubt, however, that he was in fact, as Blair later charged, on an "embassy among the Northern manufacturers"; and Governor James Hamilton, Jr., at least, thought he acted with Calhoun's sanction.[41] Blair was soon denouncing a coalition between Calhoun and Clay, which on the surface seemed not improbable. The truth was, however, that while Calhoun, Clay, and McLean were all in opposition and might have succeeded had they combined their strength, no one of them would defer his claims to another, and between Calhoun and Clay there remained an as yet unbridgeable ideological gulf.[42]

5

The Cabinet reorganization, weighted as it was in favor of Van Buren, should have been enough; but the puppeteers of the Kitchen Cabinet were not satisfied. The publication in May of letters from Branch and Ingham, stating their side of the affair,[43] probably convinced the Jacksonians that the dismissed Secretaries would have to be discredited also, lest public opinion be turned in their favor. Be that as it may, a newspaper controversy began which reached a climax with a bitter exchange of letters between Eaton and Ingham on June 17, 18, and 20.[44] Eaton accused his former colleague of inspiring slander against Peggy in the *Telegraph,* and challenged him to a duel. Ingham tossed off the challenge, after which Dr. Philip G. Randolph, Eaton's brother-in-law, who was also Chief Clerk in the War Department and Acting Secretary of War, forced entrance into Ingham's room. Later in the day, according to Ingham's account, Eaton, Randolph, Major Lewis, Colonel John Campbell, Treasurer of the United States, and Major Thomas L. Smith, Register of the Treasury, lay in wait for him, armed, at the Treasury building. Having been warned, Ingham provided himself with a bodyguard when he went to his office to wind up his official business, and was not molested. In the evening, however, the conspirators "paraded until a late hour on the streets" near Ingham's lodgings, "threatening assault on the dwelling."[45] Before dawn the next morning Ingham set out for his Pennsylvania home, and rumor had it that Eaton followed as far as Baltimore.[46] Ingham, of course, reported the matter at once to Jackson, who passed the letter along to those named. They denied it categorically, and the administration press played up the cowardice of Ingham's flight.[47]

Berrien was also challenged by the former War Secretary for the same offense, and by way of rejoinder he published his version of the quarrels in Jackson's Cabinet.[48] Others embroiled in the battle of printer's ink were Branch, the erstwhile Navy Secretary, and Colonel Richard M. Johnson, who had played the role of *amicus curiae* in the controversy between Jackson and the anti-Eaton faction. As a new explosion threatened, Kendall was hastily assigned the task of making out a case for Eaton.[49] The resulting document was published in the *Globe* for September 13, 1831, over Eaton's signature. It received the prominence that only a controlled press could give it, being printed in large type, set in column-and-a-half width, and taking up the whole of the first three pages of the paper and half of the fourth.[50] It had been widely circulated within the Jackson ranks before publication, but only McLane seems to have found any objection to it. He feared that it would serve only to touch off another internecine struggle within the party;[51] but to its authors such an outcome was not unwelcome. Berrien replied promptly and caustically;[52] and because of the nature of Eaton's references to him, Calhoun also felt called on to reply. He did so in the Pendleton *Messenger,* reprinted in the *Telegraph* for October 28.[53]

Even after that, sporadic attacks and sorties continued; but for the most part the administration forces were content to drop it. They had achieved what they wanted. Calhoun was in opposition; his followers were out of the Cabinet and for all practical purposes out of the party; and events in South Carolina promised to make better anti-Calhoun copy than even Peggy Eaton.

CHAPTER VIII

CALHOUN JOINS THE NULLIFIERS

1

THE younger leaders of the State Rights and Free Trade party in South Carolina had no intention of letting their fight against the tariff be sidetracked by Calhoun's conservatism, or by his Presidential aspirations. For two years they had been held in check, supporting a reform administration that did not reform, and now Great Britain threatened to complete their ruin with a retaliatory duty on cotton.[1] They had lost ground since their failure to win a two-thirds majority in the state legislature in the fall of 1830 and they did not mean to fail again. Shortly after news of the Cabinet shake-up reached South Carolina, Governor Hamilton and McDuffie met to plan their own strategy. Calhoun was not consulted nor informed, and neither Hayne nor Hammond was taken fully into their confidence. The upshot of the discussion was an "accidental" visit of McDuffie to Charleston, where Hamilton arranged a public dinner in his honor on May 19, 1831.[2]

The general tenor of the toasts was incendiary, and McDuffie's speech was even more so. For three hours he talked, his big-boned, spare frame leaning a little forward, long black hair disheveled, with deep-set blue eyes under heavy brows dominating a grim and rugged face. McDuffie was the finest orator among the Nullifiers—finer even than Hayne; and his was the only intellect among them that approached Calhoun's for sheer power of abstract reasoning. On this occasion he was "almost seemingly inspired," and delivered himself of a "superb and gigantic effort which . . . struck a damp in the hearts" of his opponents.[3] The speech was designed as the opening gun in a campaign to win the legislature for a convention in 1832. "In the course of a fortnight," wrote Hamilton, while McDuffie was preparing his text for publication, "we shall move on our State rights associations and not only attempt to make 'Nullification easy' but succeessful too."[4]

Up to that time the leaders of the party had stuck closely to the

Virginia and Kentucky Resolutions and to the *Exposition and Protest* of 1828. They had emphasized the conservative nature of their remedy, which over and over again they had insisted was constitutional and nonviolent. They had repudiated disunion and revolution, insisting only that the Constitution was and was intended to be a compact between sovereign states.[5] McDuffie went much farther than any of them had yet gone. The line previously followed, under Calhoun's guidance, was in effect to say to the Federal Government: We are patiently suffering great wrongs, for which we demand redress. If we cannot get it from you, it will always be possible in the last resort to fall back on the sovereignty of our state, declare your law unconstitutional, and refuse to enforce it. McDuffie no longer addressed the general government at all. He turned directly to his fellow South Carolinians and called on them to nullify the tariff, leaving the impression that he cared little whether the means were peaceable and constitutional or not. The episode may well have been consciously designed to blast Calhoun out of the middle of the road. In any event, that was its primary effect—that, and the wrecking of Duff Green's deal with the New England manufacturers.

In a thoughtful and compelling valedictory in the *Southern Times,* which he was quitting as editor, Hammond tried to undo the damage, and Duff Green devoted columns in the *Telegraph* to the same purpose. The Washington editor praised McDuffie, but called his arguments "too refined to be practical." He reviewed his own conversations and correspondence on the tariff, from which he concluded that the manufacturers themselves desired a change; and then he addressed himself directly to the South, giving it as his "decided opinion, formed upon better information than Mr. McDuffie can possess, that a conciliatory tone . . . will secure an amicable adjustment of this question, upon terms that will be mutually advantageous." He called for "wisdom, moderation, and perseverance" and declared the true policy of the country to be that advocated in Calhoun's tariff speech of 1816. But in private he gave full rein to his annoyance, writing caustically to Hamilton to inquire if they "were all crazy at McDuffie's dinner" and if they "intended to start into open rebellion and insure the empire of the whore of Washington." Hamilton, on the other hand, thought Green's scheme for compromising with the Northern manufacturers would ruin Calhoun, who could not have one face north and another south of the Potomac.[6]

None knew it better than Calhoun himself. He did not require the needling of the Columbia *Telescope,* with the portly shadow of Dr. Cooper behind its editorial chair, to convince him that he must go with his state or be abandoned by it.[7] He had not been forewarned of McDuffie's intention, but he realized only too well that the speech had precipitated a crisis that he alone could meet. He prepared openly to join the Nullifiers, hoping still that it was not too late to bring the movement back within the bounds he had originally marked out for it. He hoped too that his Northern friends could sustain him but was prepared to lose them if they could not.[8]

Hayne was chosen to rally the party to nullification as a conservative, constitutional, and peaceful remedy. The occasion was a great mass meeting in Charleston on July 4, 1831. McDuffie was not repudiated, but Hayne skillfully explained the doctrine of state interposition in terms as far removed as possible from the language used by the volatile Congressman in May. He ridiculed the notion that nullification would dissolve the Union. Scarcely six months earlier Georgia had nullified a decision of the Supreme Court in the first of the Cherokee cases, but Georgia was still in the Union. Pennsylvania had done likewise in the earlier Olmstead case, but the Union still stood firm. The derivation of the doctrine from the Kentucky and Virginia Resolutions was stressed, and great names such as Pinckney and Sumter were associated with it.[9]

The Union party also held a meeting in the same city on the same day, the feature of which was the reading of a letter from Andrew Jackson. The President declined an invitation to attend the meeting personally, but he commended the cause. He made clear by implication that he regarded those of the other faction as advocating disunion, and gave what could be taken as a promise that any move to nullify the tariff would be met by force. The enlightened citizen should know, the President declared, "that high and sacred duties which must and will, at all hazards, be performed, present an insurmountable barrier to the success of any plan of disorganization, by whatever patriotic name it may be decorated, or whatever high feelings may be arrayed for its support."[10]

Although he had sustained Georgia in her refusal to carry out the Supreme Court's ruling in the Tassel case[11] and had gone so far as to withdraw the United States troops from that state at the demand of Governor Gilmer,[12] Jackson was preparing to take drastic action against the Nullifiers in South Carolina. It cannot be demonstrated that the distinction arose out of his quarrel with Calhoun, but it is not unlikely. The President had stated more than once that only the Supreme Court could determine whether an act of Congress was unconstitutional; but during the summer of 1831 he took great pains to see that the constitutionality of the tariff of 1828 did not get to the Court for a decision. The Holmes case, trumped up by McDuffie for the purpose of testing the law, was about to come to trial. The defendants had refused to pay duty on certain imported goods on the ground that the law was invalid. The United States Attorney in Charleston resigned rather than bring suit on the posted revenue bonds. Jackson's first inclination was to refuse the resignation and impeach the officer, but he decided on second thought merely to appoint a more pliant prosecutor. In the meantime he proposed to send "a private agent to look and enquire, and take the necessary testimony to expose all who are engaged in this act of intended Treason against our Government." He had been informed that "Calhoun is at the bottom of this thing," and that apparently was enough to convince him that the Union was threatened.[13] James A. Hamilton, who was then United States Attorney in New York, gave Jackson detailed advice as to how the suit might be managed to avoid sending it to a jury or, failing that, to restrict the evidence to the single point of the validity of the bonds.[14] The latter procedure was followed; the Nullifiers lost their case, and with it all chance of getting a Supreme Court ruling on the tariff.[15] The direct interference of the President in the affair was not known to the Nullifiers, but it was known to the Unionist leaders and it strengthened their hands.

2

It was while all this was going on, and immediately prior to the clarification of issues at the party rallies of July 4, that the Pendleton *Messenger* announced the forthcoming publication of a statement on nullification by the Vice President.[16]

The statement was dated July 26, 1831, and has come to be known as the Fort Hill Address.[17] It was calm, logical, and sane, towering far above the controversial broadsides of the day. Like the *South Carolina Exposition and Protest,* which it resembles in content,[18] it belongs rather to the literature of political thought. The arguments need not be repeated here, save that once more Calhoun turned the State Rights dogma into a vehicle for developing a complete theory of government designed to balance the conflicting pressures of economic interests. To the simple majority rule with which Jackson's political philosophy began and ended, Calhoun added the principle of the concurrent majority of the same society polled by dominant interest groups, and identified the states in the latter capacity.[19]

Writing carefully for a general audience, he used concrete illustrations and common terms; but he developed his argument so skillfully that the doctrine of nullification, or state interposition as he preferred to call it, followed inevitably from his premises. He denied, as Hayne had done, that there was anything revolutionary in it, or that it was in any manner fraught with violence. The Constitution was a compact between sovereign states by which the exercise of certain powers was delegated to a general government created for that purpose. If the parties to the compact could not judge of its infraction and interpose to arrest the exercise of powers not delegated, then they had submitted their property, their liberty, and their lives to an irresponsible monster, over which they had no control. The mode of redress, when the Constitution was patently violated and all lesser means had failed, was for one or more of the injured parties to interpose to halt the operation of the unconstitutional law. The general government could then appeal, if it so desired, to the constitution-making power—the states—and the will of three fourths would be final.

Calhoun knew perfectly well that by publicly accepting nullification he was sacrificing all possibility of achieving the Presidency in 1832—perhaps of ever achieving it.[20] The personal hazard involved in the step he readily conceded, as he conceded also the futility of mere argument to change men's minds where their interests were involved. He was driven on by his own fanatical conviction that he was right, and that truth must ultimately prevail. "I know not how it will be received to the North," he wrote to Maxcy, "tho I suppose not with much approbation. My first and great object was to state my opinions clearly, and with critical regard to truth; to which I have made all others subordinate. Of their truth, I have not the least doubt, as time will prove. We have much to learn in political science. The rule of the majority & the right of suffrage are good things, but they alone are not sufficient to guard liberty, as experience will teach us."[21]

And to Samuel Gouverneur he wrote with even greater assurance of rectitude: "I know I am right. I have gone over the whole subject, with more care, than I ever did any other; and feel that I cannot be mistaken. . . ."[22] In addition to his political friends, Calhoun mailed copies of the Fort Hill Address to Taney, Cass, and Woodbury of the new Cabinet.[23] Three thousand copies of it were printed for use as campaign literature within the state, along with a thousand copies of Hayne's July 4 speech.[24]

The Fort Hill Address was a very important document, for Calhoun and for the nation. The prestige and distinction of its author meant that nullification must thereafter be taken seriously, by its opponents as well as by its friends. The subject was presented in the best possible light, under the highest possible auspices, and it could not be ignored. Nor was it. The doctrine was so plausibly derived and so cogently reasoned that those who claimed descent from the old Republican party of 1798 found it difficult to reject; and it was presented with such obvious good faith, such impersonal detachment, such evident love of country, that it was exceedingly difficult to make a case for disunion or treason against those who held it. Even most of those who thought Calhoun "fatally wrong" conceded his sincerity, his patriotism, and his ability; and all conceded his courage.[25]

Even Blair and the Jacksonian editors who followed in his wake found it expedient to wait until the direct impression made by Calhoun's address had been dulled by time and commentary before launching new thunderbolts against the Vice President. Thereafter, however, the *Globe* lost no opportunity to advance the charge of treason. Disunion is treason; nullification is disunion; Calhoun is the high priest of the Nullifiers. So ran the syllogism, stretched out through issue after issue, reprinted in paper after paper, with now and then an article praising Van Buren's high-minded patriotism by way of contrast.

The attack on nullification and on those who supported it was largely a matter of partisan politics; but the doctrine itself was not partisan in purpose. The South was already a conscious minority, and the interpretation of the Constitution advanced by Calhoun in the Fort Hill Address was the only interpretation under which her economic interests could be secured. Well in advance of his time he had come to grips with the paradox of a society divided in interest between industry and agriculture, where a subsidy to the one was automatically a tax upon the other. His own solution was to subsidize neither, but the same problem has been solved in an age less sparing of the public purse by subsidizing both.

3

During August and September of 1831, while the country was debating his political theory and assessing his merits as a Presidential candidate, Calhoun was having personal difficulties to match his public troubles.

Late in July or in the first few days of August Floride suffered a miscarriage which left her ill and shaken for six weeks or more.[26] She was still ill late in August when the Carolina highlands were drenched by days of pouring rain. The bursting bolls of upland cotton were beaten from the plants, the Fort Hill plantation suffering with its neighbors. The Seneca River overflowed its banks, and Calhoun watched helplessly while fifty acres more of cotton on the bottom lands were submerged in the swirling yellow flood. All but three acres of his corn also were lost, and only fifty acres of cotton survived disaster. The losses were similar, though not so heavy, on the lands he still owned at Bath, near Willington. Altogether it meant that the plantations would not break even for the year.[27]

It was in the midst of rain and floods and illness, when nerves perhaps were a little raw or discipline a little lax, that Aleck, a house servant, slipped away into the woods after Floride had threatened him with a whipping. Calhoun guessed rightly that he would make for the plantation at Bath and wrote to his brother-in-law to be on the lookout. He wanted the overseer told, if Aleck should be taken, "to have him severely whipped and sent back immediately. . . . He had offended your sister, and she threatened him, with a severe whipping. He ran away to avoid it; and has left us without a house servant, except females."[28] Floride was still ill, after a monthlong siege, and may well have had further cause for worry in the tense political situation so closely affecting her quiet, self-assured husband; but even at best she managed the domestic slaves not too skillfully. She was inclined to be lax and easygoing, and then when things threatened to get out of hand, imperious and slightly panicky.

Aleck was almost immediately caught by Major Armistead Burt, who in 1828 had married Martha Calhoun, daughter of the Vice

President's brother William. To Burt, at Abbeville, Calhoun wrote his thanks, and gave explicit directions as to the punishment to be meted out, to forestall any repetition of the incident. ". . . I wish you to have him lodged in Jail for one week, to be fed on bread and water and to employ some one for me to give him 30 lashes well laid on, at the end of the time. I hope you will pardon the trouble. I only give it, because I deem it necessary to our proper security to prevent the formation of the habit of running away, and I think it better to punish him before his return home than afterwards. I will send for him the last of next week."[29]

This incident has often been singled out to instance the degrading nature of the slave system, and as evidence of a vindictive strain in Calhoun's character. Out of its context it appears considerably worse than it was. Those who regard the punishment as excessive will find that the slave codes of the day enjoined penalties considerably more severe, and those who are revolted by corporal punishment will find that brutality in the treatment of labor was by no means peculiar to the master class of the South.[30] We cannot expect a man of Calhoun's conservatism to depart so radically from the mores of his time as to give up corporal punishment. It is enough that he applied it rarely and without unusual harshness. Without condoning the incident, it may be better understood, and so may the political obstinacy of the South, if we explore a little farther into the background.

4

If any specific period may be fixed, it was probably in 1831 that the South began to assume toward its peculiar institution an attitude that was a mixture of panic and resignation, and toward the free states an attitude compounded of resentment and distrust. The Missouri Compromise debates of 1820 had revealed that the average Southern slaveowner no longer looked to eventual emancipation and the ultimate extinction of slavery, but had come to regard the institution as necessary to his own existence. By 1830 it appeared to him more necessary still, for though cotton output had doubled in the decade, the slave population had increased only slightly more than 25 percent. The demand for Negroes increased with the spread and intensification of cotton culture, and the availability of slaves became in itself a limiting factor in the Southern economy.

It was during the same decade that the plantation system, stimulated by improvements in cleaning and spinning machinery, began moving toward the vast impersonal enterprise it was to become by 1850. The number of slaves per owner rose steadily and the personal relation between master and slave began to be lost. It was in a sense a phase of the industrial revolution, which during the same period was fixing the factory system upon the North. In each case the tendency was toward increasing the number of workers responsible to a single entrepreneur or capitalist. The essential difference lay in the nature of the workers. In the South a plantation might consist of one white family, two or three overseers, and hundreds of slaves, miles removed from any kind of help. Yet the slaves had to be kept in physical vigor to perform their tasks. The plantation owner had all the cares of the manufacturer, with a lower rate of return, far greater responsibilities, and an appalling weight of fear and moral obloquy hanging like the sword of Damocles above his head.

The industrial revolution, however, brought consequences broader and more far-reaching even than the multiplication of mechanical power and the concentration of capital. Not only were science, industry, and commerce given a new and vaster impulse, but every phase of human activity found new stimulation. The American and French Revolutions marked the beginning of a new freedom and a larger self-expression for the common man, who sought a greater measure of control over his rulers, mechanical as well as human, and felt himself entitled to a larger share of the product of his toil. Everywhere men were experimenting, seeking, testing, pursuing eternal truth as they had not done since the Renaissance. For a generation or more the continent of Europe was beset by revolution, political, intellectual, and economic. In the United States the same restless ferment, the same release of energy, was absorbed in the westward surge, in the extension of economic frontiers, in the rapid growth of an indigenous culture, and in what came to be known as the Great Awakening. The industrial age had begun, and with it more leisure for the middle class. Men and women had time to think; and in New England and the Northwest, peopled by New England stock, the heritage of Calvinism turned their thoughts naturally into moral channels. The year 1830 saw an unparalleled religious revival sweep through the Northern and Middle States. The energy and enthusiasm of conversion were quickly turned into channels of reform—temperance, woman suffrage, but most dynamic of all, the abolition of slavery.

In 1829 a free Negro, David Walker of Boston, published an impassioned "Appeal . . . to the Colored Citizens of the World" that shocked the South into an acute awareness of its insecurity. The moribund American Anti-Slavery Society came suddenly to life; and in January 1831 appeared the first number of William Lloyd Garrison's *Liberator*. The *Liberator* was inflammatory throughout, using simple illustrations that would carry a message even to the illiterate slave, should it ever fall into his hands. To the South it was incitement to rebellion, and the rebellion came in Virginia before the year was out. It was on August 21, 1831, that Nat Turner and seven other slaves ran amuck in Southampton County, and in twenty-four hours' time had killed and mangled fifty-one whites. The effect was to sear into the consciousness of every Southerner a mortal fear, and a mortal hatred of those whom he held responsible for planting the seeds of revolt in the minds of his slaves.

It was immediately after news of Nat Turner's rebellion had reached him that Calhoun ordered thirty lashes for his own runaway slave, and we may be sure that the reaction of other masters would have been the same. Through the inspired fanaticism of Nat Turner the Negro throughout the South gained confidence and became aware, however vaguely, of his own power. He had learned that white men could be terrified, and killed, by blacks. It was shortly after Turner's rebellion had been put down that a copy of the *Liberator* fell into the hands of Governor Floyd, who exclaimed, "If this is not checked it must lead to a separation of these states."[31]

Editors in the North as well as in the South protested against the incendiary character of the Walker pamphlet and of the *Liberator*, and all seemed to agree on a connection between these publications and the "late awful tragedy enacted in Virginia." Niles echoed the thought, if not the words, of Floyd when he declared that "Free labor and slave labor *cannot* abide together."[32] Hayne wrote to Harrison Gray Otis, then Mayor of Boston, to solicit his aid in keeping Garrison's paper out of the hands of Southern slaves;[33] and Floyd swore that he would not rest until slavery was abolished in Virginia. An emancipation plan was actually introduced into the Virginia legislature in January 1832, and after vigorous debate it passed the assembly, only to fail in the upper chamber by a single vote.[34]

Even in Virginia, where slavery long had been economically on the decline, it was too late; and in South Carolina Cooper, Turnbull, C. C. Pinckney, William Smith, and others had already formulated the moral defense of slavery as a positive good.[35] In the theory of nullification Calhoun had also formulated the political defense of slavery. Just as the industrial North and East required a government strong enough to levy and collect the protective import duties on which their prosperity was founded, so the South required a government too weak to interfere with her system of labor. Even before the tariff issue was settled, the question of slavery had moved to the fore as the crucial problem on the solution of which depended the permanence of the Union.[36]

CHAPTER IX

THE USES OF POLITICS

1

BEFORE the Fort Hill Address appeared Calhoun's Presidential campaign was making seemingly good progress in the North where he had a host of enthusiastic partisans. On August 9, 1831, he was nominated in New York City at an exuberant meeting in Broadway House. The hall was packed and the crowd of well-wishers filled the stairways and overflowed into the street, despite heavy rain and the fact that the meeting had been announced only the preceding day.[1] Calhoun himself, knowing that he had taken an unpopular stand on the constitutional issue, no longer had any idea that he could be elected, but he did look forward to Jackson's defeat. He expected to carry the South himself and thought the rest of the country would divide between Jackson and Clay. In such a contingency there was a strong possibility that the election could be thrown into the House, where the South Carolinian's followers might well hold the balance of power.[2]

Duff Green continued to be the most active of Calhoun's supporters. When Gilmer's plans for a Calhoun paper in Richmond fell through, Green proposed that Richard K. Crallé, editor of the Lynchburg *Jeffersonian and Virginia Times,* should take over the assignment; and with the aid of Governor Floyd the necessary funds were raised.[3] Early in September Green visited New York and New England for general electioneering purposes, and specifically to see if the Antimasons could be induced to nominate Calhoun at their convention scheduled for September 26. The visit only confirmed what Calhoun already knew—that there was no chance unless there was conclusive evidence that at least the entire South would sustain the views expressed in the Fort Hill Address.[4] The only evidence that was forthcoming, however, was a close victory for the Nullifiers in the Charleston city election.[5] Virginia, split into factions, still hung back.

As for the Antimasons, they were playing the field. The strength of the movement was undoubtedly overrated, but it was in the hands of a shrewd group of politicians who knew what their bargaining power was. Among the leaders were Thurlow Weed, the Rochester editor who had outmaneuvered Van Buren in 1824, and beetle-browed, hook-nosed young William H. Seward, who was just rising to power in New York politics. Calhoun declined to be a candidate, but permitted Alexander Hamilton to attend the convention in his interest.[6] The Antimasonic nomination eventually went to William Wirt, but both Hamilton and Green insisted that this result had been brought about by Calhoun's friends. The Vice President, in their partisan view, was the real choice of the convention. The Fort Hill Address had made it impossible to nominate him, but Wirt would be withdrawn in his favor whenever the situation justified such a move.[7] As Blair's cries of "treason" gained volume and circulation, however, Calhoun lost rather than gained in strength. By November the Antimasonic leaders were hoping to unite both Calhoun and Clay behind Wirt.[8]

The names of Calhoun and Clay were often coupled in the fall of 1831, and if there was no basis for Blair's repeated charges of a coalition between them, it was not because both men hadn't thought of it. Both were in difficult positions. Calhoun was Vice President in an administration that had repudiated him, and the self-avowed champion of a minority cause. Clay was in retirement in a state in which the Jacksonians showed steady gains. Within his own party, moreover, there was discontent, as younger men shouldered their way forward; and the Kentuckian realized that only a bold gamble would save him. So at the last minute John J. Crittenden, long a personal friend and political supporter, was withdrawn as the National Republican candidate for the Senate, and by a shaky margin Clay himself carried off the palm. It enabled him to secure the party nomination for President in December.

Calhoun, meanwhile, had repeated in correspondence the views on internal improvements he had expressed to Hammond in March, so that they might be known to anyone who had use for them; and they did not differ radically from Clay's. Clay, for his part, wondered if the more moderate tariff men could not be brought to accept a reasonable compromise. He gave tacit endorsement to the aims of the South-West alliance in November when his leading paper in the South, the Richmond *Whig,* came out for a liberalized land policy and tariff reform. It was generally expected that when Congress met, the supporters of Calhoun and Clay would find enough common ground for a working coalition.[9]

2

On his way to Washington to attend the first session of the Twenty-second Congress, Calhoun arranged his route to coincide with his political interests. He stopped over at Raleigh, North Carolina, long enough to attend a public dinner in his honor; and he stayed two days in Richmond, only reaching the Capital on the seventh or eighth of December.[10] In Richmond he discussed his theories, his hopes, and his fears at length with Governor Floyd and with Richard K. Crallé, who was then preparing to move the *Jeffersonian* to the Virginia capital. He was preoccupied with nullification and was certain that South Carolina would invoke that remedy if the tariff were not greatly modified. He also took note of the charges of disunion leveled against him and his followers, and denied flatly that any state had a right to secede from the Union over a dispute with the general government. Only a conflict between parties to the constitutional compact could end in secession, and then only after an adverse decision by the three-fourths majority required to amend the instrument. Calhoun was equally emphatic that he would make no arrangement with Clay, and that so far as Jackson was concerned he would act only on the defensive.[11]

Washington was in a fever of political excitement that even a protracted spell of bitter weather could not chill. Henry Clay, fresh from his successful gamble in Kentucky, and named on December 13 as National Republican candidate for President of the United States, was much in evidence. His long straight hair was now almost white, but he carried his head high, his voice was still melodious, and his manners were charming.[12] Despite a long period of uncertain health, his step retained something of its old-time spring, and his eyes twinkled as of old. Other new Senators included Isaac Hill of New Hampshire, lame and frail of body but robust of mind and will; George M. Dallas of Pennsylvania, once a leading partisan of Calhoun but for the time being a Jacksonian; William L. Marcy of New York, long an intimate and trusted henchman of Van Buren; Willie P. Mangum, veteran State Rights Democrat from North Carolina; and polished, gentlemanly Stephen D. Miller of South Carolina, who had come late into Calhoun's camp but would follow all the way. In the House the most talked-of newcomer was plump, bald, saturnine John Quincy Adams. His tongue was more caustic than ever, his learning more prodigious, and his prejudices and his temper were no whit softened by advancing age. Two years earlier he had thought his career at an end; but Old Man Eloquent was still to be born, and he would yet climb to greater heights than any he had previously known.

Calhoun was still on the road, somewhere between Richmond and Washington, when Jackson's third annual message was read to Congress on December 6. This time it was not Duff Green, the public printer, who distributed advance copies to the press, but lean and dour Francis Preston Blair of the *Globe*.[13] The message was moderate and conciliatory in tone, and in content all Calhoun himself could have asked. The President forecast the payment of the public debt within another year, and with that prospect in view called upon Congress to modify the tariff at the present session. "A modification of the tariff, which shall produce a reduction of our revenue to the wants of the government, and an adjustment of the duties on imports with a view to equal justice in relation to all our national interests . . . is deemed to be one of the principal objects which demand the consideration of the present congress." There was no mention whatever of the scheme for distributing the surplus so reprobated by the South; and even the Bank question, with Van Buren no longer at his elbow, the President was content to leave "for the present to the investigation of an enlightened people and their representatives."[14] The South was jubilant, and the South Carolina delegation prepared to carry out Jackson's request for a reduction of the tariff to revenue needs.[15]

The report of the new Secretary of the Treasury, Louis McLane, cast some doubt on Jackson's sincerity, or on that of McLane himself. He recommended that the reduction of the tariff to revenue needs be accomplished by eliminating duties altogether on some items rather than by a general reduction on all items. But the articles he singled out for continued protection included precisely those most necessary to the South: wool and woolens, iron, and hemp. Clay had offered a similar scheme as a basis for compromise earlier in the year, and McLane now boasted that he had cut the ground from under the great tariff champion and secured the credit for the administration. The Treasury Secretary also recommended disposing of the public lands "at a fair price" to the states in which they lay. Between the two proposals he had effectively forestalled any rebirth of the South-West alliance in the hands of Clay and Calhoun.[16]

Actually there was little danger of such a union being brought about. Before the McDuffie dinner of May, Calhoun might have accepted a tariff compromise somewhat along the lines proposed. The scheme differed only in degree from his own suggestions made to Hammond in March. But South Carolina had since rejected halfway measures, and the sharp rise of antislavery propaganda had added to the gravity of the situation. It was no longer merely the tariff that was at stake, but an interpretation of the Constitution which would permit a defense of slavery. To establish that interpretation it was necessary either that the tariff be modified in clear response to South Carolina's demands, or that the law actually be nullified by state action. So Calhoun told McLane that only a general reduction on all imported articles would satisfy the South, and advised the Nullifiers to prepare for the worst.[17]

For a time the antitariff forces made overtures to Clay, holding out the *quid pro quo* of support in his Presidential campaign from the Calhoun party in the South;[18] but the Kentuckian was no longer interested. He could not afford to make concessions to Calhoun's political theory, and he had found a better issue than the tariff on which to base his campaign. Clay's issue was recharter of the Bank of the United States. If recharter were passed just before the election, he reasoned, Jackson could not veto it without losing the support of the moneyed interests the country over. If he did not veto it, on the other hand, he would lose the backing of the articulate anti-Bank group in the West. Either way it would be a campaign issue, and either way Clay would be the one to profit by it. It was, moreover, a question on which the Nullifiers, the Antimasons, and even the Jacksonians themselves were split, offering an excellent opportunity to recruit the disaffected from other parties.

3

It was neither the tariff nor the Bank that brought about the first *rapprochement* between the Clay and Calhoun forces, but the nomination of Martin Van Buren to be Minister to Great Britain. The former Secretary of State had been at his post in London since September, but the appointment had been made after Congress adjourned and so had not yet been before the Senate. Jackson sent in the nomination on December 7, 1831, but no action of any kind was taken for three weeks. Then on the twenty-seventh the question was referred to the Committee on Foreign Relations, of which Tazewell was chairman.[19]

The interim was long enough to permit lively speculation. It was recalled that Van Buren's instructions to McLane, when the latter had gone to England at the beginning of Jackson's term, had been deeply resented by the National Republicans. The instructions had been in effect a public repudiation of the foreign policy of Adams and Clay and were regarded by many as truckling to Great Britain. There was therefore ample reason why the Clay partisans might prefer to see Van Buren rejected; and after the Seminole correspondence no one could doubt the animosity that existed between the Calhoun and Van Buren factions. Yet partisans on both sides agreed that to reject the little Dutchman would be to make him a martyr, with the probable consequence of assuring his nomination for Vice President on the Jackson ticket; and Jackson himself informed his favorite that such would be the case.[20]

The curious part of the business was that Van Buren's own followers, although they obviously could not vote against him in the Senate, were as eager for his rejection as were the partisans of Clay and Calhoun. It was the faithful Cambreleng who explained to his chief why his own friends were earnestly seeking his defeat. "I know you will be annoyed at such a result," he wrote, "but it's the only thing that can remedy your error in going abroad—it's the only thing that can prevent the election in 1836 from going to the House when the largest state in the Union will be most assuredly beaten."[21] In short, Van Buren's martyrdom was to make him President in 1836. The opposition, up to a certain point, reasoned in very similar fashion but arrived at an opposite conclusion. If he is rejected, argued Duff Green, "the Concern is then compelled to take him on the Baltimore Convention or he is utterly down & forever. If he runs on the Jackson ticket and is elected vice President he enlists against him the animosity of all those who have been encouraged to hope that they might be smuggled into the Presidency and he will be easily beaten down as the candidate for the succession. Say that

Jackson dies or resigns & Van should come in—We then charge him with usurpation—being smuggled in & we make him more odious than he now is."[22]

Tazewell reported on the nomination from the Committee on Foreign Relations on January 10, presumably favorably since the committee had an administration majority. The matter was dropped for another week, which was devoted mainly to a discussion of the tariff. It was on January 17 that John Holmes, Senate veteran from Maine, revealed the opposition strategy. He moved a resolution returning the nomination to the Committee on Foreign Relations, and instructing the committee to investigate the causes of the present Cabinet unheaval with special reference to Van Buren's part in it.[23] The move was adroit enough to be worthy of the genius of the Little Magician himself. Because it insinuated that the President had not given the true reasons for the Cabinet dismissals, the administration Senators were forced in defense of Jackson to vote against the resolution. By so doing, however, they would appear to be voting down an investigation and would expose Van Buren to the imputation that his record would not bear examination. Discussion was sharp, and amounted to a general airing of all the charges Calhoun and his supporters had leveled at the little New Yorker since the Seminole affair broke.

When the case for the opposition had been fully outlined, Holmes urbanely consented to let his resolution lie on the table for the time being, and the Senate proceeded to consider the nomination itself. A motion was presently made that it too be tabled. Webster strolled out of the chamber, creating a tie which Calhoun broke in the affirmative. Almost immediately some hint of this leaked to the press, although all proceedings were of course in executive session.[24] When the injunction to secrecy was lifted late in the month, Blair charged that the plan had been conceived by "a more wiley brain than that in the head of John Holmes"; and Jackson named names, or rather called them. "I have no hesitation in saying," he wrote to his old friend John Coffee, "that Calhoun is one of the most base hypocritical and unprincipled villains in the United States."[25]

The nomination as debated in executive session on January 24 and 25 and on the latter day, again by Calhoun's casting vote, it was rejected, 24-23.[26] Tazewell and Tyler, although neither cared much for Van Buren, voted with the administration on what both regarded as a purely party question;[27] but Hayne, Miller, Gabriel Moore of Alabama, and George Poindexter of Mississippi—the four who were known as Calhoun's men—voted with the Vice President and the National Republicans against confirmation. Clay and his following based their stand on the pusillanimous character of Van Buren's instructions to McLane, but the Calhoun faction placed their opposition on the ground that the former Secretary had been a corrupting and distracting influence in the government. At one point in the debate Forsyth had alluded so unmistakably to Calhoun that the Vice President had felt called on to answer. The exchange indicated, if it did nothing else, that old animosities had not been forgotten.[28]

With the perspective of hindsight it is easy to say that the rejection of Van Buren was bad politics for those who did it, that it played directly into the New Yorker's hand, and that it did indeed make him President according to the plans of his followers. Yet the performance was not quite so stupid as it has sometimes been made to appear. Calhoun was undoubtedly too optimistic if Benton overheard him correctly: "It will kill him, sir, kill him dead. He will never kick, sir, never kick."[29] But political optimism was an essential part of his nature. Besides, he had no other choice, nor had his partisans. As Duff Green pointed out at the time, everyone knew Calhoun's opinion of Van Buren's character, and his belief that the former Secretary of State had been responsible for his own quarrel with Jackson. In those circumstances he could hardly have voted to confirm the Minister without losing both his own self-respect and the respect of his enemies. Neither could he evade the issue; for Clay and Webster, who were themselves publicly committed, would see to it that the Vice President also went on record.[30]

It is true that the close friends of Van Buren rejoiced in the result, and that more than one outsider agreed that his martyrdom would mean the Presidency. But the friends of the opposition also rejoiced in victory; and the violence of the denunciations in the *Globe* and even in the Richmond *Enquirer* create a suspicion that some of Van Buren's friends had doubts.[31] In short, Clay and Calhoun both conceded that the rejection would make Van Buren the Jackson nominee for Vice President. They did not concede, in January 1832, that the Jackson ticket would be elected; and it was not unreasonable to suppose that a defeat at the polls, even if only for the second place, would be, if not a mortal, at least a crippling blow to the Red Fox.

ROBERT Y. HAYNE

GENERAL JAMES HAMILTON, JR.

FRANCIS PRESTON BLAIR

JOEL ROBERTS POINSETT

Sketch of Fort Hill, showing Calhoun's office

Sketch of the interior of Calhoun's office

4

Van Buren's defeat indicated a temporary union of expediency between Calhoun and Clay, if no more. It appeared to bear out the line of attack that Blair had been following for months, and he opened up again with renewed vigor. Calhoun, Clay, and Webster were likened to the triumvirs of ancient Rome and accused of seeking to split the Union into parts so that each might rule a portion. Blair's complete lack of restraint threatened to become a liability to the Jacksonians, and for a time they considered replacing him with Kendall.[32]

Duff Green not only denied in the *Telegraph* that there was any understanding between Calhoun and Clay: he denied that Calhoun was a candidate for the Presidency.[33] In both particulars, as of February 1832, he was probably correct. Even so sanguine an individual as John C. Calhoun must have realized by that date that he had no Presidential prospects of his own, even though he waited until May to make public withdrawal from a contest he had never formally entered. While the tariff was being debated in the Senate the Vice President was inclined to lay at Clay's door responsibility for the sectional conflict then reaching a crisis.[34] Clay was equally suspicious of the South Carolinian and regarded as "flagitous" the disposition of Calhoun's followers "to purchase support to the anti-tariff doctrines, by a total sacrifice of the public lands to the States within which they are situated."[35] Both men were aware, however, that should the election go to the House, it would be within the power of Calhoun's partisans to make Clay President.[36]

Calhoun's friends in Virginia started Philip P. Barbour as a rival to Van Buren for the Vice Presidential nomination on the Jackson ticket for a similar reason. Barbour's principal claim was that he had expressed for Calhoun "the highest respect . . . as a man of talent, integrity and a gentleman."[37] The Virginians did not hope to elect Barbour and they certainly did not mean to vote for Jackson. They simply wanted another man in the field in hopes of preventing any candidate from getting a majority. A Vice President could then be chosen by the Senate, where the combined Clay and Calhoun forces represented a majority.[38]

The *Jeffersonian and Virginia Times,* meanwhile, was moved from Lynchburg to Richmond, still under the editorship of Richard K.

Crallé. The avowed purpose of the paper was to advocate what Governor Floyd called the "true States Rights principles" and what Calhoun referred to as "the old Whig doctrines of '98."[39] Duff Green printed the prospectus of the paper in the *Telegraph* and secured pledges of subscriptions from Calhoun's friends in Congress.[40] On the last day of February he sent Floyd, who was handling the finances for the *Jeffersonian,* a draft for $1,000, and promised $2,000 more "upon a few days notice."[41] The first issue appeared on March 29, 1832. It would, according to Green, "supply the place which the apostacy of Mr. Ritchie has vacated."[42]

Coincident with the appearance of Crallé's paper came the first explicit move toward political union between Calhoun and Clay. Who made the first overture is not clear. Each side preferred to have it appear that an offer was made by the other. The fact remains, however, that late in March Governor Floyd found an occasion to explain away the harshness of his previously expressed opinion of Henry Clay. Shortly thereafter Calhoun himself had an interview with one of Clay's close political friends, which was followed up by Duff Green. The proposal Green made was that Calhoun would be formally presented as a candidate for the Presidency late in the summer if his friends believed he could carry three or four states in the South. Chief of these was to be Virginia, and to insure a Calhoun victory there his sponsors wanted the Clay ticket withdrawn. They believed the Vice President could carry also the two Carolinas, Georgia, and possibly Alabama and Mississippi. If he could win only Virginia, the Carolinas, and Georgia, however, it would be enough to throw the election into the House, where Clay would be chosen. The success of the whole scheme depended on the support of the Clay party in Virginia.

Clay conceded that the scheme would probably work, even if it had been motivated by "the desperate condition of Mr. Calhoun's prospects," and he hastened to consult Francis Brooke, foremost of his own lieutenants in Virginia. He wanted to know how much strength Calhoun had in that state and whether the Clay partisans there could be induced to accept such an arrangement.[43] At the same time Green noted a "strong predisposition to Calhoun among Clay's & Wirts friends," and found the Clay supporters anxious that Calhoun should run,[44] a circumstance indicating that the overtures were not exclusively on Calhoun's side. Clay thought seriously enough of the proposition to make a flying trip to Virginia just after the middle of April, spending three or four days with Brooke and other party leaders.[45]

In the end the proposed deal came to nothing. Clay probably remembered too vividly the public reaction to his earlier bargain with Adams to risk another of the same sort. There must, too, have been a price attached to the support of Calhoun's followers in the House, and it was undoubtedly a price that would have to be paid in advance: modification of the tariff at the current session of Congress. Clay still thought he could win the election on the Bank issue if Wirt's friends would give him a little help; and the South Carolina excitement had made Calhoun a questionable ally. Late in May Duff Green announced again that Calhoun was not a candidate and had resisted becoming one for twelve months past. Calhoun was enough of a realist to know that no man who held the opinions he had avowed could hope for the votes of more than a very small fraction of his fellow citizens, and he placed his refusal to become a candidate squarely on that ground. "In other words," said Ritchie, "the grapes are sour. . . ."[46]

The advantages of an arrangement such as that proposed between Calhoun and Clay were broached again from time to time,[47] and the respective followings of the two men actually did join forces against Van Buren in North Carolina.[48] The principals, however, made no further effort to unite before the 1832 election.

CHAPTER X

THE BANK, THE TARIFF, AND THE ELECTION OF 1832

1

AFTER the defeat of Van Buren, Congress divided its time between the Bank recharter and modification of the tariff. Both were major political issues for opponents of the administration. It was Clay and his adherents who wanted to assure the continuance of the Bank of the United States. It was Calhoun and the Nullifiers who wanted the tariff revised. The two questions were debated concurrently, and now and again they almost appeared to merge. The political stakes will be a little clearer, however, if we examine them separately. First, then, the Bank.

It was over the Bank question that ponderous and durable Thomas Hart Benton abandoned the South-West alliance to Clay and went over unreservedly to the Jacksonians. There was an old feud with the Bank in Benton's past, but he could have forgotten that, as he forgot his old feud with Jackson. He was moved in part, undoubtedly, by personal conviction; but in part also, like Webster and Calhoun and Van Buren, he chose to follow the popular will in his own state. It was during the session of 1831-1832 that Benton emerged as the outstanding foe of the Bank and the leading champion of "hard money." He earned for himself the profound gratitude of the Jackson party, and in time would earn also the nickname of "Old Bullion," which he wore proudly to the end of his days. The leading defenders of the Bank in the Senate were Webster and Clay, and in the House McDuffie. The Nullifiers, as a party, were indifferent to the question, and Calhoun's followers took sides according to their own judgment.

Nicholas Biddle himself was still reluctant to raise the Bank question when Congress met. Webster and Clay, both on occasion attorneys for the Bank, pressed hard for a formal memorial praying for recharter; but Secretary McLane thought it sure to lose at that session. The President, he argued, would regard any move in that direction before the election as hostile and would therefore certainly veto it if it passed. He tabulated the opinions of the members to show that there would not be two thirds in either house prepared to override the negative.[1] Thomas Cadwalader arrived in Washington just before Christmas as Biddle's personal representative, and his reports, based on long conversations with McLane and influential members of both houses of Congress, were not encouraging.[2] At length, however, both Cadwalader and Biddle yielded to the judgment of Webster and Clay. On January 9, 1832, the memorial was duly presented, by Dallas in the Senate and McDuffie in the House.[3]

Clay had consciously selected the Bank as a political issue, but Biddle much preferred to keep it out of politics, and for some time he carried water precariously on both shoulders. His spokesmen in Washington sought to learn from friendly Cabinet members and from the President himself what modifications in the Bank charter would make the institution acceptable to Jackson. They offered freely to make all necessary concessions, and even suggested the political wisdom of making the recharter an administration measure. Biddle was thus ready without a qualm to sell out Clay and Webster if he could come to terms with Jackson; and he was equally ready to double-cross Calhoun. For one of the ways in which the Bank was to be made palatable to Jackson was by insinuating through inspired articles in the press that it was really the Vice President and his partisans who opposed the institution. The entire Cabinet except for Taney was on the side of the Bank, so it probably looked easier than it was.[4] In late February Biddle was actually shown a statement of the President's wishes with respect to the Bank charter, and agreed to everything.[5] It all lent credence to the suspicion that the real foe of the Bank was Martin Van Buren, who was not present to twist the old General to his will. At any rate Benton suddenly began to play for time, while Van Buren hurried home from England.

It was at Benton's instigation that A. S. Clayton of Georgia proposed in the House that the Bank be investigated.[6] Investigation meant delay, but the friends of the Bank could not object without implying that the institution had something to conceal. Clayton's resolution was debated for the better part of two weeks and was then passed with the active support of McDuffie. Here was politics with a vengeance! McDuffie's purpose was to delay the Bank vote until after the tariff had been decided, thereby putting the State Rights party in position to bargain with the Bank supporters for concessions on the tariff. The tactics were too clear, however, and both the Bank lobbyists and the Jacksonians moved quickly to forestall the desired outcome. Biddle's board of strategy proposed to start another Bank bill in the Senate, which they did; and the Speaker named to the Bank investigation group both McDuffie and John Quincy Adams, chairmen respectively of the Committees on Ways and Means and on Manufactures. The investigation was to take place in Philadelphia, and all action on the tariff would therefore be effectively suspended until the chairmen of the two committees concerned with it should return.[7] McDuffie of course could have declined to serve, but Adams' absence alone would have halted consideration of the tariff. Cambreleng was also of the investigating party, no doubt to look after Van Buren's interests.

The special committee left for Philadelphia late in March, and Biddle presently rushed incognito to Washington, where he had a long conference with Jackson and McLane.[8] When the group returned in April, they disagreed as to what they had discovered, save that they had not found any evidence of corruption. More time was lost while majority and minority reports, including a separate report by Adams, were prepared and printed. Then Biddle took over the reports as campaign documents of his own.[9]

The advocates of tariff reduction and the friends of the Bank in the House were still jockeying for position late in May, when the Bank recharter reached the floor of the Senate. Biddle himself arrived in Washington at about the same time—this time without concealment—to direct his lobby in person, and Webster gave the Bank president great credit for the success of the bill.[10] It was even hinted that loans were freely made to members, some of whom went home to avoid casting an unfavorable vote, while others who had been opponents changed both minds and votes.[11] It is hardly likely, however, in view of the party divisions in Congress at that time, that either Biddle's influence or his loans were actually needed. At least they were not in the Senate. The vote came on June 11 and the Senate approved recharter 28 to 20. The National Republicans were united, with such stanch Jacksonians as Dallas and Wilkins of Pennsylvania and Smith of Maryland voting with them. Among Calhoun's partisans, on the other hand, only Poindexter voted for recharter, with Hayne, Miller, Moore, and the two Virginians on the side of the administration.[12]

It was the end of June before the House got around to consideration of the bill passed by the Senate. Then after only three days of debate, the lower chamber also voted recharter of the Bank of the United States, by a majority of 107 to 85.[13] When the bill went to the President for signature on July 3, however, it was generally conceded that there would be a veto.[14] On Sunday, July 8, Van Buren appeared in Washington, going directly to the Executive Mansion; and on Tuesday, July 10, the veto message was received. The order of events was not coincidence.[15]

Webster and Clay, who had reserved their principal thunder for just this contingency, argued for the Bank on July 11, 12, and 13, ably seconded by Ewing of Ohio and Clayton of Delaware. Only Benton saw any point in speaking on the other side. The veto could not possibly be overridden, and the speakers were only fixing the issue and preparing some of the literature for the coming Presidential campaign.[16] Blair was doing likewise. "It is difficult to describe, in adequate language," declared the *Globe* on July 12, "the sublimity of the moral spectacle now presented to the American people in the person of Andrew Jackson. . . ."

Two days later the President signed the tariff of 1832, and this time it was South Carolina that found language inadequate.

2

The tariff controversy, by 1832, was beyond reasoning. The cleavage was too deep for argument. Intelligent men on each side thought those on the other side bent on their destruction, and each side thought the other willfully, obstinately, and maliciously wrong. Many, perhaps most, of the members of Congress, and innumerable plain citizens the country over, thought the contest had gone far enough and that it was time for compromise; but everyone wanted the concessions to come from interests other than the one he paricularly represented. The belligerent attitude of South Carolina only stiffened the resistance to change on the part of the manufacturing states. By 1832 the charges of Blair and the Jackson press, through constant repetition, had begun to assume the outward aspect of truth; and Northern men who should have known better began to believe that the South Carolina doctrines actually were intended to rationalize a separation of the slave states from the Union.[17] At a time when the highest statesmanship was needed, an issue that threatened the very existence of the nation was made a matter of partisan and sectional politics.

Among those who were convinced at the start of the session that the tariff must be reduced was John Quincy Adams, chairman of the House Committee on Manufactures. Adams would maintain the duties as they were until after the payment of the public debt, but in this he met no objection from the South. The South, in fact, regarded him as on their side and commended him for it.[18] The ex-President did not, of course, go quite that far. He would "certainly not consent to sacrifice the manufacturing interest," but he did believe that "something of concession would be due from that interest to appease the discontents of the South"; and he suggested to McLane that the Treasury should offer a compromise plan.[19] His own section repudiated it and the weight of economic pressure began slowly to bear against a compromise.[20]

The tariff debate, meanwhile, had got off to a flying start in the Senate. Revenue measures cannot originate in the upper house but they can always be discussed by calling them resolutions instead of bills. So on January 9, 1832, Senator Henry Clay of Kentucky, father of the "American System" and National Republican nominee for President of the United States, introduced a resolution to abolish duties on foreign articles not coming into competition with domestic productions. Wines and silks were excepted, but the duties on these were to be reduced. The scheme would scarcely affect the revenue and would actually increase the inequality of which the South complained. Worse still, as Hayne patiently explained, the principle of protection was retained, although he and those with whom he acted held it to be unconstitutional.[21] Duff Green predicted inevitable nullification if the protective policy were not abandoned; John Tyler and Samuel Smith shook their heads and gave the protectionists more ammunition by talking of eventual separation of the states if sectional interests could not be reconciled.[22]

When Clay's resolution came up for debate on January 16, Hayne moved an amendment that would have reduced the tariff to the revenue level after payment of the public debt. He was willing to allow reasonable time for gradual reduction on those articles in direct competition with American manufactures, but all duties were eventually to be equalized. It may be assumed that this was also Calhoun's position. At least it was consistent with that taken by McDuffie in the House, and Calhoun specifically commended McDuffie's stand.[23] It was also, significantly enough, the compromise position of twelve months later.

The Senate chamber was crowded for Hayne's speech. He was always popular with the galleries, and he did not disappoint them this time. His auditors, according to the *Globe,* left "with better auguries for the restoration of harmony among the different sections of the Union than they brought with them. The spirit of compromise, in which Mr. Hayne advocated the interests of the South, impressed very favorably some of those who are identified with the opposite policy." Yes, the *Globe!* and Blair went on to rejoice that the country's wounds were soon to be healed.[24] Could it be that Jackson himself, with neither Van Buren nor Eaton at hand to whisper in his ear, was ready to make such concessions on the tariff as would satisfy the South? If so, his intentions lasted only briefly. One of the Van Buren men must have pointed out to the old chieftain that, if the administration supported such a compromise as Hayne wanted, Calhoun would inevitably get the credit for it: Calhoun, who had been advocating precisely that for years, but who according to their own propaganda was threatening to break up the Union and was certainly the greatest knave alive. So the orders went out and Blair was soon at it again, charging that Calhoun did not really want any adjustment of the tariff lest he have no excuse to nullify. On February 2 Clay replied to Hayne and closed the door to compromise.[25]

3

In the House, where the Committees on Manufactures and on Ways and Means were working on rival bills, things moved more slowly, and there was a long interruption while the special committee to investigate the Bank sojourned in Philadelphia. Adams continued to work for modification well into March, but found the members of his committee not in agreement on any single point.[26] It was after the outcome of the Senate debate had convinced him that the tariff could not be modified at that session anyway that he decided to call South Carolina's bluff. He professed still to regard the system as impolitic and impracticable, but "as the South Carolina nullifiers have given notice that *if* the Tariff is not modified this Session, *they* will act," he inclined to the opinion that it would be as well "to give them the opportunity to make good their threat."[27]

Calhoun was equally sure after the Senate debate that there would be no satisfactory adjustment of the tariff at that session, but he also knew that South Carolina was not bluffing. The point had simply been reached at which one side or the other had to give in, and the South, because she was a permanent minority, could not yield without at the same time yielding every future point on which her interests might differ from those of the majority. "All history proves," he wrote to Crallé in April, "when the parts of a community are placed in the relation, now existing between the South and the other sections, reason is perfectly impotent to stay the course of injustice and oppression. If no conservative principle be found in the Constitution, to arrest the natural course of events, in such cases, the end must be a revolution or an entire change of system." The conservative principle, as he had already explained on numerous occasions over the past four years, was state interposition or nullification, and the time was rapidly approaching when it would have to be invoked as the only alternative to surrender.[28]

Neither Calhoun nor his followers stopped trying, but by the time the House Committee on Manufactures reported a tariff bill late in May the situation was hopeless. It was as though both sides saw only disaster ahead but each held the other responsible and itself powerless to interfere.[29] Adams presented the committee's bill on May 23, like one washing his hands of the whole affair. It was based, he said, on a new report by the Treasury, but no member of the committee was pledged to support any part of it. As for himself, he admitted privately that he thought it would be lost and that he did not care one way or the other.[30]

Through the rest of May and all of June the tariff bill was debated in the House, with the Southern wing trying desperately but unavailingly to gain concessions. Their minimum requirements were restated by Green in the *Telegraph* for May 24, much as Hayne had detailed them in the Senate. The surplus revenue must be eliminated and the tax burden must be equalized so far as possible, but as much time might be taken to make the adjustment effective as the North required. The evidence is sketchy but such as there is indicates that through June, up to two or three days before the bill was passed, Calhoun and Adams were working together to find some acceptable common ground. Twice during the interval Calhoun dined with Adams, and both times Webster also was of the company. On the first occasion Clay, Poindexter, and Hayne were among the guests; and on the second, McDuffie, Silsbee, and Verplanck of New York. On June 25 Adams notes visiting McDuffie and Calhoun and discussing constitutional questions at length. The notes give no indication of the ground covered, but the selection of guests could hardly have been purposeless.[31]

As the bill moved on its tortuous and tumultuous way to final passage, it was clear that no essential change would be made to placate the South. The administration members made the bill their own and fought every attempt at amendment. Ritchie pleaded with Van Buren to hasten to Washington and stop the madness before it was too late. "Should Congress rise without adjusting the Tariff, on liberal principles, Hamilton & Hayne, Calhoun & McDuffie will help S. Carolina to adopt nullification. . . . The whole South is indignant at the opposition & obduracy of the Tariffites. Virginia is now cool; but very excitable, and determined not to send a man or a musket to put down S. Carolina.—Events may hurry us farther. . . ."[32] And Hayne spent fruitless hours arguing with Jackson himself.[33] The bill passed the House on June 28, by a vote of 132 to 65. It came up in the Senate the following day and, though debate was stormy, it passed on July 9, 32 to 16.[34] In both houses the vote was large enough to override a veto, had Jackson been disposed to offer one.

Both Jacksonians and National Republicans talked of the new law as though it were a final settlement of the question and the fixed and unalterable policy of the country. For the purposes of Clay and Van Buren had alike been served. The bill was so equivocal and involved that no one could be sure on the face of it whether it was good or bad. The tariff men could say they had made concessions, and the South could not prove until the revenue had actually been collected that they had not. By then the election would be safely over.

4

The Democratic convention met in Baltimore on May 21 and 22, 1832, and unanimously endorsed the President for a second term. Van Buren, who had "reluctantly" consented to accept the second place on the ticket in the interest of his own vindication, was duly nominated for Vice President, though with something less than unanimity. The convention then adopted a resolution recommending that each delegate report to his constituents as he thought proper. There was to be no general address to the public, such as the National Republicans and the Antimasons had issued. All shades of opinion were represented and the party managers were too shrewd to attempt a platform of common principles. Theirs was a party of men rather than of measures. Van Buren, like Jackson, was to be all things to all people.[35]

As the stormy session of Congress neared its close, Calhoun withdrew and Tazewell was again elected President pro tempore of the Senate.[36] This time the Virginia Senator accepted the honor and presided over the remaining week of the session. It was a victory for Calhoun, but on the score of legislation the victories were all Clay's. The tariff was so like the one he had originally proposed as to be indistinguishable. The Bank recharter had passed; and even the veto, so he believed, was in his interest.[37] The South Carolinians were once again reduced to the impotency of protest. Except for three who were of the Union party, the members of the state's Congressional delegation signed a sober address to their constituents, reviewing the history of tariff legislation. They suggested no remedy but expressed their "solemn and deliberate conviction that the protective system must now be regarded as the settled policy of the country, and that all hope of redress from congress is irrevocably gone."[38]

Before the end of July the political alignments were clarified as they had not been since Jefferson's time. The Bank veto brought Biddle and all the economic power he represented into the Clay fold.[39] Leading Jackson papers, including the powerful New York *Courier and Enquirer,* were swung over to the opposition under pressure from the commercial interests.[40] Those manufacturers who had flirted with the Calhoun faction came scurrying back to Clay, and the basic political division along economic lines seemed almost to be restored. The National Republicans now stood for the moneyed interests and the conservative middle class just as the Federalists of Hamilton's day had stood; while the Democrats professed to represent the propertyless, the small landholders, and those who worked with their hands. These are, of course, generalizations to which there are many exceptions; but the only significant exception was the South. By temperament and interest the Southern planter should have been on Clay's side. He was as conservative as any man alive, and his was at once the landed and the commercial class of his section. Had it not been for Garrison and the antislavery agitators, he might have voted the National Republican ticket in spite of the tariff. The abolitionists reminded him that he could neither sustain by his suffrage nor condone by his tolerance any system of government based on the sovereignty of the majority in the national legislature. He could not, therefore, be satisfied with either Jackson or Clay. So the South was indifferent or divided, Jackson won a thumping victory, and Clay learned four years late that those who wield the economic power in any community are always numerically in the minority.

Calhoun undoubtedly expected, when he left Washington, that South Carolina would go through with nullification. It is probable that he had also decided at that time to come into the Senate when his term as Vice President expired, or perhaps even earlier. In the Senate he would be the active leader for reform, in the sense in which the South understood the term, and could wield a considerable influence.[41] Whichever side won the election, he expected to be in opposition, and so he advised his supporters to take no part in the contest. Late in August, however, Duff Green brought the *Telegraph* out against Jackson.[42] He could not come out in support of Clay; but as various Clay editors ordered copies of his anti-Jackson *Telegraph Extra,* Green made peace with those who had once been his bitter foes. He saw no reason why the friends of Calhoun, as individuals, should not vote for Clay, or why they should not make common cause against Van Buren. Green was soon on friendly terms with James H. Pleasants of the Richmond *Whig* and Oran Follett of the Buffalo *Daily Journal,* and Blair was again croaking hoarsely that Calhoun, Clay, and Webster were a new Triumvirate seeking to subvert the government and divide its territories among themselves.[43]

By election day the issues had been so thoroughly confused that few voters could have been sure just what any of the candidates stood for, had done, or meant to do; but Andrew Jackson was still the hero of the masses. When the ballots were counted, the old General had won 219 electoral votes to 49 for Clay, 7 for Wirt, and 11 cast by the South Carolina state legislature for John Floyd of Virginia and Henry Lee of Massachusetts. Wirt had carried only Vermont; and Clay had won no more than Massachusetts, Rhode Island, Delaware,

Kentucky, and 5 of the 8 votes of Maryland. Martin Van Buren's total was 30 electoral votes short of Jackson's votes, because Pennsylvania had preferred Senator William Wilkins for the second office.[44]

The election, in the eyes of most observers, settled two points: internal improvements at the expense of the general government and a nationally chartered bank were both unconstitutional.[45] The tariff was still unsettled, but South Carolina was rapidly preparing to force that issue.

CHAPTER XI

SOUTH CAROLINA INTERPOSES

1

THE passage of the tariff of 1832 put local politics in South Carolina back where they had been before the ice water of Calhoun's Fort Hill Address. The middle-of-the-roaders were again pushed aside by the fire-eaters and Fourth of July orations were revolutionary battle cries. The leading conservatives, like Calhoun and Hayne, were still in Washington, and it was such as Governor Hamilton and Robert Barnwell Rhett who dominated the occasion. Rhett's speech at Walterboro was a manifesto and a call to arms; and the generally favorable reception it received indicated how far the state had drifted since the same orator's first Walterboro address of four years earlier.[1] The average South Carolinian was no more interested in dialectics than the average man has ever been anywhere. He simply knew that for five years his leaders had been threatening to do something about the tariff if the duties were not reduced. Once more Congress had acted, and the duties remained prohibitively—he believed unjustly—high. The state elections coming on in October offered the best chance the state would ever have to redress its own wrongs. If the people were apathetic it was not the basic issue but the spate of words that was at fault; so the younger leaders tried sharper and more warlike words.[2]

The growing belligerency of the younger leaders gave color of truth to the charges of the opposition. It was easier for the Unionists at home and for the Jacksonians everywhere to argue that nullification meant rebellion when so many of the Nullifiers seemed to think so themselves. As the battle for control of the state legislature gathered headway in July and August, the issue of convention or no convention was largely forgotten and the simpler, more comprehensible resistance or submission took its place. Resistance, at one extreme, meant the peaceful, constitutional interposition of the sovereignty of the state to arrest the tariff; at the other it meant revolution or civil war. Submission also held different meanings for different people.

Some, like Drayton, were willing to accept the tariff of 1832 as at least a gesture in the direction of compromise; others, like Cheves, merely thought that South Carolina should not act alone, and wanted a convention of the Southern States.

Outside of South Carolina there were a few sober and thoughtful reactions, particularly in Virginia; but for the most part Blair set the tone for the press, and Jackson himself gave Blair his cue. So far as the President was concerned, the grievances of which the South complained had been removed by the tariff of 1832. It therefore followed that the "whole attempt at nullification is an effort of disappointed ambition, originating with unprincipled men who would rather rule in hell, than be subordinate in heaven."[3] Blair amplified the theme, with oblique references to "another Vice President, who involved himself in intrigues to exclude the favorite of the people from the Chief Magistracy, and on failing, conspired against the Union. . . ."[4]

Charge and countercharge fanned the flames of excitement and worked the state up to fever pitch. It was when things threatened to boil over and it seemed as though rebellion would be the order of the day that Calhoun again intervened, with a carefully timed exposition of his own conservative views. His statement took the form of a letter to Governor Hamilton, dated August 28, 1832. Hamilton published it in the middle of September so that it could be read and would still be fresh in mind by election day. It must have come as something of a shock to the cynical among the Unionists, who had expected the Vice President to abandon his followers and "astonish the natives with another somersault."[5] For the letter to Hamilton was again a defense of nullification as a peaceful, legitimate, and constitutional mode of redress. Calhoun was so sure of himself, so confident that he was right, that he thought his newest exposition would settle the question once and for all, "at least as far as reason has anything to do with settling political questions."[6] Even the Unionists conceded that he was "entitled to some credit for the skill with which he has put together his materials," although the argument they regarded as a "paltry affair."[7] Daniel Webster was more generous when the letter came into his hands. He found it "by far the ablest and most plausible, and therefore the most dangerous vindication of that particular form of revolution" which had yet appeared. Webster knew that it would have to be answered and proposed to do it himself, in the form of a letter to Chancellor Kent of New York. He gave up the project, however, when he learned that Calhoun was to come into the Senate, where they would undoubtedly debate the issue in person.[8]

In the Jackson press the cries of "treason" only grew the louder, and the President ordered both land and naval garrisons at Charleston replaced with men who had not been exposed to the virus.[9] Yet all Calhoun sought was to stop the collection of tariff duties until the question of constitutionality could be determined by a convention of the states or by the submission of an amendment; that, and to restrain the warlike enthusiasm of his followers. He was not trying to destroy the Union: he was trying to save it from those who professed to be its best friends. On the day of the South Carolina election he wrote Maxcy that nullification would win; "but," he hastened to add, "any movement will be made with the view of preserving the Union. The end aimed at will be a general convention of all the States,"—not just the Southern States, as some of the Unionists wished—"in order to adjust all constitutional differences, and thus restore general harmony. We have run nearly fifty years on the first tack. It is a wonderful run; but it is time to bring up the reckoning, in order to take a fresh departure."[10] Jefferson himself had said as much, after the Missouri Compromise, and not even Francis Preston Blair yet dared to call Thomas Jefferson a traitor.

2

In the constitutional literature that had grown up since 1789 there was ample justification for the step South Carolina was about to take; but there was also a solid and substantial precedent given by Andrew Jackson himself, and so recent that not even the dullest could have forgotten it. It was early in 1832 that the last of the Cherokee cases reached the Supreme Court of the United States, whose decision was nullified by the state of Georgia. The Unionists insisted that the Georgia case was different, but if Calhoun's careful plans had been followed in South Carolina, the two cases would have been identical. The Georgia case will therefore bear some examination.

In her anxiety to rid herself of the Indians, Georgia had passed in 1830 a series of proscriptive laws designed to obliterate entirely the Indian sovereignty in the state. The laws of the Cherokee Nation were pronounced null and void, Indians were forbidden to testify in court in any case involving a white man, and white men were forbidden to reside among the Indians except under license from the Governor. The tribe had sought an injunction in the Supreme Court to restrain Georgia from executing her laws; but this was denied by a divided court in 1831, on the ground of inadequate jurisdiction.[11]

The controversy reached the high court again in February 1832. In the new case Samuel Worcester and a number of other missionaries, who had been for some time residing among the Cherokees under license from the Federal Government, were arrested by Georgia authorities because they had not obtained the necessary permission from the Governor. They were convicted by a Georgia court and sentenced to four years at hard labor. All except Worcester and one sturdy companion accepted pardons from the Governor and agreed to abide by the laws of the state. Worcester carried his case on appeal to the Supreme Court. The American Board of Foreign Missions, which had sent him to the Cherokees in the first place, retained William Wirt and John Sergeant as counsel for the missionary—one of them Antimasonic nominee for President of the United States, and the other Vice Presidential candidate on the National Republican ticket. The cause of the missionary, and through him of the Cherokees, was thus associated with the opposition to the administration. The notoriety of the case and the fame of the counsel were such that fifty or sixty members of the House and a handful of Senators forsook their official duties to attend the Court; and the case was hotly debated in the House itself.[12]

The decision was handed down early in March by the Chief Justice, with only Baldwin dissenting.[13] The Court held that the laws of Georgia were of no force or effect in the territory of the Cherokee Nation, and declared the act of the state under which the defendant had been convicted to be void. The decision created "a very strong sensation in both houses" of Congress, but no one believed that Georgia would accept the judgment or that Jackson would compel her to do so.[14] It was in relation to this case that the President is said to have remarked, "Well, John Marshall has made his decision, now let him enforce it."[15]

Whether Jackson said any such thing or not doesn't matter. What does matter is that no attempt whatever was made by the administration to carry out a judgment of the Supreme Court that happened to conflict with the sovereignty of a state. It is true that in Georgia there was no convention, no ordinance, and no mobilization of militia; but it is true also that the sovereignty of the state was at least tacitly recognized as paramount to that of the Federal Government, expressed through one of its three co-ordinate branches. From the incident the Nullifiers took new heart; for if Jackson would not interfere in Georgia, surely he could not justify interference in South Carolina.

What they forgot was that Jackson's prejudices were all the justification he needed.

3

The South Carolina elections of 1832 were colorful, spirited, and often violent. Following the lead of the Nullifiers, the Unionists had organized political clubs of their own. The two parties had their own emblems—a blue cockade and palmetto button for the Nullifiers; an American eagle for the Unionists. Feeling ran high. Friends of years' standing bowed stiffly to each other on the street, but did not speak. The young hotheads brawled in the alleys or coldly shot at each other on the dueling ground, according to their social caste. The women were as pugnacious as the men, and did everything but make lint in anticipation of more serious fighting.[16]

As the campaign worked up to its climax, both sides were driven to extremes. The Unionists, by election day, were upholding the protectionist policy, and the Nullifiers were skirting the edges of outright rebellion.[17] In popular sentiment, however, the Nullifiers had all the best of it. They won a close victory in the Charleston city elections in September, and in the state elections the following month the margin was overwhelming. The popular majority was only about 6,000 out of some 40,000 votes cast; but the heavy Unionist vote was concentrated in a small number of districts. Pendleton, where the Nullifiers doubled the vote of their Unionist opponents, was typical. In the legislature the majority was a little over two thirds in the lower house and nearer three fourths in the senate.[18] Governor Hamilton was in Pendleton at the time of the election, undoubtedly to confer with Calhoun as to strategy; and his proclamation calling an extraordinary session of the legislature for October 22 was actually prepared before the election results were known.[19]

The legislature convened as called and received its orders from the Governor. There was, Hamilton declared, no further hope of redress from Congress. The tariff of 1832 was as bad as any tariff had ever been, and had been pronounced by both major parties to represent the final and settled policy of the country. Argument and protest had availed nothing, while the economic ruin of the state proceeded before their eyes. He would offer no suggestions as to a remedy, but the people had clearly spoken on one point. The Governor asked that the popular will be heeded and a convention be called to consider the situation.[20] Within three days a convention bill was passed by votes of 31 to 13 in the senate and 96 to 25 in the house. The event was celebrated with artillery fire and music. The band, with quaint humor, played "Yankee Doodle."[21]

Members of the convention were chosen after a whirlwind campaign in which the disheartened Unionists scarcely tried; but even had they made a fight of it, the result would have differed only slightly. The convention represented the propertied classes rather than the rank and file, and its members had been chosen on the basis of the same limited suffrage as the regular elective officers of the state.[22] Because of his position as Vice President of the United States, Calhoun had not permitted his own name to be put up as a delegate, but he was almost the only leader of the party who was not a member of the convention. Governor James Hamilton, Jr., and his father were both present. So also were Senators Robert Y. Hayne and Stephen D. Miller and ex-Senator William Smith; McDuffie, Barnwell, and J. K. Griffin of the Congressional delegation; Chancellor William Harper; and three of the ever-present Pinckneys—Charles Cotesworth, William C., and the veteran Federalist of other days, Thomas. Other great names in South Carolina history included Pierce M. Butler, R. J. McCord, F. H. Elmore, Armistead Burt, and Robert Barnwell Rhett, who for another year or so would still be called R. Barnwell Smith. The small group of Unionists included Alfred and D. E. Huger, Henry M. Middleton, Benjamin F. Perry, and Judge John Belton O'Neall.[23] Predominantly the members of the convention were men in middle life, with a handful of Revolutionary veterans and very few young men.

4

When the convention met on November 19, Governor Hamilton was elected president, and Isaac W. Hayne, nephew of the Senator, was chosen secretary.[24] There is no evidence to show that Calhoun was in Columbia during any part of the convention session, and it is hardly likely that he was. His presence would have been seized upon by the Jacksonians and used for political purposes, to the possible detriment of the cause for which he was working. Even had there been no such reason, his own sense of propriety would probably have kept him away.[25]

The convention began its work with the appointment of a Committee of Twenty-one to draft an Ordinance of Nullification. On the committee were Hayne, Miller, Barnwell, Griffin, and McDuffie; Colonel Pierce M. Butler; Robert J. Turnbull; and for the Unionists, Judge O'Neall and Henry Middleton.[26] Disregarding the small Unionist minority that wanted no nullification at all, the principal differences of opinion in the committee were as to the time of application and whether a threat of secession should be included in the ordinance. The Twenty-one agreed at the first meeting, on November 20, that the tariff as a whole should be declared to be unconstitutional, rather than to single out and make exceptions for those articles on which duties were already at the revenue level. On the time of application there were two distinct opinions. The radical wing wanted the ordinance to be immediately effective. The conservatives, following Calhoun, wanted to give Congress one more chance by selecting a date to correspond with the payment of the public debt. The secession question found the group divided into three factions. Hayne and McDuffie favored a declaration that the state would be automatically out of the Union should force be used against her. Another alternative, defended by Barnwell, was merely to threaten secession in case coercion should be attempted; and still a third faction, led by Colonel W. C. Pinckney, wanted no reference to secession at all.[27] It is with this last position that Calhoun would have agreed. The date of application was finally compromised, with February 1, 1833, being chosen. The secession question was left to a subcommittee which followed the views of Hayne and McDuffie. And after another stormy session of the committee, a clause requiring a test oath of allegiance to the state was inserted.[28]

By November 22 the Committee of Twenty-one had finished its work and offered to the convention four documents. These were a Report, prepared by Hayne; the Ordinance of Nullification itself, drafted by Chancellor Harper; an Address to the People of South

Carolina from the vigorous and barbed pen of Robert J. Turnbull, whose "Brutus" papers had first aroused the state in 1827; and an Address to the People of the United States, for which McDuffie was responsible, but which incorporated parts of a draft by Calhoun.[29] The Report was a comprehensive review of tariff legislation and its effects in the cotton states. The Address to the People of South Carolina emphasized once more the peaceable and constitutional nature of the action being taken and minimized the danger of coercion by the Federal Government. The people of the other states of the Union were asked to believe that South Carolina acted in no unfriendly spirit toward them, and were offered a concise statement of the principles which she held to justify her course. The Ordinance of Nullification declared the tariffs of 1828 and 1832 to be null and void, and forbade the collection within the state of duties levied under them. It provided also that no appeal could be taken to the Supreme Court of the United States; prescribed for all civil and military officers of the state an oath to enforce the Ordinance and the laws that might be passed under its authority; and proclaimed that the use of force by the Federal Government would be looked upon as dissolving the bonds of union between South Carolina and the other states.

The Ordinance went farther than Calhoun had intended it to go. His plan had been merely to declare the tariff unconstitutional by convention, and to have the legislature prohibit the collection of the duties. Enforcement was to be entirely through the courts, with proceedings being taken against any officer who attempted to collect the duties. The officer would then have to seek a writ of error; and if the Supreme Court ruled in his favor, the decree would simply be ignored. The whole arrangement was designed to parallel exactly the Georgia case, in which Jackson had already tacitly condoned the nullification of a Supreme Court ruling. If the President resorted to force, then the Federal Government and not South Carolina would be the aggressor.[30]

The Ordinance was adopted on November 24, 1832, by a vote of 136 to 26.[31] The Report and the two Addresses were also approved, and twenty thousand copies of each document were ordered printed. The Nullifiers then signed the Ordinance, the Unionists refused to sign it, and the convention adjourned. The legislature took over from there, passing all laws necessary to put the Ordinance into effect. Over the test oath there was a sharp struggle in the senate, but it was finally approved.[32] For the security of the state in the event of coercion, which none of the Nullifiers regarded as a serious possibility, an act reorganizing the militia was also passed.

The work was completed at a party caucus on the evening of November 27, where it was unanimously agreed that Hayne should be the next Governor. It was also agreed, but only after some bitter words, that Calhoun should replace Hayne in the United States Senate, with Hamilton being reserved for military command in the event of armed conflict.[33] Despite Hayne's brilliant record as Senator, this arrangement was the only one possible in these circumstances. Desirable as it was to send Calhoun to Washington to defend the state from the attacks that were certain to come, it was even more necessary to have in the Governor's chair someone who commanded the highest degree of respect both in and out of the state, and whose conservatism could be relied on to check any display of belligerency. It was up to South Carolina to prove that her remedy was peaceful, and in the last analysis the responsibility lay with the Governor. Aside from Calhoun himself, Hayne was the only man who met the requirements, and he had also the indispensable advantage of friendly personal relations with Andrew Jackson. In short, it was because Hayne's services were required at home rather than because Calhoun's were demanded in Washington that the former was not returned to the Senate. Had the purpose been merely to make a place for Calhoun, it would have been Miller rather than Hayne who gave way.

5

It was at first understood that, in view of the overwhelming sentiment in the state in favor of the measures adopted, the Unionists would not oppose, but would go along with the majority. By prearrangement, however, the Unionists met in a convention of their own on December 10, and before they adjourned they had placed themselves in outspoken opposition. In this change of attitude Poinsett was the moving force, and behind Poinsett stood the grim, uncompromising figure of Andrew Jackson.[34]

Poinsett, with an admirable understanding of Jackson's character, had informed the President immediately after the victory of the Nullifiers at the polls that any failure of the Federal Government to suppress the insurrection in South Carolina would be a triumph for Calhoun.[35] Jackson reacted as Poinsett must have known he would: he directed the Secretary of War to alert the forts in Charleston Harbor against surprise attack and ordered the forts defended "to the last extremity."[36] And immediately after the passage of the convention bill by the South Carolina legislature, George Breathitt, brother of the Kentucky Governor, was sent to Charleston in the guise of a postal inspector. He was actually, however, to be a spy for the President, with orders to learn the strength of the forts and the purposes of the Nullifiers. He was to work with Poinsett, Drayton, and the Collector of Customs in Charleston.[37]

Breathitt found his assignment already accomplished by Poinsett, who seemed to know, even before the convention met, what steps would be taken and what the lines of cleavage would be. He knew that McDuffie would favor secession if coercion were attempted by the Federal Government, and he knew that Calhoun opposed this step. He undertook to supply the President—using Breathitt as messenger—with the names of "disloyal" officers, both in the military services and in the civil administration. He suggested the advisability of sending some small vessels of war to Charleston, ostensibly for repairs; and he called for arms and ammunition, including grenades, for his own Unionist followers. All in all, he managed to create the impression that the "loyal" South Carolinians could handle the situation themselves with adequate matériel and the moral support of the Federal Government.[38]

The administration was well aware that hostilities, if begun by the Federal authorities, would arouse for South Carolina the sympathy of other states and perhaps render coercion impossible. Every precaution was therefore taken to let the overt act come from the Nullifiers. When it came, Calhoun was to be held responsible.[39] Even while Poinsett played all the changes on Jackson's antipathy for Calhoun, and while the President moved swiftly and efficiently to reinforce the military and naval commands in the recalcitrant state, the *Globe,* under Kendall's personal guidance, came out for a reduction of the tariff to revenue needs. It was, of course, a plain admission that the tariff of 1832 had not, as McLane and Jackson claimed, removed the grievances of the South; but Kendall now wanted to play a different game, and he was never one to stickle over consistency. It was presumably Kendall himself who wrote a series of editorials in the *Globe* on the blessings of union and the horrors of civil war, designed to isolate the nullification leaders. The rank and file, the *Globe* announced, had been willfully deluded into the belief that nullification was not hostile to the Union, which their leaders had all the time meant to destroy. Thus the plain people of South Carolina were offered a way of escape and at the same time were promised full relief from the oppressive laws of which they complained. They had only to abandon Calhoun and McDuffie to the noose, and all would be well. Even Hamilton and Hayne might be pardoned, for old friendship's sake.[40]

If the Nullifiers were aware of the reaction of the administration, they ignored it and proceeded to carry out the plans already made. On December 3 the state legislature cast South Carolina's Presidential vote for John Floyd of Virginia. On December 10, the day the Union convention met in Columbia, Hayne was elected Governor of the state by a vote of 123 to 26; and two days later Calhoun was chosen United States Senator, 121 to 28. Calhoun then resigned the Vice Presidency on December 28, 1832.[41]

CHAPTER XII

THE DUKE OF PENDLETON

1

CALHOUN'S contribution to the nullification movement was twofold: he rationalized the doctrine; and by his personal prestige and the sheer weight of his character he restrained the impetuous, convinced the doubters, and guided a potentially revolutionary outburst into conservative and nonviolent channels. To his opponents he was himself the very personification of nullification, its originator, and the moving force behind it. In jeering reference to his power they called him the Duke of Pendleton and alleged that South Carolina sneezed when Calhoun took snuff. Yet he held no state office, had no patronage to dispense, and was not in a position of economic dominance. By 1832 and increasingly thereafter South Carolina did his bidding and showered her honors upon him; yet he never controlled a political machine of the type Van Buren wielded, nor appealed as Jackson did to the imagination of the masses. His hold over his own state and eventually over most of the South was based on sheer intellectual leadership. In the long run he never failed to convince his fellows that what he sought was for their good and that their interests were safer in his hands than they would be if entrusted to anyone else.

It is true that Calhoun's family connections were powerful, but their power was based less on economic or social standing than on political prestige, and that was largely his own doing. There were many relatives, such as Patrick Noble, Francis W. Pickens, and Armistead Burt, who made distinguished names for themselves in politics; but without exception they were younger than he, and owed their political beginnings in varying degrees to his influence. Although he acquired considerable property through his wife's family, Calhoun was never more than able to make ends meet, and in comparison with the great low-country plantations his holdings were trivial. It was neither weight of property nor skill in political manipulation that enabled him to prevent revolt in South Carolina after the tariff of 1832, and that made him thereafter the almost undisputed master of the state—it was intellectual pre-eminence and force of character alone.

In the nation as a whole, such leadership as his had become all but impossible because every downward extension of the suffrage brought with it less respect for the qualities he had to offer; but in South Carolina, where less than 10 percent of the population were qualified to vote, the political structure in the ante-bellum years approximated Jefferson's aristocracy of talents. For half a century the state was ruled by men who rose to power by ability alone. Some of them, like the Pinckneys, the Allstons, the Hugers, had deep-rooted family connections; others, like Cheves, McDuffie, Petigru, came from the most humble of origins. In a state noted for her aristocracy the paradox held good that ability rather than wealth or family was the key to honor and preferment.

Calhoun had a scholar's mind, at home with books and happiest when dealing with abstract principles; yet in the affairs of his farm and of his family he was eminently practical, and was on occasion capable of descending from the heights to take part in the rough-and-tumble of practical politics as well. He was always sure of himself, slow to be guided by the advice of others, confident of his own powers to the point of bigotry. Yet he did not repel, as self-assured men are apt to do, but impressed all who met him with his personal charm, his graciousness, his conversational gifts. He could be as dogmatic as any New England parson, and as unyielding as the granite hills; yet he could shift his ground with lightning speed when it became untenable, and usually he knew before his fellows when the time to shift had come. He was ambitious in the best sense of the term, seeking his own advancement not for the sake of power but because he would interpret the honors of office to mean that he had won the gratitude of his countrymen and had merited reward at their hands. Yet he said more than once—and demonstrated over and over again by his actions—that what he called his sense of duty was stronger than his ambition. By that he meant that he would pursue the course his own reason charted, hopeful that it would meet eventually with public approbation, but willing to accept the consequences if it did not.[1]

There was in Calhoun's character a strong element of Calvinism, softened and modified by the impact of his own wide-ranging mind, but a dominant force nonetheless. It is true that he had abandoned many of the stricter tenets of the Scotch Presbyterian faith in which he had been reared. He was among the founders of the Unitarian Church in Washington, and at home in Pendleton he regularly attended the Episcopal Church, through community of interest and associations. About the divergences and niceties of creeds he cared little. We are told, however, that he believed "in a particular Providence to the very hairs of one's head,"[2] and in his own way there is little doubt that he did. In him it was not blind faith, but a rational conviction that the universe itself demonstrated the existence of a power and intelligence transcending man and his follies, and it was this conviction that enabled him to travel his often rugged political road in tranquillity and peace. In the midst of the greatest fight of his career he was able to write that he had "never lost an hour's sleep, nor a meal" through anxiety or fear.[3] He came to look on all life as a struggle against evil, and to regard the reward as more in the struggle than in the victory.[4] Having done what his reason told him was right, he could accept defeat with composure and resignation. His sense of duty was never impeded by any wish to avoid the test of battle. He believed that right was absolute and knowable, and sure in the end to triumph.

The austerity that marked Calhoun's public life was softened in the family circle, where he was affable and unreserved. Yet even in his most intimate contacts he was always a man set apart, neither lonely nor alone, but individual and unique. The unblemished purity of his life was remarked by all who knew him, and a great personal simplicity was in part the secret of his power. He was at once cheerful and grave, almost if not quite without a sense of humor; yet people of all conditions and degrees instinctively trusted him and felt at home in his presence. This feeling was especially true of children and the childlike of all ages. It was also true that those who knew him best—the intimates of his household, the neighbors, the friends of his school days—were those who loved and respected him most. Above all, his personal integrity won and held his followers. Whatever they might say in the heat of political battle, or might later write to justify themselves at his expense, the number of Calhoun's antagonists who really questioned his sincerity, his honor, his political or personal honesty, or his deep and abiding affection for his country and its institutions was few indeed.[5]

2

The gleaming white house that was the Calhoun home stood on top of a knoll, surrounded and all but obscured by towering cedars and ancient oaks. Pillared porticoes faced north and east, and from the wide verandas one could see billowing miles of forest land patched and crisscrossed with the red earth of cultivated fields, or perhaps the snowy white of cotton ready for the harvest. To the west and south of the house the fields and woodlands of the Fort Hill estate sloped down two hundred feet or more to the snaky, mud-saturated Seneca River a mile or so away. Far to the north and northwest rose the jagged lines of the Allegheny and the Blue Ridge Mountains, changing in color and mood and even outline with the changing seasons and the varying conditions of light and atmosphere. On a clear day one could see mountain peaks in four states.

The house itself, from the day the Calhouns first made it their permanent home in 1826, was constantly in process of construction. With Floride Calhoun building was a passion and eternal remodeling a necessity of life. Rooms and wings were added, doors and windows were cut or boarded over, stairways were introduced and removed for greater symmetry or convenience; but always the house grew in spaciousness and comfort. A short distance in front of the north portico the ground fell away sharply for perhaps a dozen feet, and at the foot of the slope was a spring of cool, clear water. A springhouse covered it, but was so built as not to rise to the level of the knoll on which the house stood; and the rocky cliff behind it had been partially hollowed out to form a sort of cave where butter, milk, cheese, and other dairy products were cooled and stored. Close by were flower beds, the kitchen garden, and the orchards, where it was said that every kind of flower or vegetable or fruit that could be grown in that latitude was found. Most prominent among the orchard fruits were those that could be readily dried or preserved, such as apples, peaches, and figs; but there were many others. Calhoun even experimented with oranges.[6]

Calhoun's study, or office, or library—it was variously called by all three names—was a separate building: a square, one-story frame structure directly south of the mansion, perhaps fifty feet or so away. A narrow porch with four columns faced the house, and squarely in the center was a single door. Inside the building consisted of one plain, Spartan room. Bookcases and maps took the place of wall covering and the only decorative note was a pair of antlers from some luckless stag shot in the near-by woods, by Calhoun himself or more likely by one of his numerous connections. To this building Calhoun kept the key, and no one else entered it when he was not there. It was here that he kept his books, wrote letters, reports, and no doubt occasional speeches; and here that he received friends and neighbors and the great and near-great of the political world as they chanced to visit Pendleton. It was here in all probability that the Fort Hill Address and the letter to Governor Hamilton were written, and here that Hamilton, Noble, McDuffie, Hammond, and the other nullification leaders who visited Calhoun in the summer and early fall of 1832 talked over their strategy with their acknowledged leader.

Beyond the garden to the southeast and about an eighth of a mile from the house were the slave quarters: a row of stone houses joined together to form a single barracklike structure, with gardens in the rear and a large open space in front. There were quarters here for eighty to one hundred Negroes, each family having its own house or unit. At a later date, and very probably from the beginning or near the beginning of Calhoun's management, a number of the slaves had small patches of land which they were allowed to cultivate in their spare time, the proceeds being their own. These individual plots were plowed with the other farm lands, then were planted and cultivated by their respective proprietors. Most of the Negroes enjoying this privilege, which was probably a matter of seniority, raised cotton and were as shrewd as the white planters in driving a bargain for it. They were said to be well up on the market prices at New York and Liverpool.[7]

Calhoun was very particular about the character of his slaves, and would not purchase one until a complete and thorough investigation had been made.[8] He was particular also about their health and welfare. He would not, for example, permit them to go into the fields without shoes when the weather was chilly. It sometimes happened that a cold spell struck before the winter supply of shoes had been received, but Calhoun accepted the loss of time without a murmur.[9] Most of the slaves were born on the place, and all of them were called "Calhoun" after their owner. To outsiders, at least, they appeared to be happy and contented, fond of their master and kindly treated. They attended church on Sunday or spent the day as they pleased. Usually there was a Negro minister or lay preacher on one of the plantations in the area. Marriages among the slaves were gala affairs, with dancing and singing and celebrating in which the Negroes from all the neighboring farms joined. Where the bride and groom belonged to different owners, the party was held at the plantation house of the bride's owner. In such cases some settlement was usually arranged between the owners so that the couple would not be separated. The house servants in particular were treated with great tenderness, especially by the women of the household; but all of them were nursed in illness and cared for as though they were children.[10] It was once said of him that the most convincing argument Calhoun could offer in defense of slavery was his own plantation.[11]

The plantation, or farm, as Calhoun preferred to call it following the upcountry custom, was a model of scientific agriculture far in advance of the times, as well as a small self-sustaining community in itself. In addition to the house and slave quarters, there was the normal complement of barns and outbuildings. In the early 1830's Calhoun also built a gristmill for grinding his own corn and small grains, and a ginhouse for ginning his cotton. These were located at the base of a steep slope, where a tumbling stream could be diverted to form a millrace. On the river there was a private wharf where bales of cotton could be loaded on flatboats and floated down the Seneca and the Savannah to Augusta, and where supplies of various sorts could be received by water.

At this date the farm included some five hundred and fifty acres, of which more than half were in cultivation and the rest in pasture and woodland. Save on the broad river bottoms the slopes were steep; yet nowhere on Calhoun's land were there any traces of the scars and gullies that already marred the face of the South. Calhoun estimated in 1832 that erosion was costing South Carolina alone some twenty million dollars a year,[12] but on his own farm he had solved the problem. It was a solution that differed only in terminology from the best usages of today. On all the upland fields he himself surveyed and staked out "guard drains" or hillside ditches to prevent the too rapid runoff that carried away the soil, and the fields were plowed in furrows parallel to these ditches—in other words, with the contours of the ground. He also followed a system of crop rotation to prevent exhaustion of the soil. Peas were used as a soil-building crop to follow corn, but Calhoun speeded up the process on the rich bottom fields by planting the two crops simultaneously, so the pea vines covered the ground from which the cornstalks rose.[13]

For the most part the bottom lands—perhaps one hundred and twenty acres—were devoted exclusively to corn, with the rolling hills given over to cotton and pasture, and the steeper slopes to orchard trees or left in native woods. In all the products of the farm the emphasis was on quality. The cattle were red Devons, which Calhoun had introduced in that section of the state; the numerous saddle and carriage horses were carefully selected, and even the hogs were of superior breed. Calhoun was also the first in the area to plant Bermuda grass for pasturage, and he experimented constantly with plows and coulters and other varieties of farm machinery. Despite the low prices for cotton during the high-tariff years and the relatively high labor cost entailed by the slave system, he would undoubtedly have made money from the place had his political activities permitted him to devote full time to its management.

3

Calhoun's personal habits were regular and orderly. He rose at four or five in the morning, depending on the season, rode or walked for an hour over the farm, then read or wrote in his study until breakfast, which was served about eight o'clock. The rest of the morning was spent in the study, except on Fridays, when he generally rode to Pendleton village. He was always back for dinner, however, somewhere between two and three in the afternoon. The period from sundown till dark would be spent in the fields, and the evening was devoted to family and guests.[14] Often there was music, a darky strumming on a guitar and singing with the inborn melody of his race; and always there was talk, ranging over all the categories of thought and all the fields of human knowledge, but always coming around to politics. Calhoun talked freely of his hopes and aspirations, and analyzed for all who wished to hear the political currents and movements of his time.[15]

Although Calhoun himself was temperate, even abstemious, in the matter of food and drink, the hospitality of Fort Hill was lavish. The cuisine included everything the South afforded, together with im-

ported wines; yet the prevailing atmosphere was one of s
and even the most ordinary of dishes impressed those wh
them. It was breakfast that sent one English visitor into ec
breakfast of "excellent coffee with delicious cream, and tha
national dish of South Carolina, snow-white hominy brough[illegible] to
table like maccaroni, which ought to be eaten, with lumps of sweet fresh butter buried in it."[16] The "grits" were cracked in Calhoun's own mill, from corn raised on the Seneca bottoms, and the butter and "delicious cream" also were produced on the place. So too were the beef and pork and fowl of dinner menus, and even the game was shot in the near-by woods.

Though there were disappointments and frustrations, the family life was cheerful and happy, primarily because Calhoun's own temperament made it so. Floride's special province was the home, and by all accounts her management of domestic concerns was superlatively good. Her accomplishments were social and domestic; and as long as the household was running smoothly, its rooms filled with guests, and her brood of noisy, growing children happy, she was content. So widely reputed was her skill in domestic matters that her old house servants were eagerly sought for after the Civil War.[17] Beyond the kitchen garden, however, her interests did not extend. She understood little of the operation of the farm, was easily imposed on, and during her husband's long absences in Washington she was inclined to leave everything to the overseer. For politics and intellectual pursuits, which together with agriculture absorbed Calhoun's major energies, she cared nothing at all.

Calhoun quickly got into the habit of asking one of his relatives—most often a brother-in-law—to drop by Fort Hill for a few days now and then when he was away, to make sure that all was going as he wished. After 1830 it was generally Floride's younger brother, James Edward Calhoun, to whom he turned for advice and assistance, despite the proximity of the older brother, John Ewing, whose plantation seat was only two miles from Fort Hill. During the years that Calhoun sat in Monroe's Cabinet and for the first term of his Vice Presidency, it had been John Ewing who managed most of the financial and business transactions in which members of the family had a joint interest. After Calhoun took up his permanent residence at Pendleton in 1826, however, a gradual change became apparent. Personal relations remained friendly, but men whose interests and habits differed as widely as those of John Ewing and John Caldwell Calhoun were not likely to grow more intimate on closer acquaintance. Calhoun was Spartan rather than puritan. He never condemned another because of an undue fondness for drink, or cards, or horse racing. But he was not likely to rely on such a man for business judgment or the management of money, cousin and brother-in-law or not. The other neighbors must have felt much the same way, for though John Ewing was perhaps the largest property owner in the district, his perennial campaigns for a seat in the state legislature during the 1830's were humiliatingly unsuccessful.[18]

John Ewing Calhoun was dissipated, extravagant, and in money matters unreliable. He spent much time in Charleston, and even when he was at Pendleton he interested himself in little except the pursuit of pleasure. He had a race track built on his place at Keowee, and it was whispered about among the Negroes that his horses were shod with silver shoes, so prodigal was he of his more than ample means. Even when he undertook some useful enterprise, such as the establishment of a "woollen manufactory" in 1829, he soon lost interest and the venture petered out.[19]

With James Edward relations were far more intimate. One of Calhoun's own sons had been named for his Uncle James in 1826. The correspondence between the two men grew steadily broader in its scope as James Edward matured; and when he took an indefinite furlough from the Navy in 1829 to try his hand as a planter, it was Calhoun who advised him as to lands and crops and tools. Until something else could be found, it was on Calhoun's own original plantation, Bath, near Willington, that James Edward settled. He eventually purchased the place, after he resigned his naval commission late in 1833, and incorporated it together with adjoining lands into a single plantation known as Millwood.[20]

James Edward had a sturdiness of character that both set him apart from his brother and drew him close to his sister's distinguished husband. Time and again, when Calhoun was tied up in Washington and Floride was at Fort Hill, the older man would write to James in response to letters from Floride. "Your sister writes to me," begins a typical appeal, "that my overseer is not doing well, and that my business is very backward. I have written to your brother John to go over, and to give some attention to my affairs; but you know how indifferent he is both as to his own, and other people's business. . . . I would consider it a singular favour, if you would make a visit to Pendleton, and bestow a few days attention to my affairs. . . . Should you find it in your power, without material injury to your own business (I would not want it otherwise) do for me in every respect, as you would for yourself. . . ."[21] It was one of many such requests, to which James Edward invariably responded with promptness and efficiency. Calhoun, for his part, made purchases and handled commissions for his favorite brother-in-law in Washington and other cities that he had occasion to visit.[22]

James Edward sometimes seemed to have more influence with Floride than her husband did, and he was the only one who could exert any influence at all on his mother. "Old Mrs. Calhoun" as she was usually called by the neighbors, to distinguish her from her daughter, made her permanent home at Pendleton. In fact, she was the real owner of Fort Hill, which her son-in-law merely rented from her. Sometimes she lived with the John C. Calhouns, sometimes with the John Ewing Calhouns, sometimes in Pendleton village, but perhaps most frequently at a small house she had built for herself called Cold Spring. Cold Spring was a mile or so from Fort Hill, in the direction of Keowee. As she advanced in years, the old lady grew more eccentric and more difficult to handle. She would flounce out of one or another of the houses she frequented without a word of explanation and take up her quarters somewhere else. She would take unreasonable whims, would become obsessed with fancied slights, or would simply want to be by herself; yet she was not strong and required more care than she would allow.

A characteristic incident occurred in the fall of 1830, after old Mrs. Calhoun had been living quietly for some time at Fort Hill. One evening in October she did not return to the house, and Calhoun found on investigation that she had gone to Cold Spring. She had also dismissed her overseer and was determined to run the place herself. Calhoun could do nothing with her. "The thing is vexatious," he wrote to James Edward, "but we must not omit to do all that is practicable to make her situation as comfortable as possible." So James came up to Pendleton and stayed at Cold Spring with his mother until things appeared to be in running order.[23] Calhoun prepared to take Floride and some at least of the children to Washington, and was on the point of departure when his mother-in-law had another outburst of obstinacy. Calhoun and John Ewing talked it over, and they decided Floride should unpack her baggage and stay home.[24]

Calhoun was singularly unruffled by these domestic disturbances, even when they were closer to him than his mother-in-law. Floride had inherited enough of her mother's eccentricities so that she was coming to be known as a "character" in her own right. She was inclined to be suspicious and to distribute blame freely for whatever displeased her; yet Calhoun not only did not quarrel with her, he would not permit others to quarrel with her. He was so reticent about his private life that references are very, very few. There is one, however, that is so revealing for both Floride's character and for his own that it must be noted, though it occurred many years after the time here under discussion. Andrew, the oldest son, had quarreled briefly with his mother, and Calhoun believed Andrew to be entirely in the right. He nevertheless wrote: "As to the suspicion & unfounded blame of your Mother, you must not only bear them, but forget them. With the many good qualities of her Mother, she inherits her suspicious & fault finding temper, which has been the cause of much vexation in the family. I have borne with her with patience, because it was my duty to do so, & you must do the same, for the same reason. It has been the only cross of my life."[25]

Andrew Calhoun once told a friend that he had never heard his father speak impatiently to any member of the family;[26] yet Andrew himself had probably given as much cause as any of them. Calhoun must have been sorely disappointed when Andrew left South Carolina College without graduating in 1832, but he never gave any indication of it. He showed every evidence of pleasure when on January 3, 1833, Andrew was married in Columbia to Eugenia Chappell, the daughter of one of Calhoun's old colleagues of his Congressional days, and shared his son's grief when Eugenia died after scarcely a year of marriage.[27]

4

Calhoun was pre-eminently a public figure and the very intensity of his nature, the strength of his convictions, the evangelical qualities of his mind, made it inevitable that the bulk of his time would be absorbed in political pursuits. Yet he was devoted to his family and always felt happier when at home on his farm. When away in Washington he was a faithful correspondent, writing weekly letters to his wife and at short intervals to the older children, his own brothers, and his brothers-in-law. His frequent complaints on that score indicate that he received fewer letters than he wrote. Very little of this family correspondence has been preserved, but there is enough to give a relatively clear picture of the family interests and relationships. Floride wrote faithfully but omitted much that her husband wanted to hear. James Edward kept his brother-in-law informed as to details of the plantation affairs whenever he got up to Pendleton. But more and more, as she grew older, it was Anna Maria who kept her father up to date, and she soon became his favorite correspondent.

Anna Maria had already had some schooling in Edgefield, where she lived in the family of Francis W. Pickens, before she entered a more advanced institution in Columbia in the winter of 1831-1832. She was then fourteen years old. The decision had not yet been made when Calhoun left Pendleton in November, and he learned of it from his wife rather than from his daughter herself. He affected pique when he wrote her on December 30, 1831. "I have been waiting some time to hear from you, but see that as usual you stand on the ceremony of the first letter, even with your father." He quickly forgave her, however, and went on in a tone of gentle banter: "I do not know, that I ought to censure you for your aversion to writing, as I believe it is in some degree hereditary; but you ought to recollect, that the great object of education is not only to cultivate our faculties, but to learn to control our dispositions; to restrain those that are too strong, and strengthen those, that are too weak. Among the latter, I am sure you will place your disposition to correspond." He discoursed briefly on the art of letter writing, and its desirability in a lady. "In your case, with your vivacity, and good sense, all that you want is *practice;* and I must insist on your extending to me during the winter, a full share of your practice." He wanted to know all about the school, the friends Anna made, the studies she undertook. He had sent money for her to Colonel Chappell (whose daughter Eugenia was perhaps already engaged to Andrew Calhoun) and had asked the Colonel to "hold it in his hand and disburse it for you." Calhoun had many friends in Columbia, but he hoped Anna would visit only a few families and would not go to large parties. "It will be time enough two, or three years hence to go into company."[28] He sent her a proof of an engraved portrait of himself, but she did not like it because it did not do him justice to her partial eyes.

An account of Anna's activities was quickly forthcoming. She had not really stood on ceremony, it seemed, for the letter was dispatched before she had heard from her father. He undertook to set an example of punctuality and answered the very next day. He was obviously pleased with his daughter's letter and with her attitude toward her studies and toward her first venture in living away from her family. He even found it necessary to check her natural gregariousness with an admonition to "form a general acquaintance with all, but be familiar with but few, well selected and worthy of your friendship."[29]

Over the next two or three years, until Anna was old enough to come to Washington with her father, the correspondence between them was faithfully carried on. Calhoun's letters to his daughter reveal a facet of his nature that is to be found nowhere else. He advised as to her studies, restrained or encouraged her youthful enthusiasms as the need might be, fell in with her whims and fancies but always brought her back to the serious business of molding her character and equipping her mind. On his side letters were not always promptly answered because of the pressing demands on his time, but he would accept no such excuse from her. "I know," he explained, "that you acquire so rapidly, that you cannot in fairness be entitled to put in the plea. You see from what I write, that I shall expect a prompt acknowledgement of this my letter; and, when I tell you how much pleasure it affords me to hear from you, my dear child, I am sure your compliance will be as cheerful as I doubt not it will be prompt. You will, at all events, not be able to get off with your old excuse, that you have no aptness at letter writing. Your last letter is remarkably well written. . . ." He urged on her the study of dancing and music, and noted the importance of posture in walking and sitting.[30]

Calhoun expressed suitable pleasure when Anna quickly rose to the head of her class, but seemed even more pleased that under the rigid discipline of a boarding school she had overcome her aversion to early rising. "We lose time, pleasure and health by late sleeping. Life is a journey. If we lose the morning, it will require hard and fatiguing travel to reach our stage. . . . The greatest effort will scarcely regain the loss of a single hour in the morning." He promised to buy her the music she had requested, and noted her new-found ambition to be a singer. "Give a full and fair trial to your voice, but unless it should prove at least pretty good, it would be an useless consumption of time to attempt to become a Singer; but do not dispair till you have made a fair trial." He commented, too, on what must have been an imperious demand that he tell her about politics. "I am not one of those," he assured her, "who think your sex ought to have nothing to do with politicks. They have as much interest in the good condition of their country, as the other sex, and tho' it would be unbecoming them to take an active part in political struggles, their opinion, when enlightened, cannot fail to have a great and salutary effect."[31]

Always Calhoun addressed Anna Maria as an adult and as an equal, and as time went on she became more and more his political confidante. It is not surprising that, when she accompanied him to Washington a few years after this time, a New England visitor found her among the most persuasive and intelligent advocates of the Southern point of view.[32]

Within two years Anna was taking over many of her mother's household tasks, and most especially that of looking after the younger children. She continued to write faithfully to her father, and he continued to ask for more letters still. "I am sure," he chided her early in 1834, "if you saw the number of letters I had to write, you would not expect from me a regular exchange of letters, one for one, but would write me two, or three for my one, that you received." Her mother's letters, he explained, he always answered immediately, no matter what else he had to do, but other letters had to wait sometimes. It did not mean that he enjoyed hearing from her any the less. Anna's letters, he insisted, gave him "a great deal of news, that I get from no other quarter. You cannot write too often, or too fully."[33] She wrote him long accounts of the younger children, and how they progressed in their studies. He expressed his pleasure and commended her skill as a teacher. "I am particularly gratified, that Cornelia has become fond of her books, as I had almost dispaired, that she ever would. The mode you have adopted proves, that you are not a little skilled in the knowledge of the operation of the human mind."[34]

The pert, eager, black-eyed youngster, whose mind so resembled her father's, had come to be his main link with the side of his home life that he missed most sorely, and he took pains to tell her so. "Were it not for your letters," he began, "there are a thousand incidents that are daily occurring, where every incident, even the smallest, is interesting to me, of which I should remain ignorant. Your Mother and

Brother write me on grave subjects of business, or what relates to the welfare of the family; but you fill up the interval with those little, but to me interesting details, which it is so agreeable to an absent father to know. Were it not for you, I would not have heard a word about the Humming birds, their familiarity, the vines, their blooms, the freshness of the spring, the green yard, the children's gardens, and finally Patrick's mechanical genius and his batteaux, every item of which excited agreeable associations, but accompanied with painful recollection of my long absence, from those so dear to me."[35]

Anna was also coming to supply another very important place in her father's life. She was coming to give him the intellectual companionship that Floride, with her complete lack of interest in politics, had never been able to offer. It was Anna, in her sixteenth year, who stood fast at Calhoun's side in the nullification fight, and who thereafter throughout the remainder of his life shared his political battles and seconded his aspirations and his hopes.

CHAPTER XIII

KING ANDREW

1

WHEN Congress assembled on December 3, 1832, the Senate was again under the necessity of electing a President pro tempore. Tazewell had resigned his seat late in October, on the ground that as part of a hopeless minority he could accomplish nothing for his state.[1] Calhoun was still in South Carolina; but it was already known in Washington, and pretty generally over the country, that he was to replace Hayne as Senator and so would not return to the chair of the Senate.[2] The President pro tempore, therefore, would be the permanent presiding officer for the remainder of the Congress; and whoever held that post would be automatically barred from taking more than a nominal part in the stormy debates over the tariff and nullification that were anticipated. It was for that reason that George Poindexter, who had been Tazewell's closest competitor for the honor at the previous session, withdrew his own name before the balloting started.[3]

The voting quickly concentrated on Hugh Lawson White of Tennessee and John Tyler of Virginia, with Tyler throwing his own strength to White on the fifth ballot. The arrangement meant that the President and the acting Vice President would be from the same state, but Tyler was willing to trust that situation to White's sense of propriety.[4] So apparently were the other Senators. On the whole, the choice was excellent. White was the candidate of the administration but he was in every way acceptable, both to the National Republicans and to the Nullifiers. Although a close friend of Jackson's, the Tennessee Senator had steadfastly refused to accept office at the hands of the President. Lean, dour, puritanical, he was a man who would follow his conscience wherever it led him. The decisions of the chair would be inflexible but impartial, and the small band of State Rights Democrats would have their full strength available on the floor.

The brief sitting on December 4 was devoted to the reading of the President's message. Calhoun, Clay, and Webster, the giants who were to dominate the proceedings of the next three months, were not yet in Washington; and it looked for a time as though they would have little to do when they came, so mild, moderate, and conciliatory was the message. After the usual summary of foreign relations, the President congratulated the country and the Congress on the payment of the public debt. It was, he declared, an occasion that called for prompt reduction of the revenue to the needs of the government. He expressed the hope that the reduction could be so accomplished as to "remove those burthens which shall be found to fall unequally" on any of the great interests of the nation; and he recommended that "the whole scheme of duties be reduced to the revenue standard as soon as a just regard to the faith of the government and the preservation of the large capital invested in establishments of domestic industry will permit." Less than six months earlier he had accepted the tariff of 1832 as the permanent policy of the country. He now denied that the protective system had ever been intended as more than temporary and incidental, and with ironic understatement noted that it tended "to beget in the minds of a large portion of our countrymen a spirit of discontent and jealousy dangerous to the stability of the union."

Jackson ended his passage on the tariff with a reference to the obstruction of the revenue collections "in one quarter" of the country and expressed the hope that prudence, patriotism, and good sense would solve the difficulty. He left the impression that, should it become impossible to execute the existing law at any point, he would lay the matter before Congress.

Having gone so far, the President went farther still and made his own the rest of Calhoun's original platform. He recommended that the public lands ought to be sold for no more than enough to cover the expense of administering the land system, and suggested that the disposal of the soil ought to be surrendered to the states. The only other important reference in the message was one questioning the safety of the public money on deposit in the Bank of the United States and its branches.[5]

The tone and substance of the message could not have been wholly unexpected. Led by the *Globe,* the administration press had been emphasizing tariff reduction for ten days or more; and the press reflected fairly accurately the popular wish, so far as it could be learned. Particularly in New York there was a strong desire to adjust the duties to pacify the South, with Van Buren's partisans trying to outdo Clay's. Van Buren himself was understood to have declared a general amnesty for all his old foes, excepting only Calhoun. Now that the election was safely won and no votes could be lost in Pennsylvania, the Vice President-elect was out to get for himself any credit there might be for securing a modification of the protective system.[6] On the day the message was read, the *Globe* called for reduction of the tariff to "the standard of a safe and prudent, moderate, but adequate revenue.—Not because that measure is demanded by menaces; but because it is just in itself, and is due to the feelings of an important section of the country. . . ." Three days later Blair was even arguing that the election was a clear victory for tariff reduction and that Calhoun had forced through the Ordinance of Nullification solely to get credit for the adjustment.[7] The tariff, in other words, was to be reduced, and each side hoped to make political capital of it.

The reaction to Jackson's tariff proposals was generally favorable. The South was pleased and relieved. The high-tariff men, to be sure, were inclined to feel that their interests had been surrendered "to the nullifiers of the South and the land-robbers of the West";[8] and Southern spokesmen felt that a vast deal of suffering and ill feeling might have been spared had Jackson shown half the zeal for tariff reform in 1829 that he now showed three years later. Even Duff Green, who no longer denied that his paper was the organ of the Nullifiers, praised the message, complaining only that Jackson had not been explicit on state interposition.[9]

He did not have long to wait for his answer. On December 10 the President issued a Proclamation against the Nullifiers. Relief turned to dismay, and pleasure to hot indignation. In terse and commanding prose the Proclamation declared that the National Government was sovereign and indivisible, that no state could refuse to obey the law, that no state could leave the Union. It closed with a direct appeal to the people of South Carolina, who were told they had been led by deluded or designing leaders to the brink of treason; and it left no doubt that the whole force of the United States would be used if need be to collect the duties in the rebellious state. The argument of the Proclamation was that of Webster in the second reply to Hayne, and of John Marshall in half a dozen leading decisions of the Supreme Court. It was written, however, in the language of the layman, and it compressed all that the great champions of nationalism had said into a fraction of the space they took to say it.[10]

Yet able and powerful as it was, it went too far for its purpose and its time. Its reasoning, though cogent and compelling, destroyed not nullification alone, but the whole theory of State Rights from which the doctrine of interposition had been derived. When it proclaimed the government to be no federation but a consolidated whole with sovereign power vested in the majority, it went far beyond the purposes of the founding fathers, and ran directly counter to widely accepted beliefs of the time. The net effect, therefore, was not to isolate the leaders in South Carolina but to arouse all those who feared concentrated power, by whomsoever exercised. New party lines were drawn, and the Nullifiers found support where none had been expected.

Jackson himself probably failed to grasp the finer points of political theory involved, but his understanding of the reactions of the common man was, as usual, incomparable. As Benton put it, the "mass of the people think the Union is attacked, and that the Proclamation is to save it, and that brief view is decisive with them."[11] Yet farseeing men the country over realized that to establish the political philosophy of the Proclamation meant in the end the abolition of slavery and probably the destruction of the Union. In four short years Jackson had led his party from bitter opposition to the "consolidating" tendencies of John Quincy Adams to a form of authoritarianism that outdid even the Alien and Sedition Acts of Adams' father. The individualistic democracy of the frontier lost ground to the cult of power so dear to wealth and property. The South, with its common interest and its common fear, began to coalesce, and sectional cleavage began to assume an ideological content. If any single date can be fixed as that on which a given event was predetermined, the Civil War became inevitable on December 10, 1832.

2

The various steps taken by the administration after the passage of the Ordinance of Nullification in South Carolina fit together into a well worked out pattern. The Proclamation was a warning that the state would be crushed if she persisted in opposing the law, but the annual message had contained an explicit promise that the law would be changed. Jackson informed his aides that he meant to have the leading Nullifiers "arrested and arraigned for treason," and indicated that military force would be used if needed.[12] Yet a member of the Cabinet, acting unofficially and incognito but on the President's orders, pointed out the danger of victory for either side and asked Virginia to act as mediator. The Cabinet member was Lewis Cass, the Secretary of War, and his overtures were made through Thomas Ritchie of the Richmond *Enquirer.*[13]

If Cass was indeed following privately given orders from the President, then the Proclamation was largely bluff; and the masterly caution of the Secretary's military preparations seem to bear this out. He sent Major General Winfield Scott, the second ranking officer in the Army, to take command in South Carolina, with orders to stay out of trouble at almost any cost. Again and again Cass emphasized to Scott the "anxiety of the President to avoid, if possible, a resort to force." He was, of course, to repel attack, but he was to lean over backward to avoid giving any possible provocation for attack; and nowhere in Scott's orders was there ever a word about arresting anybody, for treason or anything else.[14]

The *Globe,* meanwhile, with the rest of the administration press tagging in its wake, hammered endlessly on the theme that nullification was treason and Calhoun the archtraitor, who had failed to win the Presidency of the whole Union and so sought now to break it that he might rule at least a part. The real purpose of the Nullifiers and the actual state of affairs in South Carolina were carefully concealed, while it was made to appear that Jackson had all along intended to reform the tariff and relieve the people of the South from their unjustly heavy burden of taxation.

The strategy, in short, was to yield the point but to destroy Calhoun. His danger was personal, physical, and very real, and no one knew it better than he did.

3

More than a month was allowed to pass before Jackson followed up his Proclamation—a month in which the reaction of all sections and classes could be ascertained and a majority in Congress could be lined up. The Proclamation had split the Jackson ranks wide open, but it had split the opposition also. Ritchie praised the Proclamation as well as the annual message; Benton "could not concur" in some of its doctrines, but was willing to accept it because he expected Jackson to destroy the Bank; Sam Houston, in Texas, read the document "with much pride and inexpressible satisfaction." Floyd saw civil war as now inevitable; to the Nullifiers it was "the black Cockade Federalism of '98 revived fearfully invigorated by its long sleep, and . . . destined to bring about another reign of terror." Cambreleng denounced it, and Van Buren himself tried to get Jackson to tone down some of the doctrines he had expressed.[15]

The National Republicans were similarly divided. Webster placed himself under the administration banner, but Clay found many things in the Proclamation that he could not stomach. Philip Hone, who spoke for the mercantile class in New York, meant the highest praise when he called it "just such a paper as Alexander Hamilton would have written and Thomas Jefferson condemned." One New England disciple of Hamilton thought the South would be driven from the Union; but another thought the Proclamation a meaningless gesture to cover up the discomfiture of the administration. Hezekiah Niles, the high priest of the American System, called Hayne's official answer "a very ably written and strong paper"; and Judge Story, whose famous *Commentaries* were almost ready for the press, thought that Jackson had expressed "the true principles of the Constitution." For the abolitionists, Garrison pronounced the Proclamation "an exceedingly powerful and eloquent exposition of the Constitution and Laws."[16]

Such was the state of feeling when news reached Washington that Calhoun was on his way to the Capital. It was almost universally believed that Jackson would have the South Carolinian arrested as soon as he arrived and would make short work of his trial for treason. And all too many, thanks to the misrepresentations of the *Globe* and its satellites and the unguarded tongue of the President, believed him guilty and were only too willing to see him hanged.

Calhoun did not actually leave South Carolina until two weeks after his election to the Senate, although Congress was already in session. The reason for the delay, however, was not any fear of Andrew Jackson but the serious illness of Mrs. Calhoun, brought on perhaps by the nervous strain of the past weeks.[17] It was December 22 before Floride's health was so far restored as to permit her husband to leave. He stayed briefly in Columbia to confer with Hayne, and reached Raleigh, North Carolina, on December 30. From Raleigh he went to Richmond, and arrived in Washington on January 3. Everywhere he was an object of curiosity, often of apprehension and disdain. Crowds gathered to look upon him as years before they had looked at Aaron Burr. So thoroughly had the *Globe* done its work that Calhoun was regarded as a man whose mad ambition would stop at nothing; and prejudice against him, even in the South, was bitter. He was aware of Jackson's threats against his person and fully conscious of the hostility he met along the way, but he remained outwardly calm and undaunted. Tall, erect, with flashing eyes and rugged features crowned by a shock of dark wiry hair, he was a commanding—even a noble—figure as he faced hostile mobs and asked no quarter. His passionate sincerity was so obvious that even lifelong foes, after seeing him, accorded him grudging admiration.[18]

In Raleigh he talked for hours to shifting crowds in the great hall of the hotel. He tried to explain what nullification meant and assured his audience that there would be no breach of the peace in South Carolina unless citizens of the state were attacked by Federal troops.[19] In Richmond he attended, as guest of Governor Floyd, a session of the Virginia legislature, which was debating a report of its special committee on Federal relations.[20] News of his progress preceded him to Washington, but no hostile demonstration greeted his arrival. In that city where he had lived so long and was so intimately known, it was beyond the power even of Andrew Jackson or Francis Preston Blair to paint him in the image of a Catiline. "However he may now err," wrote Margaret Bayard Smith, who was both an old friend and an old political foe, "he is one of the noblest and most generous spirits I have ever met with. I am certain *he* is deceived himself, and believes he is now fulfilling the duty of a *true patriot.*"[21]

Right or wrong, deceived or a little more clearheaded than his fellows, Calhoun's courage was superb. Alone, unfaltering, with head erect and steady eyes, he walked slowly and deliberately into the Senate chamber at noon on Friday, January 4, 1833, and presented his credentials as Senator from South Carolina. For almost eight years he had sat in that same chamber as presiding officer. A dozen of the forty-eight men who then constituted the Senate of the United States had served with him in Congress during the trying years of the War of 1812, and still others had been his friends and partisans in bygone Presidential campaigns. A few stepped up and shook his hand, but most of them held back. The galleries were crowded, but ominously still, as Calhoun stood before the President pro tempore, raised his right hand, and in a solemn, clearly audible voice took the oath to uphold and defend the Constitution of the United States. Others congratulated him then, and the ice was broken.[22]

The question of tariff reduction was already before both houses of Congress, with every indication of administration support. It would not be the administration, however, nor Martin Van Buren, who would get the credit for modifying the long-contested protective policy. It would be John C. Calhoun, and the South thereafter would be his.[23] In the House a sweeping tariff-reduction bill hastily prepared by the Committee on Ways and Means, and called the Verplanck bill after the committee's chairman, reached the floor on January 8.[24] The Verplanck bill was understood to be a Van Buren measure and to have the full support of the administration.[25] Even to Calhoun the road to peace looked relatively clear, until Stephen D. Miller touched off another explosion by presenting to the Senate on January 11 resolutions of the South Carolina legislature denouncing Jackson's Proclamation.[26] The following evening Silas Wright of New York, who had just arrived in Washington to take the seat in the Senate vacated by Marcy's election as Governor, called on the President. Because the new Senator was a confidential friend of Van Buren's, Jackson talked freely and made no secret of his intention of disciplining Calhoun, Hamilton, and Hayne. He expected to save the rest of the South by reducing the tariff, but South Carolina he apparently preferred to punish. He seemed to feel, in fact, that anyone who sought to save Calhoun from the noose was trying to disgrace both the country and Andrew Jackson.[27]

Calhoun did not know, of course, that Jackson had so recently repeated his threats when he introduced on January 14 a resolution calling on the Executive to lay before the Senate copies of the Proclamation, the counterproclamation of Governor Hayne, the South Carolina Ordinance, and other documents in the nullification controversy.[28] It would have made no difference, however, had he known that the hangman awaited him outside the door of the Senate chamber. His was the same stubborn Scotch-Irish stock as Jackson's own, and he was no more likely to yield a conviction than was the President. In the normal order of procedure, Calhoun's resolution would have been called up for argument the following day. He acquiesced, however, when Felix Grundy asked him to let the matter rest.

According to the Tennessee Senator, the documents requested were already on the way, together with a message from the President, and were expected on the seventeenth.[29]

Anticipating no important business on the intervening day, Calhoun came late to the Senate, only to find that the documents had already arrived and the President's message was being read. And what a message it was! Calhoun sat rigidly in his seat, his eyes blazing with mounting fury as he listened. The doctrines of the Proclamation were repeated, and Jackson was asking bluntly for power to make them good. He wanted no less than authority to alter or abolish ports of entry where duties could not be collected, power to remove causes from state to Federal courts at his discretion, and authority to employ military force to execute the laws. The language of the message was carefully guarded, not asking outright for the powers in question, but suggesting the revival of long-dead statutes under which in times of Federalist dominance they had existed. There was nothing guarded, however, in the direct reference to South Carolina. The state was declared to be "in the attitude of hostile preparation" and ready for "military violence," and the President announced his intention to regard "aggression . . . as committed when it is officially authorized, and the means of enforcing it fully provided."[30]

When the reading was over, Grundy moved reference to the Committee on the Judiciary, but Calhoun was on his feet as soon as the motion had been made. For almost sixteen years he had not taken part in legislative debates, and he was to speak now without preparation because he had not expected the question to arise for another day. He was, moreover, out of order, because he meant to speak not to Grundy's motion but on the message itself. This he conceded at the outset, throwing himself on the indulgence of the Senate. No one objected, and for perhaps half an hour he held the floor.

Rarely if ever has a maiden speech in the Senate or in any other legislative body been made under more trying circumstances, or impressed itself more forcefully upon those who heard it. Calhoun's usually mobile features were expressionless as chiseled granite, his body rigid and tense as that of an animal at bay. Only his lips moved, but from them poured a torrent of words with incredible rapidity: words of biting scorn and passionate rejection. His expressive eyes, now black as coals, now flaming with the intensity of his excitement, darted restlessly about the room. The very bonds of language were powerless to chain his feelings. He was defiant, impassioned, and superb.[31]

He changed no opinions as to the right or wrong of South Carolina's action, but he won for himself the respect if not the admiration of his foes. Original Jackson partisans who would have hanged him ten days before rushed up to grasp his hand, and men in the galleries wept unashamedly.[32] Jackson was told that Calhoun's speech had failed, and promised again to "strike at the head" as soon as the first overt act should be committed.[33] Webster felt a little sorry for a man he regarded as broken, and resolved to avoid any personal unkindness.[34] But John Tyler, scion of the old Virginia school and as independent as any man alive, was jubilant. "Calhoun met the thing," he wrote gleefully to Floyd, "in a style which I have never heard surpassed—his manner was different from anything I ever heard from him before—warm—impassioned—burning—He repelled with indignation the charge of his State desiring a dissolution. . . . Rely upon it that he is more than a match for all opponents."[35] Even Churchill C. Cambreleng, although his sympathies certainly lay elsewhere, was inclined to agree with Tyler's conclusion.[36]

So were the Senate, the Congress, and the country itself divided over the character and motives of one man. There was no middle ground, no compromise, no no-man's land. He attracted, or he repelled; he convinced, or he antagonized; he was loved, or he was hated. He was the pure and unsullied patriot, ready to sacrifice position, honors, life itself for the liberties of his country; or he was the very image of Lucifer—the archangel fallen, damned forever to the bottomless pit by his own overmastering ambition. Toward Calhoun indifference was impossible.[37]

Calhoun himself said nothing about his speech, but he credited the President's message with advancing his own cause. For the message had completed the work the Proclamation had begun, and had so aroused the Southern members of both houses that a united South was certain within six months if the tariff was not modified. When that happened, the "doctrines of 98" would be successful again, and would "again save the Republick." Calhoun had been unable to trace the still persistent rumor that his own arrest had been ordered, but he did not doubt that Jackson, like Macbeth, saw in his dreams "the image of a Crown."[38] With his every exercise of executive indiscretion, Jackson forced his opponents closer together. Differences of opinion on tariff, bank, or public lands were less important than agreement on the preservation of constitutional government. Clay merely echoed Calhoun when he wrote that nothing was any longer certain save that "the will of Andrew Jackson is to govern."[39]

Within a week Calhoun was on the offensive, carrying the fight to the administration. On January 21 the Judiciary Committee reported a bill authorizing the use of force to collect the revenues, and the next day William Wilkins of Pennsylvania, the committee chairman, sought to fix a time for debate. Wilkins proposed a lapse of only two days; Miller sought to postpone the whole question until the tariff had been acted on. After some discussion, Monday, January 28, was agreed to, but immediately Calhoun was on his feet. The Force Bill rested on the same constitutional theory as the message and the Proclamation. The South Carolina Senator offered a set of three resolutions, carefully designed to challenge that constitutional theory.[40] The Force Bill, it had just been agreed, would not be debated for another week, but Calhoun might call up his resolutions the next day. If he could center the discussion on them rather than on the bill, he would have the right to the final speech. If, moreover, he could get his resolutions adopted, the Force Bill would collapse without a hearing because it would then be patently unconstitutional. He had not presided over the Senate for eight years without learning how to take every advantage offered by its rules.

In introducing his resolutions, Calhoun spoke briefly—again for no more than half an hour. The emotional excitement of his earlier effort was gone. He was terse, concise, and icily calm. There was not a superfluous word or thought, and no possibility of doubt in his challenge. "But two modes of political existence can long endure in our country; the one that formed, by the framers of our admirable constitution, a federal system, uniting free and independent States in a bond of union for mutual advantages, and to be preserved by the concurrent consent of the parts; or a government of the sword. The choice is before us." The administration forces, already divided and ill at ease over Jackson's highhanded methods, were threatened with a rout at the hands of this one man alone. For they had not only to win the support of both houses of Congress, they had to keep public opinion on their side as well; and Calhoun's courageous, singlehanded battle no less than his clear, incisive words was making it harder day by day to justify forcible intervention in South Carolina.[41] The power to coerce one state was the power to coerce them all; and there was hardly a state in the Union that had not been at one time or another in opposition to the general government.

4

In South Carolina the belligerent attitude of the administration served only to make the party cleavage sharper and the danger more real. Jackson's Proclamation set the state legislature aflame. Defiant resolutions were immediately passed, and the Governor was instructed to issue his unyielding counterproclamation and to mobilize the militia. The timorous resigned themselves to bloodshed and financial ruin.[42] Hayne's proclamation came on December 20 and the following day he named his military aides, including James H. Hammond and Francis W. Pickens. Detailed instructions for mobilization and arming of the state troops were issued the day after Christmas.[43] Yet even as he gave orders for raising a South Carolina army, Hayne continued to insist that he and his party wanted neither disunion nor civil war. "We have been compelled to nullify," he wrote privately to a New York correspondent, "after 10 years of patient endurance & remonstrance, as the only means left to cause our complaints to be attended to."[44]

As there had been from the start, there were conservatives and radicals within the Nullification party—conservatives like Hayne, who would call out the militia but would take every precaution to avoid a clash and accept any reasonable compromise on the tariff as a victory; and radicals like Rhett who wanted to strike the first blow by seizing the government arsenals.[45] Fortunately the conservatives were in command; and when the Virginia legislature sent Benjamin Watkins Leigh to Columbia as an official emissary from that state with instructions to urge postponement, they turned it to account. They wanted Virginia, should they yield to her mediation, to guarantee her support if the tariff was not modified; but they saw that Leigh's mission could be used to play for time.[46]

So it fell out that shortly after Leigh's arrival in South Carolina the effective date of the Ordinance was deferred until the fourth of March. The postponement was the work of a State Rights party meeting in Charleston on January 21 and had no semblance of legality about it. The action met, however, with popular approval. It was the date Calhoun and Hayne had sought from the convention in the first place, and so the Governor discreetly took the party vote as binding without seeking to reassemble the convention to vote on it.[47] Almost immediately thereafter news arrived that the Force Bill had been reported from committee, and excitement flared again. Sober South Carolinians saw no alternative but to withdraw from the Union if the Force Bill passed and tariff reduction did not.[48] The demand for arms exceeded "*five times over* the number in possession of the State," and two emissaries were sent north to purchase more.[49]

The Unionists formed military companies of their own, armed from the Federal arsenals with weapons issued by General Scott. Now and again clashes between Unionists and Nullifiers seemed imminent, but always they were avoided by the extraordinary caution and self-restraint of the latter.[50] There was, however, a subtle change in the atmosphere. Where Poinsett had earlier assured Jackson that South Carolina could put her own house in order, with the aid of government arms, he conceded by mid-January that the revenue laws could not be enforced except at the point of Federal bayonets. His own followers, most of them, would not move against their fellows. As the Nullifiers gained the upper hand, Poinsett cast caution to the winds and begged the President to strike the first blow.[51] While Calhoun's stature grew with each move he made in the Senate and with every threat Jackson hurled against him, Poinsett writhed and pleaded with the President not to make a martyr of his enemy.[52]

When Jackson later showed genuine relief at the prospect that the Ordinance of Nullification would be repealed, Poinsett went so far as to urge no tariff reduction until the following session of Congress, lest the Nullifiers be the ones to reap the profit from it.[53] If Jackson's perceptions had been as quick as his temper, it would have been clear to him from the start of his correspondence with Poinsett that the South Carolina Unionist leaders were far more eager for a clash of arms than the Nullifiers.[54] It is not those in power, but those who have been rejected at the polls, who seek external aid for an appeal to the sword.

The crisis was over for all practical purposes by early February, and the state settled back to await the turn of events in Washington. The conservative wing of the State Rights and Free Trade party had gained its original purpose with the postponement of the effective date of nullification until after Congress had adjourned, and Virginia's intervention had enabled them to save face at the same time. The rank and file of the Unionists were less hostile as the end both parties sought seemed about to be achieved. The Force Bill, should it pass, would be another complication, but Calhoun's position was getting stronger every day. When men left their guns at home and concentrated their attention on the incoming mails, the danger of civil war was past.

CHAPTER XIV

COMPROMISE AND CONSOLIDATION

1

ALTHOUGH there was little sympathy for nullification outside of South Carolina, there was a very general feeling among people of all classes that the tariff was too high. The desperation of South Carolina was only a forerunner of what might be expected from the entire South if some notice was not taken of the protests that had been mounting since 1824. A majority of the public men of the day recognized the real threat to the Union that lay in this long aggravated discontent. It was this feeling that made Calhoun's position strong, for any reasonable adjustment of the tariff would be his victory, regardless of the sponsorship of the measure.[1]

The strategy of the administration was to reduce the tariff promptly to the revenue level, but to maintain the principle of protection. The State Rights group, following Hayne's proposal of the previous session, favored a less precipitate reduction of the duties so as to inflict no unnecessary hardship upon the manufacturers, but insisted on abandonment of the principle. The manufacturers, for whom Webster and Adams served as spokesmen, wanted to retain the protective principle and hang onto as much as possible in the way of duties. No one of these three factions commanded a majority, but there was among them enough in common to make compromise possible.

The tariff from 1816 on had been Henry Clay's own special hobby and private preserve. Clay, moreover, had lost prestige by his crushing defeat at the polls in November, and the younger leaders of his own party were seeking frankly to put him on the shelf.[2] His sole opportunity—perhaps the last he would ever have—to retain control of his party and continue in a position of national leadership lay in his willingness to sacrifice the measures for which he had so long fought, and figure as the compromiser. He grasped eagerly for the role, and it may be said that no man in the country at that time was better qualified to play it.

Clay reached the Capital just as Jackson's Proclamation against the

Nullifiers offered new luster to the crown reserved for the peacemaker. After the Proclamation, the man who engineered an acceptable tariff adjustment could also claim to have averted civil war and appear as the savior of the Union. The Kentucky Senator probably had some sort of tariff scheme in his pocket when he got to Washington. At any rate he left almost immediately on a business trip to New York and informed Webster, whom he met in Philadelphia, that he had drafted a compromise tariff bill. He did not reveal the details, however, until both men were back in the Capital, perhaps because he realized that Webster would probably desert him on that issue.[3]

Nothing had come of the negotiations between the Clay and Calhoun factions in the spring of 1832 because Clay had then believed he could win the election without Calhoun's support. His confidence was rudely shattered when the ballots were counted, and by December he was ready to make concessions. Almost from the start of the session of Congress, a "marked familiarity and good will between the Nullifiers & the opposition" was in evidence.[4] Clay revealed something of his plans early in the game to Judge Brooke of Virginia, who passed the good word along, as it was doubtless intended he should, to Calhoun's Virginia followers. Floyd heard it from Brooke around Christmastime, and we may be sure he so informed Calhoun when the South Carolinian passed through Richmond a few days later.[5]

Just when Calhoun and Clay got together on a personal basis cannot be certainly determined, but it could not have been long after the former's arrival in Washington. Tyler talked to Clay and other protectionists before January 10, when he wrote to Floyd that he expected the disputed principle to be yielded and the tariff to be gradually reduced over a seven-year period; and Calhoun wrote on the same day to his brother-in-law that the prospect for a satisfactory adjustment was good.[6] Details were not yet fully matured when Jackson's message of January 16, asking for authority to coerce South Carolina, speeded up the discussions. Within a few days of that date a general understanding was probably reached. Clay agreed to a gradual reduction of all duties to the revenue level and to abandonment of the principle of protection; Calhoun pledged acceptance by South Carolina and repeal of the Ordinance of Nullification.[7] It is significant that Calhoun, with his deep-rooted aversion to sudden change, rejected the Verplanck bill because it would be too hard on the manufacturers. He refused to accept what would have been a sweeping victory for the South because he believed that no permanent peace could come out of total victory for either side.[8]

Clay waited just long enough after the opening discussion of the Force Bill to let the administration members fully appreciate the difficulties in which they were involved by this appeal to force. Then on February 11, 1833, he gave notice that on the following day he would ask leave to introduce a bill to modify the tariff.[9] The chamber was packed when the Senate convened on February 12, but for once even the ladies were silent as Clay rose to speak. His manner was grave, his language simple, sincere, conciliatory. He wanted to heal the rift that everyone had seen widening between North and South. The tariff, good or bad, was the cause of that rift. He proposed, therefore, that the duties be gradually reduced year by year until they stood at a uniform 20 percent ad valorem in 1842, thereafter to remain at that level. Some items were to be placed at once on the free list, and others in 1842. When the 20 percent level was reached, all duties were to be laid only "for the purpose of raising such revenue as may be necessary to an economical administration of the Government."[10]

Forsyth, in the role of administration floor leader, opposed on the ground that it was a revenue measure, which could originate only in the House. In the course of his remarks the Georgia Senator cast aspersions at Clay and was promptly taken to task by Sprague and Holmes for the National Republicans and by Poindexter for the Nullifiers. Then Calhoun rose and swept the suddenly silent chamber with that compelling, hypnotic glance which never failed to impress those on whom it fell. All who loved the Union, he declared, must desire an end to sectional conflict. The bill which the Senator from Kentucky was asking leave to introduce was intended to restore harmony. He approved of the purpose and the principles of the bill and should support it. The galleries burst into thunderous applause, and for a few minutes pandemonium reigned.[11]

Behind this compromise bill lay many things, including a very genuine desire on the part of both Clay and Calhoun to heal the sectional breach and restore harmony. Both men realized the calamitous consequences should Jackson be allowed to use force in South Carolina. Both men wanted to get the tariff out of politics. Both were anxious to take credit away from the administration for settling the vexed question. In addition Clay was fighting to retain the leadership of his party, and Calhoun to escape between the horns of his own personal dilemma. With letters from all parts of the country indicating that a compromise was sincerely desired by all the interests concerned, the situation was made to order for both men, and the question of who had the upper hand is largely irrelevant.[12]

Clay's bill was taken up the day after its introduction, and it was agreed that it should be referred to a select committee of seven, representing different sections of the country. Although the select committee was moved by Felix Grundy of Tennessee, it was Clay who at Grundy's instance was named chairman, the other members being Calhoun, Clayton of Delaware, Dallas of Pennsylvania, Grundy, William Cabell Rives who had replaced Tazewell from Virginia, and Webster.[13] Clay was accused of stepping over the Potomac after votes, and Calhoun was no less roughly handled; but the new version of the South-West alliance held firm and was ratified by votes within a week. On February 15 the National Republican favorites, Gales and Seaton, were elected printers to the House, defeating Blair in a bitter two-day struggle; and shortly thereafter Duff Green was re-elected printer to the Senate.[14] Calhoun was no longer isolated nor alone.

2

If the tariff compromise was to save face for Calhoun and the Nullifiers, the Force Bill was equally to save face for Andrew Jackson. For the President had made much of his determination to preserve the Union and had made it clear that he meant thereby the use of an army to collect the tariff duties in South Carolina. If Congress denied him the necessary powers, it would be in the nature of a rebuke that would be all the harder to take because administered primarily by Calhoun. The Force Bill, therefore, became the leading measure of the administration, with all the patronage and power of the Executive being brought to bear to secure its passage. Even tariff reduction, vital as it was to a peaceful settlement of the conflict, was made to depend so far as the party was concerned on the previous enactment of the Force Bill.[15]

All this was clearly understood before the debate began, and it was also well understood that the real champion of the administration in the Senate would not be any of the leading Jacksonians, but the incomparable Daniel Webster.[16] The Force Bill was but the logical carrying out of the theory of government enunciated by Webster in his second reply to Hayne and incorporated by Livingston into Jackson's Proclamation. It was the old Federalist doctrine, and Webster had no choice but to sustain it.

The Force Bill reached the Senate floor on January 28, after a preliminary skirmish over Calhoun's resolutions. Grundy had moved on January 23 to substitute a set of resolutions more in keeping with the views of the administration, in what was a clever bit of parliamentary jockeying; for Grundy's amendment would take precedence for purposes of debate over Calhoun's original motion, and it would therefore be Grundy's resolutions rather than Calhoun's that would be argued. When the question came up on the twenty-eighth, Calhoun tried unsuccessfully to get Grundy to withdraw his amendment, and then consented to lay the whole business on the table so that the Force Bill itself could be argued.[17] He would have preferred to debate the resolutions first, but he was not going to do anything that might delay consideration of the tariff compromise on which he and Clay were already in substantial agreement.

From then on until its actual passage on February 20, the Force Bill occupied the major portion of the time of the Senate, gradually working up to its thundering climax. Everybody knew that the real debate would be the inevitable clash between Calhoun and Webster; but each of the two wanted the other to speak first, so as to gain the advantage of rebuttal. One after another the other gladiators took each his turn on the floor, and the debate grew in interest with each passing day. For three weeks the galleries were crowded, and those who attended derived "an acquaintance with the nature and operation of our institutions, and the character and concerns of the various parts of the Union" that could not have been "learned from books for years."[18] The audience always included at least one member of the Cabinet, Cass being the most frequently in attendance, presumably to serve as eyes and ears for the President.

The bill was introduced by William Wilkins of Pennsylvania, chairman of the Judiciary Committee, whose ultimate reward was the Mission to Russia. Wilkins held the floor for two days, suffering frequent interruptions from Calhoun. Then George M. Bibb of Kentucky took two days to denounce the measure and was followed in turn by Theodore Frelinghuysen of New Jersey, Bedford Brown of North Carolina, and John Holmes of Maine. John Tyler of Virginia took up the cudgels on February 6, with the best speech made thus far; but the audience grew only the more restless as one after another the Senators had their say and the field narrowed. Webster was "understood to have made great preparation" and his supporters did not conceal their conviction that Calhoun feared the contest, would strain too hard, and be annihilated.[19]

By this time Willie P. Mangum of North Carolina, George M. Dallas of Pennsylvania, Stephen D. Miller of South Carolina, and Gabriel Moore of Alabama had all taken a turn on the floor. The Senate was already sitting in evening sessions, but the audience remained faithful. It was becoming increasingly clear that Webster could outsit Calhoun in their contest for the final speech, and it was conceded after the brilliant performance of William Cabell Rives on February 14 that Calhoun himself would have to reply. Rives had won the seat vacated by Tazewell in a closely fought election, carried through by the slim Jacksonian majority in the Virginia legislature; and in his argument for the Force Bill he paid back all he owed, with interest. It was then that the excitement reached its peak, for the clash of the giants was known to be at hand. At the close of the evening session on February 14 Calhoun indicated his intention to speak the following day.[20]

Webster was in the Senate chamber when the gavel fell and so, it almost seemed, was half of Washington. The small, semicircular room, with its two rows of armchairs facing the rostrum, could hardly have held another soul. The lower gallery overflowed onto the floor itself, but every available space there was also occupied. Everywhere one heard the rustle of overabundant skirts, and pink and blue and yellow bonnets dotted the room. But for the grave faces of the Senators, it might have been a fashionable tea, with all of the Capital's best society in attendance. Outside it was ominously cold—the stormiest day of the winter, with snow falling and the wind blustering across the grounds—but the storm inside was of a different and still more ominous kind.[21]

With the singular directness and lack of oratorical flourish that characterized all his speeches, Calhoun plunged at once into his theme. He denounced the Force Bill as a virtual repeal of the Constitution and a declaration of war upon his state; he denounced the manner of its presentation and the forces mobilized behind it. But he explained only so much of his own constitutional theory as was necessary to support his case, and he presented nothing that he had not repeated many times over in his published writings on the subject. In the main he stuck strictly to the bill and its implications. Many in his audience were disappointed, for they had expected a definitive defense of state sovereignty and nullification; but Calhoun knew exactly what he was doing, and a little disappointment with his performance fitted perfectly into his plans. He probably realized that Webster would have preferred to avoid the debate altogether, lest he fail to equal the grand eloquence of his second reply to Hayne.[22] He knew that Webster had been maneuvered by his own party and by the President into the key position as defender of the Force Bill, that the New Englander had made careful preparation, and that the only way he could prepare in advance a reply to Calhoun was to stick to the constitutional argument. He guessed, in short, that Webster would speak not to the Force Bill but to Calhoun's own resolutions, which would give the South Carolinian a right to reply if he himself avoided that subject in his own speech.[23]

Calhoun concluded on the sixteenth, speaking for about two hours on that day. He stood loosely beside his desk, his gaunt figure showing for once no tension; but his brilliant eyes roamed restlessly over the room as they always did when he was under the stress of nervous excitement. He was plainly tired and careworn, but his words gushed forth with the same unbelievable rapidity that was his own peculiar hallmark. His sinewy phrases were built into short incisive sentences and compact, completely ordered paragraphs. There were no superfluous words and no rolling periods. He spoke only to the minds of his hearers—never to their emotions—and so he made a perfect foil for the magnificent theatricalism of Webster. To those who only listened there was no question of the victor. It was the golden, glowing words and thrilling tones of Webster that echoed back and forth in every brain for days. But the speeches had still to be read in print, and the debate was not yet over.

Webster was apparently caught off guard by Calhoun's tactics, and he proceeded as he had planned. Almost before Calhoun's last words, consigning those who upheld the bill to the execrations of posterity, had ceased to vibrate in the chamber, Webster was on his feet. He snatched the echo from the still, somewhat heavy air, and in his deep, rumbling voice proclaimed his willingness to take his chances with posterity. By the sheer magic of his voice alone he all but lifted the audience from its seats with just those simple words; and until three o'clock, when a recess was taken, he held them spellbound. At five the Senate reconvened and Webster went on for three hours more, making the blood run hot and cold by turns. When at last he finished, the gallery, which had sat for ten solid hours, broke into wild applause and had to be cleared before the Senate could adjourn.[24]

It is little wonder that those untrained to follow argument thought Webster had overwhelmed his adversary and crushed forever the reasoning of the State Rights school. Even Webster himself was taken in by his easy conquest—for a few days. But veterans of the House who sat as visitors in the Senate gallery, and the Senators themselves, were not so sure. Calhoun had taken copious notes, and the godlike Daniel, swept away by his own enthusiasm, had left himself vulnerable.[25] Jackson was told what he wanted to hear—that Calhoun's speech "was a perfect failure" and that Webster had "handled him as a child."[26] But Benton wrote hastily to Van Buren that the bill was unwise and urged the Vice President-elect to hasten to Washington to use his influence in securing modification before irreparable damage should be done.[27]

Forsyth spoke for the bill on February 18 and Poindexter, the most skillful orator among the Nullifiers, closed for the opposition on February 19 and 20. Between these two speeches, Calhoun had requested the right to be heard on his resolutions in answer to Webster and a date had been set early in the following week. Grundy and Ewing of Ohio answered Poindexter by way of closing for the administration; and at ten in the evening on February 20, 1833, the vote was taken. The chamber was thin, and Calhoun at intervals had sought an adjournment so that the issue might be decided by a full house. The administration leaders were adamant. When it was clear that the vote would be taken regardless, Calhoun and those of his supporters who remained silently left the chamber. John Tyler alone refused to leave and cast the only vote against the bill. The final count was 32 to 1. Among those not recorded was Henry Clay.[28]

3

The select committee on the tariff did its work during the climactic week of the battle over the Force Bill. It was a week of severe strain for all concerned and it is little wonder that agreement proved impossible to reach. Webster and Dallas, representing the two leading manufacturing states, opposed Clay's compromise in its entirety. Grundy wanted to substitute an administration measure; Clayton would not accept it without in some fashion slipping the protective principle back into it. Calhoun and Rives were willing to take it as it was.[29] The committee held its meetings in the early morning when the Senate was not in session, and it was still sitting on Sunday, February 17, after days of stalemate. The debate between Calhoun and Webster on the Force Bill had terminated only the evening before, and both men were exhausted. The other members of the committee were already present when Rives and Grundy arrived at the Capitol. The two latecomers explained that they were on their way to church, but each expressed his willingness to concur in anything Calhoun would agree to.[30]

In that time of crisis it was high personal tribute from men on the other side in the bitter fight then in progress. With Rives' and Grundy's votes added to Calhoun's and his own, Clay reported the bill out of committee with no more than verbal changes to clarify its meaning and explained it to the Senate on February 19, the day before the passage of the Force Bill. At the same time, however, Clay indicated that he would offer from the floor an amendment on which the committee had been unable to agree.[31] This was the widely discussed "home valuation" clause, providing that after 1842 duties should be levied on the basis of valuation made at the port where goods were first received rather than, as had previously been the case, the port of origin.

The amendment was duly offered when the bill came up for debate on February 21, and Calhoun expressed his regret that Clay had felt himself bound to propose it. He thought it unconstitutional, since it would mean that local prices would determine the duties and there would consequently be no uniformity between states. He also thought that it would be used to defeat the expressed purposes of the bill, because the importing merchant, in order to pass the tax on to the consumer, would include the amount of the duty in his evaluation. The actual tax would thus exceed the 20 percent maximum because it would be levied on a valuation already inflated by 20 percent. He would be compelled to vote against the whole bill if this amendment were made a part of it. Clayton was equally firm that he could not support the bill without the home-valuation clause, and he made it clear that he held the upper hand. He regarded the compromise as a concession from the stronger to the weaker party; and if the Nullifiers would not accept the terms, he would move to lay the bill on the table and keep it there, leaving South Carolina to fight her own war with Andrew Jackson. He deferred the motion at Bibb's request, but the question was still hanging fire when an adjournment was taken. The next day the home-valuation amendment was passed by 26 to 16.[32]

Calhoun and all the Nullifiers voted "aye," and the sting could have been but little eased for the South Carolinian by his prefatory remarks, to the effect that he understood the amendment would not be so construed as to violate the Constitution or to include the duties themselves as an item in the valuation. Clayton, with the manufacturers' lobby behind him, and all those who wished to humiliate Calhoun ready to follow his lead, had made it the condition of passing the bill that all the Nullifiers—and especially their leader—must vote for the amendment. In part this insistence was to get the Nullifiers on record, so that they could not at some future date claim that the law was unconstitutional; in part it was pure sadism, the purpose of which was to convince the public that the Nullifiers were in so desperate a spot that they must accept any indignity to get out of it. Had Calhoun called Clayton's bluff, it is possible that the bill would have passed anyway, or that Verplanck's bill would have; but he was too anxious to restore harmony and avert civil strife to take that risk when the only cost was to his personal pride.[33]

For two or three more days the tariff bill was debated in the Senate, with Webster speaking against it on February 25 and Clay answering him.[34] Late in the afternoon of the same day, the House prepared to resume debate on the Verplanck bill when Robert P. Letcher of Kentucky, a devoted Clay lieutenant, moved to strike out all but the enacting clause and to substitute the bill then being debated in the Senate. There were objections and various parliamentary maneuvers, but the forces of the new coalition seemed completely disciplined and had unshaken control of the situation and of the House. Before members were allowed to go to their lodgings that evening the bill was sent to a third reading; and on February 26 it was passed by a vote of 119 to 85.[35] To obviate any possible constitutional question as to its origin, the House bill was substituted for that which had been under discussion in the Senate, though the two were identical in every respect; and on March 1 it was passed, 29 to 16. Before the vote was taken in the Senate Calhoun stated various objections to the bill, but affirmed his willingness to accept it as a peace offering and pledged his influence to gain acceptance for it in the South.[36]

Immediately after the passage of the compromise tariff, the Senate accepted certain House amendments to a bill that had been carried in the upper chamber late in January—a bill to appropriate for a limited time the proceeds of the sale of the public lands and distribute them among the states. It was a bill introduced by Clay and regarded by the protectionists as a part of the tariff compromise. For the protectionists held that the wording of the tariff bill—that duties could be levied only to meet the necessary expenses of government—meant that all of those necessary expenses were to be paid out of the proceeds of the tariff, unsupplemented from any other source. In this way, they hoped that 20 percent would be inadequate and protection would not be dead, or rather would be left as the home-valuation amendment left it, to local option. The other major source of revenue was the public lands, and a scheme of distribution would insure there being no revenue from that source. Calhoun opposed the measure, as he had opposed Jackson's similar proposition at an earlier date, but it was nevertheless passed. Jackson, however, allowed it to die in his pocket as the Congress came to an end.[37]

4

Webster must have realized, when Calhoun secured consent of the Senate on February 19 to call up his resolutions a week later, that he had been tricked out of the much-prized privilege of rebuttal in the constitutional debate. He must have understood then that Calhoun's speech on the Force Bill, which he was so sure he had demolished, was like his own first reply to Hayne—only bait to draw out his opponent for the slaughter. He had shunned the argument, preferring to rest on the laurels won against Hayne; but he had been forced into it willy-nilly, had fallen bodily into the trap laid for him, and was now to receive the answer that had been in abeyance since 1830. There was nothing to do but wait for the blow to fall. It fell on February 26.

Calhoun spoke for a mere two hours, but two hours were enough. For Webster, in an unguarded moment, had admitted that the whole State Rights argument would follow if Calhoun's premise was correct and the Constitution was indeed a compact between the states. The South Carolinian set out to demonstrate that point, covered by the first of his resolutions; and even the hostile *North American Review,* edited by Alexander H. Everett, brother of the Massachusetts Congressman Edward Everett, and one of Webster's warmest friends, admitted that he had succeeded.[38] Calhoun himself once said of Webster that he always knew when he was beaten in an argument and you could see that he knew it. Seated near Calhoun on this occasion was John Randolph of Roanoke, feeble and emaciated, far gone toward actual insanity, but still lucid and still the master of the perfect phrase. He had come to Washington, he said, to attend the death of the Constitution. He was no friend of Calhoun's, nor any believer in nullification, which he held to be falsely derived from the resolutions of 1798. But throughout Calhoun's speech Randolph was seen to nod his head approvingly, while his shrewd, tired old eyes sought Webster's face. A hat on a seat in front of him obscured his view, and his shrill voice was heard around the chamber: "Take away that hat. I want to see Webster die, muscle by muscle."[39] He told Calhoun that his argument was unanswerable; and Webster did not in fact attempt to answer it. He confined himself instead to a few brief remarks which were bold and stirring, but were nevertheless simply ungrounded assertions. Calhoun's speech was a conspicuous parliamentary triumph, and Randolph merely expressed what every competent observer thought.[40]

The historical confusion as to the outcome of that famous debate stems largely from the subsequent course of events. For though he lost the argument with Calhoun, it was Webster's ideas that triumphed in the end—were in fact well on the road to triumph then. Calhoun based his case on the meaning of the Constitution for those who wrote and ratified it, and in those terms his argument was basically sound, even though nullification itself was drawn from a Jeffersonian gloss rather than from the literal text of the instrument. But Webster's interpretation was the only one compatible with the existence of a great national state, in a world growing every day more nationalistic. It was the only meaning that could be sustained and permit the exploitation of the industrial revolution in America. Admittedly it meant the end of chattel slavery and the substitution of new problems of racial and labor relations, but such was the trend of the western world and to fight against it meant in the end extinction.

It was not Webster's logic that defeated Calhoun, but his stirring appeal to nationalism.

The resolutions were tabled the same day that Calhoun spoke, but they had served his turn and he was satisfied. On March 1 the Force Bill passed the House, and the same day saw the passage of the compromise tariff in the Senate. Jackson signed both bills the following day.

The text of the Force Bill—the "bloody bill" as many a Southerner called it—was printed in the *Telegraph* for March 4, 1833. It was inauguration day for Jackson and Van Buren, but Duff Green bordered his columns in black for the death of the Constitution. To Green the bill had been passed "in the mere wantonness of power" and had destroyed at a blow "all that is valuable in our institutions."[41] To McDuffie, who reflected the general attitude of the South, it was an act "to subvert the sovereignty of the States of this Union, to establish a consolidated Government without limitation of powers, and to make the civil subordinate to the military power."[42] To Calhoun it merely demonstrated the truth of his contention that the numerical majority, unchecked by any other power, would carry out its will by force without regard to minority interests.

CHAPTER XV

THE UNIFICATION OF SOUTH CAROLINA

1

CONGRESS adjourned at five o'clock in the morning, Sunday, March 3, 1833, having sat all night.[1] The session had lasted exactly three months, but it was one of the most eventful and portentous ever held. Calhoun had been present only during the last two months, but the physical and emotional strain had been enormous and he looked haggard and worn. In the slightly sunken cheeks, unnaturally bright eyes, and almost cadaverous figure a modern doctor would probably have detected signs of incipient tuberculosis, and ordered rest and quiet.

But Calhoun's work was not yet done. On February 13—was it purposely timed to coincide with the introduction of the tariff compromise?—James Hamilton, Jr., in his capacity as president of the South Carolina convention, had convoked the members of that body to reconvene on Monday, March 11, 1833.[2] The situation was still tense, for unless the convention accepted the tariff compromise and repealed the Ordinance of Nullification, everything that had been achieved in Congress would be lost. Calhoun was determined to be in Columbia when the convention met, whatever the hazards of the trip might be.

He did not wait for Jackson's second inauguration, leaving Washington either during the day on March 3 or early on the morning of the fourth. The weather was still icy cold with inches of snow on the ground, when he left Alexandria by stage. Cracked and broken by frost, the poorly surfaced road was soon impassable for the high-wheeled, top-heavy vehicle, and Calhoun switched to a sturdier but jolting and uncovered mail cart. Day and night he traveled, mostly by cart, his weary body becoming wearier by the hour, and sometimes numb with cold. But his jaw was set and his brain, as always, worked on with restless, unshakable energy. Only two months ago he had traveled this same road northward, had faced sullen, hostile crowds without flinching, and met with steady eye the accusing look of men who called him traitor. On the southward journey he was something of a hero to the few who caught glimpses of him in his hasty passage, but this time he could not stop to argue or expound. There was no time for explanation, no time for weakness, no time for self-congratulation or for fear.[3]

The convention met at noon on March 11, for an hour—just long enough to accept the resignation of Hamilton as president and elect Governor Hayne in his stead; and to appoint a Committee of Twenty-one to consider the report of Benjamin Watkins Leigh, the Virginia commissioner, as well as "all other matters connected with the subject and the course which should be pursued by the Convention."[4] Those members who were also part of the state's Congressional delegation—Senator Stephen D. Miller and Representatives Robert W. Barnwell, J. K. Griffin, and George McDuffie—were present at the opening session. Calhoun arrived during the night of the eleventh, having made in a week by mail cart a trip that usually required two by stage. He was pale, emaciated, weary to the very marrow, but sure of himself still, and confident that the convention would do what he wished.

On March 13 a committee was appointed to confer with the "Senators and Representatives lately in Congress, and now in the town of Columbia" and to ask them to supply the convention with any relevant information in their possession. The next day, however, the committee reported that the gentlemen in question deemed it unnecessary to report as a body, and referred the convention to those of its own members who had just come back from Washington.[5] Though the language was general and no names were mentioned, the meaning was clear: Calhoun did not wish to address the convention. He was undoubtedly aware that any remarks he might make would be caught up by the administration press: it would be said that he had stilled the tempest with a word, and this would be advanced as proof that he had all the time been master of the wind.

It is true that there were those among the convention members, particularly the followers of Dr. Thomas Cooper, who were dissatisfied with the compromise; and certainly it was less than the convention had originally asked. It could therefore be argued that Calhoun's failure to speak was to save face for himself.[6] The Committee of Twenty-one, however, had already reported in favor of repealing the Ordinance of Nullification before the request for explanations from the Congressional delegation was made.[7] Miller, Barnwell, Griffin, and McDuffie all were members of this committee; and if certain characteristic tricks of style mean anything, Calhoun also had a hand in drafting the committee's report.[8] Unquestionably he had talked individually to key members of the convention, and there was no question in anyone's mind where he stood or why. Surely in the circumstances he cannot be accused of reluctance to defend his course. He simply did not wish to give Jackson any vestige of an excuse to hold him responsible for what the convention did.

Repeal of the Ordinance was debated on March 14, with Miller and Barnwell both explaining the circumstances of the compromise. The following day a new ordinance nullifying the Force Bill was introduced by the Committee of Twenty-one, together with a report and resolutions commending Virginia for her mediation. Then nullification of the tariff was rescinded by a vote of 153 to 4. The Force Bill, after a two-day debate revolving primarily around the test-oath requirement, was declared on March 18 to be null and void, and later in that same day the convention was pronounced dissolved.[9]

Before the convention ever assembled, its conservative leaders were agreed that the tariff compromise would be accepted and the Force Bill nullified,[10] and their control of the situation was not shaken. Despite an undercurrent of rebelliousness on the part of some of the younger men, an astonishing unanimity prevailed. Calhoun himself never doubted the wisdom of the course pursued, and was quite sure that South Carolina—not Andrew Jackson—had preserved the Union.

2

The constitutional controversy of 1830-1833 left scars that extended far beyond the boundaries of South Carolina, or even of the South. Out of the tariff controversy, nullification, the threat of force, the half-truths and whole falsehoods of propaganda, came a new sectional solidarity. The wind of suspicion and distrust had been sown, and the whirlwind of civil war would inescapably be the harvest. In South Carolina men wore the blue cockade of the Nullifiers long after the issue had been settled. The extraordinary military preparations made to repel a possible invasion by Yankee troops were continued in effect, for the South had been convinced that she would have no more liberty in the future than she was prepared to maintain by the sword.[11]

The split in interest between North and South was already too deep to be removed by any alteration in the revenue laws. It stemmed from the widely different economies of the two sections: the South with its one-crop system, its slave labor, its imperative need for world-wide markets; the North with its diversified farms, its thriving commerce, its growing, expanding, slowly dominating industrialism. It stemmed from advancing industrial technology and an enormously increased demand for cotton. The nullification leaders had been unjustly slandered when time and again they were accused of seeking to set up a Southern confederacy; but before Jackson went out of office, sober and serious men among them would be talking of just such a step and wondering if they had not erred in remaining in the Union in 1833.[12]

Calhoun was never the advocate of such a solution. Throughout his life he remained steadfast in his loyalty to the Union he loved. But as the agitation of the slave question increased through the 1830's and 40's he was driven farther and farther in the direction charted by the radical wing of his own party. He had time and again to yield a point or concede an issue, or to lose his grip and watch the fire-eaters plunge ahead on the road to ultimate disaster. Before the end, even Calhoun acknowledged that a Southern confederacy might prove to be the only solution, if sectional differences were actually incapable of reconciliation. But never did he advocate it, never did he wish it, never did he turn a finger to bring it about. He stood, indeed, as the great barrier between the South and secession from 1830 on until his death. Again and again he interposed to curb the sectional enthusiasm—the Southern nationalism if you will—of his followers; and as long as he lived the South, though she nursed and fed upon her grievances, could not be charmed nor drugged from her allegiance to the United States.

3

Calhoun's primary concern, once the Ordinance of Nullification had been rescinded, was to restore unity to South Carolina. A civil conflict within the state had barely been averted, and differences of such intensity could not be allowed to endure. Aside from nullification, which was no longer an issue, there remained two major obstacles to harmony: the personality of John C. Calhoun, and the test oath.

Calhoun himself realized that his leadership could hardly be acceptable to men who had so lately painted him with horns and cloven hoofs. To minimize so far as possible the element of personal rancor, he retired to Pendleton, while his editors exulted in the triumph of the state rather than in the victory of Calhoun. For eight months he stayed out of the limelight, while Hayne and Hamilton and McDuffie made pointed overtures to the Unionist leaders.[13] Some, like Drayton and William Smith, left South Carolina for good rather than submit to Calhoun's dominance. Others, like Poinsett and Petigru, kept up a show of opposition, but in the end gave in.[14] When the Congressional elections, deferred from the previous fall, were held in September 1833, the Unionists scarcely made an effort. Of the nine Representatives chosen, only huge, truculent James Blair from the Unionist stronghold of Lancaster was elected in opposition to the Calhoun slate. Henry L. Pinckney, brother-in-law of Governor Hayne and former editor of the strongly nullification Charleston *Mercury,* was unopposed for the seat vacated by Drayton's self-imposed exile.[15] The position of the state in national affairs was further strengthened by the resignation of Senator Stephen D. Miller because of ill health and the selection of the mercurial William C. Preston in his place.[16]

It was not until late November that Calhoun came down from the hills to take part in a public function. Robert J. Turnbull, the real father of nullification if any one man could be so designated, had died suddenly in June. The Nullifiers planned an imposing monument to his memory, and the laying of the cornerstone on November 22, 1833, was made the occasion for a great party rally in Charleston. The ceremonies started at eleven in the morning, when most of the high civil and military officials of the state and city marched in solemn procession to St. Philip's churchyard. Hayne had already taken his place beside the tomb, and there was a momentary hush when Calhoun's arrival was announced and he was escorted to his place beside the Governor. The cornerstone, with copies of *The Crisis* and Turnbull's other writings beneath it, was duly laid. Hayne spoke briefly but eloquently. There was a religious service conducted by Calhoun's Yale classmate and lifelong friend, the Reverend Doctor Christopher E. Gadsden, rector of St. Philip's and one day to wear the bishop's miter. There was a stirring eulogy by James Hamilton. The high point of the whole affair, however, was an hourlong address by Calhoun at seven in the evening, for which the auditors moved from the cemetery to the circus.[17]

The whole occasion so far as it concerned Calhoun—his delayed arrival at the churchyard; his again delayed entry at the circus, where the "immense assemblage" sprang to its feet and greeted him with "the most overwhelming bursts of applause"; the emphasis in his address on the common interests of the South and on constitutional liberty as the basis of enduring union—all this had the appearance of careful staging to serve a well-thought-out end. The Nullifiers of South Carolina, calling themselves the State Rights party, were demonstrating their own solidarity but were at the same time offering a basis on which their late opponents within the state, and Southern men generally, could join with them. They were also offering their leader in the guise that fitted him best: the conservative champion of the individual, the state, the section, against the exercise by the majority of arbitrary power. It was Calhoun's first speech since the stirring debate with Webster, and we may be sure that the presence of the party's favorite editor, Duff Green of the *Telegraph,* was not accidental.[18]

Calhoun was not, as some of the Unionist leaders professed to believe, "incessantly agitating."[19] He was exerting his whole strength and influence to compromise internal differences and preserve a Union that some of his own followers no longer believed to be worth the effort.[20] To achieve this end he was willing to efface himself, and to remain so far as possible in the background. Even the test oath he was willing to compromise when the time came, important as it seemed to his abstract way of thought.

4

It was around the test oath that the conflict between Unionists and Nullifiers centered, but the bitterness of the struggle can be appreciated only in terms of the ideological clash between the two groups. The original Ordinance of Nullification had contained a clause requiring all civil and military officers of the state to take an oath to support and carry out the Ordinance. The legislature had prescribed such an oath, in language that made allegiance to the state of South Carolina paramount to allegiance to the Union. The committee that drafted the more recent Ordinance nullifying the Force Act had sought to include a similar oath, and the issue had been hotly debated in the convention. For the sake of harmony, a substitute was accepted, declaring merely that "the allegiance of the citizens of this State, while they continue such, is due to the said State; and that obedience only, and not allegiance, is due by them to any other power or authority, to whom a control over them has been, or may be delegated by the State." It was left to the general assembly to prescribe the form of oath to be used, but Judge John Belton O'Neall of the State Court of Appeals, the leading Unionist member of the convention, made it clear that he regarded the kind of oath desired by the Nullifiers as contrary to the state constitution.[21]

On the theoretical side, the whole case for nullification was built up on the premise that sovereignty inhered in the states and that the Federal Government exercised only a delegated authority. In case of conflict between state and general governments, like that so recently terminated, there must be no question where the allegiance of the citizen belonged. The only moral justification for any such conflict was the sovereignty of the state, and if the state was sovereign the oath to support and defend it must be so worded as to transcend all other oaths. It was a question of logical consistency that could not be yielded without giving up the very basis of the argument.

It is easy enough to condemn the whole nullification movement and all that went with it in terms of the constitutional doctrines of the post-Civil War era.[22] But those doctrines were not established in the 1830's. To a large and thoughtful segment of the population—not alone in South Carolina or even in the slaveholding states—the notion that allegiance to the Federal Government could transcend the duty of the citizen to his state was to deny the whole justification for the existence of the United States; it was to concede that Jefferson and the patriots of 1776 had been wrong and George III and his Parliament right; it was to admit the legitimacy of a consolidated government, restrained only by the practical limits of the physical power at its command.[23]

There was a very practical side to the test-oath question, too. The state militia would constitute an effective army for the defense of South Carolina against any future attempt at coercion only if officers and men could be absolutely depended on to follow the orders of the Governor of the state as against those of the President of the Union. With the state even yet not fully demobilized, the problem was a very real one, which the oath would help to solve by forcing Unionist officers to resign.

When the legislature met in November 1833 the test oath was duly enacted, and at the same time an amendment to the state constitution was started to forestall legalistic criticism. Poinsett privately advised the Unionist militia officers to take the oath but to follow it with a joint statement to the effect that they did not regard it as in any way impairing their allegiance to the United States.[24] Other Unionists were bolder and under the leadership of Calhoun's one-time law student, Robert Cunningham, military companies were secretly organized. Their existence gave the state authorities grave concern and led Governor Hayne to wonder if the Unionists really contemplated civil war.[25] Before any real damage was done, however, a test case found its way into the State Court of Appeals. Lieutenant Edward M'Cready refused to take the oath and sued for his commission. A Charleston court upheld the oath and the Unionist leaders prepared, should the decision on appeal also go against them, to carry the case to the Supreme Court of the United States. A favorable decision there would again embroil the state with the federal authorities, and the whole struggle might have to be fought out over again.[26]

The case was argued with great ability in the spring of 1834. Defending the oath was thirty-three-year-old Robert Barnwell Rhett, Attorney General of South Carolina, and the man who had forced the issue in the state after the tariff of 1828. The appellant was represented by James L. Petigru and Thomas S. Grimké, the latter a former law partner of Hayne. The decision, however, followed the partisan affiliation of the judges. O'Neall declared the oath unconstitutional in an opinion that echoed the consolidationist thought of Webster and of Jackson's Proclamation against the Nullifiers; and Presiding Judge David Johnson, also a Unionist, concurred in somewhat milder language. Chancellor William Harper, who had drafted the original Ordinance of Nullification, was the third member of the court. He dissented sharply, but futilely.[27]

Hayne was immediately besieged with demands that he nullify the decision by withholding commissions from those who refused the oath, that he call a special session of the legislature forthwith, and that the offending judges be removed. Though his own popularity and influence were at stake, Hayne resisted the pressure. He consulted as quickly as possible with Calhoun, McDuffie, Preston, Hamilton, and Hammond; and all agreed on the conservative and conciliatory course. On June 12 Hayne issued a proclamation sustaining the decision of the Court of Appeals. He praised the ability with which the case had been argued on both sides, and announced that he would thenceforth issue commissions to militia officers on the basis of the pre-nullification oath.[28]

Scrupulously the Nullifiers avoided any rashness or violence and concentrated on securing the two-thirds majority that would be needed in the next legislature to pass the oath as a constitutional amendment. In the eyes of the country at large their standing rose with each new evidence of their sincerity and their willingness to abide by constitutional processes.[29]

5

Through August and September of 1834 a vigorous campaign for the state legislature was conducted, but the Unionists steadily lost ground and by mid-September they knew they were beaten. They had used the test-oath issue as a means of keeping their party alive, but the truth was that the average South Carolinian did not take it very seriously. The tariff compromise was widely accepted within the state as an honorable settlement, and by most the credit for it was given to the Nullifiers. Although their victory was the most overwhelming they had ever achieved, the Nullifiers remained conciliatory and moderate. Behind the scenes Calhoun was actively counseling peace, and his influence prevailed with the younger leaders. When the legislature met, Hamilton sought out Petigru and offered to write the disputed amendment in any way that would be acceptable to the Unionists. A compromise wording was agreed upon and the Nullifiers carried it through.[30]

To seal the bargain, McDuffie was agreed on for Governor; and though he had resigned his seat in the House only three months earlier because of ill health, he allowed himself in such a cause to be "drafted." His election was unanimous, and for the first time in almost a decade South Carolina presented a united front to the world. It was inevitable that the State Rights leaders should see in this internal unity, following long and bitter struggle, a pattern for sectional unity throughout the South. No doubt it was also inevitable that such as Duff Green should seize the occasion to focus national attention once more on the "most distinguished son of the South."[31]

CHAPTER XVI

THE HERO CONDEMNED

1

WHILE Calhoun and his partisans were struggling to bring harmony to South Carolina during the summer and fall of 1833, Andrew Jackson was busily creating a new cause for discord in national affairs, and was forging an issue on which the otherwise discordant elements of the opposition to his administration could unite. After months of argument and internal bickering within his own party, the President removed the public funds from the Bank of the United States. To intellectual descendants of Federalism like Clay and Webster, it was economic heresy that would set class against class and ultimately ruin the propertied interests of the country. To Calhoun and those who shared his jealousy of power it was another concomitant of rule by force, another exercise of arbitrary authority which followed logically from the doctrines of the Force Act and proved, if anyone still doubted, that Jackson had substituted his personal will for the reign of law under constitutional guarantees.

The removal of the deposits was probably each of these things, and more; but to the tough-willed and single-minded old soldier in the White House it was the strategic maneuver in what was to be the decisive campaign in his long war against the Bank. By July 1832 when he vetoed recharter, Jackson was convinced that the institution was bad for the country. Six months later he was also sure—and not without reason—that the Bank was hostile to him personally and had actively worked against him in the fall election. The charter had still more than three years to run, but Andrew Jackson did not believe in giving an enemy three years of grace.

In his annual message of December 4, 1832, Jackson had questioned the safety of the government deposits, and at the same time had taken the initial steps toward securing a Cabinet favorable to removal. Louis McLane did not approve of the policy, but as Secretary of the Treasury it would be his responsibility to carry it out. It was arranged, therefore, that Livingston should go as Minister to France, where a troublesome debt question was in the making, and that McLane should move up to the State Department. The Treasury post was offered to William J. Duane of Philadelphia in December 1832, although he did not accept it until the end of January and the shift was not actually made until the first of June 1833.[1]

On his third day in office the new Secretary of the Treasury was informed that he was expected to exercise the power vested in him by the Bank's charter to remove the government deposits, then amounting to about nine million dollars, as soon as new depositories could be arranged for.[2] Then Jackson left for a triumphal tour of the East, while Kendall, under instructions prepared by himself, undertook to find state banks in which the government funds might be kept.[3] Toward the end of June illness forced the President to cut short his trip; but he retired to his favorite summer retreat at the Rip Raps on Old Point Comfort, confident that the deposits would be removed and a crippling blow struck at the Bank before Congress met.

A hitch presently developed in the reluctance of Duane to carry out Jackson's will, a reluctance in which he was abetted by McLane and tacitly supported by Van Buren. The Vice President was wise in the ways in which economic power might be brought to bear on government, and he was clearly alarmed at the storm he knew the removal of the deposits would arouse. The recharter had been denied and the Bank would go out a year before Andrew Jackson himself. Van Buren expected to inherit political capital from each, and he was content to wait. But Jackson was intent on marching forth to battle without delay, and the Little Magician dared not cross him. McLane proposed, and Van Buren seems to have favored, making the order for removal effective January 1, 1834, so that the whole question could be brought before Congress. Kendall knew that Congress would block it unless McLane used his own considerable influence in its favor, and he distrusted the Secretary of State. Van Buren sought delay while he showed the plan to Silas Wright, perhaps the ablest financier among the Jacksonians and a loyal member of the Albany Regency. Wright agreed that it would be better (for Van Buren's political future, but he didn't say that out loud) to delay action until Congress met.[4] The President, with the glib and plausible Blair at his elbow, saw no reason for delay. Blair had once been a banker himself, and he had also once been a National Republican. He knew all the arguments and, better still, he understood thoroughly the psychology of Andrew Jackson. Were not scores of Congressmen and Senators in debt to the Bank of the United States? And would not a two-thirds majority be bought if the Bank retained the power and the funds to do it?

In July, at the Rip Raps, a paper setting forth the whole case for removal was concocted by the Old Hero and his chief propagandist.[5] By August the opposition press was full of it. McLane became bolder in his insistence on delay, and Duane's normally rather willowy spine became remarkably stiff. Van Buren equivocated and kept as far away from Washington as possible. But Kendall made the necessary arrangements with the state banks, while Jackson became more grim of purpose with each new criticism, each sign of weakness from a follower.

On September 15 the President announced that he would delay no longer, and three days later the July paper, now skillfully revised by Taney, was read to the Cabinet.[6] The public funds as they were paid in at the customhouses and land offices were to be deposited, beginning October 1, with designated state banks, while disbursements would continue to be made from the Bank of the United States until the government deposits in that institution were exhausted. Duane was given two days to issue the necessary order or resign. He did neither, and was curtly dismissed on September 23, Taney being named to the Treasury in his stead. The Cabinet was completed in November by the appointment of Benjamin F. Butler of the Albany Regency as Attorney General.[7]

The order to deposit no more government funds in the Bank of the United States was promptly issued by Taney in his new capacity as Secretary of the Treasury, and the administration armed for battle. It was not anticipated that Nicholas Biddle would accept the situation quietly, or even accept it at all. He did not. From the beginning of the Bank war, or at least from the time of the recharter fight of 1831-1832, Biddle had personified the Bank in Jackson's mind, while Biddle had identified the government of the United States with Andrew Jackson. Each regarded the contest as a personal battle and neither asked nor offered quarter. If the public interest suffered in this clash of egos, each would have replied, and in effect did reply, that he could not help it—it was all because the other was a scoundrel.

Calhoun followed the various steps in the Bank war from the quiet of his study at Fort Hill. The Bank was in a sense his own creation. But he believed that the institution had used its power to favor Northern at the expense of Southern commerce, and so he was prepared to restrict its control of credit. He did not question the constitutionality of the Bank, nor did he doubt the necessity of some kind of central regulation of the currency. The expediency of a national bank, however, was one thing; the removal of the deposits was quite another.

It was true that the Secretary of the Treasury was empowered under the Bank's charter to withdraw the government funds if he saw fit, but he must immediately report his reasons for so doing to Congress. The presumption was that Congress too would have to be convinced, but in this case Congress had already by an overwhelming vote pronounced the deposits safe.[8] From this alone it could be argued that the removal, on the President's express authority, was stretching the power of the Executive, but that was the smallest part of the case. The removal of the deposits left great sums of money at the disposal of the Treasury. It would be possible, and was in fact inevitable, that any bank in which part of this money was deposited would issue notes against it and generally enlarge its sphere of activities. The public funds thus became a potent engine of patronage. The depositories had been selected by the Executive alone, under terms dictated by the Treasury without legal prescription or limitation. For all practical purposes the public funds had been seized by the President—the same President who had a few months earlier asserted and made good his right to put down a sectional opposition by military force.

Is it any wonder that men who sincerely believed that the powers of the President, and of the Federal Government in all its branches, had been deliberately and carefully limited to prevent the centralization of power should see in this bald union of purse and sword the beginning of the end for the Republic? It was a union that had been fatal to liberty since time began, and there was nothing in the character of Andrew Jackson to convince those who had opposed him that it would not be again.

2

But for Jackson's removal of the deposits, the coalition between Calhoun and Clay might have gone no farther than the tariff compromise which gave it birth. For with the passage of that act the purposes that brought the two men together were accomplished. Clay, a badly beaten Presidential candidate, recaptured the leadership of his party; Calhoun extricated himself from a difficult and possibly dangerous situation. Certainly at the time Congress adjourned on March 3, 1833, there were no commitments between them as to any joint action in the future.[9] That, however, the political foes of neither man could be expected to believe.

The South Carolina Unionists, left stranded by the compromise, could hardly be blamed for believing that a bargain had been struck whereby Calhoun was to "ride behind Clay."[10] Nor was it out of character for Jackson to see in the association of these two enemies of his own every evil that he had previously blamed on either. In March he thought that the tariff compromise had been deliberately arranged to create a large surplus revenue, which was to be used to corrupt Congress and secure a recharter for the Bank; two weeks later the President foresaw the Bank influence being corruptly used to secure the election to his own office of either Clay or Calhoun—he was not sure which; and finally he charged the coalition, as he had earlier charged the Nullifiers, with seeking to destroy the Union and set up a Southern confederacy.[11]

The evolution of Jackson's attitude toward the principals in the prospective alliance of opposition forces was exactly paralleled by the editorial policy of the *Globe*. Blair began immediately after the inauguration, with the Bank of the United States as the major object of attack. The Bank was in due time associated with Calhoun through his early sponsorship of it, and the Carolinian himself was charged once more with treasonable intentions.[12] While the President toured the pro-Bank Eastern states and received an honorary degree from conservative Harvard, Blair concentrated on "exposing" the conspiracy by which the South was to be taken out of the Union. The truth of the charge, the *Globe* assured its readers, was admitted by the Nullifiers themselves, for they were even then distributing medals bearing the legend, "John C. Calhoun, first President of the Southern Confederacy." There were no such medals, as Blair himself was eventually compelled to admit, but the story helped to discredit Calhoun with Clay's Northern followers.[13] In May the Jackson oracle began indoctrinating its readers to believe that the slave question was being deliberately agitated in the South as a new excuse for destroying the Union; and the various elements of the hypothetical Calhoun conspiracy were skillfully woven together during the month of June. In July, coinciding exactly with Jackson's return from New England, the Bank once more became the center of attack. By carefully pointed inference Biddle was then revealed as the power behind the insidious coalition of Nationalists and Nullifiers.[14]

In this final conclusion there was an element of truth. Throughout the summer and fall of 1833 Biddle worked heroically to bring Clay and Calhoun together, and it was probably his influence more than that of any other man that ultimately brought Webster to cast in his lot with the other two. Biddle did not underestimate his foe. He knew that the overthrow of Jackson would require the combined strength of the opposition, but combination for many months seemed highly improbable.

Webster had not supported the tariff compromise, had taken the lead in passing the Force Act, and had received overtures from the administration not unkindly.[15] At the same time the old-line Federalists showed a disposition to substitute Webster for Clay as the head of the strong-government, pro-business party. The Massachusetts Senator appeared for a time to have two roads to the White House opened before him, and he dallied with them both.[16] During March and April Biddle used his economic hold over Webster, who was both attorney for the Bank and deeply in debt to it, to forestall an open rupture with the National Republicans.[17] When Webster started an electioneering tour of the West, however, Clay became suspicious and made advances toward Calhoun and the State Rights Democrats.[18] A correspondence between the Kentucky Senator and Governor Floyd of Virginia continued for several months. Copies of the letters were sent by Floyd to William C. Preston (who was Mrs. Floyd's nephew), and were presumably shown by him to Calhoun.[19]

The Nullifiers, for their part, preferred to keep free from all alliances unless they could see tangible gain for themselves. In ideology they were poles apart from both Clay and Webster, and saw no virtue in entering into a coalition that would simply elevate one or the other of these to the Presidency.[20] Biddle saw the point before his political friends did and approached the Nullifiers through Thomas Cooper on the ground most likely to appeal to them—executive usurpation. At the same time he condemned the Proclamation, which the majority of the Bank party upheld.[21] The Nullifiers did not take the bait, or perhaps Cooper was not in their councils. When Clay gained momentum as the Bank candidate in late October, Duff Green publicly announced that the differences in principle between the Kentuckian and the State Rights party were insurmountable, and began weighing the relative strength of Benjamin Watkins Leigh and Judge John McLean.[22] Calhoun himself, in his Charleston speech on the occasion of the Turnbull ceremonies, made it clear that there could be no union of State Rights and tariff parties save on the principles of the former.[23]

To Biddle these differences among the elements of the opposition threatened to be fatal, and he was still laboring indefatigably to bring about an understanding even after Congress had met. "I only repeat what I have said again & again," he wrote to Webster on December 15, "that the fate of this nation is in the hands of Mr Clay Mr Calhoun and yourself. It is in your power to save us from the misrule of these people . . . but you can only do it while you are united. It is for that reason that every honest man is anxious that you three should not be alienated from each other. . . ."[24]

3

In spite of the insinuations of the *Globe* and the strenuous exertions of Nicholas Biddle, the leaders of the opposition were still far from any kind of union among themselves when Congress met on December 2, 1833. Calhoun's first concern, when he took his seat a few days later, was to define his position and that of his followers with relation to the other parties. In the Senate the State Rights group remained small in numbers, but for prestige and individual ability its members stood high in a body of unusual distinction. Their political power, too, was out of all proportion to their actual strength, for the Jacksonians and the National Republicans were almost evenly divided. "No measure can be taken but with our assent," Calhoun wrote before the session was two weeks old, "where the administration and the opposition parties come into conflict." In the House the Jacksonians still held the upper hand, but Calhoun's followers were "a good deal stronger" than they had been in the previous Congress, both numerically and in terms of internal solidarity.[25]

Personal relations between National Republicans and Nullifiers were cordial,[26] and the two groups showed admirable discipline in every matter of joint concern. Beyond that, however, the State Rights partisans would not go, regardless of the bait held out to them as a party and as individuals. "We are aware of the danger," Calhoun wrote after the first month of the session, "of our merging into one or both of the great parties now contending for the Presidency. We . . . are determined to preserve our seperate existence. . . . If there is to be Union against the administration, it must be Union on our own ground. . . ."[27]

The opposition was in clear control when it came to organizing the Senate, and the selection of committees was quickly taken from the hands of the Jacksonian President pro tempore, Senator White of Tennessee. There was a delay of some ten days while Webster flirted with the administration, but Van Buren rejected the overtures of the New England champion, and Biddle cracked the whip. By December 16 the opposition forces had closed ranks and the committees were chosen by ballot without a hitch.[28]

Calhoun took no committee assignment at all, and Clay contented himself with the last place on Public Lands. As former Cabinet members, each would have been entitled by custom to the chairmanship of the committee in the field of his experience; but both wanted to be free to act independently on the floor. All of the committees were made up with opposition majorities, but since the removal of the deposits was certain to be the major issue of the session, the greatest care was bestowed on the personnel of the Committee on Finance. Webster was made chairman, in part as a conciliatory gesture after his attempted bolt, in part no doubt because Biddle wished it. The other members were Tyler of Virginia, Ewing of Ohio, Wilkins of Pennsylvania, and Mangum of North Carolina. Ewing was a thoroughgoing partisan of Clay, and Wilkins was a whole-hog Jackson man. The other two, though not Nullifiers, were State Rights Southerners who could be counted in the Calhoun camp.[29] Shortly thereafter Webster wrote his often quoted note to Biddle suggesting that if the Bank wished to continue his services a retainer would be in order.[30] Before the end of January he was back unreservedly in the conservative fold and his friends were busy denying that he had ever left it.[31]

In the lower house it was a different story. Andrew Stevenson was re-elected Speaker by a large majority, and committees were so made up as best to serve the President's program. Calhoun's friends were pretty generally left out altogether. James K. Polk of Tennessee held the key position as chairman of Ways and Means[32] and also served as administration floor leader. George McDuffie by common consent became spokesman for the opposition.

4

The strategy of the opposition was necessarily to emphasize executive usurpation, on which all of the leaders could agree. The Bank was to be kept in the background until the larger battle had been won.[33] It was Clay who directed the political course of the coalition and who led its sorties on the floor of the Senate; but the issue was Calhoun's. Through the long nullification struggle he had made himself the undisputed champion of individual liberty and of minority interests against the arbitrary power of the majority. Less than a year before, in his debates with Webster on the Force Bill, he had pointed out and decried the trend of the government toward dictatorship; but the National Republicans had scoffed at the idea and had abetted the trend to the extent of voting into the President's hands the power to use military force to coerce a domestic minority.

It was much easier for the party of the economically well-to-do to see dictatorship in the removal of the deposits than it had been to see it in the failure to reduce the tariff, or even in the threatened subjugation of South Carolina. They objected vehemently, but the more they objected the closer they were driven to Calhoun's ground. As the session progressed, Calhoun's strength steadily rose. Much of the old prejudice against him vanished. He was not only the "most confident man in either house"; he was the intellectual leader of the anti-Jackson forces.[34]

The Jacksonians too accepted the issue of executive power. It fitted the President's conception of his office. For Andrew Jackson, deep down in his subconscious mind and sometimes consciously as well, did not think of himself as administering a government. He was leading an army, which he called a party and which he confused now and again with the "people." An army did not compromise with its foes; it battled to extermination. Neither was there any halfway house for loyalty, in Jackson's mind. You were for him or against him. If for him, you obeyed orders without question; if against him, you were a species of traitor to your country, to be annihilated as promptly and as thoroughly as possible. The second term found the old General more difficult than ever to reason with, and more than ever likely to be guided by the advice of those who fawned on him.[35] But he was most formidable when defending himself and his course against direct personal assault, and it was the frontal attack that Calhoun and Clay had chosen to make. Since Jackson had ordered the removal on his own authority, the issue was necessarily a personal one; but for the time being it served the political purposes of the opposition leaders better than any other would have done. To destroy Jackson would be to destroy Van Buren and to leave the succession open to one of themselves.

The President's message of December 3, 1833, was followed the next day by a careful exposition in which the Secretary of the Treasury stated his reasons for removal of the government deposits from the Bank of the United States. The line of justification was already familiar from the earlier publication of the paper read to the Cabinet on September 18, and from the unwearying efforts of the *Globe*. But though it added nothing new to the argument, Taney's report did offer precisely the point of departure that the coalition sought for its attack on the administration. Three weeks were devoted to organization and preliminary skirmishing. Then on the day after Christmas Clay introduced two resolutions which were to fix party lines for the remainder of Jackson's term. The wording was modified from time to time in the course of three months of debate, but the import did not change. One resolution pronounced the reasons offered by the Secretary of the Treasury for removing the deposits to be unsatisfactory. The other enounced that in the whole proceeding the President had assumed power both unconstitutional and dangerous.[36] For three days Clay spoke to these resolutions, and his speech was a mighty philippic against power. When he finished on Tuesday, December 31, the tumult in galleries and lobby was so great that it could be stilled only by ejecting the visitors.[37]

At approximately the same time that Clay opened the opposition batteries against the President in the Senate, memorials and petitions began to appear, depicting the economic distress of the memorialists and praying that the deposits be restored. They arrived singly at first, then in batches, and finally in floods. They came from substantial citizens in all parts of the country, and in most cases the distress they depicted was real, though probably exaggerated. To what extent it was also necessary was another matter. With the public deposits gone and his Bank scheduled to close its doors in two years' time, Biddle had no choice but to restrict credit preparatory to balancing his books. The degree of restriction required, however, was a matter of judgment which undoubtedly involved political as well as financial considerations.[38] Calhoun was probably not aware of the extent to which his political allies were playing the Bank's game. Biddle was quite willing to use the lanky and confident Carolinian but did not altogether trust him. Jackson, however, saw exactly what was happening and where it must lead. He saw his own support dwindling under the pressure of public opinion in the home district of each individual Congressman, and he called on his partisans to stop debating and vote while they still retained a working majority in the House.[39]

The opposition strategy might well have been completely successful had not Biddle overplayed his hand. Proud, confident, as egotistical and extroverted as Jackson himself, and quite as obstinate, "Czar Nick," as his enemies called him, actually did before the fight was over pretty much what Jackson accused him of doing before he did it. He tightened the screws on business to impress Congress with the sufferings of the mercantile community, and refused to relax the pressure lest any evidence of prosperity be interpreted favorably for the financial policy of the administration.[40] Even Webster could not persuade him to modify his course. He had joined battle with the Hero of New Orleans, and he would not yield an inch. Let the merchants fail, let the banks break, let the people suffer! "The relief, to be useful or permanent, must come from Congress & from Congress alone. If that body will do its duty, relief will come—if not, the Bank feels no vocation to redress the wrongs inflicted by these miserable people. Rely upon that. This worthy President thinks that because he has scalped Indians and imprisoned Judges, he is to have his way with the Bank. He is mistaken. . . ."[41] The State Rights Senators, already unwilling to give the Bank permanent existence, were ready by the end of the session to repudiate Biddle entirely.

The financial distress, however, was not wholly Biddle's doing.

Part of it, including some of the seeds that were to germinate and flower into the Panic of 1837, was the direct outgrowth of Jackson's financial policy. For the government funds had been placed in the "pet banks" without adequate safeguards or controls, or indeed seemingly any idea of the probable consequences. As long as the Bank of the United States received the notes of other banks in payment of government dues, it could exercise some kind of control over these various banks. They were in its debt, and if they departed too far from conservative standards, Biddle could exert intolerable pressure merely by presenting their notes for redemption. When the Bank of the United States ceased to be the fiscal agent of the government, however, it lost its power to regulate the bank paper that constituted in fact the currency of the country. The depository banks used the public money not as a deposit but as though it were windfall capital of their own, expanding credit in keeping with their new-found resources and their unaccustomed freedom from restraint. If most of their loans went to good Jacksonians, it was no doubt because the latter were more enterprising or perhaps more needy than their politically conservative fellows. In the normal course of business the government deposits in the Bank of the United States were presently exhausted and the Treasury began issuing drafts on the pet banks. All of them were shocked, and many were unable to pay. Hard pressed as it was in Congress, the administration could not let its hand-picked agents collapse, so the banks were bolstered and propped up and lectured on their duties; but reform was no more than temporary.[42]

In addition to the public pressure, many prominent members of the Jackson party saw political as well as economic ruin for themselves in the continuance of the administration policy. Behind the scenes the substantial merchants of New York pleaded with Van Buren to save the country before it was too late. Others among the original Jackson men were inclined to blame Van Buren for the whole affair. In the middle of the Bank war there were persistent rumors that the Cabinet was at work on a new bank scheme; and there may well have been some basis for them, although they were categorically denied by the White House. Jackson was no more able to capitulate than Biddle.[43]

As the panic spread and the public pressure increased, the strength of the opposition in both houses grew. In the lower chamber it amounted only to a change of party allegiance by the waverers. In the Senate it included actual change of men. John Black, elected to fill a vacant seat from Mississippi, arrived just before Christmas; and Alexander Porter, chosen to fill the unexpired term of the late Josiah S. Johnston of Louisiana, took his seat early in January. Both joined the opposition.

More significant and of greater weight in the political scheme of things was the action of Virginia. The loyalty of the state had been badly shaken by the Force Act, and after the removal of the deposits not even Jackson's popularity nor Van Buren's skill could hold in line the Old Dominion that had sired Jefferson and Randolph. A State Rights majority was returned to the legislature in the fall of 1833. In January, Littleton Waller Tazewell was elected Governor to succeed Floyd, and a few weeks later the legislature passed resolutions instructing Virginia's Senators to work for restoration of the deposits to the Bank of the United States. The Bank, to be sure, was pronounced unconstitutional, but the assumption of power over the public funds by the President was sharply condemned.[44] Senator William Cabell Rives, who had been one of the administration leaders, could not consistently follow these instructions. In line with tradition, he resigned his seat and Benjamin Watkins Leigh, lately emissary to the Nullifiers, was sent to replace him.[45]

The debate on Clay's resolutions, meanwhile, had steadily progressed, with only necessary interruptions for other business, and the vote was taken at the end of the day on March 28, 1834. The battle throughout had been highly unequal. The weight of numbers and of ability were both on the side of the opposition, and the weight of conviction overwhelmingly so. For in spite of their impassioned speeches, the majority of the administration members condemned the removal of the deposits as heartily as did Clay and Calhoun, and privately admitted as much outside the Senate chamber.[46] It was under Jackson that the triumph of party discipline over personal volition became the rule rather than the occasional exception in Congress. The Treasury's reasons for removal of the deposits were pronounced "unsatisfactory and insufficient" by a vote of 28 to 18. The resolution that "the President, in the late executive proceedings in relation to the public revenue, has assumed power not conferred by the constitution and laws, but in derogation of both" was adopted by a count of 26 to 20.[47]

The two who switched votes were William Hendricks of Indiana and John P. King of Georgia. In addition to these, Samuel McKean of Pennsylvania and Gabriel Moore of Alabama, the latter one of Calhoun's original Nullifiers, admittedly voted against their convictions in sustaining the administration; and two others of the opposition, Samuel Bell of New Hampshire and Ezekiel Chambers of Maryland, were absent. These votes alone would have given the opposition a two-thirds majority, but even this would not have been the measure of real sentiment. But for the trammels of party, at least in the opinion of the senior Senator from Virginia, the President would have commanded only four votes.[48]

Jackson, for some strange reason, was surprised by this result, and even a little hurt, but he was still a fighter and he answered as a fighter should. He set Butler, Taney, and Kendall to work on a written protest to be sent to the Senate;[49] and in the House, where he still held a slim majority, he tightened the rein of party with urgency and vigor. New York City was voting for Mayor and Aldermen on April 8, 9, and 10, and a defeat for the administration there would be a disastrous blow to Van Buren. So on April 3 the word went down to the party leaders in the House, and the hesitant and the timid were whipped into line.[50] The next day four resolutions sustaining the administration were forced to a vote by a margin of 114 to 106. The resolutions, which had been under debate for some time, had originated with the Committee on Ways and Means. The first, opposing recharter of the Bank, and the fourth, providing for an investigation into the causes of the current economic distress, were passed by substantial majorities. The second, opposing restoration of the deposits, was carried by a majority of 15; and the third, endorsing the pet banks, commanded a majority of only 12 votes.[51]

Close as the margin was, it represented to the hard-pressed President a "glorious triumph" and the "overthrow of the opposition in the House."[52] The news, with prefabricated conclusions from it, reached New York just in time to be cried abroad before the polls opened; and the administration, whether due to this cause or not, achieved enough success to call it victory. C. W. Lawrence, a popular merchant running on the Jackson ticket, defeated the Van Buren apostate, Gulian C. Verplanck, for Mayor by 179 votes in a total of more than 35,000; but the opposition carried a majority of three on the fifteen-man Board of Aldermen.[53]

5

The long debate over Clay's resolutions went far beyond the question of removing the deposits. The whole field of executive power was explored, and with each new argument Calhoun's stand against consolidation appeared more sound and his earlier speeches more prophetic. It was ironical but it was true that within a year after the passage of the Force Act many of those who voted for it were willing to condone even nullification to save themselves from Caesar. Calhoun watched this shifting tide, and he was jubilant.

It was Calhoun's first and only speech against removal of the deposits, delivered on January 13, 1834, that heralded the change of sentiment in favor of his party and his views. He began by conceding the right of the President to remove one Secretary of the Treasury and to appoint another in his stead; and he gave to the incumbent full credit for ability and character. But he denied categorically the right of the Secretary to remove the deposits on the grounds stated, and came as near to demonstrating his point as the inadequacies of language would permit. He touched on the broader problem of the government's responsibility for maintaining a uniform currency and promised to discuss that question when a suitable occasion offered. But the crux of his speech was the curbing of irresponsible executive power.

Calhoun reiterated once more his often repeated insistence that he belonged to neither of the great parties then contesting for political control. He acknowledged with thanks Clay's expression of confidence "that the small party who were denounced at the last session as traitors and disunionists" would be found now "standing in the front rank and manfully resisting the advance of despotic power." It was an indication that the character and motives of the Nullifiers were at last beginning to be understood, and it was high time. For the struggle being waged against executive dominance differed in no essential from the earlier contest against legislative omnipotence, and if it should succeed it would be only because the firm stand taken by South Carolina had secured an adjustment of the tariff and had thereby made possible united action.[54]

Like most of Calhoun's speeches, this one defies abridgment. In form, in sentence structure, in reasoning, it is so concise that it must have required intense concentration on the part of his fellow Senators to follow it. Clay and Benton, who had made the opening speeches for the prosecution and defense, respectively, had each held the floor for three days. Yet Calhoun made more impression on friends and foes alike in an hour and a quarter than both together. His own comment was only that his speech, "notwithstanding the nullification it contains," had been "well received . . . by all parties";[55] but that was understatement. It was still a subject of animated discussion six weeks after it was delivered, and it was notable that the Jackson forces did not even attempt an answer. Neither was it printed in the *Globe,* where it might corrupt the faithful. Duff Green was not the only one who saw in the widespread and favorable response, particullarly that of the Northern press, new hope for the South Carolinian's Presidential prospects.[56]

Calhoun himself preferred to read in the reception accorded his speech the approaching triumph of his constitutional views, and he advised his partisans to steer clear of Presidential politics. "We have a great battle to fight for liberty and the Constitution, and there is time enough to determine to whom the honors shall be awarded. . . . Better—far better for us, that those in power should remain there against our consent, than that we shall put others there, who do not agree with us, with our consent. Our doctrines are spreading rapidly, and you must not be surprised to see them in the ascendant before two years. . . ."[57] Calhoun was always oversanguine where his own beliefs and prospects were concerned, but this time he did not misjudge the situation. Even Clay, who firmly believed in national supremacy, was convinced that the perpetuation of the Jacksonian doctrines could mean only despotism or the dissolution of the Union;[58] and the Pennsylvania legislature received petitions calling on the state to interfere, after the manner of South Carolina, before the President assumed despotic powers.[59]

6

Jackson never thought of himself as a despot. He was always, in his own eyes, the servant of the people, doing only what they wished—or would wish presently after Blair had explained it to them in the *Globe*. If he could not always square his actions with the letter of the Constitution, he had men around him who could. It took the combined efforts of Kendall, Taney, Butler, and probably Blair and Donelson as well, nearly three weeks to justify the removal of the deposits on the sole authority of the President of the United States, at a time of no financial crisis and only two months before Congress was to meet. The Protest, received in the Senate on April 17, 1834, was an ably conceived and well-written document.[60] It argued that Clay's resolution of censure did, in effect, charge the President with an impeachable offense but gave him no chance to defend himself. Should impeachment charges be brought, moreover, they would have to come from the House, and the Senate, which had thus already committed itself, would have to sit in judgment on them. There was also an adroit popular appeal. Incorporated into the text of the Protest were resolutions from the legislatures of Maine, New Jersey, and Ohio favoring removal of the deposits, and it was pointed out that four of the six Senators from these three states had voted to censure the President for doing only what the legislatures to which they owed their seats wanted done.

The Protest was read, and immediately Poindexter was on his feet to move that it be not received. He was ably seconded by Sprague of Maine and Frelinghuysen of New Jersey, two of the four Senators alluded to in the document. Benton defended the President, announcing that he would not rest his efforts until the resolution of censure had been expunged from the records of the Senate. The following day Leigh, Clayton, and Calhoun were heard, and their arguments apparently struck home. At any rate, on the next legislative day, Monday, April 21, a new message from the President was read. The original Protest had been, or might be, misunderstood. To set the record straight, Jackson now specifically denied that he had ever asserted or meant to assert any control over the public funds not granted him by law, and disclaimed ever having denied to Congress the right to prescribe the place or places of deposit for the public treasure.[61] It was in fact a considerable retraction, but the Senate was in no mood to be cajoled. Poindexter moved that the supplement too be rejected, and laid on the table a set of resolutions sharply condemning the Protest as a breach of the privileges of the Senate.[62]

The situation was not improved by the discovery that the language of the Protest had been modified by the President's secretary after it had been read to the Senate, and that it was the modified version that had been printed and had gone forth to the country.[63] The net effect of the whole affair, however, was merely to reopen the debate on executive usurpation, and to supply more arguments and illustrations to the opposition. Webster did not fail to point out that half the Cabinet—the Secretaries of State and Treasury and the Attorney General—had not yet been offered to the Senate for confirmation, although the session was already five months old. The debate continued for perhaps two weeks, after which Poindexter's resolutions were adopted.[64] By a vote of 27 to 16, the Senate denied the power of the President to question its actions, and thereby upheld the condemnation it had previously extended to his own.

CHAPTER XVII

THE WHIG COALITION

1

IT WAS probably inevitable that factions working toward the same end should draw together and should come to be considered by their opponents, if not by themselves, as a single party. The passage of Clay's resolutions of censure against the President was the first major success of the coalition of National Republicans and Nullifiers, and from that event the emergence of the Whigs as a national party is usually dated.[1] Negotiations had undoubtedly been going on among the various leaders for a considerable time, but the sphere of their joint action was strictly limited. Calhoun never yielded the separate identity of his own partisans. Neither Calhoun nor Clay nor Webster was willing to renounce his own Presidential aspirations in favor of one of the others, while Judge John McLean was the choice of at least a portion of the Antimasons and dissident Democrats who found their way into the Whig fold.[2] Considering the elements of which the party was formed, and the prominence, ability, and accepted ambitions of its leaders, it is surprising that it accomplished as much as it did.

There must have been some general agreement as to program at the start of the session in December 1833, but each of the three opposition leaders expected to predicate his own rise on Jackson's fall, so the program could not look too far ahead. Clay assumed from the outset that he would be the Presidential candidate of the combination, by virtue of his leadership of the largest element in it, and he counted on the tariff compromise to make him acceptable to the South.[3] But Webster thought it was his turn. He was the choice of New England, probably the favorite of the Bank, and was receiving his share of quiet encouragement in the cotton belt.[4] As for Calhoun, the more he saw his own standing rise, the less was he disposed to permit his strength to be merged with that of Clay or Webster or even McLean. The trend in his favor set in after his January 13 speech on the deposit question. The plaudits were still coming in when he wrote to Van Deventer than he had never, so far as he could judge, occupied "a more elevated stand in the confidence of the intelligent and virtuous. The clouds are breaking away and my motives and character begin to be understood."[5]

As the session wore on, however, the need for closer integration must have been obvious to all of the opposition leaders. The evidence is fragmentary, most of it coming from John Quincy Adams, who could be as cryptic as any man living when recording a political "arrangement"; but such as it is, it indicates a great deal of discussion in the early part of March. Calhoun was host on March 8 to a group that included Preston and Warren R. Davis of South Carolina, the mountainous Dixon H. Lewis of Alabama, Benjamin Watkins Leigh who had taken his seat as Senator from Virginia only three days earlier, Willie P. Mangum of North Carolina; and of the National Republicans, ex-President Adams, Senator Samuel Southard of New Jersey, who had been Secretary of the Navy in the Cabinets of Monroe and Adams, and Senator Peleg Sprague of Maine. They talked far into the night, and the talk was of politics. Three days later Benjamin Gorham and Edward Everett were the hosts, and the guests included their Massachusetts colleagues Adams, Levi Lincoln, and Senator Nathaniel Silsbee; Calhoun and Preston; and Henry Clay. On March 12 the performance was again repeated, with Robert B. Campbell, freshman Representative from South Carolina, doing the honors.[6] Although all of these were ostensibly social gatherings, they were notable for bringing together prominent members of the State Rights and National Republican parties. There were undoubtedly other similar gatherings of which we have no record because they did not include Adams.

The obvious purpose of such political dinners was to bring the two major factions of the opposition into agreement on a long-range program—a program that would look at least as far ahead as the Presidential election of 1836. All the evidence points to failure in this main objective, and to Calhoun's insistence on his own party principles as the reason for it. Meetings and negotiations were probably still in progress when Duff Green prepared to launch a new Calhoun-for-President campaign as the only remaining alternative. He forbore to "raise our flag" publicly until he could do so without embarrassing Calhoun's action in Congress, but behind the scenes he

CALHOUN, ABOUT 1834
by W. S. Blanchard

HENRY CLAY NICHOLAS BIDDLE

ROGER B. TANEY THOMAS HART BENTON

worked vigorously. His campaign was aimed at the elimination of Clay.[7]

2

Green was already writing letters, buttonholing politicians, and filling the columns of the *Telegraph* with extravagant praise of the South Carolina Senator when circumstances gave Calhoun an opportunity to explain what he stood for in the way of policy.

Although executive usurpation was the common theme of the opposition throughout the session, the very measures that gave it color forced a consideration of the whole question of banking and currency. On this point there was little agreement. The administration was committed to its system of state banks, and the National Republicans wanted to recharter the Bank of the United States; but the Nullifiers, who held the balance of power, were sharply disagreed among themselves.

In order to preserve a united front at least until the resolutions of censure had been passed, the currency issue was kept rigorously in the background by the coalition leaders; but Nicholas Biddle, fluttering like an anxious mother hen through the lobbies of the Capitol, grew impatient of delay. A bill was accordingly prepared to continue the existing bank for another six years after 1836, but waiving its exclusive privileges. The deposits were to be restored and the directors were to be authorized to begin distributing capital to stockholders three years before the new expiration date by way of winding up their concerns. This project was to be launched, with special publicity in New York and other centers, as the alternative to the administration's system of state banks.[8]

There was every indication that the scheme was to be made the core of the opposition program, but it was well advanced before Calhoun learned of its existence. He had previously discussed his own views with members of the Clay group and also with administration leaders, and he had said enough on the currency problem in his January 13 speech against removal of the deposits to let both sides know that he agreed with neither.[9] In the circumstances the National Republicans could hardly be expected to take him into their confidence. When he heard of the plan, however, he immediately sought an exchange of views with Webster who had the bill in charge. Personal relations between the two men had been strained since their clash over the Force Bill a year earlier, but Calhoun did not hesitate on that account to send word through a mutual friend that he would like to explain why he disapproved. Neither did Webster hesitate to call on his old adversary at once, and the whole currency question was fully and amicably discussed. Neither convinced the other, but Calhoun agreed not to take the floor in opposition. He insisted, however, that he would have to state his own views for the record.[10] He did so on March 21, 1834, after Webster had argued the case for a national bank, Leigh had pronounced such a bank unconstitutional, and Wright had defended the pet banks favored by the administration.[11]

The speech was throughout conciliatory, statesmanlike, without rancor or partisanship. Calhoun's objection to the project of the National Republicans was that it was an evasion rather than a solution of the problem. It meant that the Bank could be used as a campaign issue in two more Presidential elections, and that until it had served this purpose no effort would be made to come to grips with currency inflation. He did not believe that reform could be long postponed without plunging the country into economic chaos.

The problem as he saw it was not whether the public funds were to be disbursed by one bank or many banks or any bank at all. The problem was to recover the control of the circulating medium which was the constitutional responsibility of the Federal Government. The legal currency at that time was certain specified gold, silver, and copper coins. The circulating medium, however, actually consisted almost exclusively of notes issued by some four hundred and fifty banks incorporated by twenty-five separate and distinct authorities. The aggregate capital of these banks was at least $145,000,000 and their notes in circulation exceeded $70,000,000; yet there was less than $15,000,000 in metallic currency in the country, and the bulk of that lay in the vaults of the Bank of the United States. Both banks and bank notes were increasing in number far beyond any proportionate growth in population or volume of business enterprise. The ratio of paper to metal, already far beyond the limit of safety, was becoming steadily greater; discounts rose in proportion, and the purchasing power of paper declined. If the process were allowed to continue, there would come a time when the banks no longer even pretended to redeem their notes in gold, the notes would be worthless, and the intricate operations of the commercial world would collapse.

The remedy Calhoun believed to be the restoration of a safe ratio between paper and specie: to increase the amounts of metal and decrease the paper in circulation; and he thought the best agency for achieving this end would be some kind of bank. As he put it, he would "use a bank to unbank the banks, to the extent that may be necessary to restore a safe and stable currency." When that object had been attained, however, he saw no reason why the Treasury could not manage its own transactions without banking assistance. In this solution Calhoun's innate and deeply rooted conservatism was strongly in evidence. While he recognized the evils of the existing system and visualized a better one, he would not make any sudden transition from one to the other. The change must be made slowly over a period of years so that currency would not be unduly disrupted and business could proceed with certainty as to future policy.

The particular kind of bank—national or state, new or old—that would best serve the purpose he had outlined Calhoun was willing to leave to the decision of others. As a talking point he suggested a new Bank of the United States, modified and limited, and chartered for twelve years. That period would allow time to change the system with a minimum of shock. It would also overlap the span of the recently modified charter of the Bank of England, and permit full advantage to be taken of British experience.

Calhoun concluded with an appeal to his fellow Senators to put partisanship aside and act to arrest the economic crash of which he warned them. The State Rights Senators, he knew, believed a national bank to be unconstitutional, but that should not prevent them from voting for a temporary renewal designed to break the connection between the banks and the government in the least harmful fashion. They held the tariff, too, to be unconstitutional, but had voted for the compromise of 1833. The National Republicans need have no scruples. They had no doubts as to the power of Congress to charter a bank, and the commercial and manufacturing interests they particularly represented stood to lose most by the explosion that was certain to follow a continuance of the existing course. As to the administration members, they professed to be the advocates of a metallic currency. The measure proposed would restore such a currency in the most effectual way, "gradually and slowly, and to the extent that experience may show that it can be done consistently with due regard to the public interest."

If either of the dominant parties would offer a constructive program of monetary reform, it could be carried with Calhoun's aid, and he offered his support on that question to either side that would assume the responsibility. He realized that he would have a better chance of achieving his purposes by working with a strong party than by playing his hand alone. But that did not blind him to the opportunity his position—and the failure of administration and opposition leaders alike to grasp the issue—gave him. If he could point the way to an acceptable and workable compromise on the currency question that would take the bank issue out of politics, he would not only have performed a signal public service: he would have restored himself to a position of national leadership and elevated the small circle of his followers into a major party.

Calhoun's speech had a profound effect. The pompous and portly Benton, who rode the hobby of a metallic currency until he earned the nickname of "Old Bullion" and the less flattering sobriquet of "Gold Humbug"—Benton, who avowed that Jackson could do no wrong, and roared down all who disagreed, was the first to offer commendation. He rose as Calhoun took his seat and "expressed his satisfaction that the Senator from South Carolina had restored the debate to the elevation that belonged to the Senate."[12] The blindly partisan *Telegraph* was extravagant in its praise; but it was not long before Green was able to quote equally flattering comments from papers devoted to the fortunes of the National Republicans, and even of the administration.[13] Calhoun himself was touched and heartened by the reception accorded to his views by men of all parties, both in Washington and back in his home state, and saw in this new cordiality further evidence that the State Rights philosophy was gaining ground, though he had been careful not to commit that party to his personal views.[14] He accomplished nothing positive at once, but he so changed the direction of the Senate's thinking that Webster moved almost immediately to table his own motion, which was not again revived.[15]

The only constructive move of a long-range nature with respect to the currency question was made almost incidentally in the House. It came in the course of a fruitless debate on the deposits, and was made by William Fitzhugh Gordon, a State Rights Representative from Virginia. What Gordon did was to offer by way of amendment to an administration bill for regulating the deposit banks a detailed version of the plan Calhoun had mentioned as an ultimate possibility. The proposal was simply that those who collected the revenue should also hold and disburse it: that the Treasury retain and pay out its own funds, substituting drafts on the Treasury for bank notes to avoid the frequent transportation of specie.[16] The scheme was important because it was in essence the Independent Treasury plan which was to form the core of Van Buren's financial policy three years later. Where Gordon got the idea is not certain. Condy Raguet, Philadelphia editor and economist, had conceived a similar plan which he sent to Senator Hugh Lawson White near the end of March 1834, nearly three months before Gordon's proposal was made. White and the Virginia Representative roomed at the same place, and the latter undoubtedly saw Raguet's outline. We know, however, that Gordon prepared his bill in consultation with Calhoun, who had made his own currency speech a week before the date of Raguet's letter to White; and there is some evidence that Calhoun discussed the plan also with prominent Virginians on his way to Washington before the session opened in December 1833. In all events, it is clear that whether the South Carolina Senator conceived the plan himself or merely saw merit in it when it was suggested by others, he was willing to have the Independent Treasury put into the records by one of his partisans. He did not urge it himself because he did not believe that a system so radically different from that previously in use could be suddenly invoked without producing an upheaval in the commercial world. He preferred to hold it in reserve as one of the possible lines of approach after the currency had been restored by slow and gradual means. When he became the champion of the Independent Treasury in 1837, it was after the banks had been effectually "unbanked" by panic, specie payments had been suspended, and there was nothing else to lose.[17]

3

A week after Calhoun had proclaimed his own political platform in his currency speech, he and his supporters acted with the National Republicans to pass the resolutions censuring the Executive for removing the deposits. When he argued on April 9 for repeal of the Force Act, however, he was once more on his own. Clay even took the floor on the other side, and with pointed reference to the incident wrote to his Virginia confidant, Judge Brooke, that the "nullifiers are doing us no good here."[18] Jefferson's birthday saw a great rally of the State Rights party in Philadelphia, probably arranged by Duff Green, at which McDuffie, Preston, and Poindexter were the guests of honor, Calhoun having declined to go.[19]

While the State Rights orators were receiving "incessant marks of public respect" in the Pennsylvania metropolis, Clay made another speech in the Senate, April 14. In it he referred to a general revival in various places of the party names of the Revolution—Whig and Tory—to denote the partisans of liberty and the adherents of prerogative and power. Clay was merely recognizing a usage that had gradually grown up over the past two years, without much regard for any particular set of principles. The leading Southern paper of the National Republicans had gone by the name of the Richmond *Whig* since its origin in 1824, and had lately absorbed the Virginia organ of the Nullifiers, Crallé's *Jeffersonian and Virginia Times.*[20] Duff Green had used the term "Whig" as early as March 1832 to designate the State Rights opposition to the tariff, and it had made some headway with the Nullifiers.[21] After Clay gave the name his seal of approval as a label for the combined anti-Jackson forces, various editors claimed it for themselves, including Green and James Watson Webb of the New York *Courier and Enquirer,* once a Van Buren sheet but now pro-Bank and pure Federalist.[22] But the State Rights ticket in the Virginia election of the winter of 1833-1834 called itself "Whig"; and there was a "Whig" ticket in the New York City elections of early April. By the summer of 1834 the term was in common usage everywhere, and it meant the Clay-Calhoun-Webster coalition.[23]

To Calhoun it meant no such thing. Again and again he took pains to explain publicly and privately that although he co-operated with the Whigs in many particulars, he was not one of them, and was just as ready to co-operate with the administration whenever it presented measures of which he could approve. In his currency speech of March 21 he made explicit reference to "the State Rights party . . . of which I am proud of being a member, and for which I entertain so strong an attachment."[24] To Governor Tazewell he explained his position in equally unequivocal terms a few days later. "We do not constitute the opposition," he wrote, "but a small independent party, condemning the general course of the administration, while we differ widely with the opposition in principle & policy. The danger in our position is absorption by one, or the other party, or partly by both. . . ."[25] When Clay presented in the Senate on May 2 a report from the Committee on Public Lands, Calhoun stated that while he would vote to print as many copies of the report as Clay desired, his opinion of the accompanying bill, which he had opposed at the previous session, remained unchanged.[26] And on May 6, speaking against the reception of Jackson's Protest, he took note of Clay's earlier use of the term Whig and dissociated himself from it. He agreed with the Senator from Kentucky that the revival of the party names of the Revolution was a happy indication "of a return to those principles that lie at the foundation of liberty," but as for himself, he wished "no change of party designations." "I am content," he explained, "with that which designates those with whom I act. It is, I admit, not very popular, but is at least an honest and patriotic name. It is synonymous to resistance to usurpation—usurpation, come from what quarter and under what shape it may; whether it be that from this Government on the rights of the States, or the Executive on the Legislative department." He was, in short, a Nullifier and intended to remain so.[27]

Indeed, long before the session of Congress was over Calhoun was convinced that his allies of the coalition were no more disposed to carry out the reforms he deemed essential than was the administration. "The Nationals, I find," he wrote to his brother-in-law toward the end of May, "are as much inclined to extravagance in disbursements as ever. If the administration were out of the way, a conflict would be unavoidable with them on the appropriations, and I do not know, that it can be avoided as it is." At the same time he pointed out to Governor Tazewell that the rising course of expenditures and dwindling revenues under the tariff compromise would probably be used at some not too distant date as an excuse for reviving the protective policy.[28]

4

However they might disagree in policy, the two groups that came to be designated as Whigs acted together with increasing consistency in matters of practical politics. In February and again early in May they united to reject Jackson's nominations for reappointment of four government directors of the Bank—the four who had served as administration spies in Biddle's camp.[29] Toward the end of May they joined to delay action on the nomination of Andrew Stevenson of Virginia to be Minister to Great Britain until Stevenson resigned as Speaker of the House. Then they outgeneraled the administration forces and elected a Speaker of their own.

It was on June 2, 1834, that a new Speaker was chosen. The leading candidates were James K. Polk and John Bell, both of Tennessee and both understood to be administration men. The National Republicans tended to favor Bell as the more moderate of the two, knowing that they had not the strength to carry a man of their own choosing; and the Nullifiers supported Richard H. Wilde of Georgia. In devious ways, however, the Nullifiers had been given to understand that Polk opposed Van Buren's claims to the Presidential succession, so they prepared to reward him with their votes at the proper moment, on a signal to be given by Warren R. Davis of South Carolina. The contest was close, with administration votes dividing between the two Tennesseans in seemingly well-regulated proportions. After each ballot a bulletin with the result was carried to the Senate chamber. As Van Buren was reading one of these bulletins, Willie P. Mangum of North Carolina, shrewd and wise in the ways of politics and men, noticed a fleeting change of expression on the usually perfectly controlled features of the Vice President. He concluded instantly that his party had been tricked, and himself rushed to the House to tell Davis to hold up the State Rights vote. At the psychological moment Wilde was dropped, and Bell—not Polk—was elected Speaker of the House by the combined strength of the Whig coalition.[30]

The "panic session" was now rapidly drawing to a close, with the Whigs firmly in the saddle in the Senate, and through Bell in control of the organization of the House. June 23 saw the names of Roger B. Taney and Benjamin F. Butler finally submitted to the Senate, the one to be Secretary of the Treasury, the other Attorney General of the United States. The next day, with a minimum of debate, Butler was confirmed, but Taney was summarily rejected by a majority of 28 to 18. A few minutes later a vote was taken on Stevenson, and he too was rejected, by the margin of a single vote.[31] Louis McLane, who had now served as Secretary of State for more than a year, saved himself from a similar fate by resigning on June 18 without waiting for his name to be sent in.[32] Taney also resigned as soon as his confirmation failed, leaving the two top Cabinet posts vacant.

With June 30 already fixed for the adjournment of Congress, the President had little time in which to act, but seemingly even he feared to let the appointments lapse until the intersession. On June 27 he sent in the names of John Forsyth of Georgia, administration floor leader in the Senate, to be Secretary of State, and Levi Woodbury of New Hampshire, the Secretary of the Navy, to succeed to the Treasury Department. Both were confirmed at once. The next day Mahlon

Dickerson, former Senator from New Jersey, was named to the Navy post vacated by Woodbury, and he too was confirmed. The new arrangement gave a firm grip on the Cabinet to the designated successor of the President, Martin Van Buren.[33]

At the evening session of the Senate on June 28, the Vice President, according to custom, did not appear. The coalition thereupon elected George Poindexter of Mississippi as its President pro tempore.[34] It was Poindexter's distinction to be one of the two members of the Senate with whom Van Buren was not on personal good terms—the other was Calhoun—and to be more cordially disliked by Andrew Jackson than any other member of Congress.

On the face of it, the combined forces of the opposition were victorious all along the line. In reality, however, they had lost ground. For Biddle's tactics in squeezing the public to spite Jackson had boomeranged. Democratic victories in local elections, particularly in New York, meant that the Bank as a political issue was dead. After Congress adjourned, Whig leaders in both Boston and New York threatened public exposure if credit restrictions were maintained. Biddle denied, of course, that restrictions had ever been ordered, but he at length conceded with the utmost good temper that business had so far improved as to permit some expansion.[35] It was already too late. Biddle's own policy had led many who were otherwise indifferent to agree that the Bank had too much power. Van Buren had judged rightly that the old agrarian democracy of the South, even though it opposed and deplored the doctrines of the Proclamation and of the Force Act, still feared and hated even more what Jefferson and Taylor had branded as the "money power."[36] Southern men who had championed the Bank were on uncertain ground, and this undoubtedly had something to do with McDuffie's decision later in the year to resign his seat in the House.[37]

Calhoun's own position remained strong because he had taken a clear and unequivocal position on the currency question, and because he was the acknowledged leader of the faction, however small, that held the balance of power in the upper house of Congress. For the moment he was stronger than either Webster or Clay, but he would remain so only to the extent that he could keep his following from choosing sides in the Presidential contest—at least until the principles for which they stood could be made a clear issue in the campaign.[38]

The "Bank panic" was in fact the true test of Jackson's leadership, and he had won. Right or wrong, he had never wavered, never doubted, never cast a backward glance; and his unshakable determination was the measure of his power. When people are uncertain and confused, they will rally around those who appear decisive; and the strength of conviction of one man can give strength to a multitude.

5

The term Whig came to be generally applied to the whole coalition before the year was over, and was reluctantly accepted as a party designation even by the Nullifiers, though they never consented to a genuine merger with Clay. The Whigs succeeded the old Federalists as the party of property and the political haven of "the wise, the rich, and the good." The State Rights men were the party of property in the South; but more and more, as the abolitionist crusade gained momentum, their interests narrowed and property came to mean only one thing.

In contrast to the emphasis of the Whigs on property and their appeal to the middle and upper classes, the Jacksonians put their faith in the common people. Not that any Jacksonian had been known to reject any property that came his way. He thought, in fact, that more of it ought to move in that direction, and this change of destination for the nation's wealth was one of the feats of helmsmanship he expected from Old Hickory. The Democrat, in the eyes of his Whig neighbors—like the Jeffersonians in the eyes of the Federalists of an earlier day—was lawless and violent, as befitted the follower of a military chieftain. It seemed only natural to men of means, who were by nature timid and by training a little myopic, that the year that saw the birth of the Whig party should be marked by riots and disorder. The two events were natural antitheses.

It was Jackson, as usual, who provided the issue, and the issue was—himself. He was aggressive to the point of arrogance, never willing to count the cost, always slashing his way ahead. Often he went too far, often he was wrong, occasionally he was absurd; but he always had men around him who could mitigate or even capitalize his errors, and invariably the people supported him. Jackson was a pocket-sized Paul Bunyan and a drawing-room Mike Fink rolled into one, with a dash of Davy Crockett and a large leaven of Scotch shrewdness. His enemies called him a frontier bully, and in many ways he was. What his enemies failed to appreciate was that in a growing, expanding, gambling, ebullient country like the United States of the 1820's and 30's, the frontier bully was a national hero.

The issue was Andrew Jackson and all his works. "Big Bully Bottom" Benton had virtually announced as much on the last day of the session when he introduced a resolution to expunge from the Senate Journal the censure of the President.[39] At the local level the party managers went to work to change the complexion of state legislatures so that hostile Senators could be turned out.[40] Van Buren himself drafted more than one leader for the *Globe;* and Jackson set about exposing the "hippocrites in our own ranks who wish to favor the designs of the opposition."[41] Chief among these "hippocrites" was John Bell of Tennessee, now Speaker of the House of Representatives.

As an issue the Whigs wanted nothing better. It was, in fact, probably the only one on which they could agree. Their difficulty was to find a man who would be equally acceptable to tariff and antitariff states, equally pleasing to consolidationists and Nullifiers, and sufficiently moderate to draw off a portion of the Jackson following. Calhoun, Clay, Webster, and McLean each had his partisans. Calhoun still insisted, however, on the separate identity of his party. Duff Green vetoed an opposition convention in Virginia because it would include Clay and Webster men, and lost no opportunity to advance the claims of the South Carolinian.[42] There were many who shared Green's enthusiasm, but who knew as Calhoun himself knew that he stood no chance. Ability, experience, character could not outweigh in the popular mind the unfavorable verdict of the party press. Men would not vote their convictions but their prejudices.[43]

While the Whigs bickered among themselves, the Jacksonians gained steadily among the masses. These gains were evident by the middle of August in Virginia, where a grass-roots campaign was being waged against the re-election of Leigh to the Senate. The Richmond *Whig* thereupon declared itself ready to give up Clay for the good of the party, and called on the *Telegraph* to give up its preference for Calhoun.[44] Green quibbled and for a month the two editors argued with each other. The name of Daniel Webster was meanwhile put in nomination in Massachusetts by Edward Everett; and in Ohio Louis McLane was suggested as a suitable compromise.[45] Green saw danger in these new names, particularly that of Webster, who was almost as objectionable to the Nullifiers as Van Buren himself.[46] Eventually the editor agreed to support anyone who would advance the principles for which the *Telegraph* stood. He would take Clay or Benjamin Watkins Leigh. But the effect of the concession was lost by the succeeding argument, which went to prove that neither of these, but Calhoun alone, was ideologically sound.[47] Calhoun agreed explicitly as to adherence to principles but urged his editor to drop the Presidential question altogether.[48]

Election returns began to trickle in after the middle of October. The Jacksonians won the state legislature in New Jersey, and the new majority promptly elected Garret D. Wall to the Senate to replace Frelinghuysen.[49] In Virginia the Whig majority was so reduced that Leigh secured his re-election by a bare two votes. The Jacksonians won in Pennsylvania, where there was another Senate vacancy to be filled; and in the crucial New York election of early November they swept their ticket into office by imposing majorities.[50] For all this a Whig victory in Massachusetts was small compensation; and even that was soon followed by another Jackson triumph in Georgia.

The Whigs at last realized what they were up against, and began to look seriously for a neutral candidate. Tyler proposed Governor Tazewell of Virginia, and Duff Green gave the proposition sympathetic publicity, if not outright support.[51] The perennial candidacy of Judge John McLean gained new support, and Clay, Adams, and Calhoun were approached in his behalf.[52] The scramble among the Whigs was still in progress and getting nowhere, to the vast amusement of the Jacksonians, when a new menace loomed up on the Presidential horizon.

On December 29, 1834, the members of the Tennessee delegation in Congress—with Polk, Grundy, and Cave Johnson alone absent—asked Senator Hugh Lawson White if he would acept a nomination for President. The next day the Senator, one of Jackson's oldest friends, who had so far been a party man on controversial issues, authorized the use of his name.[53] For this masterly stroke John Bell, who had been threatened by the President with political ruin just a few months before, was primarily responsible. White was a Democrat, perhaps the most respected of them all, and his candidacy was ostensibly for the party nomination against Van Buren. Yet he had all the qualifications the Whigs required. Jackson was loath to let him go and offered him second place on the Van Buren ticket with the reversion of the first, before he swept his old friend out-of-doors.[54]

CHAPTER XVIII

THE USES OF POWER

1

THE issue of executive power which brought the divergent elements of the opposition together after the removal of the deposits was far more real to Calhoun than it was to his allies of the Whig coalition. South Carolina had looked down the guns of warships sent to Charleston harbor at Jackson's command, and had seen her cities threatened by an army under the orders of the President. To men reared in the traditions of the American Revolution this was tyranny, and the circumstance that it was supported by the majority merely indicated that enough partisans to make a majority had been coerced, cajoled, or bought. The issue was thus broadened by the State Rights leaders to include not only executive power itself but also the means by which it was achieved and sustained, and the whole question was carried back one farther step to the earlier contest over the nature and location of sovereignty. It was immaterial in Calhoun's thinking whether the supreme power was exercised by Congress or by the President. If it was exercised without safeguarding the liberties and interests of the minority it was irresponsible, and unless it could be in some manner restrained it would be fatal to republican institutions.

The confusion and cross-purposes, the sectional hostility and personal antagonisms, that characterized the second term of Jackson's "reign" were largely by-products of a basic difference in political faith. The underlying issue was stated in the Great Debate of 1830 and clarified in the restatement of 1833. With the Proclamation against the Nullifiers and the Force Act, Jackson took his stand on the side of unified national sovereignty. The opposition was necessarily based, tacitly or overtly, on the philosophy of the Fort Hill Address. Because Clay and Webster were ideologically closer to Jackson than they were to Calhoun, it was inevitable that the South Carolinian would eventually emerge as the real leader of the opposition.

The basic issue was fought out under different guises between the fall of 1834 and the election of Van Buren two years later. Time and again the lines of battle crossed and friends and foes found themselves acting together. Policies and personalities were often confused, and the Jackson press—as venal as any this country has ever known—did an extraordinary job of obfuscation. It is nevertheless possible to reduce the more general partisan struggle to three main points of dispute, which will be more meaningful if treated individually. First in time, though it overlapped the others, was the contest over the uses of executive power: the tactics used by the administration to consolidate its position and to perpetuate its rule. The second area of conflict centered around the strategy of the opposition, which sought under Calhoun's guidance to curb the will of the President by sharply restricting the major instrument of power at his command—the patronage of office. The third was the sectional struggle between the slaveholding states and the Northern abolitionists, which served to clarify the constitutional issue underlying the battle against executive power and to split the older party groupings along new lines of cleavage.

2

It was Martin Van Buren himself who pounded the gavel that called the Senate to order on December 1, 1834. It was highly unusual for the Vice President to be in the chair at the opening of a session of Congress; and in this instance it deprived the President pro tempore, George Poindexter of Mississippi, of an honor he believed rightfully his. This seemingly trivial incident was one link in a long chain of circumstances that was now nearing its disgraceful end. In itself it is not important, but it throws a searching light on the methods of Jacksonian democracy, and these methods account for much of the bitterness that characterized the next two years. Poindexter was a man of brilliant parts, immoderate habits, and violent temper. More than any other among the Nullifiers—more even than Calhoun—he had aroused the personal wrath of the President;[1] and when Jackson was angry he acted first and considered afterward. Jackson had visited Tennessee in the summer of 1834, shortly after Poindexter had been elected President pro tempore of the Senate. The Mississippi Senator was also on his way home; and as luck would have it, the two men arrived at an inn along the route at the same time. Jackson pointedly insulted his foe and followed it up, when the Senator was out of earshot, with some ugly and thoroughly slanderous remarks about his wife. Poindexter eventually heard of it, through the activities of the Jacksonian editor of the Baltimore *Patriot,* to whom he addressed a letter. This masterpiece was so studiously insulting to the President of the United States, in his private capacity, as to be in fact a challenge. Certainly Jackson himself had gone to the dueling ground on less provocation.[2]

From late September until two weeks before Congress convened, this controversy filled the papers, with Jackson maintaining a discreet silence while his editors made specious denials and equivocal excuses. At the same time, however, his political machine used every resource at the command of a powerful and wealthy administration to secure Poindexter's defeat in the campaign he was then waging for re-election. Bad blood there was in abundance by the time the Senate met, and the President pro tempore found himself deprived of the honor of presiding.

Although he was careful not to say so, Van Buren's early arrival was probably on Jackson's orders, and was intended to be interpreted as it was. Why else should the cautious Dutchman have carried a brace of loaded pistols everywhere he went, even into the Senate chamber? The Vice President was still wearing his side arms when the Newburgh (New York) *Telegraph,* widely believed to be under his control, stated explicity that his prompt arrival in the Senate was for the reason Poindexter inferred. The latter, moreover, in true Jacksonian phrase, was referred to as a "bloated mass of corruption." Poindexter demanded a disavowal of both intention and press comment and received both, in language cold, formal, and utterly correct.[3] For the moment the incident was closed, but for the moment only.

The Senate meanwhile had listened with decidedly mixed emotions to the President's message, had organized itself, and was getting down to serious business. The weight of Jackson's wrath lay not on "Poins" alone, but revealed itself to the Senate as a whole in the presence of new faces and vacant seats. The administration maintained its grip on Georgia and Pennsylvania, where Forsyth and Wilkins, both "promoted" for party services, were succeeded respectively by Alfred Cuthbert and James Buchanan. Whig stalwart Peleg Sprague of Maine, who had already gone against the wishes of the majority in his state legislature, saw no further prospect of keeping up the fight. He resigned a month after the session began and was presently replaced by an undeviating Jacksonian, John Ruggles. Parallel circumstances brought Robert H. Goldsborough into the Senate from Maryland in place of Ezekiel Chambers.

Calhoun was not on hand for the reading of the President's message, but he had ample time to read and digest it before he reached Washington. An olive branch was held out to one portion of the opposition with the suggestion that, since the country was free from debt and at peace with the world, the time had perhaps arrived to settle "those principles in our domestic policy, which shall be best calculated to give stability to our republic, and secure the blessings of freedom to our citizens." There was a well-merited slap at the Bank of the United States, in which the President did not fail to make the most of Biddle's change of face on the credit question; but boasting was soon followed by a tacit admission that the public funds were not soundly placed in the state banks. The President had taken responsibility for the transfer on himself, but he now wanted Congress to assume it by enacting legislation to regulate and control the deposit banks. He acknowledged, grudgingly, that the affairs of the Post Office were almost as bad as a Senate investigation begun at the previous session intimated; and he redefined his position on internal improvements, with lip service to state sovereignty.

But the heart of the message—the grenade that Jackson always managed to contrive when the controversies that waged endlessly around him seemed about to subside—was the passage on French relations. The treaty negotiated by William Cabell Rives and ratified early in 1832 stipulated that France was to pay twenty-five million francs, then equivalent to about five million dollars, in reparation for spoliations arising out of the Napoleonic wars. In return, the United States was to reduce duties on certain French wines. The duties had been duly reduced, but though nearly three years had passed since ratification of the treaty, no installment of the debt had yet been paid. The French Assembly had repeatedly failed to make the necessary appropriation. Jackson now proposed that the United States "take redress into their own hands." Congress would be adjourned before any action taken by France could be known, but the President saw no reason why he should be hampered on that account. He asked for a law authorizing him to make "reprisals upon French property, in case provision shall not be made for payment of the debt, at the approaching session of the French Chambers."[4]

This sudden belligerent rattling of the sword might have a number of meanings. It might be simply the direct and forthright diplomacy of an old soldier whose patience was quickly exhausted. It might be the technique of a partisan leader who regarded his party as an army and knew that armies—especially volunteers—quickly disintegrated when there was no enemy in sight. It might be a red herring, designed to unite the party and the nation against a foreign foe to cover up the unhappy consequences of the Bank war. Each of these views had immediate supporters in the Senate, but the point on which all agreed was that Jackson had made foreign relations the dominant theme of the session. When the selections were made, therefore, Clay accepted the chairmanship of that committee. The method was by ballot, as it had been in the previous session, and this single change was the only significant one.[5]

Calhoun again had no regular committee assignment, though his work as chairman of a Select Committee on Executive Patronage (as we shall see in the following chapter) determined the Whig legislative program for the remainder of Jackson's term.

3

Jackson's sharp attitude toward France was influenced by the advice of the man most intimately familiar with the situation—Edward Livingston, who had been Secretary of State when the French treaty was ratified, and had now been Minister to France for almost two years. Louis Philippe had assured Livingston again and again that the money would be paid; but the truth was that the treaty was unpopular with the masses and the King's own position was none too secure. The Minister concluded that a little pressure would be helpful, and in the summer of 1834 he suggested to Jackson the suspension of intercourse with France—a proceeding that would in no way hurt the United States but might well cripple French industry.[6] It was just such advice as might have been expected from the intellectual father of the Force Act, and it exactly suited Jackson's temperament. The President was already thinking seriously of the idea when he learned that the French Chambers had been prorogued until December 29. He at once concluded that the action had been deliberately taken to prevent news of another rejection reaching Washington while Congress was in session, and determined to ask for provisional legislation in order to overawe the Chambers.[7]

Whether his request had the desired effect or not is a moot question; but there was no question about the effect it had on an already truculent opposition. The Senate Foreign Relations Committee, composed of Clay, King of Georgia, Mangum, Sprague, and Tallmadge of New York, went into session on the matter as soon as its organization was completed; while Duff Green made daily comments in the *Telegraph* under the heading "War with France." Little else was discussed in the cloakrooms, and no business of importance was transacted on the floor until this was disposed of.

Clay presented an extremely able and conciliatory report on January 6, 1835. The committee concurred entirely with the Executive as to the justice of the claim, and in their determination to collect it; but they insisted that peaceable means should be exhausted before belligerent ones were resorted to. The report concluded with a resolution to the effect that it was inexpedient to grant authority to the President to make reprisals against French property.[8] A week later the report was debated, with Clay taking the lead. There were actually three separate views on that question as on most others. The Jackson men were "very warlike"; the Nullifiers insisted that it was nothing but a debt; and the National Republicans wanted to be as firm as possible without risking war. In spite of these divergences, the debate was exceptionally moderate. All groups seemed genuinely anxious to find a formula on which they could agree. Calhoun, in fact, stated it in precisely those terms, declaring his hope that "there would be unanimity in the views of honorable Senators on this important subject, and that such phraseology of language would be used as would indicate it."[9]

The resolution was modified to read "That it is inexpedient, at present, to adopt any legislative measures in regard to the state of affairs between the United States and France"; and in that form was unanimously adopted at the conclusion of a single day of argument, January 14.[10]

As soon as Jackson's message reached Paris the French Minister in Washington was recalled and Livingston was offered his passports. He declined them but surrendered his official functions to his secretary and left Paris. The opposition press in that city, meanwhile, began quoting the opposition press in Washington, arguing that the President's message did not reflect the true sentiment of the American people.[11] The action of the Senate tended to confirm this view, and Clay's report went far toward appeasing French sentiment. The

House of Representatives also debated the question at length and did not reach an agreement until the last day of the session. When they did, it was largely the doing of John Quincy Adams, who saw in the President's action much what he had seen in Jackson's Florida invasion of fifteen years earlier—a positive type of diplomacy that would command the respect, and in the end the acquiescence, of European nations. The House, therefore, resolved that "the treaty of the 4th of July, 1831, should be maintained, and its execution insisted on." As in the Senate, the vote was unanimous.[12]

One more maneuver in connection with the French debt should be recorded. In the normal course of legislation the House had passed and the Senate had approved a bill making annual appropriations for the military establishment; but a Senate amendment had made it necessary to return the bill for further action in the lower chamber. On the last day of the session the fortification bill turned up again for Senate action. The amendment had been amended, adding three million dollars to the appropriation, which sum was to be spent at the discretion of the President, should the defense of the country require it before the next meeting of Congress. To those who, like Calhoun, distrusted Jackson's motives, this was merely a prelude to involving the country in war while Congress was out of session. It was the indirect approach after the direct approach—the power to make reprisals against French commerce—had been denied. The Senate therefore rejected the amendment. The House insisted, the Senate again refused, and as the minutes ticked away, a conference committee agreed on a lesser sum.

The conference report, however, never reached a vote. It went first to the House where Cambreleng, who had been chairman of the conference committee, refused to present it because it was unsatisfactory to him personally. Dixon H. Lewis of Alabama, a Calhoun partisan, then took the report from Cambreleng to present it himself. A roll call revealed that a quorum of the members did not answer to their names, but the opposition charged that a quorum was nevertheless present. The House was still bickering when the Senate tired of waiting and adjourned; so not only the amendment but the whole fortification bill was lost.[13] Jackson of course blamed the failure on his enemies in the Senate, but the Whigs held the administration members in the House responsible.[14]

The loss of the fortification bill, no less than the action of Senate and House on the President's request for provisional powers, was accepted in France as a conciliatory move. The Chambers, accordingly, voted the appropriations necessary to pay all installments of the debt then due, with interest. A proviso was added, however, that the payments were to be made "only after the French government shall have received satisfactory explanation as to the message of the president of the United States, dated December 2, 1834."[15]

4

The fate of the fortification bill no doubt reflected in some measure the general reaction of opposition members to the tactics adopted by the administration in a matter of quite another kind.

It was on the morning of January 29, 1835, that Warren R. Davis, Representative in Congress from Pendleton District, died after a brief illness. He was a close personal and political friend of Calhoun's, and Calhoun had been with him all night. So had Francis W. Pickens, who now held McDuffie's seat in the House. It was directly from the deathbed of their friend that these two went to their respective places in Senate and House, where they pronounced brief eulogies and moved the customary period of mourning.[16] The funeral was held from the Hall of Representatives at noon the next day, with President, Cabinet, and both houses of Congress present.

The procession had just passed out of the rotunda of the Capitol when a man stepped in front of the President, drew a pistol, and snapped the trigger at point-blank range. The weapon did not go off but before he could be overpowered, the man drew another and tried again. The second pistol also failed to go off. The assailant, whose name was Richard Lawrence, was immediately taken into custody and the pistols were confiscated. The weapons were of a type set off by percussion caps. In both cases the caps had exploded but the powder failed to ignite, a circumstance that might or might not have been accounted for by the dampness of the day. Francis P. Blair, who seemed always to be at the President's heels, drew the charge from one of the pistols on the spot and declared it to be fully and properly loaded. Both weapons were then turned over to the proper authorities, to be held as material evidence. The next day, however, the one still retaining its charge was fired by the President's secretary, with the United States Marshal and the United States Attorney for the District of Columbia in attendance.[17]

Even while Lawrence was being seized, Jackson had loudly expressed the opinion that the would-be assassin was a tool of Poindexter's, and that the Mississippi Senator was responsible for the whole affair. Poindexter, of course, was immediately informed of the President's remarks, and on January 31 sent a note to the White House asking if the charges attributed to Jackson had in fact been made. His letter was returned without comment.[18]

On the very day that the second pistol was fired, and thus rendered worthless as evidence, Blair came out in the *Globe* with a barbed insinuation that Lawrence had been inspired to attempt the assassination of the President by speeches he had heard in the Senate, and particularly by certain remarks of Calhoun's.[19] The South Carolina Senator had the passage read into the record on the next legislative day. To his mind it merely confirmed all he had ever charged against the administration. For was not the *Globe* an official paper, which expressed the views of the Executive himself? And did not this paragraph show once again that by one means or another the Senate was to be silenced? Senators were not to criticize, because they might later be called to judge as an impeachment court. They might not condemn lest they inspire thereby the assassination of the condemned. And if they did so far forget themselves as to express opinions, they were called on to expunge them from their journals. "Did they not see, clearly as the light of heaven, the march to irresponsible power?"[20]

The Jacksonians of course could not be expected to see any such thing, but they did see that the approach was wrong and they changed it forthwith. The administration press switched its emphasis to the miraculous nature of the President's escape, but the opposition sheets countered that it looked more like humbug. A miracle at that time would be so convenient for a hard-pressed administration, which could then declare its policies divinely sanctioned and all opposition impious. And since the pistols had been discharged, it was no longer possible to determine whether they had in fact been properly loaded on the fatal day.[21] The prisoner, being clearly insane, was quite unable to give any assistance in resolving the matter.

It was at this point that Blair went back to Poindexter as the most acceptable villain. Within two weeks he had ferreted out two witnesses who swore they had seen Lawrence and Poindexter in conversation three days before the shooting and on various other occasions. Blair also secured affidavits from these witnesses and placed the affidavits in the President's hands. Thereafter they were freely shown to visitors at the White House and their substance, in magnified and bepurpled form, was not long in finding its way into the papers. As it presently appeared, it was no less than a charge against Poindexter of conspiracy to assassinate the President of the United States, and the President himself was presumed to be the author of it.[22]

Poindexter was inclined to agree with Senator Tyler, who wrote of the charge: "If true, he deserves to be hung; if false, his accusers would disgrace the gallows."[23] The Mississippi Senator immediately requested a Senate investigation and refused to occupy his seat until he had been exonerated. The task did not take long. A committee consisting of Nathan Smith of Connecticut, Mangum, King of Georgia, Wright, and Tyler was selected by ballot on February 21 [24] and began at once to gather evidence. The *Globe* was quite put out by this development, complaining that as Poindexter was involved only in his personal capacity, the Senate was not concerned. Blair also tried to discredit the committee in advance as being packed with Poindexter's friends.[25] It was notable, however, that Wright and King were administration wheel horses and that the committee's report, made on February 26, was unanimous. The verdict was that "not a shade of suspicion rests upon the character of the Hon. George Poindexter" in connection with the matter under investigation.[26] There was a spontaneous burst of applause from the galleries, and Poindexter resumed his seat.

The full text of the report was presented on March 2, the earliest that it could be copied. It showed conclusively that the entire charge rested on the two affidavits, which were proved by other evidence and admitted under cross-examination to be wholly perjured. The exoneration of Poindexter was then unanimously voted by the Senate.

It was the following day that the fortification bill was lost.

5

As the Twenty-third Congress came to an end, the two opposition factions in the Senate again divided offices. John Tyler, representing the State Rights wing of the coalition, was elected President pro tempore, while the public printing went to Clay's editors, Gales and

Seaton of the *National Intelligencer*.[27] Mutual collaboration, however, was not unity. Behind the common front against executive "usurpation" lay a fundamental divergence of views which made agreement on a Presidential candidate impossible.

The administration forces tolerated no such differences. Their leaven was the patronage and power of office, and immediately after the adjournment they prepared to make the most of these advantages. The Virginia elections for Congress and for the state legislature were held in April 1835, and Virginia, like New York and Pennsylvania, was a key state, with parties nearly evenly divided. It is in such circumstances that a political machine operates most effectively, and the Jackson machine was used in this instance with skill and cunning. Returns were slow to come in, with many individual contests in dispute; but the final tally showed the Van Buren Democrats with a minimum preponderance in the legislature of two votes over all other parties.[28]

From Virginia the Jacksonians moved on to Baltimore, where Van Buren was duly nominated, on the orders of his chief, by as unrepresentative a convention as ever met. Blair was in the convention city to set the stage well ahead of the May 20 opening date, and he remained to pull the strings, but there was little need of his services. The delegates understood their duty too well to want reminding. The party propagandist devoted most of his time to making peace between two rival Pennsylvania delegations and to quieting an incipient revolt on the part of the Virginians. The political bosses of the Old Dominion felt that their party services justified a substantial reward, and they sought to secure it by putting William Cabell Rives on the Van Buren ticket for Vice President. Blair flattered them that their great champion was too badly needed on the floor of the Senate, where the new Jackson legislature would soon contrive to send him, to waste his talents in the presiding officer's chair. But the truth was that the Vice Presidential nomination had been promised to Richard M. Johnson of Kentucky in a bid for Western votes. It mattered little to Jackson that the battle-scarred slayer of Tecumseh was unacceptable to the South because of his Negro mistress and mulatto daughters. He was a party man, through and through, and his reward had been earned. His nomination was duly carried, but even Jackson's will could not make it unanimous. Johnson received only 178 votes to 87 for Rives.[29]

The nominations came as a surprise to no one, least of all to Calhoun. The South Carolinian saw in this open designation of his successor by the President, however, the final proof that Jackson had indeed abandoned the democratic process. The procedure fitted perfectly into the picture of executive power that Calhoun and his own partisans had long since painted, and it tended to confirm the worst fears of the South, already alarmed over the abolitionist crusade. To men jealous of the liberties of their country, it made little difference whether the Chief Magistrate elevated his successor to power by military force or by the use of executive patronage, save that force might be easier to resist. Nor did it matter that the heir apparent had publicly denied any hostility toward the peculiar institution of the South: he would owe his election to Northern votes, and the abolitionists would soon hold the balance of power in the dominant Northern states.[30]

By the summer of 1835 the Presidential campaign was well under way with the Democrats united and the Whigs reduced to squabbling factions. From the start the Whig campaign was negative. They were against Van Buren, but aside from that they had no principles nor aims in common. In default of a candidate on whom they could agree they concentrated on sectional favorites and hoped only to throw the election into the House, where Van Buren could conceivably be blocked. Calhoun and Clay, the real leaders with national followings, had stepped aside. Webster was the candidate of New England. General William Henry Harrison, who was a military hero and had no enemies, was the choice of the Western Whigs; and the South, it was hoped, would give its support to Hugh Lawson White.

It was White's campaign that gave the Whigs new ammunition in their battle against executive power, for the President concentrated his personal efforts against his former friend. Though he had twice offered the Tennessee Senator a Cabinet seat, Jackson now likened him to Aaron Burr, and dubbed him for the ears of the faithful the "Tennessee Brutus."[31] To every member of the state legislature the President sent, under his own frank and sometimes addressed in his own hand, successive issues of an *Extra Globe,* filled with abuse of White and carrying Benton's floridly rhetorical blasts against the resolution of censure. These activities, Jackson explained, did not constitute interference in local politics, but only the fulfillment of his own Presidential oath to uphold and defend that Constitution which the Senate had so grossly violated.[32] Yet White had not voted for the censure, nor even against the administration on any party issue. He had merely yielded to the urging of some of his fellow citizens that he run for President!

The party lines were hardening by the time Congress met in December. The Antimasons of 1832 were drifting to one or another of the Whig candidates according to their sectional allegiance, while the Locofocos—the radical wing of the New York Democrats—were moving to Van Buren.[33] The Nullifiers, however, remained uncommitted, and their silence was eloquent as to the ideological differences among the Whigs. As the slave question increasingly monopolized the attention of the South it became more clearly evident that the only firm defense of slavery lay in the compact theory of the Constitution; and even White, slaveholder though he was, had voted for the Force Act.

6

Jackson's seventh annual message, sent to Congress on December 8, 1835, was again largely devoted to relations with France. After the French Chambers had made payment of the debt conditional on a satisfactory explanation of Jackson's bullying, Livingston had sailed for home. His son-in-law and secretary, Thomas P. Barton, had been left in Paris as Chargé d'Affaires, but had been given specific instructions by his government. He was to "ask for the final determination of the French Government," and if arrangements to pay the installments then due were not made forthwith, he was to demand his passports. No further word had yet been received, but the President promised a special communication as soon as Barton had been heard from.[34]

The language of the message was very moderate, for Jackson, and by no means revealed the true state of his feelings. His own draft, which his advisers somehow prevailed upon him not to use, asked bluntly for power to grant letters of marque and reprisal and was replete with such terms as "insulting," "degrading," and "dishonorable." The draft would have left France no alternative but war. It was almost as flagrant a challenge to the Senate of the United States, to which Jackson assigned full responsibility for the "defenseless" state of the country.[35] The message as actually delivered was less bellicose, specifically disclaiming any intended menace in that of December 1834, and being careful to add no further provocation to that which already existed.

For the next six weeks there was no official news, although the press continued to carry disquieting rumors. Then on January 18 Jackson exploded his promised special communication. The French answer to Barton's request had not been satisfactory. Diplomatic intercourse between the two countries had ceased, and it had been publicly announced that a French fleet was outfitting and destined for American waters. The President flung back defiance which he wanted Congress to back up without delay. He asked for a nonimportation act, and for "large and speedy appropriations" for the Navy and for the coastal defenses.[36]

In the half century since the Revolution two Americas had come into being: one young, eager, cocky, and certain that the United States could thrash the world; the other careful, conservative, with many ties abroad, and aware that civilization antedated the Mayflower. To the former Jackson was already the symbol of the hopes and aspirations of the common man; he became now the personification of the national honor. To the latter Jackson was already an ambitious and self-seeking demagogue who now revealed the means by which he meant to elevate himself to imperial estate. After the message of January 18 it was no longer possible to regard the French question as merely "a ruse of the administration to call off the people from attending to their domestic demerits."[37] The affair was serious, and might be fatal.

James Buchanan, whose diplomatic experience consisted of two years as Minister to Russia, was conceded the role of administration spokesman on foreign affairs, though his ponderousness and lack of humor made him a perfect foil for Clay. The message read, he lumbered to his feet to express the approbation of his party for the vigorous and manly course the President had elected to pursue.[38] His fulsome language required some kind of rejoinder from the opposition, lest they perchance be thought to agree. In his capacity as chairman of the Committee on Foreign Relations Clay would be required to report officially later, and hence it was inadvisable to commit him now. It was therefore Calhoun who rose to voice an impromptu dissent. He had had no previous knowledge of the contents of the message, or even that there was to be a message on that day, so he was unprepared with documents or citations save as memory provided them. He needed no others.

Calhoun explained that he had come to Washington convinced that war would be avoided. He thought the cause too trivial for war and had faith that great, enlightened nations closely bound by ties of friendship would not resort to so extreme a measure. He now feared that the situation in which the country was placed must be regarded as the "result of a deliberate and systematic policy." He did not charge the President with aiming from the start toward war, but he believed the course chosen to be the one most likely to bring about that end. He was aware that his own position would be misconstrued as treasonable opposition to his country's cause. He felt, nevertheless, that he must speak the truth as he saw it. In his eyes the truth was that the responsibility for the conflict, should it come to that, would lie with the United States rather than with France.

There was something like a gasp from the assembled Senators, but Calhoun rushed ahead in his quick, nervous way, not deigning to notice. The course of events as he reviewed them looked very different from the same events as summarized by the President. Calhoun recalled, as Jackson had not, that when the treaty was under negotiation Rives had been warned repeatedly that it could not be carried out without a vote of the Chambers, and that such a vote might be impossible to get. He recalled that the American Minister had been urged to delay the signing until the Chambers met so that they might be consulted in hopes of avoiding the very situation that had since arisen, but Rives had been unwilling to delay. He recalled also that Rives had then boasted of his diplomatic triumph and the President himself had published the boast. A further irritation had been thoughtlessly or willfully provided by the Secretary of the Treasury, who cleared a bill for payment of the first installment of the French debt through the Bank of the United States, although he knew perfectly well that no appropriation had been made by the Chambers and that the bill could not be paid until it was. In the circumstances Calhoun thought that Louis Philippe and his ministers had shown uncommon zeal and skill to bring the matter within eight votes of passage. Success appeared certain despite these obstacles when the President again chose the exasperating course with his messages of December 1834 and this which had just been read.

Briefly Calhoun reviewed the prospects of a conflict in which all the advantages lay with France. In a "just, honorable, and necessary war" he would meet such consequences without fear, but this war would hazard life and property and the liberty and institutions of the nation for a point of etiquette. "I say the liberty and institutions of the country. I hold them to be in imminent danger. Such has been the grasp of Executive power, that we have not been able to resist its usurpations, even in a period of peace; and how much less shall we be able, with the vast increase of power and patronage which a war must confer on that department?"[39]

Calhoun showed on this occasion as on many others great moral courage. He was not called on to speak at all, yet speak he did, and deliberately in defense of the unpopular side. Indeed, had his fears proved correct and war been the result, his stand would have been construed inevitably as treason.

The members of the opposition very generally believed that Jackson wanted yet another Presidential term, and that in the event of war he would be a candidate. Some went so far as to charge that the French crisis had been deliberately manufactured for that very purpose; and Calhoun had moments of disgust in which he too believed it. No one in the Senate really wanted war, Van Buren's partisans least of all—of that he was sure. Yet he saw the war spirit slowly mounting and feared that when the hysteria was high enough the war message would be sent in and Congress would meekly bow to the command of its master. The spoils party would be supplanted without change of personnel by the military party, and the cycle from despotism to despotism would be completed in two generations. "We have been moving along," he wrote to Governor Tazewell a few days after his speech, "in such a beaten and almost hopeless track of baseness & corruption, that I have had little spirit to write to any friends. But the disease is now coming to a head, and the terrible reaction of all the vice, folly & corruption of this the most vicious, mad and corrupt administration, that ever disgraced the government, is about to recoil on the country with fearful disaster."[40]

The fears of the opposition were in no wise set at rest when administration members immediately called up a resolution earlier offered by Benton to use the surplus revenue for military purposes. The tension rose from day to day. The Jacksonians accused the Whigs of imperiling the safety of the nation; the Whigs charged the party in power with seeking war as a means of perpetuating its hold, and of inventing this means of using the surplus to avoid reducing the revenue.[41] Things were near the cracking point when Congress was informed on February 8 that Great Britain had offered to mediate the dispute with France and that the President had accepted the offer.[42]

7

Although the tension was eased somewhat, the debate was by no means ended; and perhaps the very removal of the threat of danger lent added sharpness to the succeeding interchanges. It was on February 17 that Silas Wright, who spoke on occasion for the White House, announced that the danger of war might be considered past. In the course of his remarks he referred ungently to the opposition and to certain members of it in particular, including the senior Senator from South Carolina. Calhoun replied at once—to Wright, to Buchanan, to virtually all who had preceded him in the monthlong debate.

Calhoun allowed himself large latitude. He was happy to know that there would be no war. He was glad also to see such zealous champions among the administration members of the permanent system of fortifications. He recalled how bitterly those who adhered to the same party had attacked him when that very system of fortifications was planned and built under his direction when he headed the War Department. He inquired what the state of the country's defenses might be had they then succeeded and he failed. And he congratulated them on their wholehearted, though somewhat tardy, conversion. It confirmed his faith that "justice must in the end prevail."

He moved on then to predict once more the coming economic catastrophe: "an explosion," he anticipated, "the like of which has scarcely ever been witnessed in any country." He traced the causes to the removal of the deposits, "that most lawless and unconstitutional act," with the unprecedented expansion of bank credit that followed, not omitting caustic reference to the surplus revenue. After ruminating for a while on the nature of the banking system and its abuses, he caught up a reference Wright had made to Jackson's popularity and to the "power and talents of the opposition, which it had successfully resisted." The opposition, he declared, was essentially weak, and almost anyone could have overcome it, with the patronage at the disposal of the President. For the opposition was made up of antagonistic elements, whose incongruous union always broke down in the face of victory.

At this frank admission there were smiles from the Democratic leaders, but they did not smile for long. Calhoun set off on another tack, tracing the steps in Jackson's rise to power, his two-faced course on the tariff, and his betrayal of the South which yet would not unite to thrust him out because she had put him in. He noted the emergence of a party "held together, not by principle, or by a system of public policy, but by the hopes of personal gain and advancement"—the New York system, now ascendant in the Union. Jackson, however, would soon be out of power and there would be a change, either of policy or of men.

He transfixed Van Buren with those great, glittering eyes whose lightnings were the most conspicuous feature of his face, and poured forth at once his challenge and his scorn. The "President's nominee" would never successfully play Jackson's game. With all his objections to Jackson, Calhoun "could not deny him many high qualities: he had courage and firmness, was bold, warlike, audacious; though not true to his word, or faithful to his pledges." He had, moreover, deserved well of his country for his military services. Not so the chosen successor. "He is not . . . of the race of the lion or the tiger; he belonged to a lower order—the fox; and it would be in vain to expect that he could command the respect or acquire the confidence of those who had so little admiration for the qualities by which he was distinguished."[43]

CHAPTER XIX

CURBING EXECUTIVE PATRONAGE

1

THE threat of foreign war as a means of quieting domestic opposition; the use of slander to destroy the effectiveness of critics and rivals; the perpetuation of a dynasty by the designation of a successor—all these were accompaniments of absolutism familiar since the dawn of recorded history. Jackson, of course, had not consciously planned his course to create this appearance, and he repudiated indignantly the inferences drawn from it. Yet no political realist with any knowledge of history or of human nature could fail to make just those inferences, and only the incurably naïve could fail to see danger in what he inferred.

Calhoun had long since formulated an utterly realistic political theory in which the central theme was the struggle between rival interests for control of the machinery of government. It was a struggle in which offices, contracts, subsidies, and legislative stimulants to favored economic interests were the rewards of victory and also the instruments by which the victors consolidated their power. Jackson's practice was merely living proof of Calhoun's generalization, and the South Carolinian would have been dull indeed if he had not sought to apply the remedy his theory pointed out. Patronage was the means of perpetuating political power, so the patronage should be curbed.

It was fully in keeping with the times, and consistent with his known and often repeated views, that Calhoun should ask an investigation of the extent of executive patronage, the reasons for its recent increase, and ways of reducing it. His resolution to that effect was approved on January 6, 1835, the same day that Clay's report on French relations was presented. Calhoun requested a committee of six members, to be composed of two from each party, thus emphasizing again the actual division of the Senate into three rather than two groups. The administration members, of course, saw this request as merely to insure a two-to-one majority for the opposition. The principle was nevertheless accepted and an exceptionally able committee selected by ballot. Calhoun, as mover of the resolution, was chairman, with George M. Bibb of Kentucky the second member representing the State Rights wing of the Whigs. The National Republicans were Southard and Webster; the Jacksonians Benton and King of Georgia.[1] The whole proposal was a shrewd way of publicizing the growth of executive power, but the selection of Benton as one of the committee's members was a stroke of genius. For Benton, in 1826, had been chairman of just such a committee, on which Van Buren and White also had served, but the practices that the voluble Missourian and his colleagues had then condemned in Adams had since been immeasurably extended by Jackson with their approval and support.[2]

Calhoun approached his subject in the broadest possible light, treating not only the appointments to office but also the expenditure of public funds as part of the executive patronage. It was, indeed, to the revenue that the larger part of the report was devoted. For despite the progressive reduction of the tariff under the compromise of 1833—still, to be sure, a relatively minor item—the revenues of the government were increasing in spectacular fashion. Yet the public debt, previously the largest single item of expenditure, had been liquidated. A surplus well in excess of needs was steadily accumulating in the pet banks, where it was being used for speculative purposes. Since most of the speculation was in public lands, the process operated to increase the revenue still farther, and to build up the surplus at a constantly accelerating rate. The pet banks had at first been encouraged to lend money freely as an offset to the contraction of credit by the Bank of the United States. This in itself had an inflationary effect, even without the additional impetus of a generally expanding economy. Prices rose fantastically, and particularly the price of real estate; but the price of the public lands was fixed by law. Inevitably there was a rush to purchase public lands. The speculator bought with bank paper which he paid to the land office, whence it promptly returned to the bank in the form of a public deposit, only to be re-lent to a new speculator who repeated the process. Land sales that had averaged a little over a million dollars a year prior to 1830 amounted to almost four million in 1833, the last year for which Calhoun had figures. They would continue to climb to five million in 1834, fifteen million in 1835, and twenty-five million in 1836.[3]

ANDREW JACKSON, ABOUT 1835
by Ralph E. W. Earl

Antislavery drawing from the *Liberator,* May 3, 1834

It was the beginning of this process that Calhoun observed and linked with the growing tendency toward centralizing the powers of government in the hands of the Executive. His own views were undoubtedly well formulated before he raised the question in the Senate and were discussed privately with intimates, although they were not offered to his committee until all the necessary statistics had been received from the Treasury and other departments.[4] When the relevant material was in hand, however, Calhoun seems to have been able to convince all of his colleagues except Benton, despite the "astounding novelty" of some of his proposals.

The report was presented to the Senate on February 9, 1835, with Preston and Southard reading it from the clerk's table. The reasoning was close and the statistics voluminous; but the gist of the argument was that there were then in the employ of the executive branch of the government 60,294 persons, plus 39,549 pensioners, or a total of 100,079 individuals who with their families were directly dependent on the public treasury, compared with a total of only 55,777 in the same categories in 1825. In the same period the revenue had risen from twenty-eight million dollars to thirty-seven million dollars, and the expenditures, exclusive of payments on the public debt, from thirteen million dollars to twenty-seven million dollars. The increase had been progressive and was considerably greater than the increase in population. Additional sources of patronage were identified in the award of government contracts and in the disposal of Indian lands, while the influence of the Executive was shown to be still further increased by the expectations he was able to hold out to those not yet employed but hopeful.

The primary reasons for the great increase of patronage, in the eyes of Calhoun and the majority of his committee, were the Jacksonian practice of displacing officeholders for partisan reasons and the removal of the deposits from the Bank of the United States, with the subsequent assumption of control over the public funds by the Executive. The remedies were to get rid of the surplus revenue, to make officeholders less dependent on the President, and to establish legal control over the public funds. These three remedies were reduced to specific legislative proposals.

The revenue, in so far as it stemmed from customs duties, could not be sharply reduced without upsetting the tariff compromise, which Calhoun was unwilling to countenance. The next best thing was to render the surplus unavailable to the government until such time as the revenue could be reduced to the level of necessary expenditures. When Jackson had proposed the distribution of the surplus in his first annual message, Calhoun had strenuously opposed the measure, on the ground that it would be used as an excuse for maintaining the tariff. He still regarded the principle as unsound. In the present circumstances, however, he believed it preferable that the excess funds should be in the state treasuries than that they should remain in the control of the Federal Government where they must serve to concentrate still further a power already dangerously concentrated. Calhoun offered, therefore, a joint resolution to amend the Constitution by specifically authorizing distribution of the surplus revenue among the states until the year 1843, when the reduction of the revenue under the compromise would reach its maximum. A bill to regulate the deposit of public money in the state banks was also proposed, both as a means of limiting the control of the President over these funds and as a means of curbing the speculative uses to which they were being put. The third of the committee's recommendations was a bill to repeal the provisions of the act of May 15, 1820, which limited the terms of various public officers to four years.[5]

Calhoun had made judicious reference to Benton's patronage report of 1826, and he now suggested that copies of this earlier analysis, which agreed so fully with that of his own committee, be printed. There was a sharp debate before ten thousand copies of each report were ordered—a debate in which Poindexter attacked the administration, Benton attacked Calhoun's report in lieu of offering a minority report of his own, and Calhoun, with an air of the utmost astonishment that the Senator should have changed his mind, read back to Benton the points the latter had so cogently made nine years before.[6]

The joint resolution proposing a constitutional amendment got nowhere. The Whigs could not command anything approaching the necessary two-thirds majority, and the Jacksonians, though distribution had once been their own policy, opposed all the recommendations of Calhoun's committee on principle. The proposition did, however, win the support of other State Rights partisans, among them some who had been as vigorous as Calhoun himself in denouncing Jackson for his early advocacy of a similar scheme.[7] The other two proposals met with better success. Both were fully and at times bitterly debated, but the repeal of the four-year law was passed on February 21, by a vote of 31 to 16, with Benton for sweet consistency's sake voting aye. The bill to regulate the deposits was approved on February 27, by 28 to 12.[8] Both measures were lost in the House, where the administration still held the numerical advantage; but both were destined to reappear, together with the distribution scheme, in the succeeding Congress.

The true significance of the Senate debates on executive patronage lay, perhaps, in the margins by which Calhoun's measures to reduce the President's influence were passed. Democrats voted with the Whig majority on both bills, and the Whigs themselves showed more integration and better teamwork than theretofore. The argument for both propositions was so clear that administration members could not oppose without conceding the point at issue—that the influence of the Executive was overriding. Benton, because of his 1826 report, was in the worst dilemma, and though he yielded to the inevitable and voted with the majority he made his displeasure quite clear.

After Calhoun had opened the debate on February 13, 1835, Benton spoke against the whole course proposed, although in committee he had objected only to distribution of the surplus. Calhoun replied sharply, quoting once more from Benton's own past professions and accusing the Missouri Senator of desiring to retain the surplus revenue as a gigantic slush fund for keeping his party in power. In the course of his remarks, Calhoun referred to those who held office at the will of the President as "corrupt sycophants and supple instruments of power"—a phrase he had used in his report without objection from Benton. On this occasion, however, the latter chose to regard it as a personal insult. In the circumlocutory fashion common to parliamentary debate he charged Calhoun with deliberate falsehood. Poindexter raised the point of order, Van Buren upheld the speaker, and Webster appealed from the decision of the chair. The wrangle lasted some two hours, during all of which time Calhoun sat motionless in his seat while his colleagues debated his veracity. At last the decision was reversed and Benton declared out of order. Calhoun then took the floor again and gave his opponent such an unmerciful tongue-lashing that Benton must have had the hide of a rhinoceros to stand up under it. For two or three days there was talk of an impending duel, but the affair was somehow patched up. Benton said no more on the subject for the rest of the session, but he was still smarting when he wrote his memoirs twenty years later.[9]

For the remainder of the debate Silas Wright and Felix Grundy came forward as the champions of the administration, while Hugh Lawson White expressed the view of the moderate or borderline Jacksonians. He too had been a member of the 1826 committee and had joined in the much discussed report then made. He had, he told the Senate on February 16, approved certain principles then, and he approved them still. He praised the President and referred to his own consistent support of the administration. He hoped still to be with his political friends when this vote was taken, but if not, he would at least be with his political principles.[10] It was on that same day that Jackson rewarded his old friend's devotion to principles by reading him out of the Democratic party.[11]

Calhoun himself acted as floor manager for the bill to repeal the four-year law, which came up first; Webster carried the load for the bill to regulate the deposits; but Nationals and Nullifiers supported both. The Whig program was slowly taking shape, and it is significant that the recharter of the Bank, or even the restoration of the deposits, was no longer part of it. It is also significant that, though it was still premature, the Independent Treasury scheme was again brought up in the House, by William Fitzhugh Gordon of Virginia. This time it reached a vote, and though only a handful approved it, Francis W. Pickens was one of them.[12]

2

Those who had been skeptical of Calhoun's analysis of executive patronage when the report was under discussion in the Senate were given a practical demonstration during the next few months. The Whig majority in the Virginia legislature was reversed by the elections of April 1835, and a month later Van Buren was unanimously nominated for President by a convention of officeholders and pensioners. The party machine was then directed with almost equal success to the elimination of individual Whig Senators—by direct replacement if an election was due; if not, by "instructions" that would force resignation. There were many changes when the Twenty-fourth Congress met in December 1835 and most of them favored the administration.

Jackson had at last triumphed over Poindexter, who was replaced by Robert J. Walker. Garret D. Wall, chosen by the New Jersey legislature immediately after the Democratic victory in the fall of 1834, at last succeeded Frelinghuysen whose term had expired in March. Samuel Bell, veteran National Republican from New Hampshire, was out and Henry Hubbard, Jacksonian Congressman, promoted to his place. The vacant seat left by the death of Nathan Smith of Connecticut was filled by John M. Niles, founder and pro-Jackson editor of the Hartford *Times*. George A. Waggaman of Louisiana, who had gone down the line with the Whig coalition, was not returned, and the vacancy was eventually filled by Robert C. Nicholas, a Jackson Democrat. Nathaniel Silsbee of Massachusetts had voluntarily yielded his seat to John Davis without change of political allegiance; but a similar shift in Kentucky was more significant. There courtly George M. Bibb, who though consistently in opposition had identified himself rather with Calhoun than with Clay, was defeated by a state legislature under Clay's control. His successful opponent was John J. Crittenden.

The Whigs still held a majority in the Senate, but their ranks had been thinned, and would be broken when "instructions" from Virginia came in. There were two new candidates for statehood too, and the patronage of the administration would have been used to little purpose had both not shown Jackson majorities. The presumptive Senators from Michigan, chaperoned by Benton, were already seated though voteless on the floor, and Arkansas was ready to send two more good Democrats to join them whenever the formalities were over. When Jackson sent his first major appointments of the session to the Senate late in December it was with the moral certainty that his party would be in the majority by the time the vote was taken. Heading the list was Roger B. Taney to be Chief Justice of the United States in succession to John Marshall who had died during the summer. Philip P. Barbour was nominated for Associate Justice, and Amos Kendall for Postmaster General.[13]

It was little wonder that Van Buren was in high feather, wandering about the chamber chatting with friends and foes alike, and in the evenings giving frequent dinner parties of fabulous proportions.[14] Nor was it astonishing that the Whigs, although they had organized the Senate and controlled its legislative course, were demoralized and subdued. Clay continued as chairman of the Committee on Foreign Relations; Webster remained chairman of the Committee on Finance; and Ewing of Ohio, a Clay Whig, took Poindexter's old spot at the head of Public Lands.[15] Again Calhoun had no regular committee assignment, but made his contribution outside the area of routine legislation. This time it was as chairman of a Select Committee on Incendiary Publications, appointed December 21, 1835, but the discussion of this phase of his activities belongs properly in another chapter.

In the House of Representatives, too, the elections had strengthened the administration. Polk was chosen Speaker over Bell with votes to spare, and Van Buren's spokesman, Churchill C. Cambreleng, became chairman of the key Committee on Ways and Means. Blair was easily elected printer to the House over all competitors.[16]

As the full power of the Executive made itself felt in the changing political composition of Congress, the Nationals sank into apathy and the effective leadership of the opposition forces passed to the Nullifiers. In the Twenty-fourth Congress it was Calhoun who directed the Whig coalition in the Senate, while in the House the antiadministration leadership was seized by a group of able youngsters from the South: Francis W. Pickens and James H. Hammond of South Carolina, Dixon H. Lewis of Alabama, and Henry A. Wise of Virginia. The issue was still the power of the Executive, but men who held with Webster and Clay that the general government was sovereign could not logically object to an exercise of executive power, however arbitrary, that was sustained by a Congressional majority. The State Rights members were under no such restraint.[17]

3

Aside from the question of French relations and the defense preparations thereby entailed, the major problems of the session were financial and most of them grew directly or indirectly out of the Bank war. Jackson had himself recognized some of the attendant evils when he asked in the annual message for legislation to regulate the public deposits. The greatly increased returns from the sale of public lands, however, were not linked in the President's mind with the speculative use of the public funds on deposit with the pet banks. He attributed the phenomenon to the rapid spread of agriculture, which he commended. The Whig leaders saw closer connection between land sales and irresponsible finances, and the two questions were ultimately merged.

Clay set the stage for the wide-ranging debates of the latter part of the session on December 29, 1835, when he reintroduced once more his favorite land measure—a bill to distribute among the states the proceeds from the sale of public lands for the years 1833-1837 inclusive. It was essentially the same measure that Jackson had pocket-vetoed in 1833, but the existence of a twenty-million-dollar surplus arising in large part from those very land sales gave it greater urgency than it had then had.[18] When Clay had finished a brief explanation of the nature, purpose, and history of his bill, Calhoun took the floor to introduce again the three measures growing out of his patronage report of the previous session: the bill to repeal the four-year tenure law, the bill to regulate the public deposits, and the joint resolution to amend the Constitution so as to provide for distribution of the surplus. The proposed amendment was read a second time and made the special order for January 18. It was on that day, however, that the French crisis reached its peak, and the amendment was never called up. It could not, in any circumstances, have been passed. The repeal of the four-year law fared better, passing the Senate by a narrow margin on February 3, but it was never brought to a vote in the House.[19]

The land bill and the regulation of the deposits were far more important to the administration than any other part of the Whig legislative program. Action on these, therefore, was deliberately delayed. The Jacksonians expected to control the Senate before the session was over, as they already controlled the House, and the bills could then be rewritten according to their own wishes. The real point at issue was the control and disposition of the surplus revenue, which was expected to reach thirty million dollars before the middle of 1836.

Since the removal of the deposits this huge excess of government funds had constituted a gratuitous addition to the capital of the deposit banks, whose use of it had led even the administration that placed it there to seek a halt. The only other alternatives were to spend the money for some useful purpose or to turn it over to the states to spend. Jackson's Maysville Road veto had closed the door to one use—a door that Van Buren had lately proposed to reopen by constitutional amendment.[20] To spend the money for fortifications, as Benton desired, was equally objectionable to the Whigs, since it would constitute both a threat to peace and a potent source of patronage. The states, on the other hand, could use the money for the public works barred to the Federal Government, with benefit to all concerned. When Calhoun proposed to amend the Constitution to permit distribution for a limited time, he anticipated that the states would use the funds so provided to build railroads, and it was generally understood that such would be the case.[21] This fact alone accounts for much of Van Buren's opposition to the scheme, for the commercial supremacy of New York, in so far as it stemmed from trade flowing through the Erie Canal, would be challenged by competing routes to the West.

It was around the middle of March 1836 that the Democrats achieved their preponderance in the Senate—to be precise, on March 14, when William Cabell Rives took the seat Tyler had surrendered as Senator from Virginia. Other vacant seats had been filled through January and February, until the balance of power finally shifted. The administration signalized its triumph the following day when the new Senate majority confirmed the Supreme Court appointments of Taney and Barbour and gave its approval to Kendall for Postmaster General. Calhoun voted against the confirmation of Taney, then left his seat before the other votes were called.[22] The Whigs still controlled the committees, but the Democrats were equal to the occasion, as they demonstrated some two weeks later. On March 31 Walker of Mississippi introduced Benton's favorite measure, to lower and graduate the price of the public lands and to grant pre-emption rights to actual settlers. He knew that the Committee on Public Lands would not report the bill favorably, so he moved reference to a special committee of five, to be named by the chair. There were sharp objections from Calhoun and Clay, but the motion carried and what amounted to a new land committee was appointed. Walker was its chairman, and it included three Democrats to two Whigs.[23]

For the next month discussion centered around the public lands. Party lines were presently inextricably crossed by the sectional issues involved. Walker's bill was abandoned in favor of amending Clay's. The question of the surplus was inevitably raised and entered freely into the arguments. Finally, in amended form, the bill was passed by the Senate on May 4. Calhoun voted against it, as he had on each of its many appearances since he entered the Senate, but Buchanan and other Democrats were in the affirmative.[24] The bill was finally abandoned in the House because the distribution of the surplus accomplished the same purpose in more general terms.

One interruption in this debate, though it came to nothing, has some importance as revealing the direction of Calhoun's thinking at this time. Benton proposed a resolution late in April to the effect that after a given date nothing but specie—gold and silver—should be received in payment for the public lands. Benton's purpose was to get more metallic currency into circulation, and Webster denounced it as irresponsible tampering. Calhoun, however, saw many advantages in it, particularly that it might serve in some degree as a check to speculation. He did not know how the settlement and prosperity of the West might be affected by it, but he was willing to be guided by the views of the Western Senators.[25] Calhoun was steadily pursuing a policy—more broadly still, he was following out the implications of a political philosophy—rather than seeking a party program. Again and again he displayed his willingness to act with either party or both as he could fit the measures offered into his own conception of the public good.[26]

4

The land debate was almost over in the Senate when Silas Wright on May 2 submitted an amendment to Calhoun's deposit bill. It was in fact a substitute, which liberalized the terms on which the deposit banks were to hold the public money, but restricted the use that might be made of it by requiring that the surplus was to be invested in interest-bearing state securities. It was at least a step in the direction Calhoun had charted in his proposed constitutional amendment, and he at once moved to push it still farther toward his own original proposition. He offered a further modification, to the effect that the surplus should be deposited with the states in proportion to their population, subject to being returned on demand but without interest.[27]

For some reason which Calhoun did not at once perceive, Wright then grew very cool toward the bill he had virtually made his own. On one pretext or another he postponed bringing it before the Senate, until at last Calhoun called it up himself on May 25. A week later, on the South Carolinian's motion, the bill was referred to a special committee of nine members, chosen by ballot. Wright thus became chairman, with Calhoun, Webster, King of Alabama, Buchanan, Shepley of Maine, Leigh, Hendricks of Indiana, and Ewing of Ohio serving with him. Despite its administration majority, and against the wishes of its chairman, the committee in effect restored Calhoun's original bill, with its more rigorous controls over the deposit banks, and added to it his amendment for depositing the surplus with the states. In this last provision, however, there was an important modification. The deposits were not made returnable on request, but each state was to give to the Treasurer of the United States a certificate of deposit representing the amount received. These certificates were a species of promissory note, negotiable by the Treasury for what they would bring. Though still called a deposit, the transaction had been converted into a loan.[28]

In the subsequent debate Wright tried to separate the regulation of the banks of deposit from the disposal of the surplus, although he had himself first put them into the same bill. Failing that, he lost interest in the whole subject, but members of his own party kept it alive. It was only when the bill came to a final vote on June 17 that the motives behind Wright's hesitation were fully clear. He had sought to split the bill so that Jackson could veto the distribution provision while retaining the regulatory sections; but a majority of his own party would not accept this arrangement. Southern and Western men saw in the surplus revenue the capital they so badly needed to challenge by way of railroad and canal the commercial supremacy of New York, and they would not give it up no matter how it might affect Van Buren's prospects.

The Democrats were now as badly split as the Whigs, with William Cabell Rives, disappointed in his Vice Presidential hopes, and Nathaniel P. Tallmadge of New York leading the dissidents. Both spoke out on the floor for the old Republican doctrines of economy and responsibility in government before a vote on the bill was taken. The final count was 38 to 6, with only Benton, Grundy, Cuthbert, and Wright remaining loyal to Van Buren's cause. The two Mississippi Senators also voted in the negative, but in their case it was because of a special provision in their state constitution.[29]

"The effect," wrote Calhoun, "has been a complete disorganization of parties for the present. The President is furious, and threatens to veto the bill. . . . The Globe took a decided stand against it, and Mr Van Buren is understood to be warmly opposed; but all in vain." The schism was perhaps not permanent, but it was deep, and it sprang from causes more fundamental than the rivalry of Benton and Rives for the party succession. There was, Calhoun thought, a "growing conflict between the more honest portion of the party, and the real plunder and humbug portion, who are willing to go all lengths. They have arrived at a point at which it is difficult for these two portions to go on together much longer."[30]

In the House of Representatives the deposit bill was taken up on June 20, well ahead of its normal turn. The Van Buren following sought, as they had in the Senate, to split the bill into its components, while Chief Justice Roger B. Taney drafted a veto message for the President which held the deposit of funds with the states to be unconstitutional.[31] At the last minute, however, Jackson changed his mind. It must have been clear that the majority of his following favored the distribution, and to veto it would have made the cleavage within the party perhaps irreconcilable. Richard M. Johnson, the party nominee for Vice President, carried the word to the faithful in the House on June 21. He carried also an amendment to the deposit section, making the funds returnable on demand and restoring much the same language Calhoun had used in the first place. The House sat on into the evening, passing first the amendment and then the bill itself by large bipartisan majorities.[32] The amended bill came back to the Senate on June 22 and was promptly approved, after Calhoun had assured the doubters that no Secretary of the Treasury would ever ask to have any part of the deposit returned.[33] Jackson signed it without comment the following day, his only indication of annoyance being to permit the *Globe* to editorialize on the subject before the fact of his signing was communicated to the Senate.[34]

Calhoun rejoiced. To him the bill was the "most decisive measure that has ever been adopted to regulate the Government," and one that would go far "to restore the ascendancy of the States, and effect a deep political reform."[35] He saw it both as a means of redressing the balance of power between Federal and state governments, upset since the Force Act, and as a lever for loosening and ultimately for eradicating the spoils philosophy. The mere fact that the Jacksonians were divided among themselves on the issue was enough to indicate to the South Carolina Senator that the net result would be good. Others were not so sure. Duff Green found it necessary to devote three columns to defending Calhoun's course against those who could not understand why he now saw such cause for congratulation in the passage of a measure he had sharply opposed on many earlier occasions.[36] Governor McDuffie protested against the continuation of a system that made distribution necessary; and the South Carolina legislature at first refused to accept its allotted share of the public funds.[37]

CHAPTER XX

THE OUTPOST YIELDED

1

It was in the middle 1830's that the antislavery agitation reached crisis proportions and became a major political issue. It coincided in point of time with the settlement of the tariff controversy and with the battle against executive power as represented by Jackson's policies, foreign and domestic; and basically it involved the identical principles that underlay these otherwise unrelated events. For as long as the government was accepted as federal in character slavery could never be more than a local institution. Once the Nationalist doctrine gained the ascendancy, however, the labor system of the South became equally the responsibility of the North.[1] Domestic slavery was protected by the Constitution of the United States, but the Constitution meant whatever the sovereign power determined that it should mean. If the sovereignty lay with the Executive, or with a partisan majority in the national legislature, slavery could and would be abolished whenever it seemed politically expedient to the stronger party. If on the other hand the sovereignty lay with the states, then abolition could be forever blocked by the South. The nullification episode had shown that the general government could be successfully resisted, but unity alike in thought and action was required. So Calhoun sought to align the South behind the State Rights dogma, and the Jacksonians used the official power at their command to keep the South politically divided.

The antislavery literature that came from the Northern centers was violent and abusive, growing more so as the tide rose. It aimed frankly at the complete destruction of slavery and scoffed at the problems abolition posed for the South. The picture was always overdrawn, often utterly false, but it was stated convincingly with the weight of moral purpose and usually the names of clergymen behind it.[2] An emphasis on sexual lewdness and physical brutality was calculated to infuriate intelligent Southerners, whose moral plane was at least as high as that of their critics; while literature designed to incite the slave to revolt could hardly fail to elicit prompt and outspoken response. It came—from pulpit and college classroom, in the press and in the halls of Congress.

Some, like Thomas R. Dew of William and Mary College and the redoubtable Duff Green, sprang to the defense of slavery as a positive good; and it is perhaps significant that among the historical works on which Dew relied to prove the naturalness and beneficence of the institution were the very books that had nourished Calhoun's young mind in his first student days. Others, like Thomas Ritchie, tried to quiet their own fears by firmly announcing that the "clamor about the slaves" could not continue. The venerable James Madison insisted that the Northern people would not intermeddle with slavery because their own self-interest "as merchants, as ship-owners, and as manufacturers" lay "in preserving a union with the slaveholding States"; and the *National Intelligencer* protested that the South was perfectly safe because, as everyone agreed, there was no constitutional power to interfere.[3]

Calhoun was among the first to realize that the antislavery movement had little or nothing to do with the self-interest of manufacturers and merchants. He saw it for what it was: the product of a religious fanaticism that could never be stopped by argument or by appeal. It went hand in hand with the great revival of 1830; it was fed by a world-wide movement for social reform; and it was enormously stimulated by emancipation in the British West Indies in 1833. When the Missouri Compromise had sharply posed the issue in 1820, Calhoun had deplored the tendency of the South to believe in a Northern conspiracy to free the slaves. He had pleaded then for mutual trust and understanding between the sections. But he had added one significant qualification. "Should emancipation be attempted it must and will be resisted at all costs," he had then written, "but let us be certain first that it is the real object, not by a few, but by a large portion of the non slave holding states."[4]

By the beginning of 1834 it was no longer possible to doubt that emancipation was the end sought, nor that those who sought it would in time control a majority of the Northern states. Those states were closely divided into two major parties, with the abolitionists allied to neither but ready to give political support in return for concessions to their point of view. Calhoun comprehended as few of his contemporaries did the relentless, driving, uncompromising quality of the puritan mind, and he undertook to stop the crusade before the moral fervor that lay behind its propaganda swept all the free states before it. Yet in the very stubbornness of his opposition he added strength to the movement he designed to check. His too was a puritan mind, and saw no middle way.

He had no doubt that the abolitionists would eventually merge with one or the other of the parties struggling for power in the states in which they worked. Their own ends required a strong, consolidated government to carry them out, so that they were most likely to go over to the party whose views already inclined that way. By consequence abolition eventually would become a Whig principle, and the South would be forced back toward the Democratic fold.[5]

The Twenty-third Congress found the abolitionists strong enough to count Senators and Representatives in their service, and the stage was set to make slavery a political issue. The first move was to be the introduction of a bill for emancipation in the District of Columbia. Calhoun could consider such a step only "as the commencement of the work of immediate emancipation over the whole [of] the South, to which event it will certainly lead, if not promptly met by the entire slave holding states, with the fixed determination to resist at any hazard."[6] No such bill was brought up in the session of 1833-1834, doubtless by agreement between the Northern and Southern wings of the anti-Jackson coalition; but there were petitions in both houses, at that session and the next, which were referred to the respective committees on the District.

The literature of the abolitionists, already adapted by a crude picture technique to reach slaves who could not read, was meanwhile being spread in ingenious ways throughout the Southern States. One method was to attach simple pictographs to products of Northern manufacture which were to be sold in the South. Another was to send bundles of pamphlets and papers to Southern agents to be personally distributed through a sort of underground. Mailing lists were compiled from city directories and other sources. The purpose of all this literature was to apprise the slave that his bondage was unjust if not illegal, that he was exploited and abused, but that he had thousands of white friends to the North who were actively at work to secure his deliverance from a cruel servitude. Nat Turner's rebellion was still fresh in Southern minds, and they reacted with a zealous fury equal to that of the abolitionists themselves. Let these infamous pictures and simple texts actually reach those for whom they were intended and terror would stalk the South. There would be blood and slaughter bred of mutual fear, the cotton states would be economically ruined for generations to come, and the Union itself would be dissolved.

Before we judge the slaveholders of the old South too harshly, let us recall how completely and utterly they were themselves in bondage to a system they did not create but had come to accept through generations of familiarity. Their livelihood came from their plantations, and these were worked by slaves. One white family might live in the midst of several hundred blacks and miles from any kind of help. Generally the slaves were well treated and loyal to their masters. They were valuable chattels, representing over the whole South close to a billion dollars of capital. To beat and starve and chain them, as the abolitionists insisted was the universal rule, would have been sheer madness on economic grounds alone. But the slaves themselves were too illiterate and too naïve to appreciate these points and they were possessed, as is their race today, of vivid and colorful imaginations. Let the seed of revolt be but sown and who could foresee the end?

2

Feeling ran high throughout the South by the time Congress adjourned in March 1835, and the bitter partisan struggle then in progress served only to inflame still more already outraged sentiments. Van Buren was about to be nominated for the Presidency, and he was a Northern man subject perhaps to abolitionist pressure. Thomas Ritchie undertook to find out where the New Yorker stood. Silas Wright replied that his friend did not believe Congress had any constitutional power to interfere in the relation between master and slave in the states, and that it would be impolitic to abolish slavery in the District of Columbia.[7] To Calhoun it was a dangerous evasion, for the *power* to abolish slavery in the District was conceded by implication, and to yield that power would be in the end to yield a crucial outpost in the slavery fight. To admit that Congress had the power to abolish slavery in the District would mean that sooner or later, when the pressure had become strong enough, that power would be used, and it would be the opening wedge for emancipation in the states.

Conditions were ripe for an explosion, and the match was applied in Charleston in July when thousands of copies of incendiary abolitionist tracts and pictures arrived by steamboat from New York. These publications were addressed to respectable citizens of Charleston, including clergymen of all denominations, and to post offices throughout the Southern and Southwestern states. The material was immediately impounded by the Charleston postmaster, Alfred Huger, pending specific instructions from the Postmaster General; but the city was aroused as it had not been since the days of nullification. A mob was persuaded to disperse on assurance that the tracts would not be delivered except on orders from Washington, but a few unruly spirits broke into the post office that night. The offensive matter was confiscated and burned in the streets.[8]

Unionist and Nullifier came together at last without reservations and joined to set up a citizens' committee of twenty-one to handle the situation. For some weeks the administration of the city was virtually in the hands of a five-man subcommittee headed by Robert Y. Hayne, and it is high tribute to Hayne's prestige and political skill that there was no further violence.[9]

Huger's report went to Amos Kendall, who had succeeded Barry as Postmaster General in May, and Kendall was almost as indignant as the Charlestonians. He called the papers involved in the episode "most flagitious" and privately advised Southern postmasters to intercept all such matters in the future, delivering it to none but those who would step forward and avow themselves bona fide subscribers. As a long-range solution Kendall wanted specific authority given to the Post Office Department to bar incendiary publications from the mails.[10]

Though undoubtedly offered with the intention of quieting the South, Kendall's advice, as soon as it became known, served to stir up another hornets' nest. Since the Force Act the State Rights men had seen the specter of absolutism in every new assertion of national power; and they saw in this proposal no solution but only an aggravation of their troubles. If the Post Office were empowered to decide what should and what should not be admitted to the mails, the *United States' Telegraph* and the Charleston *Mercury* could be as easily excluded as Garrison's *Liberator*. They countered by proposing that each state decide for itself what matter was fit for its citizens to read and that postmasters be held liable for violations of state laws.[11] Following Calhoun's lead, the conviction was growing among Southerners that only the sovereignty of the states could save them in the end from social and economic ruin. To protect that sovereignty from encroachment, therefore, was their primary political duty.

Again the younger and more impetuous among Calhoun's following talked unguardedly of dissolution and swore they would "sacrifice a thousand unions" before they would ruin themselves and witness the desolation of their homes.[12] Calhoun maintained his customary attitude of moderation and saw hope in the evidence that the South was at last uniting. He was aware that many in the slave states were ready to resist abolition "even to the extent of disunion" if necessary, but for himself he was not yet willing to concede the necessity. He hoped and believed that measures far less extreme would be enough. He had chosen his course by September of 1835 and was sanguine of success. "I see my way clearly on the Slave question and I do not fear an entire triumph on our own conditions; to be followed by unbounded prosperity in the South and a universal rise in property of every kind. . . ."[13] The first step was concerted action, so the Charleston *Mercury* called for a Southern Convention to consider the abolition crisis, and the *Telegraph* endorsed the call. The *Globe,* of course, professed to see in all this only additional evidence of Calhoun's desire to set up a Southern confederacy with himself at its head.[14]

The convention did not materialize that year, but Southern Governors showed a considerable degree of unanimity without it. McDuffie of South Carolina and Tazewell of Virginia were the most articulate, demanding that the Northern States take steps to suppress incendiary publications originating within their borders. And Governor William L. Marcy of New York, after consultation with Van Buren, told his own legislature that these Southern demands were no more than just.[15] The South, disaffected since 1830 when Jackson failed to reduce the tariff, and mistrustful of Van Buren for his part in that failure, was to be wooed back into the Democratic fold.

3

Following the advice of the Postmaster General, Jackson asked in his annual message of December 1835 for a law to prohibit the circulation of incendiary publications through the mails.[16] In the normal course such a recommendation would have gone to the respective committees on Post Offices and Post Roads, but in the Senate Calhoun moved reference to a special committee. The strategy was lost on no one. Four of the five members of the standing committee were from states in which abolitionist sentiment was strong and vocal. This was a question, not of party politics but of sectional interests, and the South could not trust Senators from New England or the Northwest, however well-intentioned, to see it her way. The proposal was debated with considerable realism and the division was close, but it carried. A committee of five was then selected by ballot. Calhoun of course was chairman, the others being King of Georgia, Mangum of North Carolina, Davis of Massachusetts, and Linn of Missouri. It was a committee as thoroughly packed on the slaveholding side as the Post Office Committee was on the side of the free states.[17]

A report on incendiary publications, together with a bill designed to prevent their circulation, was presented to the Senate on February 4, 1836. How far the thinking of members of the committee may have been colored by partisan politics was not clear, but the report was admittedly the work of Calhoun alone, fully concurred in only by Willie P. Mangum. It was a minority report, presented with the consent though not the assent of the majority; and the accompanying bill was similarly supported only by the two Carolinians. It is perhaps indicative of Calhoun's personal dominance at the time that the majority of his committee, though they believed him wrong, did not even attempt to substitute their views for his.[18]

Calhoun praised the President's stand against "these unconstitutional and wicked attempts" to destroy the peace and harmony of the country, and hoped with him that the nonslave states would use every power they possessed to hinder the dissemination of incendiary documents, but took sharp issue with Jackson's request for a law to bar such materials from the mails. The objection was based on constitutional grounds—that Congress could not interfere with the freedom of the press by forbidding circulation any more than it could by forbidding publication. A parallel with the Sedition Act of 1798 was drawn, and Madison's report on it cited as final proof that the general government could not abridge freedom of the press in any manner whatsoever.

No more could Congress be given the power to decide what might or might not be incendiary, for if they could forbid the one they could enforce the other. Some future Congress, dominated by abolitionists, could compel circulation of the very materials most hurtful to the

South. Here again was Calhoun's conviction, arrived at in 1828, that a majority was under no practical restraint; and his solution was the same as it had been then. The internal peace of the states, he now argued, was their own responsibility alone. Only the states could be trusted to decide, each for itself, what papers and pictures were dangerous to its security. The authority of Congress extended only to aiding upon request in the enforcement of any legitimate state law, and even then no farther than its delegated powers would permit. Among the permissible limits within which Federal assistance in the enforcement of state laws might be requested were the commerce power and the transmission of the mails.

The interpretation of the Constitution on which all this rested was explicitly stated in the body of the report: "That the States which form our Federal Union are sovereign and independent communities, bound together by a constitutional compact, and possessed of all the powers belonging to distinct and separate States, excepting such as are delegated to be exercised by the General Government, is assumed as unquestionable." When Calhoun had stated the same proposition in his debate with Webster in 1833 it had not only been questioned: it had been utterly denied. To him, however, it was still unquestionable. "The compact itself expressly provides that all powers not delegated are reserved to the States and the people. To ascertain, then, whether the power in question is delegated or reserved, it is only necessary to ascertain whether it is to be found among the enumerated powers or not. If it be not among them, it belongs, of course, to the reserved powers. . . ."

Calhoun turned then, with the frank realism that was so characteristic of his political thinking, to the nature of the evil his committee was combating, and of the institution whose existence was at stake. The professed object of the abolitionists, he declared, "is the emancipation of slaves in the Southern States, which they propose to accomplish through the agency of organized societies, spread throughout the non-slaveholding States, and a powerful press, directed mainly to excite in the other States hatred and abhorrence against the institutions and citizens of the slaveholding States, by addresses, lectures, and pictorial representations, abounding in false and exaggerated statements." The whole campaign was based on the belief that slavery in any circumstances was an unmitigated evil, and should be abolished regardless of the consequences.

He then launched into a defense of slavery as it existed in the South. In language reminiscent of John Randolph of Roanoke in the days of the Missouri Compromise, he argued that two races so different in character and culture, and so nearly equal in numbers, could not exist side by side without precipitating a conflict that would end in the elimination of one or the other. Social and political equality between the races he held to be impossible. "No power on earth can overcome the difficulty. The causes lie too deep in the principles of our nature to be surmounted. But, without such equality, to change the present condition of the African race . . . would be but to change the form of slavery. It would make them the slaves of the community instead of the slaves of individuals," and the community would feel no such responsibility for their welfare as their masters felt. Even if a war of extermination could be avoided both races would feel insecure, and the former slaves would look to the other states for protection against their former masters. Thus they would become tools in the hands of the political majority for controlling the Southern States. The South could not submit, and the Union would be destroyed.

Returning to the immediate subject of the inquiry, he noted the disastrous effects of the abolition literature on both sections of the country. Because of the tendency of this type of publication to incite servile revolt, the South must "resort to the most rigid discipline and severe police, to the great injury of the present condition of the slaves." In the North, where the incendiary books and papers were freely circulated, the minds of coming generations would be poisoned against their Southern brethren. "But, as hatred begets hatred, and animosity animosity, these feelings would become reciprocal, till every vestige of attachment would cease to exist between the two sections; when the Union and the Constitution, the offspring of mutual affection and confidence, would for ever perish." Nor did he fail to add a warning of a different sort: "A very slight modification of the arguments used against the institutions which sustain the property and security of the South and make them equally effectual against the institutions of the North. . . . It would be well for those interested to reflect whether there now exists, or ever has existed, a wealthy and civilized community in which one portion did not live on the labor of another. . . ."

The accompanying bill provided that postmasters should not knowingly accept for transmission to any state, nor deliver if received, any publication forbidden by the laws of the particular state. The general government was to enforce the law, but the states were to determine for themselves, each in its own case, what the law should be.

The report made a profound impression, in and out of Congress. Calhoun's sincerity was not questioned, and his analysis of the evil and of the consequences of allowing it to persist won wide acceptance. Neither his defense of slavery, to which his committee colleagues had particularly objected, nor his interpretation of the Constitution, was essential to the major conclusion: that the continued circulation of the kind of literature being ground out by the abolitionists would in the end be fatal to the permanence of the Union.[19] The report was a factor, however, in further straining the bonds that held the Whig coalition together. The old National Republicans, through their sectional ties, their relation to the manufacturing interest, and especially through the outspoken antislavery leadership of their ex-President, John Quincy Adams, were being pushed willy-nilly into the arms of the abolitionists, and their arrangement with the Nullifiers was becoming a liability. Such a stand as Calhoun had taken might well ruin the Presidential chances of Henry Clay in 1840, for Clay also owned slaves. So the National Republican press ignored the report so far as it could, and did not conceal its dissatisfaction with the political implications raised in it.[20]

When Calhoun's bill on incendiary publications was called up early in April, John Davis of Massachusetts, though he had been a member of the special committee, opposed it on the floor. Another committee member, John P. King, Jacksonian from Georgia, supported the bill but took sharp issue with Calhoun's constitutional reasoning and accused the South Carolina Senator of playing politics. It was at this precise time that Rives of Virginia and Tallmadge of New York were beginning a rebellion against Van Buren; but Calhoun did not yet know it. He defended his course in mild and conciliatory language, and continued to work as he had been working from the start—to keep slavery out of politics, not to put it in. When Grundy offered a feasible substitute for the bill on April 30, he accepted it. So did Van Buren a month later when he gave the casting vote to pass the bill to a third reading—a bit of strategy engineered, in all probability, by Calhoun to get the Democratic candidate on the record. The bill lost, 25 to 19, when it came up for final passage on June 8, but James Buchanan and Silas Wright voted aye.[21]

4

The circulation of incendiary publications was only one aspect of the slavery controversy. More important in the strategy of the abolitionists were petitions from ever larger groups of respectable citizens asking Congress to abolish slavery and the slave trade in the District of Columbia. The normal procedure up to 1836 had been to refer all such documents in either house to the standing Committee on the District of Columbia, where they were promptly forgotten. The first abolition petitions of the session in the Senate were presented by Thomas Morris of Ohio on January 7, 1836. This time Calhoun was instantly on his feet, demanding that the petitions be read. When the reading was over, he called for the question on receiving them and in a few brief remarks launched an attack on the abolitionists that was to end for him only with his life, and for his followers only with the blood bath of civil conflict.

With vehemence but without gestures, he stated his case. His height was perhaps magnified by his slenderness and by his thick, bushy hair, still dark in color and relatively short, so that it seemed to stand straight up. His dark, deeply sunken eyes dominated a strongly marked face, beginning to show traces of emaciation. A New England observer, seeing him in action for the first time on this occasion, found "nothing amiable in his countenance, but the contrary. The strongest expressions are: mind, energy and malignity." He spoke "with great force, but not with ease . . . expressing much by the muscles of his face, and his deep, dark eyes."[22] He seemed an evil genius, no doubt, to many who heard him speak in defense of slavery; but there were others, no less honest or sincere, who thought he gave to everything he touched "the impress of unsurpassed, if not unequalled, greatness."[23] It was an issue that, once men's passions were aroused, admitted of no middle ground. The theological absolutism of the abolitionists was matched by an equally unyielding logical absolutism in the South. To each side the other was at first mistaken, then malignant, and finally vicious with the viciousness of those who have been already damned and have no more to lose.

Calhoun turned passive resistance into positive opposition. The petitions under discussion, he insisted, "contained a gross, false, and malicious slander" on eleven states of the Union. The petitioners asked, moreover, for a violation of the Constitution; for he held that

Congress had no more jurisdiction over slavery in the District of Columbia than it had over slavery in the states, and he warned that the South could never consent to make the District an opening wedge for general emancipation. He did not doubt that the abolitionists well understood the effect of this agitation: it would end in the disruption of the Union, and he would not have it so. "Nothing can, nothing will, stop these petitions but a prompt and stern rejection of them. We must turn them away from our doors, regardless of what may be done or said."[24]

The question of receiving or refusing to receive the petitions was warmly debated, but there was neither sectional nor partisan agreement as to what should be done. Some upheld the right of petition, others denied any right to petition for an unconstitutional object. Some insisted that Congress had power to abolish slavery in the District of Columbia, but ought not to do so unless the local inhabitants wished it; others denied the power. The discussion was twice postponed, so that it was January 19 before the full-scale debate came on.

The day chosen followed immediately after the Senate had heard what the Whigs regarded as Jackson's war message against France. Partisan feeling had never been higher, and for the moment the slavery debate served as a kind of sedative. In the face of threats both at home and abroad men representing all sections and all points of view sought earnestly to reach a peaceful solution of this most disrupting of all domestic problems. The opening argument by Leigh of Virginia was careful, moderate, and conciliatory. Leigh believed with Calhoun that the petitions under discussion and the incendiary publications then being studied by a special committee were simply two sides of the same shield. To demonstrate his point he quoted almost identical language from Dr. Channing's latest book and from one of the petitions whose reception was at issue. The theme of both tract and prayer was that those who held slaves were butchers, pirates, and reprobates.[25]

Silas Wright answered in the role of administration spokesman. He was certain that the petitions to which the South so bitterly objected represented the sentiments of only a fragment of his fellow Northerners—a small and ignorant minority; but he thought that proper respect for this minority required that the petitions be received. He would then vote to reject the prayer of the petitioners. Calhoun could not see that it was any more respectful to a small minority at the North to receive and reject than it would be not to receive; and he thought the latter course the only one that was respectful to the overwhelming majority in the South. The prayer was unconstitutional, and they could refuse to receive the petitions on that ground without any violation of the right of petition.[26] But the point of unconstitutionality was precisely the point that the Van Buren following dared not admit, lest it cost them too many votes in the Northern and especially the New England States.

Debate on the reception of abolition petitions was resumed in the Senate after Calhoun's report on incendiary publications had sharpened and clarified the whole slavery controversy, and continued sporadically until early March, when the Senate voted 36 to 10 to receive. All the negative votes were from the South, and they included Jacksonians, Whigs, and Nullifiers. Two days later the prayer of the petitioners was rejected, 34 to 6.[27] The true significance of the voting was perhaps its revelation that in New England at least the abolitionists were already too strong to be opposed by their Senators. The Southern contingent began pulling closer together, regardless of party ties. Enemies of yesterday made common cause today if both held slaves. Hugh Lawson White, the Whig candidate for President in the South, and Daniel Webster, who was the choice of those same Whigs in New England, were farther apart on this question than such ancient foes as Calhoun and Andrew Jackson. Community of economic interest was coming to be the basis of party affiliation.

The first set of petitions had scarcely been disposed of when Webster offered others on March 16, moving according to previous custom that they be referred to the Committee on the District of Columbia. Willie P. Mangum was instantly on his feet, moving that the petitions be not received and calling at once for yeas and nays. Mangum's motion took parliamentary precedence over Webster's. There was further but subdued debate. Then Leigh moved to table the motion not to receive, and this was done without a division. In this casual fashion a solution was found that proved satisfactory to the Senate for years to come. Thereafter, without debate, the question of reception was regularly raised and as regularly tabled.[28]

5

The slavery controversy was fought out simultaneously and in similar terms in the House of Representatives, but with results very different from those in the Senate. Almost as soon as the House was organized the fight began. December 16, 1835, saw the first of an endless procession of abolition petitions received and laid on the table by an overwhelming majority.[29] The next day routine business interposed, but the eighteenth opened with another of the same type. It was at this point that young James H. Hammond made his first appearance on the floor of the House and took to himself the leadership of the South on that vexed and vexing question. The motion he made cannot be regarded as spontaneous or personal. He shared a mess with Calhoun, Preston, Pickens, and Thompson of his own state, and we may be sure the course to be followed in both houses was carefully planned in advance in one or another of the rooms at Mrs. Lindenberger's house on Capitol Hill. Calhoun had been satisfied as to the course that ought to be followed on the slavery question as early as September, and he was far too competent a political general to leave his lieutenants in the dark.

It was, then, the planned strategy of the Calhoun group that Hammond was following when he moved that the petition then before the House be not received. Prior petitions had been tabled or their prayers rejected, but this treatment had in no way restrained the introduction of new ones. He would therefore ask the House "to put a more decided seal of reprobation upon them" by rejecting the petition itself rather than simply denying the prayer of the petitioners.[30] This move set off a major debate involving the rules of the House, Presidential politics, and sectional pressures. The Calhoun group, as we have already seen, believed that the abolitionists were deliberately concentrating on the District of Columbia as an opening wedge rather than as an end in itself. They therefore denied categorically that Congress had any power to legislate on the subject, in the District or anywhere else. They wanted to stop the agitation before the pressure got too strong for Northern members to stand up against.

Hence these moves to "stop the petitions at the threshold." By refusing to receive them at all, on the ground that the end sought by the petitioners was a violation of the Constitution, they hoped to establish that point so clearly that the agitation would cease. At the same time, for their own preservation, they wanted to commit the Northern Van Buren men on the issue. Van Buren himself had been driven to the point of making a stronger and stronger case against the expediency of abolition in the District but remained unrecorded on the actual constitutional question.

The state of feeling of the Southern contingent in Congress on the whole slavery question was too obvious to be overlooked. Even many of those who offered the explosive memorials thrust upon them by their constituents believed the net result would be fatal. "It appears to me," wrote John Fairfield of Maine, "if the abolitionists, or those who get up these petitions, many of them at least, knew what mischief they were doing, that they would abstain. The South will not have that question meddled with, and if we persist in attempting it, a dissolution of the Union must follow."[31] The South—or many intelligent spokesmen for it—was not so sure that the abolitionists acted in ignorance. There were Southern men by 1836 who thought the abolitionists were consciously and deliberately trying to break up the Union, perhaps in the interest of a foreign power.[32] Absurd, of course, but no more absurd than Northern charges going back to 1830 that Calhoun was seeking to destroy the Union. Each side was bent on achieving, or preserving, something it held more important than any possible political consequences.

Through the six weeks or so that the general argument precipitated by Hammond was carried on, he was in regular touch with the older and more experienced members of his party—the veterans of nullification. Unquestionably the day-to-day progress was talked over with Calhoun, who raised the same issue in the Senate on January 7. He was not following Hammond's lead, as some of the latter's more enthusiastic friends seemed to think,[33] but both were working in terms of a general plan. The fight on the petitions came up first in the House, because the question normally received much more attention in that body, whose members were both more numerous and more likely to be directly responsive to their constituents. The other element of the same program—the fight on the incendiary publications—had to be brought up in the Senate, where the Whig coalition still held a majority and Calhoun could count on getting a friendly committee. In both cases and in both houses the all-important thing was unity of purpose. The leaders were prepared to "meet the question boldly in every shape in which it can be brought up and the more directly the better," provided only that the South could "be brought to act and vote together on the issue actually presented." They feared "nothing from discussion or excitement, nor even from misrepresentation." The only thing they feared was division among themselves.[34]

But politics still cut across sectional lines. Van Buren could not much longer stand out against the pressure for a commitment one way or the other on the constitutional power of Congress over slavery in the District of Columbia. The best way to relieve the pressure was to split the South on the same issue; and that, with his customary deftness, Van Buren did in the way most damaging to his opponents. For it was Henry L. Pinckney of South Carolina, Nullifier, former editor of the *Mercury,* intimately connected with the Calhoun leaders and so far as the country knew one of their own preferred spokesmen, who was chosen as the wedge to split the slave states. Perhaps the idea was his own; perhaps it was shrewdly planted; but certain it is that the resolution out of which came the notorious "gag rule" of the House was not discussed in advance with Calhoun or with the other Southern leaders. Only Pickens saw it ahead of time, and he pleaded with his colleague not to offer it. It was discussed prior to introduction, however, with the Van Buren strategists, and probably modified by them.[35]

Pinckney indicated on February 4, 1836, that he would offer a resolution on the question of abolition in the District of Columbia. Only three days earlier Hammond had maintained in a long, careful, fully documented speech that the power of Congress to legislate for the District of Columbia did not extend to the subject of slavery, and had based on this argument his insistence that the petitions under consideration since the beginning of the session ought not to be received. He had no intimation that Pinckney believed otherwise. He probably knew, before the resolution was read on February 4, what it contained, since Pickens had been told; but even Pickens had not seen the full text, as modified by the Van Buren strategists. The clerk read as follows:

"*Resolved,* That all the memorials which have been offered, or may hereafter be presented, to this House, praying for abolition of slavery in the District of Columbia, and . . . every other paper or proposition that may be submitted in relation to that subject, be referred to a select committee, with instructions to report that Congress . . . ought not to interfere in any way with slavery in the District of Columbia. . . ."[36] The constitutional right to interfere in the states was specifically denied, but the resolution conceded by implication the *right* of Congress to interfere in the District, even while denying the expediency of doing so. It was Van Buren's position, but it was not the position of Calhoun, nor Hammond, nor Pickens; it was not the position of South Carolina or the South.[37]

For the next four days the Calhoun group tried to get Pinckney to abandon his ground, and for a time they thought they had succeeded. On February 8, however, Pinckney called up the resolution and argued for it on the floor. It was Hammond who answered, in bitterness and scorn. He said nothing of his colleague's motives, but his restraint was eloquent. So too was his terse summation of the Calhoun view: "We deny the power of this House to act upon the subject at all, and desire to exclude it entirely and forever from these walls. My colleague calls upon you to legislate upon it, and thereby yields you the power to act upon it. . . . I believe the adoption of the gentleman's plan of settling this controversy will give [the Union] one of the most fatal blows it has ever received. For I assure this House that a Union based upon the principles of that resolution cannot stand. We cannot give up rights and consent to hold our property at your will. We cannot give up the constitution, and consent to repose our all upon the tender mercies of this House, to be withdrawn whenever they may deem expedient."[38]

The protest was vain and futile. The Van Buren forces wanted it the way it was, and they controlled the House. The resolution was split into four parts, to be separately voted on, but each was carried. The reference of all petitions to a select committee was adopted, 174 to 48, with Hammond, Pickens, Wise, and the other Calhounites voting no. That Congress had no power to interefere with slavery in the states was affirmed, 201 to 7, with J. Q. Adams and Edward Everett among the seven; but on this as on the remaining parts the Calhoun group refused to vote. The inexpediency of interfering with slavery in the District of Columbia was upheld, 163 to 47, but the reasons why it was deemed inexpedient were acceptable only to 127, with 75 not satisfied.[39] A committee of nine members to receive the petitions and to make the prescribed report on them was then ordered, with Pinckney as its chairman and moving spirit. Also a member of the committee was a future President of the United States and loyal Van Buren supporter, young Franklin Pierce of New Hampshire.

A week after the adoption of the Pinckney resolutions, another petition for the abolition of slavery in the District was submitted to the House by one of the Massachusetts members. Wise, ignoring all that had gone before, promptly moved that it be not received and asked if it was in order to debate the question. Now it had certainly been the intention of those who passed the first of the Pinckney resolutions that all future petitions of the same sort were to be referred automatically to the select committee; but Speaker Polk ruled otherwise and told the Virginia hotspur he might go ahead. The decision of the chair was challenged, and debated for the remainder of the day. It was debated again after the lapse of a week, a vote was taken, and the decision was reversed by 147 to 56. Polk seemed greatly pleased by the whole affair, and doubtless was, for it had been arranged by the Van Buren majority for his convenience. The Speaker's original decision favoring the views of the Calhoun group was for the benefit of his constituents, who also thought that way. The reversal was in the interest of Van Buren's election.[40]

The mail from the South by this time was coming in, and for Pinckney it was not pleasant. The old South Carolina Unionists—the few who remained unreconstructed—found his logic irresistible, because it meant that he had broken with Calhoun. But those who spoke for the majority in the state—and it was a majority overwhelming since the post-office incident of the previous July—were shocked. Hamilton found the Charleston Representative's course "utterly inexplicable . . . except on the presumption of religious fanaticism." He was "reluctant to charge venality & corruption," but old Thomas Cooper did not hesitate. "Indeed," the latter wrote cynically to Hammond, "the immense patronage, operating upon men ready to sell themselves, & who like Paley 'cannot afford to keep a conscience,' is inestimable." Hayne, who was Pinckney's brother-in-law, was deeply regretful, but was joining with other citizens to determine on a course of action. To the younger men it was "that D—nd traitor Pinckney" and his "more traitorous resolutions." All agreed that Pinckney's public life was over.[41]

Pinckney stalled on the report of his committee as long as he could, while his Southern colleagues offered him one more chance and the Van Burenites demanded the full measure of performance, as though they had indeed already paid over their thirty pieces of political silver. It could finally be delayed no longer, and was laid before the House on May 18, 1836. It concluded with three resolutions. The first was to the effect that Congress had no power over slavery in the states. The second reaffirmed the inexpediency of interference in the District of Columbia. The third was the gag rule itself: "*Resolved,* That all petitions, memorials, resolutions, propositions, or papers, relating in any way, or to any extent whatever, to the subject of slavery, or the abolition of slavery, shall, without either being printed or referred, be laid upon the table, and that no further action whatever shall be had thereon."[42]

Wise denounced the report on the ground that he had been specifically promised by Pinckney that it would deny the constitutional power of Congress to interfere with slavery in the District. "He did not consider the report as a defense of Southern interest, nor as an expression of Southern feeling." Waddy Thompson declared that he had "listened in vain for one South Carolina argument, or one honest bursting out of the feelings of a South Carolinian," and he hoped the authorship of the report would not be taken to mean that it represented the views of his state.[43] Small chance of that!

For days the report and its resolutions were debated with rising bitterness and deepening dissension. Polk was often unable to keep order, and when the resolutions came to a division, men refused to vote and defied the rules of the House. The first resolution was adopted 182 to 9; the second, 132 to 45; and the gag rule, 117 to 68. Wise and Thompson refused to vote on any of the three. Adams and his equally obstinate New England group voted no on the first; Adams declined to vote on the second; and on the third rose in response to his name to announce amid cries of "Order!" that he held the resolution to be unconstitutional and a violation of the rights of his constituents. Pickens joined Wise and Thompson in refusing to vote on the first two, but voted against the gag rule.[44] Hammond had already been forced by illness to resign his seat, and so was not present for the finish.

The *Globe,* in a column captioned "Nullifiers and Abolitionists," congratulated the country "upon the final overthrow of the joint plot of these malcontent confederates to unsettle the Government and disturb the Union, by agitating the slave question in Congress." The *Mercury,* with more restraint and greater truth, condemned Pinckney's report because it gained nothing for the South and abandoned the very outpost that it was most important to secure. "It *yields* the constitutional right to abolish Slavery in the District of Columbia: and that is the sum total of good and evil which it has done. The abolitionists claimed nothing more, and all *the right* they ever claimed it has conceded."[45]

CHAPTER XXI

THE HERO VINDICATED

1

THE spring of 1836 found the country rising to the crest of such a boom as it had never known before. Prices had risen steadily since the Bank war until the cost of living was 60 to 70 percent above that of 1834. Commercial enterprises expanded like inflated toy balloons. Real estate values soared to fantastic levels, and interest rates went as high as 15 and even 20 percent. Cotton brought 16.8 cents a pound in Charleston, a rise of seven cents since 1832. For the country as a whole, imports during 1836 almost doubled the value of those four years earlier. Customs receipts had increased almost 50 percent since the tariff compromise went into effect, and even higher than the customs were the revenues from the sale of public lands.[1]

There were those who saw in all this only the evidence of lush prosperity, and others like Calhoun who realized only too clearly the artificial nature of the accumulating wealth. By both groups the situation was generally linked with the questions of the currency, the regulation of the deposit banks, the public lands, and the surplus revenue which were occupying the attention of Congress. On the nature of the disease, if it was a disease, and on the remedy, however, there were wide divergences of opinion.

Jackson's own reasoning on the question was as direct and uncomplicated as his reaction to nullification had been. Prices were too high because there was too much bank paper passing for money; but as long as the government accepted it, it was legal tender, no matter how worthless in fact. The answer was not to accept it. Get the country back on gold and silver currency and all would be well. Benton proposed in April that Congress require payment for public lands in specie only, and Calhoun agreed that such a measure would probably reduce speculation. The proposal was not acted on, but as soon as Congress adjourned the Missouri Senator carried it to the White House. Jackson saw in it not only a curb to speculation but a move in the direction of a hard-money currency, and he made it his own. On July 11, 1836, at the President's instance, the Secretary of the Treasury issued the Specie Circular. After August 15, only gold, silver, "and, in the proper cases, Virginia land scrip" were to be received as payment for the public lands, save only that for another four months actual settlers and bona fide residents of the state in which the purchase lay might continue to give paper for quantities up to 320 acres.[2]

The move was immediately challenged by the *United States' Telegraph,* which pointed out that whether such was the intention of the President or not, the Specie Circular would "play into the hands of those speculators who have already invested largely in the public lands."[3] The effect was much as forecast. Specie drained from the Eastern commercial cities to the West, and presently went into hiding because people thought the government must distrust the banks. Without specie public lands could not be bought from the government, but millions of acres had already passed into private hands, and these were sold and resold at constantly mounting prices, paid for in inflated bank paper and adding still further to the speculative boom.[4]

Another factor in hastening the impending crash was the initial operation of the deposit bill. Among the regulations imposed on the pet banks was one limiting the amount of public money to be held by any bank to three fourths of the total of its capital. Many of these institutions held considerably larger sums than were now permitted, and were compelled to call in loans on short notice. At the same time preparations had to be made to shift the first installment of the surplus revenue to the state treasuries on January 1, 1837, which meant that still larger sums must shortly be called in and surrendered by the depository banks.[5] The result was still further pressure on an already overextended money market.

With the Presidential election only a few months away, the disordered economy of the country and the measures taken to cure it were bound to become partisan issues. The Specie Circular was an administration measure, so it became the chief whipping boy of the Whigs. The deposit act, on the other hand, was largely Calhoun's doing; and though many Democrats had supported it and Jackson had reluctantly given it his assent, it presently became an object of criticism for the Van Buren party. To Calhoun the Specie Circular, though he would have accepted it as an act of Congress, was just another instance of arbitrary and unauthorized power on the part of the President. The deposit act, by contrast, marked a swing away from the consolidating tendencies of the preceding years, and not the least of its virtues was the fact that it owed its passage to the "steady and firm co-operation of a majority of the friends of the administration in both houses."[6] Van Buren agreed that the bill became law because of the "partial diversities of opinion among the friends of the administration," but in guarded language he expressed his own disapproval of it.[7]

2

Another factor in both economic and political situations was Texas. Ever since the Sabine River had been established as the southwestern boundary of the United States by the Spanish treaty of 1819, Westerners had looked with covetous eyes at the broad plains stretching away to the Rio Grande. When the Missouri Compromise of the following year established the principle of simultaneous admission to the Union of slave and free states, the South too began to consider Texas as potential American soil, for there was no other territory adapted to the slave economy which could be used to balance the extended reaches of the north and central West.

The acquisition of Texas was one of Jackson's favorite projects, toward which he had worked from his first inauguration. Poinsett had sought at the President's instigation to buy the region from Mexico, and Anthony Butler, who went to the Mexican capital in 1829 as Jackson's personal agent but remained as envoy, added bribery and intrigue to the routine methods of diplomacy. Sam Houston, with or without Jackson's connivance, contemplated for a time the private conquest of the country by filibusters and Indians, operating from bases in Arkansas; and by 1833 the huge Tennessean was in Texas actively engaged in promoting a revolution against Mexico.[8]

The Mexican Government, meanwhile, had abolished slavery in 1829, partly in the hope of discouraging Americans from settling in Texas. Large land grants, however, had already been made to Stephen F. Austin and others associated with him, and it soon became evident that the existing labor force was inadequate for their development. Austin secured modification of the decree to except Texas, but Mexican restrictions against settlers from the United States continued in force until revoked by Santa Anna in 1833. The Mexican dictator probably thought only to keep Texas quiet until he had secured his grip on the rest of the country, but his action opened the way for a tide of adventurers and speculators who would in due time become revolutionaries. As early as February 1833 Houston notified Jackson that an independent government would ultimately be set up. A year later he predicted that within twelve months Texas would be "acting in all things" as a sovereign state, and that within three years all ties with Mexico would be severed. Before the end of 1835 he was frankly advertising in American newspapers for volunteers to help "liberate" Texas, offering "liberal bounties of land" in return. "Let each man come with a good rifle, and one hundred rounds of ammunition, and to come soon."[9]

The ostensible purpose was to defend the original constitution of Mexico against the "usurpations" of Santa Anna, who had recently taken steps to disarm the too belligerent Texans. The question of annexation to the United States, however, was never far below the surface. It was Houston's avowed purpose from the start, and rumors of negotiations to that end got into the American press with increasing frequency as Texas moved on toward armed revolt.[10] The timing was well-nigh perfect. The fever of land speculation sweeping the United States brought capital and powerful vested interests to the support of the rebels, and the current agitation of the slave question in Congress could not fail to arouse Southern sympathy for a territory out of which four or five slave states might be carved. Stephen F. Austin was in Philadelphia negotiating a substantial loan from Nicholas Biddle (whose bank was now a Pennsylvania corporation) when news of the massacre at the Alamo shocked the United States.[11] A month later came Houston's smashing victory over Santa Anna at San Jacinto, and the independence of Texas was assured.[12]

The frank activities of the Texans in recruiting men and collecting funds in the United States, the open sympathy of the bordering states, and the strategic placing of an American army under General Edmund P. Gaines, Commander of the Southern Division, on the east bank of the Sabine all lent color to the suspicion in Mexico and elsewhere that the United States would go to war to prevent the reconquest of the province. This new show of military force came close on the heels of the settlement with France, but its sectional character created among partisans a "state of singular confusion."[13] Preston of South Carolina, uncompromising opponent of Jackson and of the French "war," offered to the Senate a petition from Philadelphia praying for recognition of Texan independence.[14] Caustic John Quincy Adams charged that military appropriations were designed for war against Mexico, to annex territory and extend slavery.[15] Intermittently through May and June of 1836 the Senate received memorials and debated recognition of the newborn republic, aware that recognition might be taken in Mexico City as a declaration of war. Some, like Thomas Ritchie of the Richmond *Enquirer,* called for outright annexation.[16] As the session of Congress neared its close, the Senate Foreign Relations Committee, consisting of four members from slave states and one Democratic rebel (Clay, King of Georgia, Tallmadge, Mangum, Porter), brought in a resolution calling for recognition of Texas whenever "satisfactory information shall be received that it has in successful operation a civil Government, capable of fulfilling the obligations of an independent Power." This resolution was adopted without a dissenting vote on July 1.[17] Calhoun spoke for it and made it clear that he regarded recognition as a prelude to ultimate admission to the Union.[18]

Congress had scarcely adjourned before news reached Washington that General Gaines had crossed the Sabine River. Amos Kendall, who served by turns as goad and rein to the President, urged the southern commander's immediate recall. He thought war with Mexico over Texas more than likely as an eventuality and not particularly to be deplored, but the time was not yet. In the meanwhile he hoped the United States Government would "maintain such an attitude as not only to be right but to appear so before the world," which already held the United States responsible, not unreasonably, for the whole Texas revolution.[19] In his reply to Kendall, Jackson explained that Gaines had crossed the river under orders. He had in fact been ordered to occupy Nacogdoches, two thirds of the way to the Neches River, which Jackson claimed as the true boundary intended by the Spanish treaty. The President was critical of Gaines, who had not actually gone as far as he was ordered to go; and to save the appearance of neutrality he had canceled the General's requisitions on the Governors of near-by states for militia. But Gaines was not ordered back to the east of the Sabine; he was, on the contrary, given new instructions authorizing him to enter Texan or Mexican territory if necessary in pursuit of hostile Indians.[20] Jackson was also in familiar correspondence with his old friend and protégé, Sam Houston, who was inaugurated as President of the Republic of Texas on October 22.

3

Through the spring and summer of 1836 the administration press, led by the *Globe,* aimed its broadsides at Calhoun. The protective tariff, the distribution of the surplus, and the agitation of the slavery issue were all laid at the door of the South Carolina Senator, and it was insinuated that the single purpose behind them all was the ultimate disruption of the Union. The net effect, and perhaps the only effect that was seriously intended, was to breathe new life into all those who opposed Calhoun in his native state. There were individual Unionists still unreconciled, and there were those among the Nullifiers themselves who chafed under a party discipline as rigorous as Jackson's own. Those who complained most loudly conceded Calhoun's genius, his patriotism, his qualities of mind and heart, but they resented his tendency to dictate party policies without consultation and they professed to believe that his ambition stood in the way of real harmony in South Carolina.[21] There were many otherwise friendly who believed that Calhoun had had his day and that it was time he stepped aside.

Calhoun had in fact been toying, for more than a year, with the idea of retiring from public life, but the very qualities to which his more ambitious followers most objected made it impossible for him to give up the fight. He saw far more in the party battles of the day than just another Presidential campaign. To him the survival of the South was at stake. He had never for a moment lost sight of the relation between a national government vesting sovereignty in the majority and the ultimate goal of the abolitionists, and he would not—by his very nature he could not—surrender the leadership to men who might yield the constitutional issue for temporary economic or political gains. Neither could he give up the reins to hotheaded youngsters who might seize the first provocation to take the state and ultimately the South out of the Union.

Cautiously he steered his course between the two extremes, and beneath the velvet glove that controlled his partisans there was a grip of steel. His self-assurance was complete. He expected those who agreed with him to follow his lead. Those who did not agree were given an opportunity to change their minds, but if they proved obdurate they were eliminated. Calhoun himself could not be convinced, nor led to change his mind, by the arguments of others. He had to convince himself. This he could and sometimes did do, but always with a new twist or embellishment or direction that made the argument peculiarly his own. By the late summer of 1836 the outlook for all he sought and all he hoped seemed black indeed. The Whigs were apathetic in the face of the powerful Democratic machine, the tide of abolitionist publications was rising to staggering proportions, the South was divided and insecure. Yet Calhoun refused utterly to believe that the Union could not be preserved, and insisted that the whole effort of his party be devoted to seeking constitutional measures of redress. He conceded that even these might fail, but still they must be tried.[22]

Affairs in South Carolina were at their lowest ebb when a planned and calculated revolt was launched against Calhoun's leadership. Henry L. Pinckney was its spearhead and it was backed by the Van Buren machine. On August 19 Pinckney announced his candidacy for re-election to Congress in a long letter to his constituents. His case was compounded of self-justification for the course he had pursued on the slavery petitions, of recantation of his old allegiance to the Nullifiers, and of abuse of Calhoun. Consciously he appealed to the Unionists of other days and sought to run as their candidate.[23] The powerful *Courier* backed him, for no better reason than to mortify Calhoun;[24] and the *Mercury* announced the rival candidacy of Isaac E. Holmes for the Nullifiers.

In Calhoun's mind it was clear that Pinckney had to be defeated, not because he had revolted against the party leadership—although that would have been cause enough—but because he had conceded the right of Congress to abolish slavery in the District of Columbia: because he had willfully surrendered a crucial position in a war of extermination. It made little difference to Calhoun personally who replaced the erring Congressman, but he saw danger in revival of the Unionist party, especially on such an issue. So he approached the old Unionist leaders and offered to take as his candidate any man they chose to put up. They selected Hugh Swinton Legaré, whose chief virtue was that he had been out of the country during the nullification fight and so had fewer personal enemies than Poinsett, who would have been the logical choice. Then Isaac Holmes and Colonel William Dubose successively declined a formal nomination from the State Rights party. Both based their refusals on the need for unity if Pinckney was to be beaten, and Dubose went on to urge his party to give support instead to the "accomplished and eloquent Legaré."[25]

On October 7 the *Mercury* announced a Nullification ticket, headed by Legaré, and the next day published a Unionist ticket identical in every way except for the candidate for state senate from the Charleston District. Poinsett appeared on the Unionist slate for this position, but because the Pinckney ticket also included Poinsett's name the Nullifiers would not back him. The election was held three days later, and Legaré won the major contest by a shaky margin of less than a hundred votes.[26]

Back of the Pinckney purge lay an issue more important than local politics. For the Unionist leaders realized as clearly as Calhoun that the only safety for the South lay in denying the power of Congress to interfere with slavery anywhere. Old differences could be and were forgotten in the face of the long-range threat to the economic security of the section and the stability of the Union offered by Pinckney's stand. Petigru and Calhoun buried the hatchet together, and the revolt so far as South Carolina was concerned was over.[27] In national affairs Calhoun was already the symbol not of his state alone but of the entire South at a time of deep and critical sectional division. However South Carolina might rebel against him, she would be weaker when he was gone; however the South might resist his leadership, he pleaded her cause with a skill and cogency that no other could hope to match. His experience, his sincerity, the tremendous force of his own convictions, raised him to a pre-eminence that could not, after nullification, be successfully challenged.[28] It may be, as has been charged, that Calhoun's uncompromising stand on slavery made the Civil War inevitable; but it can be argued with at least equal plausibility that his unflinching defense of minority interests, and his consistent refusal to accept the ultimate alternative of secession, prevented civil war in his lifetime.

The Congressional election in the Charleston District was more important to the South than the Presidential contest, though most Southerners were probably not aware of it. There at least a principle was at stake, whereas there was no real issue between Van Buren and his Whig opponents. It was Calhoun who stood for a political philosophy opposed to that acknowledged by the party in power—not Harrison, nor White, nor Webster. The campaign scarcely rose above a personal level and the Whigs were beaten before ever they went to the polls.

Jackson left for Tennessee as soon as he could get away and personally stumped the state for Van Buren. A month before the election he thought his favorite would carry every state in the Union except Massachusetts, Vermont, and South Carolina. He proved an unreliable prophet. To his intense chagrin, White carried Tennessee by 10,000 votes, and even carried Jackson's own district by 43 to 18.[29] White also carried Georgia; and South Carolina, through her state legislature, gave her electoral vote to Willie P. Mangum and John Tyler. Webster carried only Massachusetts, but Harrison showed unlooked-for strength, winning in Vermont, New Jersey, Delaware, Maryland, Kentucky, Ohio, and Indiana, for a total of 73 electoral votes. Van Buren, however, had 170, counting three in dispute from Michigan—a safe majority of the total. Richard M. Johnson did not fare so well, falling one short of a majority on the most liberal basis, and throwing the election of Vice President, for the first and only time, into the Senate.

As soon as the results were known, Mangum and Alexander Porter of Louisiana followed an example earlier set by Benjamin Watkins Leigh and resigned their Senate seats. All three had disregarded the instructions of their respective legislatures, and their usefulness was over. The opposition sought to regroup its defeated forces, but the alliance of Nationals and Nullifiers was at an end. The Whigs, after 1836, were no longer a coalition but a single party, inheriting the strength and the weaknesses of the two parties of property that had preceded them. Calhoun stood alone, watching the internal conflict of the Democrats, watching the spreading economic shadow that would soon be panic, watching the progress of the abolitionists, and preparing to trade political strength for the protection of the South.[30]

4

When Congress met on December 5, 1836, for the last short session under Andrew Jackson, the administration had a clear majority in both houses. The election had paved the way for the old Hero's public vindication, of which Benton's expunging resolution was the authentic symbol.

Aside from the official whitewashing of the President, the major business of the session was again financial. Jackson himself was so alarmed at the disordered state of the currency and the uncontrolled speculation in lands which was engulfing the country that he was almost ready to retrace his own steps. When preparing his annual message late in November 1836 he seriously considered recommending a national bank. It was, to be sure, to be set up in the District of Columbia and was to be chartered on "real banking principles" in contrast to those which animated Nicholas Biddle's "monster"—but it was nevertheless to be a bank. Jackson seems to have contemplated confining this proposed institution to the functions of deposit and exchange, and his thinking at this time was probably one of the steps by which the Democracy worked itself around to the Independent Treasury scheme that came out of the panic.[31]

Jackson's advisers dissuaded him from any mention of a new bank. At least he did not mention it. But the financial portions of the message were curious indeed in the light of the policies laid down in previous years. A brief review of the second administration was illuminating in its candor. "The Government had," declared the President, "without necessity, received from the people a large surplus, which . . . was deposited in sundry banks. The banks proceeded to make loans upon this surplus, and thus converted it into banking capital; and in this manner it has tended to multiply bank charters, and has had a great agency in producing a spirit of wild speculation. The possession and use of the property out of which this surplus was created belonged to the people; but the Government has transferred its possession to incorporated banks, whose interest and effort it is to make large profits out of its use. This process need only be stated to show its injustice and bad policy." He forebore to mention that the "Government" guilty of this injustice was for all practical purposes himself, and that the "bad policy" was his own.

He went on to denounce the deposit act of the previous session, though he had signed it. The government possessed no power to collect revenue for the purpose of giving it to the states, and the act in question was being treated by them as a deed of gift. In this case he graciously conceded a "partial change in my views upon this interesting subject," but spoiled the effect by insisting that his recommendations of 1829 and 1830 had been misunderstood. He had only meant distribution as a temporary expedient to get rid of a dangerous surplus, and he had meant to do it by constitutional amendment. The Jackson of 1829 and 1830, as expounded by the Jackson of 1836, sounded for all the world like the Calhoun of 1835!

There was only one right thing to do, the President continued, and he had meant to do it all the time—reduce the revenue to the wants of the government. Now he sounded like the Jackson Calhoun had supported for the Presidency in 1828, but it was a little late in the day. Late in the day, too, to call loudly for tariff reduction to pare down the surplus. If he had begun his first Presidential term with tariff reduction, there would have been no surplus and a great many unfortunate wounds would not have been inflicted on the body politic. He must have anticipated some such retort when he wrote the message, for he hastened to insert a justification: "the condition of the manufacturing interest" had been such when he took office "as to create an apprehension" that duties could not be reduced at that time "without extensive mischief." He knew that was very lame, also, so he hurried on to something he could denounce with his accustomed freedom from apologies. He had much to say about inflated bank paper, referred to the good effects of his Specie Circular, and called for the return of a metallic currency to the land. The message ended with a commendation for the "prosperous condition" of the executive departments, and for the "ability and integrity with which they have been conducted."[32]

Blair had paved the way in the *Globe* for just such a message, with steady attacks on the tariff compromise of 1833, denunciations of the deposit act, and praise of the Specie Circular. For the next three months the tariff and the deposit act continued to be skillfully associated by the party editor and were made to appear as the joint and probably corrupt handiwork of John C. Calhoun.

5

The Democratic schism of the previous session had prevented action on the expunging resolution at that time, to Benton's annoyance and disgust. The election, however, had whipped the dissidents back into line, at least for the moment, and on December 7, the day after the President's message had been read, the Missouri Senator gave the long-familiar notice: as soon as enough Senators were in their seats he would introduce a resolution to expunge from the Journal the resolution of March 28, 1834, censuring the President for the removal of the deposits.[33] He waited a month in hopes of getting the Michigan Senators seated in time to swell the Jacksonian majority, but early in January 1837 he decided to proceed with the forces already at his disposal.

The expunging resolution was called up on January 12, 1837, read, and once more expounded by Benton, his deep voice booming like the broadside from a seventy-four. The debate, if such it may be called, occupied that day and the next. It consisted mainly of extravagant praise for Andrew Jackson and all his works by those Senators who owed their seats to legislative "instructions," and sharply ironical replies from the opposition. When one impassioned Jacksonian invoked fire from heaven to burn the polluted page of the Senate Journal, Gabriel Moore of Alabama, whose seat was already forfeited to his convictions, suggested that a sunglass might do it. He could think of no more fitting way to finish the farce.[34]

Twilight had already fallen on Friday, January 13, 1837, when Calhoun rose, to hold the floor for a brief three minutes. His seat was in the first row, just before the presiding officer's desk. He had only to turn around to sweep the darkening room with his deep-set, scourging eyes. He scarcely moved, but his short, incisive sentences fell like stinging nettles, and more than one Senator refused to meet his gaze as the scornful words poured shame and humiliation on a Senate that had become a mere rubber stamp for power.[35]

To the gaunt, stubborn, avenging fate, half Roman tribune and half disembodied intellect, that was John C. Calhoun, there were some questions so plain that they could not be argued, and this was such a one. The measure was a palpable violation of the Constitution; for the Senate was required to keep a journal and a portion of that journal was now to be destroyed, for no better reason than that the President willed it so. "We all know," he told his fellow Senators, "how these legislative returns have been obtained. It is by dictation from the White House. The President himself, with that vast mass of patronage which he wields, and the thousand expectations he is able to hold up, has obtained these votes of the State Legislatures. . . ." Briefly he reviewed the circumstances, and held up to scorn the paltry arguments of the resolution's defenders; but he knew that no reasoning, however sound, would change the issue. "The day is gone; night approaches, and night is suitable to the dark deed we meditate. . . . Other preceding violations of the constitution (and they have been many and great) filled my bosom with indignation, but this fills it only with grief. Others were done in the heat of party. Power was, as it were, compelled to support itself by seizing upon new instruments of influence and patronage; and there were ambitious and able men to direct the process. Such was the removal of the deposites, which the President seized upon by a new and unprecedented act of arbitrary power; an act which gave him ample means of rewarding friends and punishing enemies. Something may, perhaps, be pardoned to him in this matter, on the old apology of tyrants—the plea of necessity. But here there can be no such apology. Here no necessity can so much as be pretended. This act originates in pure, unmixed, personal idolatry. It is the melancholy evidence of a broken spirit, ready to bow at the feet of power. The former act was such a one as might have been perpetrated in the days of Pompey and Caesar; but an act like this could never have been consummated by a Roman Senate until the times of Caligula and Nero."[36]

In hushed and shamefaced silence the Senate adjourned until Monday, January 16.

Benton feared even then that there would be defections from the tight Jackson ranks. Many Democrats were manifestly unhappy, and the rivalry between him and Rives, which had flared into open revolt six months before, might well burst out again. Not that he feared for Rives, but there were others whose hero worship showed signs of cooling, now that Jackson would no longer be the dispenser of patronage. So the Missouri Senator, whose pockets always seemed to be well lined, was host on Saturday evening at Boulanger's, with all the administration Senators as his guests. There, mellowed by good wine and oysters, and subdued by argument and threats, they were pledged to take the expunging resolution precisely as it was, and to prevent adjournment on the next legislative day until it had been passed. The meeting was sometimes stormy, and Benton was forced to yield the point of actual obliteration in favor of black lines and words; but by midnight, when the group filed silently out of the famous Washington restaurant, the pledge had been given.[37]

The Senate met at noon on January 16 at usual, with expunging the order of the day. Clay, leaning indolently against his desk, delivered one of those sarcastic tirades of which he was past master. Buchanan, in his heavy humorless way, made answer. Others on both sides said their pieces, and Webster, the greatest orator of them all, read in his thrilling, vibrant voice a protest for himself and his colleague, John Davis. Since four o'clock the committee rooms had been laden with food and drink—hams, turkeys, beef, wine, coffee, pickles—provided by the senior Senator from Missouri, so that no member of his pledged band might make hunger an excuse to absent himself.

When Webster had finished Benton called for the vote, cracked the party whip, and enjoyed the fruits of his victory. The count was 24 to 19, in a Senate then numbering fifty members. It was late in the evening when the vote was finished. Most of those who had voted "nay" filed silently from the room, and a few of those who voted "aye" went with them. There were only twenty-five Senators on the floor when the clerk, to a chorus of hisses from the galleries, drew the black lines with Benton's pen and wrote across the hated resolution that it had been expunged by order of the Senate. After the added farce of arresting a spectator, refusing him a hearing, and letting him go, the Senate adjourned. Benton pronounced the night's work "very good," but young Henry A. Wise, watching from the gallery, "looked at Rives and thought of Virginia and wept." The losers held their heads high, but the party Senators who voted for expunging "looked more like culprits, than victorious leaders."[38]

Benton presented the expunging pen to Jackson, who promised to leave it in his will to its original owner. The President was as delighted as a schoolboy released with apologies from penance after school. He gave a dinner at the White House for the Senators who did the deed, and being too ill himself to attend, he placed the ponderous and jubilant Benton in the chair.[39] Richard K. Crallé, another Virginian, was now editor of the *Telegraph,* and his account the next day was a bitter thing to read. On the eighteenth, in a black-bordered box, he listed the names of the expungers. "The following individuals," so the legend ran, "received from the hands of Martin Van Buren the *accolade,* on the night of the 16th January, 1837, and are received into the order as 'KNIGHTS OF THE BLACK LINES.' "

6

The tactics used to line up the administration forces behind the expunging resolution accomplished their immediate purpose, but in the long run they very nearly destroyed the party. Men who were following a course which they knew to be wrong, but from which they could not escape, were likely to be more than ready to assert independence in other matters. So it proved, at least, in this case. Even before the disgraceful performance of January 16 had been played out the Democratic rift had been reopened, and the Senate turned from the President's vindication to find the opposition, abetted by rebellious Jacksonians, again in control.

The first break came on a Whig motion to repeal the Specie Circular. When the proposition was first debated, Rives offered an amendment which was a complete substitute. It converted the resolution into a bill requiring all dues of the government to be paid only in gold or silver or in the notes of specie-paying banks. The further condition was added that these banks, to have their notes accepted, must issue none in denominations less than a prescribed minimum, which was to rise from five to twenty dollars over the next four years. Jackson was furious. He dispatched Blair forthwith to the Senate with an oral message for the Virginia rebel and all those who supported him, but there was no visible change in sentiment.[40]

Rives's bill was referred not to the Committee on Finance, of which the shrewd and utterly loyal Silas Wright was chairman, but to the Committee on Public Lands under Walker of Mississippi. Walker was soon in the camp of the rebels, and so was almost everyone else. Benton and Wright held firm to the end, but the bill passed on February 10, by 41 to 5. Calhoun did not vote because he had no opportunity to explain his reasons, which meant that his vote either way would have been qualified. The bill also passed the House by a thumping majority.[41] It was only two days before the end of the session, however, and Jackson applied another of his infuriating pocket vetoes.[42]

Calhoun's efforts to extend the deposit act to any surplus accruing during 1837 turned the wrath of the administration back in his direction. He had asked reference to a special committee on the explicit ground that Wright's Committee on Finance would be unfavorable. Despite the strong Democratic majority the vote on the referral was a tie, which Van Buren broke in favor of his friend.[43] The administration press, and Benton on the floor of the Senate, then began a series of steady attacks on the South Carolina Senator, charging that by his refusal to abandon the tariff compromise he was deliberately seeking to perpetuate a surplus so that it could be distributed among the states. Yet Calhoun had stated on the floor again and again, and had written publicly and privately, that he much preferred reduction of the revenue to deposit of the surplus; and he stated it once more on January 12, when he agreed to a consideration of the public-land question before his own bill came up. The postponement was to give the Committee on Finance an opportunity to report on reduction of the revenue. Though Calhoun now stood unattached to any party, his influence was so strong that the administration singled him out for special attention.[44]

Churchill C. Cambreleng, meanwhile, who remained chairman of the House Committee on Ways and Means, and who shared with Wright the intimacy and confidence of Van Buren, had introduced on his side of the Capitol a bill to reduce the tariff to a uniform 20 percent, "any thing in the act of 2d of March, 1833, to the contrary notwithstanding." The reduction was to take place in three increments, beginning September 30, 1837 (the governmental fiscal year then began on October 1) and becoming fully effective one year later.[45] Wright's report on reduction of the revenue, presented orally on January 27, followed the same pattern. Clay protested this presumptive violence to the tariff compromise, and Calhoun called on the South to observe the agreement faithfully as long as the manufacturers abided by it. In the subsequent debates Calhoun exposed the dubious parts taken by Wright and Van Buren in the passage of the reprobated act of 1828, and Clay detailed the negotiations that led up to the compromise.[46]

Though Wright proclaimed that the compromise of 1833 was dead, Webster found a "general disposition to leave things, for the present" as they were, and Webster's was the authentic voice of the manufacturing interest. Calhoun spoke with equal authority for the South, and for private consumption he called this tariff reduction move of the two New Yorkers "all a humbug, never intended to be carried into effect. The only object is to weaken and deride the South."[47] Wright's bill, in much modified form, did pass the Senate, but the whole matter was quietly sidetracked in the House.

Calhoun's bill to extend the deposit act to cover any surplus in the Treasury on January 1, 1838, never came out of the Committee on Finance, but the identical provision reappeared three or four days before the end of the session as a rider on a fortification bill from the House of Representatives. After a pungent exchange of doubtful compliments between Calhoun and Wright, the provision was struck out by the Senate. The House disagreed, the Senate held firm, and a conference committee got nowhere at all. So in the final hours of the Congress and of the administration, fortifications and distribution alike were lost.[48]

Clay's land bill fared no better in committee than Calhoun's deposit bill. When the land question came up for debate on January 12, it was Walker's bill to limit sales to actual settlers that was laid before the Senate. For some three weeks it was debated with warmth and vigor until its author on February 3 pronounced it so altered by amendment that he could no longer support it. The next day it was recommitted, but not before Calhoun had blamed the unbridled speculation in lands on the financial policies of the administration and had accused highly placed officials of taking part in it. "Does any man here entertain a doubt that high officers of Government have used [the deposits in the pet banks] as instruments of speculation in the public lands? Is not the fact notorious? Is not one in the immediate neighborhood of the Executive among those most deeply concerned? . . . Is it not well known that several officers in the Departments purchased lands to sell on speculation, with funds officially under their own control?"[49] The land bill reached the floor again on February 7, in revised form. At this point Calhoun remarked that it did no one any good as it was, and offered as a substitute the conditional cession of the public lands to the states in which they lay. The substitute was rejected handsomely, 28 to 7.[50]

The next day was devoted to an official count of the electoral votes for President and Vice President of the United States. There was a wrangle over the vote of Michigan, but it did not matter. Van Buren had a clear majority without it, and Johnson could not muster a majority with it. In the balloting by the Senate for Vice President, Johnson was chosen by 33 votes to 16 for Francis Granger of New York, the leading Whig candidate. The Senate at that time numbered fifty-two members, and all were present. The three who did not vote were Calhoun, Preston, and White.[51] Van Buren, it should be remarked, had paid his farewells to the Senate on January 28, leaving the chair to William R. King of Alabama, the President pro tempore.[52]

Calhoun introduced his land-cession amendment as a separate bill on February 9 and a considerable debate on it took place, with Webster and Clay, his late allies, both opposing. It was on the heels of this debate that the Carolinian took the floor for another purpose.

He had the clerk read a letter received from the President of the United States "within the last forty-eight hours." It was a brusque demand in the well-known Jackson manner that Calhoun either retract his remarks of February 4, implicating the Executive in land speculation, or lay charges before the House so that the President could be tried. The letter quoted the version that appeared in the *Congressional Globe* rather than the more accurate account given by the reporters of the *National Intelligencer,* and was accompanied by two affidavits from spectators testifying to the correctness of the report. Jackson was always fond of affidavits.[53]

Calhoun repeated his charges, and many others he had made against Andrew Jackson over the past five years. His reference to "one in the immediate neighborhood of the Executive" had been to John McLemore, a relative of the President by marriage. Then he bluntly accused the President of a breach of the privilege of the Senate. "I, as a legislator, have a right to investigate and pronounce upon his conduct, and to condemn his acts freely, whenever I consider them to be in violation of the laws and of the constitution. I, as a Senator, may judge him; he can never judge me." Again he was Calhoun the Roman tribune, defying Caesar and warning his people that their liberties were in danger.

There was tension in the Senate when he resumed his seat. Felix Grundy, for twenty-five years a personal friend though often a political foe, was first to break it. He had not understood Calhoun to accuse Jackson personally of speculating, or to say anything exceptionable, and he deplored the "long continued and unhappy differences and misunderstandings" between the President and the Senator from South Carolina. Walker followed with a similar protestation. He had been an attentive listener on the occasion to which the President referred, but had heard nothing uttered by the Senator that could be criticized. No administration supporter denied the breach of privilege, but they preferred to gloss over the incident and so no move was made on the majority side to defend the prerogatives of the Senate. Clay rebuked the Democratic members for it. He could do nothing himself but commend Calhoun's course, but the majority had it in their power to vindicate the independence of the Senate. The challenge met only with the same cowed silence that had accompanied the expunging of a few weeks earlier.[54]

It was on the final day of the Congress that a special House Committee on the Executive Departments presented reports which were printed and widely circulated by way of finis to the Reign. The majority commended the administration and whitewashed Jackson. The minority, consisting of Wise of Virginia, Lincoln of Massachusetts, and Campbell of South Carolina, condemned both with vigor and evident satisfaction. The committee had held hearings over a month's time and had heard statements from twenty-eight witnesses. Calhoun himself had been asked to appear, but had ignored the summons. Pickens had testified, however, and had made sure that Calhoun's views were properly spread on the record. Some witnesses, like Reuben Whitney, whose activities on behalf of the Treasury in connection with the deposit banks were both mysterious and notorious, refused point-blank to come. But the net result was to add an impressive volume of evidence to Calhoun's patronage report of 1835, and to add new names to the list of those whom Jackson called his enemies.[55]

CHAPTER XXII

THE CALHOUN CLAN

1

IT MUST have been in the fall of 1834 that Anna Maria decided to go to Washington. She was then nearing eighteen, a beautiful girl by any standard, clever, lively, and accomplished in all those matters of music, dancing, literature and such that were expected of the daughters of cultured households. In addition, Anna had a deep and thoroughly partisan interest in politics, which her father had nurtured and upon which he looked with considerable pride. It was probably her political rather than her social impulses that prompted her to revisit the Capital, where she had not been since she was a child. Whether she personally engineered the invitation or not we do not know, but certain it is that in ample time for plans to be made Calhoun was urged by Virgil Maxcy to bring his charming daughter with him when he came up for the December meeting of Congress. She could stay with the Maxcys, and Mrs. Maxcy would be responsible for her welfare.

Calhoun declined the invitation. He would not have time to devote to his daughter; she was too young; and all the other excuses were doubtless offered. But Anna had too much of her father's own temperament to be put off when she had made up her mind. She went to Washington, accompanied by Maria Simkins, her schoolmate and daughter of another of Calhoun's lifelong friends. The problem of chaperone was solved with equal ease: her mother was prevailed on to go too.

As things worked out, Anna really preceded her parents. Calhoun had planned to leave Pendleton before mid-November and to make most of the trip by steam, the power that was already revolutionizing the older America. The railroad was in flourishing operation from Hamburg, across the Savannah from Augusta, to Charleston, and from the latter city a line of packet boats went to Norfolk and Baltimore. The whole trip could be made in five or six days. At the last minute, however, urgent business matters arose, and the packet, which sailed only every four weeks, departed without the Calhouns. The next one was not until December 6. Congress would convene on the first, and Anna wanted time to visit some friends in Virginia.

At this point Francis W. Pickens came to the rescue, probably not without prompting from Anna, who was then visiting in the Pickens home at Edgefield. Mrs. Pickens, it should be noted, was the former Eliza Simkins, sister of Anna's school friend. Pickens himself was a cousin of Calhoun's and was highly regarded by the older man, both for his personal qualities and for his considerable political services during the nullification fight. He had now been rewarded with an election to Congress to fill out McDuffie's unexpired term, and he was anxious to be on hand promptly. He offered to take the girls along with him, and the offer was quickly accepted. They were on their way when Calhoun wrote to Maxcy to explain the change of plans, and to place the girls in Mrs. Maxcy's care until Floride's arrival.[1]

It was just as well that Floride had yielded to her daughter's entreaties. Socially the winter of 1834-1835 was one of the gayest the city had known in many years. The lioness of the season was Harriet Martineau, young English authoress and social reformer, who arrived in Washington in the middle of January and remained a total of five weeks. Miss Martineau did not care for Washington, which she found "straggling out hither and thither," with its houses a quarter mile apart. She did not like to "cross ditches and stiles, and walk alternately on grass and pavements." Neither did she like the weather, but the people, even those she did not approve of, she found interesting.[2] Among those who particularly pleased her were Clay and Webster. Calhoun also showed her marked attention, his mess giving her a dinner, and we may be sure that Mrs. Calhoun was in every way a charming hostess.[3] Miss Martineau, it should be explained, was very deaf. She could hear only through a speaking tube, so her conversations were necessarily limited to one person at a time. In the Senate and Supreme Court she watched rather than listened.

There is no reason to believe that Harriet Martineau did not, at the time, reciprocate Calhoun's kind feelings. At least they were often in each other's company, she seemed to others to be pleased with his conversation, and she accepted letters of introduction from him before starting South. It was only after her Southern trip, where she saw nothing good in the system of labor there employed—after her own abolitionist leanings had come to the fore and after Calhoun had come out as the champion of the slave states and of slavery—that her judgment was altered. This is a necessary caution, for the Calhoun she describes in her *Retrospect of Western Travel* (1838) is not the Calhoun she actually knew early in 1835. The man she describes as a "cast-iron man, who looks as if he had never been born and never could be extinguished" is a caricature, so overdrawn that she herself would not have recognized it three years earlier.[4]

2

The Southern plantation in its heyday was the center of social activity as well as the primary unit in the economy of cotton. Fort Hill had rooms to spare, the summer climate was mild and stimulating, and as the children grew up the friendships and the visitors multiplied. It was no more than to be expected that after her first season in Washington Anna Maria would bring some young friend home with her for a visit, nor was it surprising that the guest should be Margaret Green, daughter of the editor whose life seemed dedicated to the task of making Calhoun President. The Calhouns and the Pickenses, including Floride and Anna, Eliza Pickens and her sister Maria Simkins, and the attractive and exuberant Margaret Green, left Washington on the steamboat as soon as Congress adjourned in March of 1835.[5]

It was probably a gay party, for the boat was crowded with Southern members and their ladies, including gallant John Tyler, courtly Willie P. Mangum, and William C. Preston whose extraordinary conversational gifts and great personal charm had not yet been withdrawn from the support of his Senate colleague. The Calhoun party arrived in Norfolk on March 8,[6] proceeding in all probability by boat to Charleston, and thence to Pendleton by rail and stage or private carriage.

The girls stopped off at Edgefield where Pickens lived, and remained until late in April. Andrew, who still made his home in Columbia, passed through Edgefield toward the end of that month and escorted his sister and her friend to Fort Hill.[7]

If Andrew and Margaret had met before, it was only as the children of fathers who were friends and associates in a common cause. This time everything was different. It was spring, for one thing, and spring at Fort Hill was something to be deeply felt and not lightly forgotten. It was more than a year since Eugenia's death, and Andrew was quite normal again. He was probably especially vulnerable at that time and place. Details are meager, but Margaret's visit lengthened out past midsummer, and Andrew still lingered at Fort Hill.[8] The next spring Andrew came to Washington, and they were married there on May 5, 1836.[9] Only four days earlier the bride-to-be had been crowned queen of the annual May-day festival in Georgetown, where she ruled over the 160 girls who took part in the ceremonies.[10]

By summer the young couple were back at Fort Hill, where they were to remain until Andrew could be properly settled as a planter on land of his own. They were still there a year later, when Margaret presented Calhoun with his first grandchild, a boy born late in May 1837. The child died early in the following year.[11]

3

Andrew's marriage took place only two weeks after the death of Floride's mother—hardly a "decent" interval among God-fearing Calvinists. It is possible, of course, that the news did not reach Washington before the wedding. It is certain that it came too late to permit a change of plans without great inconvenience. The old lady's death had been expected for some months. It was because of her infirmity that Floride had not accompanied her husband and daughter to Washington in the winter of 1835-1836, and was therefore not present at the wedding of her eldest son.

Old Mrs. Calhoun was seventy-one when she died, still stalwart in the Presbyterian faith, still ruggedly independent, as erratic and unpredictable as she had ever been, and more than ever obstinate in her vagaries. She was visibly failing by the spring of 1835,[12] but for six months she refused to admit that anything was wrong. Then in late July, when Patrick Noble and Francis W. Pickens were both guests at Fort Hill, she decided to make a will. Of this intention she said not a word to her daughter or son-in-law, but directed Anna Maria to summon James Edward to her presence. It was from Pickens that Calhoun learned what was afoot, and that Noble was to draw up the document. He wrote at once to James urging that he come up immediately. He had no idea what Mrs. Calhoun's intentions were, and so far as he and Floride were concerned any disposition of the property acceptable to the others would be approved. But James knew more about his mother's affairs than anyone else, and he also knew her eccentricities. If he did not come after she had asked for him, that alone might influence her judgment.[13]

James Edward came, completed the business, and took his leave; but the problem of old Mrs. Calhoun was by no means solved. As the fall drew on and the session of Congress approached, Calhoun sent another hurried appeal to his favorite brother-in-law. The old lady was so feeble that he dared not leave her unattended. He had planned to take Floride, Anna, Cornelia, and William with him to Washington, while the older boys went to school at Willington, but it now appeared that John Ewing would be absent much of the winter in the lower country. He saw no solution except that James Edward take his mother to live with him for the period of Calhoun's absence, but he realized that she would probably refuse.[14] She did. So in the end Floride and the younger children stayed home, and the dutiful James probably took up his own quarters at Fort Hill while Calhoun and John Ewing were both away.

Old Mrs. Calhoun died at Cold Spring on April 21, 1836.[15] The will she had so secretively made eight months before was promptly declared invalid, and the distribution of her considerable estate was left entirely in the hands of her three children: John Ewing, extravagant, dissipated, reckless of his own property and that of others; James Edward, abstemious and prudent as Calhoun himself, a skillful manager whose every venture prospered, but whose native shyness kept him out of society and had kept him so far unmarried though he was nearing forty; Floride, gracious and charming most of the time, but stubborn and occasionally unreasonable, quick-tempered, and emotionally unstable, with no adequate scale of values for material things and careless of the value of time.

The estate was still unsettled when fall came around once more, and Calhoun knew that if no understanding were reached before he had to leave for Washington another winter would pass before anything could be done. Land prices meanwhile were rising beyond all semblance of relationship to values, and the panic which he had been predicting for two years past was clearly on its way. Such of the property as they meant to liquidate would have to be disposed of quickly or it could not be done at all. Again Calhoun turned to James Edward, who wisely contrived some kind of an agreement with his brother.[16]

Fort Hill, which he had hitherto merely rented from his mother-in-law, went outright to Calhoun. No doubt this was James Edward's doing, and may well have been a contributing cause of the friction which presently developed between Calhoun and John Ewing, for the property had actually been registered in the latter's name in accordance with his mother's invariable custom.[17] Whatever the background may have been, the whole estate was divided three ways, with Floride's share, including the Fort Hill plantation, actually going to her husband. For a year or more thereafter John Ewing Calhoun did not speak to his brother-in-law, though James Edward and John Caldwell remained as close as they had always been. It was again James Edward who arranged with John Bonneau for the sale of Bonneau's Ferry, old Mrs. Calhoun's Cooper River plantation, while John Ewing drank even more heavily than usual and for a time in mid-1837 appeared to be a hopeless wreck.[18]

4

James Edward Calhoun was far more than his brother-in-law's agent in business matters. He was a personal and political confidant, and was the friend as well as the uncle of Calhoun's children, who loved nothing better than to stay with him for indefinite months. Anna Maria kept house for him on her visits, and teased him unmercifully on his bachelorhood. She called him the "Hermit of Millwood," and insisted that innumerable charming ladies would like nothing better than to take her place as housekeeper, though she was sure none would do a more devoted job.[19] Anna was more pleased than anyone else when early in 1839, at the ripe age of forty-two, Uncle James finally succumbed—the more so as the bride was her own best friend, Maria Simkins.[20]

James Edward seems to have been a man of singular tact. Not only did he have better success than anyone else in curbing the more extravagant whims of his mother; he exerted a similar influence over his sister, and Calhoun often enlisted his aid when Floride was moved to embark on one of her periodic building sprees. One instance is typical of many. In the spring of 1838, while Calhoun was in Washington, Floride wrote from Millwood where she was visiting that she meant to start an addition to Fort Hill as soon as she got home.

Calhoun urged her to wait until he returned to Carolina, but took the wise precaution of writing James at the same time, to solicit his co-operation. "I have long since learned by sad experience," he explained, "what it is to build in my absence. It would cost me twice as much and the work then will not be half as well done."[21]

James Edward numbered among his neighbors in Abbeville District all three of Calhoun's brothers, Armistead Burt whose wife was Calhoun's niece, and George McDuffie, who was close to being a foster son of William Calhoun.[22] With all of these Calhoun kept in close touch, but only his letters to James Edward survive. Almost invariably they contain messages for or references to the others. Whenever he planned to be in Abbeville on business, or to pass through the town on his way to Washington, he would write in advance to James Edward, or to Burt, to make sure that the various members of the clan knew he was coming. Often there would be urgent appeals: he must see his brother William, or brother James, or brother Patrick, but would be in Abbeville only a few hours. It was James Edward's function to round up the desired brother and get him to the appointed place at the designated time.

Most revealing, perhaps, are Calhoun's letters during the first half of 1838, when his younger brother Patrick suffered a breakdown after illness, and for a time appeared to have lost his reason. "Write me fully and early, and let me know in particular how brother Patrick is. . . ."[23] So he instructed Armistead Burt, who lived nearest to the invalid, when he first learned that Patrick was ill. Then in the spring came the breakdown, and talk of an asylum as a last resort. Calhoun made plans to hurry home as quickly as possible, urging meanwhile that Patrick must on no account be locked up unless his mind was completely gone. Such a step would otherwise be too great a cruelty.[24]

Floride had established herself with James Edward to be near by in case of need, and a few days after Calhoun's advice was given his wife wrote hurriedly that the case was indeed hopeless. Calhoun then wrote to Mary, Patrick's wife, and in greater detail to James Edward, his ever-faithful reliance in time of trouble. "I have just received Mrs. Calhoun's letter . . . which has deeply affected me for the condition of my brother Patrick. I have written to Mary, that unless there should be in the meantime some decided change, I think he ought to be sent to the Asylum. I advised her as soon as she receives my letter to send for William & James and come to some immediate decision. I do hope you will ride over as soon as you get this. Your advise and aid may be of great service. Take my brother James in your way. The condition of the family demands consolation & sympathy under so heavy a dispensation.

"I will write you again shortly, when my mind is more at ease. I am too much grieved to touch on any other subject, but that, which has caused this communication. . . ."[25]

It took both courage and a complete disregard of self for a man of Calhoun's political prominence—a man who still hoped to be elected President of the United States—to advertise to the world that he had a mentally unbalanced brother; yet that is precisely what his advice to put Patrick in the asylum meant. Fortunately for all concerned, it proved unnecessary. Miraculously, Patrick began to improve and by midsummer there was hope, though it was the spring of 1839 before complete restoration of his faculties was assured.[26]

One or another of Calhoun's brothers and their families were often among the guests who usually filled the beautiful white-pillared mansion to overflowing from the time its owner returned from Washington each spring or summer until he left again for a new session of Congress as winter approached. Other relatives included Nobles and Pickenses and Burts, and Calhouns of varied generations and pursuits. There were always young people about, for Calhoun was especially fond of their society. His own children were in and out, and as they grew older they collected their own friends and brought them home. The young people of the neighborhood came, too, at first perhaps with their parents, but presently on their own: Sloans and Lewises and Simpsons and Adamses and a dozen others. Often of an evening the rug would be rolled up in the spacious parlor and the young people would dance, while one of their number played the piano or perhaps one of the Negroes fiddled or strummed on a banjo or guitar.

5

As the Calhoun children grew up, they came to hold a larger and larger place in their father's world. He was never too busy to enter into their games and their studies, never too preoccupied with politics to weigh and consider the individual affairs of his sons and daughters, to acquaint himself with their friends, to promote in every way he could their happiness. Children and young people trusted him instinctively and felt at ease in his presence. He never talked down to them, or patronized them, or regarded their interests with disdain.

At the time of Andrew's second marriage the youngest of the children was not yet seven years old. On formal occasions he was called by his full name, William Lowndes, but mostly his brothers and sisters, the neighbors, his mother, and even his father called him Willie. James Edward, at ten, was Willie's most frequent companion, next to Dave Sloan on the adjoining plantation, and both of them showed a great partiality for their Uncle James Edward, with whom they visited at every opportunity. James was usually called "Junior" to distinguish him from that same uncle, and even his father's letters to him are so addressed. John Caldwell, on the other hand, though legitimately entitled to a junior after his name, was rarely so designated. In the family he was always Johnny. Three years older than James and two years younger than Pat, Johnny usually consorted with the older brother rather than the younger. All of the boys had their initial schooling at Pendleton Academy.

Youngest of the two surviving girls was Martha Cornelia, always called in the family by her middle name. She was twelve in 1836, a year younger than Johnny and two years older than James. Partially crippled from infancy, she received her education at the hands of tutors, with her sister Anna Maria carrying not a little of the burden. There is no doubt that Cornelia was indulged and petted by the whole family. She became a voracious reader, largely because she could not play as other children did, and so she was always given first choice of the papers and periodicals that came into the house.[27] Lest she become introverted and warped, she was made part of the social life of Fort Hill to the extent of her powers, and as soon as she was old enough to enjoy it, her father took her frequently to Washington with him.

Calhoun never gave up hope that Cornelia might be cured, and he spent much time and money in the search for specialists. In the winter of 1837-1838 he found a doctor in Baltimore who thought the girl's crooked spine could be straightened, and he wrote forthwith to Anna to bring her younger sister to Washington as soon as possible. For a time there was improvement, and Cornelia submitted to the treatment for a solid year, but there was no permanent cure.[28]

Patrick, second to Andrew among the boys but nearly ten years younger, was sixteen just before Van Buren's inauguration. At Calhoun's request the South Carolina delegation in Congress recommended the boy for an appointment to West Point. As soon as the new Secretary of War, Joel R. Poinsett of South Carolina, was installed, Calhoun wrote personally to ask the first favor he had ever sought in connection with the institution he had done so much to foster. A political enmity of ten years' standing between the two men was forgotten on both sides, and Pat entered the Academy in the summer of 1837.[29] He moved at once to the head of his class, and in the spring of 1838, when Anna and Cornelia were both in Washington, Calhoun managed through Poinsett to get his son a leave of absence to visit the Capital. Anna was allowed to write the young cadet of his good fortune. She quoted their father that the trip was a reward for good behavior. It had been under negotiation for some time, but Anna and Cornelia had been sworn to secrecy until everything was sure and the proper papers had been signed.[30] Nowhere was there any hint of reproach, but only praise for scholastic accomplishment and affection for a son and brother. Yet Calhoun and Anna both knew that Patrick, on holiday in New York the previous winter, had shown a taste for night life and a lack of skill at cards; and that he had borrowed freely from a cousin of his mother's, J. E. Boisseau, a New York commission merchant, to pay his debts.[31] There would be many such occasions in the future, but from Calhoun at least there would never be reproach or blame.

After that date—indeed, from 1835 on—there was scarcely a session of Congress when one or another of the Calhoun children was not in Washington. Their father loved them all, urged them to write to him, schemed and devised to work in visits from them without interfering with their schooling; but of them all it was Anna Maria whose presence gave him the greatest pleasure.

6

Between Anna Maria and her father there was a rare bond of sympathy, an extraordinary degree of understanding, which deepened and broadened with the years. After her first visit to Washington in the winter of 1834-1835, Calhoun was never completely happy unless Anna was with him. When they parted they wrote long and gossipy letters to each other, letters filled with advice and personal detail, but filled also with politics and philosophy and humor. It was often on

Anna that Calhoun relied to persuade or coax or cajole her mother or her brothers into doing what he wanted done. It was Anna who tramped or rode with him over the damp red earth of the fields in the early morning, as the corn on the bottoms and the upland cotton ripened for the harvest; Anna who sat in the Senate gallery when his great speeches were delivered; Anna who filed and preserved his correspondence, who sprang to his side when he was under attack, who nursed him when he was ill. Her mind was a feminine duplicate of his. More than anyone else in the family, it was Anna who understood him and his ideals. More than anyone else on earth she worshiped John C. Calhoun, and he adored her as men rarely love their daughters.

After Andrew's wedding it was not the bride and groom but Anna Maria who went to Niagara Falls. When the session of Congress was over, she had embarked on a tour of the Northern States for her own enlightenment. With what companions and chaperones we do not know, but she could have covered remote byways and still never have been far from one or more of her father's friends. She was delighted with the whole trip, but especially so with the Falls.[32] We may be sure, also, that her visit served in some measure a useful purpose. The slavery controversy was at its furious peak, and pamphlets were issuing almost daily from New York and New England presses branding all Southern women as licentious and degraded, in mind as well as morals. It was undoubtedly good for Northern politicians who wavered on the slavery issue to see and talk to a genuine Southern woman.

After Anna's return to South Carolina she visited for a time with her Uncle James Edward at Millwood; then went again to Washington for the last and most subservient session of Congress under Andrew Jackson. She found Washington society dull that winter. As her father's daughter she was excluded from administration circles where, as she informed her uncle, the "ugly and disagreeable" Miss Blair was much courted.[33] Anna's humor was of the puckish variety, for everyone knew—even bachelor Uncle James in the South Carolina hinterland—that Elizabeth Blair was the reigning beauty of Washington. Anna took comfort from a rumor that Blair would be turned out when Van Buren became President, but it was all in good fun. She did not aspire to be a belle in the nation's Capital, but only to be herself—which was to say a carbon copy of her father.

In that she succeeded very well; and she presently outdid Miss Blair in a romantic way, also.

Anna did not accompany her father to the special session of 1837, nor did she go with him for the opening of the regular session in December, being then at Millwood housekeeping for her Uncle James. Calhoun wrote her a full account of his trip on his arrival: how a foot of snow had fallen during the night after he left Raleigh, and how beautiful it was. "Every twig & branch was burthened with a weight of snow, heaped up the whole length 3 or 4 inches high. The pine bushes looked like white masses, piled up like hay stacks. . . ." But at Gaston, North Carolina, where he had planned to take the railroad, he found the trains unable to move against the drifts of snow across the tracks.[34] Upon his somewhat delayed arrival in Washington Calhoun went first to Brown's Indian Queen Hotel, and his impulse was to remain there. He missed the companionship of a mess, however, and within a week or so had moved to Mrs. Page's boardinghouse on the Avenue, opposite the Centre Market. There a small mess was formed with John Campbell, one of the South Carolina representatives, Mrs. Campbell, her sister, and a protégée, "Miss Lee, of Leesburgh," who was also a friend of Anna's.[35]

But the mess was dull, and the austere, reserved South Carolinian, who seemed to some of his contemporaries to have no emotions, was desperately lonely. Before Christmas he wrote to Anna that he missed both her and her friend Maria Simkins. "You must both come on in the spring and have our old family Mess reconstituted. It was the most pleasant I ever had. . . ." And on January 1, perhaps while the party men were milling around at Van Buren's first New Year's levee, Calhoun wrote again, with greater urgency. He wanted Anna to "come on with Francis" (Pickens) if he had not already left. He was sure she would find Washington more pleasant than Millwood, and her presence would "add much to my happiness." He would manage the expense somehow. By that time Calhoun was aware of the serious nature of his brother Patrick's illness, which was probably the reason for Anna's continued residence at Millwood; so he left the final choice to her own sense of duty, but he made unmistakably clear what he wanted. "I feel deeply the pain of absence from you. . . ."[36] There was further delay while Anna arranged for her mother to take her place at Millwood, but early in April Anna was in Washington.[37]

It was probably immediately after her arrival that she met Thomas

Green Clemson. Clemson was then thirty-one years old, with dark wavy hair and dark eyes that looked far away. He was handsome by the standards of his time, and striking if only because he stood a good six feet six inches tall, but it was probably none of these things that attracted Anna Calhoun. It was more likely that she saw through the passionless shell of intellectual preoccupation, so like her father's own, to the genius and vitality and vision that lay beneath. Clemson was a mining engineer, trained at the famous French School of Mines, and he was also a chemist of no mean ability. His business in Washington was to confer with Dr. Lewis F. Linn, United States Senator from Missouri. Late in 1837 Linn, Clemson, and two other partners had bought the LaMotte lead mine in Missouri, and Clemson was to examine the property in the spring of 1838.

It was in April that he left for the West, not intending to return. He could have seen little of Anna in three weeks at most, but he had seen enough. He was back in a month or two, ostensibly to help his partners raise money. There was a sentimental parting early in July when Anna left with her father for Fort Hill. Then ardent letters followed the twenty-one-year-old girl to her home, and by mid-August Clemson was complaining with all the bitter impatience of a lover that it had been a long six weeks since he had seen her, that he had written near a dozen letters in that time, and he had heard from her not one word in answer. He heard eventually, however, and the wedding was set for November 13, 1838.[38]

The ceremony was performed at Fort Hill on the evening of the appointed day by the Reverend William T. Potter of the Episcopal Church in Pendleton.[39] It was a gala affair, with friends and neighbors and members of the Calhoun clan from miles around among the guests. Andrew and Margaret were there, and so were Duff Green and his wife, who were on their way to Florida. The Greens, whose residence was now in Baltimore, probably brought Cornelia with them. She had been left in their charge when Calhoun and Anna had set out for South Carolina in July because she was still under the care of her Baltimore physician.[40] Calhoun's brother William, at least, was there,[41] and presumably James also, though Patrick was still too ill to travel. Floride's brothers, of course, were present, with scores of cousins and kinfolk of indefinite degree.

The young couple departed shortly for Philadelphia; Calhoun and Floride were off to Washington before the end of the month; and in

December the plantation was deserted completely when the boys went to spend Christmas, and as much more time as they could get away with, at Millwood with Uncle James.[42]

Anna's marriage in no way altered her relationship to her father. She was, to be sure, less often with him, but she wrote with the same intimacy and freedom. Her thinking continued to follow his pattern, and her life to be ordered by his standards. Her personality was an extension of his, and without conscious effort her adoration was communicated to her husband, although his also was a strong personality and an independent, even at times a truculent, nature. Though Pennsylvania born and bred, and trained in Europe, Clemson became wholly Southern in feeling and sympathy as well as residence, and in due time would place his great abilities at the service of the Confederacy.

7

It was in the winter of 1834-1835 that Calhoun first contemplated retiring from public life to devote himself exclusively to his "domestick duties," by which term he comprehended all his other interests in so far as they bore on the problem of increasing his means and making it easier to launch seven children in careers of their own. It was probably the abolitionists who kept him in the Senate, finally. He was undoubtedly sincere when he explained to his cousin Francis Pickens in the summer of 1835 why he had decided to attend another session of Congress, in spite of his personal inclinations. The "ambitious impulses" of his earlier life, he insisted, had long since subsided. He saw no personal gain, but rather loss, in his return to Washington; yet he felt himself to be the only barrier between the South and the onslaughts of the abolitionists. Let the South submit, so he believed, and she would eventually be abandoned to the blacks. On that issue he saw no Southern leader ready or able to take his place. He saw rather many able public men who would inevitably contest with one another for the mantle as it slipped from his shoulders, and he feared that in their personal rivalry the cause would fail.[43] The Pinckney resolutions of the following winter showed how well-founded his fear was.

Calhoun devoted himself to his nonpolitical interests, building up his affairs as though he would indeed be able to give them full attention in the course of another year or two. He continued to experiment at Fort Hill with crops and fertilizers, to combat droughts and floods, erosion and soil exhaustion. He was late to the meeting of Congress in the winter of 1837-1838 because he had lost his overseer and he would not leave until everything was again in running order.[44] In Washington early in 1838 he procured some Siberian spring wheat, which he sent to James Edward with instructions for planting.[45] In recognition of his achievements in agriculture over a period of years he was elected in the fall of 1839 president of the Pendleton Farmers' Society.[46]

Through Missisippi friends in Congress Calhoun learned of the successful manufacture in that state of cottonseed oil, and when he returned from Washington in the spring of 1837 he brought full details with him, which he turned over to James Edward. James studied the process, and at his request Calhoun procured an oil press from the North the following winter.[47] In the spring of 1838 he ran across a Philadelphian, skilled in the manufacture of cotton and in the handling of textile machinery, who contemplated settling in the South. Calhoun sent the man to James Edward, to McDuffie, and to other Southern friends. The depression had brought down the price of machinery and of skilled labor, and he conceived the time propitious for setting up such enterprises in his native state.[48] Again, in the fall of 1839, at Calhoun's instigation, Clemson studied the operation of an iron works near Clarksville, Georgia, and James Edward began prospecting for iron ore on recently acquired mountain lands along the Tupelo River.[49]

Through the same period Calhoun was extending his own holdings in the Georgia gold region around Dahlonega, and was increasing the scale of his operations. He had first interested himself in gold mining in September 1832 when Andrew had purchased an interest in the O'Bar mine, in what later became Lumpkin County. The transactions are obscure, but the property was apparently reconveyed to its original owner later in the same year. At least the tract as a whole, consisting of some 239 acres, was sold for six thousand dollars to David C. Gibson late in November 1832. On July 25, 1833, Calhoun repurchased the O'Bar mine from Gibson for the original purchase price.[50] There is a record of no further acquisition, nor of any serious mining operations, until 1835. In May and December of that year, and in September 1836, Calhoun added small tracts to his total, two of them

ANNA CALHOUN CLEMSON
probably by De Block

THOMAS G. CLEMSON

GEORGE McDUFFIE

FRANCIS W. PICKENS

FRANKLIN H. ELMORE

by way of sheriff's sales.[51] The really important purchase was made in September 1835. On that occasion he bought out one of three partners "in the best lot of all in the gold region." This lot was about twenty acres, crossed by a rich vein which entered the main deposit near the center of the property. The vein had been worked on a small scale for two years, and without the use of machinery had yielded an annual average of five hundred pennyweights, or twenty-five Troy ounces, of gold to the hand. Calhoun saw no reason why the yield should not be progressively better as the main deposit was approached. "The lot is completely cleared & prepared for operation & I take possession & go into profitable operation at once with experienced miners & tried overseers. I gave $4,000 to be paid out of the proceeds of the mine, and can furnish my quota (20 hands) without diminishing my crop here next year. . . ." Calhoun's partners in the venture were Colonel F. Carter and Captain Clay.[52]

It was at Calhoun's invitation that G. W. Featherstonhaugh, well-known British geologist, visited the Georgia gold region in the late summer of 1837, and later made a general mineralogical survey of the Carolina mountain area.[53]

8

Calhoun was known as a competent businessman, who met his obligations punctually, never speculated or gambled, and never assumed financial obligations for others except members of his own family. The family, however, was large; and as the children grew up and married, they proved to be a heavy drain on his resources. He once said, toward the close of his career, that he allowed each of his children a "portion" of seven thousand dollars when they settled in life;[54] and so far as the records of his dealings are available this appears to be substantially correct, although that sum was not always directly bestowed.

The first heavy drain on his resources came in the late 1830's following the marriages of Andrew and Anna Maria. The proceeds from his most profitable Georgia mine holdings were committed to the payment of his investment in the property, so that his only real source of income at that time was his farm and his inheritance from his mother-in-law. The property acquired from old Mrs. Calhoun's estate appears to have been liquidated as promptly as possible,[55] and it was probably the source from which he drew the sums spent on Andrew's account. The whole situation was complicated by the panic of 1837 and the subsequent prolonged depression. Calhoun's resources were not equal to Andrew's needs, and in the end it was Thomas Clemson who came to the rescue. From that time forward intra-family debts were a fruitful source of friction.

After his marriage Andrew spent the better part of three years locating suitable lands on which to set up for himself as a planter. Fort Hill was his base of operations, with Margaret dividing her time between the Calhoun farm and her father's home in Baltimore. For a time Andrew considered emigrating to Texas, and probably visited the Lone Star Republic, but he eventually abandoned the notion. He spent much time in Alabama, where Calhoun urged him to buy, and was in that state when his first-born child died.[56] By the fall of 1838 he had become discouraged with the prospects west of the mountains and had begun to explore his own native state, being careful not to locate too close to his father's place.[57] Almost immediately thereafter, however, the precise thing he sought became available in Marengo County, Alabama, and he seized upon it. The plantation was called "Cane Brake," and the price was twenty thousand dollars. There was no time to lose if Andrew was to get a crop in before the spring planting season of 1839 ended. Clemson raised the money in Philadelphia on a short-term note for which he pledged the joint credit of Calhoun, Andrew, and himself; and Calhoun probably supplied the necessary cotton hands, mules, and equipment out of the Fort Hill complement. The deal was closed in March 1839.[58]

A recession, meanwhile, following a partial economic recovery after the panic of 1837, had once more strained private credit to the breaking point as new and heavy pressure was put on the money market. The Calhouns had undoubtedly meant to substitute a long-term note, negotiated in South Carolina, for the note Clemson had given in Philadelphia, but they were unable to raise the necessary funds. Toward the end of April, with the due date approaching, Calhoun was frantic. "It is of the utmost importance," he wrote to his son-in-law, "that the note should not be protested. My publick station, and the relation I bear to the banking question, much more than even my private credit, make it essential that our engagement should be met; and I would rather submit to any sacrifice, than to fail to take up the note."[59]

The loan had probably been negotiated with the Bank of the United States of Pennsylvania, and the wily Biddle would have liked nothing better than to get a financial hold over the foremost champion of the Independent Treasury. Clemson did not need Calhoun's prompting to see the potentialities of the situation, and somehow raised the money on his own credit, leaving Andrew Calhoun, or Andrew and his father jointly, indebted to him for twenty thousand dollars before he had been in the family six months.[60]

The Calhouns had meanwhile returned to Fort Hill as soon as Congress adjourned in March 1839, coming by steam packet from Baltimore to Charleston to make the trip as easy as possible for Cornelia.[61] The trip took less than three days, despite six hours lost between tides while the vessel was stuck on a sand bar off the Carolina coast. Floride and Cornelia seem to have taken the voyage as a matter of course, but Calhoun felt called on to boast on his own account to Anna that he had lost only one meal, and had "the prospect of making a sailor at last."[62] The journey was completed by railroad to Aiken, the nearest point on the line, where one of the Fort Hill Negroes met them with carriage and horses.

It was shortly after their return that Clemson was offered the position of State Geologist by the Governor of Pennsylvania. Calhoun advised him to take the place, both for the four-thousand-dollar salary it paid and for the professional advancement it promised, and he thought Clemson was inclined to do so.[63] Nothing came of it, however, and by May Calhoun was advising his son-in-law as to the purchase of "a gang of negroes," clearly indicating the intention of the young couple to settle in the South.[64]

The Clemsons were at Fort Hill in the summer of 1839 and shared with the Calhoun family one of the worst outbreaks of fever the district had known. Only Floride, Johnny, and Cornelia escaped. Patrick was so ill that for a time his life was despaired of; but it was Anna who fared worst. Already ill with fever, she gave birth to a daughter on August 13, and was herself barely out of danger when the child died three weeks later.[65]

When Calhoun left for Washington in November, Clemson accompanied him as far as Charleston, while Anna and Floride went to Millwood to stay for a time with James Edward and Maria. It was shortly thereafter that Clemson settled his affairs in Pennsylvania and took over the active management of the Fort Hill plantation.[66]

CHAPTER XXIII

THE LOUISVILLE, CINCINNATI AND CHARLESTON RAILROAD

1

ALTHOUGH his fear of consolidation had long since led Calhoun to abandon his earlier championship of internal improvements by the Federal Government, even for military purposes, he never abandoned his earlier conviction that the hope of permanent union lay in easy and rapid communication and commercial intercourse among the various sections of the nation. As the fury of canal building subsided with the practical success of the railroad in the early 1830's, Calhoun, like many of his contemporaries, began to think in terms of railroads rather than turnpikes and inland waterways; but the purposes to be served and the routes to be followed remained in his mind essentially as he had outlined them in 1819.[1] When a project for connecting Charleston and Cincinnati by rail took shape in 1835, he hailed it joyfully, but he was already far ahead of those who planned the venture.

The possibility of a railroad connection with the West, using inclined planes and stationary engines to supplement the mobile power of the locomotives in crossing the mountains, had been under consideration for some time. Various tentative routes between Charleston and the Ohio River had been roughly surveyed in 1832 by Colonel Stephen H. Long of the Topographical Engineers, and delegates from Tennessee and the two Carolinas had met to consider the matter in the fall of that year.[2] In October 1833 the tracks of the South Carolina Railroad were brought into Hamburg, opposite Augusta on the Savannah River. The question of a branch line to Columbia, which would be a key point on any transmontane route, was being seriously agitated when a rail connection between Charleston and Cincinnati was again proposed, this time by citizens of the Ohio city.[3]

After preliminary investigation to determine the feasibility of the route—probably amounting to no more than an examination of Colonel Long's map—the Cincinnati group formally proposed the project to the citizens of Charleston. The Charleston Chamber of Commerce referred it to a special committee of its own, which reported favorably.[4] The newspapers at both ends began to play it up and to associate with it as many distinguished names as possible. In Charleston a committee of fifteen, with Robert Y. Hayne at its head, was named to consider ways and means. A similar group in Cincinnati was headed by Whig Presidential candidate William Henry Harrison.[5]

Calhoun took no part in these early moves for a railroad through the mountains, but he was nevertheless taking active steps to connect the South and the West by rail. In February of 1835 he had presented to the Senate his report calling for a constitutional amendment to permit distribution of the surplus revenue among the states until the tariff should reach its minimum under the compromise act of 1833. He had not specified at the time that he expected the Southern and Western states to use the money that would thus be placed at their disposal for railroad building, but such was the universal belief. Calhoun publicly expressed that view later in the year;[6] and anyone who doubted that such would be the case need only have followed the persevering last-ditch opposition of the New York delegation to the whole distribution scheme to be fully convinced. New York had no thought of sharing the rich commerce of the West, then flowing to her wharves through the Great Lakes and the Erie Canal, with Charleston or any other city.

The use to which the money would be put, if the surplus were actually distributed, was undoubtedly clear in Calhoun's mind before he proposed the measure. Each state would have a share. Each would have money to invest. Why should they not work together to tighten their own bonds of union? He had once proposed to use the Bank dividends and bonus for this purpose. He would now use the surplus revenue and thus make the tariff itself contribute in the end to the benefit of the South. He had intended to broach the question in the summer of 1835, preparatory to waging a fight for distribution at the next session of Congress, when the dangerous turn taken by the antislavery agitation led him to concentrate all his energies in that quarter for the time being.[7]

For the details of his railroad project Calhoun probably recurred to his own report on roads and canals made early in his War Department days. His mind was orderly and comprehensive. He saw things not as fragments but as wholes; and the agitated connection between

Charleston and Cincinnati, whatever route it followed, could never be more than a fragment in the great network of transportation lines he envisaged. This network, save that railroads dominated over canals, river channels, and highways, came very close to the scheme he had proposed in 1819, which had in its turn been an extension and modification of Albert Gallatin's program of 1808.

The essence of Calhoun's earlier proposal for a system of military roads and canals, disregarding the intracoastal waterway and the Maine to Louisiana highway which had no bearing on the present problem, had been three main east-west routes, linking the Hudson with the Great Lakes, the Chesapeake Bay area with the Ohio River, and the Charleston-Augusta area with the Tennessee River. West of the Appalachians these routes were to be supplemented and continued by a canal from Lake Michigan to the Illinois River, which would connect the Great Lakes with the Mississippi, and a road from New Orleans to the Tennessee. Since this plan first had been advanced in 1819, the northern route had become a reality by completion of the Erie Canal, and railroads were already pushing out toward Lake Erie from both New York and Albany. The central route was served by the National Road, over which freight passed in five days between Baltimore and Cincinnati; and this was rapidly being supplemented by the Chesapeake and Ohio Canal, already advanced as far as Williamsport, and by the Baltimore and Ohio Railroad which was in operation as far as Harpers Ferry. On the southern route, however, only the Charleston and Hamburg railroad was functioning. There were also short, unconnected sections of rail lines operating in Georgia, but these had been deliberately built on a narrower gauge than the South Carolina road.

Calhoun proposed to carry the Charleston and Hamburg line across the Savannah to Augusta, join the scattered sections of Georgia railroads into a single standard-gauge line, which would cross the Tennessee River near Lookout Mountain and proceed from there to Nashville. From the Tennessee metropolis a rail line was to follow the Cumberland River to its mouth, cross the Ohio in that vicinity, and proceed thence by two branches, one north to Lake Michigan, one northwest to the Mississippi opposite the mouth of the Missouri. Cincinnati would be reached by a separate branch from Nashville; and another branch, from the head of navigation on the Tennessee, would proceed to Memphis, where it would join a road already under construction from New Orleans. Still another branch was to cross Georgia to Columbus, where it would join projected roads from Montgomery and Pensacola.[8]

When the Cincinnati project came to popular focus in the summer of 1835 Calhoun wrote to John S. Williams, one of the prominent sponsors of the movement in the Ohio city, to praise the idea of connecting the Western country with the South Atlantic ports, and to outline his own grandiose plan: "the most important and magnificent work in the world."[9] Williams answered by sending a pamphlet describing the project developed in Cincinnati. The route followed as straight a line as the terrain would permit between the two terminal cities, crossing the mountains through the valley of the French Broad River, near Asheville, North Carolina. Calhoun replied that he had supposed this route impractical because of the formidable nature of the mountains, but if it were feasible from an engineering point of view, he saw much to recommend it—not as a substitute, however, but as a supplement to the route he had in mind.[10] With the panic still a year and a half away, and the prospect of an annual windfall from the Federal Government in the form of a share of the surplus until 1843, he was probably justified in seeing no reason why both roads should not be built.

None of this altered in the least his conviction that the "true direction will be to extend the Athens [Georgia] railroad to the head of steam navigation on the Tennessee; and thence to Cincinnati."[11] It was a conviction resting not alone on the fact that it was easier to turn the end of a mountain chain than to cut across it at its highest point. The road so built would not be an end in itself, but an integral link in a larger plan. He would make Charleston the ocean terminus not merely for the commercial region centering around Cincinnati, or even especially for that, but rather for the remoter West whose multiplying commerce then wound its tortuous way through the Great Lakes to New York or floated down the Mississippi to New Orleans and made the hazardous detour to Europe around the tip of Florida.

2

The citizens' committee under Hayne's able and energetic leadership made excellent progress. With five thousand dollars appropriated to its use by the Charleston City Council, James Gadsden, A. H. Bris-

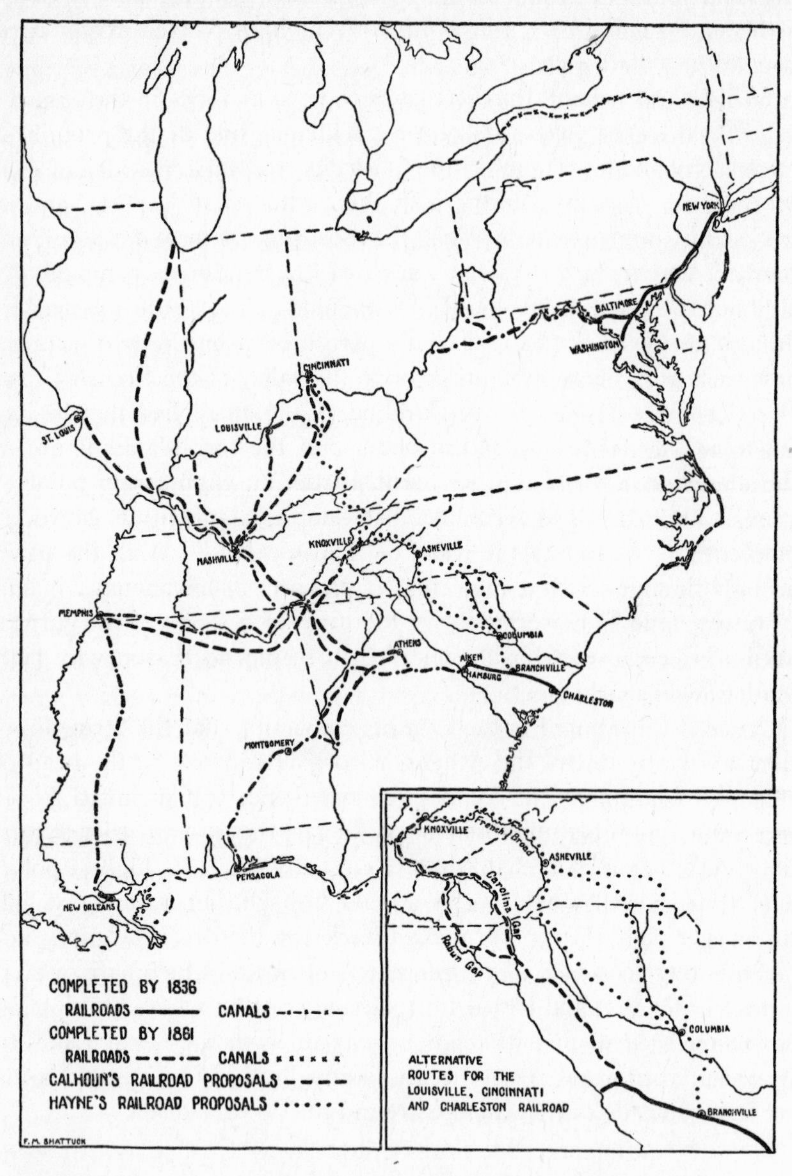

MAP SHOWING MAJOR RAILROAD CONNECTIONS BETWEEN SOUTH AND WEST AS PROPOSED BY CALHOUN IN 1835 AND AS ACTUALLY BUILT BEFORE THE CIVIL WAR.

bane, and James G. Holmes—among the most distinguished engineers in the state—were hired to examine the projected route of the railroad. When the legislature met in December, a survey was officially authorized and ten thousand dollars were appropriated to finance it, under the direction of a commission whose members included Hayne, Patrick Noble, and Abraham Blanding. At the same time an act of incorporation was passed, chartering the Cincinnati and Charleston Rail Road Company, with a capital stock of six million dollars. The company was to be organized whenever stock to the value of four million dollars had been subscribed, the books to be opened the third Monday in October 1836. There were to be twenty-four directors, three each to be chosen from among the stockholders in the states of Ohio, Kentucky, Tennessee, North Carolina, and South Carolina, and nine to be selected at large.[12]

Under prodding from the South Carolina commissioners, the legislatures of North Carolina and Tennessee passed similar acts, but the Kentucky legislature attached conditions. The road must pass through Lexington, and both Louisville and Maysville were to be served by branch lines. Kentucky insisted, moreover, that she be given six members of the Board of Directors instead of three. The South Carolina sponsors did not like it but had no choice in the matter. They acceded, and the road was chartered as the Louisville, Cincinnati and Charleston Rail Road Company.[13]

These preliminaries out of the way, the South Carolina engineers were joined by others lent by the War Department, and the detailed survey was begun in April 1836. It was notable, however, that no other state joined South Carolina in providing funds for the reconnaissance.[14]

While the survey was still in progress a convention was arranged to meet in Knoxville on July 4, 1836, where representatives of all of the interested states could pool their ideas and come to a working agreement as to plans. It was to this convention that the South Carolina commissioners submitted their report.

The composition and procedure of the Knoxville convention at once revealed some of the stresses underlying the project. There were some 380 delegates altogether, 81 of them from South Carolina, but only 6 from Ohio where the whole movement originated. Georgia, which would not be served at all by the road as conceived in Cincinnati, sent almost as many delegates as Kentucky and considerably more than

North Carolina. Tennessee, which straddled any route that might be chosen and was the scene of the meeting, accounted for a third of the total number; but there were scattering representatives from Virginia, Alabama, and Indiana, all far removed from the contemplated route.[15]

Temporary chairman was former Senator John Williams from the host city, whose career had been chiefly notable for his steady opposition to Andrew Jackson; but the permanent president was Robert Y. Hayne, whose old opponent of the nullification days, Joel R. Poinsett, was also among the delegates from South Carolina. There were those who believed the presidency of the convention would have gone to Calhoun, had he been able to attend;[16] but he did the cause perhaps greater service by remaining at his post in Washington to see the distribution bill through Congress.

The report of the South Carolina commissioners, summarizing the engineering surveys, was the major business of the convention. Only the most difficult parts of the proposed route had been examined by instrument, and that only to the extent of ascertaining if a practicable grade could be achieved. The failure of the states other than South Carolina to provide funds for the work had necessarily kept it to an irreducible minimum. According to the commissioners' report, however, the engineers were unanimous in approving the passage of the mountains by way of the French Broad River and the Cumberland Gap. After reference to a committee of forty-five, which reported favorably, the delegates also gave their unanimous approval to this route, qualifying it, however, to the extent of approving branch lines that would carry the road into Georgia, Alabama, Virginia, and Indiana.[17]

When it was all over Hayne appealed eloquently for financial support, resting his case as he had from the start on the necessity for breaking down sectional barriers; but it was his subsequent toast to the South and West that revealed the clue to his thinking. "We have published the banns—if anyone know aught why these two should not be joined together, let him speak now, or forever hold his peace."[18] It was the old project for a political alliance of the South and West: a project that went back to the election of 1828, lay at the bottom of the Webster-Hayne debate, and formed an essential part of the background for the fight against the tariff and for the quarrel between Jackson and Calhoun. The wedding had never quite come off, for every time a day had been set Martin Van Buren had cozened the sturdy bride with promises and presents, and the groom, surrounded by his retinue of slaves, had been left waiting at the church.

This time Hayne proposed to try community of interest instead of horse trading, but it still remained to be seen how deeply the interest of either section was actually involved in the Louisville, Cincinnati and Charleston Railroad. Only the port of Charleston and its hinterland would benefit commercially in the South, even if the freight from Cincinnati proved equal to expectations. The remoter but expanding West would probably continue to seek its markets through the Mississippi or the Lakes, to the commercial benefit of New Orleans and New York. And once the B & O had crossed the Alleghenies, no sentiment on earth would keep the exportable produce of the Ohio valley from the wharves of Baltimore.

3

On a clear day one could stand on the terrace in front of the north portico of Fort Hill and see in the distance the long, jagged line of the Blue Ridge Mountains. With a glass it was possible to discern the outlines of the valleys whence foaming streams emerged to become the familiar rivers of the uplands: the Tugaloo, the Keowee, the Saluda. Calhoun often studied the southeastern rim of the Appalachian rampart in this way, and from the peculiar formation of the mountains just a compass point west of north he judged there must be a passage through the ridge. He talked of it from time to time with men he met from the mountain country, both Carolinians and Georgians. He found many who had heard of such a gap; he even found a few who had been through it, and who told him it could be reached by following one of the westerly branches of the Keowee.

When the railroad to Cincinnati was under discussion in 1835 Calhoun naturally thought of this mountain pass, which he called the Carolina Gap to distinguish it from the Rabun or Georgia Gap a little to the west of it, but he made no point of it because he thought the preferable course for the road would be a wide curve through upper Georgia to the Tennessee. When the engineers began their survey of possible mountain routes, however, he thought this pass too should be explored. A hasty reconnaissance was made of the Rabun Gap, which was summarily pronounced inferior to the French Broad route, but the Carolina Gap was not surveyed. The nearest approach to it was a trip to the vicinity made by Hayne and Captain Williams of the Topographical Engineers in May of 1836. They found no practical route, but Calhoun insisted that they had not been guided to the proper spot.[19]

When the Knoxville convention chose the French Broad route without a dissenting vote, Calhoun was suspicious and alarmed. He did not believe, in spite of the commissioners' report with its bland assertion of unanimity on the part of the engineers, that the mountains could be successfully passed at that point. Even if they could, who was to say until the survey had been made that it could not be more easily and cheaply done by way of the Carolina Gap? Calhoun was undoubtedly aware that Colonel Gadsden had some doubts that had not been alluded to by the commissioners, and had withdrawn from the survey.[20] Certainly it was not solely a wish to oblige that brought Gadsden to Pendleton early in September where he joined Calhoun and Colonel William Sloan for a personal exploration of the Carolina Gap.[21] The examination only confirmed Calhoun's suspicion that the original selection of the French Broad route had been due to local pressure rather than to topographical suitability. He believed, in short, that the stockholders and the state were about to be made the victims of an economically unsound railroad, when a sound one could just as well be built, and he prepared to bring the matter out into the open.

In a long and detailed letter to the editor of the Pendleton *Messenger*—his friend Frederick W. Symmes, who also represented Pendleton in the state legislature—he described the Carolina Gap route and its advantages over the passage by the French Broad. The route followed the White Water, a tributary of the Keowee, to its source, crossed a divide to the headwaters of the Tuckasegee, and descended that stream to its junction with the Little Tennessee. If the grade were not too steep, or the obstacles to laying the road otherwise insuperable—and he insisted that it would be found to meet the test in all particulars—Calhoun saw every advantage with this pass. A line drawn from Charleston to St. Louis led straight through the Carolina Gap, taking Nashville on the way. He left it to others to determine whether the route would "in any degree sacrifice the immediate object of the road, to connect Charleston with Louisville, Lexington and Cincinnati"; but it was clear that his own object was to push on to a much farther west.[22]

Calhoun was by this time thoroughly aroused, and he went to great lengths to force a reconsideration of the railroad route. His personal following was mobilized to stimulate public opinion and get a favorable board of directors when the road was organized. Meetings were got up by Calhoun lieutenants at the familiar Calhoun strongholds: Pendleton, Abbeville, Edgefield, and other upcountry towns. The superior advantages of the Carolina Gap route for serving the interests of Georgia and Tennessee were skillfully impressed upon influential railroad enthusiasts in those states. Friends in South Carolina and elsewhere were primed to buy the minimum fifty shares of stock required to qualify for the board of directors. Addresses from citizen groups, newspaper articles, and personal meetings were all directed toward the forthcoming session of the legislature. The Calhoun spokesmen in this as in more strictly political affairs were James Edward Calhoun, Francis W. Pickens, Armistead Burt, George McDuffie, and Patrick Noble.[23]

A resolution favoring the Carolina Gap route was adopted by the citizens of Pendleton and forwarded to Hayne. The latter replied with considerable dignity that no route had been finally chosen, and that all passes through the mountains would be fully explored before any selection would be made.[24] But the Pendleton *Messenger* quoted some unguarded language in the formal "address" of a meeting in Columbia, signed by men prominent in the origins of the road, which seemed to mean that the company had been committed to the French Broad route before any survey had been made or any organization perfected, as the *quid pro quo* for a charter to do business in North Carolina.[25]

The issue was further confused at this point by the publication of a lengthy statement from Colonel A. H. Brisbane, one of the three engineers originally appointed by the city of Charleston to select a route. Though it only appeared in the *Courier* on October 20, Brisbane's letter, addressed to his fellow citizens of Charleston, was dated September 28, 1836. He had, so he declared, just received the official reports of the Knoxville convention, and was distressed to note that his own recommendation in favor of the Rabun Gap had been suppressed. He had been over the whole ground again with instruments, under the auspices of the state of Georgia, and Lieutenant White of the Topographical Engineers, who had been on the French Broad survey, had gone with him. They agreed there was no comparison between the two routes. The Rabun Gap to the Little Tennessee showed grades of forty to fifty feet to the mile; the French Broad route could only with the greatest difficulty be reduced to two hundred feet to the mile. Brisbane then went on to predict that a road through the Rabun or some other westerly gap to the Little Tennessee, or a lower road through northern Georgia, would certainly be built—by Georgia alone if the other states did not co-operate. And he argued forcefully that lower building and operating costs due to its easier grades would give to such a road an insurmountable competitive advantage over any line that might be built by way of the French Broad River.[26]

This controversy was in full swing when the stock of the Louisville, Cincinnati and Charleston Railroad was offered to the public on October 17, 1836. It was almost inevitable that the sales, in the circumstances, would be disappointing, and the minimum of four million dollars required by the charter was attained only through the personal purchases of Wade Hampton of Columbia. Of this sum, $3,343,200 was raised in South Carolina.[27] The total subscription was far short of the amount that would be required to build the road.

Some such response must have been anticipated by the backers of the project, for they did not await the outcome of the stock subscription before proposing that the railroad be associated with a bank. After testing out the idea in the newspapers, a formal memorial to that effect was prepared for the legislature.[28]

Calhoun watched this new turn of events with even greater concern than he had felt over the summary choice of route. He denied flatly that he was maneuvering for the presidency of the road, that he was a candidate for it, or even that he would accept it if offered unless it came as the "decided wish" of the company and would not bring him into conflict with his friends.[29] The long-standing struggle with the South Carolina Unionists had only recently been resolved, and it had taken all the political strength he could muster to crush the Pinckney revolt in the fall elections. Calhoun was not seeking any further causes of conflict within the state or out of it. He hoped only that the railroad question could be so managed as to avoid splitting the state into parties and making it a political issue.

Calhoun hurried to Columbia for the opening of the state legislature near the end of November, and probably had a hand in the preparation of Governor McDuffie's annual message. Whether in Calhoun's language or his own, McDuffie expressed dissatisfaction with the terms of the railroad charter which gave to South Carolinians so small a voice in an enterprise which they were to finance so largely. He recommended against a subscription by the state until the route was agreed on, the surveys made, and the work begun; and he voiced a strong objection to any tie-up between the railroad and a bank.[30]

In the face of the Governor's hostility, the legislature modified the charter, eliminating Ohio entirely, reducing Kentucky to a par with the other states in the matter of directors, and absolving the company of any obligation to enter the state of Kentucky at all if the modified charter were not accepted there. The railroad bank, however, was passed despite McDuffie.[31] When Calhoun left Columbia for Washington, it was in the belief that the enterprise was degenerating into a stock-jobbing scheme, but he retained enough faith to insist that Armistead Burt and James Edward Calhoun attend the organization meeting scheduled for Knoxville in January.[32]

The lines were being drawn for a showdown over the route of the railroad, and, in a broader sense, over what kind of a railroad would be built. The contest was certainly not, however, as it has long been represented, a struggle between high-minded nationalism on Hayne's part and narrow sectionalism on Calhoun's. Both alternatives linked South and West, if that was nationalism; both would join portions of the South if that was sectionalism. Calhoun and Hayne had both been Nullifiers, if that was narrowness; but neither the older party lines nor those more newly drawn seemed to have any bearing on the case. Poinsett, who had bitterly opposed the Nullifiers, and the *Southern Patriot,* which fed the Pinckney rebellion, were both on Calhoun's side in the railroad contest.[33] No, it was not that Calhoun was bent only upon unifying the South while Hayne sought greater understanding between sections through commercial intercourse. The real point at issue was local self-interest. Calhoun's route—either the Georgia road or the Carolina Gap—would serve only the Charleston area and a small portion of southern South Carolina, whereas Hayne's route would give rail service to Columbia, Greenville, Spartanburg, and the growing area between. Hayne conceded as much in his report of the following year. Neither the legislature nor the people of South Carolina, he declared, would ever "consent that the resources of the State shall be applied to a road running on the Southern border of the State to Augusta, and at that point leaving our State entirely. . . . A road carried through Columbia and from thence by the best route . . . to the mountains, will interest the whole State. . . ."[34] The route through Georgia would in fact serve the purpose of intersectional intercourse far better than the French Broad route to Cincinnati because it would serve larger hinterlands in both South and West. It would also have a better chance of survival for this very reason, and because it would face less in the way of competition. The people of South Carolina, however, would not support it, because it would not pass through the most populous portion of their own state.

4

Calhoun had no sooner left Pendleton in late November 1836 than Captain Williams began to survey the Carolina Gap, and in a remarkably short time reported the grade too steep.[35] Calhoun insisted that the less favorable side of the pass had been deliberately chosen, and ultimately secured a resurvey by Major William G. McNeill, who had been selected by the directors of the company as chief engineer; but it was September 1837 before the work could be done, and by that time it no longer mattered.[36]

The organization meeting of the railroad had been held in January 1837 as scheduled, but under the original charter, since the other states had not had time to pass on the modifications imposed by the South Carolina legislature. Kentucky, therefore, had six directors, and Ohio, Tennessee, North Carolina, and South Carolina had three each. Since South Carolinians held five sixths of the stock, however, it was a foregone conclusion that the six directors at large would be chosen from that state, giving her nine out of twenty-four. Calhoun and Hayne were both among the nine, with Hayne then being chosen president of the company by unanimous vote of the board of directors. Neither Calhoun nor Hayne was personally present at the meeting, the former being in Washington and the latter detained by his duties as mayor of Charleston. At the same meeting the French Broad route was definitely selected—but not so definitely as to end the controversy.[37]

The board did not meet again until October, and in the interim panic stalked the land. The banks suspended specie payments, business slowed to a standstill, and old political enmities were forgotten in a common cause. Calhoun was again prevented from attending the meeting, this time by the special session of Congress called to cope with the economic crisis; but the seed he had planted was beginning to bear fruit. It was still apparently assumed by most of the directors, and was treated as immutable in Hayne's public utterances, that the French Broad route was final; and as though to reaffirm this official approval, the October meeting was scheduled for Flat Rock, North Carolina. An opposition to this route, however, had been slowly rising since Calhoun's letter to the *Messenger* the preceding fall. It reached its peak and found perhaps its definitive expression on September 30, 1837, when James Gadsden published an open letter to the stockholders of the railroad. Timed for the board meeting and the stockholders' meeting to follow it, Gadsden's letter virtually settled the question so far as public opinion was not prejudiced by the economic advantage of a location along the line.[38]

Gadsden pointed out—what had been in Calhoun's mind from the start—that it was foolish and dangerous to stake such an undertaking on a commercial connection with Cincinnati. The Baltimore and Ohio Railroad, the Chesapeake and Ohio Canal, and the combined canal and railroad project then being pushed by Virginia to join the James and Kanawha Rivers—all these lines would tap the Ohio Valley long before the Charleston road could hope to approach its terminus, and the commerce of Cincinnati would naturally and logically find its outlets at Baltimore and Norfolk. Charleston must seek more distant reaches of the West, moving on not from Cincinnati but from Louisville. The obvious and only economical route was through northern Georgia to the Tennessee River—the route Calhoun had proposed in 1835. Gadsden did not criticize the French Broad route as such, but he delivered a telling blow against it just the same. "It is not from a *particular Gap,* or a *single elevation in the mountains,* however favorable . . . that we can designate a route on a long line of 700 miles of road. . . . It is from the sum of the elevations, and depressions throughout the entire line of route; it is from the number, and altitude of the inclined places, contrasted with the length of levels, that we can arrive at certain and satisfactory results. . . ." Gadsden then went on to show that no part of the Charleston-Cincinnati route had yet been surveyed in detail, as it would have to be before the line could be laid out, whereas the Georgia route had been fully surveyed to the Tennessee River. The one route, moreover, would take eight to ten years to build, even under the most favorable conditions, and would have to be half completed before it would yield any financial return at all. The other would be completed and in operation in two or three years.

The wily engineer had not addressed his appeal to the stockholders in vain. James Hamilton, on his way home from the Flat Rock meeting, told Calhoun that the French Broad route was abandoned in favor of purchasing the existing Charleston and Hamburg road, merging with Georgia railroad interests, and extending the line through Georgia to the Chattahoochee and the Suck.[39] Before the end of October it was official. To quiet rumors and let the public know what was to be done, Hayne issued a preliminary report to the stockholders through the press.[40]

The language was carefully guarded, but the meaning was unmistakable. The stockholders had resolved that the French Broad route was entirely practical, and was the best route from Charleston to Cincinnati. They expressed their firm intention to build a railroad by that route. But they would not even survey the ground, much less build the road, through North Carolina, Tennessee, or Kentucky, unless and until those states were prepared to finance the work. They could not drop the whole idea without forfeiting their charter, but they came as close to it as the law allowed. It had also been agreed, as Hamilton had reported to Calhoun and as Gadsden had urged, that the Charleston and Hamburg road should be purchased, and linked at Augusta with the Athens road, which was then to be carried to the navigable waters of the Tennessee under a Georgia charter. To pacify the upcountry South Carolinians, who had invested heavily in the venture, the road was to be carried at once from Branchville to Columbia and eventually, perhaps, beyond that to the state line. That was all. Hayne insisted throughout that the Georgia scheme was an adjunct and not a substitute, but he must have known as well as Calhoun did that they would never raise enough money to build them both, even if both could find profitable business.

Calhoun was jubilant, as well he might be;[41] though it was not wholly a change of heart that had led to the conversion of the directors, nor entirely the merits of the Georgia route that motivated the purchase of the Charleston and Hamburg line. Under the terms of its legislative authorization, the Southwestern Railroad Bank could not be chartered until the outstanding stock of the Louisville, Cincinnati and Charleston Railroad amounted to eight million dollars, and the company was given only until December 1, 1837, to double its resources. Private capital was scarce, and the fourth quarterly installment of the surplus revenue had been held up by Congress at the special session. The desired sum in stock certificates, however, could be secured in one transaction by purchasing the South Carolina Canal and Rail Road Company, whose stock then became stock in the L, C & C.[42]

5

Another meeting of the board of directors of the railroad was scheduled for Columbia on December 1, to ratify the purchase of the Hamburg road. Calhoun did not get away from Fort Hill in time to attend, but did expect to see Hayne and others before he went to Washington. Presumably he did see Hayne. Certainly he saw Hamilton; and when he left for the regular session of Congress it was in the conviction that the affairs of the L, C & C, save for its banking connection, were as he would have them.[43]

The backers of the French Broad route, however, had by no means given up the project. Consisting mainly of residents of South Carolina north of Columbia and east of Greenville, the most populous portion of the state, they wielded considerable political pressure, which was reinforced by the whole North Carolina group. The South Carolina legislature, after the purchase of the Hamburg line and the apparent change of direction, subscribed a million dollars to the stock of the road and guaranteed the two millions that must be borrowed to pay for the properties of the South Carolina Canal and Rail Road Company. Tennessee followed suit with a stock subscription of $650,000, and both Tennessee and North Carolina confirmed the grant of banking privileges. Hamilton was dispatched to England to borrow the necessary two million dollars, and preparations were made to set up a Southwestern Railroad Bank. When the legislatures of North Carolina and Kentucky both showed signs of being ready to purchase stock, however, the French Broad route was hastily brought back into the center of attention.[44] The board of directors met in Lexington, Kentucky, late in August 1838 and authorized further surveys in the area of the Cumberland Gap. They would, as Henry Clay remarked at the time, "get more soft words than money in Kentucky";[45] but the soft words were persuasive. By October preparations were again getting under way to build the road originally approved at Knoxville in 1836, which in two and a half years had still not advanced to the stage of detailed surveys.

More firmly than ever Calhoun believed the project to be economically unsound, and he took the only course left open to him to stop it: he resigned as a member of the board of directors. Officially he attributed his action to the pressure of other duties; but in a private letter to Hayne he minced no words. He did not doubt Hayne's sincerity, but his own conviction that the Cincinnati road would prove a "complete and disastrous failure" was too deep to be overcome. He still believed that rail connection with the West was of vital importance, both politically and commercially, but he remained equally certain that "we ought to look to the Tennessee instead of the Ohio, and much farther to the West than Cincinnati or Lexington. . . ."[46]

Hayne replied immediately. He regretted the disagreement the more because the road was probably doomed to failure without Calhoun's support, but he refused to yield an inch of the ground he had taken. The invitation had come from Cincinnati, which seemed to him sufficient justification for retaining that city as the western terminus, despite the spectacular failure of the Cincinnatians to give the road any financial support. And he held that the action of the various state legislatures in chartering the road had unalterably fixed its route. That route, he went on, had been carefully selected by "Colonels Gadsden and Brisbane and Mr. Holmes" who had "reported decidedly in favor of the route by the French Broad River as affording a passage for a Rail Road 'unexampled in the topography of the world.'" Then followed a review of the action of the Knoxville convention and the whole subsequent history of the project.[47] It was an able and persuasive defense, but it ignored Brisbane's charge that his own report in favor of the Rabun Gap had been suppressed. It also ignored Gadsden's careful qualification that one gap in the mountains did not necessarily mean that a seven-hundred-mile railroad passing through it would be feasible, and the same engineer's publicly expressed preference for the Georgia route. It evaded the hard economic fact that the competing lines must reach Cincinnati and pre-empt the trade long before the Charleston road could be built; and it ignored Calhoun's plea for rail connection with the young expanding West beyond the Mississippi.

Hayne's letter went far toward saying that if the road failed, it would be Calhoun's fault for opposing it. The latter agreed that failure would be calamitous, but he could not let the issue stand as Hayne had left it. He wrote again, earnestly and at great length. He did not wish to weaken public confidence in the management of the road. It was for that reason that he had not expressed his disagreement with the route in his resignation, but only in his private letter to Hayne. He would not willingly forfeit the charter of either railroad or bank, nor violate pledges given to other states. But he realized, as apparently Hayne did not, that even if each state concerned did her full share and the road were built as planned in the minimum of time, it would be doomed in the end to succumb to the competition of other more advantageous avenues of trade. He conceded Hayne's point that the French Broad route was preferred by a majority in South Carolina, but to his mind that was merely another instance "of important undertakings defeated through selfish and local feelings."[48]

With his resignation from the board of directors, Calhoun sold his own stock in the Louisville, Cincinnati and Charleston Railroad.[49]

6

The Southwestern Railroad Bank opened its doors on January 1, 1839, with Abraham Blanding, who had consistently supported Hayne in the affairs of the railroad, as its president.[50] Calhoun was no longer interested. His energies, such as could be spared from Senatorial duties, the plantation, and the Georgia mines, were by that time devoted to furthering communication with the West by rail and water, and he was already consulting with leading citizens of Illinois and the more distant West in furtherance of the plan.[51]

His attention was sharply recalled to the affairs of the L, C & C when Hayne died very suddenly late in September 1839, after an illness of only five days. South Carolina had not quite absorbed the shock before Blanding also died. The directors' meeting, which Hayne had been attending when stricken with fever, had revealed that the financial affairs of the company were chaotic. The economic depression which had engulfed the country more than two years earlier had steadily drained individual resources. Railroad stocks, bought on installments, in many cases could not be redeemed. An increasing number among the stockholders were for abandoning the whole project, and the company had been kept alive by only a narrow margin at Hayne's last meeting with the board.[52]

Though he no longer had any financial interest in the road, Calhoun was concerned for his many friends and relatives who were deeply committed. At the same time he saw an opportunity to redirect policies which he considered so unsound as to doom the whole enterprise to certain failure. His object, he believed, could best be accomplished by the election of Gadsden to the vacant presidencies of both bank and railroad, and he so instructed James Edward.[53] Calhoun was of course aware that Gadsden's election to the railroad presidency would be bitterly opposed by all those who had supported Hayne's efforts in behalf of the French Broad route. He knew also that his own endorsement would be a handicap rather than a help in the same quarter. He depended on the votes of Edgefield and Abbeville stockholders to carry through his plans; but he preferred that James Edward, on whom he relied to organize the move, should take no personal hand in the matter lest his own agency be inferred. Of the ultimate route of the road he said nothing, save to repeat his own lack of confidence in the one previously selected and to express the hope that conflicting views might now be harmonized in the interest of all concerned.[54]

The directors met in Columbia early in December 1839, and a strong movement for Gadsden was backed by Calhoun's friends. He was defeated, however, by Vardry McBee of Greenville, who was able to unite the votes of North Carolina stockholders with those in South Carolina who wanted rail connections extended north from the state capital.[55] The financial pressure and the growing conviction that the route to Cincinnati through the French Broad Valley would be economically disastrous were too strong for the new president, and they must eventually have proved so even for Hayne. McBee resigned after a few months, and Gadsden was duly chosen. Before the end of 1840 all thought of going beyond Columbia was publicly abandoned, and Calhoun enjoyed a ghoulish victory. "Thus ends the humbug," he wrote to Andrew, "with a debt of several millions on the state, great loss to those concerned, and the loss of credit and mortification to the projectors. If I could triumph, when state and friends have suffered, what a triumph I would have."[56]

CHAPTER XXIV

VAN BUREN JOINS THE NULLIFIERS

1

THE fourth day of March 1837 was mild and clear, though snow still gleamed from the hills across the river and lay in the shady spaces around the Capitol. The streets and parks and avenues of Washington were jammed with people as they always have been on inauguration day, but this time the crowd was singularly quiet.[1] Andrew Jackson was going home, and there was a sense of impending disaster in the air. Van Buren had never fired the popular imagination as the old General had. True, he was Jackson's personally chosen heir, if that was any comfort, but he was no rugged and indomitable warrior. He was smooth and smiling and tricky, like Nicholas Biddle.

Promptly at noon Van Buren stepped forward on the eastern portico of the Capitol, delivered a brief and carefully worded inaugural address, and took the oath of office from Chief Justice Roger B. Taney. But the cheers were cheers of parting for Andrew Jackson, and Jackson's was the triumph. He had lived to witness "the glorious scene of Mr. Van Buren, once rejected by the Senate, sworn into office, by chief justice Taney, also being rejected by the factious Senate."[2] With stately dignity the old General bowed his white-maned head to the crowd and withdrew. Three days later he was on his way to Nashville, and to retirement. It was the end of an era.

Van Buren's position was peculiarly difficult. Though he had concurred in, if he had not himself determined, the policy of his predecessor, it must long since have been clear to his shrewd judgment where that policy led; and he was now faced with the necessity of arresting and in some instances reversing Jackson in order to maintain himself. He had inherited all of Jackson's enemies, and he was only too well aware that alone he could not stand against them. He had kept Jackson in power by taking over for his own purposes the Adams-Clay alliance of North and West; but with Jackson gone he could no longer hold the West, where Harrison had shown unlooked-for strength, and it would be but a matter of time before the elements that had joined forces to pass the compromise of 1833 were welded into a full-fledged political alliance of South and West. Even at that moment a direct rail connection for commercial purposes between the two sections was in prospect, and it would indeed be a bond of steel.

So Van Buren gave up the West to Clay and Harrison, hoping they would fall out, and sought to breathe new life into the older combination of North and South—of planters and plain Republicans—which he had himself so effectively wielded in 1828. In the states that dominated the North—New York, Pennsylvania, and New Jersey—he controlled a powerful and smoothly operating political machine that would do his bidding at least for the next four years. But the South he could win to his cause in only one way: by adopting the Southern position on the explosive abolition question, which would commit him in the end to the whole philosophy of State Rights.[3] So Forsyth of Georgia remained in the State Department, Woodbury of New Hampshire in the Treasury, Dickerson of New Jersey in the Navy post, and Butler of New York in the office of Attorney General. But the War Department, vacant since September when Cass had become Minister to France, went to Joel Roberts Poinsett of South Carolina. The North and South shared similarly in the important diplomatic posts. George M. Dallas of Pennsylvania went to Russia, and Henry Wheaton of New York to Prussia. The Belgian post went to Virgil Maxcy of Maryland. Andrew Stevenson of Virginia was already in London, and John H. Eaton, with a triumphant Peggy at his elbow, was at Madrid. Only Cass at Paris and Postmaster General Amos Kendall were from the West.[4]

The inaugural address was a glorification of the national history, but with a special tribute to the astuteness of the founding fathers in assigning their respective spheres to general and state governments. With the slave question alone did the new President touch on a contemporary issue, and there he upheld the property rights of the South. No act of Congress tampering with slavery in the District of Columbia, he declared, would receive his sanction.[5]

For the time being, although he was present at the inauguration, Calhoun offered no comment. His opinion of the past and present administrations, however, could be read by anyone who did not already know it in the editorial column of Richard K. Crallé's *Reformer,* which had succeeded the *Telegraph* less than two weeks earlier. In Crallé's view Jackson's two terms in office had merely aggravated and intensified all the abuses of which the General himself had complained in Adams. Elected to reform the government, he had corrupted it, and by naming his successor he had transformed it from a republic to a hereditary monarchy. Crallé anticipated no change of policy under Van Buren, and he pointedly rejected the President's bid for Southern support on the slavery issue. Like Pinckney, Van Buren had sacrificed the outpost. He had based his opposition to abolition in the District of Columbia on expediency rather than on the Constitution, and those who acknowledged Calhoun's leadership would have none of it.[6]

It was not without significance that Poinsett had been elected to the South Carolina state senate on the Pinckney ticket in 1836, or that Thomas Ritchie of the Richmond *Enquirer* was among the distinguished visitors at the "coronation." Van Buren's bid for Southern support was directed to those who opposed Calhoun rather than to the actual leader of the South. Calhoun saw the President's weakness, and prepared to crush him.[7]

It was then that economic retribution intervened. The new crisis forced new measures, and created political alliances that would have been unthinkable in March.

2

The economic heritage of the Jackson administrations was even more important than the political in its influence on the future. The rising inflation of the preceding two or three years reached its peak about the time of Van Buren's election. The huge surplus revenue of the Federal Government, on deposit with the pet banks since 1834, had formed a revolving fund for land speculation. The Specie Circular in the summer of 1836 had merely hastened the inevitable collapse by driving gold and silver out of circulation, and early in 1837 the downward spiral began. In New York, where the commercial life of the nation already centered, the false front of prosperity was crumbling. Bread riots in February were followed a few days after Van Buren's accession by the collapse of a prominent Wall Street banking house. Other failures followed in quickening tempo and before the end of April suburban real estate had dropped to 10 percent of its value six months earlier. In South Carolina cotton dropped from eighteen cents in February to thirteen cents in March, and by the end of May was down to eight cents.[8] Everywhere the picture was one of increasing misery and spreading ruin through the spring of 1837.

Blair stoutly defended the Specie Circular and blamed the panic variously on the Bank of England, the distribution of the surplus, the defeat of the fortification bill, and on what he chose to regard as the unjustified agitation of the abolition question for the sole purpose of disunion by the senior Senator from South Carolina.[9] Incessantly the *Globe* rang all the changes on the old Jacksonian theme—the democracy of numbers against an aristocracy of wealth; but the *National Intelligencer* and the Whig press generally saw Jackson's "ignorance, perversity, and mismanagement" as the real cause of the catastrophe. The weak despaired; the strong sought an avenue of escape.[10] Calhoun foresaw the complete overthrow of the banking system, unless the British Government should intervene with its superior resources, and blamed the past administration which "by its folly and vice has lost all control for good over the banks and the currency." Even members of Van Buren's official family regretted, now it was too late, that the Specie Circular had not been at least suspended.[11]

The crisis came to a head on the eighth and ninth of May when a prolonged run on the New York banks drained them of a million dollars in specie. On the tenth, by mutual agreement, the banks were closed and specie payments were suspended. Other cities either had suspended already or immediately did so. The Charleston banks held out until the eighteenth, but at last they too ceased to redeem their notes in gold and silver.[12] In the larger cities order was kept by Federal troops reinforcing the local police. With banker, merchant, and common man alike demanding succor from the government, Van Buren on May 15 issued a proclamation calling Congress to meet in special session on the first Monday in September.[13]

3

The suspension of specie payments left the Government of the United States in a most embarrassing position. Since 1834 the pet banks had been the sole financial agents for collecting, keeping, and disbursing the public revenues; but the act of 1836 regulating these depositories required that they redeem their notes in gold and silver.

When they ceased to do so, they ceased automatically to be legal depositories. So the middle of May found the government with no place to put its money and no machinery for paying its obligations. There was nothing for it but that the various Collectors of Customs must retain in their own possession the sums paid in duties, and the land agents the sums paid for public lands. Disbursements were made by Treasury draft on the former depository banks, which the Secretary "hoped" they would honor. If they did not, however, the Collectors were authorized to perform banking functions to the extent of making payments on government obligations.[14]

The situation sharply underscored the utter inadequacy of the financial legislation, or lack of it, under which the Treasury had been operating since Jackson first undertook to do without the Bank of the United States. It precipitated a sweeping reconsideration of the relations between the government and the banking system, in which politician and publicist, planter and merchant, industrialist and banker each took a hand.

Side by side with this wide-ranging economic reanalysis, which occupied the months between the suspension of specie payments and the meeting of the special session of Congress, went a thoroughgoing political realignment around the issue of economic recovery. There were new parties, and new names for old ones. The Locofocos, originally merely the lunatic fringe of the New York Democracy, began to infiltrate into the party councils. The antiforeign reaction to economic crisis produced the normal result in the form of a Native American party, whose natural conservatism led it in the direction of the Whigs. The real division, however, was clearly between those who believed the road to recovery lay through re-establishment of a national bank and those who did not, the latter again being split into two groups. One of these, for which Rives made himself spokesman, wanted to continue the Jacksonian system of depository banks, with more rigid controls. The other, which came shortly to be identified with Calhoun, favored the Independent Treasury scheme first proposed in Congress by William Fitzhugh Gordon of Virginia in 1834.

The Whigs were of course the champions of a national bank. To them the whole economic crisis was all directly traceable to Jackson's war on the Bank of the United States and the way out of the difficulty was clearly to restore the *status quo ante*. Most of the South Carolina leaders had gone along with the Whigs since 1833-1834, primarily because of their common aim—the defeat of Jackson; but there were influential spirits among them who were finally ready to amalgamate, now that the Jackson party in the person of Van Buren seemed ripe for destruction. Chief of the group was Senator William C. Preston, who had already refused to follow Calhoun's lead in the fight on the abolition petitions, and had been for some months seeking a pretext for an open rupture. With the onset of the panic, Preston espoused the cause of a national bank. So did James Hamilton, Jr., after a fashion; and Governor Pierce M. Butler arrived at the same place by endorsing the Whigs.[15]

Calhoun, with his deeper insight into the nature of the political process, analyzed the situation in a very different fashion. For ten years he had been fighting against the centralization of power in the general government because he had come to realize that the constitutional system of checks and balances within the Federal structure offered no effective bar to absolutism save to the extent that actual sovereignty remained with the states. The Whig party, with Clay, Webster, and Harrison for its chiefs, was irrevocably committed to the consolidationist position, and for that reason alone would in time be committed also to abolition. To amalgamate with a party grounded in such principles would be to surrender all he had stood for since he first went into opposition to the Adams administration in 1826. He could not and would not do it, and no possible political reward—not even the Presidency itself—could move him. He refused flatly to accept the second place on a Harrison ticket for 1840; he refused all promises of the Presidential succession at the hands of the Whigs thereafter; and he refused to permit the Southern Whigs to put him in independent nomination.[16]

He was a Nullifier, not a Whig. He knew that the State Rights philosophy was the only sound basis the American political structure afforded for opposing an administration whose sins were the fruits of power, and he knew that the Whigs would never occupy that ground. The Whigs, in fact, were more deeply tainted with consolidationism than even the Jacksonians, for with them it went back in legitimate line to Hamilton and the elder Adams. The Democrats were recent converts and might yet be weaned away from the unnatural doctrines to which Jackson had committed them. So he urged his followers to stand firm and to seek the economic and political redemption of the country rather than their own advancement. If his friends chose not to follow him, he was ready to step off the public stage. These views, together with a suggestion that perhaps the best hope lay in a reorganization of the original Jackson party, were embodied in the summer of 1837 in two long letters to Duff Green, who was acting as intermediary for the Whigs. Green saw the point, and a slightly touched-up paragraph from one of Calhoun's letters, placing the welfare of the nation above personal ambition and partisan feeling, presently appeared in a New York paper. It was widely copied, and it served to apprise both the rank and file and the leaders of the administration that Calhoun's co-operation might yet be secured if the policies advanced were such as he could approve.[17]

The question of policy was actually being determined at about that same date. Earlier in the year William M. Gouge of Philadelphia had argued cogently in a widely circulated pamphlet that the government could get along without banks by making the Treasury itself a bank of deposit and disbursement for its own funds.[18] By request, he stated his views more succinctly for the President's confidential use. Others consulted, in addition to members of the Cabinet, included Silas Wright and Churchill C. Cambreleng, long the personal financial and commercial advisers of Van Buren; Chief Justice Taney, whose agency had been decisive in destroying the Bank of the United States; and, through an intermediary, William C. Rives.[19] Taney and Rives still favored revision of the deposit bank system, but the consensus was for the Independent Treasury. The alternatives were still under consideration at the White House when the Raleigh *Star* republished Calhoun's currency speech of 1834, with its program for "unbanking the banks." Other papers copied it, and Crallé called attention to it in the *Reformer*.[20] Van Buren had, therefore, good reason to suppose that if he adopted the Independent Treasury plan, there was a fair chance of securing Calhoun's support, even though he could not count on Rives and Ritchie.

The President made up his mind, probably before the end of July. At any rate, the *Globe,* after several weeks of preparation by way of denouncing the banking system, came out on August 16 with a reprint of Gordon's 1834 speech on the Treasury scheme and an editorial approving it. Opposing the plan was the *Madisonian,* newly established organ of the Rives-Tallmadge faction; but the *Reformer* was carefully noncommittal.[21] So was Calhoun himself, but before he left his home for Washington toward the end of August he made clear to friends, particularly to McDuffie, that he preferred a complete separation of the Treasury from the banking system.[22]

4

When the special session met on September 4, 1837, the actual division of parties was in doubt. In terms of the affiliations of the previous Congress the administration commanded small majorities in both houses; but in fact the insurgent Democrats led by Rives of Virginia and Tallmadge of New York in the Senate and by Garland of Virginia in the House held a balance of power. Should these "seceders," as Blair called them, go over to the Whigs, the administration could carry its program only by uniting with the Nullifiers. The Vice President himself was in the chair of the Senate when the session opened, and a printer to that body had already been chosen, so there was no immediate occasion for a test of strength in the upper chamber. In the House, however, Polk won his re-election as Speaker with a scant three votes to spare.[23] Still more indicative was the contest for printer to the House, where neither Gales and Seaton, backed by the Whigs, nor Blair, supported by the administration members, could command a majority. The Democratic insurgents threw their own strength to Thomas Allen, publisher of the *Madisonian,* and after a three-day battle Allen was chosen by a switch of Whig votes.[24]

In the choice of committees the presiding officers of the two chambers had no choice but to follow the older party cleavages, but the selections were in reality Van Buren's, with the two crucial positions going to his own close friends: Cambreleng retained his post as chairman of Ways and Means in the House, and Wright continued as chairman of the Senate Committee on Finance. Neither Calhoun nor Clay received any assignment at all, and Calhoun's political friends received places of only trivial importance.[25]

The business of the session was outlined in the President's message, read by the clerks of the respective houses at noon on September 5. Van Buren was no longer noncommittal, but clear and unequivocal with a concrete program to offer. A review of the economic crisis which had necessitated the calling of Congress three months ahead of the regular time was followed by the recommendation of various measures to afford temporary relief. These included permitting the mercantile community to defer payment on duty bonds, an indulgence already granted *per interim* by executive order; the adjustment of claims against the former deposit banks; the issuance of Treasury notes to take care of the immediate obligations of the government; and postponement of the fourth installment due to the states under the deposit act because there was no longer any surplus to distribute. The core of the message, however, and that to which everything else was merely contributory, was the Independent Treasury—a system whereby the "collection, safe-keeping, transfer and disbursement of the public money" would be managed by officers of the government without the aid or intervention of any bank or banks.[26]

The reaction was what might have been expected. To the ever-fluent Blair the message was "a second declaration of independence . . . an imperishable monument to the genius, firmness, probity and patriotism of its author." The *Intelligencer* condemned it lock, stock, and barrel. The *Madisonian,* whose editor was still contesting for the post of printer to the House, was loud in its praise, but assumed that the President would of course yield his own preference if Congress agreed on a different plan.[27] The Calhoun press, as though waiting to be told what to think, offered no comment; but Calhoun himself, although as yet he made no public statement, took an immediate stand on the major issue.

"Van Buren has been forced by his situation and the terror of Jackson to play directly into our hands," he wrote to James Edward shortly after the appearance of the message, "and I am determined, that he shall not escape from us. . . . I have taken my stand. I go against the chartering of a United States bank, or any connection with Biddles, or any other bank. I go in a word for a complete seperation from the whole concern. So far I have come to a fix[ed] determination. Beyond that I wait for developement; and shall come to no conclusion, till I see the whole ground. . . ." He knew that Preston would go with the Whigs for a national bank, and that some, at least, among the South Carolina Representatives would do likewise, but he would fight that fight when he came to it.[28] To Anna Maria he wrote at the same time, with genuine relief. He acknowledged the delicacy of his position, which was causing great speculation in Washington, but he found the role he meant to play far more congenial than his previous association with the Whigs. "It was impossible for me to go with the leaders of the nationals. We disagreed on almost all points except resistance to Executive usurpation. We could not part on a point better for me, than the one on which we now seperate. I stand now on my own bottom, with no influence acting on me but a rigid adherence to those great principles, for which I have made so many sacrifices."[29]

Within two or three days the rumor was flying about Washington that the Nullifiers and their chief meant to support the Independent Treasury, and on September 14 the rumor was confirmed in the *Reformer.* In a long editorial on that day Crallé explained how Van Buren had been forced by circumstances to the State Rights position. The editor—and by implication his principal—still distrusted the motives and purposes of the President, but approved the financial program and would support it in spite of the source whence it came.[30]

5

It was a full week before Congress got down to business, the interval being occupied with organizational matters, while the administration leaders reduced the President's recommendations to specific legislation. The Senate then took the initiative, and over a period of four days Wright introduced six measures which together constituted Van Buren's program for economic recovery. In the order of their introduction these bills provided: (1) for postponing deposit with the states of the fourth installment of the surplus revenue; (2) for an issue of Treasury notes; (3) for further postponing payment on duty bonds; (4) for adjusting outstanding claims against the former deposit banks; (5) for storing merchandise in public warehouses pending payment of duties; and (6) for imposing "additional duties as depositories, in certain cases, on public officers."[31] The last of the six was the core of the whole financial policy—the bill to make the Treasury independent of banks. It authorized under suitable safeguards the retention and disbursement of public funds by Collectors of Customs, Surveyors of Land Offices, Postmasters, Directors of Mints, and others entrusted by law with the handling of public money. The offices of these various fiscal agents would become in effect both banks of deposit and extensions of the Treasury, and so the bill came to be known as the subtreasury bill.

Up to this time Congress had been marking time. The administration leaders, Wright and Benton in the Senate, Polk and Cambreleng

MARTIN VAN BUREN
by Henry Inman

Calhoun speaking in the Senate, 1838

in the House, had been feeling their way, not knowing with certainty who was on their side. The lines began to form on September 14, the day the subtreasury bill was offered in the Senate. The special order of the day was the bill to postpone the fourth installment of the deposits; but Rives, who secured the floor, did not speak to the point at issue. He complained instead that no measure had been offered specifying what kind of money might be received in payment of the public dues. It was a subtle way of injecting the bank question, and Wright clearly so understood it, replying simply that the Finance Committee had now reported all the bills it intended to propose. Rives then asked an adjournment until Monday—it was early Thursday afternoon—to allow time for study.[32]

At this point Calhoun entered an earnest plea for promptitude and boldness, speaking somberly of the gravity of the emergency they had been called together to meet. He spoke also of the specific remedies proposed, but the reporter could not hear him. We may guess, however, what he said, for it was later that same day that the *Reformer* appeared with its editorial endorsement of the Independent Treasury. Rives' protest was set aside. The postponement bill was debated, amended, and ordered to be engrossed. The following day it was passed by 28 to 17, Calhoun going with the administration, Preston with the Whigs.[33]

It was on Saturday, September 16, that Calhoun really showed his hand. The bill to issue Treasury notes was before the Senate, when the South Carolinian asked bluntly what the administration intended to do about separating the government from the banks. There was no alternative, he insisted, between the Bank of the United States desired by the Whigs and a Treasury completely independent of the banking system. He recalled that he had so argued in 1834, but had stated then that the existing arrangement could not be abandoned and the new one created all at once without precipitating economic catastrophe. The catastrophe had come anyway; there was nothing now to lose by the change, and everything to gain. But whichever alternative was chosen—a new national bank or an independent Treasury—all measures for economic recovery must stem from it and revolve around it. The Treasury note bill under discussion fitted neither as it stood. If a bank was to be re-established, there should be no issue of Treasury notes at all, but a loan from the bank; if the banking connection was to be completely severed, the relation of these Treasury notes to the legal currency of the country must be defined. He moved, therefore, that further consideration be postponed until Monday, to give him time to prepare an amendment. The postponement was carried over the protest of Wright and Benton, and the Senate adjourned for the remainder of the week end.[34]

The news was quickly spread about the Capital that Calhoun would speak on Monday, September 18, on the divorce of bank and state. Everyone knew that the occasion was momentous, for it meant that the most powerful single individual in public life was going to take a position on the great issue of the day, and on the position he took might well depend the future of the administration and of the Democratic party.

He spoke to a crowded Senate and to overflowing galleries, and it was not mere egotism when he later said that in that moment he had held the fate of the country in his hands.[35] With the almost equal division between the two great parties, he and the small group that would be guided by his will could turn the balance either way. He did what might have been expected of a man so confident of his powers, so jealous of his fame: he charted a course of his own choosing and bade the administration follow if it would sustain itself.

His thesis was that the connection between the government and the banks was in fact broken and could not for at least four years be restored even if it were desirable to restore it. The system of depository banks had failed too miserably to be again considered, and the President was pledged to veto any re-establishment of the Bank of the United States. The only alternative was for the government to handle its own financial transactions. It must, however, go farther; for the great function the national bank had performed had been to supply a stable currency. Without the bank, the government itself must regulate the circulating medium. In the course of his speech Calhoun analyzed as clearly as it had ever been done in the Senate the nature of money and credit, and the role of the government with relation to each. He traced also various passages from recent history, to make his own position clear, and pledged his support to any measure of relief not inconsistent with the principles he had steadily maintained.[36]

Calhoun then offered his promised amendment to the Treasury note bill. For the next calendar year he would accept the notes of specie-paying banks for three fourths of the dues of the government, but would decrease the proportion each year until 1841 when all payments to the Treasury must be in the "legal currency of the United States, or in such notes, bills, or paper issued under the authority of the same, as may be directed to be received by law." Benton immediately rose to offer a hard-money proviso of his own, but he expressed his complete accord with the purpose sought by Calhoun's amendment. In so doing he accepted in behalf of the administration the conditions attached to the Carolinian's offer of support.[37]

Thereafter things moved with increasing rapidity. Bills to postpone payment on duty bonds and to settle claims against the former pet banks passed the Senate the next day, along with the Treasury note bill. By agreement Calhoun's amendment was detached from the latter measure and added instead to the subtreasury bill itself. Benton's hard-money clause was also incorporated so that legal currency was now defined as gold or silver coin or "such notes, bills or paper" as the government might issue or authorize.[38] It was around this amendment that the main battle centered, for there in essence lay the whole purpose of separating bank and state. The amendment placed in the hands of the Treasury the exclusive power to regulate money, and by so doing deprived the banks of what had been a very profitable prerogative.

As the debate lengthened out, Preston identified himself with the Whigs in opposition, where he was presently joined by Rives of Virginia and Tallmadge of New York. But Wright, Benton, and the Van Buren inner circle let the Carolina champion have his way. Though he had no contact with the White House and sought none, the leadership of the administration forces on the financial question passed inexorably to Calhoun. Before September was over he was sure of victory. He and his new-found allies, he thought, had given "a mortal blow to the union of the political and money power" and had fair prospect to "unite & liberate the South, provided the States right party shall be true to itself & its principles"—provided, that is to say, the State Rights party would follow John C. Calhoun into the Van Buren camp! Yet he yielded nothing of principle, and even gloried in his past differences with those who now followed his lead. When Preston charged him with deserting the Whigs he retorted that he had never been a Whig nor anything else but "an honest Nullifier." In general he lost no opportunity to drive home the fact that the administration had come to his ground rather than he to theirs.[39] It was the sort of humiliation for which Van Buren could not, and did not, forgive him.

The amendment passed the Senate 24 to 23 on October 3, and the next day the subtreasury bill also passed in its amended form by 26 to 20.[40]

On the other side of the Capitol the political pattern was the same. It was Francis W. Pickens who introduced the subtreasury bill in the House of Representatives, rather than Cambreleng or any other member of Ways and Means;[41] and such State Rights champions as Robert Barnwell Rhett of South Carolina and Robert M. T. Hunter of Virginia, both freshman members, were among the foremost in its support. The balance of parties, however, leaned in the other direction. The Whigs and the Democratic insurgents, led in the House by Garland of Virginia, gained the upper hand, and the subtreasury was tabled by 120 to 107 on October 14.[42]

Two days later the special session came to an end, having passed four acts for the relief of the country. The deposit with the states of the fourth installment of the now nonexistent surplus had been postponed; payment on duty bonds had been postponed; provision had been made to adjust the outstanding claims against the deposit banks; and an issue of Treasury notes had been authorized to serve as a circulating medium in lieu of the bank notes that had ceased to be legal tender when specie payments were suspended.[43] On the debit side the relation of the government to the banking system remained unresolved. The new union of Nullifiers and Democrats had been unable to pass the subtreasury bill; but so had the opposition been unable to restore a banking connection.

6

The intense bitterness with which the advocates and the opponents of the subtreasury scheme regarded each other was not wholly due to the inflamed state of party feeling. It can be fully understood only in the light of an imperfect comprehension of fiscal economics shared by protagonists on both sides, and in the setting of class distrust that was the heritage of Jackson's Bank war. Assuming with Calhoun that there was no real alternative between the Bank of the United States and the Independent Treasury, the irreconcilable convictions of the two groups were something on the following order:

A small group of theorists, like William M. Gouge and Condy

Raguet, with whose work Calhoun was thoroughly familiar, argued for the subtreasury on the ground that it was economically feasible and that it was desirable in the abstract for the government to have complete control over the currency. Popular support for the measure, however, was generated solely as an inverted opposition to the Bank of the United States. All the old Jackson arguments against the Bank—that it used the credit of the government for its own profit, manipulated currency and credit for the sole benefit of a moneyed aristocracy, and that it was in fact a "monster of corruption"—were used to win to the new scheme the laboring and artisan classes, the farmers, the salaried, and in general all those of small or moderate means who could be persuaded that Biddle's Bank had ruined them, or inevitably would ruin them if re-established.

By the same token, the subtreasury was opposed by all those who profited, or thought they profited, by the operations of a national bank and, by simple transference, any bank. Intelligent and able men believed in all sincerity that unless the funds of the government were deposited in banks, the whole banking system would collapse; and that unless bank notes passed as currency, business would be impossible. Credit was completely identified in the minds of the business community with the banking function, and to destroy banks was to destroy credit. "Nothing can be more monstrous," wrote James Louis Petigru at the time of Calhoun's public endorsement of the subtreasury, "than to support a scheme for doing away with bank paper and of course with credit, and ruining all who are in debt. It is awful—it is so sudden—and of Mr. Calhoun so unexpected."[44] It was equally impossible for Preston to understand how Colhoun could honestly believe "that the only true currency is *inconvertible* but receivable gov't. paper." [45] In his view a Treasury note should pay interest, like a bank note, and should be redeemable in specie at the current rate of exchange—a rate to be determined by the law of supply and demand.

Naturally the Whigs, as the party of property and business generally, were aghast. They did not try to see in the Independent Treasury anything except the deliberate destruction of their interests, and they bitterly upbraided Calhoun for thus lending himself to the cause of chaos—of nihilism—of anarchy. The man who had fought with them against Jackson's Jacobinism was now the very god of the Jacobins, and they could, of course, see no reason for it but political corruption.[46] That Calhoun had in fact pointed out the advantages of the subtreasury at a time when the Democrats were unalterably opposed to it made no difference; nor were they moved by the fact that William Fitzhugh Gordon, who had twice introduced the measure in the House during the Bank fight, had then called himself a Whig. It was simply unthinkable to the average propertied man of the 1830's that the government could possibly transact its business in any other way than through banks.

The very nature of the opposition drove the administration step by step toward the camp of the Nullifiers. The economic interests that were certain to desert the party in the North could be balanced only by united support in the South; but the defection of the Rives bloc meant that Van Buren could not carry the South without Calhoun's aid. The Carolinian's speech of September 18 offered the President an opening, and he seized it. In the *Globe* of that very evening Blair devoted his entire editorial column to an admiring summary of Calhoun's remarks, and no one would have guessed that the same editor had devoted the better part of the preceding six years to calling the man he now extolled a traitor. Thereafter the *Globe* was eloquent in his praise, while the halter was deftly shifted to the necks of Rives and Tallmadge. Before the end of September the *Madisonian* was in open opposition, having announced its shift in an editorial entitled "We have met the enemy and we are theirs"; and two weeks later the Charleston *Mercury* gave grudging support to Van Buren, in so far as the President "had become a Calhoun man."[47]

There were those in the Democratic party who feared that Calhoun's support would do more harm than good; and there were others who bitterly resented the South Carolina Senator's calm assumption of leadership.[48] But the official party line as laid down in the *Globe* was one of deference and respect toward the new ally; and the credo of the Democracy as proclaimed in the first number of the "official" *Democratic Review* was one to which Calhoun could subscribe wholeheartedly.[49]

Decisive Whig victories in New York in the November elections only threw Van Buren the more completely upon the South, which was to say upon Calhoun.

7

Back in South Carolina Calhoun faced mutiny. For years his following had been coached and cajoled and goaded into deep and abiding hatred of Andrew Jackson, and Van Buren they had been taught to hold beneath contempt. Yet Calhoun now told them to support the party they had learned to hate and the man they most despised. Somehow, between his return to Carolina late in October and the meeting of the legislature six weeks later, Calhoun had to convince his party that their principles would be safe and their political future secure only by breaking the Whig alliance of the past four years and going back to the party at whose hands they had suffered so much. Even the old Unionists, who had consistently supported Jackson, now refused to stay with the Van Buren party, because as solid and substantial citizens they could not stomach the subtreasury. That in itself should have been evidence enough to the Nullifiers that it was Van Buren and not Calhoun who had changed his ground.[50]

The fight had begun in Washington when the entire South Carolina delegation in the House, excepting only Pickens and Rhett, followed Preston in opposition to the subtreasury. Back on the local ground, Governor Pierce M. Butler also bolted, and so did James Hamilton, and Hayne. Even the faithful McDuffie lost his enthusiasm when Calhoun was out of sight.[51] For a time only the *Mercury,* now edited by Rhett's brother-in-law J. A. Stuart, and the Pendleton *Messenger* supported Calhoun's position in the state. The *Reformer* in Washington unwittingly gave a text to the opposition with a severe criticism of Preston, and the junior Senator soon became the rallying point for opponents of the subtreasury as well as for those personally hostile to Calhoun.[52]

The seeds of revolt were already rooted in Charleston where the errant Pinckney was re-elected to his old post as Mayor even before the special session met; and the great prestige of Langdon Cheves was presently added to the opposition scale. Calhoun, on the other hand, was powerfully aided by Poinsett.[53]

At no time was Calhoun dismayed, or doubtful of the issue. He prepared his lieutenants for the struggle before he left Washington, and sounded "publick sentiment" on his way home. The principal leaders he saw personally, but left largely to them the details of the campaign.[54] As usual, he relied more on the power of reason than on political manipulation, and published a complete exposition of his views and his reasons for them in the form of a letter to certain citizens of Edgefield who had invited him to join them in a public dinner.[55] This "Edgefield letter," as it came to be called, is in its way an extraordinary document. It is both a political testament and an amazingly frank treatise on practical politics. Calhoun was asking the State Rights party, and the South generally, to leave the Whigs and to go with Van Buren. He thought it only fair to tell them why.

Briefly he retraced the theme of the past ten years: How Congress had overstepped what he firmly believed to be the true meaning of the Constitution and had exercised sovereign powers not rightfully assigned to it, in order to establish and sustain the protective tariff; how this legislative usurpation had been overthrown by the interposition of South Carolina; and how the Nullifiers had then made common cause with the National Republicans to prevent the President in his turn from making good a claim to similarly sovereign powers. The coalition was for this single purpose only, because the very executive encroachments against which it was directed were no more than the logical consequence of the principles to which the Nationals themselves adhered.

The coalition had been successful. The administration had given up its claims to unconstitutional powers, and had so far altered its course as to stand now on the principles it had invoked to defeat the National Republicans in 1828. The Nullifiers were thus forced to reconsider their own position. In continued alliance with those same National Republicans, now going under the name of Whigs, they could undoubtedly crush the administration, but to do so would be merely to restore the system they had with such difficulty destroyed. The Whigs believed in the consolidation and centralization of the powers of government. The first fruit of that consolidation would be an immense new national bank, which would operate as the last one had against the interests of the planting states. A union of political and financial power would follow, and then renewal of the protective system itself.

It seemed to Calhoun as important as it had ever been to restrain the tendency of the government to consolidation, and therefore as essential to oppose the policies of Clay and Webster now as it had been to oppose those of Jackson half a dozen years before. In his mind the basic question was still a question as to the location of sovereignty, and he was more firmly convinced than ever that to yield the point in favor of any branch of the general government would mean economic and social catastrophe to the South. So he called on his followers to forsake the Whigs and on the Southern adherents of the administration to reoccupy the old State Rights ground. He offered his own principles as a rallying point for all who opposed "consolidation, or the overaction of the central government" and predicted that parties would "again be formed on the old and natural division of state rights and national, which divided them at the commencement of the government, and which experience has shown is that division of party most congenial to our system, and most favorable to its successful operation."

Calhoun knew, of course, that his motives would be questioned. He anticipated in the letter itself, in fact, all the criticisms that would presently be leveled at him. But for all this he professed to care nothing, and threw himself upon the judgment and good sense of his fellow South Carolinians for vindication.

It is no wonder that the Whig leaders bitterly resented this Edgefield letter and savagely denounced Calhoun for it. To them it was worse than desertion: it was apostasy, and might well rob them of all the ripe fruits of victory. Yet the Whig denunciation was unfair, for they had known all along that Calhoun would not unite with them on policy. It is not surprising, either, that the letter has sometimes been given a purely sectional interpretation, for Calhoun speaks in it with complete frankness of the overmastering importance of uniting the South. Yet it is plain from the context that he does not mean uniting the South for disunion, or for any other purpose than that of protecting its dominant interest; and all his contemporaries—Whig, Democrat, Federalist, or what you will—agreed that the protection of the interests of its citizens was the chief purpose of government. The motive of purely personal ambition is equally difficult to sustain, for there is not a scintilla of evidence to show that at this time he had any more to hope for from the Democrats than from the Whigs.

Whatever hidden motive or meaning there may have been in Calhoun's explanation, it was not perceived by the people of South Carolina, for whom the letter was primarily intended. They accepted it in good faith for what it plainly said. Calhoun himself was in Columbia early in December, where his reception was enthusiastic. Resolutions endorsing the subtreasury were prepared for the legislature, and he wrote jubilantly that his course would "be sustained by a triumphant majority say 3 or 4 to 1." He erred on the side of caution. The majority was better than ten to one.[56]

CHAPTER XXV

THE OUTPOST RECAPTURED

1

POLITICAL lines were still fluid, but the main currents at least were well defined by the time Congress reconvened for the regular session early in December 1837. When Van Buren wrote his first annual message, read on the fourth, he knew where his strength lay, and what elements would have to be won over in order to convert the minority of the special session into a majority in the lower house. The subtreasury was boldly recommended once more, but the President qualified it carefully in deference to the violence of prevailing opinion on the question. "If a majority of Congress see the public welfare in a different light; and more especially if they should be satisfied that the measure proposed would not be acceptable to the people; I shall look to their wisdom to substitute such as may be more conducive to the one, and more satisfactory to the other." This was more like the Little Magician, and there was further legerdemain in his subtle appeal to the West, where except for New England his greatest weakness lay. He proposed a new pre-emption law to validate the claims of all those who had "seated themselves on the public lands, without authority" since the last such law was passed; and he recommended "preparatory steps" toward graduating the price of the public lands.

On the slavery question the President had nothing at all to say, but his acknowledged spokesmen in the Senate were soon to be forced, willy-nilly, to Calhoun's position.

The reception of the message revealed nothing new, but indicated a certain tightening of party and sectional lines. To J. Q. Adams it was a deliberate sacrifice of Northern freedom to Southern slavery, with "the purchase of the West by the plunder of the public lands" thrown in. Philip Hone, who was in Washington for the occasion, found in the message "all the abominable doctrines" of September, and lamented, "Was ever a commercial people cursed with such rulers?" But the Charleston *Mercury,* still devoted to Calhoun's interests, confined its comment to a single line: "The President is firm in adhering to his true policy."[1]

Both in and out of the party there was more interest in what Calhoun was going to do than there was in Van Buren's policy recommendations. Neither of the South Carolina Senators was present when the session opened, and Calhoun, as had been consistently the case since he entered the Senate, was given no regular committee assignment. Preston was assigned the third place on the Committee on Manufactures, but clearly was considered a Whig and was rendered harmless by association with four subtreasury Democrats. Calhoun took his seat on December 18, and Preston, who was already in the city, called on him. He too apparently wanted to know what Calhoun was going to do. He was cordially received, but he did not call again and was soon openly in the Clay camp. Legaré went even farther, carrying his hostility to the point of rudeness when he publicly snubbed his state's most distinguished son on the steps of the Capitol.[2]

With members of the administration, too, Calhoun's personal relations were irregular. He did not call at the White House, and in fact had not spoken to Van Buren on a personal basis since early in 1831. With Poinsett, however, the old political squabble seemed fully made up, and the Secretary of War was probably Calhoun's primary contact with the administration. He was also on friendly terms with Mahlon Dickerson, the Secretary of the Navy, and undoubtedly with Levi Woodbury, who had once been a close friend. If he found the city dull it was not because he was any longer a social outcast, but because he missed Anna Maria.[3]

Politically, he was execrated by those whom he had so recently left, and distrusted by those with whom he now acted. He held in his own person, for the moment at least, the balance of power in a shaky administration at a critical time, yet he stood virtually alone, refusing now to amalgamate with the Democrats as firmly as he had previously rejected union with the Whigs. He sought neither popularity nor power, but only to do his duty as he saw it, "with fidelity & intelligence, and to stand with a fair character in after times."[4] His calm insistence that he had not changed or altered his views, but stood where he had always stood, willing to act with anyone who sought the same ends, merely infuriated his critics, who would not or could not understand the broader philosophy behind everything he did. "His misfortune is," wrote one of his friends at that time, "that being taller than other people, he looks over their heads, & deceives himself by supposing they can see as far as he can."[5]

2

Calhoun's first opportunity to amplify the basic principles on which he acted came unexpectedly and, so far as he and his followers were concerned, without premeditation. It arose out of a sudden and violent resumption of the slavery controversy, which will be clearer if the background is sketched in a little more fully.

The slavery debates in Congress in the early months of 1836 had underlined the growing predominance of the North in numbers and in economic power. To those who were willing to face realities it was obvious that if ever the line between political parties became a geographical one, the free states would command a majority. When that happened, the theory of the Constitution built up by Marshall and Webster and made effective by Andrew Jackson would justify the dominant section in doing as it would with Southern property in the name of humanity and religion. In retrospect it is easy enough to say that the South actually had only one course open to her—to make what terms she could with power, and prepare to yield her peculiar institution with as good grace as she could muster. But the nature of the attack, the political traditions of the people, and their social and economic heritage alike forbade so obvious a solution. They had never acknowledged the claims of the majority to sovereign power; they had never conceded the right of the general government to interfere with property of any sort; and above all they so resented the libelous caricature of themselves given currency in the abolitionist tracts that dispassionate discussion was impossible.

The net result of the antislavery crusade was to unite the South and inevitably to give new impulse to the separatist spirit that had never been far beneath the surface. Calhoun's error was his belief that both slavery and the Union could be preserved. "The constitution," he wrote in 1836, "has placed in our power ample means, short of secession, or disunion, to protect ourselves. All we want are harmony and concert among ourselves to call them into effectual action when the necessity comes."[6] He was still thinking in terms of the nullification fight and the peaceful interposition of state sovereignty; but many of his own followers were already postulating an ultimate withdrawal from the Union. This trend was one of the things that spurred him on and gave greater urgency to his arguments on the slavery question. He had to consolidate his own grip on the South, if only to keep her in the Union. Once a separatist movement took hold under younger and more radical leadership, he realized that he would be powerless to stop it.[7]

Prior to the election of 1836 the Van Buren managers did their utmost to keep slavery from becoming an active political issue. It was nevertheless injected into the election in South Carolina where Pinckney's surrender of the constitutional ground against abolition in the District of Columbia was the explicit reason for his defeat. Immediately thereafter the slave question came up again in a new guise with dispatches from Texas to the effect that the Texan Congress had voted to join the United States; and by a largely sectional vote the Senate resolved to recognize the Lone Star Republic with its slave-based economy.[8] In this fashion Texas became an integral part of the slavery debate and served to fix the direction of the contest for the next decade and a half.

It was at approximately the same period that Calhoun completed the transition in his own thinking on the slavery question. Nearly twenty years had passed since he had conceded the equality of men to be a just and noble ideal, but one that was impossible to attain in the South.[9] He was now driven by his environment, his purposes, but most of all by the inner compulsion of his own logic, to deny even the ideal. Calhoun was essentially an intellectual who preferred to fight his battles with intellectual weapons. The economic arguments of the abolitionists could be met by figures; the political arguments by invoking once more the compact theory of the Constitution. But his own stern Calvinist heritage would not let him rest content to defend on economic and legalistic grounds an institution morally wrong.

Perhaps it was that very heritage which influenced subconsciously his answer; for Calvin had taught the doctrine that redemption is only for the chosen few, while the mass of mankind is doomed from all eternity. Here was a class structure rigid, unyielding, and ordained by God. Given such a society, was it too much to conclude that the Elect might well be masters and the damned be slaves? Whatever Calhoun did he rationalized; whatever he sought he buttressed with an intellectual justification. So he re-examined the institution of Negro slavery in the Southern States, and found it not evil but good in itself, given the nature of man, the soil and climate of the region, the physical and mental characteristics of the two races concerned. He began the moral defense of slavery in his report on incendiary publications in 1836, and within a year the doctrine was firmly intrenched in his intellectual armory. He held it "an inevitable law of society that one portion of the community depended upon the labor of another portion, over which it must unavoidably exercise control"; and he argued that where the class division was between two widely dissimilar races the relationship of master and slave was the only relationship that would enable the two races to live together in peace.[10] To abolish slavery—even to talk of abolishing slavery—would upset the equilibrium and set the two races at each other's throats. The Congressional battle was not just a squabble over the freedom of the press or the right of petition, nor in the long run even over the meaning of the Constitution except in so far as that was a measure of defense. "Our fate, as a people, is bound up in the question. If we yield we will be exterpated; but, if we successfuly resist, we will be the greatest and most flourishing people of modern time. . . ."[11]

3

The debates in Congress in 1836 and 1837 over the reception of abolition petitions, and particularly the gag rule adopted in the House, served only to inflame still further the crusading zeal of the abolitionists, while the simultaneous broaching of the Texas question added to their political strength. It was the Texas Revolution and the subsequent request for admission to the Union that enabled Adams to conjure up the Slave Power bogy, by which the South was represented as seeking the rich lands beyond the Sabine only to extend her slave-built empire and fasten her dominance upon the North.[12] Through 1837 the abolitionist presses multiplied and the antislavery societies increased. Almost invariably the agitators were condemned by their own communities, but riots, interrupted meetings, and broken presses only brought new converts to the cause. A turning point was reached on November 7, 1837, when Elijah P. Lovejoy, abolitionist editor in Alton, Illinois, was killed by a mob while trying to defend his press.[13]

The popular reaction to the Lovejoy murder indicated something of the political strength of the antislavery movement in the Northern

States, and brought a corresponding zeal to the Southern defense of the institution. Among those who took Lovejoy's part was Thurlow Weed, veteran editor at forty of the Albany *Evening Journal.* Weed had attached himself in 1824 to John Quincy Adams and played an important part in Adams' election. From National Republican he became an Antimason and was now a Whig, but he was leaning heavily toward abolitionism. The bulk of Northern sentiment, Whig and Democratic alike, held that the South approached the slave question as fearlessly and as intelligently as the North, and held the abolitionists to be the sole aggressors.[14] But editors like Weed, local politicians bidding for marginal support like William H. Seward, and a growing handful of very able Congressmen and Senators under Adams' lead were bent on making abolition not only the faith of the North, but also the platform of the Whigs.

The financial crisis filled up the special session of 1837; but with the Lovejoy murder still occupying space in the press, the slavery theme was back in prominence when Congress met again in December. This time it was quick-witted William Slade of Vermont who took the initiative in the House with a new line of attack. On December 18, 1837, he presented petitions in the familiar form for the abolition of slavery and the slave trade in the District of Columbia and announced his intention of speaking to them. The gag rule had not yet been reenacted that session, so that Slade could not be prevented from speaking. He did as he had promised, and with a vengeance, two days later, moving that his petitions be referred to a special committee with instructions to bring in a bill to grant the prayer of the petitioners.

Slade then launched into a wholesale attack on the whole institution of slavery, in a vein of invective eloquence calculated to be most aggravating to the South. Legaré expostulated, others interrupted and called him to order, but he could not be stopped, either by the Speaker or by the House. He ignored the chair and shouted down his critics. With Pickens still absent, the leadership of the South Carolina delegation was seized by dynamic young Robert Barnwell Rhett, who was serving his first term in Congress but was a veteran of the state legislature—one of the radicals whose appeals to action had been a constant threat to Calhoun's conservative course during the nullification fight. While Slade was speaking, Rhett prepared two amendments which he proposed to offer to Slade's bill if such a bill ever reached the floor. The first declared that since the Constitution had "proved inadequate to protect the southern states in the peaceable enjoyment of their rights and property," it was expedient "that the said constitution should be amended or the union of the states dissolved." The second called for a committee of two members from each state to report on the "expediency and practicability" of carrying out the first. He did not, of course, expect them to be adopted, any more than he expected Slade's proposed bill to pass without them, but it was a striking way of posing the issue and the alternative.[15]

As Slade proceeded with his tirade, members gathered in groups on the floor, ignoring the orator but keenly alert to the explosive possibilities of his attack. At last Henry A. Wise of Virginia made himself heard above the din, and invited the Virginia delegation to retire with him to a committee room. Hopkins Holsey of Georgia followed suit, and Rhett announced that the South Carolina delegation had already consulted and agreed to a three o'clock meeting in the District of Columbia Committee room. As the Southern delegations started walking from the hall, someone moved an adjournment, and it was quickly carried. Then Campbell of South Carolina mounted a chair and called on all the members from slaveholding states to join the South Carolinians in the District Committee room, which they did.[16]

At this impromptu meeting 64 out of 106 Southern members were said to be present. They came together again at seven in the evening, with the Senators also in attendance. One account says that every Senator and Representative from a slave state then in Washington was present excepting only Thomas Hart Benton and Henry Clay. The session lasted until midnight, but it brought no unanimity of action. Calhoun pleaded earnestly for a Southern convention to consider the whole question, determine what course was necessary, and take the required steps; and Rhett joined in the plea. But where Calhoun merely conceived the Southern States as falling back on their sovereignty and using the immense pressure that unity would give them to compel an acceptance of their approach to the problem by the general government, Rhett thought in the language of the amendments he had drafted to Slade's bill: amendment of the Constitution or dissolution of the Union.

Calhoun's approach was no more successful than Rhett's; nor could he even win a majority for his proposition that Congress should refuse to receive the abolition petitions. His only victory was the appointment of a committee of one from each slave state to consider steps to be taken to prevent future infractions of what they all regarded as Southern rights. The consensus of the meeting favored the gag rule, and a resolution to that effect was forced through the House in another stormy session the following day.[17]

Although they did not follow his program, Calhoun was the dominant figure in the meeting. Where others were confused and groping, he was sure of himself, and sure of his course. He was clearly the real leader of the South, with no challenge to fear save that from the young disunionists.

4

Calhoun's point of departure was that the Constitution, rightly interpreted and understood, gave ample power to the Southern States to protect themselves. It did not need to be amended for that purpose, and the Union did not need to be dissolved unless flagrant and repeated violations of the compact by the North, under the abolitionist spur, forced its termination. The House by re-enacting the gag rule had again departed from the constitutional ground, but the damage might still be rectified in the Senate.

The slavery issue had already been raised in the upper chamber before the storm broke at the other end of the Capitol. One of the familiar petitions was offered December 18, the day on which Calhoun took his seat, by Garret D. Wall of New Jersey, and was handled according to the practice established in 1836. Before the question of reception was tabled, however, Clay reviewed the whole procedure and wondered if it would not be better to refer such memorials to a committee and make a full report, to quiet the public mind. He thought the extraordinary multiplication of these documents represented rather a belief that the right of petition was in danger than a genuine growth of abolition sentiment.

All this, in Calhoun's eyes, was willful blindness. He had no doubt that the petitions sprang from "a spirit of fanaticism, which was daily increasing," and which if not met effectively would in the end destroy the Union. "Grant the reception of these petitions and you will next be asked to act on them." It was precisely what would happen in the House two days later, but Calhoun did not know it then. He knew only that the agitation was "not to be stopped by reports on paper, but by action, and very decided action." The first object of the South, whose very existence he held to be involved, must be to preserve herself. Her second object was to preserve the Union, which could be done, he was convinced, only by steady and firm resistance to encroachments.[18]

The next day Benjamin Swift of Vermont took a new tack in the antislavery fight, offering not petitions from citizens, this time, but resolutions from his state legislature—resolutions protesting against annexation of Texas or the admission of any new slave state to the Union; affirming the constitutional power of Congress both to abolish slavery in the District of Columbia and to outlaw the slave trade between the states; and instructing Vermont's Senators and requesting her Representatives to work toward these ends.[19]

It was a "new and bold step, and from a higher quarter," which could not be met in the customary way. Calhoun moved a postponement to give the South time to consult, and the resolutions were temporarily withdrawn. Whenever they should come up, however, Calhoun knew that "the whole question must assume to us a new and momentous form." "I think," he wrote to his brother-in-law on December 20, "the sooner the issue is made the better for us and the country; but how it is to be brought on, I am not prepared to say. I think a Southern Convention at the earliest period that the South can be brought [to] act indespensible."[20] On the very day he wrote, the crisis was precipitated by Slade's challenge to the Southern members in the House.

His defeat on the Southern convention and his failure to block the gag rule at the December 20 meeting, together with the radical disunion sentiment there displayed by a small but aggressive minority, were probably the decisive factors in Calhoun's choice of means for combating the Vermont resolutions. What he did was to prepare a series of resolutions of his own, setting forth his theory of the Constitution much as he had done in 1833, and expounding the obligations and limits imposed by that instrument with respect to slavery. He went behind the immediate problem to the broad principles involved and tried once more to commit the Senate to the constitutional theory of nullification. The resolutions were introduced on December 27, 1837.[21]

In 1833 Calhoun had sought to establish an interpretation of the Constitution in terms of which the Force Bill would have been a clear violation. In the face of a hostile majority, he failed, but his resolutions were not voted down—they were simply passed over. He was now attempting the same strategy, but with far better chance of success. The Southern members had to sustain him or abandon their common cause; and the Democrats had to go along, regardless of sectional ties, because his support represented the only hope they had of carrying their own program of economic recovery and reconstruction.

The first resolution simply restated the compact theory of the Constitution and declared that each state had entered the Union voluntarily "with the view to its increased security against all dangers, *domestic,* as well as foreign." The second contained the reserved powers theory of the 1836 report on incendiary publications: that the states severally retained "the exclusive and sole right over their own domestic institutions and police," and condemned as "tending to weaken and destroy the Union itself" intermeddling with these institutions "under any pretext whatever, political, moral or religious." The third affirmed that the general government was the agent of the states, and was obligated "to resist all attempts by one portion of the Union to use it as an instrument to attack the domestic institutions of another. . . ." The fourth placed domestic slavery among the institutions not to be attacked or meddled with. In the fifth resolution any effort to abolish slavery in the District of Columbia or the territories under pretext "that it is immoral or sinful" was declared to be "a direct and dangerous attack on the institutions of the slaveholding States." The sixth and final resolution condemned as tending to weaken the Union and discriminate among its members any refusal on antislavery grounds to extend the territories of the Union or to admit new states.[22]

Considering the magnitude of the question and the past history of attempts to commit the Senate to this same constitutional theory, the debate on Calhoun's resolutions occupied surprisingly little time. The South Carolinian was gaunt and haggard from illness and overwork, but throughout the debate he remained the skillful floor leader of a tightly knit, thoroughly disciplined majority—this in the same Senate where five years before he had battled for the same cause alone, politically dead, morally damned, and ready in many eyes for the hangman's noose. The resolutions were called up on January 3, 1838, and Calhoun stated the issue as he understood it. On one side he saw "a portion of the people of the North, who assert and maintain that our domestic institutions are sinful and immoral. On the other we claim our institutions as secured to us under the Constitution, which we will not suffer them to interfere with." The South, he thought, had two possible courses: "the one to repel attack and aggression; the other to stay the tide, if possible," by some such means as the resolutions he was sustaining. He solemnly reiterated that he was a "firm, unflinching friend of the Union," despite gross and shameful misrepresentations to the contrary. He wanted all friends of the Union to come forward now. "If the resolutions were defective in principle, let them be voted down; if incorrect in phraseology, let them be amended; but he would ask those who believed them correct to give them their cordial support."[23]

As the discussion proceeded along more general lines, Calhoun passed over the petitions for abolition as less important than the crucial fact that the South "had been assailed upon the principle that slavery was wicked, and immoral." He saw the abolition spirit as only another manifestation of "that fanaticism that had carried thousands of victims to the stake . . . the opinion that the faith of one man was criminal in the sight of another."

The first and second resolutions were slightly altered, with Calhoun's consent, and both were passed, the first 32 to 13, the second 32 to 9. Webster stated his disagreement with the constitutional theory and voted no, but did not offer to reopen the 1833 debate. Clay voted for both, and the administration forces formed a solid phalanx behind Calhoun. The third resolution was debated for three days, but all amendments except such as Calhoun himself approved were voted down. He was in complete command of the situation, and on January 6 the third resolution also passed, 31 to 11.[24] How Andrew Jackson would have thundered if he had been there! For this was the same Senate that had passed the Force Act at his command, now solemnly affirming in effect that the Nullifiers had all along been right!

Calhoun was pleased. He conceived that he was carrying the fight to the free states, where the agitation started, and at the same time forcing Northern Democrats "into conflict with the abolition and consolidation parties."[25] But by the same token, as would presently appear, he was forcing Southern Whigs into conflict with himself, and Northern Whigs into the arms of the abolitionists.

The fourth resolution, modified somewhat in language but not at all in meaning, was taken up on January 9, and passed by 35 to 5.[26]

When the fifth came up immediately afterward, however, Clay moved a substitute, more narrowly restricting the issue, and a battle of the Titans began. By the time the Senate adjourned at five o'clock Calhoun and Clay were hurling charge and countercharge of inconsistency and disunion at each other's heads; and oddly enough, they were no longer talking about slavery, but about the late Bank of the United States.[27] For the next two days the battle continued, and Calhoun again defended his attitude toward the Union. "It had pleased Providence . . . to cast his lot in the slaveholding States. There were his hopes, and all that was near and dear to him. His first duty was to them, and he held every other, even his obligations to this Government and the Union, as sacred as he regarded them, subordinate to their safety. . . ."[28]

It is such unguarded admissions as these that constitute the only evidence for Calhoun's alleged conspiracy against the Union. Call it narrow localism if you like, but it is this same kind of localism that has always formed the core of resistance to the totalitarian state. The patriots of the Revolution loved their country, too, and called it England until it became a clear-cut choice between their ancient allegiance and their native soil. No government would ever be changed if men did not hold liberty, or faith, or property, or local ties more dear. No government that has not respected these contravening loyalties has ever been aught but despotism, nor ever will be.

Clay's substitute was further modified by Buchanan, and in the form of two separate resolutions was passed, the first on January 10, by 36 to 8; the second the following day, by 35 to 9. In this final form, the first of the two substitutes condemned moves to abolish slavery in the District of Columbia as dangerous to the rights and security of the people of the District, as a violation of faith with Maryland and Virginia, as a "just cause of alarm to the people of the slaveholding States," and as tending to "disturb and endanger the Union." The second substitute, put through on January 11, declared that any attempt by Congress to abolish slavery in any territory in which it then existed "would create serious alarm and just apprehension" in the slave states. The repudiation of the moral criticism of slavery was abandoned, but Calhoun voted for both. His own sixth and final resolution was tabled on January 12, by a vote of 35 to 9, on Preston's motion, because the same ground was covered in his own pending resolution on the annexation of Texas.[29]

5

The actual issue was almost hopelessly confused by the political cross-purposes of the primary actors involved and by the growing belligerency of the South in response to the more vicious slanders of the abolitionists. Calhoun believed that his resolutions had in large measure recaptured the ground that Pinckney had given up, because the compact theory of the Constitution would in itself prevent any move toward emancipation, in the District of Columbia or elsewhere; but he knew that there were those in his native state, including men whom he numbered among his friends, who were "preparing for revolution" without compunction or regret.[30] Webster thought that Clay and Calhoun together were attempting "what they attempted in 1833, to make a new Constitution."[31] Clay saw in the whole episode only a shrewd move to advance Calhoun's political interests, and adversely to affect his own.[32]

Yet the resolutions were not so abstract, nor the discussion of them so unprofitable, as Clay professed to believe, and the Constitution Calhoun was expounding was nearer to that envisaged by the founding fathers than Webster's version of it. It was, at all events, the only interpretation of the document that stood the slightest chance of stopping the antislavery agitation, and Calhoun knew his people well enough to realize that unless the agitation were stopped in one way or another it would lead in the end "to the overthrow of one of the most admirable Governments that ever existed."[33]

Twenty-five years earlier Calhoun had said in Congress that "*government is protection,* and that it cannot exist where it fails of this great and primary object."[34] It was New England that had been unprotected then. Now it was the South, and he knew that the *status quo* could not long endure. Yet still he did not seek, nor wish, but dreaded the alternative. "I[n] speaking of abolition," he chided his impetuous daughter, "you say it is better to part peacably at once, than to live in the state of indecision we do. That is a natural and common conclusion, but those, who make it up, do not think of the difficulty involved in the word; how many bleeding pours must be taken up in passing the knife of seperation through a body politick, (in order to make two of one) which has been so long bound together by so many ties, political, social and commercial. We cannot and ought not to live together as we are at present, exposed to the continual attacks and assaults of the other portion of the Union; but we must act throughout on the defensive, resort to every probable means of arresting the evil, and only act, when all has been done, that can be, and when we shall stand justified before God and man in taking the final step."[35]

On the same day that Calhoun wrote those lines to Anna, his political creed—a creed that he hoped and believed would make that "final step" unnecessary—was publicly restated. The *Reformer* had followed the *Telegraph* into oblivion, and its place was taken by still another journal, the Washington *Chronicle*. The element of continuity was again supplied by Crallé, who served as editor. The first issue appeared January 25, 1838, with an editorial confession of faith that was both Crallé's and Calhoun's. The editor declared his purpose to be "the support of the State Rights doctrines of 1798. . . . The disturbances engendered by sectional interests, and the conflicts of jurisdiction between the Federal Government and the States might have been avoided, had we carefully observed the counsels contained in these celebrated resolutions . . . the Constitution [has] become, in theory and practice, essentially and dangerously changed. We should not, perhaps, greatly err were we to say that, a majority of the people of the United States, now believe that their common government is one created by the people *en masse,* and based on the will of an absolute majority;—the States bearing the same relation to the Federal Government that counties do to the States. Than this there cannot be a more dangerous error—it is of the very essence of consolidation; and has already led to incalculable evils. It has enabled selfish and designing men . . . to strike at the Union through a vaunted devotion to the interests of the *whole people.* It has warmed into life the fatal spirit of sectional jealousies; and armed it with the most powerful and deadly weapons. Abolition, blind and bigotted, careless of the present, and reckless of the future, is, unquestionably, the offspring of this fatal delusion. So also was the tariff, and other systems which have contributed so much to scatter dissention, and weaken the bonds of Union.

"So long as this dangerous error retains its hold on the public mind," Crallé continued, "there will be, as all men of reflection must perceive, a constant struggle on the part of the minority to protect its rights against the encroachments of the majority." He saw the only hope for the continued existence of the nation in the removal of the cause of sectional strife, and to this end he pledged his paper and his own best efforts. He would be the partisan of no individual, but only of the State Rights philosophy, supporting all measures consistent with it, and opposing all that tended in the direction of consolidation. Like Calhoun, he saw the best chance of achieving his purpose in a rebirth of the party that had stood in opposition to Adams in 1827.[36]

CHAPTER XXVI

THE DEMOCRATIC COALITION

1

By the time the subtreasury bill, incorporating Calhoun's legal-tender amendment, came up again at the regular session of 1837-1838 the administration Senators were thoroughly compromised. They had placed themselves perforce squarely behind the Carolinian on his State Rights-antiabolitionist resolutions, and however they might feel about it personally they had no choice but to stay behind him still. At the special session Van Buren had staked his administration on the subtreasury, and Calhoun was not inclined to give the Senate an opportunity to exercise its wisdom on a substitute. On the ground that members were already familiar with the measure, he met every delaying tactic, and forced it to the floor on January 31, 1838.[1]

The Whigs wisely permitted the Democratic rebels to open for the opposition, which Rives did on February 2. By way of confirming and consolidating his previous position, the Virginia Senator now proposed an amendment substituting for the subtreasury scheme a system of carefully regulated state banks.[2] The debate centered around this amendment for the next two weeks, but the arguments were largely irrelevant. The administration members upheld the subtreasury and denounced the Bank of the United States. The Rives proposal was precisely what they had themselves advocated after Jackson removed the deposits, and they could not consistently attack it now save by indirection. The Whigs, for their part, neither upheld the state banks nor denounced the subtreasury. Their arguments were personal, and the target was Calhoun. Clay in particular was "very impudent" and the South Carolinian expected at no very distant date to "have a round with him."[3] In the Senate and in the press the Whig case was slowly worked up and directed to a single focal point, beginning with the groundless charge in December that Calhoun had expressed disapproval of the subtreasury on his way to Washington for the special session.[4]

Publicly, at least, Calhoun ignored these personal attacks and stuck strictly to the point at issue. When he conceived that enough had been said on Rives' amendment he took the floor on February 15, contrasting the state bank and subtreasury systems in a "speech of great power, and more than usual animation."[5] In his direct and incisive fashion he sloughed away the chaff, held up the real alternatives for all to see, and recapitulated the relative advantages and disadvantages of a national bank and an Independent Treasury. His speech was the starting point for the remainder of the debate, and if the administration had doubted or hesitated, it did so no longer. A few hours after its delivery the *Globe* was on the streets, with a leading editorial in which Blair pronounced it "the most splendid and powerful intellectual effort" of Calhoun's career. "We consider his speech as decisive of the question," the editor concluded. "Mr. Rives' substitute is annihilated."[6]

The next move was up to the opposition, and Clay himself was the indicated champion.

2

In Clay's speech of February 19, 1838, all the pent-up animosities of the past five months and the carefully suppressed bitterness of years' standing came to a focus and burst with overwhelming vehemence on the head of John C. Calhoun. The brilliant Kentuckian began with the subtreasury, but he was not replying to anything his antagonist had said on the Senate floor four days earlier. He was answering, with accumulated and compounded interest, Calhoun's great speech of September 18, 1837, with its open announcement of a change of sides; and more particularly still, he was answering the Edgefield letter. For months he had been preparing, awaiting his opportunity, and when it came he took every advantage of it.

A week-end postponement had served to advertise the event. The Senate chamber was jammed to the limit of its small capacity, and Clay's performance was all that any audience could have desired. He was pleading, gentle as the dove, and the next minute a raging lion; his words were as the soft south wind and the roaring North Atlantic gale. He denied, denounced, ridiculed—did everything, in fact, but answer the argument. It was all strictly parliamentary, but when he took up the Edgefield letter he overreached himself. He did not confine his charges of apostasy to Calhoun's recent break with the

Whigs, but went back to the early days of their careers, when side by side they had done so much to force the War of 1812 upon a reluctant administration. Then with cutting sarcasm and a cavalier disregard for truth, the Kentucky orator followed their two careers to that day and hour; and in every point where they diverged, Calhoun appeared politically and morally at fault. The final conclusion was that from motives which yet remained to be disclosed, but by innuendo had personal ambition behind them, Calhoun had sold out to Van Buren.[7]

Calhoun rose immediately to give notice that he would answer in due time. He had not wished to interrupt while Clay was speaking, but he now accused the Kentuckian bluntly of perverting and misstating the arguments. He intended, he announced, "to pay his respects to that Senator at the first opportunity, both with respect to his argument and his personal attack on him; and when he did so, the debt between them should be fully cancelled."[8]

It was almost three weeks before the account was squared, a delay due in part at least to an unexpected and shocking incident that showed again how high partisan and sectional feelings ran. On February 24 (Saturday of the week Clay had opened with his devastating attack on Calhoun) Representative Jonathan Cilley of Maine was killed in a duel by Representative William Graves of Kentucky. Graves was a Clay Whig and Cilley that rare anomaly, a New England Nullifier, who had broken with Jackson when the Proclamation was issued. The cause of the duel was a matter of punctilio, involving criticisms made by Cilley in the House of newspaper articles by James Watson Webb of the New York *Courier and Enquirer*. Webb's demand for an explanation had been refused on the ground that a member of Congress was not accountable to the press; whereupon Graves had injected himself into the fray on Webb's behalf.[9]

Graves' initial letter, so framed as to make a duel inevitable, and the challenge itself were both actually drafted by Henry Clay, though that fact was carefully concealed for more than four years. Crittenden was also involved behind the scenes. Publicly concerned were Representative Henry A. Wise of Virginia, who acted as Graves' second, and George W. Jones, delegate from Wisconsin Territory, who performed the same service for Cilley. The duel was a thoroughly barbarous affair, fought with rifles at eighty yards. There were two exchanges of fire before the fatal one, but the combatants refused after each exchange to be reconciled.

The whole affair was inexcusable, and certainly would never have occurred if partisan feeling had been less bitter.[10] The Justices of the Supreme Court expressed their disapproval by refusing to attend the funeral, and Congress eventually passed an antidueling law. The most conspicuous immediate result, however, was a distinct softening in the temper of the debate when Calhoun and Clay resumed their hostilities.[11]

Calhoun's following thought Clay's speech of February 19 "in very bad spirit," revealing primarily that he felt Calhoun to be in his way. "They have always felt so towards one another," Hammond confessed, "but have been both too wise to show it."[12] Calhoun himself thought Clay's effort "in the main very feeble and personal" and was preparing to give him "as good as he sent" when the Graves-Cilley duel interrupted things for the time being.[13]

It was March 10 when Calhoun finally took the floor. Again the time and occasion had been duly advertised, and again the Senate chamber was filled to overflowing. The doors were left open so that hundreds who jammed the corridor outside could hear, even though they could not see, and hundreds more could not get near enough even to hear. The House could not secure a quorum, and its members too found their way into the smaller Senate chamber, where privilege allowed them to find places on the floor if they could. Even John Quincy Adams was there, sitting beside his one-time Secretary of State, and it was just as well, for Adams too was included by indirection in Calhoun's remarks. Clay had left himself wide open when he elected to go back a quarter of a century to begin his personal allusions; for his own career was more vulnerable than Calhoun's, and the latter took full advantage of that fact.

According to Benton, Calhoun's reply to Clay was consciously patterned after Demosthenes' Oration on the Crown, which he says the South Carolinian restudied in the interval during which his speech was being prepared, and the resemblance is indeed marked. The contrast between Calhoun and Clay as speakers was never more clearly brought out than in this debate. The Kentuckian was a master of gesture, of tone, of fine nuances in sound as well as in meaning. He had to be seen as he moved restlessly about the Senate chamber to be fully appreciated, and no written record of what he said could do him justice. Calhoun on the other hand stood rooted in one spot, scarcely moving a muscle, except that his brilliant, hypnotic eyes darted from one face to another; yet in his eyes alone he managed to convey almost as much of scorn or triumph as Clay conveyed by changing tone and co-ordinated movement. Calhoun's voice was even and steady, a little harsh, not at all rich or rolling. He still spoke, when excited, with incredible rapidity, but this time he had himself well under control and paced his remarks so all could follow. Clay's speech was rich in imagery and his words were colorful, his periods tending to be long and rhythmical. Calhoun's was concise and sharply pointed, with never an excess word, and periods so short at times as to sound clipped and staccato. He relied almost entirely on content, logical arrangement, clarity of structure, for his effects, and hence his speeches may be read today with far more pleasure and comprehension than those of most of his contemporaries.

Calhoun followed the same formula Clay had adopted, replying first and most briefly to the arguments, such as they had been, on the subtreasury. He had little difficulty in demonstrating that the Kentuckian, in his eagerness, had refuted not the points made by his opponent but hypothetical arguments devised by himself for the sole purpose of demolishing them. Calhoun professed himself unwilling to waste the time of the Senate on such trivia and hurried on to the main body of his own speech. There his theme was that Clay, unable to combat the subtreasury by logic, had resorted to one of the most ancient of subterfuges—the *argumentum ad hominem.*

The remainder of the time was consumed by Calhoun in a detailed and in the main successful defense of his own career and an attack on Clay's which was the more effective for its restraint. At every point where Clay had accused him of inconsistency, he had the secretary of the Senate read excerpts from his 1834 speeches on the removal of the deposits and on the limited recharter of the Bank—speeches made when he and Clay were on the same side. In no case was the charge borne out, least of all the most unworthy of them—that he had enlisted under the Van Buren banner for an as yet undisclosed price—which the Kentuckian had based on the Edgefield letter. Excerpts from that letter too were read, and again Calhoun asked his fellow Senators if the facts sustained the charge.

Then he turned to Clay, deep scorn flashing from his dark animated eyes and echoed in his biting words. "I pick up the shaft, which fell harmless at my feet. I hurl it back. What the Senator charges on me unjustly, *he has actually done.* He went over on a memorable occasion, and did not leave it to time to disclose his motive." Old John Quincy Adams, at whom the shaft was also leveled, did not move a muscle but he poured venom into his diary that night.

Before Calhoun was through he had reviewed his own career from the war with England up to the day he spoke, and he found nothing in it—neither his vote for the tariff of 1816, nor his sponsorship of the second Bank of the United States in that same year, nor anything he had since done—that was inconsistent with the philosophy he now professed, the philosophy of the Kentucky Resolutions and the principles of 1798.

Clay immediately answered, Calhoun rejoined, and for some time there was an impromptu give-and-take in which Preston joined against his colleague. It was Calhoun, however, who held the stronger position throughout and who terminated the discussion when he saw fit. Before the exchange was over Clay had abandoned most of his own ground and was more than ready to call it quits.[14] As even some of his own partisans admitted, Clay had been "but a child in Mr. Calhoun's hand."[15] The *Globe* and the *Chronicle* were also in perfect agreement as to the outcome. The vindication had been triumphant, and the effect was better still, for Calhoun had never lost his calm dignity of bearing, but Clay had let anger lead him to extravagance.

Two days later Webster took up the argument against the subtreasury, and like Clay he selected Calhoun for his antagonist. In the eyes of the opposition the Carolinian was the great champion of the administration program, who must be overcome at whatever cost. It is probable that even Wright and Benton, who resented Calhoun's presence on their side, were happy enough to see him rather than themselves cast in so uncomfortable a role.

Webster also followed Clay in his resort to personalities, but his touch was deft and light. It is said that he provoked laughter even from the all but humorless Calhoun himself.[16] Webster was far more effective than Clay had been, both in his arguments against the subtreasury and in his attack on Calhoun, because like his antagonist he maintained his dignity. But he based his argument against the subtreasury on the completely mistaken ground that it would destroy credit; and in his efforts to show Calhoun's inconsistency he dwelt overlong on the Carolinian's defense of a national bank in 1816, when he had himself opposed.[17]

Calhoun replied to Webster in ten days' time, justifying his third appearance in the debate on the ground that again he had been personally attacked and so was entitled to defend himself. As the tone of Webster's speech had been altogether different from Clay's, so was Calhoun's reply to Webster very different from his reply to Clay. Webster had been explicit in his expression of personal regard and in his insistence that his attack on Calhoun's record was political and not personal. Calhoun acknowledged the distinction graciously. "Indeed," he declared, "there never has been between the Senator and myself the least personal difference; nor has a word, having a personal bearing, ever passed between us in debate prior to the present occasion, within my recollection, during the long period we have been in public life—except on the discussion of the Force Bill and Proclamation; which, considering how often we have stood opposed on deep and exciting questions, may be regarded as not a little remarkable."

He then took the Force Bill and the Proclamation as his point of departure. Webster, like Clay, had built his whole battle plan on Calhoun's alleged desertion of the cause as victory was about to be achieved, but it was not Calhoun's cause that would have been victorious: it would have been those very doctrines of consolidation and power that Webster had championed for Jackson and that Calhoun had so strenuously opposed. "Yes, I repeat, it would have brought in the Senator and his consolidation doctrines, which regard this government as one great National Republic, with the right to construe finally and conclusively, the extent of its own powers, and to enforce its construction at the point of the bayonet; doctrines which at a blow sweep away every vestige of State Rights, and reduce the States to mere petty and dependent corporations. It would also have brought in his policy, bank, tariff, and all."

Calhoun's defense against Webster was as dispassionate as though it were someone else whose course had been attacked and not his own. He held to the high level of broad principles of government, in terms of which alone he claimed consistency, and showed with the incisive clarity of which he was so great a master that the philosophy of power had descended to the Whigs while he continued to hold, as he had always held in the past, that liberty was the great end of government. On the personal side, he dispensed with sarcasm, and sought, as Webster himself had sought, to avoid the cutting phrase that must leave a lasting wound. Webster's record was far more vulnerable than even Clay's, and he needed no tricks of oratory to reveal his opponent's weakness.[18]

A young army officer stationed in Washington at this time without too much to do managed to listen to the whole debate, which he reported afterward to a South Carolina friend at West Point: "I fancy that there are very few subjects on which we now differ—in some opinions about politics we didn't use to agree but if you have stood fast we do now. I have come over. . . . I am as good a nullifier now as you would wish to see. . . . I heard the great Debate between Clay & Calhoun & between Webster & Calhoun—I heard them much discussed in conversation also: I was decidedly of opinion that Calhoun beat them all out & out. . . . Ever since I heard those speeches I have been an ultra sub Treasury man. . . ."[19]

3

Although Webster, Clay, and Rives carried the burden of the fight against the subtreasury on the floor of the Senate, the most effective weapons against the measure were wielded elsewhere, and it was Nicholas Biddle who called the turn. Early in February the Tennessee Senators were instructed by their legislature to vote no, and the Pennsylvania legislature, under Biddle's lash, soon took a similar course. Each of these states had one Whig Senator, so that only the votes of Grundy and Buchanan were affected, but those two were almost enough to turn the tide. Clay urged Biddle to seek instructions in New Jersey to change Wall's vote, while he himself tried by way of Richmond to convert William H. Roane, the junior Senator from Virginia.[20]

Even after the loss of Grundy and Buchanan, Calhoun believed the bill would pass by a small margin.[21] He was probably still of that mind when one of the stalwarts on his own side suddenly deserted. Rives's amendment substituting the state bank system for the subtreasury had just been voted down on March 21 when Alfred Cuthbert of Georgia claimed the floor. In his pleasant Irish brogue Cuthbert told of the pain it gave him to differ with his party, claimed the right—that Calhoun especially had to grant him—of honest conviction, and moved to strike out the twenty-third section of the subtreasury bill. It was the section defining legal tender and providing that the use of bank notes should gradually be discontinued: in short, Calhoun's amendment of the special session, without which the bill became a mere temporary expedient—without which there was no real separation of bank and state and no genuine solution of the currency problem.[22]

The next day, in his reply to Webster, Calhoun vindicated to the best of his ability the complete divorce of the government and the banks; but on the twenty-fourth Cuthbert's amendment was adopted, 31 to 21. The administration leaders held firm but enough waverers joined the Whigs to make the vote decisive. Calhoun then announced in a brief but penetrating speech that he could not support the subtreasury with the legal tender clause no longer a part of it; and when the bill was passed to a third reading a few minutes later, he voted no. He also voted no on the final passage of the amended bill, which occurred on March 26. The vote was 27 to 25, with the waverers back in line now the bill had been emasculated. Of the professed Democrats only the "instructed" Grundy and Buchanan joined Calhoun in opposition.[23]

The result left some doubt as to the sincerity of the administration's wish to separate bank and state, but it left none on the score of Calhoun's complete independence from all party ties. The Whigs rejoiced, as well they might; Calhoun predicted a new wave of inflation, the renewal of a government connection with the banks as they resumed specie payments, and in due time another shock "more terrifick than that, which we have lately experienced."[24]

During April and early May the New York banks and most of those elsewhere resumed specie payments, but Biddle held the still powerful Bank of the United States of Pennsylvania aloof from the general movement. To resume while the subtreasury bill was still under consideration would have been in his eyes a surrender. The emasculation of the measure in the Senate was not enough to satisfy Biddle's long-starved ego, and he began marshaling his forces to crush it altogether in the House. At the same time he tried to trick the government into a new business relationship with his institution by a disingenuous offer to pay at once the sums still owing the Treasury on its liquidated stock instead of holding to terms calling for payments spread over the next three years.[25]

Calhoun had given up the fight no more than Biddle. The supporters of the subtreasury in the House were prepared to stake everything on the omitted section,[26] and through April and May Calhoun moved "heaven, earth, & ——— to obtain Southern votes" for it. He reasoned with individual members, as he had argued at home the previous fall, that an Independent Treasury would free the South of her commercial dependence on New York and other Northern cities. His "plausibility, & endless perseverence," combined with the patronage of the Executive, had accomplished far more before May was over than the Bank men had believed possible. Even Nicholas Biddle's nephew, Representative Charles Biddle Shepard of North Carolina, was undecided.[27] Calhoun might, indeed, have accomplished all he sought in spite of Biddle's greater resources for persuasion, had it not been for the open defection of Preston, Legaré, and Waddy Thompson, the last representing Calhoun's own district in the House.[28]

The repeal of the Specie Circular on May 31 was hailed by Biddle as the first fruit of his own campaign against the financial policy of the administration, and he redoubled his efforts. John Sergeant, again representing a Philadelphia constituency in the House, was asked to tabulate the probable vote on the subtreasury, and to let the bank president know how many more votes were needed. "Perhaps," Biddle added with a cynicism born of long experience, "we may prove to some of our Penna. members, that their course is injurious to the state & to themselves." June 25 saw the bill beaten on third reading, 125 to 111, and Biddle took full credit for it to himself.[29]

Calhoun's last bid for victory had been a special session of the South Carolina legislature late in May which reaffirmed the resolutions of the winter in favor of the subtreasury and declared that any public servant refusing to promote that policy would be pursuing a "course injurious to the welfare and prosperity of the state." The stroke was engineered by Rhett and Elmore through their respective brothers in the legislature and was generally supported by the former Unionists.[30] It was not enough. Only Campbell, Legaré and Thompson voted against the policy adopted by their state, but the margin of defeat was fourteen votes.

4

The sharp clash over the abolition issue with which the session opened and the sectionalism inherent in the subtreasury fight would in themselves have been more than ample to strain still farther the already strained relations between North and South. The Texas question was equally dangerous to the future harmony of the country, however, and it was inevitable that it too would be aired while partisan feeling was at its height and individual tempers were ragged. Each of these issues had its bearing on the others, and added something to the net effect.

It was William C. Preston who injected Texas into the already potentially explosive situation in the Senate. Calhoun's State Rights resolutions were still being debated when on January 4 Preston introduced a resolution of his own calling for annexation. With diabolical ingenuity he called it "re-annexation," and based his case on the allegation that the Rio Grande was the true boundary of the United States under the Louisiana Purchase and had so remained until surrendered by the treaty of 1819 with Spain—a surrender "of evil precedent and doubtful constitutionality."[31]

For the moment Preston was content to let the matter rest, knowing that he could call up his resolution whenever he chose. He delayed until June 14, at a late hour of the day when many seats were empty. Samuel Southard moved to table the resolution on that ground and Calhoun agreed, adding that he favored the purpose but opposed the preamble. Preston then made it clear that he thought Southard and Calhoun, both of whom had been members of Monroe's Cabinet when the "evil precedent" was established, were trying to evade the issue. The exchange between Calhoun and Preston that followed dripped with acid. Southard, caught in the cross fire, withdrew his motion to table, but it was renewed by Norvell of Michigan and carried, Calhoun voting no.[32]

The Texas question was not allowed to come up again in the Senate, but was simultaneously being argued in the House, in the form of a report from the Committee on Foreign Affairs. On the same day that Preston called up his resolution in the Senate, Waddy Thompson in the House moved to instruct the Foreign Affairs Committee along similar lines. He would have the committee report a joint resolution "directing the President to take the necessary steps for the annexation of Texas to the United States as soon as it can be done consistently with the treaty stipulations of this Government."[33] There was undoubtedly collusion between the two South Carolina insurgents, and one of their purposes was certainly to embarrass Calhoun in his battle for the subtreasury. What they succeeded in doing, however, was to arouse all the never-too-well-concealed suspicions of John Quincy

Adams, who as Secretary of State had negotiated the treaty of 1819.

Adams had already conjured up the myth of a Southern conspiracy against the Union, and the annexation of Texas, sponsored like nullification by South Carolinians, fitted his canvas to a T. He filibustered for three weeks until the session ended. The net result of his efforts was to raise to fever pitch the already aggravated hostility between the sections. In the North feeling ran so high that Nicholas Biddle's board of directors refused to sanction a Texas loan, and Texas itself withdrew its petition to be annexed.[34]

5

Behind the scenes, as well as openly in the halls of Congress, the Van Buren administration wooed the Nullifiers through the session of 1837-1838. The sarcastic side digs at nullification in which not so very long ago it had been the delight of the Jacksonians themselves to indulge were now regarded as out of order and were instantly rebuked by presiding officers who gave allegiance to Jackson's hand-picked heir.[35] The administration-sponsored *Democratic Review* devoted twenty pages of its April issue to a sympathetic pen portrait of Calhoun in a conscious effort to welcome him back to the party.[36] It was all so obvious that the Calhoun press felt called on to issue a qualification, lest the position of the South Carolinian be misunderstood. "In supporting the divorce of the government and the banks," warned the Pendleton *Messenger* late in May, "we do not conceive that State Rights men are identifying themselves with the administration. We may unite with them in this measure, as we did with the Whigs in resisting executive usurpations without committing ourselves to their support any further than we conceive their measures to accord with our principles."[37]

And indeed it was entirely true that Calhoun did not feel any obligation to go all the way with Van Buren's program. When the President made his gesture toward the West in the form of a liberalized land program, Calhoun voted no on both the pre-emption bill and the bill to graduate and reduce the price of the public lands. By the same token his own substitute measure, ceding the lands under certain conditions to the states in which they lay, continued to be unpalatable to the administration members, and got no farther than reference to committee.[38]

The administration spokesmen ignored the differences of view and after Congress had adjourned they continued their efforts to bring Calhoun more completely and fully into the fold, even to the extremity of abandoning their own position and adopting his. In supporting the State Rights resolutions of January the administration had come over on the slavery question. It was already in the Calhoun camp on the financial program. Both groups claimed true allegiance to the "old Republican doctrines" of 1798. Where, then, lay their differences? Through the summer and fall of 1838 clear up to the off-year elections Blair and the Van Buren press endeavored to show that there were none. There was, to be sure, a vast conspiracy against popular government which had been undermining free American institutions for twenty years, but it no longer appeared to be the work of ambitious and designing men at the South called Nullifiers. That all but forgotten word was not even mentioned. The conspiracy now appeared to have been fostered all along by Federalists, masking under various guises such as National Republicans and Whigs, but always including the archconspirators Henry Clay, Daniel Webster, and Nicholas Biddle. It was now these iniquitous Federalists who had created an octupuslike bank, who had aroused and still egged on the abolitionists, who sought to drive a wedge of misunderstanding and distrust between North and South.[39]

Just before the earlier state elections were held, the *Globe* reprinted excerpts from an address by General John A. Dix of the Albany Regency to a convention in upstate New York, and from a letter of Calhoun's to a State Rights rally in Richland District, South Carolina. "Without communication with each other," exulted Blair, "it will be seen that Mr. Calhoun and General Dix delineate the doctrines of the present day, deriving them from their origin at the foundation of the Government, as if the same head and hand directed the pencil. . . ."[40]

None knew better than Calhoun what value to place on praise from Francis Preston Blair, or on the growing savagery of the attacks on his character and motives that now filled the Whig journals. "In times so degenerate," he wrote to his old Yale classmate, Micah Sterling, "when there is so little of truth and sincerity, he, who speaks and acts as he really thinks, is almost sure to deceive everybody. I speak from experience. . . . Had I gone with the crowd and the current of the times, and aimed at advancing my popularity and influence, instead of struggling to preserve our free institutions and the liberty of the country, I could have passed for a first rate patriot; at least equal to Mr. Clay or Mr. Webster. What is really remarkable is this. Almost all allow me to possess abilities and sagacity, and yet, altho' I have done the most unpopular acts, of which I could not but see the consequences, even in performing them, I have been charged with motives of popularity and ambition."[41] Obsessed as he was with his own theory of government and his application of it to the Constitution of the United States, he saw himself as the great champion of reform. The government in his eyes had been corrupted both by the consolidationism of the National Republicans and by the spoils philosophy of the Jacksonians, and in the bitterness of sectional conflict he saw the inevitable fruit of these departures from what he regarded as true principles.

Van Buren's weakness and the dynamism of Calhoun's own strength of character and conviction had placed the South Carolinian in the dominant position, and he no longer doubted the ultimate triumph of his views. Nor did he relinquish hope that in spite of all the factors that would bear against him, his fellow countrymen would yet recognize his merits and elevate him to the highest office in their gift. The conclusion of his letter to Sterling indicates that the ambition he had long put aside was stirring once more. "What may be my fate in taking the course I have," he went on, "my friends take much more interest in it than I myself do. I look to nothing beyond the discharge of my duty. As to the Presidency, I would not accept it, unless I was called by the publick voice *to reform the government & restore it to its prestine purity & vigour*."[42] In the almost desperate overtures of the Democrats he could hardly fail to see a premonition of this public call, and so he held tenaciously to his identity and to his principles. Let them come to him, and if they came it must mean an approval of what he stood for and of what he was.

The off-year elections in the fall of 1838 only strengthened Calhoun's hand, for the results bore out all he had foretold of the political strength and tactics of the abolitionists. In New York the Whigs made a conscious bid for abolitionist support with the nomination of William H. Seward for Governor, and Seward won. In Ohio the incumbent Whig Governor was defeated because he had defied the abolitionists and delivered up to Kentucky authorities an antislavery agitator.[43] In the North and West generally the Whigs showed gains, with an accession of abolitionists to their ranks, while the Democrats held on grimly in the South. It was only in South Carolina and Alabama where the Calhoun faction was in firm control, however, that the administration won clear-cut and decisive victories. Where Van Buren had made his bid for Southern support on halfway measures, or on any ground other than Calhoun's thoroughgoing defense of slavery and of state sovereignty, he had lost. Calhoun read the implications of this as clearly as Van Buren. He began to hope that the South could find adequate protection through political channels, and he began to wonder if the logical man to succeed Van Buren in the White House might not, perhaps, be John C. Calhoun.[44]

6

Of all the state elections in the fall of 1838 none held more interest or more national significance than those in South Carolina; for South Carolina was the microcosm where Calhoun's leadership was to be tested. On the outcome there would depend in large measure whether the Van Buren administration would continue its progress in the direction of "Southern principles."

Calhoun did not wait for the adjournment of Congress on July 9, but returned home immediately after the defeat of the subtreasury in the House. He blamed that defeat, not on Nicholas Biddle who took personal credit for it, but on the activities and votes of two dissident South Carolina Congressmen, Legaré and Thompson, and he was determined that neither should be re-elected. His first move was to enlist the aid of Poinsett.[45] He continued to insist that he and his followers did not belong to the administration and that the separate identity of the State Rights party must be maintained; but in so far as purposes were identical, it was clearly to the advantage of both to get together. In the defeat of Thompson and Legaré they shared a common aim.[46]

The campaign got under way immediately with no quarter asked or given. Late in July certain citizens of Richland District, of which Columbia was the principal city, got up a barbecue for Preston. They were charged by the anti-Preston faction with political motives and were soon forced to extend the scope of the affair to include Elmore, the Representative from the district, and Calhoun, the other Senator; but only Preston came. Calhoun declined in a letter blunt to the point of rudeness, which was widely circulated. The affair, he said, had been arranged to honor Preston, which could mean only that those responsible wished to commend the junior Senator's course in Congress. For his part, Calhoun held Preston's course detrimental to state and nation. He emphatically did not approve it and would attend no dinner with those who did.[47] He was in no way mollified by a toast upholding his own claims to the Presidency, and was plainly delighted to be able to pronounce the dinner a failure. The State Rights party in the same Congressional district then tried to get up another dinner to heal the breach, but this too he declined, taking the opportunity, however, to restate the case for the subtreasury. Preston cordially reciprocated Calhoun's ill feeling in his own prompt declination.[48]

A political dinner in Greenville on August 28 precipitated hostilities of another kind. This invitation Calhoun accepted, and spoke for an hour and a half in defense of the subtreasury. Because it was in his own district, Waddy Thompson also was present, and made an immediate unscheduled and ungentle reply. Calhoun rejoined sharply, and two days later Thompson called the senior Senator to account. He stated his own understanding of the situation and his recollection of the language both had used, and wanted to know if Calhoun had intended the offensive remarks he had made or if he might consider them withdrawn. Calhoun replied somewhat testily that he had of course intended his remarks, but that they had been applied at the time to a proposition different from that to which Thompson now attributed them. In the absence of a verbatim report, or even a summary one, of the actual speeches, it is impossible to say now where the real truth lay, but Calhoun's qualification was sufficient to prevent further personal hostilities.[49]

Thompson thereafter shrewdly insisted that he was an administration man, that he opposed the Bank of the United States, and that his admiration for Calhoun was boundless. The issues were thoroughly confused as Thompson proved more than a match for successive candidates hand-picked to run against him, and to Calhoun's intense mortification he was triumphantly re-elected by a large majority.[50] Henry L. Pinckney also won re-election as Mayor of Charleston early in September, and for a time things looked out of hand. Calhoun roamed the state like a troubled spirit, campaigning as he had not done for years; and a new State Rights paper, the *South Carolinian,* was set up in Columbia, with Calhoun virtually dictating its policies.[51]

Although Waddy Thompson remained invincible, the tide elsewhere began to turn in September. On the nineteenth of that month a Democratic Independent Treasury ticket was announced in Charleston, with Isaac Holmes for Congress and Daniel E. Huger, a one-time Unionist, for the state senate. The *Courier* continued to represent Legaré as the administration candidate, and the issue was further confused by putting Huger on the Legaré ticket as well as on the Holmes ticket; but it was a losing battle. The die-hard Bank men among the old Unionists—"Mr. Petigru's little army of centurions without soldiers," the *Mercury* called them—rallied to Legaré, but through Poinsett the full weight of the administration was thrown behind the other ticket. The *Globe* took a hand in the business just before the balloting, officially condemning Legaré as belonging to the opposition, and in the final count Holmes's victory approached a two-to-one margin.[52]

In less publicized contests Calhoun was completely victorious. Preston, of course, would remain in the Senate until his term expired, and Thompson would be back to plague the delegation in the House; but both would now be forced to throw themselves wholly upon the Whigs. The legislature was overwhelmingly under Calhoun's thumb, and with the exception of Thompson he could call the tune for the state's Congressional delegation after the fourth of March.

CHAPTER XXVII

ADMINISTRATION SPOKESMAN

1

BY THE end of 1838 the struggle in South Carolina was over, and in the nation as a whole the prospects of the Nullifiers were better than they had ever been. Calhoun was the almost absolute master of his state and was on the way to being master of the South. The government was moving as rapidly in the direction of his own political views as under Jackson and Adams it had moved away from them. The great reform about which he had been talking and writing for ten years seemed at last about to be consummated. That it would be Martin Van Buren, whom he disliked and distrusted, who would be in the eyes of the country and of history the instrument of the reform seemed to Calhoun unimportant in comparison with the desirability of the object to be achieved.[1]

Many factors besides the political ones discussed in the preceding chapter had combined to give direction and momentum to the administration. Nicholas Biddle, as usual, had overplayed his hand. When the Treasury and War Departments accepted credit in the Bank of the United States of Pennsylvania as payment for bonds due in 1838 and 1839, he rejoiced too loudly in what he regarded as a victory. He had consistently refused to resume specie payments, and this alone made the action of the administration inconsistent. More important, however, was the fact that by accepting credit, the government had in effect made Biddle's Bank once more a depository. He was easily convinced that Van Buren had surrendered, and with unparalleled effrontery proceeded to tell the Secretary of State what he wanted in the President's annual message. He hoped there would be no more of "this worn out foolery of Mr. Calhoun," by which he meant the subtreasury.[2]

Even had he won the victory he supposed, Biddle was not yet in position to dictate terms to the Government of the United States, and he was politely rebuffed. Forsyth replied promptly that the message was already in final form and that the President's views as to the management of the public funds remained unaltered.[3] It was not Biddle's arrogance alone, however, that made it impossible for Van Buren to reverse his course. Public opinion still held with Andrew Jackson that a national bank was a monster of corruption; and the South was now sure that Biddle's Bank in particular had more than a nominal connection with the abolitionists. Had they not interfered successfully when the Bank would have aided Texas? And was not John Sergeant, Pennsylvania Congressman and once National Republican candidate for Vice President, attorney both for the Bank and for the Pennsylvania Abolition Society?[4]

The *Globe* emphasized the role of the abolitionists in the New York elections, moving on to a triple alliance of "Federalism, Fanaticism and Bankism";[5] and in principle the argument was sound. For only under the constitutional theory of Federalism could the abolitionists hope to achieve their purpose; and the power of a national bank derived from the same centralist view of the fundamental law. It was not accident that made the Whigs the advocates of the Bank, or led the abolitionists to seek political action in the Whig fold; and the nearer the Whigs advanced to the old Federalist position, the more were the Democrats driven by the necessities of partisan politics to be antifederalist. They were soon to learn, if they did not know already, that there was no middle ground between consolidation and state sovereignty.

As the issues were slowly clarified and the sectional nature of the alignments was revealed by the elections of the summer and fall of 1838, Van Buren drew politically and personally closer to the South. A third Southerner entered the Cabinet when Felix Grundy of Tennessee replaced Butler as Attorney General in a shift that also saw Mahlon Dickerson of New Jersey yield the Navy Department to J. K. Paulding of New York. Unheralded, but perhaps most significant of all, on November 27, 1838, Abraham Van Buren, the President's eldest son, married Sarah Angelica Singleton of Sumter District, South Carolina. George McDuffie's deceased wife had been an older sister of the bride; and so McDuffie's small daughter (who one day would marry General Wade Hampton) would call Martin Van Buren's son her uncle.

2

Van Buren's second annual message, read on December 4, 1838, was no more than a restatement of the policies he had so far pursued. He noted the substantial progress of economic recovery which he attributed to the relief measures of the special session. He recommended once more the Independent Treasury, being careful to protest his innocence of any hostility toward banks as such. He acknowledged the pre-emption act of the previous session and repeated his request that the price of the public lands be scaled down.[6] Again he said nothing about slavery, in the District of Columbia or elsewhere, but again his partisans would be forced to support substantially the Calhoun position.

This time the clash occurred in the House of Representatives, where the gag rule had been re-enacted at every session since 1835. The organization of the House was completed on December 10, and that same evening a party caucus worked until midnight on a new set of resolutions to deal with the abolition petitions. They were introduced the following day by Charles G. Atherton of New Hampshire. The government was declared to be one of limited powers, with no jurisdiction whatever over slavery in the states. It was then asserted, correctly, that the ultimate purpose of petitions and memorials for the abolition of slavery in the District of Columbia and the territories was abolition in the states; that Congress could not discriminate among the states, nor do by indirection what it could not do directly; and that therefore Congress had no jurisdiction over slavery in the District of Columbia or the territories. After the preliminaries, the gag rule was reaffirmed. Though the pattern was somewhat different, the general conclusion and the net effect were the same as in the resolutions Calhoun had driven through the Senate the previous session: Congress had been forbidden to tamper with slavery anywhere. Adams and his growing band of followers put up their usual sharp struggle, but the administration members stood solidly behind their caucus agreement and the Atherton resolutions were adopted.[7]

The tendency of all this was to make the slavery question a party issue: to identify the Whigs with abolition, and to cut off thereby not only the entire slaveholding South but also conservative and substantial citizens throughout the North and West whose natural inclinations would have placed them in the party of property but who could stomach the fanatical abolitionists no more than could the South. The course of Adams and his cohorts on the Atherton resolutions alarmed the Whig leaders in the North as much as it annoyed the Southern members of the party, like Wise and Garland, who had consistently supported the successive gag rules.[8] Clay presently tried to undo the damage by taking a stand himself against the abolitionists, but it was already too late to appease the South.

The Atherton resolutions, meanwhile, were declared unconstitutional by the legislature of Vermont in a rider attached to antislavery resolutions of the familiar type. Senator Prentiss from that state asked early in January that the Vermont resolutions be printed; but Calhoun, alert for the slightest reference to the forbidden topic, was instantly on his feet. King of Alabama and Lumpkin of Georgia joined in his protest and the motion to print was tabled, 29 to 8.[9]

On this question Clay avoided casting a vote, but he was not able to withstand the pressure from influential Whigs, both North and South, for long. He chose his opening carefully and on February 7, 1839, he spoke to a memorial offered by himself. It came from leading citizens of the District of Columbia and protested vigorously against external agitation of the slavery question in the District in opposition to the will and the desires of those who would be affected by it. Many of the signers were Clay's own friends of long standing, and it is a fair guess that he himself inspired the document to give him a suitable sounding board. Be that as it may, he came out with a ringing denunciation of the abolitionists and denied categorically any power in Congress to interfere with slavery wherever it existed.[10]

Calhoun sardonically complimented the Kentuckian on his conversion, recalling that Clay had prevented the inclusion of a similarly unequivocal declaration in the resolutions of the previous year. He had listened to the Senator on this occasion with great pleasure, and he considered that the danger to the South was now over.[11] So did the South generally, but the common feeling was that Clay's bid had come too late. He had seen the light too recently and some of the company he kept was still objectionable. Van Buren was safer, because he was now so deeply committed that he could not change his mind. The President realized his advantage and made the most of it. The Whigs were carrying water on both shoulders, and if they did not stumble it would not be any fault of Francis Preston Blair. With an eye on both buckets, the editor pointed out that the Whigs had used the abolitionists to win the New York elections and had then renounced the alliance lest it cost them the South and make Baltimore rather than New York the center of the Western trade.[12]

3

The final session of the Twenty-fifth Congress produced only routine legislation. It had been obvious since the failure of the subtreasury bill in June 1838 that the opposition commanded a majority in the House, while the administration with its State Rights allies controlled the Senate. The program laid down in the President's message was therefore primarily for future reference and to allow Democratic members to make speeches for home consumption. Calhoun made three, devoting himself as usual to broad principles of representative government. The importance of these speeches lies in the circumstances of time and place. The Twenty-sixth Congress, except for Virginia and a few scattered individual districts, had already been elected, and the returns indicated a strong probability that Calhoun and his State Rights party would hold the balance of power in both Houses. Van Buren could hope to succeed in his program only with Calhoun's aid, and in January and February of 1839 the South Carolina Senator laid down the conditions on which he would return to the Democrats. They amounted to unconditional surrender.

Calhoun's first effort, on January 16, was in opposition to the administration-sponsored bill to graduate and reduce the price of the public lands. It was a question that had been agitated for a decade by Western members. First Clay, then Benton, then Walker had essayed the role of spokesman for the West. The precise nature of the proposals had varied from time to time, but the general idea had been much the same, whether sponsored by Western Whig or Western Democrat: the price of the public lands was to be reduced, and a differential scale was to be established. As long as poor land cost as much as good, the settler would inevitably push on until he found the most satisfactory conditions—lands richer or more level or better watered—leaving behind him less desirable acres untouched. There were thus large unsettled regions alternating with thriving communities. The problems of transportation and local government were unnecessarily complicated and the states concerned were becoming greatly alarmed.

Calhoun had consistently opposed the graduated price as a solution to the problem, and he opposed it now. He had favored at least from the beginning of Jackson's administration an outright cession of the public lands to the states in which they lay. He was prepared to offer adequate compensation to the older states in the form of a percentage or in some other manner, since they had originally surrendered the lands for nothing. He would set up standards and conditions, but basically his position was that the sovereignty of the states required that they control the lands within their own borders. This proffered cession had been an important element in the abortive alliance of 1830, when the South had thought to win with it Western votes against the tariff. A new alliance of South and West was now in the making, with railroad communication and port facilities among the projected bonds of union, but the major inducement was still to be Southern votes to give control of the public lands to the Western States. In return the South was to gain the support of the West in her fight against the abolitionists.

Calhoun rested his case on what he called justice to the West, and on wisdom, which in this instance as in so many others was another name for expediency. In justice he held the states entitled to their lands, and this was no more than consistent with the State Rights philosophy he professed. In wisdom he wanted Congress to cede the lands as an act of right before the balance of sectional power swung so far to the West that the new states could make their own policy and vote it through. The West was young and at times ill-mannered, but the day was not far distant when the public-land states would hold a majority of the seats in Congress.[13]

Calhoun realized, although he did not emphasize it in this speech, that the ultimate fate of the South with her great economic and moral burden of slavery would in the end lie in Western hands, and he desperately wanted those hands to be friendly. Thomas Hart Benton, on the other hand, regarded himself as the leader of the public-land states, and he meant to be the beneficiary of any bargain driven with them. He had been a party to the original South-West alliance of 1830, and he saw as clearly as any of the South Carolinians that one of the by-products of this new movement would be to make Calhoun President. This same result might also follow from a perpetuation of Van Buren's temporary union of South and North. Benton therefore worked stubbornly against both. His own hopes lay in the exclusion of the South, because in that way only could he exclude Calhoun.

When Calhoun next took the floor, on January 30, 1839, it was to protest against a presumptive violation of the compromise of 1833. The occasion was Benton's request for leave to bring in a bill to repeal the salt duty and fishing bounties, but he used the opportunity to review the whole tariff question. He would not alter any duty until the progressive reductions came into full force in 1842. The whole subject could then be reviewed in the light of existing conditions. The measure Benton proposed was to reduce a tariff, but there were others who talked already of the renewal of the protective system and who denounced the compromise on that account. Having thus made his opening, he restated the political philosophy of the Nullifiers.

The compromise of 1833, he declared, which Senators would now like to be rid of, had terminated "one of the most dangerous controversies that ever disturbed the Union." The danger was not, as some believed, of dismemberment. "It is a *Federal Union*—an Union of *Sovereign States;* and can be as effectually and much more easily destroyed by *consolidation* than by *dismemberment*. . . . The constant struggle is to enlarge, and not to divide; and there neither is, nor ever has been, the least danger that our Union would terminate in dissolution. But the danger on the opposite side is imminent, as was foreseen, from the first, by our wisest statesmen and most ardent patriots; and never was this danger more menacing than when the gallant and patriotic state he represented, gave the blow that led to the compromise. That blow was not to destroy, but to save the Union;—not for disunion, but against consolidation;—and most effectual did it prove." Nullification, he argued, and nothing else had broken the protective system. He would fight against any renewal of that system, but he hoped that when the time for reconsideration came it would be done in a spirit of liberality and justice, "to promote the interest and harmony of the whole."[14]

It was on February 22, just ten days before the expiration of the Congress and the halfway point in Van Buren's term, that Calhoun pulled all the loose threads together, gave a complete and rounded exposition of his views and purposes, and stated explicitly the price of his future co-operation. The occasion was a bill introduced by John J. Crittenden, Clay's Kentucky colleague, providing that employees of the Federal Government should be dismissed from the service for interfering in elections. Calhoun expressed his complete sympathy with the purpose intended but he saw a better way to limit the patronage and reduce the corruption of the government. That was to restrain its powers within their proper constitutional limits.

Calhoun then offered a concise and keenly discerning analysis of the opposing schools of political thought as they had grown up in the United States since the adoption of the Constitution. The national or Federal school he identified with Hamilton, and with Jefferson the State Rights Republican school, but the labels were nominal and for convenience only. The analysis was an excellent and accurate rendering of the distinction between power and liberty in the state. He showed how Hamilton's policies all had been directed toward the single end of a strong, consolidated, unified nation, and how the national bank, the public debt, the tariff all had been instruments and consequences of this view. The opposing philosophy of Jefferson had aimed at so limiting the powers of the government that it could not infringe the liberty of the individual, the preservation of which was regarded as the very purpose for which governments existed. He showed how the end had been sought by balancing the state governments against the national, by permiting no growth of constitutional powers by construction, and above all by keeping the vast economic power of wealth out of the hands of political rulers.

Jefferson, though he had charted the course, had not been able to carry out the measures needed to pursue it. The Federal school had gained the upper hand, and its policies were openly proclaimed by the younger Adams. The first step toward reform had necessarily been Adams' overthrow. The second step had been the discharge of the public debt, which he credited to his friend and colleague, the lamented William Lowndes, who had devised the sinking fund. The source of those vast revenues by use of which the government consolidated its power had next to be removed, and that was done by the Compromise Act of 1833 and the Deposit Act of 1836. The overthrow of the Bank of the United States came next, to be followed by complete separation of bank and state, of political and money power.

So far had they come on the road to reform. What next was required? His own aim, Calhoun declared, was fixed. "It is no less than to turn back the Government to where it was when it commenced its operation in 1789; to obliterate all the intermediate measures originating in the peculiar principles and policy of the school to which I am opposed, and which experience has proved to be so dangerous and uncongenial to our system; to take a fresh start, a new departure, on the State Rights Republican tack, as was intended by the framers of the constitution." Much progress in this direction had already been made but enough remained to be done to constitute a program for the future. Most important and most difficult of the tasks yet to be accomplished was to free the government from any connection with banks. Next would come the revision of the tariff at the expiration of the Compromise Act, on the principle that no duty should be laid except to support with due economy the constitutional wants of the government. He would then put a final end to internal improvements at Federal expense, and to the "extravagant waste on, what we are pleased to call the pension system, but which has departed from every principle justly belonging to such a system." When the administrative arm of the government had been overhauled, the task would be done; the trend of half a century would be reversed, and a new start could be made. To hold firmly to the new course, however, one further measure would be needed. The new states must be placed, with respect to the public domain, on the same footing as the old. As long as the public lands remained in control of the Federal Government they would constitute a source of power and patronage, by means of which the government might again be turned into the old Federalist road.

Having said so much, Calhoun appealed directly to the administration leaders. He would not presume to advise them. The responsibility for directing the government was theirs, and so also must be the choice of policy. A great opportunity lay before them. "Take, then, your ground boldly; avow your object; disclose your measures; and let the people see clearly that you intend—what Jefferson designed to do, but, from adverse circumstances, could not accomplish—to reverse the measures originating in principles and policy uncongenial to our political system—to divest the Government of all undue patronage and influence—to restrict it to the few great objects intended by the constitution—in a word, to give a complete ascendency to the good old Virginia school over its antagonist, which time and experience have proved to be foreign to our system—and you may count with confidence on their support, without looking to any other means of success. Should you take such a course at this propitious moment, our free and happy institutions may be perpetuated for generations; but, if a different, short will be their duration."[15]

With this speech Calhoun completed his intellectual pilgrimage from liberalism through conservatism to reaction. Where once he had looked confidently toward the future he now looked back to a golden age that lay buried in the past—an age when no one questioned the morality of slavery and cotton brought forty cents a pound. For a decade he had been following a course charted by his own political philosophy, perhaps without fully realizing the implications of what he did, and he had now arrived at the predestined end. He had developed a doctrine in terms of which he could logically defend the vested interest of a minority, but it is precisely in the defense of vested interests against the encroaching forces of change that the essence of reaction lies.

The official answer to Calhoun's appeal would not come until the President stated his policies to the new Congress in December 1839, but the unofficial answer came at once. "We never heard a more philosophical, and, at the same time, statesmanlike discussion of a subject," wrote Francis Preston Blair in that evening's *Globe*. "The history of our institutions and the Administration which had given them an oblique and wrong direction—the causes and consequences of all that had signalized our political career, were associated in their natural order, and portrayed with a pencil of light."[16] The doctrines, as Calhoun had emphasized early in his speech, were the same as those of his patronage report of 1835, which Blair had then found highly unpalatable. They were in favor now, and the accolade was duly bestowed. Though the session had passed without significant legislation of any sort, Calhoun was fully justified in calling it "on the whole the most satisfactory I have seen for many years."[17]

4

The elections of 1838, with their Whig and State Rights victories, were a prelude to the Presidential campaign of 1840, and from that time until the election itself the Presidential question was never far below the surface. It constituted, in fact, one of the major—perhaps the only remaining—barrier between Calhoun and Van Buren, for Calhoun had not committed himself on the President's re-election, and steadfastly refused to do so.

Clay meanwhile was intensely active, seeking to build a Whig majority in Congress and to bind the party to himself as its leader. Even as Van Buren sought to bring the Nullifiers back to the Democratic fold, Clay made overtures to the dissatisfied and rebellious among the old Jackson men. Most important of these was William Cabell Rives, who had acted steadfastly with the Whigs since the special session. Despite his vote to expunge the resolution of censure early in 1837, Clay decided that Rives should be re-elected to the Senate by the Whigs, and in December of 1838 he set the party machinery in motion to that end. The stumbling block was John Tyler, who had a far better claim to the gratitude of the party than Rives. To secure the election of the latter by the Whig-dominated Virginia legislature, Tyler was promised the Vice Presidential nomination, but even then his friends remained suspicious—so much so that they blocked any election at all until after the Whig convention had met early in December 1839. When Tyler received his promised reward, Rives was duly returned to the Senate as a Whig.[18]

The Virginia Congressional elections in the spring of 1839 were indicative of what would be the future trend over the South. The administration won twelve out of twenty-one seats against the combined Whig and Conservative Democratic forces, and the Whig victors included Robert M. T. Hunter and Henry A. Wise, both of whom went with Calhoun on the slavery question. Hunter in fact had run and had been elected on an out-and-out State Rights, subtreasury platform, and counted himself a Calhoun man.[19]

Calhoun himself continued to refuse any active partisan role, but it is not without significance that he felt free to suggest to Poinsett Federal appointments to be passed on to Van Buren.[20] It is also significant that the *Globe* in the course of the summer went still farther than it had yet gone in the direction of espousing the State Rights cause. Blair came perilously close, in fact, to an actual endorsement of nullification itself—certainly as close as a man who still called himself Andrew Jackson's friend could dare to venture. Editorials were not published in the *Globe* without Van Buren's approval, and it was in effect the President himself who completed the editorial plural when Blair gave to the State Rights party "our warmest admiration and esteem" for their "noble and disinterested support of the true principles of the Constitution. Some of us," he continued, "may differ as to the remedy to be employed in cases of flagrant infraction of reserved rights, but we all agree in the importance of maintaining them in their full integrity, secure alike from open outrage or sophistical infringement. All the little influence or ability which we may possess, shall be exerted to this end, so that the necessity may never again recur for a harsh remedial interposition."[21]

5

Calhoun knew his own political strength too well not to make the most of it, and well before the new Congress met he advised his friends as to the role they were to play in the organization of the House. For Speaker he would be satisfied with any man on whom his followers and the administration could agree, but he wanted a fair understanding in advance as to the appointment of committees. Specifically, he wanted to know what the administration would expect if the Van Buren men helped elect a State Rights Speaker, and conversely what his followers could count on if they threw their strength to a man chosen by the party in power. He wanted no further embarrassments or misunderstandings about their position, and he urged his friends to be in Washington before the session began so that a course of action could be planned such as would best advance their own principles.[22]

A caucus was held some time before the session opened on December 2, and the administration leaders showed a flattering eagerness to accommodate their allies. It was apparently agreed without difficulty that Francis W. Pickens, who was personally closer to Calhoun than any other member of the House, should be supported as the regular Democratic candidate for Speaker. Unfortunately for himself, however, Pickens was not yet in Washington, and there were rival ambitions and jealousies within both the State Rights party and the South Carolina delegation. Before he arrived to speak for himself, Pickens' name was withdrawn by Dixon H. Lewis of Alabama and Robert Barnwell Rhett. Lewis' selection was then blocked by the Benton wing of the party, who undoubtedly would have prevented Pickens' election also. Benton feared with reason that a Calhoun Speaker would add immeasurably to the South Carolinian's strength as a Presidential rival in 1844. The caucus finally agreed on John W. Jones, a Van Buren Democrat from Virginia who had followed the State Rights party lead on the slavery question.[23]

The actual balloting in the House was delayed almost two weeks while the evenly matched Whig and Democratic parties wrangled over the seating of five members from New Jersey. Five Whigs held certificates of election from the Governor; an equal number of Democrats claimed the same seats on certification by the New Jersey Secretary of State. The House could not elect a Speaker until some kind of settlement was made, because both sides wanted the votes of the New Jersey delegation. The clerk, presiding in the absence of a Speaker, was clearly unable to cope with the rising disorder. After three days of confusion Adams asked the House to take the situation into its own hands, and in response Rhett moved that Lewis Williams of North Carolina, senior member of the body, be elected chairman pro tempore. Williams declined. Rhett then substituted Adams, put the motion himself, and announced the Massachusetts maverick elected. Adams proved unequal to the task, and confusion was compounded with ill temper.[24]

All business of both houses meanwhile was held up because the President could not send in his annual message until a Speaker had been chosen. Only after ten days of wrangling was it agreed that neither New Jersey delegation should vote, permitting a ballot to be taken on Saturday, December 14. Jones, the administration's caucus candidate, got 113 votes to 102 for John Bell, supported by the Whigs; but 118 were necessary to elect. The five additional votes that would have given the place to Jones were thrown away on other candidates by five members of the South Carolina delegation.[25]

Six ballots were taken that day, but Jones' total did not rise above 113, and on the sixth try fell to 39. Bell never exceeded his initial 102. On the third ballot the Whigs shifted to William C. Dawson of Georgia, and on the fifth to Hunter, whose high total was 68. Most of these came from the Whig side of the House, but notable among those who voted for the Virginian was Pickens. The contest was resumed on Monday, and the result of a new caucus among the Democrats was evident. On Monday's first ballot—actually the seventh—the strength of the administration was thrown to Lewis who received 110 votes, climbing on the eighth ballot to Jones' high mark of 113. There Lewis also stopped, and in his case the five votes that were thrown away were those of Benton Democrats. The break finally came on the eleventh ballot, when the State Rights party switched abruptly to Hunter, making his total 119 and giving him the Speakership of the House.[26]

Though the Whigs had voted almost solidly for Hunter, his victory was not theirs. He was an avowed State Rights and subtreasury man, and many thought him a full-fledged Nullifier. Calhoun had not in any sense engineered Hunter's election, and regarded it himself as distinctly a political accident. Yet Hunter was for all that a Calhoun man, and the confidence of the South Carolinian in him was not misplaced.[27] He was to prove an able and resourceful lieutenant for the remainder of Calhoun's life.

It was another week before the contested New Jersey election was set aside long enough to complete the organization of the House. The President's message was finally heard, however, on December 24. Only after that, on December 30, were the committees of the House announced by the new Speaker. They were carefully made up with every evidence of fairness between parties, both as to chairmanships and as to members. It was notable, however, that wherever important or controversial legislation might be at stake a Calhoun Nullifier held the balance between Whigs and Democrats on the committee. Ways and Means, which would shortly bring in the subtreasury once more, showed Jones of Virginia, recently the administraton's choice for Speaker, as its chairman. There were three other Democrats, four Whigs, and Robert Barnwell Rhett; but the balance was tipped more definitely in favor of the Nullifiers by appointing as one of the Whig members a State Rights Georgian, Mark Antony Cooper, who was soon voting with the administration.[28]

6

On his way to Washington for the session, Calhoun rode from Richmond with Senator William H. Roane of Virginia, who strongly urged a resumption of personal relations between the South Carolinian and the President. According to Roane, the President was ready to make the first advance, but could do so only if the two should encounter each other by chance. In the circumstances, he wanted Calhoun to take the initiative and leave his card at the White House on his arrival. Calhoun declined but explained that he had from the days of the special session meant to restore personal relations with Van Buren as soon as he was satisfied as to the long-range policy of the administration. He would wait, in short, for the annual message, which would be the answer to his appeal of February.[29] He was confident, however, before he had been in Washington a week that the message would be "thoroughly state rights," and we may assume that he had been so assured by a member of the administration—Woodbury or Poinsett or Grundy. He was also sure, from his reception en route and in the Capital, that he had never been stronger personally, nor stood on more solid ground than he did then.[30]

The message, when the delayed organization of the House finally permitted its delivery, was satisfactory both as to principles and policy. The leading recommendation was again the subtreasury, the arguments for which were developed in much greater detail than in previous messages. The legal-tender clause, which had become in later versions of the bill a specie clause pure and simple, was specifically mentioned and insisted on.[31] The graduation of the price of the public lands was again mentioned, but only in a sentence and without such insistence as to preclude the substitution of Calhoun's plan if he could get Congress to accept it. In general the message called for rigorous economy in government and strict regard for the constitutional separation of powers.[32]

Calhoun immediately carried out his promise, and with Roane as intermediary he called at the White House. The interview must have been a little trying for both the Senator and the President, and both retained reservations, but they did accomplish by it what both wanted above all else: they united the Democratic party as it had not been united since Jefferson's time. He had come, Calhoun told the President, to remove their personal differences, since Van Buren's course had removed their points of conflict in politics; and Van Buren graciously accepted the offer. Neither man had changed his opinion as to the original cause of their estrangement, but both were willing to forget, temporarily, for the sake of a common undertaking. Neither doubted that the public would be served by the reunion; and each knew that his own personal future lay largely in the hands of the other.[33]

No pledges were given or asked. Immediately thereafter, however, Hunter named the standing committees of the House, as though he had been waiting for the outcome of this interview. A few days later Blair, already printer to the Senate, was chosen printer to the House with the support of the Calhoun faction, although Duff Green himself had sought the position.[34] The subtreasury was rushed through the Senate in three weeks' time, before members could be instructed against it by their legislatures, and presently became the law.[35]

Calhoun also broke his long silence on the Presidential election. The Whig convention had been held the first week in December, with William Henry Harrison being nominated to oppose Van Buren. Between the two, Calhoun saw no reason to hesitate, and advised his followers that only Van Buren's re-election would give some prospect of achieving the reforms so long sought by the State Rights party.[36] At the same time Calhoun moved from unofficial to official administration spokesman. He insisted still that he himself did not desire the Presidency, and expressed once more the hope that he might retire to private life at the expiration of his term in 1841. In the minds of his fellow South Carolinians, however, and to well-wishers all over the nation he was now the logical man to succeed Van Buren in 1844. It was he more than any other individual who had brought the party back to its proper base, had rid it of corruption and double-dealing, had given it a policy and a program. It was he who had unified and reforged the fragments that had survived the Jackson orgy. The ends he had sought in the election of 1828 had at last been gained, and it was no more than right that he should lead the party he had so largely made.[37]

In truth the flux was over, or so it seemed, and the principles secure. The federal structure of the government had been reaffirmed, with powers so limited and circumscribed that a new tariff was unthinkable. The states stood forth as the guardians of their own reserved rights, including the right to own and trade in slaves. External economic influences on the government had been reduced to a minimum by balancing the planter and trader interest of the South against the manufacturing and banking interests that had so long been dominant. On these principles the new Democratic party advanced its claims to power, calling itself the party of Jefferson and claiming Andrew Jackson, if only for the sake of the amenities, as one of its own.

In reality, however, it was a new and different party that bore little kinship to the purposes of either of its heroes. For the times had changed, and with incredible rapidity were changing still. The frontier was now the Pacific Ocean, where Oregon was already clamoring for territorial status. The railroad in ten years' time had all but made the stagecoach a museum piece. Already one could go from Washington clear to New York by rail, in a matter of some twelve hours. Steamships now plied the ocean on regular runs. Cotton production was pushing two million bales a year, quadrupled since 1820.

An ingenious New England blacksmith named Davenport had contrived to make electricity turn a wheel; and Samuel F. B. Morse held patents on the magnetic telegraph for the exploitation of which he was then seeking capital. The American himself was changing, too. Already too big for his breeches, he was more cocky than ever before, and thought nothing of challenging Great Britain, France, and Mexico all at once. The Eastern mountains had not confined him, and neither would the mightier ranges of the West, nor the plains and deserts that lay between. He was also developing a moral sense and an uneasy conscience over slavery. Democracy was the magic word that would reconcile all differences and lead all true believers to the promised land at last.

In the new Democratic party, under the State Rights banner, Van Buren and Calhoun would march briefly side by side, hating each other with the hatred of jealousy on the one side, of frustration on the other, and complete lack of comprehension on both. But for both, if all went well, the alliance meant personal success. Van Buren hoped, with Calhoun's aid, to retain his office for four years more. Then, twenty years after his first bid for the Presidency, Calhoun—older, wiser, chastened, but still unbowed and confident, and infinitely stronger—might hope to reach at last the summit of his own ambition. Not the empty honors of a Southern confederacy, but the high reward of the first office in a harmonious Union.

So he had dreamed in 1821 and again in 1829. So as the wonderful century entered its fifth decade he permitted himself to dream once more. Yet the dream was not the same. When first he had sought the highest office in his country's gift it was with buoyant ambition to lead an adolescent nation on to greatness. He sought it now to protect a portion of that nation against the onslaughts of the rest, and to dam up by the force of his own intellect and will the quickening current of the stream of change.

NOTES, BIBLIOGRAPHY AND ACKNOWLEDGMENTS

NOTES

CHAPTER I

[1] The following account of Jackson's inauguration and reception is drawn in part from a variety of sources, but main reliance has been placed on Margaret Bayard Smith, *The First Forty Years of Washington Society,* 290-298 (cited hereafter as Mrs. Smith); George R. Gilmer, *Sketches of Some of the First Settlers of Upper Georgia,* 244-245; the *United States' Telegraph,* Mar. 5, 1829; and contemporary correspondence, including Daniel Webster to Mrs. Ezekiel Webster, Mar. 2, 4, 1829, in *Writings and Speeches of Daniel Webster* (National Edition), XVII, 472, 473; Joseph Story to Mrs. Story, Mar. 7, 1829, W. W. Story, *Life and Letters of Joseph Story,* I, 563; and James Hamilton, Jr., to Van Buren, Mar. 5, 1829, Van Buren Papers.

[2] There are many contemporary descriptions of Calhoun, but the best for this period is probably that of Thomas Hamilton, *Men and Manners in America,* II, 146-147. Contemporary evidence does not confirm the recollection of the Rev. Charles Cotesworth Pinckney, "John C. Calhoun, from a Southern Standpoint," *Lippincott's Monthly Magazine,* LXII (July 1898), 82, that Calhoun had iron-gray hair at this date.

[3] *National Intelligencer,* Feb. 3, 1829.

[4] Mrs. Smith, 288.

[5] The enthusiastic editor of the *United States' Telegraph* estimated the visitors in the city at 30,000; and conservative Judge Story thought the crowd on the Capitol grounds could not have been less than 10,000. Mrs. Smith, herself given to exaggeration, thought the figure of 20,000 attending the reception was too large, but James Hamilton, Jr., also put it at between 15,000 and 20,000.

[6] Charles M. Wiltse, *John C. Calhoun, Nationalist, 1782-1828,* 346-351, 362-364; William Smith to Stephen D. Miller, Jan. 13, 1827, Chesnut-Manning-Miller Papers.

[7] Calhoun to Jackson, July 10, 1828, J. S. Bassett, ed., *Correspondence of Andrew Jackson,* III, 415; Wiltse, *Calhoun, Nationalist,* 379.

[8] It cannot be proved that Jackson himself accepted Van Buren as his successor earlier than the winter of 1829-1830, but it is certain that the original Jackson men—the party nucleus from Tennessee—were committed to the New Yorker as early as 1826. Alfred Balch, in a letter to Van Buren (Nov. 27, 1828, Van Buren Papers), speaks of organizing a Van Buren party in Tennessee "two years ago," and makes a similar reference in a letter to John McLean, Oct. 26, 1835, McLean Papers. Indeed, it is hardly credible that the Crawford partisans could have been swung over to Jackson, whom they had been disciplined for years to abominate, without some such understanding. It was not until 1831 that Calhoun himself awoke to a full realization of what had been going on. See his "Reply to Eaton," *Niles' Weekly Register,* XLI, 179 (cited hereafter as *Niles*); also in R. K. Crallé, ed., *Works of John C. Calhoun,* VI, 435 ff. It was common talk in Washington, however, well before Jackson's inauguration, that the old General himself intended to be guided by Van Buren and to advance him for the succession. See, *e. g.,* Charleston *Courier,* Feb. 16, 1829, quoting Alexandria *Gazette,* February 10.

[9] Calhoun to [Micah Sterling], Jan. 7, 1829, Calhoun Papers, Library of Congress; to Virgil Maxcy, Jan. 13, 1829, Maxcy Papers. Cf. Clay to Francis Brooke, Dec. 26, 1828, C. Colton, ed., *Works of Henry Clay,* IV, 215; and John Bailey to J. B. Davis, Dec. 18, 1828, *Proceedings of the Massachusetts Historical Society,* XLIX, 217.

[10] *United States' Telegraph,* Jan. 8, 10, 12, 19, 1829; Duff Green to Ninian Edwards, Jan. 6, 1829, E. B. Washburne, ed., *The Edwards Papers,* 379-381.

[11] Late in January 1829 Eaton tried to induce Kendall to run for printer to the Senate, assuring him that he could be elected; but Kendall declined, to avoid giving offense to Green. William Stickney, ed., *Autobiography of Amos Kendall,* 281, 304. More revealing is a letter from Silas Wright, New York Congressman and Van Buren lieutenant, to his chief, Dec. 9, 1828, in the Van Buren Papers. "Much discussion is being had as to the Printer," he wrote from Washington. "It is said here, and I now suppose it is true, that Duff Green is favorable to and in the interest of Mr. Calhoun. This I did not suppose when I came here, but yet it seems to me we cannot avoid making Duff printer without bringing on a quarrel now which I think should be delayed at all Events for the present." See also James A. Hamilton to Van Buren, Feb. 12, 1829, Van Buren Papers.

[12] Daniel Webster to Ezekiel Webster, Feb. 5, 1829, Webster's *Writings,* XVI, 186-187; to Mrs. E. Webster, Feb. 19, 1829, *ibid.,* XVII, 470.

[13] William Coleman to James A. Hamilton, Mar. 18, 1829, James A. Hamilton, *Reminiscences,* 127.

[14] Duff Green to William Ingalls, Dec. 11, 1828; to Isaac Hill, Dec. 17, 1828, letter book, Green Papers. See also *United States' Telegraph* for December 1828 and January 1829; and W. B. Bryan, *History of the National Capital,* II, 210-211.

[15] Joseph Story to George Ticknor, Feb. 11, 1829, *Story,* I, 565.

[16] *United States' Telegraph,* Jan. 19, 1829; D. Webster to E. Webster, Jan. 17, 1829, Webster's *Writings,* XVII, 467; and Feb. 5, 1829, *ibid.,* XVI, 187.

[17] *United States' Telegraph,* Feb. 11, 12, 1829.

[18] Silas Wright to Van Buren, Dec. 9, 1828, Van Buren Papers; G. C. Verplanck to Van Buren, Dec. 6, 1828, *ibid.* Also Duff Green to Theodore Lyman, Dec. 7, 1828; to Ninian Edwards, Dec. 23, 1828, letter book, Duff Green Papers.

[19] Calhoun to Patrick Noble, Jan. 10, 1829, J. Franklin Jameson, ed., *Correspondence of John C. Calhoun,* 269-270. (Cited hereafter as *Correspondence.*)

[20] James Hamilton, Jr., to Van Buren, Jan. 23, Feb. 13, 1829, Van Buren Papers; Robert Y. Hayne to Van Buren, Feb. 14, 1829, *ibid.* Also William A. Ingham, "Samuel D. Ingham," *Bucks County Historical Papers,* IV, 27. I am discounting the statement of James A. Hamilton (*Reminiscences,* 102) that Ingham came to Washington hoping to be made Comptroller. It is not compatible with the circumstances and cannot be reconciled with the contemporary correspondence, including Hamilton's own.

[21] Van Buren to James A. Hamilton, Feb. 2, 1829, Hamilton, *Reminiscences,* 92. The two Hamiltons are not to be confused. James A. Hamilton, son of Alexander Hamilton, was a prominent figure in New York politics, who had been closely associated with Van Buren since 1826 or 1827. James Hamilton, Jr., was the typical high-spirited South Carolinian of the story books, an outspoken Nullifier who regarded Calhoun as too conservative. In the letter cited Van Buren asks the New York Hamilton to tell the South Carolina Hamilton that he differs from him only in reversing choices for Treasury and Navy.

[22] James A. Hamilton to Van Buren, Feb. 13, 1829, Van Buren Papers.

[23] See his "Reply to Eaton," *Works,* VI, 443. James A. Hamilton states in his *Reminiscences,* 101, that Calhoun was consulted on one occasion by Jackson, that he urged the nomination of Tazewell for Secretary of State, and that Jackson then indicated to Hamilton that he intended to disregard the advice. Hamilton does not mention this incident, however, in the almost daily letters he was writing to Van Buren at the time, and it seems most probable that after a lapse of years he remembered as a private audience with Calhoun what he described at the time as a dinner, at which the Cabinet was not discussed. Hamilton's letter to Van Buren, Feb. 18, 1829, Van Buren Papers, indicates that no interview between Calhoun and Jackson on the Cabinet had taken place up to that date; and the composition of the Cabinet was admittedly complete and generally known around Washington by February 19.

[24] James A. Hamilton to Van Buren, Feb. 18, 1829, Van Buren Papers; James Hamilton, Jr., to Van Buren, Feb. 19, 1829, *ibid.;* J. A. Hamilton, *Reminiscences,* 99.

[25] James Hamilton, Jr., to Van Buren, Feb. 19, Mar. 25, 1829, Van Buren Papers; E. K. Kane to Van Buren, Feb. 20, 1829, *ibid.;* James A. Hamilton to Van Buren, Feb. 21, 1829, *ibid;* William Cooke to Virgil Maxcy, Mar. 10, 1829, Maxcy Papers, second series.

[26] See Calhoun, *Works,* III, 52-53. Also Wiltse, *Calhoun, Nationalist,* 365-374.

[27] J. C. Fitzpatrick, ed., *The Autobiography of Martin Van Buren,* 250-251.

[28] Jackson to White, Apr. 9, 1831, Jackson's *Correspondence,* IV, 258-260, recapitulating the circumstances; Eaton to White, Feb. 23, 1829, in Nancy N. Scott, *Memoir of Hugh Lawson White,* 266.

[29] Thomas P. Govan, "Berrien and Jackson," *Journal of Southern History,* V, 448.

[30] Eaton's "Reply," *Niles,* XLI, 50. "It was the confidence I had in major Eaton and his recommendation of Branch and Berrien that induced me to appoint them in my Cabinet." Memorandum in Jackson's hand, probably September 1831, Jackson's *Correspondence,* IV, 343. See also C. P. Van Ness to Van Buren, 1832, Van Buren Papers: "Eaton . . . was not satisfied with going himself into a place that he ought not to have had but crowded in, by his management, Branch and Berrien. . . ."

[31] It was two years later, when the rivalry between Calhoun and Van Buren had become an open quarrel between Jackson and Calhoun, and the Vice President had been read out of the party along with Ingham, Branch, and Berrien, that the myth of his agency in creating the Cabinet was concocted, to be handed out by Jackson's prince of propagandists, Francis P. Blair, in private correspondence as well as in the *Globe.* "Calhoun has been plotting from the hour the President reached Washington, and I believe before, to have the immediate management of affairs by means of fastening on the President a Cabinet of his own creatures. Ingham, Branch, and Berrien were, with the liberal feelings which influence the President always toward those whom he considers his friends, appointed to gratify the wishes of Calhoun. Calhoun was not satisfied, but wanted to get McDuffie or Hamilton made secretary of war, and for this reason began to undermine Eaton." Blair to his sister, Mrs. Gratz, Feb. 23, 1831, *Atlantic Monthly,* LX (August 1887), 191. This is also the line taken by Kendall in the manuscript he prepared for Eaton, and published as the latter's "Reply." See *Niles,* XLI, 49-64.

[32] J. A. Hamilton to Van Buren, Mar. 6, 1829, Van Buren Papers; J. M. Clayton to Caleb S. Layton, Mar. 9, 1829, Clayton Papers; O. H. W. Stull to Henry

Clay, Mar. 28, 1829, Clay Papers; Joseph Story to William Fettyplace, March 1829, *Story,* I, 564; Charleston *Courier,* Mar. 21, 1829. Also Hamilton, *Reminiscences,* 100-101; Ben Perley Poore, *Perley's Reminiscences of Sixty Years in the National Metropolis,* I, 98; Francis P. Weisenburger, *The Life of John McLean,* 67.

[33] Clay to Francis Brooke, Feb. 21, 1829, Clay's *Works,* IV, 222; Webster to E. Webster, Feb. 23, 26, 1829, Webster's *Writings,* XVI, 187-188, 188-189; Ritchie to McLean, February [?] 1829, McLean Papers; Ritchie to Van Buren, Mar. 27, 1829, Jackson's *Correspondence,* IV, 17-18 n. Also Mrs. Smith, 281-283, 287.

[34] William Wirt to William Pope, Mar. 22, 1829, John P. Kennedy, *Memoirs of the Life of William Wirt,* II, 228. See also R. M. Johnson to Jackson, Mar. 9, 1829, Kentucky State Historical Society, *Register,* XXXIX (October 1941), 359; and Van Buren, *Autobiography,* 229-230. The Pendleton *Messenger,* which usually reflected Calhoun's views, commented on March 11: "We have never understood that Mr. Branch, Mr. Eaton, or even Mr. Ingham were considered first rate men. Mr. Van Buren's talents are undoubtedly of a high order, and have been, we believe, more respected than his political integrity. Mr. M'Lean is unexceptionable, and Mr. Berrien is no doubt a good appointment."

[35] Jackson to John C. McLemore, April 1829, Jackson's *Correspondence,* IV, 19-21; to John Coffee, May 30, 1829, *ibid.,* 38; to Richard K. Call, July 5, 1829, *ibid.,* 50.

[36] Van Buren, *Autobiography,* 256, 259-260.

[37] Calhoun to Tazewell, Apr. 14, 1829, Calhoun Papers, Library of Congress.

[38] James Hamilton, Jr., to Van Buren, Apr. 28, 1829, Van Buren Papers.

[39] Duff Green to the public, *United States' Telegraph,* Mar. 6, 1832. Also Calhoun's "Reply to Eaton," *Niles,* XLI, 179. According to Calhoun, he told Eaton he regarded Gadsden as being as well qualified as Van Deventer, and could not object to him.

[40] Calhoun to Maxcy, Jan. 13, June 21, 1829, Maxcy Papers; Maxcy to Calhoun, June 1, 1829, *Correspondence,* 810. Other letters from Maxcy relative to this appointment are in *ibid.,* 794-814 *passim.*

[41] C. F. Adams, ed., *Memoirs of John Quincy Adams,* VIII, 116. (Cited hereafter as Adams, *Diary.*)

[42] *Ibid.; United States' Telegraph,* Mar. 20, 1829.

CHAPTER II

[1] Mrs. Smith, 252-253.

[2] Cambreleng to Van Buren, Jan. 1, 1829, Van Buren Papers.

[3] Calhoun's "Reply to Eaton," *Niles,* XLI, 178-179. Also in *Works,* VI, 435-445.

[4] *United States' Telegraph,* Jan. 16, 1829.

[5] Description drawn from Queena Pollack, *Peggy Eaton, Democracy's Mistress, passim.*

[6] The broad outlines of the Peggy O'Neale story have been told too often to require specific citation. It is told from Peggy's point of view by Queena Pollack in her *Peggy Eaton, Democracy's Mistress;* from Jackson's in Marquis James, *Andrew Jackson, Portrait of a President;* and from the moral pinnacle of the opposition in Pauline Wilcox Burke, *Emily Donelson of Tennessee.* There are contemporary versions in Adams, *Diary;* in Poore, *Perley's Reminiscences;* in

Van Buren, *Autobiography;* and in the social and political correspondence of the period.

[7] Calhoun to James Edward Calhoun, Mar. 16, 1829, Calhoun Papers, Clemson College.

[8] Calhoun's "Reply to Eaton," *Niles,* XLI, 179. Eaton contended, when the controversy was at its height in the fall of 1831, that both Mr. and Mrs. Calhoun had left cards at his residence while he and Mrs. Eaton were in Philadelphia, and that Mrs. Calhoun's later decision not to call was therefore a reversal. Eaton's "Reply to Branch, Berrien, etc.," *Niles,* XLI, 52. This assertion Calhoun flatly contradicted. Where the question is one of personal veracity, unsupported by reliable testimony either way, the biographer is privileged to choose sides with his own subject. In her autobiography, written in 1873, when she was well past seventy, Peggy tells the same story, with embellishments, but there is so much in the volume that demonstrates an inaccurate memory that all of it must be discounted unless otherwise verifiable. See Margaret Eaton, *The Autobiography of Peggy Eaton,* 54-55. Also "Peggy O'Neal; or the Doom of the Republic," *Southern Review,* XII (January 1873), 217.

[9] Hamilton, *Reminiscences,* 70.

[10] Branch's "Exposition," *Niles,* XLI, 5. Jackson denied that Branch had so warned him. See his Memorandum in Jackson's *Correspondence,* IV, 343.

[11] Mrs. Smith, 288-289.

[12] See p. 25 above.

[13] Jackson to Gen. John Coffee, Mar. 19, 22, 1829, Jackson's *Correspondence,* IV, 13-15.

[14] Calhoun to Tazewell, Apr. 14, 1829, Calhoun Papers, Library of Congress; *United States' Telegraph,* Mar. 18, 1829.

[15] Wiltse, *Calhoun, Nationalist,* 342; Ernest Ingersoll, "The Calhoun Summer Home," *Scribner's Monthly,* XXI (April 1881), 892-895. See also A. G. Holmes, "John C. Calhoun," *Southern Magazine,* II (1936), No. 10.

[16] Andrew P. Calhoun to Calhoun, May 6, [1829], Calhoun Papers, Clemson College; Calhoun to Rev. Jeremiah Day, President of Yale College, Sept. 1, 1829, Calhoun Papers, Yale University Library; University of South Carolina Alumni Records, South Caroliniana Library.

[17] Calhoun to Virgil Maxcy, Aug. 21, 1829 (fragment), Maxcy Papers.

[18] Adams, *Diary,* VIII, 159.

[19] Van Buren, *Autobiography,* 342.

[20] Barry to his daughter, May 16, 1829, *William and Mary Quarterly,* XIII (April 1905), 239-241.

[21] Van Buren, *Autobiography,* 342.

[22] Virgil Maxcy to Calhoun, Apr. 6, 1829, *Correspondence,* 794.

[23] Maxcy to Calhoun, May 7, 1829, *ibid.,* 801.

[24] Branch's "Exposition," *Niles,* XLI, 7; also Maxcy to Calhoun, June 1, 1829, *Correspondence,* 810.

[25] Branch, *op cit.,* 5.

[26] Jackson to John McLemore, May 3, 1829, Jackson's *Correspondence,* IV, 30-31.

[27] *Ibid.* Also Jackson to Call, July 5, 1829, *ibid.,* 51, where he uses the expression, "hired slanderers of Mr. Clay."

[28] Call to Jackson, Apr. 28, 1829, *ibid.,* 28-29. When the controversy reached its climax in 1831, other presumably reliable witnesses made similar statements. According to Adams, Eaton "had lived very openly with [Mrs. E.] during the life

of her former husband." *Diary,* VIII, 356-357. And Governor John Floyd of Virginia wrote that "Mrs. Eaton was, whilst I was in Congress, considered as a lady who would be willing to dispense her favors wherever she took a fancy." C. H. Ambler, ed., *The Life and Diary of John Floyd,* 125. (Cited hereafter as Floyd, *Diary.*) In a later entry Floyd says, "I know, myself, that all is true which has been said of her." *Ibid.,* 149. Even Amos Kendall, who admittedly prepared not a little of the propaganda on Eaton's side, was, according to his later admission, convinced at the time he prepared it that his "confidence had been misplaced." Kendall, *Autobiography,* 360.

[29] Call to Jackson, July 18, 1829, Jackson Papers, second series. See also Jackson's *Correspondence,* IV, *passim.*

[30] Most important of the documents in the case are Jackson to Ely, Sept. 3, 1829, Jackson's *Correspondence,* IV, 67-68; Memorandum by Donelson, Sept. 3, 1829, *ibid.,* 68-72; Van Buren to James A. Hamilton, Sept. 24, 1829, Hamilton, *Reminiscences,* 147-148; and Van Buren, *Autobiography,* 339 ff. See also Charleston *Courier,* Sept. 9, 1829.

[31] Duff Green to Rev. J. N. Campbell, Oct. 19, 1829, letter book, Green Papers.

[32] See Eaton's letters to Emily Donelson, Apr. 8 and 9, 1829, and Donelson's reply, April 10, in Jackson's *Correspondence,* IV, 29-30 n. The quarrel is told in detail in Burke, *Emily Donelson,* I, 179-190.

[33] Branch, "Exposition," *Niles,* XLI, 6.

[34] Alexander R. MacDonnell, "John McPherson Berrien," *Georgia Historical Quarterly,* XVII (March 1933), 7-8.

[35] Barry to his daughter, Nov. 27, 1829, *William and Mary Quarterly,* XIII (April 1905), 243; Van Buren, *Autobiography,* 347-348.

[36] Van Buren, *Autobiography,* 348-349.

[37] Jackson to Gen. Call, July 5, 1829, Jackson's *Correspondence,* IV, 51-52; to John C. McLemore, Nov. 24, 1829, *ibid.,* 88-89; to John Overton, Dec. 31, 1829, *ibid.,* 108-109.

[38] The quoted language is that of Adams, *Diary,* VIII, 185.

[39] Thomas Patterson to Henry Clay, Dec. 13, 1829, Clay Papers.

[40] The *United States' Telegraph,* Dec. 15, 1829, announces the play for the following day. In her *Autobiography,* 90-92, Peggy says her husband told her the whole sordid business was concocted by Calhoun.

[41] Mrs. Smith, 311; Charleston *Courier,* Jan. 14, 1830.

[42] Daniel Webster to Warren Dutton, Jan. 15, 1830, Webster's *Writings,* XVII, 483.

[43] Van Buren, *Autobiography,* 351-355; Jackson memorandum, Jackson's *Correspondence,* IV, 123-124.

[44] Webster to Dutton, *loc cit.*

[45] Berrien to Johnson, July 7, 1831, *Niles,* XL, 382-383; Ingham to Johnson, July 13, 1831, *ibid.,* 383-384; Branch, "Exposition," *Niles,* XLI, 5-7; Van Buren, *Autobiography,* 354-356.

[46] Jackson memorandum, Jan. 29, 1830, Jackson's *Correspondence,* IV, 123-124.

[47] Adams, *Diary,* VIII, 184.

CHAPTER III

[1] The numerous efforts that have been made to demonstrate the contrary, the most plausible being those of Marquis James, *Andrew Jackson, Portrait of a*

President (1937), and Arthur M. Schlesinger, Jr., *The Age of Jackson* (1945), remain unconvincing. It does not seem to me to be possible to fit either the actions or the professions of Jackson's two terms of office into any kind of pattern save that of opportunism, and of give and take between the forces battling for the upper hand. Those who have succeeded in giving Jackson either a consistent policy or an intelligible political philosophy have been able to do so, in my opinion, only on the basis of incomplete analysis or misinterpretation of essential facts.

[2] James Hamilton, Jr., to Van Buren, Feb. 19, 1829, Van Buren Papers.

[3] J. D. Richardson, ed., *Messages and Papers of the Presidents,* 999-1001.

[4] *Illinois Intelligencer,* Dec. 6, 1828.

[5] Duff Green to H. Lane, Dec. 28, 1828, letter book, Green Papers; to Edwards, Jan. 6, 1829, *Edwards Papers,* 379-381.

[6] Charleston *Mercury,* July 8, 1829; Hamilton to Van Buren, July 16, 1829, Van Buren Papers; Cambreleng to Van Buren, Sept. 25, 1829, *ibid.;* T. W. Brevard to J. H. Hammond, Oct. 8, 1829, Hammond Papers.

[7] Calhoun to Maxcy, Nov. 2, 1829, Maxcy Papers.

[8] R. C. McGrane, ed., *Correspondence of Nicholas Biddle,* 63 ff. (Cited hereafter as *Biddle Correspondence.*)

[9] See Biddle's undated memorandum, *ibid.,* 93-94. McGrane fixes the date between October 1829 and January 1830. It must, however, have been after November 11, when Lewis wrote Biddle that the President would see him, and before December 8, when the message was delivered. The quotation is from W. B. Lewis to Henry Toland, Member of Congress from Pennsylvania, Nov. 11, 1829, *ibid.,* 85.

[10] Grundy to Jackson, May 22 and Oct. 22, 1829, Jackson's *Correspondence,* IV, 37, 83-84. Roswell L. Colt to Biddle, Jan. 7, 1830 (misdated 1829), *Biddle Correspondence,* 66-67.

[11] Erik M. Eriksson, "The Federal Civil Service under President Jackson," *Mississippi Valley Historical Review,* XIII (March 1927), 520; Duff Green to Calhoun, June 16, 1829, Calhoun Papers, Clemson College; McDuffie to Van Buren, June 15, 1829, Van Buren Papers; and Van Buren Papers generally for March-November 1829. The Pendleton *Messenger,* esp. May 13, June 3, 1829, sharply condemned the whole proscriptive policy.

[12] Green to Ingham, May 6, July 2, 3, 1829, letter book, Green Papers; to Calhoun, June 16, 1829, Calhoun Papers, Clemson College; Calhoun to McLean, Sept. 22, 1829, McLean Papers.

[13] Arthur B. Darling, *Political Changes in Massachusetts,* 62-84; and correspondence of Francis Baylies, *Mass. Hist. Soc. Proc.,* XLV (1911), 169-179.

[14] Duff Green to Ninian Edwards, May 26, 1829, letter book, Green Papers; to W. B. Lewis, July 11, 1829, *ibid.;* to W. T. Barry, July 11, 1829, *ibid.;* to Edwards, Nov. 4, 1829, *Edwards Papers,* 450-452.

[15] David R. Williams to Van Buren, Nov. 17, 1829, Van Buren Papers. Also in H. T. Cook, *The Life and Legacy of David Rogerson Williams,* 261-264.

[16] Calhoun to John McLean, Sept. 22, 1829, McLean Papers.

[17] Charleston *Mercury,* Sept. 30, 1829; *United States' Telegraph,* Oct. 6, 1829.

[18] *United States' Telegraph,* Dec. 23, 1829; Hamilton, *Reminiscences,* 151.

[19] Jackson's own draft of the message includes the provision for distribution of the surplus "should the constitution be found to sanction" it, but makes no recommendation for an amendment. Jackson's *Correspondence,* IV, 103.

[20] The message will be found in the usual sources: *United States' Telegraph,*

Extra, Dec. 8, 1829; *Niles,* XXXVII, 247-254; the *Register of Debates,* 21st Cong., 1st sess.; and most conveniently in Richardson, *Messages and Papers of the Presidents,* 1005-1025 .

[21] Despite the assertion of James A. Hamilton (*Reminiscences,* 151) that he drafted the message, the official copy that went to the joint session of Congress is in Van Buren's hand. Among the surviving papers of which it is a compilation, only the paragraph on the Bank is in Hamilton's hand. See Jackson's *Correspondence,* IV, 97 n.

[22] Thomas Patterson to Henry Clay, Dec. 13, 1829, Clay Papers.

[23] Charleston *Mercury,* Dec. 12, 1829; Pendleton *Messenger,* Dec. 23, 30, 1829; [R. M. T. Hunter], *Life of John C. Calhoun,* 37.

[24] Biddle to Alexander Hamilton, Dec. 12, 1829, *Biddle Correspondence,* 91. On this whole episode see R. C. H. Catterall, *Second Bank of the United States,* 176 ff.

[25] Alexander Hamilton to Biddle, Dec. 10, 1829, *Biddle Correspondence,* 88-91. The Hamilton brothers make an interesting study. James A. was a Van Buren lieutenant throughout the Jackson period. Alexander disliked and distrusted Van Buren and actively supported Calhoun for the Presidency. Yet the brothers seem to have remained throughout on good—even on intimate—terms.

[26] "Mr. Calhoun has made no demonstration of his views since his arrival at the City. Judging from his appearance, I should say, he considers every thing *lost.* . . ." R. P. Letcher to Clay, Dec. 21, 1829, Clay Papers.

[27] Endorsement by Lewis on copy of letter, Jackson to Overton, Dec. 31, 1829, Jackson's *Correspondence,* IV, 109-110 n.

[28] See, *e. g.,* Southard to Clay, Sept. 12, 1829: "My confident expectation is, that Genl. J. will not live thro' his Term—his health is very bad & I regret it—Mr. C. will be Prest. before the people elect him to the office." Clay Papers.

[29] Hamilton, *Reminiscences,* 151.

[30] John E. Wool to Francis Baylies, Dec. 8, 1829, *Mass. Hist. Soc. Proc.,* XLVI (1913), 335.

[31] Thomas Patterson to Clay, Dec. 13, 1829, Clay Papers.

[32] William L. Stone to Webster, Jan. 14, 1830, Webster Papers.

[33] Green to Noah, Mar. 25, 1830, letter book, Green Papers; to Col. Alexander Hamilton, Mar. 25, 1830, *ibid.*

[34] New York *Courier and Enquirer,* Dec. 19, 1829; James Watson Webb to Van Buren, Dec. 19, 1829, Van Buren Papers. The quotations are from the letter.

[35] *United States' Telegraph,* Jan. 13, 1830; Nicholas Biddle to John Potter, Jan. 9, 1830, *Biddle Correspondence,* 95-96.

[36] *United States' Telegraph,* Dec. 22, 1829.

[37] Lewis to J. A. Hamilton, Jan. 4, 1830, Hamilton, *Reminiscences,* 154.

[38] Jackson to Judge Overton, Dec. 31, 1829, and endorsement by Lewis, Jackson's *Correspondence,* IV, 108-109, and note.

[39] *United States' Telegraph,* Dec. 8, 1829.

[40] *Ibid.,* Dec. 21, 1829.

[41] *Senate Executive Journal,* IV, 43-44.

[42] *E. g.,* Alfred Balch to Jackson, Jan. 8, 1830: "Mr. Calhoun told us when he set up this Bank that it would give us a sound currency, would equalize exchange and be a blessing to the people." He then proceeds to abuse the Bank, and concludes with extravagant praise for Van Buren. Jackson's *Correspondence,* IV, 114-116.

[43] William L. Stone to Webster, Jan. 14, 1830, Webster Papers; Adams, *Diary,* VIII, 166, 179.

[44] *Niles,* XXXVII, 241.

[45] James Barbour to Clay, Dec. 20, 1829, Clay Papers; Richmond *Enquirer,* Feb. 11, 1830.

[46] *United States' Telegraph,* Jan. 8, 1830.

CHAPTER IV

[1] See R. G. Wellington, "The Tariff and Public Lands from 1828 to 1833," *Annual Report of the American Historical Association,* I (1911), 179-185.

[2] "This subject ["our South Western boundary"] and the public lands, are the two *levers* to move public sentiment in the West. If you have ulterior views your *tongue* and *pen* should dwell incessantly upon these two great topics." Thomas Hart Benton to Sam Houston, Aug. 15, 1829, Amelia W. Williams and Eugene C. Barker, eds., *Writings of Sam Houston,* I, 140.

[3] Jackson's activities in this regard are capable of more than one interpretation. In addition to the standard biographical and historical accounts, see Richard R. Stenberg, "Jackson, Anthony Butler, and Texas," *Southwestern Social Science Quarterly,* XIII (December 1932), 264-286; and "The Texas Schemes of Jackson and Houston, 1829-1836," *ibid.,* XV (December 1934), 229-250.

[4] *Senate Journal,* 21st Cong., 1st sess., 32.

[5] *Register of Debates,* 21st, 1st, 3-4.

[6] *Ibid.,* 4, 7.

[7] *Ibid.,* 11. The roll call is not given in the *Register,* but is in *Niles,* XXXVII, 350.

[8] C. G. De Witt, Member of Congress from Ulster County, New York, in the *Ulster Sentinel,* Feb. 17, 1830, reprinted in "The Great Webster-Hayne Debate," *Olde Ulster,* IX (November 1913), 332.

[9] *Register of Debates,* 21st, 1st, 22-27.

[10] *Ibid.,* 31-35.

[11] Webster's *Writings,* VI, 293-296.

[12] *Register of Debates,* 21st, 1st, 35-41. For contemporary comment from the Southern point of view, see *United States' Telegraph,* Feb. 11, 1830; and *Southern Review,* XI (August 1830), 142 ff.

[13] *Register of Debates,* 21st, 1st, 38. The allusion was to Dr. Thomas Cooper's speech of July 2, 1827. See Dumas Malone, *The Public Life of Thomas Cooper, 1783-1839,* 307-311.

[14] Wiltse, *Calhoun, Nationalist,* 308-309.

[15] The Webster-Hayne debates have become so encrusted with legend that it is extremely difficult to reconstruct even a relatively objective view of what actually happened and why. Being contemporary in origin, the legend should perhaps be called propaganda. The unprovoked attack on Webster and New England by Hayne is certainly the impression given by Webster's own first speech, if one has not read Hayne's, and is undoubtedly the impression Webster meant to convey. Mr. Justice Joseph Story, who did not hear Hayne's speech and could not have read it, since it was not yet published, says that the South Carolina Senator "went into an acrimonious and disparaging tirade against New England, which drew from Mr. Webster a very bold and powerful reply." (Story to Mrs. Story, Jan. 29, 1830, *Story,* II, 34.) The legend has been handed down, with embellishments, by

Charles W. March, *Reminiscences of Congress* (1850); and by Peter Harvey, *Reminiscences of Daniel Webster* (1877). Neither March nor Harvey heard the debate, and both got their material from Edward Everett, who didn't hear it either. Yet the contemporary evidence shows that those who heard both speeches were taken completely by surprise when Webster replied to Hayne instead of to Benton. It was so clear to the members of the Senate themselves that Benton was not considered out of order when he replied to Webster before Hayne did. (*Register of Debates,* 21st, 1st, 41.) The most accurate secondary account is that of T. D. Jervey, *Robert Y. Hayne and His Times,* 227-267. See also the Charleston *Mercury* for Feb. 2, 5, 10, 1830.

[16] De Witt, *op. cit.,* 334-337.

[17] Harvey, *Reminiscences,* 156.

[18] March, *Reminiscences,* 122.

[19] De Witt, *loc. cit.;* Mrs. Smith, 310.

[20] Claude M. Fuess, *Daniel Webster,* I, 374 n.

[21] *Register of Debates,* 21st, 1st, 43.

[22] *Ibid.,* 58.

[23] March appears to be the original source, stating in his *Reminiscences,* 118-119, that "constantly during the progress of the discussion, he sent notes, suggestive, illustrative and advisatory to the orator, by one of the pages of the Senate." Just how March, who was fifteen years old at the time, and not present, knew the contents of the alleged notes does not appear; but by the time Fuess retells it, without citation, in his *Webster,* I, 370, the "notes and suggestions" are sent "rather ostentatiously." There are no contemporary references to any notes at all, although there are numerous accounts of the debate by those who saw and heard it.

[24] Calhoun himself repudiated Hayne's interpretation and put the dogma on a sound footing in his Fort Hill Address of the following summer. The theory was, of course, correctly stated in Calhoun's *South Carolina Exposition and Protest* of 1828. For discussion of the point, see Jervey, *Hayne,* 292-293; and David D. Wallace, *History of South Carolina,* II, 426.

[25] Webster to William Plumer, Jr., Apr. 24, 1830, *Boston Public Library Bulletin,* VII (1902), 268.

[26] Poore, *Perley's Reminiscences,* I, 117-118.

[27] De Witt, *loc. cit.*

[28] *Ibid.; Register of Debates,* 21st, 1st, 68.

[29] George Watterston, *Gallery of American Portraits,* 75.

[30] "In his opinion the liberty and the union of this country were inseparably united." Calhoun, *Works,* II, 173. Webster had just read Calhoun's speech, because he quoted from it and inserted excerpts in his notes.

[31] A typical comment is quoted in the *United States' Telegraph,* February 18, from the Philadelphia *Gazette,* whose correspondent heard the debate: "I do not however think Mr. Hayne, *completely* overthrew Mr. Webster; but I am decidedly of opinion that Mr. Webster did not overthrow Mr. Hayne. . . ." See also *Niles,* XXXVII, 377.

[32] *Register of Debates,* 21st, 1st, 95-119, 555.

[33] *Ibid.,* 172. The bill was withdrawn on March 5, after it had been challenged as a revenue bill, and therefore not within the constitutional power of the Senate to originate. *Ibid.,* 244-245.

[34] See, *e. g.,* Adams, *Diary,* VIII, 190-191; and Clay to J. S. Johnston, May 9, 1830, Clay's *Works,* IV, 267.

[35] While the debate was going on, Hayne was generally regarded as speaking for the administration, and there is evidence that Jackson himself commended the South Carolinian. Jervey, *Hayne,* 266, 339-340; also Poore, *Perley's Reminiscences,* I, 118-119. Party sentiment was so strongly involved that immediately after the exchange between Webster and Hayne, Webb felt it necessary to bring the pro-Van Buren *Courier and Enquirer* out for Hayne, at the same time condemning Webster for all the old Federalist heresies and castigating the National Republicans for trying to provoke trouble between the Vice President and the Secretary of State. Quoted in the *United States' Telegraph,* Feb. 5, 1830.

[36] Among the other notable speeches were those of Felix Grundy of Tennessee, February 27 and March 1, *Register of Debates,* 21st, 1st, 210-220; John M. Clayton of Delaware, March 2 and 4, *ibid.,* 224-244; and Edward Livingston of Louisiana, March 9 and 15, *ibid.,* 247-272.

[37] Delegates to the Virginia Constitutional Convention of 1829-1830 included ex-Presidents James Madison and James Monroe, Chief Justice John Marshall, United States Senators Littleton W. Tazewell and John Tyler, and a host of other great names such as John Randolph of Roanoke, Philip P. Barbour, Abel P. Upshur, Benjamin Watkins Leigh, and William Branch Giles. The list included Governors, Senators, state legislators, and judges, past, present, and to be. A convenient list is in W. C. Bruce, *John Randolph of Roanoke,* I, 609-612.

[38] 4 Wheaton 405.

[39] Wiltse, *Calhoun, Nationalist,* 190-191.

[40] At the risk of belaboring the point, a few quotations may be in order:

". . . the Convention which formed this compact . . ." Josiah Quincy in the House of Representatives in 1811, arguing against statehood for Louisiana; Edmund Quincy, *Life of Josiah Quincy,* 209.

". . . the limits of the U. S. as they existed at the time of the compact." Daniel Webster to Ezekiel Webster, June 4, 1813, Webster's *Writings,* XVI, 26.

"The principles on which the national compact was founded . . ." Maryland Remonstrance against the War, Feb. 2, 1814, *Annals of Congress,* 13th Cong., 2nd sess., 1204.

"The operation of measures thus unconstitutional and illegal ought to be prevented by a resort to other measures which are both constitutional and legal. It will be the solemn duty of the State Governments to protect their own authority . . . and to interpose between their citizens and arbitrary power." Webster in the House of Representatives, Dec. 9, 1814, arguing against the conscription bill; Webster's *Writings,* XIV, 68.

It is perhaps not without interest to note that on a later occasion, after Calhoun's death, Webster came back to his 1814 stand and took substantially the same position that Hayne and Calhoun had taken in 1830. Speaking informally at Capon Springs, Virginia, June 28, 1851, he had no doubt that "if the Northern States refuse, wilfully and deliberately, to carry into effect that part of the Constitution which respects the restoration of fugitive slaves and Congress provide no remedy, the South would no longer be bound to observe the compact. A bargain cannot be broken on one side and still bind the other." Webster's *Writings,* XIII, 439.

[41] William Rawle, *View of the Constitution* (2nd edition), 296-297. The same authority explains that "every state must be viewed as entirely sovereign in all points not transferred by the people who compose it, to the government of the Union." (P. 31.) Rawle's work first appeared in 1825, and enjoyed a great enough vogue to justify its reissue without significant change in 1829. It was largely

superseded by Kent's *Commentaries,* the first volume of which was published in 1826, and by Story's *Commentaries,* which appeared in 1833, both of which expounded the Hamilton-Marshall-Webster theory of centralized power.

[42] Webster to Jeremiah Mason, Feb. 27, 1830, Webster's *Writings,* XVII, 488; to Warren Dutton, Mar. 8, 1830, *ibid.,* 493-494.

[43] *National Intelligencer,* May 21, 1830.

[44] Madison to Webster, Mar. 15, 1830, Webster's *Writings,* XVII, 496-497; to Nicholas P. Trist, Feb. 15, 1830, *Letters and Other Writings of James Madison* (Congressional Edition), IV, 61-66; to Edward Everett, August 1830, *ibid.,* 95-106.

[45] See, *e. g.,* Hayne to J. H. Hammond, Feb. 25, 1830, Hammond Papers; Eldred Simkins to Hammond, Mar. 6, 1830, *ibid.;* W. D. Martin to Hammond, Mar. 10, 1830, *ibid.;* F. W. Pickens to Hammond, Mar. 13, 1830, *ibid.;* Hayne to Hammond, Mar. 29, 1830, *ibid.* The credo of the Nullifiers was succinctly stated by Hammond in the first issue of the *Southern Times,* Jan. 29, 1830: "We are with the South. Heart and hand, soul and body, we are with the South. Yet we love and venerate the American Union. We have a holy, all-but a superstitious reverence for it. We believe there are but few among us who entertain different feelings. . . . We are too well acquainted with our interests not to know that an union, such as it ought to be, will be incalculably beneficial to us. And it is dear to us, not only from a consciousness of present good, and of future blessings, but from the events of the past. . . . There is no State that would do more than South Carolina to preserve the Union."

CHAPTER V

[1] Active participants were the following: Committee on Arrangements, Representatives Charles E. Haynes, Ga., Robert Desha, Tenn., Henry Hubbard, N. H., Thomas Hinds, Miss., Daniel H. Miller, Pa. Committee on Invitations, Senators Hugh L. White, Tenn., R. Y. Hayne, S. C., Levi Woodbury, N. H., and Representatives Thomas H. Hall, N. C., Joel Yancey, Ky., C. C. Cambreleng, N. Y. Committee on Toasts, Senators Thomas Hart Benton, Mo., Robert M. Troup, Ga., and Representative Warren R. Davis, S. C. See *United States' Telegraph,* Apr. 12, 13, 1830. Benton and Desha were understood to be the original instigators of the business. Charleston *Courier,* Apr. 21, 1830.

[2] Van Buren and Benton, both active participants, are responsible for much of the mythology connected with the dinner. Their respective memoirs, however, were written a quarter century after the event. Benton had changed sides in the interim, and Van Buren had forgotten or found it convenient to ignore the sequence of events. See Van Buren, *Autobiography,* 409-417; and T. H. Benton, *Thirty Years' View,* I, 148-149.

[3] *United States' Telegraph,* Mar. 16, 1830; Green to John T. Mumford, Mar. 22, 1830, letter book, Green Papers; to Mordecai Noah, Mar. 24 (not sent), 25, 1830, *ibid.*

[4] "Calhoun is forming a party against Van Buren, and as the President is supposed to be Van Buren's man, the Vice President has great difficulty to separate his opposition to Van Buren from opposition to the President. . . ." Webster to Jeremiah Mason, Feb. 27, 1830, Webster's *Writings,* XVII, 488. Also Calhoun to Samuel Gouverneur, Mar. 30, 1830, *Correspondence,* 271-272; H. Petrikin to Jackson, Apr. 2, 1830, Jackson's *Correspondence,* IV, 131-132; John Bailey to

J. B. Davis, Apr. 9, 1830, *Mass. Hist. Soc. Proc.,* XLIX, 221; James Parton, *Life of Andrew Jackson,* III, 297 ff.

[5] Van Buren, *Autobiography,* 413-414. Cf. Jackson to Coffee, Apr. 10, 1830, Jackson's *Correspondence,* IV, 134. A detailed analysis will be found in Richard R. Stenberg, "The Jefferson Birthday Dinner, 1830," *Journal of Southern History,* IV (August 1938), 334-345.

[6] *United States' Telegraph,* Apr. 15, 1830. Except as otherwise noted, the following account of the dinner is based on the *Telegraph* for Apr. 15 and 17, 1830.

[7] Van Buren, *Autobiography,* 412-415. As John Quincy Adams heard the story more than a month later, it was Daniel Miller, the Pennsylvania member of the arrangements committee, who had shown the list to his colleague, George G. Leiper. Miller read the list to Leiper "till he came to the thirteenth, when Leiper told him he had enough; he need not read any more. He then collected the whole eight together, and told them he would not sit down at the table where these toasts were to be drunk; and they all agreed to withdraw together, which they accordingly did." *Diary,* VIII, 228-229.

[8] Van Buren says the word "Federal" was inserted, after the toast was delivered, at the request of Hayne, but that Jackson had really so intended it. According to the same source, the toast was actually written in advance of the dinner in consultation with Van Buren and Donelson. Jackson had a copy of it in his pocket, but he wrote it out from memory on the back of the toast list, inadvertently omitting the word "Federal." *Autobiography,* 413-415. If so, then Jackson recopied the whole thing onto the back of another toast list, and threw the first one away. There was no insertion or alteration in it when it was handed to Duff Green, in Jackson's handwriting, for publication in the *Telegraph.* See Green's account in the *Telegraph,* Apr. 23, 1830. There is a copy in the Jackson Papers, second series, Library of Congress, in the handwriting of W. B. Lewis with an endorsement signed by Lewis identifying it as a true copy of the original that went to Green.

[9] ". . . You will see strong symptoms of *oppugnation* in the South, especially in South Carolina. There is, however, I trust, no great danger of violent irregularities. The tariff will not at present, certainly, be either repealed or reduced." Webster to J. Evelyn Denison, May 10, 1830, Webster's *Writings,* XVI, 202-203.

[10] *E. g.,* Webster to J. Mason, Apr. 14, 1830, Webster's *Writings,* XVI, 201; *United States' Telegraph,* Apr. 15, 17, 1830. Thomas Ritchie's first reaction, based not on the *Telegraph* but on letters from some of the guests, was one of enthusiasm. "The celebration excited the deepest interest, and it went off with the finest effect. . . . The principles recognized on this occasion, are the principles of Jefferson and McKean, of Clinton and Langdon—They are the principles which produced the Civil Revolution of 1800—and so long as we preserve them, the Constitution is safe, and our country is free." Richmond *Enquirer,* Apr. 20, 1830. There is no reference to Jackson's toast, which apparently did not strike Ritchie, or his correspondents, as being of any unusual significance. Neither did the strongly protariff Hezekiah Niles see any special implications in the Jackson and Calhoun toasts. If anything, he seemed to think Jackson was adopting the South Carolina doctrines. *Niles,* XXXVIII, 153-156.

[11] Webster to Clay, Apr. 18, 1830, Clay Papers. (Printed in part in Clay's *Works,* IV, 259-260.) Adams has a similar version: "The Jefferson dinner was a trick of Calhoun's against Van Buren, as the Harrisburg and Albany nominations of Jackson for re-election were a trick of Van Buren's against Calhoun." *Diary,* VIII, 222.

[12] *National Intelligencer,* Apr. 19, 1830.

[13] *United States' Telegraph,* Apr. 20, 1830.

[14] *National Intelligencer,* Apr. 21, 24, 1830; *United States' Telegraph,* Apr. 23, 1830.

[15] *United States' Telegraph,* Apr. 28, 1830.

[16] Jackson to Robert Oliver [Joel R. Poinsett], Oct. 26, 1830, Jackson's *Correspondence,* IV, 191.

[17] Benton, *View,* I, 148. Benton does not mention his own role as one of the organizers of the dinner and chairman of the toast-making committee. It is curious, too, that the strongly State Rights Senators from Virginia, Tazewell and Tyler, both declined to attend, not because of any plot to elevate Calhoun on the ruins of the Union, but because they were unwilling to "bind themselves to Gen. Jackson's car." Richmond *Enquirer,* Apr. 30, 1830. It is also noteworthy that the most militant of the antinullification editors in South Carolina, Benjamin F. Perry of the Greenville *Mountaineer,* commended not Jackson's toast but Calhoun's. Lillian A. Kibler, *Benjamin F. Perry, South Carolina Unionist,* 96.

[18] *Register of Debates,* 21st, 1st, 819.

[19] *Ibid.,* 842.

[20] A motion by William D. Martin of South Carolina on May 17 to take up McDuffie's tariff reduction bill in Committee of the Whole was defeated, 92 to 98. *Ibid.,* 1016.

[21] *Ibid.,* 427.

[22] *Ibid.,* 435.

[23] *Senate Journal,* 21st, 1st, 457.

[24] Calhoun to Van Deventer, May 12, 1830, *Correspondence,* 273.

[25] Jackson to Calhoun, May 13, 1830, Jackson's *Correspondence,* IV, 136.

[26] See Jackson to Coffee, Apr. 10, 1830, *ibid.,* 134.

[27] Richardson, *Messages and Papers of the Presidents,* 1046-1056; Van Buren, *Autobiography,* 319-329.

[28] *Senate Journal,* 21st, 1st, 468-469.

[29] *Ibid.,* 474.

[30] *Register of Debates,* 21st, 1st, 1148.

[31] See, *e. g., United States' Telegraph,* May 28, 1830; Charleston *Mercury,* June 4, 1830; *Southern Times,* June 7, 1830; Tyler to Tazewell, May 28, 1830, Lyon G. Tyler, *The Letters and Times of the Tylers,* I, 412; James Hamilton, Jr., to Van Buren, June 8, 1830, Van Buren Papers; Thomas Ritchie to Archibald Ritchie, June 8, 1830, *The John P. Branch Historical Papers of Randolph-Macon College,* I, 148; William D. Moseley to Polk, Dec. 1, 1830, *North Carolina Historical Review,* XVI (January 1939), 63.

[32] William Creighton, Jr., to Gov. Allen Trimble, [no month] 1830, *Old Northwest Genealogical Quarterly,* XI (January 1908), 35.

[33] Jackson to Col. A. P. Hayne, Apr. 27, 1830, Jackson's *Correspondence,* IV, 135-136.

[34] Jackson to Calhoun, Jackson's *Correspondence,* IV, 136. The Crawford letter is included in the various versions of the whole correspondence on the subject between Calhoun and Jackson, most convenient of which are Calhoun's *Works,* VI, 349-445; and *Niles,* XL, 11-24, 37-40, 41-45.

[35] For the earlier background, see Wiltse, *Calhoun, Nationalist,* 155-163, 362-364.

[36] Calhoun to Jackson, July 10, 1828, Jackson's *Correspondence,* III, 413-415.

[37] "On my arrival at Washington in 1818 I sought the first opportunity to enquire of Cr[awford] what part he had taken in the Cabinet Council. He then gave me substantially the same account contained in his letter to mr. Forsyth. Genl. Jackson arrived in Washington during the discussion of the Semenole Campaign in the H of Repres. On hearing that he was profuse in his abuse of Crawford I stated to many persons with the view of its reaching the Genls. eares that he was misinformed as to the part mr. Cr. had taken in the Cabinet deliberations, that it was mr. Calhoun and not Cr. who had proposed the Court martial. On returning home in the Spring of 1819 I continued to make the same statement and offered to prove it by the Prest. and his Cabinet if desirable to Genl. Jackson." Col. John Williams of Tennessee to Van Buren, Mar. 22, 1831, in Jackson's *Correspondence,* IV, 229 n.

[38] Narrative of Major Lewis, Parton, *Jackson,* III, 322 ff. Lewis says November, but Monroe did not give up his seat in the Virginia Constitutional Convention until December 8, resigning on the twelfth. *Proceedings and Debates of the Virginia State Convention of 1829-30,* 577, 620. He could not have reached Washington before December 13, and since Calhoun took over his duties as presiding officer of the Senate on December 14, he must also have been in the city at the time of the dinner. If such is the case, his omission from the guest list is probably significant. Lewis' story is corroborated by Adams, *(Diary,* VIII, 320) who got it early in 1831 from Ringgold's son-in-law; and by Major Donelson, who got it from Jackson himself about a year after the event. "It ought to be stated here," Donelson wrote on Nov. 21, 1830, "that Ringgold was interceding for Lewis favor and influence in behalf of Mr. Monroe's accounts against the Government, which are yet pending before Congress: and that it is probable he saw no better plan than that of access to the Presidents prejudice against Calhoun. Lewis was a fit and is always a ready instrument in such an operation." Statement of Andrew J. Donelson, in Jackson's *Correspondence,* IV, 205.

[39] The major sources are Calhoun's pamphlet, conveniently reproduced in his *Works,* VI, 349-445, and in *Niles,* XL, 11-24, 37-40, 41-45; Van Buren, *Autobiography,* 366-395; Narrative of Major Lewis, in Parton, *Jackson,* III, 310-330; Jackson's statement, in Benton, *View,* I, 169-180; and the collected correspondence of Jackson, Calhoun, and Monroe. The contemporary papers, especially the *United States' Telegraph* and the *Globe,* should be consulted.

[40] Houston to Jackson, Jan. 13, 1827, Houston's *Writings,* I, 71-73. For background, see Wiltse, *Calhoun, Nationalist,* 363.

[41] Quoted in Van Buren, *Autobiography,* 371.

[42] Calhoun to Jackson, May 13, 1830, *Works,* VI, 362.

[43] The time of the trip is conjecture. It had to be over a Sunday because Calhoun did not fail to appear at any session of the Senate until May 29. Monroe refers to the visit in the past tense on May 21, in a letter to Calhoun; S. Hamilton, ed., *The Writings of James Monroe,* VII, 210-212. I have therefore picked the only Sunday intervening between Calhoun's receipt of Jackson's letter and Monroe's reference to the visit.

[44] Calhoun to Monroe, May 26, 1830, *Correspondence,* 273-274; Calhoun to Wirt, May 28, 1830, *Works,* VI, 427; Wirt to Calhoun, May 28, 1830, *ibid.,* 428-429; Monroe to Calhoun, May 19, 21, 26 [27], 1830, Monroe's *Writings,* VII, 209-213.

[45] Jackson to James A. Hamilton, May 18, 1830, Jackson's *Correspondence,* IV, 137.

[46] Those who have not the time to evaluate several volumes of testimony for themselves will find a convenient summary of the evidence in Richard R. Stenberg, "Jackson's 'Rhea Letter' Hoax," *Journal of Southern History,* II (November 1936), 480-496.

[47] Van Buren, *Autobiography,* 376; Narrative of Major Lewis, Parton, *Jackson,* III, 327.

[48] The quotations are from Jackson to Lewis, Aug. 25, 1830, Jackson's *Correspondence,* IV, 176-177, but many similar passages will be found in the same volume, both earlier and later than this date.

[49] Calhoun to Maxcy, Aug. 6, 1830, Maxcy Papers.

[50] Overton to Jackson, June 12, 1830, Jackson's *Correspondence,* IV, 151-155.

[51] See Jackson to Coffee, July 20, 1830, *ibid.,* 164-165; and to Lewis, July 21, 1830, *ibid.,* 165-166.

[52] Jackson to Mary Eastin, Oct. 24, 1830, *ibid.,* 187.

[53] John C. McLemore to A. J. Donelson, Nov. 10, 1830, *ibid.,* 197 n.

[54] Jackson to Emily Donelson, Nov. 28, 1830, *ibid.,* 208. Also to Coffee, Dec. 28, 1830, *ibid.,* 215-217.

[55] Statement of Andrew J. Donelson, Nov. 10, 1830, *ibid.,* 202.

[56] *Ibid.,* 200, 204.

[57] *United States' Telegraph,* June 8, 24, 1830; Green to John McLean, June 26, 1830, McLean Papers; Green to Ninian Edwards, Oct. 8, 1830, *Edwards Papers,* 547-549. Cf. Micah Sterling to Maxcy, June 9, 1830, Maxcy Papers, second series.

[58] McDuffie to McLean, June 1, 1830, McLean Papers.

[59] Charles H. Ambler, *Thomas Ritchie, a Study in Virginia Politics,* 134-136. Cf. Adams, *Diary,* VIII, 222.

[60] Adams, *Diary,* VIII, 231.

[61] James F. Rippy, *Joel R. Poinsett, Versatile American,* 129; Charles J. Stillé, *The Life and Services of Joel R. Poinsett,* 56-58.

[62] Darling, *Political Changes in Massachusetts,* 98-129.

[63] *United States' Telegraph,* June 15, 1830.

[64] *Niles,* XXXIX, 106.

[65] *Ibid.,* 180-181.

[66] Ninian Edwards to McLean, Dec. 14, 1830, McLean Papers.

[67] Jackson to Lewis, June 28, 1830, Jackson's *Correspondence,* IV, 157-158.

[68] Jackson to Lewis, June 26, 1830, *ibid.,* 156; James A. Hamilton to Jackson, July 29, 1830, *ibid.,* 167-168.

[69] James Watson Webb to Webster, June 29, 1830, Webster Papers.

[70] Alexander Hamilton to Maxcy, Aug. 8, 1830, Maxcy Papers.

CHAPTER VI

[1] See files of the *Southern Times,* the Charleston *Mercury,* and the Pendleton *Messenger.* Also Hammond Papers, 1830 *passim;* J. Hamilton, Jr., to Van Buren, May 27, Sept. 20, 1830, Van Buren Papers; and C. S. Boucher, *The Nullification Controversy in South Carolina,* 46-87.

[2] For Cheves's views see comments of his daughter in *XIX Century,* II (April 1870), 886. Rhett is well treated in Laura A. White, *Robert Barnwell Rhett.*

[3] See especially the "Hampden" articles in the *Southern Times,* reprinted from the Edgefield *Carolinian,* actually written by Francis W. Pickens, son of Calhoun's first cousin, former Governor Andrew Pickens. See F. W. Pickens to Hammond,

Mar. 8, 13, 1830, Hammond Papers. Also Boucher, *Nullification Controversy*, 56.

[4] Pendleton *Messenger*, July 7, 1830.

[5] *Southern Times*, May 10, 1830. McDuffie explained it in similar terms to Thomas Ritchie early in June 1830. See T. Ritchie to A. Ritchie, June 8, 1830, *Branch Papers*, I, 147-148.

[6] D. L. Wardlaw to Hammond, July 21, 1830, Hammond Papers; Cook, *Williams*, 259; John W. DuBose, *William L. Yancey*, I, 50-51.

[7] William C. Preston to Hammond, July 24, 1830, Hammond Papers; Waddy Thompson to Hammond, Aug. 8, 1830, *ibid.*

[8] Charleston *Courier*, June-October 1830; Stillé, *Poinsett*, 44; White, *Rhett*, 20-21; Benjamin F. Perry, "Joel R. Poinsett," *Reminiscences of Public Men;* Cook, *Williams*, 271-273.

[9] Madison to the editor of the *North American Review*, August 1830, printed in the *Review*, XXXI (October 1830), 537-546; also in *Niles*, XXXIX, 126-128; and Madison's *Writings*, IV, 95-106.

[10] *North American Review*, XXXI, 487: "This protest has been publicly ascribed to the . . . Vice President."

[11] Calhoun to Maxcy, Sept. 11, 1830, Maxcy Papers. Also Calhoun to Maxcy, Aug. 6, 1830, *ibid.;* and Alexander Hamilton to Maxcy, Sept. 11, 1830, *ibid.* Calhoun was aware that the South Carolina excitement was being used against him personally in other sections, but he would not interfere with the progress of events. See Duff Green to Ninian Edwards, Oct. 8, 1830, *Edwards Papers*, 548.

[12] *Niles*, XXXIX, 97; *Southern Times*, Sept. 13, 1830; Charleston *Mercury*, May 15, Sept. 8, 11, 1830; Adams, *Diary*, VIII, 258; Boucher, *Nullification Controversy*, 88, 99.

[13] Boucher, *Nullification Controversy*, 102-104; Jervey, *Hayne*, 283.

[14] Wiltse, *Calhoun, Nationalist*, 389.

[15] *Southern Times*, Dec. 1, 10, 1830. Miller's election was planned during the summer. See F. W. Pickens to Hammond, June 26, July 14, 1830, Hammond Papers.

[16] *United States' Telegraph*, Dec. 20, 21, 27, 1830; Boucher, *Nullification Controversy*, 103-106.

[17] Calhoun to Maxcy, Nov. 3, 1830, Maxcy Papers.

[18] See, *e. g.*, William H. Crawford to Van Buren, May 31, 1830, Van Buren Papers; Nathaniel Macon to Van Buren, Oct. 1, 1830, *ibid.;* Hayne to Van Buren, Oct. 23, 1830, *ibid.*

[19] An early analysis of this shift will be found in *Brownson's Review*, I, (January 1844), 122.

[20] *National Intelligencer*, Dec. 30, 1830; Calhoun to James Edward Calhoun, Jan. 13, 1831, *Correspondence*, 279-280; to Hammond, Jan. 15, 1831, *ibid.*, 280-281.

[21] Richardson, *Messages and Papers of the Presidents*, 1063-1092.

[22] "A new paper (Jackson) has sprung up here within a few days past entitled 'The Globe.'—A Jackson Member (supposing me to be with my *Brother* & the administration) stated to me that its object is to supplant Duff—that 'he is to be *killed*, and they mean to have the *honor* of doing it themselves.' " F. H. Pettis to Henry Clay, Dec. 16, 1830, Clay Papers.

[23] W. E. Smith, *The Francis Preston Blair Family in Politics*, I, 69, 71-72; Blair to Mrs. Benjamin Gratz, Feb. 23, 1831, *Atlantic Monthly*, LX, (August 1887), 191.

[24] See Kendall-Green correspondence in the *National Intelligencer,* Mar. 28, 1831; and Washington *Globe,* Mar. 30, 1831. Also Smith, *Blair Family,* 60.

[25] Poore, *Perley's Reminiscences,* I, 104; Henry A. Wise, *Seven Decades of the Union,* 117; Lewis Coryell to Calhoun, July 29, 1845, Calhoun Papers, Clemson College.

[26] *National Intelligencer,* Dec. 13, 1830; Warren R. Davis to Hammond, Dec. 14, 1830, Hammond Papers; Green to Edwards, Jan. 19, 1831, *Edwards Papers,* 565.

[27] Calhoun to Hammond, Jan. 15, 1831, *Correspondence,* 280-283; McDuffie to Armistead Burt, Jan. 13, 1831, McDuffie Papers, Duke University; McDuffie to Hammond, Feb. 6, 1831, Hammond Papers. See also Green to Edwards, Jan. 19, 1831, *Edwards Papers,* 568; and Gideon Welles to Van Buren, Dec. 27, 1830, Van Buren Papers.

[28] Donald B. Sanger, "The Nullification Movement in Georgia," *Tyler's Quarterly Historical and Genealogical Magazine,* XI (October 1929), 94-106; *Southern Times,* Jan. 3, 1831.

[29] *House Journal,* 21st, 2nd, 86; F. W. Pickens to Hammond, Dec. 28, 1830, Hammond Papers; Calhoun to Hammond, Jan. 15, 1831, *Correspondence,* 280-283; Story to Mrs. Story, Jan. 28, 1831, *Story,* II, 43-44.

[30] Adams, *Diary,* VIII, 274; Charleston *Courier,* Jan. 22, 1831.

[31] Roswell Colt to Biddle, Jan. 29, 1831, *Biddle Correspondence,* 122-123.

[32] *Ibid.*

[33] Washington *Globe,* Jan. 26, 1831.

[34] Adams, *Diary,* VIII, 249-250. Cf. *ibid.,* 252-253.

[35] Floyd to Williams, Dec. 27, 1830, Floyd Papers.

[36] Adams, *Diary,* VIII, 275-277, 296-298, 304-306, 310-312.

[37] See Calhoun to Monroe, Jan. 11, 1831 (two letters), *Correspondence,* 275-278; Jan. 21, 1831 (two letters), *ibid.,* 283-284; and Feb. 4, 1831, *ibid.,* 288.

[38] John Rhea to Jackson, Jan. 4, 1831, and Mar. 30, 1831, Jackson's *Correspondence,* IV, 221-222, 254-255.

[39] Barry to his daughter, Jan. 2, 1831, *William and Mary College Quarterly Historical Magazine,* XIV (July 1905), 21-22; Felix Grundy to Daniel Graham, Jan. 24, 1831, Grundy Papers; Ephraim W. Foster to Grundy, Jan. 25, 1831, *ibid.;* William Carroll to Van Buren, Feb. 6, 1831, Van Buren Papers; R. M. Johnson to Jackson, Feb. 13, 1831, Kentucky State Historical Society, Register, XL (January 1942), 69; Jackson to Donelson, Mar. 24, 1831, Jackson's *Correspondence,* IV, 251-254; Calhoun to Grundy, June 8, 1831, Grundy Papers; Charleston *Courier,* Jan. 11, 1831.

[40] Calhoun to Hammond, Feb. 16, 1831, *Correspondence,* 289-290. Cf. Crowninshield to H. A. S. Dearborn, Jan. 7, 1831, *Mass. Hist. Soc. Proc.,* LXIII, 69.

[41] Representative W. D. Martin of South Carolina to Hammond, Jan. 10, 1831, Hammond Papers.

[42] Calhoun to James Edward Calhoun, Jan. 13, 1831, *Correspondence,* 279-280.

[43] James A. Hamilton to Jackson, Feb. 3, 1831, Hamilton, *Reminiscences,* 195; Hamilton to Van Buren, Feb. 3, 1831, Van Buren Papers.

[44] "He [Calhoun] leaves the question of publication, or rather the necessity of it, to his friends—not his political friends, but to a certain part of the So. Carolina delegation, & you will easily conjecture who they are." W. D. Martin to Hammond, Jan. 10, 1831, Hammond Papers. See also Adams, *Diary,* VIII, 313-315.

[45] See Eaton's statement in the Washington *Globe,* Mar. 26, 1831. Also Cal-

houn to Grundy, June 8, 1831, Grundy Papers; and Adams, *Diary,* VIII, 316-317, 350.

[46] Calhoun to Hammond, Feb. 16, 1831, *Correspondence,* 289-290.

[47] *Niles,* XXXIX, 457; James Watson Webb to Van Buren, Apr. 3, 1831, Van Buren Papers; Richmond *Enquirer,* Feb. 19, 24, 1831; *Southern Times,* Mar. 9, 1831; Charleston *Mercury,* Feb. 24, Mar. 11, 1831; Pendleton *Messenger,* Mar. 2, 1831; Charleston *Courier,* Mar. 4, 15, 29, 1831.

[48] A. Hamilton to V. Maxcy, Mar. 9, 1831, Maxcy Papers; Clay to Francis Brooke, Apr. 24, 1831 [misdated 1830], Clay's *Works,* IV, 262-263; J. Bernard to William C. Rives, Apr. 3, 1831, Rives Papers. See also Calhoun to Micah Sterling, Mar. 8, 1831, Calhoun Papers, South Caroliniana Library; to D. F. Caldwell, May 1, 1831, Calhoun Papers, Duke University; Allan Nevins, ed., *The Diary of Philip Hone,* 36; Mrs. Smith, 333-334.

[49] Washington *Globe,* Feb. 26, 1831; Van Buren, *Autobiography,* 366 ff; Adams, *Diary,* VIII, 404-405; Monroe's *Writings,* VII, 234-236. In 1835, when Kendall was Postmaster General and Samuel Gouverneur, Monroe's son-in-law, was postmaster of New York City, pressure was brought on Gouverneur to disavow Monroe's statement. He declined, and was dismissed as New York postmaster. The affairs of his office were in bad shape, but there is a presumption that his job might have been saved had his spine been more supple. See Calhoun to Gouverneur, May 22, 1835, *Correspondence,* 343-344; and Kendall, *Autobiography,* 349. Also *United States' Telegraph,* Sept. 17, 1836.

CHAPTER VII

[1] *Register of Debates,* 21st, 2d, 213.

[2] Wiltse, *Calhoun, Nationalist,* 324-327.

[3] *Register of Debates,* 21st, 2d, 215-310, *passim.*

[4] Adams, *Diary,* VIII, 327-328; William Prentiss to Clay, Feb. 22, 1831, Clay Papers.

[5] *Register of Debates,* 21st, 2d, 328.

[6] The controversy may be followed in the files of the *United States' Telegraph,* Washington *Globe,* New York *Courier and Enquirer,* and Richmond *Enquirer* for February, March and April, 1831.

[7] See especially the correspondence in June, July, and August 1831 between Jackson and General R. G. Dunlap, who had been a member of Jackson's party at the New Orleans celebration where Hamilton and Lewis had planned the call on Crawford. *American Historical Magazine and Tennessee Quarterly,* IX (January 1904), 83-98.

[8] See Jackson's *Correspondence,* IV, 228-236; and Benton, *View,* I, 169-180. Jackson's letters from February on through the summer are revealing documents, and must be read for any evaluation of the President's state of mind. With reference to Calhoun such adjectives as "wicked," "immoral," "profligate," and similar terms recur with astonishing frequency. See Jackson's *Correspondence,* IV, 245-345, *passim.*

[9] *National Intelligencer,* Mar. 21, 1831, quoting the Washington correspondent of the New York *Journal of Commerce.*

[10] Adams, *Diary,* VIII, 333, 337; Webster to Clay, Mar. 4, 1831, Clay Papers; John Floyd, *Diary,* 125; Frederick A. Schley to Maxcy, May 25, 1831, Maxcy Papers, second series.

[11] Floyd, *Diary,* 125-126. For contemporary description of Floyd, see Henry Barnard, "Narrative," *Maryland Historical Magazine,* XIII (December 1918), 374.

[12] W. S. Archer to Van Buren, Mar. 12, 1831, Van Buren Papers.

[13] Calhoun to Gouverneur, Apr. 16, 1831, *Correspondence,* 290.

[14] Memorandum by James H. Hammond, Mar. 18, 1831, *American Historical Review,* VI (July 1901), 741-745.

[15] Quoted in the *United States' Telegraph,* Dec. 7, 1830. The *Globe* for July 11, 1831, admits that the Cabinet reorganization was determined on at the time of the public break between Jackson and Calhoun. Also Benjamin C. Howard to V. Maxcy, Apr. 16, 1831, Maxcy Papers, second series.

[16] Adams, *Diary,* VIII, 338.

[17] See Van Buren, *Autobiography,* 396-408.

[18] Jackson's *Correspondence,* IV, 257-258, 260-263.

[19] Barry to his daughter, May 24, 1831, *William and Mary Quarterly,* XIV (April 1906), 230-232.

[20] Memorandum by Jackson, Apr. 18, 1831, Jackson's *Correspondence,* IV, 264.

[21] *Ibid.,* 264-266; Ingham to Berrien, Apr. 20, 21, May 4, 1831, Berrien Papers.

[22] Berrien to Jackson, June 15, 1831, *Niles,* XL, 304.

[23] See, *e. g.,* Jackson to Coffee, Apr. 24, 1831, Jackson's *Correspondence,* IV, 268-269; to Donelson, July 10, 11, 1831, *ibid.,* 310-311, 311-312; and to Colonel Howard, Aug. 4, 1831, Jackson Papers, second series. Also Ingham to Berrien, May 7, 1831, Berrien Papers.

[24] Van Buren to Ritchie, Apr. 16, 1831; and to B. F. Butler, same date, Van Buren Papers.

[25] *United States' Telegraph,* Apr. 20, 22, 30, May 6, June 2, 1831; John Floyd, *Diary,* 139, 140-141; Dabney S. Carr to Van Buren, Apr. 30, 1831, Van Buren Papers; Clay to Francis Brooke, May 1, 1831, Clay's *Works,* IV, 299-300; William Carroll to Jackson, May 6, 1831, Jackson Papers, second series; Tyler to Tazewell, May 8, 1831, Tyler, *Times of the Tylers,* I, 422-423; Calhoun to Maxcy, May 8, 1831, Maxcy Papers; Calhoun to Hammond, May 8, 1831, *Correspondence,* 290-292; John Floyd to John S. Barbour, June 24, 1831, Floyd Papers; William Prentiss to Clay, July 1, 1831, Clay Papers; W. S. Archer to Van Buren, Oct. 3, 1831, Van Buren Papers.

[26] Van Buren to Livingston, Apr. 9, 1831, Van Buren Papers.

[27] Jackson to White, Apr. 9, 1831, Jackson's *Correspondence,* IV, 258-260.

[28] White to Jackson, Apr. 20, 1831, *ibid.,* 267-268.

[29] Jackson to Coffee, May 29, 1831, *ibid.,* 286; to Van Buren, July 11, 1831, *ibid.,* 313; William L. G. Smith, *Fifty Years of Public Life: The Life and Times of Lewis Cass,* 244-248.

[30] As late as March 8 Jackson had written McLane asking him to remain in England another year (Jackson's *Correspondence,* IV, 246-247), indicating that Van Buren's plans were not formulated—or at least not explained to Jackson—at that date.

[31] Richmond *Enquirer,* June 10, 1831. It is noteworthy that this is well before Berrien's resignation.

[32] *United States' Telegraph,* May 19, 1831.

[33] Key to Taney, June 14, 1831, *Maryland Historical Magazine,* V (March 1910), 24-26.

[34] See, *e. g.,* John Rutherfoord to William C. Rives, Nov. 6, 1831, Rives Papers;

and R. G. Dunlap to Jackson, June 30, 1831, *American Historical Magazine and Tennessee Quarterly,* IX (January 1904), 83-85. Dunlap wanted Lewis and Kendall dismissed also.

[35] A. Hamilton to Maxcy, Mar. 9, 1831, Maxcy Papers.

[36] Floyd, *Diary,* 135; Floyd to Calhoun, Apr. 16, 1831, Floyd Papers.

[37] John S. Preston to Hammond, Apr. 17, 1831, Hammond Papers.

[38] Floyd, *Diary,* 129-141, *passim.*

[39] *Ibid.,* 142. See *United States' Telegraph,* Apr. 25, 26, 1831. Also Calhoun to Maxcy, May 16, 1831, Maxcy Papers; and James M. Broom to Maxcy, May 31, 1831, *ibid.,* second series.

[40] *United States' Telegraph,* May 12, 1831.

[41] J. Hamilton, Jr., to Hammond, June 11, 1831, *Am. Hist. Rev.,* VI (July 1901), 746-747; *United States' Telegraph,* June 18, 1831.

[42] See Calhoun to Hammond, May 16, 1831, *Correspondence,* 291; William Carroll to Jackson, June 13, 1831, Jackson Papers, second series; James Brown to Clay, June 2, 1831, *Louisiana Historical Quarterly,* XXIV (October 1941), 1155.

[43] *Niles,* XL, 201, 220.

[44] *Ibid.,* 301-303.

[45] Ingham to Jackson, June 21, 1831, Jackson's *Correspondence,* IV, 300.

[46] Adams, *Diary,* VIII, 371-372.

[47] See Jackson's *Correspondence,* IV, 300-301.

[48] *Niles,* XL, 373 ff.

[49] William B. Lewis to Jackson, July 1, 1831, Jackson's *Correspondence,* IV, 308. I am assuming that the reference is to the statement Eaton later published as his own rather than to Jackson's statement against Calhoun. A first draft of the latter document was completed in February 1831. See Jackson's *Correspondence,* IV, 228-236. Duff Green states flatly that Kendall wrote Eaton's letter. *United States' Telegraph,* Mar. 6, 1832. See also Kendall, *Autobiography,* 360.

[50] Reprinted in *Niles,* XLI, 49 ff, 57 ff.

[51] McLane to Van Buren, Sept. 6, 1831, Van Buren Papers.

[52] *Niles,* XLI, 78-82. Letter dated September 23.

[53] Also in *Works,* VI, 435-445.

CHAPTER VIII

[1] Charleston *Mercury,* Mar. 31, 1831.

[2] James Hamilton, Jr., to Hammond, May 3, 1831, *Am. Hist. Rev.,* VI (July 1901), 745; Charleston *Mercury,* May 13, 14, 19, 1831.

[3] Hamilton to Hammond, May 21, 1831, *Am. Hist. Rev.,* VI (July 1901), 746; Charleston *Mercury,* May 20, 21, 25, 1831.

[4] Hamilton to Hammond, May 21, 1831, *loc. cit.*

[5] Calhoun to D. F. Caldwell, May 1, 1831, Calhoun Papers, Duke University; B. F. Elmore to Hammond, May 16, 1831, Hammond Papers.

[6] Hamilton to Hammond, June 11, 1831, *Am. Hist. Rev.,* VI (July 1901), 746-747; *Southern Times,* May 25, 1831; *United States' Telegraph,* May 30, 1831.

[7] "If Mr. Calhoun should be a candidate and will go all the length with South Carolina, well and good; if not, South Carolina does not go with Mr. Calhoun. We want no compromising of principle, nor anything like a compromise, till the principle be fixed and settled. When that is done, then and not before, let us

sacrifice to expediency." Columbia *Telescope,* June 10, 1831, quoted in Edwin L. Green, *George McDuffie,* 106-107.

[8] Calhoun to Ingham, June 16, 1831, *Correspondence,* 294-295; to Maxcy, June 16, 1831, Maxcy Papers, second series.

[9] Charleston *Mercury,* July 13, 1831; Jervey, *Hayne,* 287-288. The Olmstead case was a dangerous precedent for the Nullifiers to invoke, for in that instance the orders of the Court had been carried out eventually by show of military force. See United States vs. Peters, 5 Cranch 115; and A. C. McLaughlin, *Constitutional History of the United States,* 343-345.

[10] Jackson to John Stoney and others, June 14, 1831, *Niles,* XL, 351.

[11] Tassel, a Cherokee Indian, was convicted of murder in a Georgia court. He claimed that the court had no jurisdiction, since the act was committed in the territory of the Cherokee Nation, and the Supreme Court agreed with him, to the extent of granting a writ of error. The Georgia authorities ignored the writ and executed the Indian.

[12] See Donald B. Sanger, "The Nullification Movement in Georgia," *Tyler's Quarterly,* XI (October 1929), 94-106, for discussion.

[13] Jackson to Van Buren, July 23, 1831, Jackson's *Correspondence,* IV, 316.

[14] J. A. Hamilton to Jackson, July 28, 1831, *ibid.,* 322.

[15] *Niles,* XLI, 119-124.

[16] Pendleton *Messenger,* June 29, 1831.

[17] Most of the newspapers reprinted it. Convenient sources are *Niles,* XL, 437-445; and Calhoun's *Works,* VI, 59-123.

[18] See Wiltse, *Calhoun, Nationalist,* 390-398.

[19] For more complete discussion of Calhoun's political theory, see C. M. Wiltse, "Calhoun and the Modern State," *Virginia Quarterly Review,* XIII (Summer 1937), 396-408; and "Calhoun's Democracy," *Journal of Politics,* III (May 1941), 210-223.

[20] Sympathy with nullification was probably stronger in Georgia than in any other state outside of South Carolina itself, but before the Fort Hill Address was published Calhoun had received from a Georgia supporter the following warning: " . . . . I have urged on many . . . the necessity of avowing our purpose of supporting you at the proper time or at least to prepare the public mind for such a course. They almost uniformly reply by asking, *is he not a nullifier?* It will be impossible to unite them in support of anyone who is tainted with nullification. No! not even against Mr. Van Buren, odious as he is." Dr. Tomlinson Fort, president of the Central Bank of Georgia, to Calhoun, July 15, 1831, quoted in Thomas P. Govan, "John M. Berrien and the Administration of Andrew Jackson," *Journal of Southern History,* V (November 1939), 464 n. The Columbia *Telescope* made the point more bluntly: "He knows unquestionably that the ground which he has taken, puts out of all hope his success, at the next Presidential election—since that success depends entirely on Pennsylvania and other northern states, that he cannot gain with these opinions." Quoted in the Richmond *Enquirer,* Aug. 16, 1831. See also Pendleton *Messenger,* Feb. 8, 1832; A. Stewart to McLean, Aug. 19, 1831, McLean Papers; William Carroll to Jackson, Sept. 1, 1831, Jackson Papers, second series.

[21] Calhoun to Maxcy, Aug. 6, 1831, Maxcy Papers.

[22] Calhoun to Gouverneur, Aug. 18, 1831, *Correspondence,* 299-300. See also to Van Deventer, Aug. 5, and to Gouverneur, Aug. 8, 1831, *ibid.,* 296-299.

[23] Calhoun to Maxcy, Sept. 1, 1831, Maxcy Papers.

[24] Jervey, *Hayne,* 291.

[25] *United States' Telegraph,* Aug. 27, 1831, reprints a page of comment from other papers. See also the same paper for Aug. 18 and 22; Richmond *Enquirer,* Aug. 16, 1831; and *National Intelligencer,* Aug. 27, 1831. There were, of course, as there always are, those who had made up their minds in advance. "Mr. Calhoun's exposé," according to his friend John Floyd, "is approved by all the real State Rights men, and I think will do him honor and be of benefit to the Country —and will enable many to see with the eyes of wisdom into many of these perplexing questions." Floyd to Duff Green, Aug. 21, 1831, Green Papers. And equally sure on the other side was Calhoun's old antagonist of the war days, William Gaston of North Carolina: "It is impossible . . . for any subtlety or sophistry to uphold a doctrine which involves such glaring and practical absurdities. What a pity that such a mind as his should be so warped from its rectitude by unholy passions." Gaston to Robert Donaldson, Sept. 3, 1831, in R. D. W. Connor, "William Gaston," *Proceedings of the American Antiquarian Society,* n. s. XLIII, 437. See also Calhoun to James Edward Calhoun, Aug. 27, Sept. 10, 1831, *Correspondence,* 301, 302-303; to Maxcy, Sept. 1, 1831, Maxcy Papers; Duff Green to Richard K. Crallé, Aug. 21, Sept. 5, 1831, *Southern History Association Publications,* VII, 167, 168-169.

[26] Calhoun to Maxcy, Aug. 6, Sept. 1, 1831, Maxcy Papers; to Samuel Gouverneur, Aug. 8, 1831, *Correspondence,* 297; to James Edward Calhoun, Aug. 27, Sept. 10, 1831, *ibid.,* 301, 302-303; to Armistead Burt, Sept. 1, 1831, *ibid.,* 301-302.

[27] Calhoun to James Edward Calhoun, Aug. 27, Sept. 10, 1831, *ibid.,* 300-301, 302-303; Pendleton *Messenger,* Aug. 31, Sept. 7, 1831.

[28] Calhoun to James Edward Calhoun, Aug. 27, 1831, *Correspondence,* 300-301.

[29] Calhoun to Burt, Sept. 1, 1831, *ibid.,* 301-302; to James Edward Calhoun, Sept. 10, 1831, *ibid.,* 302.

[30] Gamaliel Bradford, *As God Made Them,* 114-115, 123, makes much of the Aleck incident, as does Richard Hofstadter, *The American Political Tradition,* 76. The fact remains, however, that Calhoun was merely following the accepted practice of his time and place. Anyone who apprehended a runaway slave and failed to lodge him in jail was himself in violation of the law, which also prescribed whipping for the offending Negro. Corporal punishment was virtually the only one inflicted on slaves. Branding was forbidden in South Carolina in 1833, and had been rarely used before that time. There were also a very few cases of ear cropping. Detention in jail was clearly an economic waste and of dubious efficacy. Both branding and ear cropping were still in use as punishments for freemen in other parts of the country; and the lash was revived in Delaware as recently as 1935. As late as 1870 a witness at an official investigation described "an instrument for whipping children in Rhode Island [factories], consisting of a leather strap, 18 inches long, with tacks driven through the striking end." The abolitionist crusade undoubtedly added to the severity of punishments for runaway slaves in the South, with penalties up to 500 lashes, distributed over a period of time, being recorded by the 1850's. Judge O'Neall urged in 1848 that punishments be restricted to a maximum of 39 lashes "to be inflicted in portions, and at considerable intervals of time," but O'Neall was more humanitarian than most of his contemporaries. See J. B. O'Neall, *Negro Law of South Carolina,* 35; H. M. Henry, *Police Control of the Slave in South Carolina,* 52-53; Massachusetts Bureau of Statistics and Labor, *Report,* 1870, pp. 170, 181, 489.

[31] Floyd, *Diary,* 162. For the rebellion as a whole, see *ibid.,* 155-162, *passim.* For contemporary analyses of the implications of the rebellion, see Floyd to James Hamilton, Jr., Nov. 19, 1831, Floyd Papers; and Richard Pollard to William C. Rives, Jan. 30, 1832, Rives Papers. The best secondary analysis of the whole problem is Gilbert H. Barnes, *The Antislavery Impulse, 1830-1844.*

[32] *Niles,* XLI, 130, 145-146; *National Intelligencer,* Sept. 15, 1831.

[33] S. E. Morison, *The Life and Letters of Harrison Gray Otis, Federalist, 1765-1848,* II, 278-281.

[34] Floyd, *Diary,* 170-172, 173-177 *passim;* Floyd to James Hamilton, Jr., Nov. 19, 1831, Floyd Papers. There is a lengthy analysis of the slavery debates in the Virginia legislature in the *United States' Telegraph,* beginning Mar. 2, 1832. Signed "Appomattox," the articles were written by Benjamin Watkins Leigh.

[35] William S. Jenkins, *Pro-Slavery Thought in the Old South,* 65-81.

[36] *Southern Times,* Apr. 16, 1830; Calhoun to Maxcy, Sept. 11, 1830, Maxcy Papers; John Randolph to Jackson, Mar. 18, 1832, Jackson's *Correspondence,* IV, 419-422; Adams, *Diary,* VIII, 510.

CHAPTER IX

[1] *United States' Telegraph,* Aug. 11, 13, 1831; *National Intelligencer,* Aug. 13, 1831; *Niles,* XL, 417.

[2] Calhoun to Maxcy, Aug. 6, 1831, Maxcy Papers; R. Pollard to William C. Rives, Aug. 11, 1831, Rives Papers.

[3] Green to Col. S. A. Storrow, Aug. 9, 1831, Green Papers; to Crallé, Aug. 16, 21, 28, Sept. 5, Oct. 11, 1831, *ibid.;* Floyd, *Diary,* 164.

[4] Green to Crallé, Sept. 5, 11, 1831, Green Papers.

[5] *Niles,* XLI, 36.

[6] Calhoun to Maxcy, Sept. 1, 1831, Maxcy Papers. See also Adams, *Diary,* VIII, 403-404, 412-416.

[7] Alexander Hamilton to Maxcy, Oct. 3, 1831, Maxcy Papers; Green to Crallé, Oct. 4, 1831, Green Papers; James Brown to Henry Clay, Oct. 2, 1831, *Louisiana Historical Quarterly,* XXIV (October 1941), 1159; Floyd, *Diary,* 163.

[8] Adams, *Diary,* VIII, 416; Floyd, *Diary,* 168-169.

[9] Calhoun to Van Deventer, Aug. 5, 1831, *Correspondence,* 296-297; Clay to Brooke, July 24, 1831, Clay Papers; Thomas Ritchie to W. C. Rives, Oct. 26, 1831, Rives Papers; Glyndon G. Van Deusen, *The Life of Henry Clay,* 249.

[10] *National Intelligencer,* Dec. 10, 1831; Floyd, *Diary,* 171.

[11] Floyd, *Diary,* 171; Memorandum of a Conversation with Calhoun, Dec. 4, 1831, *Correspondence,* 305-306. Although unsigned, the memorandum is undoubtedly by Crallé, with whom Calhoun dined in Richmond on the date in question. Before leaving South Carolina, the Vice President had gone over all the arguments again in two documents he prepared for the state legislature. These were a Report for the Committee on Federal Relations, and an Address to the People of South Carolina, in *Works,* VI, 94-123, 124-144. Both followed the line of reasoning set forth in the *Exposition and Protest* of 1828 and in the Fort Hill Address, but neither was made public.

[12] Tyler to his daughter, Dec. 28, 1831, Tyler, *Times of the Tylers,* I, 428.

[13] *United States' Telegraph,* Dec. 6, 1831.

[14] Richardson, *Messages and Papers of the Presidents,* 1107-1121.

[15] [Hunter], *Life of Calhoun,* 41. Floyd noted that the message was "in much more subdued tones than heretofore. The old man is afraid of losing his re-election." *Diary,* 171.

[16] *Niles,* XLI, 286-296; McLane to Van Buren, Dec. 6, 1831, Van Buren Papers.

[17] James L. Clark to Hammond, Dec. 19, 1831, Hammond Papers; Calhoun to James Edward Calhoun, Dec. 25, 1831, *Correspondence,* 306-307; to A. Burt, Dec. 27, 1831, *ibid.,* 307-308; Hayne to Hammond, Dec. 29, 1831, *Am. Hist. Rev.,* VI (July 1901), 748. Cf. C. C. Johnston, Member of Congress from Virginia, to John B. Floyd, Dec. 16, 1831, *William and Mary Quarterly,* n. s. I (January 1921), 201-206.

[18] McLane to Van Buren, Dec. 14, 1831, Van Buren Papers; Morgan Neville to James Findlay, Dec. 23, 1831, Historical and Philosophical Society of Ohio, *Quarterly Publication,* I (1906), 85.

[19] *Register of Debates,* 22d, 1st, 1309.

[20] Jackson to Van Buren, Dec. 17, 1831, Jackson's *Correspondence,* IV, 385; *United States' Telegraph,* Dec. 21, 1831; *National Intelligencer,* Dec. 26, 1831.

[21] Cambreleng to Van Buren, Jan. 4, 1832, Van Buren Papers. Also John A. Dix to Dr. G. C. Shattuck, Jan. 25, 1832, *Mass. Hist. Soc. Proc.,* L, 159: " . . . so far as his friends in this State [New York] are concerned, his rejection would be decidedly gratifying to the great majority of them."

[22] Green to Crallé, Jan. 3, 1832, Green Papers.

[23] *Register of Debates,* 22d, 1st, 1309.

[24] *National Intelligencer,* Jan. 17, 1832; Washington *Globe,* Jan. 17, 1832.

[25] Jackson to Coffee, Jan. 21, 1832, Jackson's *Correspondence,* IV, 400; Washington *Globe,* Jan. 31, 1832.

[26] *Register of Debates,* 22d, 1st, 1310-1386.

[27] Tyler to John Seawell, Jan. 25, 1832, Tyler Papers; to his son, Feb. 2, 1832, Tyler, *Times of the Tylers,* I, 427.

[28] *Register of Debates,* 22d, 1st, 1378.

[29] Benton, *View,* I, 219.

[30] *United States' Telegraph,* Jan. 27, 30, 1832; Washington *Globe,* Jan. 27, 30, Apr. 14, 1832; Charleston *Mercury,* Feb. 8, 1832; Benton, *loc. cit.*

[31] John Forsyth to Van Buren, Jan. 28, 1832, Van Buren Papers; Isaac Hill to Van Buren, Jan. 29, Feb. 12, 1832, *ibid.;* R. J. Yancey to Willie P. Mangum, Feb. 11, 1832, Mangum Papers; Philip Hone, *Diary,* 67; Washington Irving to Peter Irving, Mar. 16, 1832, Pierre M. Irving, *Life and Letters of Washington Irving,* II, 480-483; William L. Mackenzie, *Sketches of Canada and the United States,* 43; William Carroll to Jackson, Feb. 20, 1832, Jackson Papers, second series; J. L. Lawrence to Clay, Jan. 30, 1832, Clay Papers; H. Niles to Clay, Feb. 3, 1832, *ibid.;* Hiram Ketchum to Clay, Feb. 12, 1832, *ibid.;* Clay to Brooke, Feb. 21, 1832, Clay's *Works,* IV, 326-327; James Brown to Clay, Jan. 24, 1832, *Louisiana Historical Quarterly,* XXIV (October 1941), 1163-1164.

[32] Green heard as early as January 1832 that the party was tired of Blair. Green to Crallé, Jan. 3, 1832, Green Papers. Early in February Cambreleng was specific: "*All*—with much *under current* with *some,*" he wrote to Van Buren on February 4, "are now unanimous for you—for the first time we held a caucus two days [ago] about a dozen of us at McLanes—all the Secretaries Barry and Taney—to try and put Kendall in Blairs place—it must be done—" Van Buren Papers.

[33] *United States' Telegraph,* Feb. 2, 6, 1832.

[34] Calhoun to Gouverneur, Feb. 13, 1832, *Correspondence,* 309-311.

[35] Clay to Brooke, Mar. 28, 1832, Clay's *Works,* IV, 330-331.

[36] The Richmond *Whig,* devoted to Clay's interests, was already predicting that in such circumstances Calhoun's following would elect the Kentuckian. Quoted in the *United States' Telegraph,* Feb. 14, 1832.

[37] Floyd to [Calhoun], Jan. 2, 1832, Floyd Papers.

[38] Such, at any rate, was the interpretation placed on the Barbour candidacy by Van Buren's Virginia managers. Andrew Stevenson to Thomas Ritchie, Feb. 4, 1832, Van Buren Papers. Cf. Green to Crallé, Mar. 12, 1832, Green Papers.

[39] Floyd, *Diary,* 179; Calhoun to Van Deventer, Mar. 31, 1832, *Correspondence,* 317; to Crallé, Apr. 15, 1832, *ibid.,* 318.

[40] Green to Crallé, Feb. 17, 1832, *Southern History Association Publications,* VII, 270. Those who pledged subscriptions may be taken as the Calhoun inner circle at that date. The list included Poindexter, 50 subscriptions; Davis, McDuffie, Harper, Barnwell, and Felder of South Carolina, 25 each; Charles C. Johnston, Thomas T. Bouldin, and Richard Coke, Jr., of Virginia, 25 each; Henry Daniel of Kentucky, 25; and Samuel P. Carson of North Carolina, 10.

[41] Green to Crallé, Feb. 29, 1832 (two letters), *loc. cit.*

[42] *United States' Telegraph,* Mar. 31, 1832.

[43] Clay to Brooke, Apr. 1, 1832, Clay's *Works,* IV, 331-333.

[44] Green to Crallé, no date [April (?) 1832], *Southern History Association Publications,* VII, 274; same to same, Apr. 6, 1832, Green Papers.

[45] Clay to Brooke, Apr. 17, 1832, Clay's *Works,* IV, 335; Brooke to Clay, Apr. 23, 1832, *ibid.* Clay left Washington on the nineteenth.

[46] Richmond *Enquirer,* June 15, 1832; *United States' Telegraph,* May 29, 1832; *Niles,* XLII, 301; Clay to Brooke, June 2, 1832, Clay's *Works,* IV, 339.

[47] *E. g.,* "A Maine Man" to Clay, June 14, 1832, Clay Papers.

[48] W[illis] H. H[aywood], Jr., to Willie P. Mangum, June 22, 1832, Mangum Papers.

CHAPTER X

[1] Samuel Smith to Biddle, Dec. 17, 1831, *Biddle Correspondence,* 143-145; Webster to Biddle, Dec. 18, 1831, *ibid.,* 145-146; Thomas Cadwalader to Biddle, Dec. 21, 1831, *ibid.,* 147-150. I cannot agree with Catteral, *Second Bank of the United States,* 215 ff, that it was Biddle himself who forced the issue.

[2] Cadwalader to Biddle, Dec. 20, 21, 22, 23, 25, 26, 1831, *Biddle Correpondence,* 146-161, *passim.*

[3] *Register of Debates,* 22d, 1st, 53-54, 1502-1529. See also Biddle to Samuel Smith, Jan. 4, 1832, *Biddle Correspondence,* 161-165; and McLane to Biddle, Jan. 5, 1832, *ibid.,* 165-169.

[4] Ingersoll to Biddle, Feb. 21, 1832, *ibid.,* 183-184. The whole story of Biddle's efforts to play off parties against one another may be read in his correspondence with Ingersoll and Horace Binney, *ibid.,* 170 ff. Cambreleng wrote Van Buren on February 5 that Taney was the "only efficient man of *sound* principles in the Cabinet." The "efficient" was added with a caret, probably in deference to Barry. Van Buren Papers.

[5] Ingersoll to Biddle, Feb. 23, 1832, *Biddle Correspondence,* 184-185; Biddle to Ingersoll, Feb. 25, 1832, *ibid.,* 185-187.

[6] *Register of Debates,* 22d, 1st, 1846; Benton, *View,* I, 236.

[7] Ingersoll to Biddle, Mar. 6, 1832, *Biddle Correspondence,* 188-190; John M. Felder, South Carolina Representative and messmate of McDuffie, to Hammond, Mar. 21, 1832, Hammond Papers; *Register of Debates,* 22d, 1st, 2164.

[8] Felder to Hammond, Mar. 31, 1832, Hammond Papers.

[9] Biddle to John G. Watmough, May 11, 1832, *Biddle Correspondence,* 190; William Findlay to James Findlay, May 26, 1832, Historical and Philosophical Society of Ohio, *Quarterly Publication,* I (1906), 86-90.

[10] Biddle to Cadwalader, May 30, 1832, *Biddle Correspondence,* 191; Webster to Cadwalader, July 5, 1832, *ibid.,* 193. Cf. "Memoir of Nathan Appleton," *Mass. Hist. Soc. Proc.,* V, 279. Appleton, who was one of them, says the friends of the Bank "took everything from Mr. Biddle. His *ipse dixit* was law and gospel to them . . . ."

[11] Barry to his daughter, July 4, 1832, *William and Mary Quarterly,* XIV, (April 1906), 233.

[12] *Register of Debates,* 22d, 1st, 1073.

[13] *Ibid.,* 3852.

[14] Biddle to Cadwalader, July 3, 1832, *Biddle Correspondence,* 192-193; Barry to his daughter, July 4, 1832, *loc. cit.*

[15] W. Creighton to Biddle, July 10, 1832, *Biddle Correspondence,* 193; *Register of Debates,* 22d, 1st, 1220; P. V. Daniel to Van Buren, July 12, 1832, Van Buren Papers.

[16] *Register of Debates,* 22d, 1st, 1222-1296, *passim;* Benton, *View,* I, 254.

[17] See, *e. g.,* "Memoir of Nathan Appleton," *loc. cit.;* Mathew Carey to Clay, Mar. 31, 1832, Clay Papers; Webster to Benjamin F. Perry, Apr. 10, 1833, Webster's *Writings,* XVII, 534-535; and William Gaston to Robert Donaldson, Dec. 8, 1833, Connor, "Gaston," 439-440. Blair had the useful faculty of being able to convince himself. See Blair to Van Buren, Jan. 28, 1832, Van Buren Papers.

[18] Adams, *Diary,* VIII, 451, 457-458, 459-460; Charleston *Courier,* Jan. 21, 1832.

[19] Adams, *Diary,* VIII, 460.

[20] "John Q. Adams has lately come out an Anti-tariff man. The Dragon stationed at Washington to guard the golden fleece of N. England seems to have had the juices of the Lethean herbs squirted into his eyes and to have consented to its being stolen by the Southern Argonauts. By what political incantations was this brought about?" Diary of Judge Charles P. Huntington of Northampton, Massachusetts, February 1832, *Mass. Hist. Soc. Proc.,* LVII, 246.

[21] *Register of Debates,* 22d, 1st, 55, 66-77.

[22] Green to Edwards, Jan. 14, 1832, *Edwards Papers,* 577-579; Adams, *Diary,* VIII, 455.

[23] Calhoun to James Edward Calhoun, Feb. 26, 1832, *Correspondence,* 312-313. McDuffie's bill called for an ad valorem duty of 25 percent from July 1, 1832, to June 30, 1833; 18¾ percent for the next twelve months; and after June 30, 1834, a uniform 12½ percent. *Register of Debates,* 22d, 1st, 1763.

[24] Washington *Globe,* Jan. 17, 1832.

[25] *Ibid.,* Feb. 1, 1832; *Register of Debates,* 22d, 1st, 257-295.

[26] Adams, *Diary,* VIII, 494.

[27] Adams, Diary entry for Apr. 5, 1832, *Mass. Hist. Soc. Proc.,* XXXIX, 518. In the published diary there are no entries between March 23 and December 1,

1832, but a few of the notes Adams jotted down for ultimate expansion into entries have been published in the volume cited. See also *Diary,* VIII, 501.

[28] Calhoun to Crallé, Apr. 15, 1832, *Correspondence,* 317-319. Also Calhoun to F. W. Pickens, Mar. 2, 1832, Calhoun Papers, Duke University.

[29] Willie P. Mangum to his wife, May 12, 1832, Mangum Papers. Cf. James Brown to Clay, May 11, 1832, *Louisiana Historical Quarterly,* XXIV (October 1941), 1166.

[30] *Register of Debates,* 22d, 1st, 3090-3092; Adams to his wife, *Mass. Hist. Soc. Proc.,* XXXIX, 519. The Treasury report, dated Apr. 27, 1832, would have reduced the revenue somewhat more effectively than McLane's earlier version, but retained all the features that made the December report objectionable to the South. See *Niles,* XLII, 188-192; and Calhoun to James Edward Calhoun, Apr. 28, 1832, *Correspondence,* 319-320.

[31] Adams, Diary entries for June 4, 14, 25, 1832, *Mass. Hist. Soc. Proc.,* XXXIX, 520-521.

[32] Ritchie to Van Buren, June 25, 1832, Van Buren Papers.

[33] Edward T. Coke, *A Subaltern's Furlough,* 110. Coke was a young Englishman traveling in the United States. He visited Washington late in June 1832, leaving the city on the twenty-sixth. He speaks of spending "several agreeable hours" with Jackson and Hayne. "The Tariff Bill formed the chief topic of conversation; but he [the President] was unable to cope with the powerful eloquence of Mr. Hayne, his more youthful antagonist."

[34] *Register of Debates,* 22d, 1st, 3830-3831, 1219.

[35] *Niles,* XLII, 234-236; Van Buren to Maxcy, Mar. 14, 1832, Van Buren Papers.

[36] *Register of Debates,* 22d, 1st, 1205-1206.

[37] Clay to Hezekiah Niles, July 8, 1832, Clay Papers.

[38] *Niles,* XLII, 412-414.

[39] Biddle to Clay, Aug. 1, 1832, *Biddle Correspondence,* 196. Cf. to William G. Bucknor, July 13, 1832, *ibid.,* 194-196.

[40] William G. Bucknor to Biddle, July 2, 1832, *ibid.,* 194.

[41] Duff Green to Crallé, July 28, Aug. 3, 1832, *Southern History Association Publications,* VII, 277-278.

[42] *United States' Telegraph,* Aug. 23, 1832; Green to Crallé, same date, *Southern History Association Publications,* VII, 278-280.

[43] Green to James H. Pleasants, Aug. 27, 1832, *ibid.,* 280; to Crallé, same date, enclosing copy of letter to Pleasants, *ibid.,* 281; to Oran Follett, Sept. 10, 1832, Historical and Philosophical Society of Ohio, *Quarterly Publication,* V (1910), 67; *United States' Telegraph,* Nov. 10, 1832.

[44] *Niles,* XLIII, 431.

[45] *Ibid.,* 177.

CHAPTER XI

[1] Boucher, *Nullification Controversy,* 174; White, *Rhett,* 24-25; Wiltse, *Calhoun, Nationalist,* 377.

[2] The procedure was justified by Isaac W. Hayne, who wrote to Hammond on June 22, 1832, that he had prepared a July 4 oration which was "piping hot." It was necessary, he explained, because "my fellow parishioners have not all the light a patriot could desire, either as to their political rights or duties. You will

easily credit that this is the case, when I tell you that a population professing five sixths of them to be Nullifiers, hesitate whether or not to elect a submission man to the next Senate." Hammond Papers.

[3] Jackson to Coffee, July 17, 1832, Jackson's *Correspondence,* IV, 462-463.

[4] Washington *Globe,* Sept. 4, 1832, and generally through August, September and October.

[5] J. L. Petigru to Stephen Elliott, Aug. 7, 1832, Petigru Papers. The letter to Hamilton is in Calhoun's *Works,* VI, 144-193.

[6] Calhoun to Patrick Noble, Sept. 10, 1832, Calhoun Papers, Library of Congress.

[7] Petigru to Elliott, Sept. 28, 1832, Petigru Papers. It was after the appearance of the letter to Hamilton that the Unionist Charleston *Courier* adopted the line that is occasionally repeated even today. It praised to the skies Calhoun's genius and ability, and charged that he was now obsessed either with "wild delusion" or "criminal ambition." "Had Mr. Calhoun," the argument ran, "brought but a tithe of that ability to the support of the institutions of his country, which he has just wielded against their stability and permanence . . ." etc. *Courier,* Sept. 29, 1832.

[8] Webster to Kent, Oct. 29, 1832, Webster's *Writings,* XVII, 526-527; Kent to Webster, Oct. 31, 1832, *ibid.,* 527; George Ticknor Curtis, *Life of Daniel Webster,* I, 433-434.

[9] Jackson to the Secretary of the Navy, Sept. 11, 1832, Jackson's *Correspondence,* IV, 474-475; to Donelson, Sept. 17, 1832, *ibid.,* 475-476.

[10] Calhoun to Maxcy, Oct. 8, 1832, Maxcy Papers. Of similar import is an excerpt, said to be from a letter from Calhoun to James Edward Calhoun, written during the nullification controversy. The letter was shown in later years to Alfred Huger, who took a copy of it. "My purpose," Calhoun wrote, "is a suspensive veto, to compel the installing, the highest tribunal, provided by the Constitution, to decide on the point in dispute. *I* do not wish to destroy the Union: I only wish to make it honest. The Union is too strong to break! Nothing can break it but the Slavery question, if *that* can. If a Convention of the States were called, and *it* should decide, that the Protective policy is Constitutional, what then? *Then give it up."* Quoted in letter, Alfred Huger to Isaac S. Nicholls, Feb. 18, 1869. Huger, at the time of the controversy, was a Unionist member of the South Carolina senate, and also of the Nullification Convention. Calhoun Papers, Library of Congress.

[11] Cherokee Nation vs. Georgia, 5 Peters 1 (1831).

[12] Adams, *Diary,* VIII, 477; *Register of Debates,* 22d, 1st, 2010-2035.

[13] Worcester vs. Georgia, 6 Peters 515 (1832).

[14] Story to Ticknor, Mar. 8, 1832, *Story,* II, 83; Adams, *Diary,* VIII, 492; Clay to Brooke, Mar. 17, 1832, Clay's *Works,* IV, 329.

[15] A. C. McLaughlin, *Constitutional History of the United States,* 429.

[16] Harriet Martineau, *Society in America,* I, 98; Boucher, *Nullification Controversy,* 164-207.

[17] The extravagances of the campaign may be followed in the files of the rival papers, especially the Charleston *Courier* and the Charleston *Mercury,* for July, August and September, 1832.

[18] For general accounts see Boucher, *Nullification Controversy,* 208-227; and D. D. Wallace, *History of South Carolina,* II, 434-453. Also Pendleton *Messenger,* Oct. 17, 1832.

[19] James Hamilton, Jr., to Patrick Noble, Oct. 9, 1832, Noble Papers, South Caroliniana Library.

[20] *Niles,* XLIII, 173-176.

[21] Johnson's narrative in Stillé, *Poinsett,* 45; Calhoun to Patrick Noble, Oct. 31, 1832, private collection of Sarah Noble Carnes, made available by Alice Noble Waring.

[22] Stillé, *Poinsett,* 45.

[23] *Journal of the Convention,* 3-7.

[24] *Ibid.,* 6-7.

[25] William M. Meigs, *Life of John Caldwell Calhoun,* I, 450, states that Calhoun was in Columbia during at least part of the session, but the letter on which he bases his conclusion, to Patrick Noble, Nov. 8, 1832 (*Correspondence,* 321-322), is actually misdated and should be 1836. See Jervey, *Hayne,* 407-408.

[26] *Journal,* 10.

[27] P. M. Butler to Hammond, Nov. 20, 21, 1832; William C. Clifton to Hammond, Nov. 21, 1832, Hammond Papers. Cf. John Chesnut to Col. James Chesnut, Nov. 20, 1832, Williams-Chesnut-Manning Papers.

[28] Butler to Hammond, Nov. 22, 1832, Hammond Papers.

[29] *Journal,* 27-78; Butler to Hammond, Nov. 22, 1832, Hammond Papers. Cf. Calhoun, *Works,* VI, 193-209.

[30] This account of Calhoun's views is third-hand, but is consistent with the other evidence and, in the circumstances, probably accurate. It was relayed to Clay by R. W. Stoddard of Geneva, N. Y., Nov. 12, 1832, who says he got it from a friend who had seen a letter from Calhoun to one of his partisans. He thinks the letter was to Van Deventer, who lived near him, and that it was intended for word-of-mouth circulation. Clay Papers.

[31] *Journal,* 23-24.

[32] A. Patterson to Hammond, June 22, 1834, Hammond Papers. Patterson says the oath was twice struck from the bill on his motion.

[33] Butler to Hammond, Nov. 27, 1832, Hammond Papers.

[34] *Ibid.; Niles,* XLIII, 291; Stillé, *Poinsett,* 45-46.

[35] Poinsett to Jackson, Oct. 16, 1832, Jackson's *Correspondence,* IV, 481-482.

[36] Jackson to Cass, Oct. 29, 1832, *ibid.,* 483. The orders were transmitted the same day by General Macomb, the commanding General of the Army, to the officer in command at Charleston. *Senate Document* 71, 22d Cong., 2d sess.

[37] Jackson to Breathitt, Nov. 7, 1832 (two letters), Jackson's *Correspondence,* IV, 484, 484-485; Jackson to Poinsett, Nov. 7, 1832, *ibid.,* 485-486.

[38] Poinsett to Jackson, Nov. 16, 1832, *ibid.,* 486-488. Cf. Petigru to Elliott, Nov. 18, 1832, Petigru Papers.

[39] Barry to his daughter, Nov. 19, 30, 1832, *William and Mary Quarterly,* XIV (April 1906), 235-236; Kendall to Van Buren, Nov. 10, 1832, Van Buren Papers; R. W. Stoddard to Clay, Nov. 12, 1832, Clay Papers; Poinsett to Jackson, Nov. 25, 1832, Jackson Papers, second series; Floyd, *Diary,* 201, 202.

[40] Kendall to Van Buren, Nov. 2, 10, 1832, Van Buren Papers; Poinsett to Jackson, Nov. 24, 29, 1832, Jackson's *Correspondence,* IV, 490-491, 491-492; same to same, Nov. 25, 1832, Jackson Papers, second series; Jackson to Poinsett, Dec. 2, 1832, Jackson's *Correspondence,* IV, 493-494; Washington *Globe,* Nov. 26, 29, 1832; *United States' Telegraph,* Nov. 21, 1832.

[41] The occasion for the delay is not clear. The resignation, addressed to the Secretary of State, is dated at Columbia, and Calhoun must have left for Wash-

ington immediately thereafter. It is most probable that he was still in Pendleton at the time of his election as Senator, and came to Columbia on his way to the Capital, for a party caucus.

CHAPTER XII

[1] On various occasions Calhoun assessed his own strength and weaknesses with considerable candor and a great deal of insight. See, *e. g.,* his letters to Virgil Maxcy, Sept. 11, 1830, Maxcy Papers; to John D. Gardiner, Mar. 25, 1833, Calhoun Papers, Duke University; to Francis W. Pickens, July 17, 1835, Calhoun Papers, South Caroliniana Library.

[2] "Journal of the Rev. A. Foster, of Willington, S. C.," Apr. 23, 1830, *Journal of the Presbyterian Historical Society,* XIII (September 1929), 291-292. See also Mary Bates, *The Private Life of John C. Calhoun,* 26; and A. B. Longstreet, "Review of Ex-Gov. Perry's Sketch of J. C. Calhoun," *XIX Century,* II (January 1870), 618-623. The passage in Perry's sketch to which Longstreet takes most vigorous exception was omitted when the sketch was reprinted in book form. Compare Benjamin F. Perry, "John C. Calhoun," in *Land of the Free,* VI (March 1869), 397-403, and *XIX Century,* I (November 1869), 417-422, with the same sketch as reprinted in *Reminiscences of Public Men.*

[3] Calhoun to John D. Gardiner, Mar. 25, 1833, Calhoun Papers, Duke University.

[4] Calhoun to Mrs. T. G. Clemson, Mar. 7, 1848, *Correspondence,* 745.

[5] Of the many estimates of his character, perhaps the most sincere are those of Mary Bates and of Judge Longstreet, cited above. Miss Bates was for some years a tutor in the Calhoun home, and Longstreet had known Calhoun intimately from the days of his own childhood. There is an excellent appraisal by an outsider in G. W. Featherstonhaugh, *Canoe Voyage up the Minnay Sotor,* II, 247 ff.

[6] Calhoun to Mrs. F. Colhoun, Apr. 9, 1827, private collection of Mrs. A. G. Holmes; Ernest Ingersoll, "The Calhoun Summer Home," *Scribner's Monthly,* XXI (April 1881), 892-895; Dave M. Sloan, *Fogy Days,* 75; "John C. Calhoun's Home Life," Anderson *Daily Mail,* Oct. 23, 1926. The last-named article is reprinted from a clipping found among the papers of William H. Trescott, who spent his latter years at Pendleton, and said to be from a Baltimore paper of August 1849. Since Trescott was well acquainted with Calhoun, the article may be presumed to have his endorsement.

[7] "John C. Calhoun's Home Life," *loc. cit.*

[8] Calhoun to A. Burt, Nov. 11, 1830, Calhoun Papers, Duke University; to Patrick Noble, Oct. 31, 1832, private collection of Sarah Noble Carnes made available by Alice Noble Waring.

[9] Calhoun to James Edward Calhoun, Nov. 17, 1833, Calhoun Papers, Clemson College.

[10] "John C. Calhoun's Home Life," *loc. cit.;* Featherstonhaugh, *Canoe Voyage,* II, 270-271.

[11] Rev. C. C. Pinckney, "John C. Calhoun, from a Southern Standpoint," *Lippincott's Monthly,* LXII (July 1898), 87.

[12] Calhoun to James Edward Calhoun, Feb. 26, 1832, *Correspondence,* 312-314.

[13] *Ibid.* Also Report of the Committee on Farms of the Pendleton Farmers' Society, *Southern Cultivator,* III (July 1845), 97-98; and Sloan, *Fogy Days,* 62-65.

[14] "John C. Calhoun's Home Life," *loc. cit.*

[15] Featherstonhaugh, *Canoe Voyage,* II, 267-269.

[16] *Ibid.* Also "John C. Calhoun's Home Life," *loc. cit.;* and Bates, *Private Life,* 11-12. Wine was ordered through Calhoun's Charleston factor, who was also Floride's cousin, John Bonneau. See, *e. g.,* Bonneau to Calhoun, Apr. 14, 1829, Calhoun Papers, Clemson College.

[17] Sloan, *Fogy Days,* 69.

[18] In 1830 he ran last in a field of thirteen. Pendleton *Messenger,* Oct. 14, 1830. He was finally elected in 1838, after he had been chastened by depression and purged by illness. *Ibid.,* Oct. 12, 1838.

[19] Pendleton *Messenger,* May 6, 1829. For financial transactions, see J. E. Bonneau to Calhoun, Apr. 18, 1828, and Apr. 14, 1829, Calhoun Papers, Clemson College.

[20] Calhoun to James Edward Calhoun, Mar. 16, 1829, Nov. 11, 30, 1830, Calhoun Papers, Clemson College. Also Feb. 26 and Apr. 28, 1832, *Correspondence,* 312-314, 319-320; and Feb. 8, 1834, *ibid.,* 332.

[21] Calhoun to James Edward Calhoun, Feb. 16, 1834, Calhoun Papers, Clemson College (published in part in *Correspondence,* 332).

[22] Calhoun to James Edward Calhoun, Apr. 28, 1832, *Correspondence,* 319-320.

[23] Calhoun to James Edward Calhoun, October 1830, and Nov. 1, 1830, Calhoun Papers, Clemson College. (The first letter is published in part in *Correspondence,* 274.)

[24] Calhoun to James Edward Calhoun, Dec. 3, 12, 14, 1830, Calhoun Papers, Clemson College.

[25] Calhoun to Andrew P. Calhoun, Apr. 12, 1847, Calhoun Papers, Duke University.

[26] Bates, *Private Life,* 9.

[27] University of South Carolina Alumni Records, South Caroliniana Library; Columbia *Telescope,* Jan. 8, 1833; Calhoun to John D. Gardiner, Mar. 25, 1833, Calhoun Papers, Duke University; to Anna Maria Calhoun, Feb. 24, 1834, Calhoun Papers, Clemson College.

[28] Calhoun to Anna Maria Calhoun, Dec. 30, 1831, *Correspondence,* 308-309.

[29] Calhoun to Anna Maria Calhoun, Jan. 11, 1832, misdated 1831 in *Correspondence,* 278-279.

[30] Calhoun to Anna Maria Calhoun, Feb. 13, 1832, *ibid.,* 311-312.

[31] Calhoun to Anna Maria Calhoun, Mar. 10, 1832, *ibid.,* 315-316.

[32] Josiah P. Quincy, *Figures of the Past,* 264.

[33] Calhoun to Anna Maria Calhoun, Feb. 18, 1834, Calhoun Papers, Clemson College.

[34] Calhoun to Anna Maria Calhoun, Apr. 3, 1834, *Correspondence,* 333-335. Also Feb. 24, 1834, Calhoun Papers, Clemson College.

[35] Calhoun to Anna Maria Calhoun, May 14, 1834, *Correspondence,* 336-337.

CHAPTER XIII

[1] Floyd, *Diary,* 199.

[2] *E. g.,* Tyler to Floyd, Dec. 4, 1832, *William and Mary Quarterly,* XXI (July 1912), 7; John Randolph to Jackson, Dec. 6, 1832, Jackson's *Correspondence,* IV, 496-497; Michael Hoffman to Van Buren, Dec. 7, 1832, Van Buren Papers.

[3] *Register of Debates,* 22d, 2d, 1-2.

[4] Tyler to Floyd, Dec. 4, 1832, *William and Mary Quarterly,* XXI (July 1912), 7.

[5] Richardson, *Messages and Papers of the Presidents,* 1154-1169.

[6] *United States' Telegraph,* Nov. 27, 28, 1832; James Brown to Clay, Nov. 5, 1832, *Louisiana Historical Quarterly,* XXIV (October 1941), 1168; Green to Crallé, Nov. 26, 1832, *Southern History Association Publications,* VII, 282.

[7] Washington *Globe,* Dec. 4, 7, 1832.

[8] Adams, *Diary,* VIII, 503. Also *ibid.,* 515; Michael Hoffman to Van Buren, Dec. 7, 1832, Van Buren Papers; Ambler, *Ritchie,* 150-151; Charleston *Mercury,* Dec. 10, 1832.

[9] *United States' Telegraph,* Dec. 6, 1832.

[10] Richardson, *Messages and Papers of the Presidents,* 1203-1219.

[11] Benton to Judge N. B. Tucker, Feb. 11, 1833, *William and Mary Quarterly,* XII (October 1903), 86-87.

[12] Jackson to Poinsett, Dec. 9, 1832, Jackson's *Correspondence,* IV, 497-498; to Van Buren, Dec. 15, 1832, *ibid.,* 500; to Cass, Dec. 17, 1832, *ibid.,* 502-503. Kendall stated in 1862 that Jackson had been offered 150,000 volunteers and meant himself to march into South Carolina at their head, but there is no evidence that Kendall's gift for prevarication grew less as he grew older. The statement was made in the course of a speech whose purpose was to recruit volunteers for the Union army, and the tale probably seemed good propaganda to the aged ex-editor. See his *Autobiography,* 631. Many volunteers were undoubtedly offered to Jackson, but he had no intention of using them, much less of leading them in person.

[13] Smith, *Cass,* 272-275.

[14] *Ibid.,* 269-271; *Senate Document* 71, 22d Cong., 2d sess.

[15] Richmond *Enquirer,* Dec. 6, 13, 1832; Benton to Judge Tucker, Feb. 11, 1833, *William and Mary Quarterly,* XII (October 1903), 86-87; Sam Houston to Jackson, Feb. 13, 1833, "Texas Letters," *Yanaguana Society Publications,* V (1940), 143-144; Floyd, *Diary,* 202-210, *passim;* J. H. Hammond to Hayne, Dec. 20, 1832, *Am. Hist. Rev.,* VI (July 1901), 751-752; Cambreleng to Van Buren, Dec. 18, 1832, Jackson's *Correspondence,* IV, 505 n; Van Buren to Jackson, Dec. 27, 1832, *ibid.,* 506-508.

[16] Clay to Brooke, Dec. 12, 1832, Clay's *Works,* IV, 345; *United States' Telegraph,* Dec. 27, 1832; Hone, *Diary,* 83-85; Diary of Charles P. Huntington, Dec. 14, 1832, *Mass. Hist. Soc. Proc.,* LVII, 252; Rufus Choate to Jonathan Shove, Dec. 25, 1832 [misplaced as of 1831], *Essex Institute Historical Collections,* LXIX, 83-85; *Niles,* XLIII, 281; Story to Richard Peters, Dec. 22, 1832, *Story,* II, 113; *Liberator,* II, 199. A wealth of other material merely confirms the cleavage within the parties.

[17] *United States' Telegraph,* Jan. 4, 1833.

[18] Pendleton *Messenger,* Dec. 26, 1832; March, *Reminiscences,* 190-192, 224-225; [Hunter], *Life,* 44; William Gaston to Hannah Gaston Manly, Dec. 31, 1832, Connor, "Gaston," 439.

[19] Gaston to Hannah Gaston Manly, *loc. cit.* Judge Gaston, a lifelong Federalist who had been a colleague and stanch opponent of Calhoun in the House of Representatives twenty years before, refused to see his old foe, and wrote bitterly of "happy prospects blasted . . . by Pride, Ambition, Perverted Ingenuity and Wicked Selfishness." Like so many of his class, he would not

concede that anyone who differed with him could possibly be honest. See also *National Intelligencer,* Jan. 7, 1833.

[20] Charleston *Mercury,* Jan. 8, 1833.

[21] Mrs. Smith, 341-342.

[22] March, *Reminiscences,* 190-191; *National Intelligencer,* Jan. 5, 1833; Adams, *Diary,* VIII, 517; [Hunter], *Life,* 44.

[23] This result must have been clear to both sides at the time. Certainly it was clear to the tariff advocates. See, *e. g.,* Barnard, "Narrative," 272.

[24] *Register of Debates,* 22d, 2d, 958 ff.

[25] *United States' Telegraph,* Jan. 7, 1833; Thomas H. Hall to Van Buren, Jan. 2, 1833, *North Carolina Historical Review,* XV (January 1938), 57; William H. Haywood, Jr., to Van Buren, Jan. 10, 1833, *ibid.,* 58.

[26] *Register of Debates,* 22d, 2d, 80; Calhoun to James Edward Calhoun, Jan. 10, 1833, *Correspondence,* 323.

[27] Silas Wright to Van Buren, Jan. 13, 1833, Jackson's *Correspondence,* V, 4 n.

[28] *Register of Debates,* 22d, 2d, 99.

[29] *Ibid.,* 99-100; [Hunter], *Life,* 45.

[30] Richardson, *Messages and Papers of the Presidents,* 1173-1195.

[31] *Register of Debates,* 22d, 2d, 100-103; Barnard, "Narrative," 283.

[32] Tyler to Floyd, Jan. 16, 1833, Tyler Papers.

[33] Jackson to Poinsett, Jan. 16, 1833, Jackson's *Correspondence,* V, 5-6.

[34] Webster to Stephen White, Jan. 18, 1833, *Am. Hist. Rev.,* XXV (July 1920), 695.

[35] Tyler to Floyd, *op. cit.*

[36] Cambreleng to Van Buren, Feb. 5, 1833, Van Buren Papers.

[37] F. Nash to Willie P. Mangum, Jan. 23, 1833, Mangum Papers.

[38] Calhoun to Ingham, Jan. 16, 1833, copy in hand of A. J. Donelson, Jackson Papers, second series. A note by Donelson says the letter had been found by a Jackson supporter in a hotel room in Harrisburg immediately after Ingham had vacated it, and was sent to the President as proof of Calhoun's "treason." It is far more likely that the document was stolen from the former Treasury Secretary. It was a method by no means unknown among the more single-minded Jacksonians. See also Calhoun to A. Burt, Jan. 16 [misdated Jan. 15], 1833, Calhoun Papers, Duke University.

[39] Clay to Brooke, Jan. 17, 1833, Clay's *Works,* IV, 347.

[40] *Register of Debates,* 22d, 2d, 174-192.

[41] *Ibid.,* 191; [Hunter], *Life,* 46; Barnard, "Narrative," 288-289; March, *Reminiscences,* 195.

[42] James L. Clark to Hammond, Dec. 17, 1832, Hammond Papers; P. M. Butler to Hammond, Dec. 18, 1832, *ibid.;* David M. Benedict to Elisha Whittlesey, Dec. 19, 1832, *Firelands Pioneer,* n. s. XV, 1109-1111.

[43] Hayne to Pickens, Dec. 21, 26, 1832, *Am. Hist. Rev.,* VI (July 1901), 752-755.

[44] Hayne to Silas E. Burrus, Dec. 29, 1832, Jervey, *Hayne,* 343-344. Also James Hamilton, Jr., to Crallé, Jan. 15, 1836, Crallé Papers, Clemson College.

[45] Barnard, "Narrative," 365, says he dined with Rhett who told him "that it was the intention of the Nullifiers to seize the arsenal at Augusta and that some weak head let it out." It may have been Rhett's intention, and even Hamilton's, but we may depend on it, it was not Hayne's, at least until hostilities had been launched by the other side.

[46] Preston to Hammond, Jan. 14, 1833, Hammond Papers. Jackson's Proclamation almost forestalled Virginia's intervention. After the Proclamation, McDuffie tried to get the Virginia legislature to drop the whole thing. "It is indeed now important that the ordinance should go into operation for the purpose of repelling the President's calumny by proving that our remedy is peaceable. Unless General Jackson announces war upon the state, by an indiscriminate attack upon men, women and children, there can be no military violence used; for the state will proceed calmly on in the civil tribunals without paying the slightest attention to the military parade or to the mad ravings of this driveling old dotard." McDuffie to Crallé, Dec. 26, 1832, Crallé Papers, Library of Congress. Also James Hamilton, Jr., to Crallé, Feb. 3, 1833, Crallé Papers, Clemson College.

[47] Hayne to Pickens, Feb. 7, 1833, *Am. Hist. Rev.,* VII (October 1901), 94; Boucher, *Nullification Controversy,* 275-276.

[48] I. W. Hayne to Hammond, Jan. 28, 1833, Hammond Papers; Hammond to R. Y. Hayne, Feb. 7, 1833, *Am. Hist. Rev.,* VII (October 1901), 95-97.

[49] Hayne to Pickens, Feb. 12, 1833, *Am. Hist. Rev.,* VII (October 1901), 97-98; J. L. Petigru to H. S. Legaré, Feb. 5, 1833, James Petigru Carson, *Life, Letters and Speeches of James Louis Petigru,* 117.

[50] Stillé, *Poinsett,* 48-49.

[51] Poinsett to Jackson, Jan. 16, 20, 1833, Jackson's *Correspondence,* V, 6-7, 8-10; Jan. 27, 1833, Jackson Papers, second series.

[52] "Let me beg you to act cautiously in the matter of the leaders of Nullification now in Washington—Do not make a Martyr of a Scoundrel—No punishment can be so dreadful to him as to have the finger of scorn pointed at him for the remainder of his miserable life." Poinsett to Jackson, Jan. 27, 1833, Jackson Papers, second series. Cf. Poinsett to Jackson, Jan. 20, 1833, Jackson's *Correspondence,* V, 8-10.

[53] Poinsett to Jackson, Feb. 28, 1833, Jackson's *Correspondence,* V, 23-24. Cf. H. St. G. Tucker to W. C. Rives, Feb. 17, 1833, Rives Papers.

[54] See Charleston *Mercury,* Jan. 29, 1833.

CHAPTER XIV

[1] Overton to Van Buren, Dec. 12, 1832, Van Buren Papers; Benton to Van Buren, Dec. 16, 1832, *ibid.;* Clay to Brooke, Jan. 23, 1833, Clay's *Works,* V, 348; *United States' Telegraph,* Jan. 5, 1833.

[2] Oran Follett to Clay, Jan. 10, 1833, Historical and Philosophical Society of Ohio, *Quarterly Publication,* V (1910), 73-76.

[3] Webster to Hiram Ketchum, Jan. 18, 20, 1838, Webster's *Writings,* XVI, 293-294; Curtis, *Webster,* I, 435-436, 454-455. Also Mahlon Dickerson to Benton, Feb. 5, 1839, and accompanying discussion between Clay and Webster, in *Congressional Globe,* 25th Cong., 3d sess., 182-183. Webster left Philadelphia for Washington on December 28, leaving Clay still in the former city. Webster to Story, Dec. 27, 1832, Webster's *Writings,* XVI, 224.

[4] Michael Hoffman to A. C. Flagg, Dec. 18, 1832, Van Buren Papers; J. M. McConnell to Clay, Dec. 27, 1832, Clay Papers.

[5] Floyd, *Diary,* 210. Floyd quotes Brooke as telling him he had received the information in a letter from Clay. Brooke will be remembered as one of the participants in the earlier efforts to bring about some kind of understanding between Calhoun and Clay.

[6] Calhoun to James Edward Calhoun, Jan. 10, 1833, *Correspondence,* 323; Tyler to Floyd, Jan. 10, 1833, *William and Mary Quarterly,* XXI (July 1912), 8-10. Tyler thought Verplanck's bill would probably pass in the House but fail in the Senate because it did not give up the protectionist principle and was too harsh on the manufacturers. "Would mortal man believe it that the manufacturers are safer in the hands of those wicked S. Carolina nullifiers, than in those of the *non descripts:* and yet it is so. I have found among the first the most conciliatory feelings. They stand upon principle—high principle. While the last seem to me to think that if they pay money enough to the South by reducing duties—they have accomplished a great affair. What in the Devil's name did our forefathers care for the two pence on tea?"

[7] Clay to Brooke, Jan. 17, 1833, Clay's *Works,* V, 347; Frederick L. Nussbaum, "Compromise of 1833," *South Atlantic Quarterly,* XI (October 1912), 343-344; McLane to Van Buren, Jan. 23, 1833, Van Buren Papers. Thomas Ritchie was at the same time urging the Virginia members to get together with McDuffie and settle their differences. Ritchie to William C. Rives, Jan. 18, 1833, Rives Papers.

[8] McLane to Van Buren, Jan. 23, 1833, Van Buren Papers. McLane noted "obvious signs of an understanding" between Clay and Calhoun, and says he knows that Calhoun "has distinctly said that the proposed bill is too rank, that its success would be victory to the South, & 'vanquishment' to the Manufacturers & that no satisfactory adjustment could be expected upon such terms!" McLane anticipated, correctly, that Clay's scheme would be substituted for the Verplanck bill, for which the Treasury Secretary himself was primarily responsible, and that Calhoun would support Clay. Calhoun's unwillingness to accept a victory that was within his grasp was beyond Jackson's comprehension, and he therefore assumed that the Nullifiers were trying to block tariff reduction in order to unite the South. Jackson to Poinsett, Jan. 24, 1833, Jackson's *Correspondence,* V, 11-12; to Van Buren, Jan. 25, 1833, *ibid.,* 12-13.

[9] *Register of Debates,* 22d, 2d, 432.

[10] *Ibid.,* 462-473, 477-478; *National Intelligencer,* Feb. 13, 1833.

[11] *Register of Debates,* 22d, 2d, 473-478; Charleston *Courier,* Feb. 18, 21, 1833.

[12] It was some years later that Clay and Calhoun each claimed to have been the master of the other on this occasion. The truth appears to be, however, that each of them needed the compromise for his own ends. If Clay needed it more than Calhoun did, it was because the Verplanck bill would probably have passed, relieving South Carolina from her difficult situation without Clay's intervention. Benton's so-called "secret history" of the compromise, while it contains some verifiable points, is for the most part demonstrably false. It is clear from the evidence cited in the foregoing pages that the Clayites and the Nullifiers were working together on the compromise at least from early January, which destroys Benton's contention that the two sides got together only after Clay's bill had been introduced and allowed to languish for some indefinite time. In view of Clay's conversation with Webster in Philadelphia in December, and his talk with Tyler early in January, no credence can be given to Benton's claim that Letcher devised the compromise and only with difficulty persuaded Clay to support it. The tale that Letcher got Calhoun out of bed to warn him of his impending arrest by Jackson is palpably absurd. Jackson had been indulging in such threats since November, but his correspondence with Poinsett demonstrates that he knew he had no authority to carry them out. Calhoun was aware of the threats, and so could hardly have been coerced into doing something he didn't want to do by a

mere repetition of them. Benton's version would make this threat the motive for Calhoun's acceptance of Clay's bill; but on his own showing the threat was made sometime *after* Calhoun had already supported the bill in the Senate. Moreover, it is hardly likely that any stand Calhoun might have taken on any bill, much less a Clay bill, would have caused Jackson to desist, had he made up his mind to arrest the South Carolina Senator. Benton is also wrong when he says that Clay and Calhoun were not on speaking terms at the time. They had at least dined together during the previous session. Benton's account is in the *Thirty Years' View,* I, 342-344. See also Barnard, "Narrative," 303, 307; Adams, *Diary,* VIII, 524; and Jervey, *Hayne,* 346 ff. Jervey thinks Benton's cock-and-bull story is belated revenge for his own exclusion from credit for the compromise. It seems more probable that his pique grew out of the fact that Clay had been slipped in in his stead as the Western member of the South-West alliance.

[13] *Register of Debates,* 22d, 2d, 484-486; *Niles,* XLIII, 407. Henry A. Wise later said, but without confirmation, that Jackson had objected to the inclusion of Clayton on the committee, and asked White to name somebody else, but the President pro tempore refused. Nancy N. Scott, *Memoir of White,* 239-240.

[14] *Register of Debates,* 22d, 2d, 1725-1726, 587-589; Adams, *Diary,* VIII, 525; William Plumer to George Ticknor, Apr. 2, 1853, recalling conversation of October 1833 with Webster, in Webster's *Writings,* XVII, 557. See also Richard E. Walker to Rives, Feb. 18, 1833, Rives Papers; and Levi Lincoln to Webster, Feb. 20, 1833, Webster Papers.

[15] Floyd, *Diary,* 214. Tyler told Floyd that McLane had specifically made the Force Bill the condition of tariff compromise. As Secretary of the Treasury, McLane was the man primarily concerned with the tariff, but he appears here and elsewhere to be wielding more than his share of the party power. It is difficult to forget, in connection with the Force Bill, that McLane was an ex-Federalist. On the score of patronage, it was well understood that vacant foreign missions (which included England and France) would not be filled until the session of Congress was over; and that new offices would be created to be filled by Van Buren. See *National Intelligencer,* Feb. 1, 1833.

[16] The legend has grown up that, as the administration forces were about to be routed by the genius of Calhoun alone, the President hurriedly sent for Webster, who put aside all personal feeling and stepped in to save the Republic. See March, *Reminiscences,* 197-200. There is no doubt, however, that Webster had already aligned himself with the administration before Calhoun ever got to Washington. Since Jackson had taken over Webster's views, there was not much else the Massachusetts Senator could do. In any event, he was a familiar at the White House and already understood to be the administration champion before the Force Bill was introduced. "The ultra federalists drive on these measures," wrote Tyler to Floyd on Jan. 22, 1833, the day after the Force Bill had been reported from committee, "and Webster will be the great champion of the administration. They must come into the closest and most fraternal embrace. I dined at the Palace, yes, palace, a few days since, and found Mr. W. there in all his glory." *William and Mary Quarterly,* XXI (July 1912), 11. Webster was, moreover, a member of the Judiciary Committee which produced the bill.

[17] *Register of Debates,* 22d, 2d, 192-193, 236-244.

[18] Washington Irving to Peter Irving, Apr. 1, 1833, *Life and Letters,* III, 50. Irving was in Washington as the guest of Louis McLane, whom he had served as Secretary in the Embassy in London. During the nullification debate the popular

author "almost lived at the capitol." Another who spent those absorbing weeks in the Senate gallery was young Henry Barnard, who was later to contribute so much to the cause of education in the United States. See Barnard, "Narrative," *Maryland Historical Magazine,* XIII, *passim.*

[19] Barnard, "Narrative," 299-300.

[20] *Register of Debates,* 22d, 2d, 519; Barnard, "Narrative," 304-305. After it was all over and the proceedings had appeared in print, Cambreleng still thought Rives's speech the ablest of the whole debate. Cambreleng to Rives, Apr. 16, 1833, Rives Papers; also H. S. Legaré to Rives, Apr. 16, 1833, *ibid.* Rives almost certainly did deliver the best argument in favor of the bill, and it is high tribute to the quality of statesmanship in the Old Dominion that it is hard to find a better speech against the bill than that of John Tyler.

[21] Barnard, "Narrative," 305; *United States' Telegraph,* Feb. 18, 1833; *Register of Debates,* 22d, 2d, 519-553. There is a good description of the Senate in session in Frances Anne Butler (Fanny Kemble), *Journal,* II, 120.

[22] Webster frankly admitted as much to his intimates. "I wish not to speak," he wrote Judge Joseph Hopkinson after Calhoun had spoken on the fifteenth of February, "but it seems unavoidable. Courage! I cannot better the matter of 1830,—nor equal it—but I will try not to show evidence of senility." Quoted in Meigs, *Calhoun,* II, 13.

[23] [Hunter], *Life,* 46; *United States' Telegraph,* Mar. 21, 1833.

[24] *Register of Debates,* 22d, 2d, 553-587; Barnard, "Narrative," 306-309; *United States' Telegraph,* Feb. 18, 1833; Charleston *Courier,* Feb. 23, 25, 1833.

[25] Barnard, "Narrative," 306-308, is the most glowing account of the debate by a thoroughgoing Webster partisan. The caustic Adams, though equally partisan, was more critical: "Mr. Webster is a very handsome speaker, but he overlabored a point as plain as day, and he hung his cause upon a broken hinge in maintaining that a Government is not a compact." *Diary,* VIII, 526. The extent of Webster's own delusion is clear from a note to Nathan Appleton, written the day after the debate. "It does not seem magnanimous," wrote Webster, "to underrate one's adversary, but, truly, between ourselves, I was greatly disappointed in Mr. Calhoun. He has little argument; or at least so it appeared to me." Webster's *Writings,* XVI, 227-228.

[26] Jackson to Poinsett, Feb. 17, 1833, Jackson's *Correspondence,* V, 18.

[27] Benton to Van Buren, Feb. 16, 1833, Van Buren Papers. Van Buren did not hasten to Washington, but he did write to Jackson by return mail to urge modification. His appeal was not in time, however, to affect the bill. See Van Buren to Jackson, Feb. 20, 1833, Jackson's *Correspondence,* V, 19-21.

[28] *Register of Debates,* 22d, 2d, 688.

[29] Webster to Nathan Appleton, February 1833, Webster's *Writings,* XVI, 228.

[30] J. S. Barbour to Calhoun, Sept. 10, 1844, Calhoun Papers, Clemson College, recalls the incident.

[31] *Register of Debates,* 22d, 2d, 602.

[32] *Ibid.,* 694-716.

[33] Clayton discusses the incident in a speech delivered at Wilmington, Delaware, June 15, 1844, and reprinted in Clay's *Works,* II, 252-259. Clay endorsed this version in a letter to Clayton, Aug. 22, 1844, *ibid.,* 259-261; and Benton drew liberally from it, with embellishments of his own, *View,* I, 343-344. Had Calhoun refused to accept the terms, Clay would probably have backed down rather than

see Jackson get the credit for easing the tension; but for that identical reason, Calhoun would not refuse.

[34] *Register of Debates,* 22d, 2d, 727-749.

[35] *Ibid.,* 1772-1811.

[36] *Ibid.,* 787-809.

[37] *Ibid.,* 234-235, 809; Clayton's speech of 1844, *loc. cit.*

[38] *North American Review,* XXXVII (July 1833), 207 ff.

[39] Charleston *Mercury,* Mar. 27, 1833; *United States' Telegraph,* Feb. 26, 1833; Barnard, "Narrative," 311, 313; [Hunter], *Life,* 46-47; John S. Jenkins, *Life of John Caldwell Calhoun,* 313; B. F. Perry, "John C. Calhoun," *Reminiscences of Public Men,* 45.

[40] William C. Preston to Maxcy, July 7, 1834, Maxcy Papers. A sketch of Webster prepared for the *National Portrait Gallery* had claimed for him an unequivocal triumph over both Hayne and Calhoun. Maxcy was writing the Calhoun sketch for the same work, and Preston wanted to be sure the claim was properly contradicted as far as Calhoun was concerned: "It is notorious that Mr. Calhouns second speech was one of the most conspicuous parliamentary triumphs ever obtained and that Randolph expressed only what every body else thought that Webster had been dying muscle after muscle throughout the whole speech."

[41] Duff Green to Crallé, Mar. 4, 1833, *Southern History Association Publications,* VII, 284.

[42] *Register of Debates,* 22d, 2d, 1903.

CHAPTER XV

[1] *Register of Debates,* 22d, 2d, 814.

[2] *Niles,* XLIV, 4.

[3] *National Intelligencer,* Mar. 7, 1833; [Hunter], *Life,* 48.

[4] *Journal of the Convention,* 82-95.

[5] *Ibid.,* 97, 99.

[6] So Jervey reasons, in *Hayne,* 352-353.

[7] *Journal of the Convention,* 96.

[8] *Ibid.,* 106-110.

[9] See *Ibid.,* 98-131; and *Speeches Delivered in the Convention . . . in March, 1833,* 14 ff.

[10] Hayne to Hammond, Mar. 6, 1833, *Am. Hist. Rev.,* VII (October 1901), 103; B. W. Leigh to Floyd, Mar. 13, 1833, Crallé Papers, Library of Congress. It was Leigh's opinion, however, that if the Force Bill had been passed without the tariff compromise, "the convention would not have paused in its course a moment."

[11] J. H. Hammond to M. C. M. Hammond, Mar. 27, 1833, Hammond Papers.

[12] ". . . had S. C. met the force bill by secession there might have been a sharp struggle, but a short one; and the whole South would soon have joined her. So I told Mr. Calhoun then. Does he not think so now?" Judge N. B. Tucker to Hammond, Feb. 17, 18, 1836, Hammond Papers. Jackson's blunt denial in the Proclamation of any right to secede was to veterans and youngsters alike a shock of rude awakening. See, *e. g.,* Nathaniel Macon to Van Buren, Mar. 2, 1833, *North Carolina Historical Review,* XV (January 1938), 59; Tyler to Pendleton, June 19, 1833, Tyler Papers; C. W. Smith to Crallé, June 30, 1833, Crallé Papers, Clemson College.

[13] Calhoun to a committee of Edgefield citizens, Mar. 27, 1833, in *Niles,* XLIV, 125-126; Wallace, *History of South Carolina,* II, 473-474.

[14] Poinsett carried water on both shoulders, appealing to Jackson and Van Buren on the ground that Calhoun was supporting Clay for the Presidency, and at the same time appealing to Webster to keep "our friend" Clay from supporting Calhoun. Poinsett to Jackson, Mar. 21, 1833, Jackson's *Correspondence,* V, 44-46; to Webster, May 24, 1833, Webster Papers; to Van Buren, July 12, 1833, Van Buren Papers. See also Kibler, *Perry,* 160.

[15] *Niles,* XLV, 36, 55.

[16] *Ibid.,* 209, 226.

[17] Charleston *Mercury,* Oct. 29, Nov. 1, 15, 25, 1833; *United States' Telegraph,* Dec. 2, 1833; *Niles,* XLV, 239-240.

[18] See Green's reference in the *Telegraph* for Sept. 4, 1834.

[19] Petigru to Legaré, Nov. 20, 1833, in Carson, *Petigru,* 127-129.

[20] P. M. Butler to Hammond, Aug. 4, 1833, Hammond Papers.

[21] *Journal of the Convention,* 117-119; *Speeches Delivered in the Convention . . . in March, 1833,* 67 *et passim.*

[22] See especially David F. Houston, *A Critical Study of Nullification in South Carolina* (Cambridge, 1896); Frederic Bancroft, *Calhoun and the South Carolina Nullification Movement* (Baltimore, 1928); and Edward S. Corwin, "National Power and State Interposition, 1787-1861," *Michigan Law Review,* X (May 1912), 535-551.

[23] See C. M. Wiltse, "From Compact to National State in American Political Thought," *Essays in Political Theory Presented to George H. Sabine,* 153-178. Also Calhoun to J. D. Gardiner, Mar. 25, 1833, Calhoun Papers, Duke University; and Lord Acton, "Political Causes of the American Revolution" (1861), reprinted in *Essays on Freedom and Power,* 196-250.

[24] Poinsett to James B. Campbell, Jan. 10, 1834, in *South Carolina Historical and Genealogical Magazine,* XLII (April 1941), 38-39.

[25] Hayne to Hammond, Mar. 31, May 20, 1834, Hammond Papers; Pendleton *Messenger,* May 28, 1834.

[26] Hayne to Hammond, Mar. 31, 1834, Hammond Papers.

[27] A. Patterson to Hammond, May [June?] 2, 1834, Hammond Papers; Elizabeth Merritt, *James Henry Hammond,* 28-30; White, *Rhett,* 28-31; Boucher, *Nullification Controversy,* 333 ff. *The Book of Allegiance* (Columbia 1834) contains full texts of the arguments of counsel as well as of the judges' opinions. O'Neall was, in fact, far ahead of the thought of his day. There was probably not a state in the Union that did not require an oath of some sort, and there was nothing in the disputed South Carolina oath that did not appear in half the others. Those of Massachusetts and New York in particular went much farther in the direction of state supremacy than did South Carolina's. See Pendleton *Messenger,* Mar. 12, 1834; Charleston *Mercury,* Apr. 30, 1834.

[28] Boucher, *Nullification Controversy,* 337-338; Hayne to Hammond, June 12, 1834, Hammond Papers; Preston to Hammond, June 12, 1834, *ibid.;* Carson, *Petigru,* 131-137; Petigru to Drayton, May 23, 1834, *ibid.,* 140; Jervey, *Hayne,* 375; Calhoun to F. W. Pickens, June 5, 1834, *Correspondence,* 338-339.

[29] Condy Raguet to Hayne, June 20, 1834, Hayne Papers; *United States' Telegraph,* June 24, 1834.

[30] I. W. Hayne to Hammond, Dec. 8, 1834, Hammond Papers; Petigru to J.

Chesnut, Dec. 9, 1834, Williams-Chesnut-Manning Papers; to Legaré, Dec. 15, 1834, Carson, *Petigru,* 167-171.

[31] *United States' Telegraph,* Dec. 16, 19, 1834; Jan. 1, 1835.

CHAPTER XVI

[1] Duane's account is in *Niles,* XLV, 236-239. See also Van Buren, *Autobiography,* 594 ff.; Kendall, *Autobiography,* 376 ff.; and Taney's manuscript account of the Bank war, in the Library of Congress. There are numerous secondary accounts of the Cabinet shuffle and its relation to the Bank war, including Ralph C. H. Catterall, *The Second Bank of the United States,* 292 ff.; and Carl Brent Swisher, *Roger B. Taney,* 210 ff. There is much valuable material in Volume V of the Jackson *Correspondence.*

[2] Duane's narrative, *Niles,* XLV, 236.

[3] Kendall, *Autobiography,* 379; Jackson to Van Buren, June 6, 1833, Jackson's *Correspondence,* V, 106-107; Kendall to Van Buren, June 9, 1833, Van Buren Papers.

[4] Kendall to Jackson, Aug. 14, 1833, Jackson's *Correspondence,* V, 156; Van Buren to Jackson, Aug. 19, Sept. 4, 1833, *ibid.,* 159-160, 179-182.

[5] Blair to Van Buren, Nov. 13, 1859, in Van Buren, *Autobiography,* 607-608.

[6] Jackson to Van Buren, Sept. 15, 1833, Jackson's *Correspondence,* V, 187; Jackson to Taney, Sept. 15, 1833, *ibid.,* 188-189. The paper itself appeared in the Washington *Globe* and the *United States' Telegraph* on Sept. 23. It is reprinted in *Niles,* XLV, 73-77.

[7] Jackson to Van Buren, Sept. 19, 23, 1833, Jackson's *Correspondence,* V, 203-204, 206-207; *United States' Telegraph,* Sept. 19, 1833; *Niles,* XLV, 65, 193, The forthcoming removal of the deposits was officially announced in the Washington *Globe* for Sept. 20, 1833.

[8] *Register of Debates,* 22d, 2d, 1936. The vote in the House was 109 to 46.

[9] Clay to Biddle, Apr. 10, 1833, *Biddle Correspondence,* 202-204.

[10] Petigru to Legaré, Mar. 5, 1833, Carson, *Petigru,* 121.

[11] Jackson to H. L. White, Mar. 24, 1833, Jackson's *Correspondence,* V, 46-47; to the Rev. Hardy M. Cryer, Apr. 7, 1833, *ibid.,* 52-54; to Coffee, Apr. 9, 1833, *ibid.,* 56; to the Rev. Andrew J. Crawford, May 1, 1833, *ibid.,* 71-72. Jackson was also inclined to blame the Nullifiers for a fire that destroyed the Treasury building! To A. Jackson, Jr., Apr. 2, 1833, *ibid.,* 48.

[12] "Mr. Calhoun and his coadjutors found their conspiracy against the Union premature. . . . The failure has induced a retrograde movement, but the project of a Southern league and separation is not abandoned. To gain time and support, Mr. Calhoun has patched up a truce with Mr. Clay. . . ." Washington *Globe,* Mar. 27, 1833. The party propaganda line is developed in the *Globe* through March, April, and May 1833.

[13] The medal story was repeated as fact, but without citation, as recently as 1930 in Fuess, *Webster,* I, 389. Kendall retailed the story in 1862, *Autobiography,* 631, but disclaimed any knowledge of the authority on which it rested. He was aware at the time, however, that the whole thing was pure fabrication. Blair first published the item in the Washington *Globe* for April 30, 1833. The *United States' Telegraph* immediately challenged him to prove it, whereupon the *Globe* for May 6 printed a letter from one Joseph B. Hinton, later identified as a member of the

North Carolina legislature, to "a friend in Washington." The letter was dated from Raleigh, N. C., April 26, which meant that the tale had found its way into the *Globe* in record time. The writer quotes a "Major Hinton," not otherwise identified but presumably a relative, as stating that the South Carolinians were passing out such medals in the upper counties of North Carolina. The Calhoun press generally branded the whole story as falsehood. See especially the Columbia *Telescope,* May 21, 1833. When the pressure became too great, Blair published on June 10 another letter from Mr. Hinton explaining blandly that he had misunderstood his informant, the Major, and it was all a mistake. It was South—not North—Carolina; badges—not medals—were involved; and there was no inscription! The "medals," in a word, were nothing at all but the familiar palmetto buttons of the Nullifiers.

[14] Washington *Globe,* May-July 1833.

[15] Webster to Livingston, Mar. 21, 1833, Webster's *Writings,* XVI, 229-230. Also March, *Reminiscences,* 250-251; and Wise, *Seven Decades,* 121.

[16] E. S. Davis to Webster, Mar. 27, 1833, Webster Papers; Dr. Bryson to Davis, Apr. 1, 1833, *ibid.;* Rufus Choate to Webster, Aug. 12, 1833, *ibid.;* Calhoun to Van Deventer, Mar. 24, 1833, *Correspondence,* 324; W. B. Lewis to J. A. Hamilton, June 22, 1833, Hamilton, *Reminiscences,* 259. See also Van Buren, *Autobiography,* 689-694, 703-704; and Curtis, *Webster,* I, 460-466.

[17] Biddle to Clay, Mar. 25, 1833, Clay's *Works,* V, 356-357; Clay to Biddle, Apr. 10, 1833, *Biddle Correspondence,* 202-204.

[18] John Floyd, *Diary,* 221-227.

[19] *Ibid.,* 232.

[20] Duff Green to Biddle, Sept. 22, 1833, Biddle Papers.

[21] Biddle to Cooper, Sept. 24, 1833, President's Letter Book, Vol. V, Biddle Papers.

[22] *United States' Telegraph,* Oct. 23, Nov. 26, Dec. 9, 1833; J. H. Hammond to W. C. Preston, Aug. 16, 1833, Hammond Papers; John Scholefield to Clay, Nov. 13, 1833, Clay Papers; Duff Green to John Floyd, Nov. 20, 1833, Floyd Papers. McLean was also dabbling with the Antimasons, and with anyone else who would dabble. See, *e. g.,* Millard Fillmore to McLean, Dec. 9, 1833, McLean Papers.

[23] *Niles,* XLV, 240.

[24] Biddle to Webster, Dec. 15, 1833, President's Letter Book, Vol. V, Biddle Papers.

[25] Calhoun to F. W. Pickens, Dec. 12, 1833, *Correspondence,* 325-326.

[26] Adams, *Diary,* IX, 67; Mrs. Smith, 345-347.

[27] Calhoun to Pickens, Jan. 4, 1834, *Correspondence,* 327-328. Also Van Buren to John Van Buren, Jan. 29, 1834, Van Buren Papers.

[28] *Register of Debates,* 23d, 1st, 19-41 *passim;* Van Buren, *Autobiography,* 674-678. Van Buren's oversubtle argument to prove that White had already been seduced over to the opposition is unconvincing.

[29] *Register of Debates,* 23d, 1st, 42-44; Clay to Brooke, Dec. 16, 1833, Clay's *Works,* V, 375; Silas Wright to E. Croswell, Dec. 16, 1833, *Boston Public Library Bulletin,* VII (June 1902), 270; E. Malcolm Carroll, *Origins of the Whig Party,* 84 ff., 102-107, 134-138.

[30] Webster to Biddle, Dec. 21, 1833: ". . . I believe my retainer has not been renewed, or *refreshed* as usual. If it be wished that my relation to the Bank should be continued, it may be well to send me the usual retainers." *Biddle Correspondence,* 218.

[31] "*Remember*—to my *certain* knowledge there was never for a moment a thought or a possibility of a union between Mr Webster & the Regency & Anti Bank—*never for a moment*." Rufus Choate to Warwick Palfray, Jr., Jan. 31, 1834, *Essex Historical Collections,* LXIX, 87.

[32] *Register of Debates,* 23d, 1st, 2136, 2160-2161.

[33] Clay to Biddle, Feb. 2, 1834, *Biddle Correspondence,* 220.

[34] Spencer O'Brien to Willie P. Mangum, Feb. 17, 1834, Mangum Papers; John Sergeant to Biddle, Feb. 27, 1834, *Biddle Correspondence,* 222-223. Also Calhoun to John D. Gardiner, Jan. 6, 1834, Calhoun Papers, Duke University.

[35] "The President is kind to me," wrote Postmaster General Barry to his daughter, Feb. 22, 1834, "but he is growing old and is irritable, acting upon impulses; listening to the stories of creatures and conforming to the counsels of men wholly unworthy of his association. Inferior men, too, by their forwardness and impudence, have his ear and confidence; such men as Major Lewis, Kendall, Blair, T. P. Moore, etc., etc. They are mercenary and selfish, and are careless of General Jackson's fame and honor." *William and Mary Quarterly,* XIV (April 1906), 238.

[36] *Register of Debates,* 23d, 1st, 58-59.

[37] *Ibid.,* 59-94.

[38] Clay to Biddle, Dec. 21, 1833, *Biddle Correspondence,* 218-219; J. A. Hamilton to Van Buren, Jan. 18, 1834, Van Buren Papers; Calhoun to James Edward Calhoun, Feb. 8, 1834, *Correspondence,* 331; Clay to Brooke, Feb. 10, 1834, Clay's *Works,* V, 377; Fillmore to Follett, Mar. 5, 1834, Historical and Philosophical Society of Ohio, *Quarterly Publication,* XI, 11; *Niles,* XLVI, 81-96; Benton, *View,* I, 415-416; R. C. McGrane, *Panic of 1837,* 4-5. The *Register of Debates* for the session is filled with memorials and petitions.

[39] Jackson to Van Buren, Jan. 3, 1834, Jackson's *Correspondence,* V, 238-239.

[40] Biddle to William Appleton, President of the Boston Branch, Bank of the United States, Jan. 27, 1834, *Biddle Correspondence,* 219-220.

[41] Biddle to Joseph Hopkinson, Feb. 21, 1834, *ibid.,* 221-222. Also Horace Binney to Biddle, Feb. 4, 1834, *ibid.,* 220-221; Biddle to J. G. Watmough, Feb. 8, 1834, *ibid.,* 221; Biddle to Charles Hammond, Mar. 11, 1834, *ibid.,* 226.

[42] Bray Hammond, "Jackson, Biddle, and the Bank of the United States," *Journal of Economic History,* VII (May 1947), 1-23; Swisher, *Taney,* 265-270.

[43] The Van Buren Papers for the first three months of 1834 are full of pleas from, or in behalf of, New York merchants. See especially James Watson Webb to Van Buren, Jan. 22; James I. Van Alen to Van Buren, Jan. 27; M. Van Schaick to Van Buren, Jan. 28 and 31; Jesse Hoyt to Van Buren, Jan. 29 and Feb. 4; and James King to Van Buren, Mar. 14, 1834. Barry, writing to his daughter, Feb. 22, 1834, blames the "derangement of the currency and suffering of the community" on the administration policy, but the policy itself he attributes to Van Buren. *William and Mary Quarterly,* XIV (April 1906), 239. Calhoun told John Sergeant late in February that the Cabinet was meeting daily on a new bank scheme, and Sergeant relayed it to Biddle, Feb. 27, 1834, *Biddle Correspondence,* 222-223. The denials, it should be noted, preceded this date. See W. B. Lewis to J. A. Hamilton, Jan. 25, Feb. 8, 1834, in Hamilton, *Reminiscences,* 269, 280.

[44] *Register of Debates,* 23d, 1st, 636 ff.; *Niles,* XLV, 436.

[45] *Register of Debates,* 23d, 1st, 807.

[46] Samuel F. Vinson to William Greene, Mar. 14, 1834, Historical and Philosophical Society of Ohio, *Quarterly Publication,* XIV, 9; John Tyler to Dr. Henry Curtis, Mar. 28, Apr. 5, 1834, Tyler, *Times of the Tylers,* I, 490-491, 492. Also Calhoun in the Senate, Mar. 21, 1834, a week before the vote: "It is now conceded, almost universally, that a rash and precipitate act of the Executive, to speak in the mildest terms, has plunged this country into deep and almost universal distress." *Register of Debates,* 23d, 1st, 1073; *Works,* II, 375-376.

[47] *Register of Debates,* 23d, 1st, 1187.

[48] *Ibid.,* 1185-1187; Tyler to Dr. Curtis, Apr. 5, 1834, Tyler, *Times of the Tylers,* I, 492.

[49] Jackson to Kendall, April [?] 1834, Jackson's *Correspondence,* V, 257-258; to Andrew Jackson, Jr., Apr. 6, 1834, *ibid.,* 259; to Coffee, Apr. 6, 1834, *ibid.,* 260.

[50] Samuel F. Vinson to William Greene, Apr. 13, 1834, Historical and Philosophical Society of Ohio, *Quarterly Publication,* XIV, 10-11. Cf. J. W. Webb to Biddle, Mar. 18, 1834, *Biddle Correspondence,* 227.

[51] *Register of Debates,* 23d, 1st, 3473-3478.

[52] Jackson to Coffee, Apr. 6, 1834, Jackson's *Correspondence,* V, 260; to A. Jackson, Jr., Apr. 6, 1834, *ibid.,* 259.

[53] Vinson to Greene, Apr. 13, 1834, *loc. cit.; Niles,* XLVI, 100, 115-117; Hone, *Diary,* 121-124.

[54] *Register of Debates,* 23d, 1st, 206-223; *Works,* II, 309-343.

[55] Calhoun to F. W. Pickens, Jan. 20, 1834, *Correspondence,* 329.

[56] William F. Gordon to Thomas W. Gilmer, Jan. 14, 1834, *William and Mary Quarterly,* XXI (July 1912), 2; Robert Allen to John Tyler, Feb. 10, 1834, Tyler Papers; J. S. Smith to Willie P. Mangum, Feb. 16, 1834, Mangum Papers; Spencer O'Brien to Mangum, Feb. 17, 1834, *ibid.;* F. Nash to Mangum, Feb. 21, 1834, *ibid.; United States' Telegraph,* Jan. 28, Feb. 11, 24, 1834. William Cabell Rives, who was regarded by the opposition as the ablest of the administration Senators, did refer to Calhoun's remarks in his own speech of January 17, the timing of which would indicate that he intended an answer, and there was some direct colloquy between the two men on the twentieth. Aside from these few references, however, Rives actually directed his arguments at Clay's speech, to which Benton had already replied. *Register of Debates,* 23d, 1st, 259-291, 297-301. Even the hostile Charleston *Courier,* or at least its Washington correspondent, was enthusiastic; Jan. 22, 1834.

[57] Calhoun to Van Deventer, Jan. 25, 1834, *Correspondence,* 329-330. Cf. to John Ewing Calhoun, Jan. 30, 1834, *ibid.,* 331; to James Edward Calhoun, Feb. 8, 1834, *ibid.;* to Tazewell, Jan. 16, Feb. 9, 1834, Calhoun Papers, Library of Congress. His constant theme in all of these letters is the imminent overthrow of the administration and an exhortation to his followers to adhere strictly to their own principles.

[58] Clay to Brooke, Mar. 23, 1834, Clay's *Works,* V, 383. Cf. Ambrose Spencer to Webster, Jan. 11, 1834, Webster Papers.

[59] *Niles,* XLVI, 85.

[60] *Register of Debates,* 23d, 1st, 1317-1336.

[61] *Ibid.,* 1393-1394.

[62] *Ibid.,* 1394-1395.

[63] *Ibid.,* 1404-1422.

[64] *Ibid.,* 1397-1398, 1711-1712.

CHAPTER XVII

[1] Arthur C. Cole, *Whig Party in the South,* 30-32.

[2] James Watson Webb to Webster, Jan. 3, 1834, Webster Papers; Millard Fillmore to Oran Follett, Feb. 1, 1834, Historical and Philosophical Society of Ohio, *Quarterly Publication,* XI, 10; S. F. Chapman to John McLean, Mar. 25, 1834, McLean Papers.

[3] Van Deusen, *Clay,* 276 ff.

[4] William Smith [one of the South Carolina exiles, now of Alabama] to Webster, Feb. 9, 1834, Webster Papers.

[5] Calhoun to Van Deventer, Jan. 25, 1834, *Correspondence,* 330.

[6] Adams, *Diary,* IX, 105-106, 108, 109.

[7] Duff Green to R. K. Crallé, Mar. 14, 1834, Green Papers. Also Daniel Bride to Green, Apr. 2, 1834, *ibid.;* George Sharswood [?] to Green, May 22, 1834, *ibid.;* George Lantsinger to Green, June 17, 1834, *ibid.*

[8] *Register of Debates,* 23d, 1st, 994-995, 1004-1005; Calhoun to Tazewell, Mar. 27, 1834, Calhoun Papers, Library of Congress.

[9] John Sergeant to Biddle, Feb. 27, 1834, *Biddle Correspondence,* 222-223; Tyler to Tazewell, June 23, 1834, Tyler, *Times of the Tylers,* I, 499; Benton, *View,* I, 469-470; *Register of Debates,* 23d, 1st, 217-218.

[10] Calhoun to Tazewell, Mar. 27, 1834, Calhoun Papers, Library of Congress; [Hunter], *Life,* 54; Calhoun in the Senate, Mar. 10, 1838, *Works,* III, 255-256. It was presumably from Tyler or Mangum, both members of the Finance Committee, that Calhoun learned of the plan, and one of these was probably his emissary to Webster, who was the committee's chairman.

[11] *Register of Debates,* 23d, 1st, 1057-1073; *Works,* II, 344-376. The basic thought of the speech had been outlined earlier in private letters. See Calhoun to James Edward Calhoun, Feb. 8, 1834, *Correspondence,* 332; to Tazewell, Feb. 9, 1834, Calhoun Papers, Library of Congress, to John Ewing Calhoun, Feb. 16, 1834, *Correspondence,* 333. There is an oversimplified account in [Hunter], *Life,* 52-53.

[12] *Register of Debates,* 23d, 1st, 1073.

[13] *United States' Telegraph,* Mar. 22, Apr. 2, Apr. 11, 1834; Charleston *Mercury,* Mar. 28, 1834.

[14] Calhoun to James Edward Calhoun, Mar. 26, 1834, *Correspondence,* 333; to Tazewell, Mar. 27, 1834, Calhoun Papers, Library of Congress; to Pickens, Apr. 15, 1834, *Correspondence,* 335.

[15] *Register of Debates,* 23d, 1st, 1144-1145.

[16] *Ibid.,* 4640-4641.

[17] In the Washington *Chronicle,* May 10, 1838, Richard K. Crallé, its editor, states that Calhoun "suggested the scheme, in our presence, to a distinguished gentleman of Virginia before the meeting of Congress in 1833." He then goes on to print in full a letter from William F. Gordon to "a member of Congress," dated May 7, 1838, which reads in part as follows: ". . . I drew the bill, which I presented to the House, as a substitute for the State Bank scheme, in *consultation with him* [Calhoun]; and although he preferred as a measure of policy, to renew the charter of the United States Bank for a short period,—in *that measure,* he looked to a *similar result. . . .*" The letter is reprinted in the Pendleton *Messenger* for May 25, 1838. See also Armistead C. Gordon, *William Fitzhugh Gordon,* 229-231; Scott, *Memoir of Hugh Lawson White,* 143 ff.; [Hunter], *Life,* 52; Jenkins, *Calhoun,* 319-322.

[18] Clay to Brooke, Apr. 17, 1834, Clay's *Works,* V, 382; *Register of Debates,* 23d, 1st, 1266-1281, 1281-1284; Calhoun's *Works,* II, 376-405.

[19] *United States' Telegraph,* Apr. 23, 1834; *Niles,* XLVI, 113, 129; Calhoun to Pickens, Apr. 15, 1834, *Correspondence,* 335-336.

[20] The merger took place in December 1833, not because of any great concurrence of views, but simply because Richmond could not support two papers in opposition to Ritchie's *Enquirer.*

[21] Green to Crallé, Mar. 12, 1832, *Southern History Association Publications,* VII, 270-271; Calhoun to Van Deventer, Mar. 31, 1832, *Correspondence,* 317; Cole, *Whig Party in the South,* 17-18.

[22] See Erik M. Eriksson, "Official Newspaper Organs and the Presidential Election of 1836," *Tennessee Historical Magazine,* IX (July 1925), 115-130. Nathan Sargent, *Public Men and Events,* I, 262, claims credit for himself, but gives too late a date—Feb. 11, 1834.

[23] Ambler, *Ritchie,* 157-158; *Niles,* XLVI, 115; Hone, *Diary,* 122-125; E. S. Abby, *Journal of a . . . Tour in the United States . . . ,* II, 135.

[24] *Register of Debates,* 23d, 1st, 1069; *Works,* II, 368.

[25] Calhoun to Tazewell, Mar. 27, 1834, Calhoun Papers, Library of Congress.

[26] *Register of Debates,* 23d, 1st, 1606.

[27] *Ibid.,* 1649-1650; *Works,* II, 424-425. The passages quoted should be compared with Calhoun's statement in the Senate, Mar. 10, 1838, in refutation of Clay's charge that he had deserted their common party: "It is . . . true that a common party designation was applied to the opposition in the aggregate, not however, with my approbation; but it is no less true that it was universally known that it consisted of two distinct parties, dissimilar in principle and policy, except in relation to the object for which they had united: the National Republican party, and the portion of the State Rights party which had separated from the administration, on the ground that it had departed from the true principles of the original party. . . ." *Works,* III, 271.

[28] Calhoun to James Edward Calhoun, May 21, 1834, *Correspondence,* 337-338; to Tazewell, May 22, 1834, Calhoun Papers, Library of Congress.

[29] *Senate Executive Journal,* IV, 361-362; 365-371; 394-398.

[30] *Register of Debates,* 23d, 1st, 4368-4373; Mangum to Bell, June 15, 1835, and Bell to Mangum, July 2, 1835, *Tennessee Historical Magazine,* III (September 1917), 198-200.

[31] *Senate Executive Journal,* IV, 426-429. Benton says the reason for Jackson's long delay in submitting Taney's nomination to the Senate was his knowledge that the Treasury Secretary would be rejected, and his desire to retain the Marylander's services as long as possible. *View,* I, 470. This argument will not, however, justify the similar delay in submitting Butler's nomination.

[32] Thomas Corwin to John McLean, June 19, 1834, *Boston Public Library Bulletin,* VII, 273-274.

[33] *Senate Executive Journal,* IV, 432, 433, 435, 442; W. A. Butler, *Retrospect of Forty Years,* 39-43.

[34] *Register of Debates,* 23d, 1st, 2122.

[35] See Biddle to William Appleton, July 4, 1834, *Biddle Correspondence,* 237-241; R. Fisher to Biddle, July 7, 1834, *ibid.,* 241-243; Biddle to J. W. Webb, July 9, 1834, *ibid.,* 243.

[36] See, *e. g.,* Nathaniel Macon, elder statesman of the Jeffersonians, to Van Buren, May 24, 1834, *North Carolina Historical Review,* XV (January 1938), 61.

Compare Alexander Hamilton to John Woodworth, Sept. 14, 1834, *Biddle Correspondence,* 244.

[37] McDuffie had determined at the beginning of the session not to stand for reelection; Calhoun to Pickens, Jan. 4, 1834, *Correspondence,* 326-327. He resigned before the year was out, using very genuine ill health as the reason. He was not so ill, however, that he could not accept election as Governor of South Carolina in December. See J. M. Felder to Hammond, June 17, 1834, Hammond Papers; McDuffie to A. Burt, May 3, 1834, McDuffie Papers, Duke University; *Niles,* XLVII, 51.

[38] Felder to Hammond, June 22, 1834, Hammond Papers; Calhoun to Pickens, July 17, 1834, Calhoun Papers, South Caroliniana Library.

[39] *Register of Debates,* 23d, 1st, 2128; Wise, *Seven Decades,* 137.

[40] Pendleton *Messenger,* Aug. 6, 1834; Wise, *loc. cit.;* Tyler, *Times of the Tylers,* I, 513-514.

[41] Jackson to Lewis, Sept. 8, 1834, Jackson's *Correspondence,* V, 289. Also Jackson to Van Buren, Aug. 8, 1834, *ibid.,* 281-282. For Van Buren's activities, see drafts in his hand and his correspondence with Blair in Volume XX of the Van Buren Papers.

[42] Green to Crallé, July 26, 1834, Duff Green Papers; *United States' Telegraph,* Aug. 2, 1834.

[43] A typical renewal of the attack is in the Washington *Globe,* July 24, 1834. See also R. W. Barnwell to W. F. Gordon, Aug. 6, 1834, Gordon, *Gordon,* 302; Frederick A. Schley to Maxcy, Aug. 11, 1834, Maxcy Papers, second series; Mangum to John Beard, Oct. 7, 1834, Charles F. Fisher Papers.

[44] *United States' Telegraph,* Aug. 20, 1834.

[45] John Spear Smith to Thomas Finley, September 1834, Historical and Philosophical Society of Ohio, *Quarterly Publication,* I, 92-95; Finley to James Findlay, Sept. 20, 1834, *ibid.,* 95-96.

[46] *United States' Telegraph,* Sept. 2, 1834. Also Pendleton *Messenger,* Sept. 3, 1834.

[47] *United States' Telegraph,* Sept. 15, 1834.

[48] Calhoun to Green, Sept. 20, Nov. 16, 1834, *Correspondence,* 341-342, 342-343.

[49] *Niles,* XLVII, 118, 150.

[50] *Ibid.,* 118, 166; Hone, *Diary,* 141.

[51] Tyler to William Fitzhugh Gordon, Nov. 9, 1834, Gordon, *Gordon,* 293-295; *United States' Telegraph,* Nov. 26, 1834; also Green to Crallé, Oct. 15, 1834, Green Papers.

[52] D. L. Disney to Van Buren, Dec. 18, 1834, Van Buren Papers; Thomas Ewing to Peter Hitchcock, Dec. 28, 1834, *Boston Public Library Bulletin,* VII, 275.

[53] *Niles,* XLVIII, 39; Scott, *Memoir of White,* 329-331.

[54] Scott, *op. cit.,* 334; *United States' Telegraph,* Sept. 19, 1836. See also letters from Polk to Cave Johnson, January-June 1835, in *Tennessee Historical Magazine,* I (September 1915), 219-227. This pair played a subtle game, pretending to support White while working for Van Buren. Scott, *op. cit.,* 253 ff.; Hugh Waddell to Polk, Jan. 7, 1835, *North Carolina Historical Review,* XVI (April 1939), 189.

CHAPTER XVIII

[1] The squabble went back to patronage distribution in Mississippi, but the final straw was probably Poindexter's closing speech against the Force Bill, Jan. 19 and

20, 1833. The speech contains a devastating satire in the form of a fictitious address of General Jackson to his troops on entering South Carolina; *Register of Debates,* 22d, 2d, 645 ff. To be fully appreciated it must be read, but we may be sure Jackson read it, and it was just the sort of thing that would have infuriated him.

[2] The letter is dated Sept. 26, 1834, reprinted in the *United States' Telegraph,* Oct. 25, 1834. The controversy may be followed in succeeding issues of this paper, through the middle of November. The Jackson press did not print all the documents. See also allusions in Van Buren to Jackson, July 22, 1834, Jackson's *Correspondence,* V, 274-275; and Lewis to Jackson, July 25, 1834, *ibid.,* 275.

[3] Van Buren, *Autobiography,* 759-762; Poindexter to Van Buren, Jan. 5, 1835, and Van Buren to Poindexter, Jan. 6, 1835, Van Buren Papers.

[4] Richardson, *Messages and Papers of the Presidents,* 1316-1342. See comment on the State Rights references in Charleston *Mercury,* Dec. 13, 1834.

[5] *Register of Debates,* 23d, 2d, 6-7.

[6] Livingston to Jackson, June 23, 1834, Jackson's *Correspondence,* V, 270-271; William B. Hatcher, *Edward Livingston,* 423-425.

[7] Jackson to Van Buren, Oct. 27, 1834, Jackson's *Correspondence,* V, 303.

[8] *Register of Debates,* 23d, 2d, 104; Appendix, 208-219.

[9] *Ibid.,* 212. Cf. Webster to William Sullivan, Feb. 23, 1835, Webster's *Writings,* XVIII, 9. The attitude of the Nullifiers was expressed in the Charleston *Mercury,* Dec. 10, 12, 1834.

[10] *Register of Debates,* 23d, 2d, 215-216.

[11] Livingston to Jackson, Jan. 15, 16, 1835, Jackson's *Correspondence,* V, 318-319; *Niles,* XLVII, 425.

[12] *Register of Debates,* 23d, 2d, 1633-1634; Adams, *Diary,* IX, 436; Hone, *Diary,* 150-151. Cf. Wiltse, *Calhoun, Nationalist,* 161-162.

[13] *Register of Debates,* 23d, 2d, 730-746, 1661-1663.

[14] Jackson to Livingston, Mar. 10, 1835, Jackson's *Correspondence,* V, 329-330; *Register of Debates,* 23d, 2d, 1663.

[15] *Niles,* XLVIII, 220.

[16] *Register of Debates,* 23d, 2d, 274, 1125-1126; Charleston *Mercury,* Feb. 5, 1835.

[17] Tyler to Robert Tyler, Jan. 31, 1835, Tyler, *Times of the Tylers,* I, 508; *United States' Telegraph,* Feb. 2, 1835.

[18] The text of Poindexter's letter, and his version of the whole affair as given in a speech in Philadelphia, Mar. 27, 1835, are in the *National Intelligencer,* Apr. 15, 1835. Also Tyler to Mrs. Tyler, Feb. 1, 1835, Tyler, *Times of the Tylers,* I, 509-510.

[19] Washington *Globe,* Jan. 31, 1835.

[20] *Register of Debates,* 23d, 2d, 275-276.

[21] *United States' Telegraph,* Feb. 2, 3, 1835; Tyler to Mrs. Tyler, Feb. 1, 1835, Tyler, *Times of the Tylers,* I, 509-510.

[22] The documents in the case are included in *Senate Document* 148, 23d Cong., 2d sess.

[23] Tyler to Robert Tyler, Feb. 23, 1835, Tyler, *Times of the Tylers,* I, 511.

[24] *Register of Debates,* 23d, 2d, 582-583.

[25] Washington *Globe,* Feb. 23, 1835.

[26] *Register of Debates,* 23d, 2d, 628-629.

[27] *Ibid.,* 697-698, 728.

[28] *Niles,* XLVIII, 186.

[29] Blair to Jackson, May 19, 1835, Jackson's *Correspondence,* V, 348-349; *Niles,* XLVIII, 226-229, 244-248; Ambler, *Ritchie,* 169-170.

[30] Calhoun to Francis W. Pickens, May 19, 1835, Calhoun Papers, South Caroliniana Library; to William F. Gordon, May 22, 1835, Gordon, *Gordon,* 297-299.

[31] Jackson to Polk, Aug. 3, 1835, Jackson's *Correspondence,* V, 357-359; to Grundy, Oct. 5, 1835, *ibid.,* 371-372.

[32] Jackson to Polk, Aug. 3, Sept. 15, 1835, *ibid.,* 357-359, 365-366; to Col. Robert Armstrong, Sept. 15, 1835, *ibid.,* 366; to A. O. P. Nicholson, *et al.,* Dec. 18, 1835, *ibid.,* 380-381; *Niles,* XLIX, 294, 337-338; Scott, *Memoir of White,* 336-342.

[33] Jabez D. Hammond, *The History of Political Parties in the State of New-York,* II, 489-490; J. Q. Adams to A. H. Everett, Dec. 1, 1835, *Am. Hist. Rev.,* XI (January 1906), 348; Thurlow Weed, *Autobiography,* I, 443; Hone, *Diary,* 184.

[34] Richardson, *Messages and Papers of the Presidents,* 1366-1396; Hatcher, *Livingston,* 446-447.

[35] Jackson's *Correspondence,* V, 377-379.

[36] Richardson, *Messages and Papers of the Presidents,* 1407-1412. Though not delivered to Congress until Monday, Jan. 18, 1836, the message was dated Jan. 15, and there is a strong presumption that administration leaders in both houses had been given an opportunity to read it over the week end.

[37] Gordon to Tyler, Jan. 15, 1836, Tyler, *Times of the Tylers,* I, 529 (italics omitted).

[38] *Register of Debates,* 24th, 1st, 169-170.

[39] *Ibid.,* 169-178; *Works,* III, 14-27, where the speech is misdated Feb. 14, 1837.

[40] Calhoun to Tazewell, Jan. 24, 1836, Calhoun Papers, Library of Congress. Cf. Samuel F. Vinson, veteran National Republican Congressman from Ohio, to William Greene, Jan. 19, 1836: "An impression seems to prevail here very generally that Jackson is desirous of running again, and that, if a French war should spring up, he would take the field again as a candidate. I have never been able to trace this impression to any definite or responsible source, and therefore do not know how much credence should be given to it. Very many of our friends believe he wants to incite a war as a means of making himself President again." Historical and Philosophical Society of Ohio, *Quarterly Publication,* XIV, 14. See also *United States' Telegraph,* Feb. 2, 1836.

[41] *Register of Debates,* 24th, 1st, 211-249, *et seq.*

[42] Richardson, *Messages and Papers of the Presidents,* 1432-1433.

[43] *Register of Debates,* 24th, 1st, 551-556.

CHAPTER XIX

[1] *Register of Debates,* 23d, 2d, 109. Benton, *View,* I, 556-557, says that Webster declined to serve and was replaced by Poindexter; also that Southard, who disapproved of the division of the Senate into three parties, did not act with the committee, although he remained a member of it. Neither of these statements is borne out by the contemporary record. The account in the *United States' Telegraph* on the day the report appeared, Feb. 9, 1835, names Webster as still one of the members of the committee. As to Southard, it is clear from his reply to Benton when the report was debated on the floor of the Senate, Feb. 13, 1835, that

he had acted with the group throughout. *Register of Debates,* 23d, 2d, 421-423. Benton further states that both he and King disagreed with the report. When Calhoun presented it in the Senate, however, he said the committee had been unanimous but for one member, and this statement was not challenged, either by King or by Benton. *Ibid.,* 361. Even Benton's opposition, as was later shown, was confined to a single point during the committee sessions.

[2] See Wiltse, *Calhoun, Nationalist,* 331-332.

[3] Edward G. Bourne, *History of the Surplus Revenue of 1837,* 15-16; McGrane, *Panic of 1837,* 43-69; [Hunter], *Life,* 55-56; *Report of the Secretary of the Treasury for 1854-1855,* 80-82.

[4] "Mr. Calhoun is at the head of a committee on Executive patronage which is virtually a committee on surplus revenue—He is broaching some measures of astounding novelty—and I think very doubtful import—As they have not been communicated to his committee as yet I am not at liberty to speak of them specifically." Preston to Hammond, Jan. 18, 1835, Hammond Papers. This seems to contradict Benton's insinuation that the report was too quickly prepared; *View,* I, 557. It had, clearly, not even been started nearly two weeks after the appointment of the committee.

[5] For discussion of this law and its purposes, see Wiltse, *Calhoun, Nationalist,* 211 and note. Calhoun's report on Executive Patronage is available in the usual sources, including *Works,* V, 148-190; *Niles,* XLVIII, 265-272; and *Register of Debates,* 23d, 2d, Appendix, 219-231. See also *National Intelligencer,* Feb. 10, 1835.

[6] *Register of Debates,* 23d, 2d, 361-392.

[7] Tyler to Tazewell, Feb. 11, 1835, Tyler Papers.

[8] *Register of Debates,* 23d, 2d, 576.

[9] *Ibid.,* 421-439; Harriet Martineau, *Retrospect of Western Travel,* I, 149; Hone, *Diary,* 150; Benton, *View,* I, 556-557. See also Charleston *Courier,* Feb. 20, 21, 23, 1835; Charleston *Mercury,* Feb. 23, 1835.

[10] *Register of Debates,* 23d, 2d, 483-491.

[11] Jackson to Balch, Feb. 16, 1835, Jackson's *Correspondence,* V, 327-328.

[12] *Register of Debates,* 23d, 2d, 1281, 1333.

[13] *Senate Executive Journal,* IV, 498.

[14] A. A. Lawrence to Amos Lawrence, Jan. 18, 1836, *Mass. Hist. Soc. Proc.,* L, 53; John Fairfield to his wife, Jan. 24, 1836, *Fairfield Letters,* 82-83.

[15] *Register of Debates,* 24th, 1st, 11-13.

[16] *Ibid.,* 1945, 1948, 1959.

[17] Calhoun to Green, Jan. 24, 1836, *Correspondence,* 356-357.

[18] *Register of Debates,* 24th, 1st, 48-52.

[19] *Ibid.,* 55, 367, 2470-2482.

[20] See Van Buren to Jackson, Nov. 5, 1834, Jackson's *Correspondence,* V, 305-307; and Jackson's Annual Message of Dec. 1, 1834.

[21] Calhoun to William C. Dawson, Nov. 24, 1835, *Correspondence,* 349-351; [Hunter], *Life,* 56.

[22] *Senate Executive Journal,* IV, 520-522.

[23] *Register of Debates,* 24th, 1st, 1028-1032.

[24] *Ibid.,* 1396.

[25] *Ibid.,* 1271.

[26] For an amplification of this view, see C. M. Wiltse, "Calhoun: An Interpretation," in *Proceedings of the South Carolina Historical Association, 1948,* 26-38.

[27] *Register of Debates,* 24th, 1st, 1383, 1577; Calhoun to Hammond, June 19, 1836, *Correspondence,* 358-361.

[28] Calhoun to Hammond, *loc cit.* I have not found a text of the bill as it came from committee, but its provisions may be deduced from the discussion in the Senate on the House amendment; *Register of Debates,* 24th, 1st, 1857-1859; and from the terms of Taney's draft of a proposed veto message, Jackson's *Correspondence,* V, 404-409.

[29] *Register of Debates,* 24th, 1st, 1821-1846.

[30] Calhoun to Hammond, June 19, 1836, *Correspondence,* 360.

[31] *Register of Debates,* 24th, 1st, 4339-4347; draft of veto message, dated June 20, 1836, Jackson's *Correspondence,* V, 404-409.

[32] *Register of Debates,* 24th, 1st, 4350-4380; R. M. Johnson to Jackson, "6 o'clock P. M.," June 21, 1836, Jackson's *Correspondence,* V, 409. The *United States' Telegraph* for July 6 says the deposit section as it appeared in the final version of the bill was filed with the Clerk of the House in the handwriting of Major Donelson, Jackson's secretary.

[33] *Register of Debates,* 24th, 1st, 1857-1859.

[34] *Ibid.,* 1870; Washington *Globe,* June 24, 1836; *National Intelligencer,* June 25, 1836.

[35] Calhoun to Armistead Burt, June 28, 1836, *Correspondence,* 361-362. Also to Hammond, July 4, 1836, *ibid.,* 362.

[36] *United States' Telegraph,* July 20, 1836.

[37] John G. Van Deusen, *Economic Bases of Disunion in South Carolina,* 155.

CHAPTER XX

[1] The terms of this analysis are essentially those used by Calhoun himself speaking in the Senate in 1849. See *Works,* IV, 518.

[2] H. H. Simms, "A Critical Analysis of Abolition Literature, 1830-1840," *Journal of Southern History,* VI (August 1940), 368-382. See also, for the whole anti-slavery controversy, Gilbert H. Barnes, *The Antislavery Impulse, 1830-1844;* and Dwight L. Dumond, *The Antislavery Origins of the Civil War in the United States.*

[3] Ritchie to Rives, June 6, 1833, Rives Papers; Madison to Clay, June 1833, Clay's *Works,* V, 364-365; *National Intelligencer,* July 9, 1833. Robertson's histories and Cook's Voyages are the titles common to Dew's footnotes and Calhoun's early reading; Thomas R. Dew, *Review of the Debate in the Virginia Legislature, 1831-32* (Richmond, 1832), reprinted in the *Pro-Slavery Argument* (Charleston, 1852), 287-490. Also see Wiltse, *Calhoun, Nationalist,* 26. Duff Green thought the publication of Dew's book would "do more to set the south right on this question of slavery than anything which could now be done. . . ." Green to Crallé, Green Papers.

[4] Calhoun to Charles Tait, Oct. 26, 1820, *Gulf States Historical Magazine,* I (1902), 98-100. See also Wiltse, *Calhoun, Nationalist,* 219.

[5] [Hunter], *Life of Calhoun,* 62.

[6] Calhoun to Pickens, Jan. 4, 1834, *Correspondence,* 327. The strategy of the abolitionists had been planned as early as 1831, but the nullification episode had forced a delay. See the *Liberator,* I, 147.

[7] Silas Wright to Thomas Ritchie, March 1835, Van Buren Papers. There are two drafts, one in Van Buren's own hand.

[8] Charleston *Mercury,* July 30, 31, 1835. The account in the *Courier* is considerably less detailed.

[9] Charleston *Mercury,* Aug. 4, 5-8, 10, 11, 1835; Jervey, *Hayne,* 379-381.

[10] Kendall to Jackson, Aug. 7, 1835, Jackson's *Correspondence,* V, 359-360.

[11] *United States' Telegraph,* Aug. 18, Sept. 10, 1835.

[12] J. H. Hammond to M. M. Noah, Aug. 19, 1835, Hammond Papers. Also Pierce M. Butler to Hammond, July 10, 1835, *ibid.;* and I. W. Hayne to Hammond, Aug. 13, 1835, *ibid.*

[13] Calhoun to James Edward Calhoun, Sept. 23, 1835, *Correspondence,* 346; Duff Green, Aug. 30, 1835, *ibid.,* 345.

[14] *United States' Telegraph,* Oct. 26, 1835; Washington *Globe,* Aug. 22, Nov. 21, Dec. 21, 1835. Benton, *View,* I, 609-623, repeats with embellishments the arguments of the *Globe,* although his speeches at the time indicate that he then shared Calhoun's view that the radical abolitionists were the real disunionists. Abolition was another of the many points on which Benton changed his mind before writing his memoirs.

[15] Maxcy to Van Buren, Nov. 22, 1835, Van Buren Papers; Rives to Van Buren, Jan. 29, 1836, *ibid.; United States' Telegraph,* Jan. 4, 1836; *Niles,* XLIX, 318-319.

[16] Richardson, *Messages and Papers of the Presidents,* 1394.

[17] *Register of Debates,* 24th, 1st, 26-33.

[18] *Ibid.,* 383-385, and Appendix, 72-77. The text of the report will also be found in Calhoun's *Works,* V, 190-208; *National Intelligencer,* Feb. 10, 1836; and *Niles,* XLIX, 408-411. See also Charleston *Courier,* Feb. 11, 1836.

[19] Calhoun to Van Deventer, Feb. 7, 1836, *Correspondence,* 358; *United States' Telegraph,* Feb. 9, 1836; D. H. Mangum to Willie P. Mangum, Feb. 15, 1836, Mangum Papers.

[20] Duff Green to Crallé, Feb. 12, 1836, Green Papers.

[21] *Register of Debates,* 24th, 1st, 1103-1108, 1124-1134, 1136-1153, 1155-1171, 1374, 1675, 1721-1737; Benton, *View,* I, 587-588.

[22] Fairfield to his wife, Jan. 7, 1836, *Fairfield Letters,* 65-66.

[23] D. H. Mangum to Willie P. Mangum, Feb. 15, 1836, Mangum Papers.

[24] *Register of Debates,* 24th, 1st, 72-74.

[25] *Ibid.,* 185-201.

[26] *Ibid.,* 201-211.

[27] *Ibid.,* 779, 803-810.

[28] *Ibid.,* 833-838; [Hunter,] *Life of Calhoun,* 58.

[29] *Register of Debates,* 24th, 1st, 1961-1964.

[30] *Ibid.,* 1966 ff.

[31] Fairfield to his wife, Dec. 22, 1835, *Fairfield Letters,* 38.

[32] Baldwin M. Hunter to M. C. M. Hammond, Feb. 1, 1836, Hammond Papers.

[33] See, *e. g.,* James L. Clark to Hammond, Jan. 16, 1836: "I see that you have made the break, and Calhoun follows in the Senate the road you in your excellent judgement had marked out in your maiden speech. . . ." Hammond Papers.

[34] R. Y. Hayne to Hammond, Jan. 14, 1836, Hammond Papers.

[35] See Pickens to the editor of the *Telegraph,* Mar. 21, 1836, *United States' Telegraph,* Mar. 23, 1836; Waddy Thompson to the editor of the *Telegraph,* Mar.

23, 1836, *ibid.*, Apr. 9, 1836. Also discussion in *ibid.*, Feb. 15, 16, 19, 20, 1836; and Charleston *Mercury*, Apr. 9, 1836.

[36] *Register of Debates*, 24th, 1st, 2482-2483.

[37] The Washington *Globe*, Feb. 17, 1836, specifically identifies Pinckney's approach with the position of the administration. The Charleston *Mercury*, Feb. 11, 1836, discusses the move from the Calhoun point of view.

[38] *Register of Debates*, 24th, 1st, 2495-2497. The *United States' Telegraph*, Feb. 10, 1836, took the same tack.

[39] *Register of Debates*, 24th, 1st, 2498-2502.

[40] *Ibid.*, 2533-2537, 2607-2621; *United States' Telegraph*, Feb. 25, 1836.

[41] Petigru to Legaré, Feb. 17, 1836, Carson, *Petigru*, 181; Hamilton to Hammond, Feb. 10, 1836, Hammond Papers; Hayne to Preston, Feb. 18, 1836, *ibid.;* J. H. Adams to Hammond, Mar. 29, 1836, *ibid.*

[42] *Register of Debates*, 24th, 1st, 2756-2757, and Appendix, 104-114.

[43] *Ibid.*, 3757-3758.

[44] *Ibid.*, 4031, 4050-4055.

[45] Washington *Globe*, May 28, 1836; Charleston *Mercury*, May 25, 1836.

CHAPTER XXI

[1] McGrane, *Panic of 1837*, 43-69; David Kinley, *The Independent Treasury of the United States*, 30. The course of the inflation in New York City may be vividly traced through the entries in Philip Hone's *Diary* during 1835 and 1836, and for the country generally in the files of *Niles' Register*. For statistics, see *Report of the Secretary of the Treasury for 1854-1855*.

[2] *Register of Debates*, 24th, 2d, Appendix, 107-108; Benton, *View*, I, 678.

[3] *United States' Telegraph*, July 13, 1836.

[4] Benton, *View*, I, 676-678; G. Van Deusen, *Clay*, 288; McGrane, *Panic of 1837*, 62-63.

[5] Report of the Secretary of the Treasury, Dec. 6, 1836, *Register of Debates*, 24th, 2d, Appendix, 77-78.

[6] Calhoun to A. S. Clayton, and others, Aug. 5, 1836, *Niles*, L, 432.

[7] Van Buren to Sherrod Williams, Aug. 8, 1836, *ibid.*, LI, 26-30.

[8] See especially Richard R. Stenberg, "Jackson, Anthony Butler, and Texas," *Southwestern Social Science Quarterly*, XIII (December 1932), 264-286; and "Texas Schemes of Jackson and Houston, 1829-1836," *ibid.*, XV (December 1934), 229-250. A more conventional account will be found in Justin H. Smith, *Annexation of Texas*, 9 ff.

[9] Houston to Jackson, Feb. 13, 1833, Houston's *Writings*, I, 274-276; to James Prentis, Apr. 20, 1834, *ibid.*, 289-290; to Isaac Parker, Oct. 5, 1835, *ibid.*, 302. The appeal for volunteers, which Parker brought out of Texas and had published in border papers, ended with a statement of principles: "support the constitution [of Mexico] and down with the Usurper!!!"—meaning Santa Anna, though by what more legitimate claim to authority Houston could call Santa Anna usurper is not clear.

[10] See Houston to Jackson, Feb. 13, 1833, *loc. cit.* A typical rumor is that in *Niles*, XLIX, 169, quoted from the New Orleans *Bee*. Annexation was undoubtedly contemplated by the original and all the subsequent land speculators from the time of the first American settlements. It was common talk in Congress, and

members of that body were not infrequently invited to take part in the speculation. See Perry, "Robert Y. Hayne," *Reminiscences of Public Men,* first series, 71.

[11] Austin to Biddle, Apr. 9, 1836, *Biddle Correspondence,* 269-271; *Niles,* L, 121-123.

[12] The battle took place Apr. 21, 1836. Houston's report is in his *Writings,* I, 416-420; and in *Niles,* L, 293-294.

[13] Duff Green to Crallé, May 6, 1836, Green Papers.

[14] *Register of Debates,* 24th, 1st, 1414-1425.

[15] Adams to A. H. Everett, May 10, 1836, *Am. Hist. Rev.,* XI (January 1906), 350-351.

[16] Ritchie to Van Buren, June 9, 1836, Van Buren Papers.

[17] *Register of Debates,* 24th, 1st, 1846-1848, 1915-1928.

[18] Calhoun's speech is not reported, but Southard, who followed him, understood him to make such a statement, and Calhoun did not challenge it. *Ibid.* See also Benton, *View,* I, 667.

[19] Kendall to Jackson, July 30, 1836, Jackson Papers, second series.

[20] Jackson to Kendall, Aug. 12, 1836, Jackson's *Correspondence,* V, 420-421; to Gaines, Sept. 4, 1836, *ibid.,* 423-424. For sharp criticism of the whole procedure, see *National Intelligencer,* Aug. 1, 5, 6, 8, 1836.

[21] E. W. Johnston to Hammond, Feb. 28, 1836, Hammond Papers. Also Johnston to Hammond, Mar. 9, 24, 1836, *ibid.*

[22] Calhoun to Francis W. Pickens, Aug. 17, 1836, Calhoun Papers, South Caroliniana Library.

[23] Pinckney's letter ran through six issues of the Charleston *Mercury,* Aug. 19, 20, 22-25, 1836. The *Courier* published only excerpts, over a two-week period. See also D. E. Huger to Col. James Chesnut, Aug. 20, 1836, Williams-Chesnut-Manning Papers.

[24] Petigru to Legaré, Sept. 6, 1836, Carson, *Petigru,* 184-185.

[25] Charleston *Mercury,* Sept. 22, 24, 27, Oct. 1, 1836. See also Poinsett's letters to J. B. Campbell through the summer and fall of 1836, *South Carolina Historical and Genealogical Magazine,* XLII (October 1941), 135-151. Poinsett pronounced Calhoun politically dead, but was remarkably hesitant about contesting the "dead" man's leadership.

[26] Charleston *Mercury,* Oct. 7, 8, 11-15, 1836.

[27] Petigru to Mrs. R. F. W. Allston, Oct. 18, 1836, Allston Papers; to Mrs. Jane Petigru North, Dec. 9, 1836, Carson, *Petigru,* 187.

[28] See, *e. g.,* James Simmons to Willie P. Mangum, Mar. 9, 1836, Mangum Papers; ——to Duff Green [1836], Duff Green Papers.

[29] Scott, *Memoir of White,* 355-356; Jackson to A. J. Donelson, Oct. 2, 1836, Jackson's *Correspondence,* V, 427.

[30] Calhoun to Hammond, Feb. 18, 1837, *Correspondence,* 367-369.

[31] Jackson to Kendall, Nov. 24, 1836, Jackson's *Correspondence,* V, 438-439.

[32] Richardson, *Messages and Papers of the Presidents,* 1455-1479.

[33] *Register of Debates,* 24th, 2d, 4-5.

[34] *Ibid.,* 416-417.

[35] Nathan Sargent, *Public Men and Events,* I, 335, describes the scene, but probably not at first hand. The Calhoun he describes, at least, belongs to the middle 1840's rather than to 1837.

[36] *Register of Debates,* 24th, 2d, 417-418. This brief speech does not appear in

the collected *Works,* but was regarded by contemporaries as a masterpiece. It is surprising that it was not included, since Crallé, then editor of the pro-Calhoun *Telegraph,* and later editor of Calhoun's *Works,* probably heard it delivered.

[37] Benton, *View,* I, 727.

[38] *Ibid.; Register of Debates,* 24th, 2d, 428-504; Charleston *Mercury,* Jan. 23, 1837; Charleston *Courier,* Jan. 23, 1837; Sargent, *Public Men and Events,* I, 343; Wise to his wife, Jan. 17, 1837, Barton H. Wise, *Life of Henry A. Wise,* 69-70; Calhoun to Hammond, Feb. 18, 1837, *Correspondence,* 368; Clay to R. P. Letcher, Jan. 17, 1837, Mrs. Chapman Coleman, *Life of John J. Crittenden,* I, 105.

[39] Jackson to Benton, Jan. 16, 1837, Jackson's *Correspondence,* V, 450-451; Sargent, *loc. cit.; Niles,* LI, 353.

[40] Jackson to Blair, January 1837, Jackson's *Correspondence,* V, 443-445; to Donelson, Jan. 11, 1837, *ibid.,* 449-450.

[41] *Register of Debates,* 24th, 2d, 21-150 *passim,* 172-204, 327-376, 562-563, 577-644 *passim,* 778, 2090.

[42] Clay to Noah Noble, Mar. 4, 1837, *Indiana Magazine of History,* XXII (June 1926), 212.

[43] *Register of Debates,* 24th, 2d, 79-89.

[44] *Ibid.,* 150-167, 376-377; *United States' Telegraph,* Jan. 4, 16, Feb. 2, 1837.

[45] *Register of Debates,* 24th, 2d, 1347.

[46] *Ibid.,* 569-577, 872-893, 902-981. Also Calhoun, *Works,* III, 43-59. Cf. Wiltse, *Calhoun, Nationalist,* 368-372.

[47] Webster to Everett, Jan. 31, 1837, Webster's *Writings,* XVIII, 25; Calhoun to J. R. Matthews, Feb. 12, 1837, Calhoun Papers, Library of Congress.

[48] *Register of Debates,* 24th, 2d, 992-1008, 1019-1021, 1022-1034.

[49] *Ibid.,* 703.

[50] *Ibid.,* 729-736.

[51] *Ibid.,* 617, 698-701, 738-739, 1656-1658; Robert Strange to Willie P. Mangum, Feb. 8, 1837, Mangum Papers.

[52] *Register of Debates,* 24th, 2d, 617-618.

[53] *Ibid.,* 753-755. The *Congressional Globe,* issued by Blair, had begun publication with the second session of the Twenty-third Congress, December 1834. It appeared weekly in contrast to the *Register of Debates,* compiled by Gales and Seaton from the daily reports in the *National Intelligencer,* but published only at the end of each session. The *Register* passed out of existence with the Twenty-fourth Congress. The incident here discussed offers an instructive illustration in reporting techniques. Calhoun's remarks are given in full in the Appendix to the *Congressional Globe,* 24th, 2d, 315, in language identical with that used in the *Register* and quoted in the text. The appendix, however, was not issued until some time after the weekly summary. The passage in question, in the weekly version, was reduced to a single sentence: "Was it not notorious that the President of the United States himself had been connected with the purchase of public lands?" (p. 153). It was this sentence that so aroused Jackson's wrath, which was no doubt aggravated by Blair's editorial comments in the Washington *Globe* for Feb. 6, 1836. "Mr. Calhoun," wrote Jackson's editor, "yesterday charged, on the floor of the Senate, that several members of the Cabinet, and a nephew of the President, had borrowed money out of the deposite banks to invest in land speculations, and looked to the land bill as a means of enabling them to profit by their purchases. He made his charge, he said, on rumor. This is the foundation upon which the assertions of this worthy Senator generally rest. . . ."

[54] *Register of Debates,* 24th, 2d, 755-760; Clay to Brooke, Feb. 10, 1837, Clay's *Works,* V, 410; Calhoun to J. R. Matthews, Feb. 12, 1837, Calhoun Papers, Library of Congress; to Hammond Feb. 18, 1837, *Correspondence,* 368; Hone, *Diary,* 242-243.

[55] *Register of Debates,* 24th, 2d, 2143, and Appendix, 189-225; Jackson to Donelson, Jan. 24, 1837, Jackson's *Correspondence,* V, 451-452; to Wise, Jan. 26, 1837, *ibid.,* 452-455; Eriksson, "The Federal Civil Service under President Jackson," *Mississippi Valley Historical Review,* XIII (March 1927), 359.

CHAPTER XXII

[1] Calhoun to Maxcy, Nov. 20, 1834, Maxcy Papers. Also to Duff Green, Sept. 20, Nov. 16, 1834, *Correspondence,* 342.

[2] Harriet Martineau, *Retrospect of Western Travel,* I, 144 ff.

[3] Mrs. Smith, 365-368.

[4] Martineau, *op. cit.,* I, 147-149.

[5] There is a great deal of inference in this, but reasonably well founded. The notice of their arrival in Norfolk, *National Intelligencer,* Mar. 12, 1835, mentions only the men of the party, but the women would hardly have been left behind. For Margaret Green's presence I rely on the fact that she was with Anna and Maria Simkins at Edgefield the following month, and would certainly not have been allowed to travel from Washington by herself. She must have been attractive because she was May Queen in Washington the following year, an honor not generally bestowed on plain girls. Her exuberance is amply attested by the only letter of hers that I have seen.

[6] *National Intelligencer,* Mar. 12, 1835.

[7] Calhoun to James Edward Calhoun, Apr. 26, 1835, Calhoun Papers, Clemson College.

[8] Calhoun to F. W. Pickens, July 17, 1835, Calhoun Papers, South Caroliniana Library.

[9] *National Intelligencer,* May 10, 1836; Pendleton *Messenger,* May 27, 1836.

[10] R. F. W. Allston to Mrs. Allston, May 8, 1836, Allston Papers.

[11] Calhoun to Pickens, July 17, 1836, Calhoun Papers, South Caroliniana Library; to James Edward Calhoun, May 29, 1837, Calhoun Papers, Clemson College; Duff Green to Andrew P. Calhoun, Jan. 22, 1838, Calhoun Papers, South Caroliniana Library.

[12] Calhoun to James Edward Calhoun, May 21, 1835, Calhoun Papers, Clemson College.

[13] Calhoun to James Edward Calhoun, Aug. 1, 1835, *ibid.*

[14] Calhoun to James Edward Calhoun, Sept. 30, 1835, *ibid.*

[15] Pendleton *Messenger,* Apr. 29, 1836.

[16] Calhoun to James Edward Calhoun, Sept. 19, 1836, *Correspondence,* 363; to James Edward Calhoun, Oct. 2, 1836, Calhoun Papers, Clemson College. The latter is published in part in the *Correspondence,* 362, where it is misdated Sept. 2.

[17] Wiltse, *Calhoun, Nationalist,* 268.

[18] Calhoun to James Edward Calhoun, May 30, July 22, Dec. 2, 1837, Calhoun Papers, Clemson College.

[19] Anna Calhoun to James Edward Calhoun, Feb. 26, 1836; Jan. 1, [1837], Calhoun Papers, South Caroliniana Library.

[20] F. W. Pickens to J. H. Hammond, Feb. 8, 1839, Hammond Papers.

[21] Calhoun to James Edward Calhoun, Apr. 21, 1838, *Correspondence,* 395-396.

[22] See Wiltse, *Calhoun, Nationalist,* 49-50, 213. When William Calhoun's wife died suddenly early in 1836, McDuffie wrote that he had "lost the most sincere & disinterested friend I had in the world, & one to whom I am bound by every tie of gratitude & affection. . . ." McDuffie to [Armistead Burt], [March 1836], McDuffie Papers, Duke University.

[23] Calhoun to A. Burt, Jan. 24, 1838, *Correspondence,* 390.

[24] Calhoun to A. Burt, May 18, 1838, Calhoun Papers, Duke University.

[25] Calhoun to James Edward Calhoun, May 23, 1838, Calhoun Papers, Clemson College. Cf. to Armistead Burt, May 27, 1838, Calhoun Papers, Duke University.

[26] Calhoun to Burt, July 2, 1838, Calhoun Papers, Duke University; to Anna Calhoun, Mar. 18, 1839, Calhoun Papers, Clemson College.

[27] Mary Bates, *Private Life of Calhoun,* 10-11.

[28] Calhoun to Anna Calhoun, Feb. 7, 24, June 9, 1838, Calhoun Papers, Clemson College. The first two letters are published in part in the *Correspondence,* 392, 393.

[29] Calhoun to Poinsett, Mar. 9, 1837, *Correspondence,* 369.

[30] Calhoun to Anna Calhoun, Dec. 24, 1837, Calhoun Papers, Clemson College, published in part in *Correspondence,* 387; Anna Calhoun to Patrick Calhoun, May 30, 1838, Calhoun Papers, South Caroliniana Library.

[31] J. E. Boisseau to Calhoun, Apr. 23, 1838, Calhoun Papers, Clemson College.

[32] Calhoun to James Edward Calhoun, Aug. 17, 1836, *ibid.;* to Francis W. Pickens, Aug. 17, 1836, Calhoun Papers, South Caroliniana Library.

[33] Anna Maria Calhoun to James Edward Calhoun, Jan. 1, [1837], Calhoun Papers, South Caroliniana Library.

[34] Calhoun to Anna Maria Calhoun, Dec. 16, 1837, Calhoun Papers, Clemson College.

[35] *Ibid.;* Calhoun to Anna Calhoun, Dec. 24, 1837, *Correspondence,* 387; Jan. 1, 25, 1838, Calhoun Papers, Clemson College (the letter of Jan. 25 is published in part in the *Correspondence,* 390-391); *Congressional Directory,* 25th Cong., 2d sess.

[36] Calhoun to Anna Maria Calhoun, Dec. 24, 1837, *Correspondence,* 387; Jan. 1, 1838, Calhoun Papers, Clemson College.

[37] B. Alvord to M. C. M. Hammond, May 1838, Hammond Papers; Calhoun to James Edward Calhoun, Apr. 21, 1838, *Correspondence,* 395-396, indicates that Mrs. Calhoun was at Millwood then.

[38] A. G. Holmes and G. R. Sherrill, *Thomas G. Clemson,* 11-14; T. G. Clemson, "Statement of the Case," Nov. 16, 1840, Clemson Papers; Clemson to Anna Maria Calhoun, July-August 1838, *ibid.* It was quite probably Calhoun himself who introduced the young couple. At least Senator Linn, who was Clemson's primary contact with Washington, was a friend and connection by marriage of Calhoun's. What the relationship was I have been unable to discover, but there are a number of letters in the Clemson College collection from Mrs. Linn to Calhoun, written in the 1840's after her husband's death, in which she addresses him as "Dear Cousin."

[39] Pendleton *Messenger,* Nov. 16, 1838.

[40] Calhoun to Duff Green, Oct. 11, 1838, *Correspondence,* 405-406. It is of course possible that Cornelia was not at the wedding, but remained in Baltimore, despite the absence of the Greens. She was there in the winter of 1838-1839,

which would have meant the fatiguing return trip had been made in a month or less.

[41] Reference in Calhoun to Anna Calhoun Clemson, Mar. 18, 1839, Calhoun Papers, Clemson College.

[42] Calhoun to James Edward Calhoun, Nov. 27, 1838, *ibid.*

[43] Calhoun to Francis W. Pickens, July 17, 1835, South Caroliniana Library.

[44] Calhoun to J. R. Matthews, Nov. 26, 1837, Calhoun Papers, Library of Congress; to Burt, Nov. 29, 1837, Calhoun Papers, Duke University.

[45] Calhoun to James Edward Calhoun, Jan. 8, 1838, *Correspondence,* 388.

[46] Pendleton *Messenger,* Oct. 11, 1839.

[47] Calhoun to James Edward Calhoun, Mar. 22, May 12, Dec. 30, 1837; Apr. 24, 1838; Calhoun Papers, Clemson College. The letter of May 12, 1837, is published in part in the *Correspondence,* 370.

[48] Calhoun to James Edward Calhoun, Mar. 27, 1838, Calhoun Papers, Clemson College.

[49] Calhoun to James Edward Calhoun, Oct. 21, 1839, *ibid.*

[50] The various deeds, dated Sept. 7 and 9, 1832, Nov. 20, 1832, and June 25, 1833, are in the Clemson Papers.

[51] One deed for a quarter interest in lot no. 817, 12th District, 1st Section, Lumpkin County, Georgia, is dated May 7, 1835, and gives the purchase price as $100. A second quarter interest in the same lot was acquired at a sheriff's sale on Dec. 1, 1835, for $75; and a third quarter interest was bid in for $12 at a similar sale, Sept. 6, 1836. Clemson Papers.

[52] Calhoun to James Edward Calhoun, Sept. 23, 1835, Calhoun Papers, Clemson College. A few lines only of this letter are included in *Correspondence,* 346. Also Calhoun to Col. F. Carter, Nov. 26 [?], 1835, *Correspondence,* 355.

[53] G. W. Featherstonhaugh, *Canoe Voyage up the Minnay Sotor,* II, 247-258, 267-269; Calhoun to James Edward Calhoun, July 7, 22, 1837, Calhoun Papers, Clemson College.

[54] Calhoun to Andrew P. Calhoun, Oct. 15, 1848, Calhoun Papers, Duke University.

[55] Calhoun to James Edward Calhoun, May 30, July 22, Dec. 2, 1837, Calhoun Papers, Clemson College.

[56] Duff Green to Andrew P. Calhoun, Jan. 22, 1838, Calhoun Papers, South Caroliniana Library; Calhoun to A. P. Calhoun, Apr. 5, 1838, *Correspondence,* 393-394.

[57] Calhoun to James E. Calhoun, Oct. 26, 1838, Calhoun Papers, Clemson College.

[58] Calhoun to Anna Calhoun Clemson, Jan. 17, 20, Mar. 18, 1839, *ibid.*

[59] Calhoun to Clemson, Apr. 30, 1839, *Correspondence,* 425-426.

[60] See statement of accounts between Clemson and the two Calhouns, Oct. 1, 1843, Clemson Papers.

[61] B. Elmore to Patrick Calhoun, Feb. 27 [Mar. 5], 1839, Calhoun Papers, South Caroliniana Library.

[62] Calhoun to Anna Calhoun Clemson, Mar. 18, 1839, Calhoun Papers, Clemson College.

[63] Calhoun to Anna Calhoun Clemson, Apr. 6, 1839, *ibid.;* to James Edward Calhoun, Apr. 14, 1839, *ibid.*

[64] Calhoun to Anna Calhoun Clemson, May 4, 1839, *ibid.*

[65] Calhoun to James Edward Calhoun, Aug. 27, Sept. 1, 1839, *ibid.*

[66] Calhoun to James Edward Calhoun, Nov. 17, 1839 (two letters), *ibid.;* Holmes and Sherrill, *Clemson*, 17.

CHAPTER XXIII

[1] Wiltse, *Calhoun, Nationalist,* 133-134, 165; *House Report* 462, 15th Cong., 2d sess.

[2] S. M. Derrick, *Centennial History of South Carolina Railroad,* 129-130. There is a copy of Col. Long's map, dated 1832, in the Map Division of the Library of Congress.

[3] *Rail Road from the Banks of the Ohio River to the Tide Waters of the Carolinas and Georgia* (Cincinnati, 1835).

[4] *Report of the Special Committee of the Charleston Chamber of Commerce, on the contemplated Rail-Road from Charleston, in South Carolina, to Newport or Covington, opposite Cincinnati, in Ohio* (Charleston, 1835).

[5] Derrick, *South Carolina Railroad,* 132-133; Jervey, *Hayne,* 385; Freeman Cleaves, *Old Tippecanoe: William Henry Harrison and His Time,* 298.

[6] Calhoun to William C. Dawson, Nov. 24, 1835, *Correspondence,* 349-351.

[7] Calhoun to J. S. Williams, July 1835, Charleston *Mercury,* Nov. 11, 1835.

[8] Calhoun to William C. Dawson, Nov. 24, 1835, *Correspondence,* 349-351; to A. S. Clayton, Nov. 24, 1835, *ibid.,* 352; to Col. F. Carter, Nov. 26 [?], 1835, *ibid.,* 353-356. Also Calhoun to J. S. Williams, July 1835, Charleston *Mercury,* Nov. 11, 1835. The scheme had been in Calhoun's mind at least since March 1831. See Hammond's Memorandum of Mar. 18, 1831, *Am. Hist. Rev.,* VI (July 1901), 741-745.

[9] Calhoun to Williams, *loc. cit.* The quotation is from Calhoun to Dawson, *loc. cit.*

[10] Calhoun to Williams, Oct. 17, 1835, *Correspondence,* 346-347.

[11] Calhoun to James Edward Calhoun, Oct. 7, 1835, Calhoun Papers, Clemson College.

[12] Derrick, *South Carolina Railroad,* 138-139, 145-147.

[13] *Ibid.,* 147-148.

[14] *Ibid.,* 138-139.

[15] *National Intelligencer,* July 22, 1836; *Niles,* LI, 109-111; Derrick, *South Carolina Railroad,* 148-149.

[16] "Mr. Calhoun is looked for very anxiously—Some say he will be here—and others apprehend that the late sitting of Congress will detain him. Should he arrive in time—he will be elected President of the convention." Thomas F. Drayton to Virgil Maxcy, June 26, 1836, Maxcy Papers.

[17] *Niles,* LI, 109-111. See also *Report of the Commissioners appointed by the legislature of South Carolina, to cause examinations, surveys and estimates to be made for a rail road between Charleston and Cincinnati* (Columbia, 1836); Derrick, *South Carolina Railroad,* 148-151; Jervey, *Hayne,* 400-403; Ulrich B. Phillips, *Transportation in the Eastern Cotton Belt,* 182-184.

[18] Quoted in Phillips, *op. cit.,* 184.

[19] Calhoun to the Editor of the Pendleton *Messenger,* Sept. 22, 1836, *Niles,* LI, 88-89.

[20] Jervey, *Hayne,* 406. The fragment Jervey quotes from Gadsden's letter to Hayne is equivocal, but seems to imply that the withdrawal was not on altogether amicable terms.

[21] Calhoun to James Edward Calhoun, August 1836, Aug. 23, 1836, Calhoun Papers, Clemson College; Sept. 19, 1836, *Correspondence,* 363.

[22] Calhoun to the Editor of the Pendleton *Messenger,* Sept. 22, 1836, *Niles,* LI, 88-89.

[23] Calhoun to James Edward Calhoun, Sept. 2 [Oct. 2], Sept. 19, 1836, *Correspondence,* 362-363; to —— [in Knoxville], Sept. 26, 1836, Calhoun Papers, Duke University; to Patrick Noble, Nov. 8, 1832 [1836], *Correspondence,* 321-322; to James Edward Calhoun, Nov. 11, 1836, *ibid.,* 364-365.

[24] Hayne to Col. F. K. Huger and others, Oct. 17, 1836, Charleston *Courier,* Oct. 19, 1836.

[25] Pendleton *Messenger,* Oct. 21, 1836.

[26] A. H. Brisbane to the citizens of Charleston, Sept. 28, 1836, Charleston *Courier,* Oct. 20, 1836.

[27] Jervey, *Hayne,* 407-409.

[28] J. Van Deusen, *Economic Bases of Disunion in South Carolina,* 230.

[29] Calhoun to Pickens, Nov. 16, 1836, Calhoun Papers, South Caroliniana Library; to James Edward Calhoun, Dec. 9, 1836, *Correspondence,* 365-367. There is some evidence that at this same time Calhoun had actually been offered the presidency of the Baltimore and Ohio Railroad, which Joseph W. Patterson was then filling *per interim* and to which Louis McLane was elected in December 1836. Duff Green was at Pendleton early in November 1836, but had not yet seen Calhoun, who was in Georgia, when he wrote to Crallé on Nov. 4: "Mr. Calhoun is from all that I can learn much disposed to quit the Senate, and if so it seems to me that he must identify himself with the Balt & Ohio Rail road or the L[ouisville] Cincinnati & Charleston Railroad. The first I understand is offered to him & urged upon him. I should prefer the first for some reasons especially if he leaves the Senate." Green Papers. No confirmation of this story has been found, either in the records of the B & O Railroad or elsewhere. Cf. Edward Hungerford, *Story of the Baltimore & Ohio Railroad, 1827-1927,* I, 186-190. It was not, however, merely one of Green's own enthusiasms, because he was much opposed to Calhoun's leaving the Senate for any reason.

[30] Charleston *Courier,* Dec. 1, 1836; Jervey, *Hayne,* 410-412.

[31] Jervey, *Hayne,* 415-416.

[32] Calhoun to James Edward Calhoun, Dec. 9, 1836, *Correspondence,* 365.

[33] *Southern Patriot,* Oct. 4, 1836; Poinsett to J. B. Campbell, Dec. 9, 1836, *South Carolina Historical and Genealogical Magazine,* XLII (October 1941), 151-153.

[34] Charleston *Courier,* Oct. 28, 1837; Jervey, *Hayne,* 443-444.

[35] Calhoun to James Edward Calhoun, Dec. 9, 1836, *Correspondence,* 365-366; to J. R. Matthews, Jan. 7, 1837, Calhoun Papers, Library of Congress.

[36] Calhoun to James Edward Calhoun, July 7, 1837, Calhoun Papers, Clemson College; Sept. 7, 1837, *Correspondence,* 378.

[37] Jervey, *Hayne,* 418-419; Derrick, *South Carolina Railroad,* 159-160.

[38] Charleston *Courier,* Sept. 30, 1837.

[39] Calhoun to James Edward Calhoun, Oct. 27, 1837, *Correspondence,* 381-382.

[40] Charleston *Courier,* Oct. 28, 1837; Jervey, *Hayne,* 443-445.

[41] Calhoun to James Edward Calhoun, Oct. 27, Dec. 10, 1837, *Correspondence,* 381-382, 385; to J. R. Matthews, Nov. 26, 1837, Calhoun Papers, Library of Congress; to James Edward Calhoun, Dec. 2, 1837, Calhoun Papers, Clemson College.

[42] Derrick, *South Carolina Railroad,* 163-164.

[43] Calhoun to James Edward Calhoun, Dec. 2, 1837, Calhoun Papers, Clemson College; Dec. 10, 1837, *Correspondence,* 385.

[44] *Niles,* LV, 40.

[45] Clay to Francis Brooke, Aug. 28, 1838, Clay's *Works,* V, 428.

[46] Calhoun to Hayne, Oct. 28, 1838, *Correspondence,* 411-412.

[47] Hayne to Calhoun, Nov. 1, 1838, Calhoun Papers, Clemson College. Quoted in Jervey, *Hayne,* 473-479.

[48] Calhoun to Hayne, Nov. 17, 1838, *Correspondence,* 412-416.

[49] Calhoun to F. H. Elmore, Oct. 7, 1839, Calhoun Papers, South Caroliniana Library.

[50] Derrick, *South Carolina Railroad,* 168.

[51] Calhoun to Sidney Breese, July 27, 1839, *Correspondence,* 430-431.

[52] Jervey, *Hayne,* 505 ff.; Derrick, *South Carolina Railroad,* 185-186.

[53] Calhoun to James Edward Calhoun, Oct. 5, 1839, *Correspondence,* 431.

[54] *Ibid.;* Calhoun to Elmore, Oct. 7, 1839, Calhoun Papers, South Caroliniana Library.

[55] Jervey, *Hayne,* 525 ff.; Derrick, *South Carolina Railroad,* 170-171.

[56] Calhoun to Andrew P. Calhoun, Sept. 25, 1840, *Correspondence,* 464; Derrick, *South Carolina Railroad,* 171-175.

CHAPTER XXIV

[1] *Niles,* LII, 18.

[2] Jackson to N. P. Trist, Mar. 2, 1837, Jackson's *Correspondence,* V, 462-463.

[3] That such would probably be his course was well understood in Washington at least a month before the inauguration. See, *e.g.,* Richard E. Parker to Van Buren, Feb. 7, 1837, Van Buren Papers; F. W. Pickens to J. H. Hammond, Feb. 17, 1837, Hammond Papers.

[4] *Niles,* LII, 17; *National Intelligencer,* July 4, 1837.

[5] Richardson, *Messages and Papers of the Presidents,* 1530-1537.

[6] *Reformer,* Mar. 3, 6, 7, Apr. 12, 1837. The paper first appeared on Feb. 22. Also Pendleton *Messenger,* Mar. 9, 1837. The Charleston *Mercury* missed its cue, and praised the slavery references in the inaugural; Mar. 9, 1837.

[7] Calhoun to James Edward Calhoun, Mar. 22, 1837, *Correspondence,* 370.

[8] Hone, *Diary,* 241-242, 248-249 ff., 253; *Niles,* LII, 209 ff.; J. Van Deusen, *Economic Bases of Disunion in South Carolina,* 155-156.

[9] Washington *Globe,* March-May 1837, especially Apr. 7, 1837.

[10] *National Intelligencer,* May 26, 1837, and generally from March on; Joseph Story to John McLean, May 10, 1837, McLean Papers; Henry Tolland to William C. Rives, May 13, 1837, Rives Papers.

[11] Calhoun to James Edward Calhoun, May 12, 1837, *Correspondence,* 370; Mahlon Dickerson to William C. Rives, May 2, 1837, Rives Papers. Also James Alexander to Rives, June 21, 1837, *ibid.*

[12] Hone, *Diary,* 256-260; *National Intelligencer,* May 12, 1837; Washington *Globe,* May 12, 1837; Charleston *Mercury,* May 16, 17, 18, 1837.

[13] Richardson, *Messages and Papers of the Presidents,* 1538-1539.

[14] Treasury Orders of May 12, 15, 1837, *Niles,* LII, 177-178.

[15] W. B. Seabrook to Crallé, Jan. 15, 1837, Crallé Papers, Clemson College; Thomas Cooper to Biddle, May 14, 1837, *Biddle Correspondence,* 278-280; James

Hamilton, Jr., to Van Buren, June 24, 1837, Van Buren Papers; Jackson to Blair, July 9, 1837, Jackson's *Correspondence,* V, 495-497; Butler to Hammond, May 30, 1837, Hammond Papers; Wallace, *History of South Carolina,* II, 472-473; U. B. Phillips, "The Southern Whigs, 1834-1854," *Essays in American History Dedicated to Frederick Jackson Turner,* 203-216.

[16] Charles P. Green to Willie P. Mangum, Apr. 26, 1837, Mangum Papers; Willis Hall to Duff Green, July 1837, Calhoun Papers, Clemson College; Calhoun to Duff Green, June 26, July 27, 1837, *Correspondence,* 372-374, 374-377.

[17] *Niles,* LII, 321. See also Calhoun to Green, cited in n. 16.

[18] William M. Gouge, *An Inquiry into the Expediency of Dispensing with Bank Agency and Bank Paper in Fiscal Concerns of the United States* (Philadelphia, 1837).

[19] Gouge to Van Buren, June 21, 1837, Van Buren Papers; Wright to Van Buren, June 22, 1837, *ibid.;* Taney to Van Buren, July 20, 1837, *ibid.;* Cambreleng to Van Buren, July 20, 1837, *ibid.;* John Brockenbrough to W. C. Rives, Aug. 5, 1837, *ibid.;* John Brockenbrough to Van Buren, Aug. 7, 1837, *ibid.* Taney's letter is also in *Maryland Historical Magazine,* VIII (December 1913), 318-326. See also Taney to Jackson, July 3, 1837, Jackson's *Correspondence,* V, 491-495.

[20] *Reformer,* July 12, 1837. After mid-May 1837 this paper appeared in conjunction with the *Merchant,* edited by Duff Green in Baltimore, but Crallé kept his Washington headquarters and date line.

[21] Washington *Globe,* especially Aug. 14, 15, 16, 1837; *Madisonian,* Aug. 26, 1837. The *National Intelligencer* had forecast on August 12 that Van Buren would adopt the plan, based on still earlier intimations in the Richmond *Enquirer.*

[22] One of the cruder tactics of the opposition was to charge, by quoting alleged conversations with unnamed persons and fragments of genuine conversations with identified persons, that Calhoun had opposed the Independent Treasury until he reached Washington, the implication being that he had then made a deal. In denying the conversations in question, Calhoun states that McDuffie knew his views before he left Fort Hill. This is borne out by a reference in his letter to James Edward Calhoun, Oct. 27, 1837, *Correspondence,* 382. Speaking specifically of the subtreasury scheme, he says that "McDuffie . . . was perfectly sound when I saw him at my house, a short time before I set out for Washington. . . ." Calhoun must, presumably, have made up his own mind before he could determine whether McDuffie was in agreement with him. For the controversy, see *Niles,* LIII, 282-283. McDuffie's "soundness" was undoubtedly induced by Calhoun's own arguments. At least the former Governor had grave doubts as late as early August. See McDuffie to Waddy Thompson, July 5, Aug. 4, 1837, McDuffie Papers, South Caroliniana Library.

[23] *Congressional Globe,* 25th, 1st, 1-4.

[24] *Ibid.,* 11-16, *passim;* Washington *Globe,* Sept. 7, 8, 1837; *National Intelligencer,* Sept. 8, 1837; *Madisonian,* Sept. 9, 1837; Blair to Jackson, Sept. 9, 1837, Jackson's *Correspondence,* V, 509-510.

[25] *Cong. Globe,* 25th, 1st, 16, 18.

[26] Richardson, *Messages and Papers of the Presidents,* 1541-1563.

[27] Washington *Globe,* Sept. 5, 1837; *National Intelligencer,* Sept. 7, 1837; *Madisonian,* Sept. 6, 1837; Hone, *Diary,* 281-282.

[28] Calhoun to James Edward Calhoun, Sept. 7, 1837, *Correspondence,* 377-378.

[29] Calhoun to Anna Maria Calhoun, Sept. 8, 1837, *ibid.,* 378-379.

[30] *Reformer,* Sept. 14, 1837. See also Charleston *Courier,* Sept. 15, 1837, whose

very able Washington correspondent (Elias Kingman) reports the rumor as of Sept. 11; and *Niles,* LIII, 33.

[31] *Cong. Globe,* 25th, 1st, 17, 22-23, 26-27.

[32] *Ibid.,* 28.

[33] *Ibid.,* 28-30, 32.

[34] *Ibid.,* 35-36.

[35] Calhoun to Anna Maria Calhoun, Sept. 30, 1837, *Correspondence,* 379-381.

[36] *Cong. Globe,* 25th, 1st, 36-37, and Appendix, 32-37; *Works,* III, 60-92. Both in the appendix to the *Globe* and in the *Works* the speech is misdated September 19. See also Charleston *Mercury,* Sept. 23, 30, 1837; Baltimore *Merchant,* Sept. 27, 1837; Charleston *Courier,* Oct. 2, 1837.

[37] *Cong. Globe,* 25th, 1st, 37.

[38] *Ibid.,* 44.

[39] Calhoun to J. R. Matthews, Sept. 27, 1837, Calhoun Papers, Library of Congress; *Cong. Globe,* 25th, 1st, 74; *Works,* III, 101.

[40] *Cong. Globe,* 25th, 1st, 96, 100.

[41] *Ibid.,* 122; Adams, *Diary,* IX, 398-399.

[42] *Cong. Globe,* 25th, 1st, 141.

[43] *Ibid.,* 147-148.

[44] Carson, *Petigru,* 190-191.

[45] Preston to Willie P. Mangum, Oct. 4, 1837, Mangum Papers. Cf. J. J. Crittenden to Mangum, Oct. 11, 1837, *ibid.*

[46] See, *e. g.,* Crittenden to Mangum, *loc. cit.* Adams referred caustically to "Calhoun's bargain and sale of himself to Van Buren," *Diary,* IX, 398. Hone wrote bitterly that Calhoun, whom he had hitherto liked, "would support the devil to lessen the political influence of New York . . . and is willing to support [Van Buren's] suicidal measures to accomplish his object," *Diary,* 282-283. The story still persisted ten years later, long after the subtreasury had demonstrated in successful operation that the fears of the Whigs were groundless, that Calhoun had justified the specie clause "in order to cripple the North." See Isaiah Townsend to Calhoun, Aug. 10, 1846, Calhoun Papers, Clemson College.

[47] Washington *Globe,* Sept. 18, 22, 1837, and following issues. If Blair's personal opinion was that revealed in his letter of October 1 to Jackson, Jackson's *Correspondence,* V, 515, it offers presumptive evidence that the turnabout was ordered by Van Buren. See also the *Madisonian,* Sept. 28, 1837; and the Charleston *Mercury,* Oct. 11, 1837.

[48] J. P. King, Georgia Senator, to a friend, Oct. 17, 1837, *Niles,* LIII, 229; Benton, *View,* II, 40.

[49] *Democratic Review,* I (October 1837), 1-15.

[50] The Unionists disowned their one-time leader, Poinsett, for joining Van Buren's Cabinet, and Petigru publicly snubbed the War Secretary in Charleston. See Petigru to his sister, July 10, 1837, Carson, *Petigru,* 189.

[51] P. M. Butler to Hammond, Dec. 11, 27, 1837, Hammond Papers; McDuffie to Calhoun, Oct. 29, 1837, C. S. Boucher and R. P. Brooks, eds., *Correspondence Addressed to Calhoun,* 155-158; Calhoun to J. R. Matthews, Nov. 26, 1837, Calhoun Papers, Library of Congress; White, *Rhett,* 34-37; Wallace, *History of South Carolina,* II, 474.

[52] Calhoun to Duff Green, Oct. 27, 1837, *Correspondence,* 383-384.

[53] Charleston *Mercury,* Sept. 6, 1837; Cheves to a Gentleman in Mississippi, Oct. 30, 1837, *Niles,* LIII, 215-217; Poinsett to J. B. Campbell, Oct. 17, 1837,

South Carolina Historical and Genealogical Magazine, XLII (October 1941), 165.

[54] Calhoun to Burt, Oct. 15, 1837, Calhoun Papers, Duke University; to Patrick Noble, Oct. 30, 1837, private collection of Sarah Noble Carnes, made available by Alice Noble Waring.

[55] Calhoun to J. Bauskett and others, Nov. 3, 1837, *Niles,* LIII, 217-218. Many other State Rights leaders had already taken the same position for the same reasons, including Tazewell, Gordon and Hunter in Virginia, and Troup in Georgia. See Tyler, *Times of the Tylers,* I, 584; and R. M. T. Hunter to T. W. Gilmer, Sept. 18, 1837, *William and Mary Quarterly,* XXI (July 1912), 79-81.

[56] Calhoun to James Edward Calhoun, Dec. 10, 1837, *Correspondence,* 385; to Anna Maria Calhoun, Dec. 10, 1837, Calhoun Papers, Clemson College; F. H. Elmore to Hammond, Dec. 11, 1837, Hammond Papers; Petigru to his sister, Dec. 20, 1837, Carson, *Petigru,* 193; *Niles,* LIII, 257.

CHAPTER XXV

[1] Adams, *Diary,* IX, 440-441; Hone, *Diary,* 292; Charleston *Mercury,* Dec. 9, 1838.

[2] William H. Haywood to Van Buren, Dec. 16, 1837, *North Carolina Historical Review,* XV (January 1938), 75-78; Preston to Tyler, Dec. 30, 1837, Tyler, *Times of the Tylers,* I, 585-587; Calhoun to Armistead Burt, Jan. 24, 1838, *Correspondence,* 389-390; Pickens to Hammond, Feb. 9, 1838, Hammond Papers; *Cong. Globe,* 25th, 2d, 15, 33; Linda Rhea, *Hugh Swinton Legaré, a Charleston Intellectual,* 162.

[3] Pickens to Hammond, Dec. 16, 1837, Hammond Papers; Calhoun to Anna Maria Calhoun, Dec. 24, 1837, Calhoun Papers, Clemson College (published in part in *Correspondence,* 387).

[4] Calhoun to Micah Sterling, Dec. 26, 1837, Calhoun Papers, South Caroliniana Library; also Feb. 26, 1838, *ibid.*

[5] Abel P. Upshur to R. K. Crallé, Jan. 23, 1838, Crallé Papers, Clemson College.

[6] Calhoun to A. S. Clayton and others, Aug. 5, 1836, *Niles,* L, 432.

[7] Nathaniel Beverly Tucker, who had urged Calhoun to take South Carolina out of the Union when the Force Bill was passed, renewed the suggestion in 1835, but Calhoun ignored the letter, or did not receive it. "That he disapproved its suggestions . . . I know," Tucker wrote later to Hammond. "But I am very desirous to know whether it reached him. I hope it did. For I would have him pass his judgment on the same subject five years hence. . . ." Tucker to Hammond, Mar. 15, 1836, Hammond Papers. Also Tucker to Hammond, Feb. 17, 18, 1836, *ibid.*

[8] *Niles,* LI, 225; *Register of Debates,* 24th, 2d, 1010-1013; Justin H. Smith, *Annexation of Texas,* 56-59, 63.

[9] Adams, *Diary,* V, 10; Wiltse, *Calhoun, Nationalist,* 196.

[10] *Register of Debates,* 24th, 2d, 566, 706-723.

[11] Calhoun to Hammond, Feb. 18, 1837, Hammond Papers.

[12] Carl Russell Fish, *Rise of the Common Man,* 299-300.

[13] See Gilbert H. Barnes, "Elijah Parrish Lovejoy," *Dictionary of American Biography.*

[14] Oran Follett to Weed, Dec. 4, 1837, Historical and Philosophical Society of Ohio, *Quarterly Publications,* XI, 11-15.

[15] *Cong. Globe,* 25th, 2d, 41; Rhett, "Address to the People of Beaufort and Colleton," *Niles,* LIII, 356-358; White, *Rhett,* 37-38.

[16] Charleston *Mercury,* Dec. 25, 1837; Charleston *Courier,* Dec. 25, 1837. Also *Fairfield Letters,* 173-174; Benton, *View,* II, 150-154; Sargent, *Public Men and Events,* II, 54-55; White, *Rhett, loc. cit.;* Robert P. Ludlum, "The Antislavery Gag Rule," *Journal of Negro History,* XXVI (April 1941), 209-211.

[17] Charleston *Mercury,* Dec. 27, 1837; Charleston *Courier,* Dec. 27, 1837; White, *Rhett,* 38-40; Adams, *Diary,* IX, 454-455; *Cong. Globe,* 25th, 2d, 45.

[18] *Cong. Globe,* 25th, 2d, 34-38.

[19] *Senate Journal,* 25th, 2d, 144. The resolutions were not actually presented until Jan. 16, 1838, after several postponements.

[20] Calhoun to James Edward Calhoun, Dec. 20, 1837, *Correspondence,* 386.

[21] *Cong. Globe,* 25th, 2d, 55; Calhoun to James Edward Calhoun, Dec. 24, 1837, *Correspondence,* 386-387; to Anna Maria Calhoun, Dec. 24, 1837, *ibid.,* 387; to James Edward Calhoun, Dec. 30, 1837, Calhoun Papers, Clemson College.

[22] *Cong. Globe,* 25th, 2d, 55; *Works,* III, 140-141.

[23] *Cong. Globe,* 25th, 2d, 73.

[24] *Ibid.,* 73-74, 76, 80-81; Appendix, 21-32, 37-41; *Senate Journal,* 25th, 2d, 106-107, 117.

[25] Calhoun to James Edward Calhoun, Jan. 8, 1838, *Correspondence,* 388.

[26] *Cong. Globe,* 25th, 2d, 38; *Senate Journal,* 25th, 2d, 122.

[27] *Cong. Globe,* 25th, 2d, 38; Appendix, 53-60.

[28] *Ibid.,* Appendix, 61.

[29] *Ibid.,* 91, 97, 98; Appendix, 60-65, 69-74; *Senate Journal,* 25th, 2d, 127, 132, 136.

[30] W. B. Seabrook to Crallé, Jan. 13, 1838, Crallé Papers, Clemson College. See also Petigru to Legaré, Dec. 17, 1837, Carson, *Petigru,* 193; F. W. Pickens to Hammond, Jan. 13, 1838, Hammond Papers; and F. H. Elmore to Hammond, [no date], 1838, *ibid.*

[31] Webster to Ketchum, Jan. 15, 1838, Webster's *Writings,* XVIII, 33.

[32] Clay to Brooke, Jan. 13, 1838, Clay's *Works,* V, 424.

[33] Calhoun to J. R. Matthews, Feb. 24, 1838, Calhoun Papers, Library of Congress; *Cong. Globe,* 25th, 2d, 177.

[34] Wiltse, *Calhoun, Nationalist,* 75.

[35] Calhoun to Anna Maria Calhoun, Jan. 25, 1838, *Correspondence,* 391.

[36] Washington *Chronicle,* Jan. 25, 1838. Crallé's editorial credo was reprinted in the Pendleton *Messenger,* Feb. 16, 1838, where attention was specifically directed to it. See also Calhoun to Armistead Burt, Jan. 24, 1838, *Correspondence,* 390.

CHAPTER XXVI

[1] *Cong. Globe,* 25th, 2d, 110-112, 118, 120, 151-152.

[2] *Ibid.,* 156-157.

[3] Calhoun to Anna Maria Calhoun, Feb. 7, 1838, *Correspondence,* 392.

[4] *Niles,* LIII, 282-283; and chapter 24, note 22, above. For the refutation, see Charleston *Mercury,* Jan. 5, 1838; and Washington *Chronicle,* Feb. 13, 1838.

[5] *Cong. Globe,* 25th, 2d, 184, and Appendix, 188-195; *Works,* III, 202-243.

[6] Washington *Globe,* Feb. 15, 1838.

[7] *Cong. Globe,* 25th, 2d, 191, and Appendix, 614-619. There are numerous accounts of this debate, but no accurate report of Clay's speech, which was care-

fully edited to delete the more offensive matter before it was printed. See Washington *Chronicle,* Mar. 21, 1838. The more readily accessible accounts are in Hone, *Diary,* 303-304; Adams, *Diary,* IX, 505-506; Benton, *View,* II, 97-118; Sargent, *Public Men and Events,* II, 34-45.

[8] *Cong. Globe,* 25th, 2d, 191.

[9] The accounts here followed are *Niles,* LIV, 5-6; and Wise, *Seven Decades,* 80-86. For the relation of Cilley to the Nullifiers, see F. W. Pickens to J. H. Hammond, Mar. 5, 1838, Hammond Papers.

[10] A duel between Wise and Gholson of Mississippi had been avoided only a month earlier by the timely intervention of Calhoun among others. See Blair to Jackson, Jan. 16, 1838, Jackson's *Correspondence,* V, 528-529, and editor's note.

[11] See F. H. Elmore to J. H. Hammond, Apr. 2, 1838, Hammond Papers. This "unhappy duel," as Elmore called it, was very probably responsible in some measure at least for the modification of Clay's language in the published version of his speech.

[12] J. H. Hammond to F. H. Elmore, Mar. 22, 1838, Hammond Papers.

[13] Calhoun to Anna Maria Calhoun, Feb. 24, 1838, *Correspondence,* 392-393.

[14] See sources cited in note 7, above. Also Washington *Globe,* Mar. 10, 12, 1838; Washington *Chronicle,* Mar. 13, 1838; Charleston *Mercury,* Mar. 14, 1838. Calhoun's speech is in *Cong. Globe,* 25th, 2d, Appendix, 176-181; and *Works,* III, 244-279.

[15] The quoted phrase is Waddy Thompson's, as recalled by Judge A. B. Longstreet, "Review of Ex-Gov. Perry's Sketch of J. C. Calhoun," *XIX Century,* II (January 1870), 622. Thompson then shared with Preston the leadership of the anti-Calhoun revolt in South Carolina, and both men were openly supporting Clay.

[16] Sargent, *Public Men and Events,* II, 49.

[17] *Cong. Globe,* 25th, 2d, Appendix, 632-641.

[18] Calhoun's speech is in *ibid.,* Appendix, 243-250; and *Works,* III, 279-326. See also Washington *Globe,* Mar. 23, 1838; and Charleston *Mercury,* Mar. 26, 1838.

[19] B. Alvord to M. C. M. Hammond, May 1838, Hammond Papers.

[20] *Cong. Globe,* 25th, 2d, 163-164, 190-191, 223, 227; Clay to Biddle, Feb. 20, 1838, *Biddle Correspondence,* 304-305, and *ibid.,* 302-304.

[21] Calhoun to J. H. Hammond, Mar. 6, 1838, Hammond Papers.

[22] *Cong. Globe,* 25th, 2d, 250-251.

[23] *Ibid.,* 259, 264, and Appendix, 265-266.

[24] Adams, *Diary,* IX, 516-517; Hone, *Diary,* 312; Calhoun to Andrew P. Calhoun, Apr. 5 [May 5?], 1838, *Correspondence,* 393; Pendleton *Messenger,* Apr. 20, 1838.

[25] Biddle to Forsyth, Apr. 30, 1838, *Biddle Correspondence,* 307-308; to Samuel Jaudon, June 29, 1838, *ibid.,* 314-315; to J. R. Poinsett, July 11, 1838, *ibid.,* 316; Hone, *Diary,* 311-312. The Bank was also, it should be added, continuing to issue and circulate notes printed from the old Bank of the United States plates, just as though its charter had never expired. It required a special act of Congress to stop the practice. See Benton, *View,* II, 67-70.

[26] Calhoun to Hammond, Apr. 18, 1838, *Correspondence,* 394-395.

[27] Webster to Biddle, May [?] 1838, *Biddle Correspondence,* 301. Also John Sergeant to Biddle, Apr. 28, 1838, *ibid.,* 305-306. With less charity than Webster, Sergeant professed to believe Calhoun's activities a mere "cloak for his ambition," but intelligent men all over the South were rapidly coming to share the view that

the South could never be commercially independent if a national bank were re-established. See, *e.g.*, Joseph Segor to Crallé, May 22, 1838, Crallé Papers, Clemson College.

[28] Calhoun to James Edward Calhoun, Apr. 21, 1838, *Correspondence*, 396.

[29] *Cong. Globe*, 25th, 2d, 478; Biddle to Sergeant, June 15, 1838, *Biddle Correspondence*, 313-314; to Samuel Jaudon, June 23, 29, 1838, *ibid.*, 314-315.

[30] *Niles*, LIV, 339; Charleston *Mercury*, July 6, 1838; Petigru to Legaré, June 1, 1838, Carson, *Petigru*, 197-198; P. M. Butler to Hammond, June 16, 1838, Hammond Papers.

[31] *Cong. Globe*, 25th, 2d, 76.

[32] *Ibid.*, 453.

[33] *Ibid.*, 451.

[34] A. T. Burnley, Texas agent, to ——, Oct. 11, 1838, Yanaguana Society, *Publications*, V, 152; J. H. Smith, *Annexation of Texas*, 63-68.

[35] *E. g.*, Adams, *Diary*, IX, 510.

[36] *Democratic Review*, II (April 1838), 65-84.

[37] Pendleton *Messenger*, May 25, 1838.

[38] *Cong. Globe*, 25th, 2d, 149, 160, 305.

[39] Washington *Globe*, July-September 1838, especially July 17, Aug. 2, 7, 24.

[40] *Ibid.*, Sept. 21, 1838. For the occasion of the Richland letter, see p. 391, below.

[41] Calhoun to Micah Sterling, July 26, 1838, Calhoun Papers, South Caroliniana Library.

[42] *Ibid.* See also Calhoun to Dr. Danall [?], Oct. 26, 1838, *Correspondence*, 406-410.

[43] Such at least was Clay's interpretation of the Ohio election. See Clay to Brooke, Nov. 3, 1838, Clay's *Works*, V, 430-431; and *Niles*, LV, 113.

[44] Cole, *Whig Party in the South*, 52-53; White, *Rhett*, 40-41. Cf. Calhoun to Hayne, Nov. 17, 1838, *Correspondence*, 416.

[45] Calhoun to Burt, Apr. 19, 1838, Calhoun Papers, Duke University; to Poinsett, July 4, 1838, *Correspondence*, 397-398; to Dr. Danall [?], Oct. 26, 1838, *ibid.*, 406-407. There is further evidence of collaboration between Calhoun and Poinsett in Charleston *Mercury*, Oct. 19, 1838.

[46] See, *e. g.*, Calhoun to Rhett, Sept. 13, 1838, *Correspondence*, 399-400.

[47] Calhoun to Joseph A. Black, *et al.*, July 24, 1838, *Niles*, LIV, 406. An account of the dinner is in *ibid.*, 359-360, 392. See also Calhoun to Duff Green, Aug. 10, 1838, *Correspondence*, 398.

[48] Calhoun to Col. R. H. Goodwyn, *et al.*, Sept. 1, 1838, *Niles*, LV, 75-76. It was this letter that Blair quoted so approvingly in the *Globe*. Also Preston to Goodwyn, Sept. 3, 1838, *Niles*, LV, 76-78.

[49] Thompson to Calhoun, Aug. 30, 1838, *Niles*, LV, 74; Calhoun to Thompson, Sept. 2, 1838, *ibid.* For an account of the dinner sympathetic toward Calhoun, by an eyewitness, see Pendleton *Messenger*, Aug. 31, 1838. Cf. Wallace, *History of South Carolina*, II, 475.

[50] Calhoun to Duff Green, Oct. 11, 1838, *Correspondence*, 405-406; to Rhett, Sept. 13, 1838, *ibid.*, 400.

[51] Charleston *Mercury*, Sept. 5, 1838; William B. Lewis to William C. Rives, Sept. 18, 1838, Rives Papers; Pendleton *Messenger*, Sept. 21, 1838; A. H. Pemberton, editor of the *South Carolinian*, to Calhoun, Nov. 1, 1838, Calhoun Papers, Clemson College.

[52] Charleston *Mercury,* Sept. 19, Oct. 3, 11, 1838; Charleston *Courier,* Sept. 27, Oct. 10, 11, 1838; Washington *Globe,* Oct. 4, 1838. See also Petigru to Legaré, Sept. 11, 1838, Petigru Papers.

CHAPTER XXVII

[1] Calhoun to Armistead Burt, Nov. 17, Dec. 24, 1838, *Correspondence,* 417-418, 422-423; to Micah Sterling, Dec. 10, 1838, Calhoun Papers, South Caroliniana Library.

[2] Biddle to R. M. Blatchford, July 31, 1838, *Biddle Correspondence,* 317; to Jaudon, Aug. 3, 1838, *ibid.,* 318-321; to E. C. Biddle, Oct. 31, 1838, *ibid.,* 334; to Forsyth, Nov. 27, 1838, *ibid.,* 335-336; [C. S. Baker] to Biddle, Aug. 11, 1838, *ibid.,* 321-323.

[3] Forsyth to Biddle, Nov. 29, 1838, *Biddle Correspondence,* 336.

[4] D. H. Lewis to R. K. Crallé, July 17, 1838, Crallé Papers, Clemson College.

[5] Washington *Globe,* Nov. 22, 24, Dec. 7, 1838.

[6] Richardson, *Messages and Papers of the Presidents,* 1700-1722.

[7] *Cong. Globe,* 25th, 3d, 23-28; Fairfield to his wife, Dec. 11, 1838, *Fairfield Letters,* 242.

[8] Harrison Gray Otis to Clay, Dec. 24, 1838, and Jan. 11, 1839, Clay's *Works,* V, 434, 438.

[9] *Cong. Globe,* 25th, 3d, 109-110.

[10] *Ibid.,* 177, and Appendix, 354-359.

[11] *Ibid.,* 177; Calhoun to Burt, Feb. 17, 1839, *Correspondence,* 423-424.

[12] Pickens to Hammond, Feb. 8, 1839, Hammond Papers; Pendleton *Messenger,* Feb. 22, 1839; Washington *Globe,* Sept. 23, 1839.

[13] *Cong. Globe,* 25th, 3d, 127, and Appendix, 95-97; *Works,* III, 360-375. In the Appendix to the *Globe* and in the *Works* the speech is misdated Jan. 15, 1839. It was delivered on January 16. See also Charleston *Courier,* Jan. 21, 1839.

[14] *Cong. Globe,* 25th, 3d, 158, and Appendix, 76-77; *Works,* III, 375-382.

[15] *Cong. Globe,* 25th, 3d, 210, and Appendix, 234-237; *Works,* III, 382-403.

[16] Washington *Globe,* Feb. 22, 1839.

[17] Calhoun to J. R. Matthews, Mar. 4, 1839, Calhoun Papers, Library of Congress.

[18] See Clay to Francis Brooke, Dec. 20, 26, 1838, Clay's *Works,* V, 432, 434-436; Tyler, *Times of the Tylers,* I, 588 ff.

[19] See Calhoun to Hunter, June 1839, *Correspondence,* 371-372, where it is misdated 1837. For correct dating, see Martha T. Hunter, *Memoir of Robert M. T. Hunter,* 71-72. The Virginia election returns are in *Niles,* LVI, 241.

[20] See Calhoun to Poinsett, Apr. 28, 1839, *Correspondence,* 424-425. Also to Duff Green, May 1839, *ibid.,* 427-429.

[21] Washington *Globe,* June 26, 1839.

[22] Calhoun to F. H. Elmore, Oct. 7, 1839, Calhoun Papers, South Caroliniana Library.

[23] This account, and the story told below, is based on many sources, most important of which are Calhoun to Anna Calhoun Clemson, Dec. 18, 1839, *Correspondence,* 436-437; F. W. Pickens to J. H. Hammond, Dec. 15, 1839, Hammond Papers; S. H. Butler to Hammond, Dec. 30, 1839, *ibid.;* P. H. Gallagher to John McLean, Dec. 20, 1839, McLean Papers; and Benton, *View,* II, 160. Calhoun himself seems unaware of the "intrigue" of which Pickens complains, but he was

of course not at the caucus, which would have been confined to House members. Gallagher thinks Benton blocked Pickens as well as Lewis, though he may have used the one to strangle the other.

[24] *Cong. Globe,* 26th, 1st, 1-50, *passim;* S. H. Butler to Hammond, Dec. 30, 1839, Hammond Papers; Sargent, *Public Men and Events,* II, 96-99.

[25] *Cong. Globe,* 26th, 1st, 51-52.

[26] *Ibid.,* 53-54.

[27] Calhoun to Anna Calhoun Clemson, Dec. 18, 1839, *Correspondence,* 436-437. Cf. George Ticknor to Charles S. Daveis, Dec. 31, 1839: ". . . Whiggery is low. I never thought much of it, and now less than ever, since the Whigs have chosen a nullifier and a sub-treasury man for Speaker." G. S. Hillard, ed., *Life, Letters, and Journals of George Ticknor,* II, 192 (1900 ed.). Also Washington *Globe,* Dec. 16, 1839; and Charleston *Mercury,* Dec. 20, 1839.

[28] *Cong. Globe,* 26th, 1st, 88-89.

[29] Calhoun to James Edward Calhoun, Feb. 1, 1840, *Correspondence,* 444-445.

[30] Calhoun to Andrew P. Calhoun, Dec. 7, 1839, *ibid.,* 434-435; to Thomas G. Clemson, Dec. 8, 1839, *ibid.,* 435.

[31] In the bill as finally passed, section 19 provides for the gradual retirement of bank notes in payment of public dues, and requires all payments to the government after 1843 to be made in gold and silver. This was Benton rather than Calhoun, but it is clear from Calhoun's speeches on the subject, especially that of Sept. 18, 1837, that he would regard a Treasury note backed by specie—gold and silver certificates they were called in a later day—as within the meaning of the law. It was not meant to exclude the convenience of paper money in business transactions, but only to be sure it was money and not some banker's credit that was passing as currency. The act is 5 *Statutes at Large* 385.

[32] Richardson, *Messages and Papers of the Presidents,* 1746-1772.

[33] Calhoun to James Edward Calhoun, Feb. 1, 1840, *Correspondence,* 444-445; to Anna Calhoun Clemson, Feb. 13, 1840, *ibid.,* 446-447; Hammond to Calhoun, Feb. 9, 1840, *ibid.,* 816-818; Van Buren, *Autobiography,* 389-392. See also the passage between Calhoun and Clay in the Senate, Jan. 3, 1840, *Cong. Globe,* 26th, 1st, 96-98.

[34] Calhoun to Duff Green, Jan. 17, 18, 1840, *Correspondence,* 438-440, 440-441; *Cong. Globe,* 26th, 1st, 157.

[35] The bill passed the Senate Jan. 23, 1840, with Buchanan, Grundy (who had just left the Cabinet to return to the Senate), and Cuthbert all voting for it. The margin was 24 to 18. *Cong. Globe,* 26th, 1st, 139-141. The Bank party made their last-ditch stand in the House, where the bill was not finally passed until June 30, by a margin of 124 to 107. *Ibid.,* 495. See also Calhoun to Clemson, Jan. 25, 1840, *Correspondence,* 441-442; to Hammond, Jan. 25, 1840, *ibid.,* 443.

[36] Calhoun to James Edward Calhoun, Feb. 1, 1840, *Correspondence,* 444-445.

[37] Charleston *Courier* and *Mercury* generally through the early months of 1840; Pendleton *Messenger,* Jan. 24, 1840.

BIBLIOGRAPHY

Only the more important materials are listed.

MANUSCRIPTS

R. F. W. Allston Papers. South Carolina Historical Society.
John M. Berrien Papers. University of North Carolina.
Nicholas Biddle Papers. Library of Congress.
John C. Calhoun Papers. Clemson College.
Calhoun Papers. Duke University.
Calhoun Papers. Library of Congress.
Calhoun Papers. South Caroliniana Library.
Calhoun Papers. Yale University.
Chesnut-Manning-Miller Papers. South Carolina Historical Society.
Henry Clay Papers. Library of Congress.
John M. Clayton Papers. Library of Congress.
Thomas G. Clemson Papers. Clemson College.
Richard K. Crallé Papers. Clemson College.
Crallé Papers. Library of Congress.
Franklin H. Elmore Papers. Library of Congress.
Charles F. Fisher Papers. University of North Carolina.
John Floyd Papers. Library of Congress.
Duff Green Papers. Library of Congress.
Felix Grundy Papers. University of North Carolina.
James H. Hammond Papers. Library of Congress.
Robert Y. Hayne Papers. South Caroliniana Library.
Andrew Jackson Papers, second series. Library of Congress.
George McDuffie Papers. Duke University.
McDuffie Papers. South Caroliniana Library.
John McLean Papers. Library of Congress.
Willie P. Mangum Papers. Library of Congress.
Virgil Maxcy Papers. Library of Congress.
Maxcy Papers, second series. Library of Congress.
Patrick Noble Papers. Private collection of Sarah Noble Carnes.
Patrick Noble Papers. South Caroliniana Library.
James L. Petigru Papers. Library of Congress.
William Cabell Rives Papers. Library of Congress.
John Tyler Papers. Library of Congress.
University of South Carolina Alumni Records. South Caroliniana Library.
Martin Van Buren Papers. Library of Congress.
Daniel Webster Papers. Library of Congress.
Williams-Chesnut-Manning Papers. University of North Carolina.

NEWSPAPERS

Baltimore *Merchant.*
Charleston *Courier.*

Charleston *Mercury.*
Columbia *Telescope.*
The Liberator.
The Madisonian.
National Intelligencer.
New York *Courier and Enquirer.*
Niles' Weekly Register.
Pendleton *Messenger.*
Richmond *Enquirer.*
Southern Patriot.
Southern Times.
United States' Telegraph.
Washington *Chronicle.*
Washington *Globe.*
Washington *Reformer.*

BOOKS AND PERIODICALS

Acton, John, Lord. "Political Causes of the American Revolution," reprinted in *Essays on Freedom and Power* (Boston, 1948), pp. 196-250.

Adams, Charles Francis. "J. Q. Adams in the Twenty-second Congress," *Proceedings of the Massachusetts Historical Society,* Vol. XXXIX (December 1905), pp. 504-553.

Adams, John Quincy. *Memoirs of John Quincy Adams;* Charles Francis Adams, ed. 12 vols. Philadelphia, 1874-1877.

Alexander, Holmes Moss. *The American Talleyrand; the Career and Contemporaries of Martin Van Buren, Eighth President.* New York, 1935.

Ambler, Charles H. *Thomas Ritchie, a Study in Virginia Politics.* Richmond, 1913

Anon. "John C. Calhoun's Home Life," Anderson (S. C.) *Daily Mail,* Oct. 23, 1926. [From clipping of 1849 in papers of William H. Trescott.]

Anon. "John Caldwell Calhoun," *United States Democratic Review,* Vol. II (1838), pp. 65-84.

Anon. "Peggy O'Neal; or the Doom of the Republic," *Southern Review,* Vol. XII (January-April 1873), pp. 213-231, 281-297.

Bancroft, Frederic. *Calhoun and the South Carolina Nullification Movement.* Baltimore, 1928.

Barnard, Henry. "The South Atlantic States in 1833, as Seen by a New Englander," *Maryland Historical Magazine,* Vol. XIII (September-December 1918), pp. 267-294, 295-386.

Barnes, Gilbert H. *The Anti-Slavery Impulse, 1830-1844.* New York, 1933.

Barry, William T. "Letters of William T. Barry," *William and Mary College Quarterly Historical Magazine,* Vol. XIII (April 1905), pp. 236-244; Vol. XIV (July 1905), pp. 19-23; Vol. XIV (April 1906), pp. 230-241.

Bassett, John Spencer. *The Life of Andrew Jackson.* 2 vols. in 1. New York, 1931.

Bates, Mary. *The Private Life of John C. Calhoun.* Charleston, 1852.

Baylies, Francis. "Baylies Papers, 1821-31," *Proceedings of the Massachusetts Historical Society,* Vol. XLVI (1913), pp. 320-338.

Baylies, Francis. "Letters, 1827-34," *Proceedings of the Massachusetts Historical Society,* Vol. XLV (1912), pp. 166-184.

Benton, Thomas H. *Thirty Years' View.* 2 vols. New York, 1854-1856.

Biddle, Nicholas. *The Correspondence of Nicholas Biddle Dealing with National Affairs, 1807-1844;* Reginald C. McGrane, ed. Boston & New York, 1919.

Biographical Directory of the American Congress, 1774-1927. Washington, 1928.

Boucher, Chauncey S. "The Ante-Bellum Attitude of South Carolina towards Manufacturing and Agriculture," *Washington University Studies,* Vol. III (April 1916), pp. 243-270.

Boucher, Chauncey S. *The Nullification Controversy in South Carolina.* Chicago, 1916.

Boucher, Chauncey S. "Sectionalism, Representation, and the Electoral Question in Ante-Bellum South Carolina," *Washington University Studies,* Vol. IV (October 1916), pp. 3-62.

Bourne, Edward G. *The History of the Surplus Revenue of 1837.* New York and London, 1885.

Brown, James. "Letters of James Brown to Henry Clay, 1804-1835"; James A. Padgett, ed. *Louisiana Historical Quarterly,* Vol. XXIV (October 1941), pp. 921-1177.

Bruce, William Cabell. *John Randolph of Roanoke.* 2 vols. New York and London, 1922.

Bryan, Wilhelmus B. *A History of the National Capital.* 2 vols. New York, 1914-1916.

Burke, Pauline Wilcox. *Emily Donelson of Tennessee.* 2 vols. Richmond, 1941.

Butler, William Allen. *A Retrospect of Forty Years, 1825-1865;* Harriet Allen Butler, ed. New York, 1911.

Calhoun, John C. "Calhoun as Seen by His Political Friends"; F. W. Moore, ed. *Southern History Association Publications,* Vol. VII (1903), pp. 159-169, 269-291, 353-361, 419-426.

Calhoun, John C. *Correspondence Addressed to John C. Calhoun, 1837-1849;* Chauncey S. Boucher and Robert P. Brooks, eds. Annual Report of the American Historical Association, 1929. Washington, 1931.

Calhoun, John C. *Correspondence of John C. Calhoun;* J. Franklin Jameson, ed. Annual Report of the American Historical Association, 1899. Vol. II. Washington, 1900.

Calhoun, John C. *Works of John C. Calhoun;* Richard K. Crallé, ed. 6 vols. New York, 1854-1857.

Capers, Henry D. *The Life and Times of C. G. Memminger.* Richmond, 1893.

Carpenter, Jesse T. *The South as a Conscious Minority, 1789-1861; a Study in Political Thought.* New York, 1930.

Carroll, E. Malcolm. *Origins of the Whig Party.* Durham, 1925.

Carsel, Wilfred. "The Slaveholders' Indictment of Northern Wage Slavery," *Journal of Southern History,* Vol. VI (November 1940), pp. 504-520.

Carson, James Petigru. *Life, Letters and Speeches of James Louis Petigru.* Washington, 1920.

Cash, W. J. *The Mind of the South.* New York, 1941.

Catterall, Ralph C. H. *The Second Bank of the United States.* Chicago, 1903.

Channing, Edward. *History of the United States.* Vols. 4-6. New York, 1937-1938.

Chitwood, Oliver P. *John Tyler, Champion of the Old South.* New York, 1939.

Claiborne, J. F. H. *Life and Correspondence of John A. Quitman.* 2 vols. New York, 1860.

Claiborne, J. F. H., ed. *Life and Times of Gen. Sam. Dale, the Mississippi Partisan.* New York, 1860.

Clark, Bennett Champ. *John Quincy Adams, "Old Man Eloquent."* Boston, 1932.

Clay, Henry. *The Works of Henry Clay;* Calvin Colton, ed. 10 vols. New York and London, 1904.

Clay, Thomas M. "Two Years with Old Hickory," *Atlantic Monthly,* Vol. LX (August 1887), pp. 187-199.

Cleaves, Freeman. *Old Tippecanoe: William Henry Harrison and His Time.* New York and London, 1939.

Cole, Arthur Charles. *The Whig Party in the South.* Washington, 1913.

Coleman, Mrs. Chapman. *The Life of John J. Crittenden, with Selections from His Correspondence and Speeches.* 2 vols. Philadelphia, 1871.

Congressional Globe. Twenty-third Congress, First Session, to Twenty-sixth Congress, First Session. Vols. 1-8. Washington, 1834-1840.

Connor, R. D. W. "William Gaston," *Proceedings of the American Antiquarian Society,* n. s., Vol. XLIII (1934), pp. 381-446.

Cook, Harvey Toliver. *The Life and Legacy of David Rogerson Williams.* New York, 1916.

Cox, Isaac J., ed. "Selections from the Torrence Papers," Historical and Philosophical Society of Ohio, *Quarterly Publications,* Vols. 1-6, *passim.*

Craven, Avery. *The Coming of the Civil War.* New York, 1942.

Current, Richard Nelson. "John C. Calhoun, Philosopher of Reaction," *Antioch Review,* Vol. III (Summer 1943), pp. 223-234.

Curtis, George Ticknor. *Life of Daniel Webster.* 2 vols. New York, 1870.

Curtis, George Ticknor. *Life of James Buchanan.* 2 vols. New York, 1883.

Darling, Arthur B. *Political Changes in Massachusetts, 1824-1848; a Study of Liberal Movements in Politics.* New Haven, 1925.

Davidson, James D. "A Journey through the South in 1836: Diary of James D. Davidson"; Herbert A. Kellar, ed. *Journal of Southern History,* Vol. I (August 1935), pp. 345-377.

Davis, John B. "Letters to John Brazer Davis"; W. C. Ford, ed. *Proceedings of the Massachusetts Historical Society,* Vol. XLIX (1916), pp. 178-256.

"Debate on Mr. Foot's Resolution," *Southern Review,* Vol. VI (August 1830), pp. 140-198.

Derrick, Samuel M. *Centennial History of South Carolina Railroad.* Columbia, 1930.

Dew, Thomas R. *Review of the Debate in the Virginia Legislature, 1831-32.* Richmond, 1832. Reprinted in *The Pro-Slavery Argument* (Charleston, 1852), pp. 287-490.

De Witt, Charles G. "The Great Webster-Hayne Debate," *Olde Ulster,* Vol. IX (November 1913), pp. 332-337.

Dictionary of American Biography. 20 vols. New York, 1928-1936.

Dodd, William E. *The Cotton Kingdom.* New Haven, 1919.

Dodd, William E. "The Emergence of the First Social Order in the United States," *American Historical Review,* Vol. XL (1935), pp. 217-231.

Dodd, William E. "John C. Calhoun," *Statesmen of the Old South,* pp. 91-167. New York, 1911.

DuBose, John W. *William Lowndes Yancey.* Birmingham, 1892.

Dumond, Dwight L. *The Antislavery Origins of the Civil War in the United States.* Ann Arbor, 1939.

Eaton, Clement. *Freedom of Thought in the Old South.* Durham, 1940.

Eaton, Mrs. Margaret L. O'Neale Timberlake. *The Autobiography of Peggy Eaton.* New York, 1932.

Edwards, Ninian. *The Edwards Papers;* E. B. Washburne, ed. Chicago, 1884.

Eriksson, Erik M. "The Federal Civil Service under President Jackson," *Mississippi Valley Historical Review,* Vol. XIII (March 1927), pp. 517-540.

Fairfield, John. *The Letters of John Fairfield;* Arthur B. Staples, ed. Lewiston, Maine, 1922.

Featherstonhaugh, George William. *A Canoe Voyage up the Minnay Sotor.* 2 vols. London, 1847.

Featherstonhaugh, George William. *Excursion through the Slave States.* New York, 1844.

Floyd, John. *The Life and Diary of John Floyd;* C. H. Ambler, ed. Richmond, 1918.

Follett, Oran. "Selections from the Follett Papers"; L. Belle Hamlin, ed. Historical and Philosophical Society of Ohio, *Quarterly Publications,* Vols. 9-11, *passim.*

Fuess, Claude M. *Daniel Webster.* 2 vols. Boston, 1930.

Goodpasture, A. V. "John Bell's Political Revolt," *Tennessee Historical Magazine,* Vol. II (December 1915), pp. 254-263.

Gordon, Armistead C. *William Fitzhugh Gordon, a Virginian of the Old School.* New York and Washington, 1909.

Gouge, William M. *An Inquiry into the Expediency of Dispensing with Bank Agency and Bank Paper in Fiscal Concerns of the United States.* Philadelphia, 1837.

Govan, Thomas P. "John M. Berrien and the Administration of Andrew Jackson," *Journal of Southern History,* Vol. V (November 1939), pp. 447-467.

Gray, Lewis Cecil. *History of Agriculture in the Southern United States to 1860.* 2 vols. Washington, 1933.

Green, Edwin L. *George McDuffie.* Columbia, 1936.

Greene, William. "Selections from the William Greene Papers"; L. Belle Hamlin, ed. Historical and Philosophical Society of Ohio, *Quarterly Publications,* Vols. 13-14, *passim.*

Hamilton, James, Jr. *An Eulogium on the Public Services and Character of Robert J. Turnbull, Esq., delivered . . . on the 22d Day of November, 1833 . . .* Charleston, 1834.

Hamilton, James A. *Reminiscences of James A. Hamilton.* New York, 1869.

Hamilton, Thomas. *Men and Manners in America.* 2 vols. Edinburgh, 1833.

Hammond, Bray. "Jackson, Biddle, and the Bank of the United States," *Journal of Economic History,* Vol. VII (May 1947), pp. 1-23.

Hammond, Jabez D. *The History of Political Parties in the State of New-York.* 2 vols. Albany, 1842.

Hammond, Jabez D. *Life and Times of Silas Wright.* Syracuse, 1848.

Harvey, Peter. *Reminiscences and Anecdotes of Daniel Webster.* Boston, 1882.

Hatcher, William B. *Edward Livingston: Jeffersonian Republican and Jacksonian Democrat.* University, La., 1940.

Haywood, Marshall De Lancey. *John Branch, 1782-1863.* Raleigh, 1915.

Henry, Howell M. *Police Control of the Slave in South Carolina.* Emory, Va., 1914.

Hibbard, Benjamin H. *A History of the Public Land Policies.* New York, 1924.

Holland, William M. *The Life and Political Opinions of Martin Van Buren.* Hartford, 1835.

Holmes, Alester G. "John C. Calhoun," *Southern Magazine,* Vol. II (1936), No. 10.

Holmes, Alester G., and Sherrill, George R. *Thomas G. Clemson: His Life and Work.* Richmond, 1937.

Holst, Hermann von. *John C. Calhoun.* Boston, 1882.

Hone, Philip. *The Diary of Philip Hone, 1828-1851;* Allan Nevins, ed. New York, 1936.

Houston, David F. *A Critical Study of Nullification in South Carolina.* Cambridge, 1896.

Houston, Sam. *The Writings of Sam Houston, 1813-1863;* Amelia W. Williams and Eugene C. Barker, eds. Austin, 1938-1943.

Hunt, Gaillard. *John C. Calhoun.* Philadelphia, 1908.

Hunter, Martha T. *A Memoir of Robert M. T. Hunter.* Washington, 1903.

[Hunter, R. M. T.] *Life of John C. Calhoun.* New York, 1843.

Ingersoll, Ernest. "The Calhoun Summer Home," *Scribner's Monthly,* Vol. XXI (April 1881), pp. 892-895.

Ingham, William A. "Samuel D. Ingham, Secretary of the U. S. Treasury," *Bucks County Historical Society Papers,* Vol. IV (1917), pp. 19-30.

Jackson, Andrew. *Correspondence of Andrew Jackson;* John S. Bassett, ed. 7 vols. Washington, 1926-1935.

James, Marquis. *Andrew Jackson; Portrait of a President.* Indianapolis and New York, 1937.

Jenkins, John S. *Life of John Caldwell Calhoun.* Auburn and Buffalo, 1850.

Jenkins, William S. *Pro-Slavery Thought in the Old South.* Chapel Hill, 1935.

Jervey, Theodore D. *Robert Y. Hayne and His Times.* New York, 1909.

Johnson, Richard M. "Letters of Colonel Richard M. Johnson of Kentucky"; James A. Padgett, ed. Kentucky State Historical Society, *Register,* Vols. 39-40 (1941-1942), *passim.*

Journal of the Executive Proceedings of the Senate of the United States. Vols. 4-5. Washington, 1887.

Journal of the House of Representatives of the United States. 20th-26th Congresses. Washington, 1828 [1829]-1840.

Journal of the Senate of the United States. 20th-26th Congresses. Washington, 1828 [1829]-1839 [1840].

Kendall, Amos. *Autobiography of Amos Kendall;* William Stickney, ed. Boston, 1872.

Kennedy, John P. *Memoirs of the Life of William Wirt.* 2 vols. Philadelphia, 1852.

Kent, James. *Commentaries on American Law.* 4 vols. New York, 1826-1830.

Kibler, Lillian Adele. *Benjamin F. Perry, South Carolina Unionist.* Durham, 1946.

King, William L. *The Newspaper Press of Charleston, S. C.* Charleston, 1872.

Kinley, David. *The Independent Treasury of the United States and Its Relations to the Banks of the Country.* Washington, 1910.

Klein, Philip S. *Pennsylvania Politics, 1817-1832: A Game without Rules.* Philadelphia, 1940.

Leggett, William. *Collection of Political Writings;* Theodore Sedgwick, Jr., ed. 2 vols. New York, 1840.

Lloyd, Arthur Young. *The Slavery Controversy, 1831-1860.* Chapel Hill, 1939.

Longacre, James B., and Herring, James, eds. *The National Portrait Gallery of Distinguished Americans.* 4 vols. New York and Philadelphia, 1835.

Longstreet, Augustus B. "Review of Ex-Gov. Perry's Sketch of J. C. Calhoun," *The XIX Century,* Vol. II (January 1870), pp. 618-623.

Ludlum, Robert P. "The Antislavery Gag Rule," *Journal of Negro History,* Vol. XXVI (April 1941), pp. 203-243.

Luther, Seth. *Address to the Workingmen of New England . . . on the Condition of the Producing Classes.* Boston, 1832.

Lynch, Denis Tilden. *An Epoch and a Man; Martin Van Buren and His Times.* New York, 1929.

Lynch, William O. *Fifty Years of Party Warfare (1789-1837).* Indianapolis, 1931.

McDonnell, Alexander R. "John McPherson Berrien," *Georgia Historical Quarterly,* Vol. XVII (March 1933), pp. 1-12.

McDuffie, George. *A Eulogy upon the Life and Character of the Late Hon. Robert Y. Hayne: delivered on the 13th February, 1840 . . .* Charleston, 1840.

McFerrin, Porter. "John C. Calhoun, Statesman and Patriot," *Methodist Quarterly Review,* Vol. LXX (April 1921), pp. 249-268.

McGrane, Reginald C. *The Panic of 1837: Some Financial Problems of the Jacksonian Era.* Chicago, 1924.

Mackenzie, William Lyon. *The Life and Times of Martin Van Buren: The Correspondence of His Friends, Family and Pupils.* Boston, 1846.

Mackenzie, William Lyon. *Sketches of Canada and the United States.* London, 1833.

McLane, Louis, ed. *Documents Relative to the Manufactures of the United States.* House Document 308, 22d Congress, 1st session. Washington, 1833.

McLaughlin, Andrew C. *Constitutional History of the United States.* New York, 1935.

Malone, Dumas. *The Public Life of Thomas Cooper, 1783-1839.* New Haven, 1926.

Martineau, Harriet. *Retrospect of Western Travel.* 2 vols. London and New York, 1838.

Martineau, Harriet. *Society in America.* 3 vols. London, 1837.

Mayo, Robert. *Political Sketches of Eight Years in Washington.* Baltimore, 1839.

Meigs, William M. *The Life of John Caldwell Calhoun.* 2 vols. New York, 1917.

Meigs, William M. *The Life of Thomas Hart Benton.* Philadelphia, 1904.

Merritt, Elizabeth. *James Henry Hammond, 1807-1864.* Baltimore, 1923.

Messages and Papers of the Presidents; J. D. Richardson, comp. 20 vols. New York, 1897-1927.

Meyer, Leland Winfield. *The Life and Times of Colonel Richard M. Johnson of Kentucky.* New York, 1932.

Miller, Harry E. *Banking Theories in the United States before 1860.* Cambridge, 1927.

Nichols, Roy F. *Franklin Pierce, Young Hickory of the Granite Hills.* Philadelphia and London, 1931.

Nullification. "Letters on the Nullification Movement in South Carolina, 1830-1834," *American Historical Review,* Vol. VI (July 1902), pp. 736-765; Vol. VII (October 1902), pp. 92-119.

Nussbaum, Frederick L. "The Compromise of 1833," *South Atlantic Quarterly*, Vol. XI (October 1912), pp. 337-349.

O'Neall, John Belton. *Biographical Sketches of the Bench and Bar of South Carolina.* 2 vols. Charleston, 1859.

O'Neall, John Belton. *Negro Law of South Carolina.* Columbia, 1848.

Parton, James. *Life of Andrew Jackson.* 3 vols. New York, 1860.

Perry, Benjamin F. *Reminiscences of Public Men.* Philadelphia, 1883.

Perry, Benjamin F. *Reminiscences of Public Men.* 2d series. Greenville, S. C., 1889.

Phillips, Ulrich B. *The Course of the South to Secession;* E. Merton Coulter, ed. New York, 1939.

Phillips, Ulrich B. *Georgia and State Rights.* Annual Report of the American Historical Association, 1901. Vol. II. Washington, 1902.

Phillips, Ulrich B. *A History of Transportation in the Eastern Cotton Belt to 1860.* New York, 1908.

Phillips, Ulrich B. *Life and Labor in the Old South.* Boston, 1929.

Phillips, Ulrich B. "The Southern Whigs, 1834-1854," *Essays in American History Dedicated to Frederick Jackson Turner,* pp. 203-216. New York, 1910.

Pinckney, Charles Cotesworth. "John C. Calhoun, From a Southern Stand-Point," *Lippincott's Monthly Magazine,* Vol. LXII (July 1898), pp. 81-90.

Pinckney, Gustavus M. *Life of John C. Calhoun.* Charleston, 1903.

Poinsett, Joel R. "The Poinsett-Campbell Correspondence"; Samuel G. Stoney, ed. *South Carolina Historical and Genealogical Magazine,* Vols. 42-43 (April 1941-January 1942), *passim.*

Polk, James K. "Letters to Cave Johnson," *Tennessee Historical Magazine,* Vol. I (September 1915), pp. 209-256.

Polk, James K. "Unpublished Letters from North Carolinians to Polk"; Elizabeth G. McPherson, ed. *North Carolina Historical Review,* Vol. XVI (1939), *passim.*

Pollack, Queena. *Peggy Eaton, Democracy's Mistress.* New York, 1931.

Poore, Ben Perley. *Perley's Reminiscences of Sixty Years in the National Metropolis.* 2 vols. Philadelphia, 1886.

Proctor, John Clagett, ed. *Washington, Past and Present; a History.* 4 vols. New York, 1930.

Rail Road from the Banks of the Ohio River to the Tide Waters of the Carolinas and Georgia. Cincinnati, 1835.

Rawle, William. *A View of the Constitution of the United States of America.* 2d ed., Philadelphia, 1829. [Unchanged, except in organization, from 1st ed., 1825.]

Register of Debates in Congress. Twentieth Congress, Second Session, to Twenty-Fifth Congress, First Session. Vols. 5-14. Washington, 1830-1837.

"Report of the Committee on Farms of the Pendleton Farmers' Society," *Southern Cultivator,* Vol. III (July 1845), pp. 97-98.

Report of the Secretary of the Treasury, on the State of the Finances, for the Year Ending June 30, 1855. 34th Cong., 1st sess., House of Representatives, Executive Document No. 10. Washington, 1856.

Report of the Special Committee of the Charleston Chamber of Commerce, on the Contemplated Rail-Road from Charleston, in South-Carolina, to Newport or Covington, opposite Cincinnati, in Ohio. Charleston, 1835.

Rezneck, Samuel. "The Social History of an American Depression, 1837-43," *American Historical Review,* Vol. XL (July 1935), pp. 662-687.

Rhea, Linda. *Hugh Swinton Legaré, a Charleston Intellectual.* Chapel Hill, 1934.

Rippy, James Fred. *Joel R. Poinsett, Versatile American.* Durham, 1935.

Ritchie, Thomas. "Letters of Thomas Ritchie—Glimpses of the Year 1830," *John P. Branch Historical Papers of Randolph-Macon College,* Vol. I, pp. 147-154.

Ruffin, Thomas. *The Papers of Thomas Ruffin,* J. G. de Roulhac Hamilton, ed. 4 vols. Raleigh, 1918-1920.

Russel, Robert R. "The General Effects of Slavery upon Southern Economic Progress," *Journal of Southern History,* Vol. IV (February 1938), pp. 34-54.

Sanger, Donald B. "The Nullification Movement in Georgia," *Tyler's Quarterly Historical and Genealogical Magazine,* Vol. XI (October 1929), pp. 94-106.

Sargent, Nathan. *Public Men and Events from the Commencement of Mr. Monroe's Administration, in 1817, to the Close of Mr. Fillmore's Administration, in 1853.* 2 vols. Philadelphia, 1875.

Schaper, William A. *Sectionalism and Representation in South Carolina.* Annual Report of the American Historical Association, 1900. Vol. I, pp. 237-463. Washington, 1901.

Schlesinger, Arthur M., Jr. *The Age of Jackson.* New York, 1945.

Schurz, Carl. *Life of Henry Clay.* 2 vols. Boston, 1892.

Scott, Nancy N. *Memoir of Hugh Lawson White.* Philadelphia, 1856.

Seaton, Josephine. *William Winston Seaton of the "National Intelligencer."* Boston, 1871.

Simms, Henry H. "A Critical Analysis of Abolition Literature, 1830-1840," *Journal of Southern History,* Vol. VI (August 1940), pp. 368-382.

Simms, Henry H. *Life of Robert M. T. Hunter.* Richmond, 1935.

Simms, William Gilmore. *The Morals of Slavery.* Charleston, 1838. Reprinted in *The Pro-Slavery Argument* (Charleston, 1852), pp. 175-285.

Simpson, Richard Wright. *History of Old Pendleton District.* Anderson, S. C., 1913.

Sloan, Dave M. *Fogy Days, and Now; or, The World Has Changed.* Atlanta, 1891.

Smith, Justin H. *The Annexation of Texas.* Corrected ed. New York, 1941.

Smith, Margaret Bayard. *The First Forty Years of Washington Society;* Gaillard Hunt, ed. New York, 1906.

Smith, William Ernest. *The Francis Preston Blair Family in Politics.* 2 vols. New York, 1933.

Smith, William L. G. *Fifty Years of Public Life: The Life and Times of Lewis Cass.* New York, 1856.

South Carolina. *The Book of Allegiance; or A Report on the Arguments of Counsel and Opinions of the Court of Appeals of South Carolina, on the Oath of Allegiance.* Columbia, 1834.

South Carolina. *Journal of the Convention of the People of South Carolina.* Columbia, 1833.

South Carolina. *Report of the Commissioners appointed by the legislature of South Carolina, to cause examinations, surveys and estimates to be made for a rail road between Charleston and Cincinnati.* Columbia, 1836.

South Carolina. *Speeches Delivered in the Convention, of the State of South-Carolina, held in Columbia, in March, 1833.* Charleston, 1833.

Sparks, William Henry. *The Memories of Fifty Years.* Philadelphia, 1870.
Stanwood, Edward. *American Tariff Controversies in the Nineteenth Century.* 2 vols. Boston and New York, 1903.
Stanwood, Edward. *A History of the Presidency;* new edition, rev. by Charles K. Bolton. 2 vols. Boston and New York, 1928.
Stenberg, Richard R. "Jackson, Anthony Butler, and Texas," *Southwestern Social Science Quarterly,* Vol. XIII (December 1932), pp. 264-286.
Stenberg, Richard R. "Jackson's 'Rhea letter' Hoax," *Journal of Southern History,* Vol. II (1936), pp. 480-496.
Stenberg, Richard R. "The Jefferson Birthday Dinner, 1830," *Journal of Southern History,* Vol. IV (August 1938), pp. 334-345.
Stenberg, Richard R. "A Note on the Jackson-Calhoun Breach of 1830-1831," *Tyler's Quarterly Historical and Genealogical Magazine,* Vol. XXI (October 1939), pp. 65-69.
Stenberg, Richard R. "The Texas Schemes of Jackson and Houston, 1829-1836," *Southwestern Social Science Quarterly,* Vol. XV (December 1934), pp. 229-250.
Stephenson, Nathaniel W. "Calhoun and the Divine Right of the Majority," *Lectures on Typical Americans and Their Problems.* Scripps College Papers, No. 3. Claremont, Calif., 1930.
Stephenson, Wendell Holmes. *Alexander Porter, Whig Planter of Old Louisiana.* Baton Rouge, 1934.
Stillé, Charles J. *The Life and Services of Joel R. Poinsett.* Philadelphia, 1888.
Story, Joseph. *Commentaries on the Constitution of the United States.* 3 vols. Boston, 1833.
Story, William W. *Life and Letters of Joseph Story.* 2 vols. Boston, 1851.
Styron, Arthur. *The Cast-iron Man; John C. Calhoun and American Democracy.* New York and Toronto, 1935.
Swisher, Carl Brent. *Roger B. Taney.* New York, 1935.
Taney, Roger B. "Taney's Correspondence with Van Buren," *Maryland Historical Magazine,* Vol. VIII (December 1913), pp. 305-326; Vol. X (March 1915), pp. 15-24.
Turner, Frederick Jackson, *Rise of the New West.* The American Nation, Vol. XIV. New York, 1906.
Turner, Frederick J. *The United States, 1830-1850.* New York, 1935.
Tyler, Lyon G. *The Letters and Times of the Tylers.* 3 vols. Richmond, 1884-1896.
"The Union and the States," *North American Review,* Vol. XXXVII (July 1833), pp. 190-249.
Van Buren, Martin. *The Autobiography of Martin Van Buren;* John C. Fitzpatrick, ed. Annual Report of the American Historical Association, 1918. Vol. II. Washington, 1920.
Van Buren, Martin. "Unpublished Letters from North Carolinians to Van Buren"; Elizabeth G. McPherson, ed. *North Carolina Historical Review,* Vol. XV (1938), *passim.*
Van Deusen, Glyndon G. *The Life of Henry Clay.* Boston, 1937.
Van Deusen, John G. *Economic Bases of Disunion in South Carolina.* New York, 1928.
Wade, John Donald. *Augustus Baldwin Longstreet; a Study of the Development of Culture in the South.* New York, 1924.

Wallace, David Duncan. *History of South Carolina.* 4 vols. New York, 1934.
Watkins, James L. *King Cotton.* New York, 1908.
Watterston, George. *Gallery of American Portraits.* Washington, 1830.
Webster, Daniel. *The Writings and Speeches of Daniel Webster;* National Edition. 18 vols. Boston, 1903.
Weed, Thurlow. *Autobiography of Thurlow Weed;* Harriet A. Weed, ed. Boston, 1883.
Weisenburger, Francis P. *The Life of John McLean.* Columbus, 1937.
Wellington, R. G. *The Tariff and Public Lands from 1828 to 1833.* Annual Report of the American Historical Association, 1911. Vol. I, pp. 179-185. Washington, 1913.
White, Laura A. *Robert Barnwell Rhett: Father of Secession.* New York, 1931.
Wise, Barton H. *Life of Henry A. Wise of Virginia.* New York, 1899.
Wise, Henry A. *Seven Decades of the Union.* Philadelphia, 1872.

PERSONAL ACKNOWLEDGMENTS

AGAIN my primary obligation is to the Library of Congress, particularly to those many individuals in the Reference Division, the Manuscript Division, the Newspaper Reference Room, and the Reading Rooms who cheerfully placed their time and special skills at my disposal during the two years and more that I worked among them. My debt to many other libraries, and to the intelligent and courteous staff members who served me with unfailing interest, is also great. I would single out in particular the Clemson College Library, where the largest collection of Calhoun Papers is housed; the South Caroliniana Library at the University of South Carolina; the Charleston Library Society; the library of the College of Charleston; the South Carolina Historical Society; the Duke University Library; and the library of the University of North Carolina. I am also under obligation to the Yale University Library, where my dealings were by way of microfilm. My obligations to institutions and to individuals for the illustrations in this volume have been acknowledged in the List of Illustrations.

To the administration and faculty of Clemson College I am further indebted for a grant from the Kress fund in aid of my researches while on the campus—a campus, I might add for the benefit of those who do not know, whose boundaries approximate those of the Fort Hill plantation as depicted in the end papers of this volume.

Among individuals who contributed to my work I owe special thanks to Mrs. Alice Noble Waring of Hughes, Arkansas, and to Mrs. Sarah Noble Carnes, for allowing me to examine and make use of their family collection of letters from Calhoun to Patrick Noble. The letters from Calhoun to Francis W. Pickens cited in this volume as in the South Caroliniana Library are here used with the generous permission of Mrs. Mary Simms Oliphant of Greenville, South Carolina.

As in the first volume of this work, Professor A. G. Holmes of Clemson College, and Mrs. Holmes, were my guides and counsellors in matters of local and state history and geography. They were also my hosts at Clemson, and my debt to them on both counts is more than can ever be repaid by mere acknowledgment.

I am further indebted to Professor Holmes for reviewing my completed manuscript, and to Mrs. Holmes for helpful comments on the two chapters dealing with personal and family matters. The manuscript was also read by Mr. Bray Hammond of the Federal Reserve System, whose profound knowledge of American financial history was generously placed at my disposal. My thanks to these critics are not less sincere for my occasional failure to adopt the suggestions offered.

On the technical side my major obligation is to Miss Frances M. Shattuck of Washington, who edited and typed my manuscript and assisted me with proof and index. Miss Shattuck is also responsible for the end papers and for the map accompanying Chapter XXIII.

C. M. W.

INDEX

INDEX

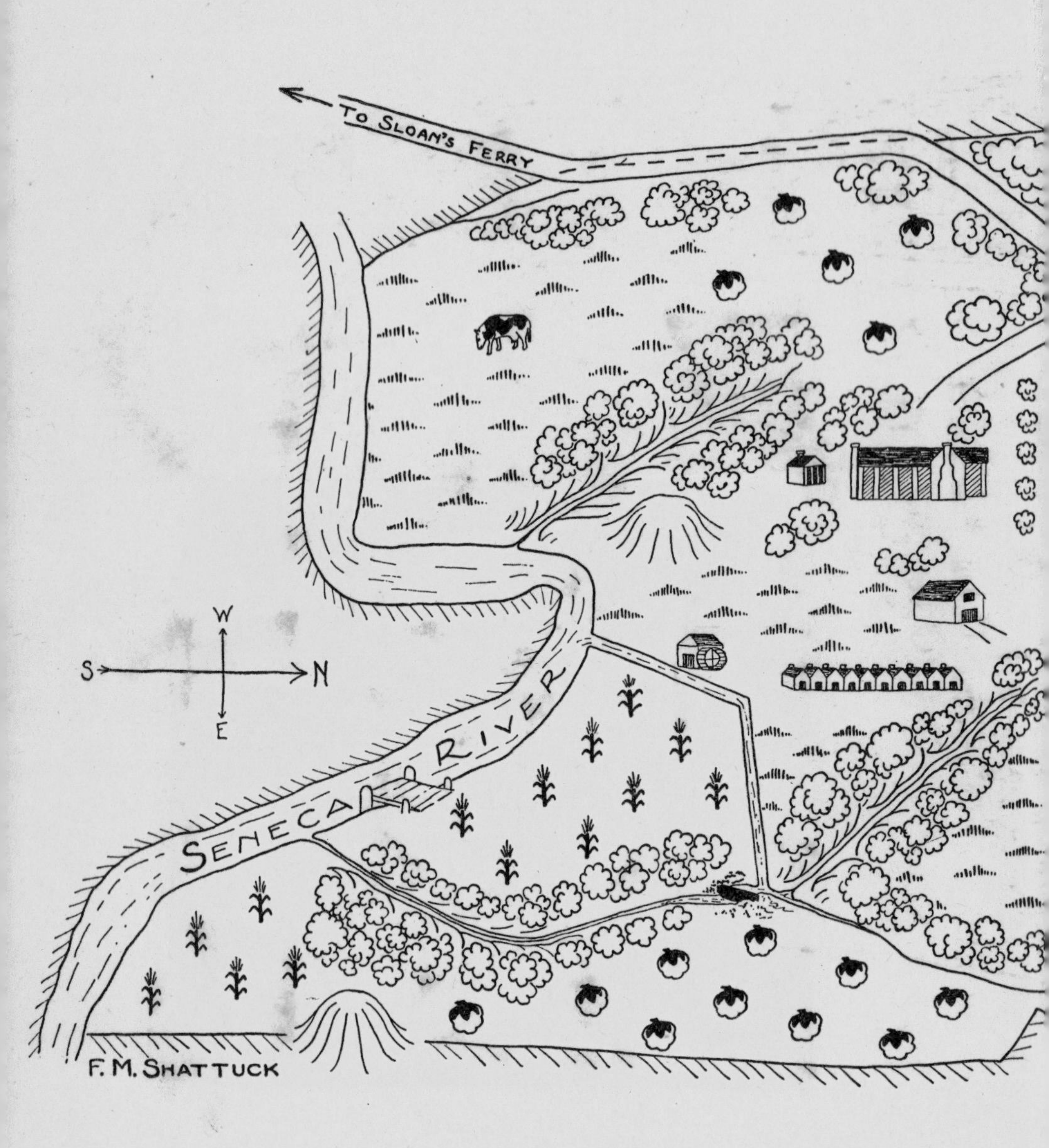
TO SLOAN'S FERRY
SENECA RIVER
W
S
N
E
F. M. SHATTUCK